Bull's Birds of New York State

BULL'S BIRDS of NEW YORK STATE

Emanuel Levine, *Editor*

Berna B. Lincoln and
Stanley R. Lincoln, *Associates*

A project of the
Federation of New York State Bird Clubs, Inc.
in association with
The American Museum of Natural History

Illustrated by Dale Dyer

Foreword by Governor George E. Pataki

COMSTOCK PUBLISHING ASSOCIATES

A division of Cornell University Press

ITHACA AND LONDON

The preparation of this publication was funded by the Division of Fish and Wildlife, New York State Department of Environmental Conservation, and the "Return a Gift to Wildlife" program.

Birds of New York State first published in 1974 by Doubleday/Natural History Press. Reissued 1985 by Cornell University Press, with supplement and corrections. *Bull's Birds of New York State* published 1998 by Cornell University Press.

Printed in the United States of America.

LIBRARY OF CONGRESS CATALOGING-IN-PUBLICATION DATA

Bull, John L.
    Bull's birds of New York State / Emanuel Levine, editor; illustrated by Dale Dyer.
      p. cm.
    "A project of the Federation of New York State Bird Clubs, Inc. in association with the American Museum of Natural History."
    Rev. ed. of: Birds of New York State. 1985.
    Includes bibliographical references and index.
    ISBN 0-8014-3404-1 (cloth: alk. paper)
    1. Birds—New York (State) I. Levine, Emanuel, 1921– . II. Federation of New York State Bird Clubs. III. American Museum of Natural History.
    QL684.N7B833 1998
    598'.09747—DC21   98-10626

Cornell University Press strives to use environmentally responsible suppliers and materials to the fullest extent possible in the publishing of its books. Such materials include vegetable-based, low-VOC inks and acid-free papers that are recycled, totally chlorine-free, or partly composed of nonwood fibers.

Cloth printing   10 9 8 7 6 5 4 3 2 1

Contents

Contents

Part II   Species Accounts   93

MAPS

Foreword

Governor George E. Pataki

As Governor of New York State, I am a strong supporter of conservation and environmental protection efforts. As a citizen, I believe one of
our most important callings is to pass on to our children an environment
that is at least as rich, as diverse, and as nurturing of life as the one passed
to us by our forebears. It is with these thoughts in mind that I welcome the
opportunity to introduce *Bull's Birds of New York State*, devoted to the documentation and full understanding of the diversity of bird life in our great
state.

Birds are, as the late Roger Tory Peterson said, "the litmus paper of the
environment." Changes in bird populations often open our eyes to problems, alerting us to a need for action. The subtle warnings of changes that
need our attention are often first noted by birders. Thus the birder is at the
forefront of our environmental protection efforts. The Federation of New
York State Bird Clubs (FNYSBC) is a prime example of our citizens' contributions to protecting the environment.

In partnership with the New York State Department of Environmental
Conservation (NYSDEC), and augmented by the Cornell Laboratory of
Ornithology, the FNYSBC completed a six-year study (1980–1985) of
breeding bird distribution in the state, documented in the 1988 publication
of *The Atlas of Breeding Birds in New York State*. These organizations are
now gearing up for a new effort starting in the year 2000, which will result
in a revised Atlas.

This partnership between the NYSDEC and FNYSBC again came into
play when it was decided to completely revise Bull's 1974 work, *The Birds
of New York State*, the result being the current volume. Part of the funding
was provided by the NYSDEC, through the Return a Gift to Wildlife tax
checkoff program; the rest was contributed by conservation-minded individuals and organizations.

Protecting habitats is a major key to the flourishing of bird populations.
In New York, we are funding the purchase of important habitat areas
through the Clean Water/Clean Air Bond Act and through the
Environmental Protection Fund. I also commend the NYSDEC's
outstanding work in the reestablishment of viable populations of
Ospreys, Peregrine Falcons, and Bald Eagles. These are dramatic success
stories!

My son, Teddy, and I are active birders. We have joined the members of
the Putnam-Highlands Audubon Society on their annual Christmas Bird

Counts. Those long days of birding and the great camaraderie will provide wonderful memories for both of us.

So, whether you watch birds on the shores of Long Island, at the Bashakill Marsh, at Niagara Falls, or just at your backyard feeder, this volume will help you appreciate what our Empire State has to offer. It will give you a historical perspective, and it will tell you what we can hope to look forward to in the future if we are vigilant stewards of our natural world.

Contributing Authors

Following each name is a list, in taxonomic order, of the species accounts written by that author. The species accounts begin on page 93.

KENNETH P. ABLE: Black Rail, Clapper Rail, King Rail, Virginia Rail, Sora, Wilson's Phalarope, Red-necked Phalarope, Red Phalarope

ROBERT ANDRLE: Black Vulture, Great Gray Owl, Snow Bunting

JOHN P. ASKILDSEN: Northern Fulmar, Black-capped Petrel, Mottled Petrel, Herald Petrel, Cory's Shearwater, Greater Shearwater, Sooty Shearwater, Manx Shearwater, Audubon's Shearwater, Wilson's Storm-Petrel, White-faced Storm-Petrel, Leach's Storm-Petrel, White-tailed Tropicbird, Red-billed Tropicbird, Brown Booby, Northern Gannet, Great Skua, South Polar Skua

EDWARD S. BRINKLEY: Red-necked Grebe, American Golden-Plover, Hudsonian Godwit, Herring Gull, Thayer's Gull, Iceland Gull, Lesser Black-backed Gull, Long-eared Owl, Northern Shrike, Hoary Redpoll

ROBERT W. BROCK: Canvasback, Redhead, Ring-necked Duck, Tufted Duck, Greater Scaup, Lesser Scaup, Franklin's Gull, Black-headed Gull, Bonaparte's Gull, Ring-billed Gull, Slaty-backed Gull, Great Black-backed Gull, Black-legged Kittiwake, Townsend's Solitaire, Western Tanager

ELIZABETH W. BROOKS: Black-billed Magpie, Boreal Chickadee, Bewick's Wren, Golden-crowned Kinglet

PAUL A. BUCKLEY: Spotted Towhee

THOMAS A. BURKE: Reddish Egret, White-faced Ibis, Azure Gallinule, Wood Sandpiper, Red-necked Stint, Little Stint, Sharp-tailed Sandpiper, Say's Phoebe, Vermilion Flycatcher, Gray Kingbird

BARBARA A. BUTLER: Turkey Vulture, Eastern Towhee

LEE B. CHAMBERLAINE: Cattle Egret, Gyrfalcon, Gray Partridge, Sandhill Crane, Caspian Tern, Red-headed Woodpecker, Red-bellied Woodpecker, Gray Jay, Common Raven, Mountain Bluebird, Varied Thrush, Prairie Warbler, Fox Sparrow

JOHN L. CONFER: Blue-winged Warbler, Golden-winged Warbler

WILLIAM E. COOK: Chipping Sparrow, Field Sparrow

MICHAEL F. COOPER: Curlew Sandpiper, Ruff, Royal Tern, Sandwich Tern, Arctic Tern, Short-eared Owl, Fieldfare, Redwing

CHAD E. COVEY: Downy Woodpecker, Hairy Woodpecker, Northern Flicker, Red-breasted Nuthatch, White-breasted Nuthatch, American Goldfinch

SCOTT T. CROCOLL: Red-shouldered Hawk, Broad-winged Hawk

KENNETH L. CROWELL: Eastern Kingbird, Purple Martin, American Pipit, Harris's Sparrow, Rusty Blackbird

WILLIAM C. D'ANNA: Boreal Owl, Chimney Swift, Ruby-throated Hummingbird, Least Flycatcher, Rock Wren, American Tree Sparrow, Black-headed Grosbeak, Brewer's Blackbird, Baltimore Oriole, Bullock's Oriole, Evening Grosbeak

JOSEPH DICOSTANZO: Pacific Loon, Common Loon, Eared Grebe, Western Grebe, Anhinga, Bufflehead, Common Goldeneye, Barrow's Goldeneye, Ruddy Duck, Purple Gallinule, Common Moorhen, American Coot, Little Gull, Mew Gull, Glaucous Gull, Sabine's Gull, Ivory Gull, Orange-crowned Warbler, Northern Parula, Black-throated Blue Warbler, Lapland Longspur, Smith's Longspur, Chestnut-collared Longspur

JEFF DODGE: Swallow-tailed Kite, White-tailed Kite, Rough-legged Hawk, Snowy Owl

JEFF DODGE AND FRANK J. NICOLETTI: Mississippi Kite, Swainson's Hawk, Red-tailed Hawk

DALE DYER: Lark Sparrow, Lark Bunting, Baird's Sparrow

STEPHEN W. EATON: American Wigeon, Hooded Merganser, Common Merganser, Red-breasted Merganser, Wild Turkey, Acadian Flycatcher, Eastern Phoebe, Chestnut-sided Warbler, Magnolia Warbler, Cape May Warbler, Black-throated Green Warbler, Blackburnian Warbler, Black-and-white Warbler, Northern Waterthrush, Louisiana Waterthrush, Hooded Warbler, Canada Warbler

STEPHEN W. EATON AND GEORGE F. BARROWCLOUGH: Dark-eyed Junco

STEPHEN W. EATON AND KENNETH C. PARKES: Ruffed Grouse, Ovenbird

WALTER G. ELLISON: Blue-gray Gnatcatcher, Veery, Gray-cheeked Thrush, Bicknell's Thrush, Swainson's Thrush, Hermit Thrush, Wood Thrush, Tennessee Warbler

KEN FEUSTEL: Northern Lapwing, Black-bellied Plover, Wilson's Plover, Semipalmated Plover, Black-necked Stilt, American Avocet, Greater Yellowlegs, Lesser Yellowlegs, Solitary Sandpiper, Spotted Sandpiper, Whimbrel, Long-billed Curlew, Burrowing Owl, Bohemian Waxwing, Cedar Waxwing

VALERIE M. FREER: Tree Swallow, Northern Rough-winged Swallow, Bank Swallow, Barn Swallow, Cliff Swallow, Black-capped Chickadee, Gray Catbird

JOHN J. FRITZ AND JOAN L. QUINLAN: Ash-throated Flycatcher, Warbling Vireo, Marsh Wren, Black-throated Gray Warbler

KEVIN C. GRIFFITH: Horned Grebe, Great Blue Heron, Great Egret, Snowy Egret, Snow Goose, Ross's Goose, Canada Goose, Brant, Barnacle Goose, Tundra Swan

JEFF GROTH: Red Crossbill, White-winged Crossbill

HELEN HAYS: Roseate Tern, Common Tern

PHYLLIS R. JONES: Blue Jay, Eastern Bluebird

STEVE KELLING: Red-throated Loon, Bobolink

MARY ALICE KOENEKE: Scissor-tailed Flycatcher, Le Conte's Sparrow

WESLEY E. LANYON: Eastern Meadowlark, Western Meadowlark

ANTHONY J. LAURO: American White Pelican, Brown Pelican, Little Blue Heron, Tricolored Heron, Yellow-crowned Night-Heron, Harlequin Duck, Oldsquaw, White-winged Tern, Northern Wheatear, Yellow-rumped Warbler

GEOFFREY S. LEBARON, KENN KAUFMAN, AND SUSAN RONEY DRENNAN: Cave Swallow

EMANUEL LEVINE: Wood Duck, American Black Duck, Mallard, Green-winged Teal, Spotted Redshank, Bar-tailed Godwit, Ross's Gull, Long-billed Murrelet, Lewis's Woodpecker

EMANUEL LEVINE AND RICHARD O'HARA: Golden-crowned Sparrow

BERNA B. LINCOLN: Yellow-nosed Albatross, California Gull

STANLEY R. LINCOLN: Yellow-billed Loon, Labrador Duck, Smew, Greater Prairie-Chicken, Corn Crake, Eskimo Curlew, Eurasian Curlew, Passenger Pigeon, Sky Lark, Brown-headed Nuthatch, Brambling, European Goldfinch

PATRICIA J. LINDSAY: Barred Owl, Northern Saw-whet Owl, Cerulean Warbler, Indigo Bunting, Painted Bunting

MICHAEL LOLYA: Buff-breasted Sandpiper, Common Murre, Thick-billed Murre, Black Guillemot, Atlantic Puffin

BARBARA ALLEN LOUCKS: Osprey, Peregrine Falcon

Contributing Authors

ROBERT E. MARCOTTE: Pied-billed Grebe, Great Cormorant, Black-crowned Night-Heron, Wood Stork, Fulvous Whistling-Duck, Greater White-fronted Goose, Mute Swan, Eurasian Wigeon, Northern Shoveler, Northern Pintail, Ring-necked Pheasant, Spruce Grouse, Common Snipe, Ancient Murrelet, Black-billed Cuckoo, Yellow-billed Cuckoo, Northern Hawk Owl, Western Kingbird, Fork-tailed Flycatcher, Ruby-crowned Kinglet, Brown-headed Cowbird, Pine Grosbeak

HARRIET T. MARSI AND GAIL M. KIRCH: Northern Harrier, Cooper's Hawk, Dunlin, White-throated Sparrow

ROBERT G. MCKINNEY: Blue-headed Vireo, Winter Wren, Nashville Warbler, Blackpoll Warbler, Rose-breasted Grosbeak

ROBERT G. MCKINNEY AND KENNETH C. PARKES: Yellow Warbler

CLAUDIA K. MELIN: Tufted Titmouse, Carolina Wren, Northern Mockingbird, Northern Cardinal

ROBERT L. MILLER: Double-crested Cormorant

NEIL S. MOON AND LAURA W. MOON: Sooty Tern

PAUL G. NOVAK: Black Tern, Loggerhead Shrike, Clay-colored Sparrow, Lincoln's Sparrow, Dickcissel

PETER G. NYE: Bald Eagle, Golden Eagle

DREW PANKO AND GERTRUDE R. BATTALY: Eastern Screech-Owl

ROBERT O. PAXTON: Piping Plover, American Oystercatcher, Willet, Laughing Gull, Blue Grosbeak

ROBERT O. PAXTON AND KENNETH C. PARKES: Forster's Tern

JOAN L. QUINLAN AND JOHN J. FRITZ: Bell's Vireo, Philadelphia Vireo, House Wren

GERRY RISING: Rufous Hummingbird, Yellow-bellied Sapsucker, Three-toed Woodpecker, Black-backed Woodpecker, Pileated Woodpecker, Olive-sided Flycatcher, Yellow-bellied Flycatcher, American Robin, Sage Thrasher, Brown Thrasher, Palm Warbler, Bay-breasted Warbler, American Redstart, Worm-eating Warbler, Swainson's Warbler, Green-tailed Towhee, Bachman's Sparrow, Yellow-headed Blackbird, Orchard Oriole, Pine Siskin

GERRY RISING AND CHARLES ROSENBURG: Barn Owl

ERIC SALZMAN: Roseate Spoonbill, American Woodcock, Monk Parakeet, Great Horned Owl, Chuck-will's-widow, Whip-poor-will, Eastern Wood-Pewee, "Traill's" flycatcher, Alder Flycatcher, Willow Flycatcher, Great

Crested Flycatcher, White-eyed Vireo, Yellow-throated Vireo, Red-eyed Vireo, Fish Crow, Brown Creeper, Pine Warbler, Kentucky Warbler, Yellow-breasted Chat, Summer Tanager, Scarlet Tanager, "Sharp-tailed" sparrows, Saltmarsh Sharp-tailed Sparrow, Nelson's Sharp-tailed Sparrow, Song Sparrow, White-crowned Sparrow, Common Grackle, Boat-tailed Grackle

ERIC SALZMAN AND KENNETH C. PARKES: Northern Bobwhite, Swamp Sparrow

ERIC SALZMAN AND CHARLES R. SMITH: Grasshopper Sparrow

KATHRYN J. SCHNEIDER: Sedge Wren, Seaside Sparrow

DOMINIC F. SHERONY: Blue-winged Teal, Cinnamon Teal, Marbled Godwit, Ruddy Turnstone, Red Knot, Sanderling, Semipalmated Sandpiper, Western Sandpiper, Stilt Sandpiper, Short-billed Dowitcher, Long-billed Dowitcher, Pomarine Jaeger, Parasitic Jaeger, Long-tailed Jaeger, Townsend's Warbler, Yellow-throated Warbler, Connecticut Warbler, Mourning Warbler, Common Yellowthroat

DOMINIC F. SHERONY AND ELIZABETH W. BROOKS: Wilson's Warbler

SHARON M. SKELLY: Gull-billed Tern, Least Tern, Bridled Tern, Black Skimmer

CHARLES R. SMITH: Upland Sandpiper, American Crow, Horned Lark, Vesper Sparrow, Savannah Sparrow, Henslow's Sparrow, Red-winged Blackbird

ROBERT G. SPAHN: White Ibis, Glossy Ibis, Gadwall, King Eider, Common Eider, Northern Goshawk, American Kestrel, Merlin, Yellow Rail, Painted Redstart

SCOTT J. STONER: American Bittern, Least Bittern

PAUL R. SWEET: Magnificent Frigatebird, Green Heron, Surf Scoter, White-winged Scoter, Black Scoter, Killdeer, Common Nighthawk, Belted Kingfisher, Prothonotary Warbler

MICHAEL L. USAI: Dovekie, Razorbill

WILLIAM WATSON: Least Sandpiper, White-rumped Sandpiper, Baird's Sandpiper, Pectoral Sandpiper, Purple Sandpiper

JEFFREY V. WELLS AND ALLISON CHILDS WELLS: Common Redpoll

DONALD A. WINDSOR: Sharp-shinned Hawk, Rock Dove, White-winged Dove, Mourning Dove, European Starling, Purple Finch, House Finch, House Sparrow

History of the Federation of
New York State Bird Clubs, Inc.

Stanley R. Lincoln, Past President

The publication of this work will mark the fiftieth anniversary of the Federation of New York State Bird Clubs as the state's ornithological organization. A short recap of the Federation's distinguished history is therefore appropriate.

After the end of World War II, it became evident that the burgeoning interest in birdwatching and ornithology required some mechanism for the birders of the state to get to know each other, to share their ideas and experiences, to jointly promote research and education in the field of ornithology, and to secure a stronger voice in bird-related conservation matters. In December 1946, the Buffalo Ornithological Society and the Genesee Ornithological Society hosted a meeting in Rochester, to which they invited all known bird clubs in the state, to discuss the feasibility of forming a statewide organization. Representatives of 10 other bird clubs and Audubon chapters joined the two ornithological societies for this historic meeting. With great enthusiasm, a planning team started the work that culminated in an organizational meeting in Amsterdam in October 1947. Temporary officers were elected, and a draft constitution and bylaws were approved for formal ratification by the charter member clubs.

On 12–14 December 1948, with all legal matters taken care of, the first formal annual meeting of member clubs was hosted by the Genesee Ornithological Society at the Rochester Museum of Arts and Sciences. The first regular officers and directors were elected, bylaws were formally adopted, and the Federation was officially under way. From the Federation's inception, two key objectives of the founding members were to start a state journal dedicated to documentation of the state's key ornithological information and to prepare and publish a new treatise on the birds of New York State to update Elon Howard Eaton's monumental two-volume work published in 1910 and 1914.

Just two years later, in December 1950, the first issue of *The Kingbird* was published, and since then it has appeared quarterly without interruption. In 1950 the organization could count 18 member clubs and had begun seeking individual members and subscriptions to help fund the cost of the journal. By the fourth annual meeting in April 1951, there were 149

Adapted from Gordon M. Meade's *The Origins of the Federation and What Happened Then,* published in *The Kingbird* in 1988, vol. 38, p. 66.

individual members, still far short of the number needed to ensure the journal's future. But succeed it did. Today the Federation has more than 40 member clubs, 90 life members, and some 700 annual members; its next 50 years look bright indeed.

The update of the state bird book, however, which from the start had been a key objective, was not realized for 26 years. Finally, with crucial assistance from the American Museum of Natural History and constant support from the Federation's leadership as well as help from many members, John Bull was able to complete his *Birds of New York State*, which was published in 1974.

The 1980s saw the Federation's most demanding project, *The Atlas of Breeding Birds in New York State*, conclude with its publication by Cornell University Press in 1988. This followed six years of fieldwork by more than 4000 volunteers working in 5335 separate 5 km "Atlas blocks" covering the entire state. The project was a superb example of cooperative effort by the Federation and its members, the New York State Department of Environmental Conservation, and the Cornell University Laboratory of Ornithology.

As the Federation enters its second 50 years, it is committed to periodically updating both the state bird book and the breeding bird atlas on approximately a 25-year cycle. Preliminary plans are already in place for an update of *The Atlas of Breeding Birds in New York State* early in the twenty-first century.

The Federation is fully aware that its established record of focusing on research and conservation to ensure the preservation and protection of our birds and their essential habitats must continue unabated. It is committed to the principle of seeking and establishing new partnership relations to cope with the challenges that the next century will surely present.

Acknowledgments

S everal years ago, I complained to fellow birder Tony Lauro that the "bible" of New York State ornithology, John Bull's *Birds of New York State* (1974), was out of date. His simple rejoinder was, "Well, why don't you write a new one?" The next day he called to badger me a bit about doing such a book, and I started to think about it. I quickly decided that I could not accomplish a task such as this on my own, but the book sounded like a reasonable and desirable project for me to undertake as Chairman of Publications of the Federation of New York State Bird Clubs.

The next step was to put the matter before the Executive Committee of the Federation, which approved the project, and an ad hoc committee consisting of myself, Berna Lincoln, Stan Lincoln, and Richard Sloss was formed. There followed several months of negotiating with the American Museum of Natural History (AMNH), which owned the copyright of John Bull's 1974 book, and Cornell University Press, as the desired publisher. Helped along by the gracious cooperation of John and Edith Bull, everything finally fell into place.

Now I had to find the people who would actually write the species accounts. Within the framework of the Federation membership, invitations were sent to active birders throughout the state, and, in a matter of a few months, a team was in place and a majority of the species had been assigned. The full list of authors appears at the beginning of this book, and they all deserve a huge round of thanks, but there are several who rate special mention. They are the ones who completed their assignments on schedule and then agreed to take on species that had not yet been placed or to take over from authors who could not fulfill their commitments. They are Robert Brock, Michael Cooper, Joseph DiCostanzo, Stephen Eaton, Robert Marcotte, Gerry Rising, and Eric Salzman. In the meantime, fund raising was under way, the effort being guided by Federation President Robert Budliger, aided by Robert Miller of the New York State Department of Environmental Conservation.

In addition to the actual authors, there were many people who were instrumental in aiding in the completion of the species accounts: Michele Alfieri, Ralph Andrews, Kathleen Brittingham, Robert Connor, Paul DeBenedictis, William Evans, Tracy Gingrich, John Gregoire, Lee Harper, Mark Kandell, Kenneth Karwowski, Richard McDonald, Kenneth Meskill, Michael Murphy, Allan O'Connell Jr., John M. C. Peterson, Chris Rimmer, and Bryan Swift.

The compilation of National Audubon Society Christmas Bird Count data was initiated by Gerry Rising and made available by John W. Shipman, with programming for that data provided by Ajay S. Shekawat.

United States Fish and Wildlife Service Breeding Bird Survey material was secured through the efforts of Charles R. Smith. In addition to his authorship of several species accounts, Smith wrote two of the introductory chapters, and he also deserves special mention for his helpful advice on many things.

Some material was taken from *The Atlas of Breeding Birds in New York State,* edited by Robert F. Andrle and Janet R. Carroll and used by permission of the publisher, Cornell University Press. This material is identified in the text.

All subspecific discussions underwent the eagle-eyed perusal of Kenneth C. Parkes, Curator Emeritus of Birds at the Carnegie Museum of Natural History, Pittsburgh, and were in some cases, where so stated, entirely written by him. To our knowledge, no other individual has made a comparable study of subspecies variations of the entire New York State avifauna, utilizing a broad range of literature and the examination of thousands of specimens housed in numerous museums.

At the AMNH, which was my home base when working on the book, many of the staff were helpful, including Christine Blake, Carole Griffiths, Jeff Groth, Shannon Hackett, Robert Rockwell, and Paul Sweet. Particular thanks are due to the Chairman of the Ornithology Department, George F. Barrowclough, who wholeheartedly backed the project and made available all the facilities of the department. Diane Treon, department secretary, was absolutely invaluable in the preparation of material and from time to time made her own subtle changes for the better.

From day one, Mary LeCroy at the AMNH cheerfully came up with an answer for every question and a solution to every problem.

Special thanks go out to my constant birding companions, Al Wollin, Sy Schiff, and Lester Feldman. Al monitored the extraterritorial data of certain species for more than a year, Sy graciously volunteered to do the indexes, and Lester gave advice on the artwork.

A word is called for about the ad hoc committee casually mentioned at the beginning of this section. Ad hoc quickly became a permanent committee, charged with the full responsibility of seeing this book through to completion, with myself as volume editor.

Dick Sloss, in his usual role of *eminence grise*, supplied the counterbalance to my more-volatile approach to things and was instrumental in the managing of budgetary matters and contractual arrangements with both the museum and the publisher.

Stan Lincoln labored uncounted hours at his computer, unifying all the material onto one master disk in accordance with the requirements of the publisher. He wrote accounts, prepared all the range material, and performed many other tasks to do with the budget and other procedural matters.

Berna Lincoln was involved in so many things, from copyediting the entire book to writing accounts, that her role cannot easily be defined. All major decisions made over the years of this work had some input from her. One of the real challenges in a work written by so many individuals is to achieve some uniformity in the presentation of raw data, such as maxima, extreme dates, and so on. Any success along those lines is solely due to her tireless efforts.

Thanks are due to Chandler S. Robbins, wildlife biologist for the U.S. Department of Interior, for a thorough and conscientious review of the final manuscript, to Peter Prescott, science editor at Cornell University Press, for guidance warmly given, to Margo Quinto, copyeditor, for remarkable exactitude and attention to detail, and to Ralph Odell for his timely assistance.

And last, I must acknowledge the patience and understanding of my wife, Mickey, during the many months devoted to the completion of this book.

I wish to emphasize here that although I, as editor, may have been the prime mover and unifying force, without the voluntary input of the more than 60 authors and the many other persons mentioned above, this work would not have been possible.

It also would not have been possible without the financial support of generous contributors. Financial support was provided by the New York State Department of Environmental Conservation through a grant from the Return a Gift to Wildlife Program, by grants from the Anne & Harry J. Reicher Foundation, and by contributions from member clubs & individual members of the Federation of New York State Bird Clubs, Inc.:

Alan Devoe Bird Club
Audubon Society of the Capital Region
Buffalo Audubon Society
Buffalo Ornithological Society
Cayuga Bird Club
Genesee Ornithological Society
Hudson-Mohawk Bird Club
Huntington Audubon Society
John Burroughs Natural History Society
Kirkland Bird Club
The Linnaean Society of New York
Lyman Langdon Audubon Society
Moriches Bay Audubon Society
The Naturalists Club of Broome County
North Country Bird Club
Onondaga Audubon Society
Queens County Bird Club

Acknowledgments

Ralph T. Waterman Bird Club
Rochester Birding Association
Rockland Audubon Society
Saw Mill River Audubon Society
Sullivan County Audubon Society
Dean Amadon
David Junkin
Harriet T. Marsi
Sally Hoyt Spofford in memory of Dr. Walter R. Spofford

EMANUEL LEVINE

Part I

Introduction

Origin and Structure of the Book

A ny book updating a state's ornithological history will be out of date before it is published. As early as about 1989, John Bull, author of *Birds of New York State*, considered a revision of his 1974 work. He sought and quickly received both an enthusiastic reception and a commitment of financial and publication assistance from the Federation of New York State Bird Clubs. Progress moved slowly on publication plans until 1992, when John, for health reasons, reluctantly concluded that he would be unable to do the necessary research and manuscript preparation.

As detailed in the Acknowledgments, the Federation, firmly believing that the work John contemplated was essential, decided to move forward on this project. It was thought fitting and proper to recognize John Bull's longstanding commitment and dedication to the birds of this state by naming this new work *Bull's Birds of New York State*.

This is a new book intended to bring the documentation of the state's ornithology as current as possible. Although this work draws on the 1974 book, all species accounts have been rewritten and brought up to date. All the introductory material, except where noted, is original with this work.

Both the 1985 reissue of Bull's 1974 volume and the frequently cited 1988 *Atlas of Breeding Birds in New York State* are still in print and available from Cornell University Press, Ithaca, New York. Readers will find those works valuable for further details and background. The Atlas provides detailed New York State distribution maps and breeding information that can only be summarized in the current volume. Likewise, Bull's 1974 epic work has much additional information on early species records and other information not duplicated here.

It should be recognized that this work is not intended to provide identification information. Any identification comments included in species accounts are either incidental in nature or offered as cautionary notes.

Sources of Data

In the past several decades, books on birds have been published in large numbers. The spate of books has been fueled by the exponential growth over the years of the number of birders, with the original spark being the 1934 publication of Roger Tory Peterson's *A Field Guide to the Birds*. Many of the published volumes are general field guides, or specialized field guides for particular groups of birds, such as shorebirds, raptors, and seabirds, or birdfinding guides devoted to particular birding "hot spots." In addition, the capacity to reach almost any part of the world with ease and the proliferation of birding tours led by experts, have prompted the publication of field guides for almost any place in the world.

However, books that are designed to document the generally prosaic and unexciting data of when and where and with what frequency birds occur are in short supply. One such classic is John Bull's 1974 *Birds of New York State*, which became the "bible" of New York birders, who relied on it to tell them what species they might expect, when they might expect to see that species, and where they might see it. Of course, there have been many publications throughout the state devoted to specific localized areas, and these continue, fueled by local clubs. Most recently, many states have embarked on breeding bird atlases such as the one completed in New York in 1985.

So, although there are many publications that cover local areas in the state, historically there have been only four that encompassed the state as a whole:

DeKay, J. E. 1844. *Zoology of New York; or, the New York Fauna*. Part 2: Birds. D. Appleton, and Wiley and Putnam, New York.

Eaton, E. H. 1910. *Birds of New York State*, part 1. State University of New York, Albany.

Eaton, E. H. 1914 *Birds of New York State*, part 2. State University of New York, Albany.

Bull, J. 1974. *Birds of New York State*. Doubleday/Natural History Press, Garden City, NY. Reprinted with 1976 Supplement by Cornell University Press, Ithaca, NY, 1985.

Andrle, R. F., and J. R. Carroll, editors. 1988. *The Atlas of Breeding Birds in New York State*. Cornell University Press, Ithaca, NY.

Some of our authors have alluded to the DeKay volume for historical data, but many references have been drawn from the Eaton work, and much more material comes from Bull's work and the Atlas. In fact, in an effort to make the text of the present book as readable as possible, the authors of the species accounts were instructed not to cite Bull (1974) as the source of the record but to insert the record without citation. The reader is therefore advised that a record with no citation comes from Bull 1974. For the same reason, and because no additional information would be found by reference to the source, citations are also omitted from the data in such sections as Maxima. Their source may be located, if necessary, by referring to the Regional Reports in the appropriate issue of *The Kingbird* as the date and place stated would indicate. Please note that *The Kingbird* was first published in 1950, and Volume 1 refers to that year. Therefore, Volume 30 would refer to 1980 and so on. Each record shows a county designation so that the Region can be identified.

If the information appears in *The Atlas of Breeding Birds in New York State*, the citation will simply be (Atlas 1988), with no author or page number, as the reader will know to refer to that particular species account in that publication.

There are also a number of records and comments followed by an individual's name and "pers. comm." or "in litt." If the reader wishes to contact that individual for further information, please write to:

Emanuel Levine, Chairman of Publications
Federation of New York State Bird Clubs
585 Mead Terrace
South Hempstead, New York 11550

The main source of new information for the last two decades was the Federation's quarterly publication, *The Kingbird*, which, in its half-century of life, has been the repository for the records and observations of the birding community throughout New York State. References to this publication are cited as, for example, (KB 28:30). In addition, authors turned to *American Birds* (cited as AB), and its successor, *National Audubon Society Field Notes* (cited as NASFN), as well as local club records. Further, information specifically applicable to New York State was compiled from National Audubon Society Christmas Bird Counts and U.S. Fish and Wildlife Service Breeding Bird Surveys and made available to the authors.

In 1977, the New York State Avian Records Committee (NYSARC) was formed by the Federation of New York State Bird Clubs to review unusual records. A "want" list was published in *The Kingbird* (28:70), along with procedural instructions and the bylaws of NYSARC. From time to time, that want list is updated in *The Kingbird*. The current *Checklist of the Birds of New York State*, published in August 1996, includes such a list by indicating with an appropriate symbol which species' occurrences should be reported to NYSARC. No new species or new breeding record may be added to the checklist without sanction from NYSARC.

Therefore, on the face of it, matters would seem simple enough. If a record of the last two decades is unusual and appears in this volume, it must have gone through NYSARC. Unfortunately, that generalization applies only to new state occurrences and breeders that were reported to NYSARC. However, there are many observers who, for various reasons, do not submit records to NYSARC but whose reports appear in accredited publications and have presumably been screened by knowledgeable persons. Therefore, the fact that an unusual record of the last two decades appears in this volume does not automatically mean it had been submitted to and acted upon by NYSARC.

Physical Boundaries

This volume has abided by the physical boundaries of the state as set forth in the 1977 Bylaws of the New York State Avian Records Committee (NYSARC) as follows:

National and state boundaries inland and on the Great Lakes, and legal marine boundaries outward to the 1000 fathom line (approximately 100 miles offshore.) The south (west) [marine] boundary extends from the Ambrose Lightship along the Separation Zone of the Ambrose–Hudson Canyon Traffic Lane to the 1000 fathom line; the north (east) [marine] boundary extends at an angle of 150 degrees (from true north) from a point midway between the east end of Fishers Island and Watch Hill, RI, to the 1000 fathom line (Reference: Coast and Geodetic Survey Chart 1108; Approaches to New York). The Hudson Sea Canyon (proper) lies just within the the the south boundary, and Block Canyon is within the north boundary; Cox's Ledge is in RI waters.

Although Bull (1974, 1976) gave no pelagic boundaries in his introductory material, in my conversations with him, he advised that his pelagic boundaries were less extensive than those established by NYSARC in 1977. So, of course, all records in Bull 1974 and 1976 fall within the purview of current NYSARC standards.

Effective Cutoff Dates

The cutoff date for Bull's 1974 volume was 31 December 1972, and for his supplement (Bull 1976) July 1975. The effective cutoff date of the present volume is generally late fall 1996, with some data into 1997. The species accounts were written by more than 60 individuals, some of whom were able to monitor their species after having completed their accounts and some who could not devote the necessary time for followup after completion.

Format of Species Accounts

Range A brief description of the species' worldwide zoogeographic distribution, with primary focus on breeding and wintering ranges as they relate to New York State.

Status A short résumé describing New York State records of relative abundance, frequency of occurrence, seasons of occurrence, and breeding information, if applicable.

Breeding If the species breeds or has bred in the state, this section covers that particular aspect in detail.

Nonbreeding If the species breeds or has bred in the state, this section covers all aspects of occurrence in the state not specifically related to breeding range, season, or activity.

Occurrence This section is used if the species does not or has not bred in the state. It covers all aspects of the species' occurrence in the state, including migration data, distribution, maxima, extreme dates, and so on. A name in parentheses that precedes the citation of the published record or museum collection is the name of the first person who reported a sighting or was responsible for the specimen. If a museum specimen exists, it is noted with the abbreviation of the museum name, followed by the catalog number of the specimen.

Remarks This section contains a discussion of subspecies, if more than one has occurred in the state. If only one form occurs or has occurred, there is no subspecific reference. This section may also contain other material the author thought might be of interest to the reader, including a summary of records from neighboring states.

Zoogeographic Regions

The word *zoogeography* simply means "the science of the distribution of animals." The world is divided into regions, as briefly described below. For a full discussion of this subject, you are referred to Thomson, *A New Dictionary of Birds*, 1964, The British Ornithologists Union, pages 205–212.

Australasian: Australia, Tasmania, New Zealand, New Guinea, the Moluccas, and Pacific Islands to the north and east.

Cosmopolitan: Worldwide, or nearly so.

Ethiopian: Africa south of the Sahara; Madagascar.

Holarctic: Nearctic and Palearctic regions combined.

Nearctic: Arctic and temperate North America (including Greenland) north of tropical Mexico.

Neotropical: West Indies, Middle America (Mexico and Central America), and South America.

Oriental: tropical Asia and islands from India and Sri Lanka east to Taiwan, the Philippines, Celebes, Lesser Sundas.

Palearctic: Europe, northern Africa (including the Sahara), and arctic and temperate Asia.

Descriptive Terms

Because this work is an extension of Bull's 1974 work, terms descriptive of frequency, occurrence, and relative abundance are in accordance with those he used, as follows:

Abundance

For those species reported annually:

Very abundant: over 1000 individuals per day per locality, often in large flocks

Abundant: 200 to 1000 individuals per day per locality

Very common: 50 to 200 individuals per day per locality

Common: 20 to 50 individuals per day per locality

Fairly common: 7 to 20 individuals per day per locality

Uncommon: 1 to 6 individuals per day per locality

Rare: 1 to 6 individuals per season

For those species of irregular occurrence (not reported annually):

Very rare: more than 6 records, but of very infrequent occurrence

Casual: 2 to 6 records

Accidental: only 1 record

Status

Resident: a species that can be found throughout the year in appropriate habitat

Migrant: a species that passes through the state on its way to and from breeding grounds and that may or may not breed in the state

Visitant: a species that appears in the state, not as a migrant or a breeder but as a seasonal occurrence on a regular basis

Vagrant: a species that appears on an irregular basis and whose normal migratory and breeding range does not include New York State

Other Terms

Allopatric: breeding areas may be contiguous but do not overlap.

Sympatric: found in same geographical areas during breeding season.

Monotypic: a species not divided into subspecies.

Polytypic: a species divided into two or more subspecies.

Nominate: the first-named subspecies of a polytypic species.

Polymorphic: a species with two or more color or size variants (morphs).

Alternate plumage: plumage during breeding season.

Basic plumage: other than breeding plumage.

Abbreviations

AB	*American Birds*
AFN	*Audubon Field Notes*
AMNH	American Museum of Natural History, New York, NY

Atlas 1988	*The Atlas of Breeding Birds in New York State*
AOU	American Ornithologists' Union
Auk	*The Auk*, publication of the American Ornithologists' Union
BBC	Breeding Bird Count
BBS	U.S. Fish and Wildlife Service Breeding Bird Survey
BBWMA	Braddock Bay Wildlife Management Area, Monroe Co.
BMNH	British Museum (Natural History) Walter Rothschild Zoological Museum, Tring, England
BMS	Buffalo Museum of Science, Buffalo, NY
BOS	Buffalo Ornithological Society
CBC	National Audubon Society Christmas Bird Count
CMNH	Carnegie Museum of Natural History, Pittsburg, PA
CUM	Cornell University Museum, Ithaca, NY
Co.	County
DEC	Department of Environmental Conservation
FNYSBC	Federation of New York State Bird Clubs
Ft.	Fort
FWC	Federation of New York State Bird Clubs Waterfowl Count
HIWMA	Howland Island Wildlife Management Area, Cayuga Co.
HLSP	Hempstead Lake State Park, Nassau Co.
HMANA	Hawk Migration Association of North America
HSP	Heckscher State Park, Suffolk Co.
HTWMA	High Tor Wildlife Management Area, Yates Co.
INWR	Iroquois National Wildlife Refuge, Genesee Co.
JBSP	Jones Beach State Park, Nassau Co.
JBWR	Jamaica Bay Wildlife Refuge, Queens Co.
JHMANA	*Journal of the Hawk Migration Association of North America*
KB	*The Kingbird*
L.	Lake
LI	Long Island
MCZ	Museum of Comparative Zoology, Harvard University, Cambridge, MA
MNWR	Montezuma National Wildlife Refuge, Seneca Co.
Mt.	Mount
Mtn.	Mountain
MVZ	Museum of Vertebrate Zoology, University of California, Berkeley, CA
NASFN	*National Audubon Society Field Notes*
NWR	National Wildlife Refuge
NYC	New York City
NYSARC	New York State Avian Records Committee
NYSDEC	New York State Department of Environmental Conservation
NYSM	New York State Museum, Albany, NY
OOWMA	Oak Orchard Wildlife Management Area, Genesee Co.

ph	photograph
PRWMA	Perch River Wildlife Management Area, Jefferson Co.
PWMA	Pharsalia Wildlife Management Area, Chenango Co.
R.	River
RMAS	Rochester Museum and Science Center, Rochester, NY
RMSP	Robert Moses State Park, Suffolk Co.
RNJB	*Records of New Jersey Birds*
SI	Staten Island
SP	State Park
TNC	The Nature Conservancy
TRWMA	Three Rivers Wildlife Management Area, Onondaga Co.
TWMA	Tonawanda Wildlife Management Area, Niagara Co.
USFWS	United States Fish and Wildlife Service
USMA	United States Military Academy
USNM	United States National Museum, Washington, DC
WHWMA	Wilson Hill Wildlife Management Area, St. Lawrence Co.
WMA	Wildlife Management Area

Note: U.S. Postal Service two-letter codes, e.g., NY, are used to designate all states and Canadian provinces.

The Physical Environment

John Bull

American Museum of Natural History

N ew York State, nearly 49,108 sq mi in area, is thirtieth in size among the 50 states. Within this area exists varied terrain ranging from sea level, where the waters of the Atlantic Ocean bathe the south-shore sand beaches of Long Island, to the 5000 ft peaks of spruce and fir in the Adirondacks, some of which tower above treeline. An overview of the physical geography of New York State is presented here. For the interested reader, more-detailed information can be found in *Geography of New York State* (Thompson 1977).

New York is bounded on the south by the Atlantic Ocean and the states of New Jersey and Pennsylvania; on the east by the states of Connecticut, Massachusetts, and Vermont; on the west by Lake Erie and a small portion of Ontario; and on the north by Lake Ontario and the Canadian provinces of Ontario and Quebec. Within the state are 62 counties: The eastern-most—Suffolk—extends as far as the Connecticut-Rhode Island state line at 72° west longitude; the southernmost—Richmond—encompasses all of Staten Island, its southernmost tip located just south of 40°30′ north latitude; the westernmost—Chautauqua—extends nearly as far as 80° west longitude; and the three northernmost counties—Clinton, Franklin, and St. Lawrence—extend to 45° north latitude.

These extremes in elevation, from sea level to over 5000 ft, together with a north-south latitudinal range of nearly five degrees and an even greater east-west longitudinal distance of almost eight degrees, produce consider-able diversity in climate, topography, and vegetation. This diversity is reflected in the correspondingly varied and large number of avian species within the temperate zone. Of the 451 species recorded in New York State, more than half (243, or 54%) have bred within the state.

Climate

Those areas nearest the sea do not have the extremes of heat and cold that occur in most of the state. The moderating effect of the ocean waters on the adjacent land areas tempers the climate in both summer and winter. Consequently, during the summer, the prevailing winds from a generally southern direction are cooled by the sea. Conversely, in winter the prevail-ing winds, from a northerly or northwesterly quarter, bring subzero temper-atures to much of upstate New York; at the same time the ocean and

11

adjacent land areas may be 20 degrees higher and even slightly above freezing because of the relatively warm seawater temperatures. Temperature differences are striking at either season only 20 miles away from the ocean. New York City and nearby inland areas may undergo a severe heat wave with temperatures in the nineties, while beachfront localities enjoy temperatures in the seventies or low eighties. Even more striking is the fact that during winter within five miles of the ocean it may be snowing, while on the barrier beaches with temperatures eight to ten degrees higher it may be raining. During snowstorms areas near the sea invariably receive less accumulation than inland areas do.

This great variance in winter temperatures has a profound effect on the birdlife, especially waterfowl and other aquatic species, which are driven out of icebound inland waters to relatively ice-free waters of the coastal bays and estuaries and to the ocean itself. The upland birds, especially those of open country, may find food more readily along the shore because of lesser amounts of snow there. Furthermore, the marine regions, with their extensive areas of salt marsh, rarely freeze over except during prolonged and severe cold waves. Finally, tidal action keeps the immediate seacoast clear of ice and snow and provides a suitable feeding area.

At the other extreme, driving winds and bitter cold during a period of precipitation make the country directly to the east of Lake Ontario, especially the Tug Hill area and the western Adirondacks, an enormous snow depository, rightly called the "snow belt" of the state, although rivaled by some regions in the western parts of the state. Accumulations of many feet of snow are not unusual. Moreover, at times the winter season is prolonged well into April.

In general, wind direction directly affects the weather. No matter what the season, the prevailing westerlies bring clear weather, whereas winds from an easterly quarter, especially if strong or of more than one day's duration, usually bring precipitation.

Within the state, factors of elevation, latitude, temperature, relative humidity, and exposure to sun and wind determine the types of vegetation to be found. The vegetation, in turn, determines the breeding bird species.

Topography

The dominant water areas of the southern portion of the state are the Atlantic Ocean and Long Island Sound, the latter separating Long Island from the mainland. In upstate New York, Lake Erie and especially Lake Ontario are the principal large bodies of water, the latter stretching from the Niagara peninsula for more than 200 miles east to where Lake Ontario narrows into the St. Lawrence River. Along the plains of Lake Ontario and the St. Lawrence Valley, agriculture is carried on extensively.

The principal mountains of the state are the Adirondacks, the Catskills, and the northern extension of the Appalachians—the Alleghenies. To the west of the Adirondacks, separated by the Black River Valley, is the Tug Hill Plateau, much less elevated than the Adirondacks. The Tug Hill upland is a plateau remnant isolated from the closely related Appalachian upland by the Mohawk lowlands and from the adjacent Adirondack highlands by the Black River Valley. With strata dropping regionally southeast from the Adirondack massif, Tug Hill owes its prominence primarily to erosional resistance of the Ordovician Oswego sandstone. Lacking significant through valleys, this upland contains some of the most extensive wilderness areas in New York. Very few roads traverse this region, except in the northern and eastern portions near the Black River. Because of the rugged terrain and poor soil, most of the farms were abandoned long ago.

The Adirondacks themselves are unique in the state in being isolated from other mountain ranges or highlands, as follows: To the north and west is the wide plain of the St. Lawrence Valley; to the east, separated from Vermont's Green Mountains, is the Lake Champlain–Hudson River lowland district; and to the south the narrow Mohawk River effectively isolates the Adirondacks from the Catskills. The highest mountains in the state are in the Adirondacks, with Mount Marcy in Essex County the highest of all—over 5300 ft in elevation. A number of lesser peaks in the Adirondacks are well over 4000 ft, most of them also in Essex County. Numerous lakes dot the Adirondacks. Glacial drift blocked their drainage systems. The remaining present-day rivers of the northern Adirondacks have their outlets into the St. Lawrence River.

The northeastern Catskills are connected with the Helderberg Plateau, the escarpment of the latter extending east nearly to Albany. To the south in Pennsylvania are the Poconos and still farther the Appalachians. The highest peaks in the Catskills are Slide Mountain in Ulster County, just over 4200 ft, and Hunter Mountain in Greene County, slightly over 4000 feet. Unlike some of the Adirondack peaks—the upper slopes of which are above the treeline—even the highest Catskill peaks are wooded to their summits, being more than 1000 feet lower than the highest Adirondack peaks.

East of the Hudson River, close to the Massachusetts state line and running parallel to it, are the Taconics, an outlier of the Berkshires. In the southeastern portion of the state south of the Catskills are the Shawangunks, which continue in a southwesterly direction into New Jersey along the east side of the Delaware River, where they are known as the Kittatinnies. Farther south in New York, the Ramapos likewise lie in a northeast-southwest direction and also continue into New Jersey. The Hudson Highlands, running in the same direction, cross the Hudson River through the counties of Putnam, Orange, and Rockland, where they are practically contiguous with the Ramapos at their southern extremity. Few of the above exceed 2000 feet. Finally, the basalt escarpment on the west bank of the Hudson River—the Palisades—extends from Rockland County south into New Jersey.

In central New York to the west of the Catskills is a broad region of elevated uplands, increasing in elevation toward the south, the highest extending into Pennsylvania. These are the Alleghenies, which in New York State run slightly over 2500 ft elevation at their highest. Altitude decreases northward and westward as the lake plains are reached, and in several spots cliff-like escarpments are a notable feature of the landscape. In the heart of this central upland region lie a series of north-south bodies of water known as the Finger Lakes. With the exception of Canandaigua Lake, glacial drift at the north end of these lakes effectively blocked drainage into Lake Ontario. However, at least one of the south-north flowing streams, the Genesee River, passing through the canyons of Letchworth State Park, Wyoming and Livingston counties, penetrates the lake plain and empties into the lake at Rochester.

A glance at the ecozone map shows how broad the Great Lakes Plain is, in some places as much as 30 to 40 miles in width. The largest freshwater marshes and wooded swamps in the state are found here; the best known and most spectacular from a wildlife point of view are Montezuma National Wildlife Refuge and Oak Orchard Wildlife Management Area. At the western extremity of the Great Lakes Plain in New York State is the Niagara River on the Canadian border. Here at the extreme eastern end of Lake Erie at Buffalo, the Niagara River flows northward through the world-famous cataract at Niagara Falls and then empties into Lake Ontario, which is considerably lower than Lake Erie. At its western edge, the Great Lakes Plain narrows significantly, south of Dunkirk in Chautauqua County, and is but a mile or so in width through much of its length. At its widest it is barely 15 miles across.

At the opposite end of the state is Long Island, well named, projecting into the Atlantic for more than 120 miles. It is by far the largest island along any coast of the continental United States, excepting the islands off Alaska.

The Ecozones of New York State

Ecozone is a recently coined word meaning "ecological zone." The pure definition of the word *ecology* is "the branch of biology that deals with organisms' relations to one another and to the physical environment in which they live."

The ecozones of the state (see the ecozone map) may be referred to in the species accounts, and in many cases the physical characteristics of that ecozone are directly related to the presence of the species. Following are brief descriptions of each ecozone as originally published in *The Atlas of Breeding Birds in New York State*.

Lowlands

Great Lakes Plain

The Great Lakes Plain, covering approximately 7206 sq mi, is a low terrain ecozone with horizontal rock formations. It is essentially a flat plain having little local relief, with the exception of the drumlin area between Rochester and Syracuse. The plain has a simple erosional topography of glacial till, modified by moraines, shoreline deposits, and drumlins. The natural vegetation consists of elm–red maple–northern hardwoods, with beech, white ash, basswood, sugar maple, hickory, hemlock, and tulip tree predominating on better drained sites. Farms and orchards predominate, with only about one-fifth of the land forested, mainly in a disrupted pattern. Climate is equable, modified by Lakes Erie and Ontario. Elevation ranges from 245 ft at the Lake Ontario shoreline to about 1000 ft, but it is mostly under 800 ft.

Erie-Ontario Plain

A large subzone of the Great Lakes Plain, the Erie-Ontario Plain borders Lakes Erie and Ontario and consists of relatively level terrain that is about 15% wooded in disrupted sections. Forests are composed of species similar to those of the Great Lakes Plain generally. Much of the area is farmland. It covers 5050 sq mi. Elevation along the Lake Ontario shore begins at 245 ft, and along the Lake Erie shore at about 527 ft. Almost the entire subzone is under 800 ft in elevation.

Oswego Lowlands

Rolling plains of about 300 sq mi, with elevation varying from 300 to 500 ft, are typical of the Oswego Lowlands, a small lowland subzone. Lake

Ontario exerts a moderating effect conducive to agriculture. Forest types of elm and red maple exist but are not extensive. Moderately productive muck soils overlie sandstone.

Drumlins

Prominent oval, elongated drumlins, generally aligned northeast-southwest and composed of glacial deposits, cover 1100 sq mi in the subzone known as the Drumlins. The area is about 25% forested and has some farming. Elevation ranges from 300 ft near Lake Ontario to a maximum of about 800 ft above sea level at the summits of drumlins.

Eastern Ontario Plains

The Eastern Ontario Plains, a nearly level area, ranges in elevation from 250 to 500 ft. Lake Ontario moderates the climate for agriculture and dairying. Elm–red maple and northern hardwoods are the dominant forest types. The subzone covers about 756 sq mi. Soils are mostly lake sediments over limestone bedrock.

St. Lawrence Plains

The St. Lawrence Plains extends over about 858 sq mi and generally is a flat and rolling plain ranging in elevation from 250 to 400 ft. Northern hardwoods are dominant in small woodlots, often in low, swampy areas. Land abandonment has resulted in considerable shrubland, and the area possesses more hills and swamp forest with elm and red maple than does the Eastern Ontario Plains. Soils of medium productivity overlie limestone and sandstone. Higher agricultural production distinguishes this area from the transition zones to the north and east.

Malone Plain

Topography in the Malone Plain varies from flat to rolling plains. The area covers about 175 sq mi, with elevation from 400 to 1000 ft. Aspen, gray birch, and paper birch make up the principal forest type. Agriculture is quite extensive but declining as land is abandoned. Clay soils cover sandstone.

Lake Champlain Valley

A lowland that covers about 288 sq mi, the Lake Champlain Valley contains natural forests of white pine, northern hardwoods, and pioneer species. Elevation ranges from 100 to 700 ft. Gentle relief and a rather mild climate owing to its proximity to Lake Champlain are characteristic, with farming prominent. It is bounded on the west and south by the Precambrian Shield and has clay soils derived from sediments of glacial lakes.

Indian River Lakes

Encompassed by the St. Lawrence Plains and Eastern Ontario Plains, the Indian River Lakes ecozone, a lowland of 241 sq mi, consists primarily of rolling hills and granite outcrops ranging in elevation from 350 to 500 ft. Precambrian granite and intruding Potsdam sedimentary sandstones underlie the shallow, poorly drained soils. Forests are a transition between northern hardwoods and oak-hickory of more southern affinity. Glacial lakes, outcrops, and rough terrain prevail in an area of chiefly recreational use.

Black River Valley

A largely agricultural area with some woodlots of northern hardwoods, the Black River Valley occupies about 350 sq mi and has an average elevation of about 1000 ft. It lies between two large second-growth forest regions and old fields, with the higher Tug Hill Plateau to the west, the Precambrian Shield on the east, the divide between the Mohawk and Black River drainages on the south, and the escarpment of the Tug Hill Plateau and margin of the flat Eastern Ontario Plains on the north. Rich loam soils cover the limestone bedrock.

Oneida Lake Plain

The Oneida Lake Plain surrounds Oneida Lake but is not named on the ecozone map. It is a largely flat plain, with elevation from 300 to 600 ft and occupying about 308 sq mi. Farming is widespread. Forests are mainly elm and red maple with swamps prominent. Northern hardwoods occur in small woodlots on the higher portions. Highly productive soils cover the sandstone and limestone bedrock. Oneida Lake helps moderate the climate.

Mohawk Valley

The Mohawk Valley, a zone of over 1840 sq mi, is characterized by a valley of variable terrain with soft sedimentary rock overlaid by glacial till. Rolling plains with gentle slopes and low local relief occur, as well as some hills with moderate slopes and higher relief. Elevation is from 500 ft to over 1700 ft. The narrow inner river valley has elevations 1000 ft below the country to the north and south. This zone generally has cooler temperature than the Great Lakes Plain. Northern hardwoods and associated species predominate, with hemlock stands in some ravines, white pine and cedar in a few swamps, and oaks on the shale slopes. Forested areas are mostly on farms and occupy less than 20% of the land. Manufacturing industries, intensive dairy farming, and a variety of crop farms are major uses of land in this area.

Hudson Valley

Rolling plains and hills bound the Hudson Valley, a 2890 sq mi depression interlaced with long, narrow stream bottomlands. Most elevations are below 500 ft and near sea level to the south. Hills and terraces overlie highly folded sedimentary rock. Hills exceeding 1000 ft above sea level rise toward the south. The climate is relatively mild. The vegetation is oak–northern hardwoods and white pine, and the Albany sand plains support pitch pines and scrub oaks. Oaks are common on south slopes, and red cedar in abandoned fields. In many places, up to 50% of the land is wooded. Several types of agriculture are practiced, there are major transportation centers, and population density is high, particularly in the north.

Central Hudson

The Central Hudson subzone, 2190 sq mi in area, is generally flat to rolling land below 500 ft but with a number of hilltops reaching over 1000 ft. Northern and pioneer hardwoods are the most extensive forest types, with some white pine and red cedar. There is a mixture of industry, residential centers, and a variety of farms in the area.

Triassic Lowlands

A small 120 sq mi zone of low relief and gently rolling plains, the Triassic Lowlands includes, on the east of the Palisades, a large igneous escarpment adjacent to the Hudson River. Soils of glacial till are deep and loamy from the underlying sandstone, limestone, and shale, with intervening lava flows protruding in some places. About 75% of the land is covered by oak–northern hardwoods forest, despite the acceleration of residential and commercial development. Climate is warm and humid in summer and mild and wet in winter. At the base of the Palisades, elevation is near sea level, but most of the area is above 200 ft, with maximum local elevation about 600 ft.

Coastal Lowlands

The Coastal Lowlands ecozone, a part of the Atlantic Coastal Plain, has very low relief, mostly below 200 ft but reaching a maximum of 400 ft. It totals 1330 sq mi. Covered by glacial drift, it is underlain by sands and clays. The climate is moderated by the ocean. Because of poor soils, scrub oaks dominate the zone, with pitch pine, the main conifer, often in the mixture. In addition, tulip tree, sweet birch, sugar and red maples, and elm occur. Much of the vegetation of the zone, as well as farmland, is being lost by rapid urban and suburban expansion, although this development is less pronounced toward the eastern parts of Long Island.

Highlands and Transitions

The highlands and transitions are composed of mountains and hills (highlands), as well as ecozones between cleared land and forest (transitions) typically having gently rolling plains and low hills.

Appalachian Plateau

A 16,770 sq mi zone, the Appalachian Plateau is mainly hill country with deeply dissected valleys, but it retains a plateau aspect, with more or less flat-topped hills and with a skyline about 2000 ft. Elevation ranges from 500 ft near the Hudson Valley to over 4000 ft in the Catskills. Water erosion largely determined the topography, with glaciers later modifying it. Escarpments exist in some places. Most of the plateau has cold, snowy winters and cool, wet summers. Northern hardwoods cover much of the zone, with oaks abundant, especially on south-facing slopes. Beech, sugar maple, basswood, white ash, and black cherry predominate; red oak is the most frequent where oaks occur. Hemlock and white pine are also found, along with many plantations of spruce and pine. About one-third of the total area is forested. Land abandonment is widespread as farming decreases.

There are 10 subzones in this largest physiographic area of the state. These are described below, generally from west to east and ending at the western edge of the Shawangunk Hills of the Hudson Valley zone.

Cattaraugus Highlands

With the exception of the valleys along the boundary with the Great Lakes Plain, the Cattaraugus Highlands subzone ranges in elevation from 1000 to 1800 ft, with a few altitudes in the southeast exceeding 2000 ft. Covering 2410 sq mi, and about 30% wooded, northern hardwoods predominate, with oaks frequently found on the south slopes. Deep valleys dissect the rather flat-topped uplands. Agricultural activity is primarily dairying.

Allegany Hills

The average town in the Allegany Hills is two-thirds wooded, with northern hardwoods covering the ridges and with more oaks on the south slopes than farther to the north. Allegany State Park covers much of this area, which totals 750 sq mi. Elevation ranges from 1400 to above 2400 ft. This subzone contains one of the very few areas in the state that was not glaciated. There is less land in agriculture than in the subzones to the north and west.

Central Appalachians

Most of the Central Appalachians, the largest subzone, lies above 1500 ft and has a few heights reaching 2300 ft and more. It encompasses 8830 sq mi. The economy is dominated by several large urban industrial areas, with the average town 36% wooded with mixtures of hardwoods, hemlocks in the ravines, and oaks on the south slopes. Agriculture is predominant in areas outside of urban communities, with much of the woodland on farms.

Finger Lakes Highlands

The Finger Lakes Highlands subzone possesses relatively level uplands dissected by deep valleys. It extends over about 1220 sq mi. Oak forests are most widespread, but there are sections of pure northern hardwoods, hemlock–northern hardwoods, and white pine. About 27% wooded, this subzone has agricultural activity of several kinds on the hills, slopes, and in the valleys. Except for the deeper valleys, elevation ranges generally from 1000 to 1700 ft, with a few points over 2000 ft.

Delaware Hills

Extensive, solid blocks of woodlands characterize the Delaware Hills, a subzone of about 670 sq mi. Forests are mainly young, even-aged hardwoods of sugar maple, white ash, black cherry, and basswood, often with hemlock. Dairying predominates. Elevation is quite variable, ranging from a minimum of 900 ft to some peak elevations up to 3000 ft.

Schoharie Hills

The Schoharie Hills subzone, covering 750 sq mi, is characterized by rolling uplands cut by deep ravines. The area is 47% wooded by oak, pine, hemlock, and northern hardwoods. Minimum altitude is 900 ft, most elevations are above 2000 ft, and some peaks reach 4000 ft. Dairy farming is the principal activity in the area.

Helderberg Highlands

Flat hilltops intermixed with steep valleys occur throughout the Helderberg Highlands, a rather small subzone of about 520 sq mi. About one-third of the land is woodland, which in many places follows the steep, shallow-soil valleys; higher lands are often in fields or shrubs. Oak and pine are found on the slopes, with mixtures of northern hardwoods elsewhere. Dairy farming is common. Elevation in the subzone, except for the lower east edge bordering the Hudson Valley, ranges from 900 to 1600 ft, although there are a few higher peaks, including one near 2100 ft.

Catskill Peaks

A rugged area of 630 sq mi dominated by erosion-resistant sandstones and few valleys and streams, the Catskill Peaks subzone is about 90% forested, mainly with northern hardwoods and some spruce and fir. Recreation and forestry are prominent, along with a few farms. In the eastern portion along the Hudson Valley zone, altitudes begin at about 500 ft. In the western part of this subzone, however, elevations are generally over 2000 ft, with many peaks topping 3000 ft, and with the highest 4200 ft. Climate is generally cool and winters severe.

Neversink Highlands

The Neversink Highlands subzone contains numerous well-known Catskills resorts. The average town is 55% wooded, primarily with northern hardwoods, black cherry, and ash but with hemlock and white pine in the ravines. Some farming contributes to the economy. The area covers about 620 sq mi, with elevation starting at 600 ft. Most of the highlands are over 1200 ft; maximum local height ranges from 1500 to 2000 ft, and a few peaks exceed this. Relief is low compared with subzones to the north.

Mongaup Hills

Relief in the Mongaup Hills subzone, an area of 370 sq mi, is quite low except in the steep southern ravines. Minimum elevation is 600 ft, but most of the area is above 1000 ft with a few heights reaching 1600 ft. The average town is 81% wooded, with mixtures of oak and red maple on the original oak-chestnut sites and with hemlock and white pine in pure stands or in mixture with hardwoods. Isolated by mountains and the Delaware Valley, and with poor soil conditions precluding extensive agricultural activities, this subzone has large amounts of land that are held for recreational purposes.

Hudson Valley

Shawangunk Hills

A part of the Hudson Valley zone, the Shawangunk Hills subzone is about 90% wooded, with generally high local relief ranging from 400 to 2289 ft. The area covers only 130 sq mi. Oaks are abundant on upper slopes and ridge tops, and tulip tree, white ash, hard maple, and hemlock, mixed with oak, occur on the lower slopes and better sites.

Manhattan Hills

Covering 500 sq mi, with elevation ranging from near sea level close to the Hudson River to over 700 ft on many hilltops, the Manhattan Hills ecozone has mild wet winters and warm humid summers. Oak and oak–northern hardwoods predominate, with pioneer trees most common as in the Hudson Highlands. Despite much recent residential and industrial development, all towns remain more than 50% wooded. The country is rolling; there are many rock exposures; and soils vary in type and depth.

Hudson Highlands

The Hudson Highlands ecozone covers 520 sq mi, and the highlands themselves are steep, rough, and stony from water erosion. Underlying igneous and metamorphic rocks are complex, with many folds and faults. Soils are shallow and acid. Elevation ranges from 200 ft to a peak of 1600 ft, with much of the zone over 700 ft; maximum local elevations are near 1000 ft, but many are as high as 1400 ft. Oak is the natural vegetation, with northern hardwoods much less abundant. About 75% of the land is forested; industrialization has spread to many small communities; and there is considerable demand for homes by commuters.

Taconic Highlands

Terrain in the Taconic Highlands, a zone 1448 sq mi, is rolling near the Hudson Valley and hillier toward the eastern border of the state. Geologically it is a very complex area, with intensely folded and faulted rocks covered with acid till. Woodlands on good soils contain white ash, tulip tree, basswood, sugar maple, black cherry, hemlock, white pine, and red oak. Those on the poorer, shallower soils are scrubby pioneer forests with gray birch, black birch, maple, and red cedar. The northern part of this zone contains successional-growth northern hardwoods, oak, and hickory, with large areas of shrubland. Elevation starts at 400 ft in the west and gradually trends higher to about 2000 ft along the Massachusetts state line.

Maximum height reaches about 2800 ft. Agriculture is the chief land use in this ecozone.

Taconic Foothills

A 40% wooded area of rolling terrain, the Taconic Foothills subzone contains forests that range from scrub pioneer types to old-growth stands of oaks and other hardwoods of a variety of species. It covers an area of 1511 sq mi, and elevation ranges from 400 to 1200 ft on many hilltops on the east. Agriculture, the main occupation, has decreased, and abandoned farmlanid is now old fields and woodlands in various stages of succession.

Rensselaer Hills

Over 67% of the Rensselaer Hills, a subzone of 180 sq mi, is wooded, with spruce and balsam fir common. Elevation begins at 700 ft, but most of the varied landscape is well above 1000 ft. Some hilltops reach 1900 ft. Predominately stony soils of low agricultural value have led to a considerable decrease in farming.

Taconic Mountains

The Taconic Mountains subzone is a very small area of 130 sq mi in two sections, with rock outcrops and shallow soils of low agricultural quality covering 67% of it. Extensive forests of northern hardwoods are mixed with white birch and oak; spruce and fir occur at higher altitudes. Elevation starts near 1000 ft, with peaks averaging over 1900 ft and the highest reaching 2798 ft.

Tug Hill Plateau

The Tug Hill Plateau is an outlier of the Appalachian Plateau. It comprises the hilly Tug Hill Transition and the largely flat and undulating Central Tug Hill and descends to lowlands on all sides.

Tug Hill Transition

The forest type in the low hills of the Tug Hill Transition is mainly northern hardwoods, with hemlock in the western section. Elevation ranges between 1000 and 1700 ft. Soils are of low productivity over Hudson River shale. Marginal dairy farms are located mostly in the southern part, and many have been abandoned. Pioneer species and the introduction of the state reforestation softwood plantations have replaced many farms in this ecozone of 1113 sq mi.

Central Tug Hill

Poorly drained soils are the reason for the large area of wetlands in Central Tug Hill, a zone covering 299 sq mi. It is mainly flat and rolling terrain, with elevation ranging from 1500 to 1900 ft. Large accumulations of snow occur on this isolated plateau from moisture-laden air of Lake Ontario. Dense forests of cut-over northern hardwoods, spruce, and fir are to be found. Severe climate and poor soils have prevented agricultural development, and much privately owned land is used for logging and outdoor recreation.

St. Lawrence Transition

About 463 sq mi in area and averaging elevations of 400 ft, the St. Lawrence Transition has soil of low to medium productivity, with a resulting decrease in farming and increase in state ownership. The area is 65% wooded, mainly with aspen, birch, and shrubland.

Champlain Transition

Lower elevations and gentle topography combined with good soil productivity make the Champlain Transition attractive for agriculture. It occupies about 268 sq mi, with elevation ranging from 300 to 1200 ft and averaging 700 ft. Forests consist primarily of aspen, birch, and northern hardwoods with some white pine, red spruce, and balsam fir. The greater amount of land used for agriculture here contrasts with eco-zones to the west and south, where much land has reverted to second-growth forest.

Western Adirondack Transition

Poor soils over Precambrian bedrock, rougher topography, and more severe climate than in the other transition areas characterize the Western Adirondack Transition. A mixture of old fields, successional forests, and farms occurs in this northern area of 1237 sq mi.

Eastern Adirondack Transition

The rolling plains of the Eastern Adirondack Transition have a more significant proportion of oak and a higher human population density than do the other transition areas. There is a high degree of land abandonment and many former agricultural clearings. The zone covers about 342 sq mi, with elevation ranging from 300 to 2000 ft and averaging 700 ft. The bedrock of granites, sandstones, limestones, and acid glacial till is covered by soils of medium to low productivity.

Western Adirondack Foothills

A large area of 3392 sq mi, the Western Adirondack Foothills ecozone is physically similar to the Central Adirondacks and Eastern Adirondack Foothills, but topography is gentler here. Average elevation is 1500 ft. Climax forest types are spruce, balsam fir, and northern hardwoods occupying, with shrubland, 85% of the area. Wetlands are characteristic of the floodplains adjacent to many rivers and streams. Logging here has created more variety in forest composition than in any other forest zone. Paper companies, hunting clubs, and large private estates own much of the land. Human settlement is rather low, but density is double that of the Central Adirondacks.

Eastern Adirondack Foothills

Hills and rounded mountains cover some 1538 sq mi of the Eastern Adirondack Foothills, with elevations ranging from 500 to 3000 ft and averaging 1400 ft. White pine, oak, and northern hardwoods typify woodlands. The abrupt eastern margin of the Precambrian Shield marks a change in typical vegetation from the spruce-fir to the west, and the area possesses a somewhat milder climate than the Western Adirondack Foothills. The zone lacks agriculture.

Sable Highlands

An isolated ecozone in the Western Adirondack Foothills, the Sable Highlands region consists of hills and rounded mountains covered by pioneer spruce, balsam fir, and northern hardwoods. About half of the land is state-owned. The area is about 277 sq mi, with elevation ranging from 1300 to 3400 ft and averaging 2000 ft. Topography and poor soils have determined land use, which is largely recreational.

Central Adirondacks

The Central Adirondacks ecozone, a large area of 3198 sq mi, is composed of hills and rounded mountains ranging from 1300 to 4000 ft. Spruce, balsam fir, and northern hardwoods are the main forest components. More than 75% of the land is State Forest Preserve; this fact largely determines land use and human population density. The eastern boundary represents the separation of the spruce-fir associations of this zone from the white pine of the Eastern Adirondack Foothills.

1. Boundaries of regions used for summaries of observations reported in *The Kingbird*. The boundaries are based on written descriptions printed in *The Kingbird*, vol. 43, no. 1, p. 37 (1993). Prepared by D. Ogurcak and J. Weber, NY Gap Analysis Project, a cooperative effort of the Department of Natural Resources, Institute for Resource Information Systems, and NY Cooperative Fish and Wildlife Research Unit, Cornell University, Ithaca, NY

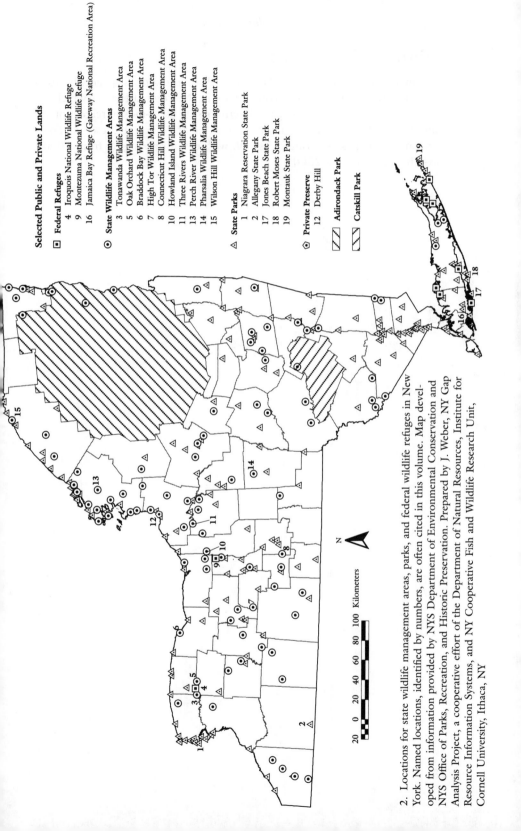

Selected Public and Private Lands

☐ **Federal Refuges**
  4 Iroquois National Wildlife Refuge
  9 Montezuma National Wildlife Refuge
  16 Jamaica Bay Refuge (Gateway National Recreation Area)

⊙ **State Wildlife Management Areas**
  3 Tonawanda Wildlife Management Area
  5 Oak Orchard Wildlife Management Area
  6 Braddock Bay Wildlife Management Area
  7 High Tor Wildlife Management Area
  8 Connecticut Hill Wildlife Management Area
  10 Howland Island Wildlife Management Area
  11 Three Rivers Wildlife Management Area
  13 Perch River Wildlife Management Area
  14 Pharsalia Wildlife Management Area
  15 Wilson Hill Wildlife Management Area

△ **State Parks**
  1 Niagara Reservation State Park
  2 Allegany State Park
  17 Jones Beach State Park
  18 Robert Moses State Park
  19 Montauk State Park

⊙ **Private Preserve**
  12 Derby Hill

▨ **Adirondack Park**

▨ **Catskill Park**

2. Locations for state wildlife management areas, parks, and federal wildlife refuges in New York. Named locations, identified by numbers, are often cited in this volume. Map developed from information provided by NYS Department of Environmental Conservation and NYS Office of Parks, Recreation, and Historic Preservation. Prepared by J. Weber, NY Gap Analysis Project, a cooperative effort of the Department of Natural Resources, Institute for Resource Information Systems, and NY Cooperative Fish and Wildlife Research Unit, Cornell University, Ithaca, NY

Adirondack High Peaks

Climax forest in the Adirondack High Peaks ecozone is spruce, balsam fir, and northern hardwoods. Topography in this rugged terrain, which includes the alpine biome, largely determines its use—mostly recreational. About 90% of the total area is included in the State Forest Preserve. The ecozone encompasses about 785 sq mi, with elevation ranging from 1000 to 5344 ft and averaging 2500 ft.

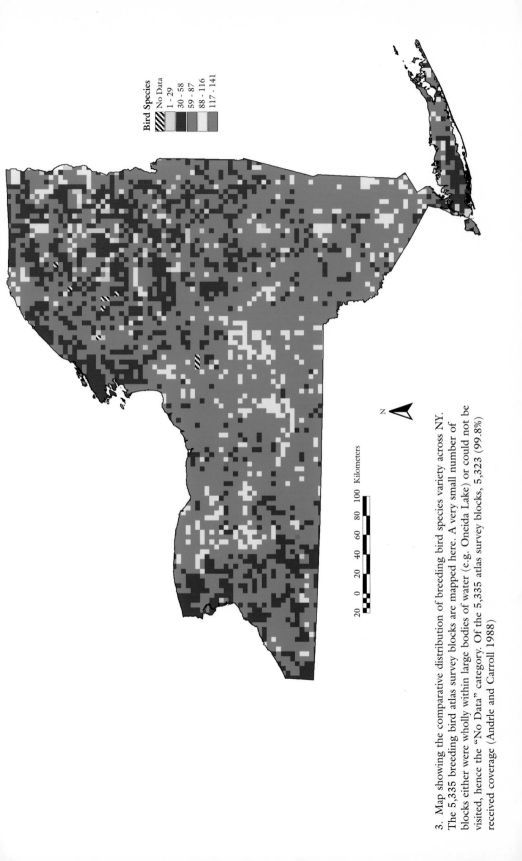

Bird Species

- No Data
- 1 - 29
- 30 - 58
- 59 - 87
- 88 - 116
- 117 - 141

20 0   20 40 60 80 100 Kilometers

N

3. Map showing the comparative distribution of breeding bird species variety across NY. The 5,335 breeding bird atlas survey blocks are mapped here. A very small number of blocks either were wholly within large bodies of water (e.g. Oneida Lake) or could not be visited, hence the "No Data" category. Of the 5,335 atlas survey blocks, 5,323 (99.8%) received coverage (Andrle and Carroll 1988)

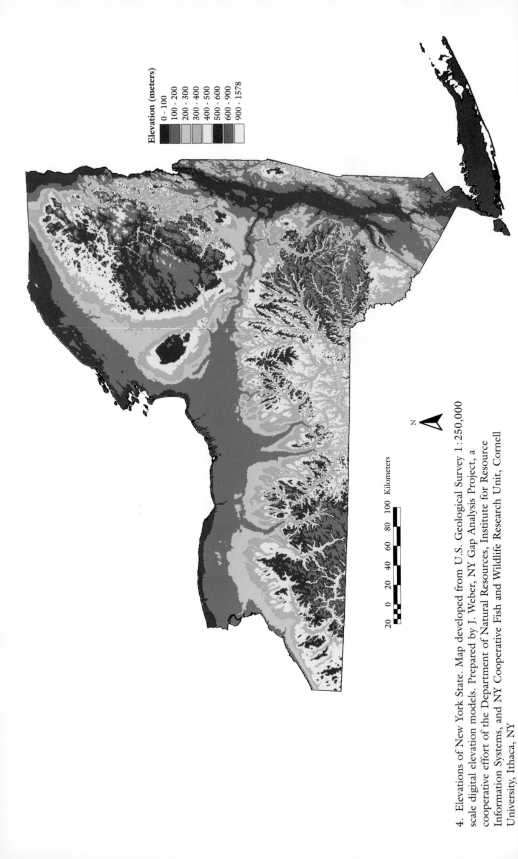

Elevation (meters)

0 - 100
100 - 200
200 - 300
300 - 400
400 - 500
500 - 600
600 - 900
900 - 1578

20 0 20 40 60 80 100 Kilometers

N

4. Elevations of New York State. Map developed from U.S. Geological Survey 1:250,000 scale digital elevation models. Prepared by J. Weber, NY Gap Analysis Project, a cooperative effort of the Department of Natural Resources, Institute for Resource Information Systems, and NY Cooperative Fish and Wildlife Research Unit, Cornell University, Ithaca, NY

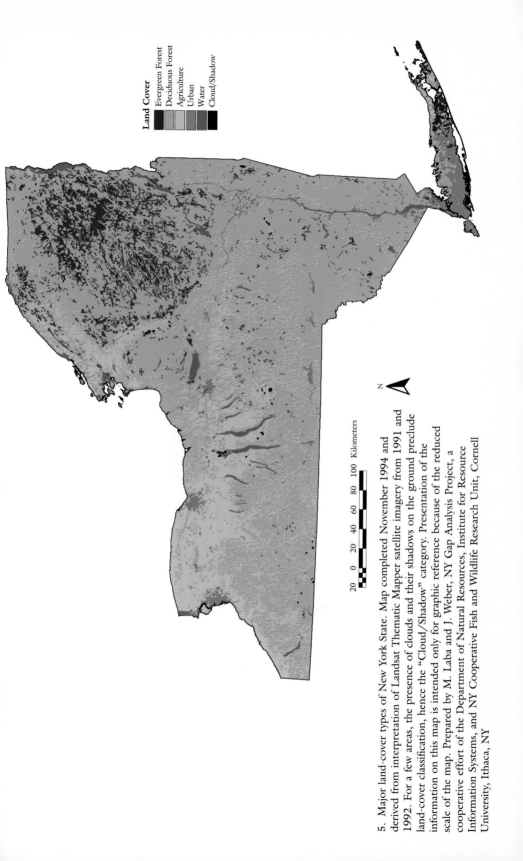

Land Cover

- Evergreen Forest
- Deciduous Forest
- Agriculture
- Urban
- Water
- Cloud/Shadow

20 0 20 40 60 80 100 Kilometers

N

5. Major land-cover types of New York State. Map completed November 1994 and derived from interpretation of Landsat Thematic Mapper satellite imagery from 1991 and 1992. For a few areas, the presence of clouds and their shadows on the ground preclude land-cover classification, hence the "Cloud/Shadow" category. Presentation of the information on this map is intended only for graphic reference because of the reduced scale of the map. Prepared by M. Laba and J. Weber, NY Gap Analysis Project, a cooperative effort of the Department of Natural Resources, Institute for Resource Information Systems, and NY Cooperative Fish and Wildlife Research Unit, Cornell University, Ithaca, NY

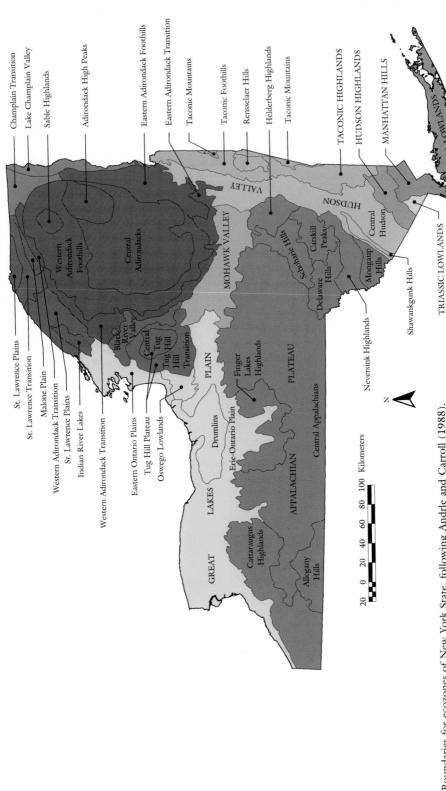

6. Boundaries for ecozones of New York State, following Andrle and Carroll (1988).
Prepared by J. Weber, NY

Gap Analysis Project, a cooperative effort of the Department of Natural Resources,
Institute for Resource Information Systems, and NY Cooperative Fish and Wildlife
Research Unit, Cornell University, Ithaca, NY

Bird Habitats in New York State

Charles R. Smith and Shari K. Gregory

Department of Natural Resources
Cornell University

I n its simplest form, habitat is where an animal lives. In suitable habitat, an animal is able to survive and find its basic needs for food, water, and shelter met in sufficient quantity and quality to allow successful reproduction and perpetuation of the species. Numbers of individuals in an area can be considered one measure of habitat quality, because numbers effectively reflect the response of a species population to the combination of environmental factors it requires for survival and reproduction (Whittaker et al. 1973). More specifically, "good" habitat can be characterized by a higher density (i.e., numbers per unit area of habitat) of individuals of species requiring that habitat, and "poor" habitat can be expected to have lower densities of individuals, all other variables being equal. But there are a lot of options for habitat use along this long continuum from good to poor habitat. High population densities can be expected in habitats that are less than optimal, even marginal, when crowding has forced species to move out of more desirable locations (O'Connor 1981). For highly mobile animals such as birds, establishing an accurate, consistently applicable definition of species-specific, "suitable" habitat can be challenging. Migratory songbirds that travel long distances, the typical "Neotropical migrants," may span the Western Hemisphere during their migrations and occupy very different habitats during the breeding season, the nonbreeding season, and at stopover locations along their migratory pathways. For the sake of simplicity, in this chapter we will undertake to characterize only bird habitats used for breeding, with occasional exceptions.

A prevailing theme of twentieth-century bird conservation has been a focus on preservation and management for rare species, one legacy from the mandates of the federal Endangered Species Act. As we look toward the twenty-first century, however, it is becoming increasingly clear that the "fine-filter," species-focused approach to conservation of biodiversity will have to be supplemented and complemented by a "coarse-filter" approach (Hunter 1990) aimed at conserving intact plant communities and the habitats they provide for assemblages of birds and other species. This shift in conservation paradigms is occurring for both ecological and economic reasons. Compared with some inventory and monitoring efforts, the costs of endangered species conservation, especially captive propagation efforts, can be substantial. The coarse-filter approach, exemplified best by the work of the Nature Conservancy (TNC), now is being expanded to landscape-scale biodiversity mapping efforts such as the national gap analysis program (Scott et al. 1993) to develop conservation plans and monitoring protocols that encompass tens of thousands of acres (Kiester et al. 1996). The approach of gap analysis, coordinated in New York State by the senior author of this chapter, relies on new interpretations of habitats and applications of advanced technologies, including computer-assisted geographic information systems (GIS), complemented by interpretations of images of the earth's surface obtained from satellites orbiting hundreds of miles in space.

Those of us who study North American birds have been beneficiaries of a generally accepted, hierarchical, standardized system of English and scientific names, maintained for more than 100 years by the Committee on Nomenclature of the American Ornithologists' Union. A generally agreed upon "taxonomy" of plant communities, identified by plant ecologists and other professionals, using standardized methods, also is an important element of any plan for conservation of plant communities and the birds and other wildlife that depend on those communities. Before we can begin to conserve bird habitats, it is necessary to have a shared vocabulary of names that communicate something about the structure and species composition typical of the plant communities that define those habitats accurately. With such a shared vocabulary and system of names, communication can be effective and efficient, and the potential for ambiguity and confusion can be reduced. Just as the name Northern Cardinal conjures up a clear mental image of that species to someone who knows birds, so also should a descriptive name applied to a habitat or plant community convey a clear image of that vegetation to those interested in habitat conservation. In New York we are fortunate to have an encyclopedia for the ecological communities of the state published by the New York State Department of Environmental Conservation (NYSDEC) (Reschke 1990) as a result of the detailed and careful work of our New York Natural Heritage Program, a cooperative effort of NYSDEC and TNC. It is the associations of plants and animals in those ecological communities that provide habitats for birds. We also are fortunate to have an emerging national standard, proposed by the Federal Geographic Data Committee (FGDC) in June 1996, based largely on the classification scheme for plant communities developed by TNC. To the extent possible in this chapter, we will follow the nomenclature and structure currently recommended by the FGDC and TNC's Natural Heritage Network.

A Historical Perspective on Habitat Change

In assessing historical changes in habitats, one first must decide when to begin. With a knowledge of the glacial history of New York, we easily can assert that there have been dramatic changes in landscapes and plant and animal communities since the last glaciers retreated, some 10,000 years ago. There even is convincing evidence that fragments of true prairie communities, a postglacial "prairie peninsula," extended well into western New York (Schmidt 1938). One of the earliest European explorers of the St. Lawrence and Great Lakes regions, Robert de Cavelier de La Salle, reported circa 1675 lakeshore landscapes "so free from forests and so full of meadows" with "wild cattle which, instead of hair, have a very fine wool" (Muhlstein 1994). La Salle's "wild cattle" most likely represented relict populations of American bison *(Bos bison)*, inhabiting remnant fragments of the postglacial, eastern prairie peninsula, documented by Schmidt (1938) and others.

But when the first Western European settlers arrived in New York, they confronted a landscape dominated by forests (Thompson and Smith 1970; Marks et al. 1992). Though sizable forest openings existed, they had resulted from beaver *(Castor canadensis)* activities, fires, severe wind storms, floods, defoliation by insects, and use by Native Americans. From his travels throughout the Northeast, John James Audubon described in his journals observations of forests damaged extensively by tornadoes and by outbreaks of fire and insects (Audubon 1834), resulting in creation of substantial openings and opportunities for responses by plants and animals to successional changes, which occur predictably in the wake of such natural disturbances. Early observers also reported that Native Americans used fire to create openings for planting crops and to drive game for hunting (Thompson and Smith 1970). Now-extinct species such as Passenger Pigeon, dependent in part on acorns and other mast from extensive old-growth forests (Haney and Schaadt 1996), were frequently observed in New York and were hunted vigorously (Bartram 1751). Species that required shrublands and open lands, however, most likely were rare on the presettlement landscape, taking advantage of ephemeral habitats that persisted for short periods after disturbances from beaver, fire, flood, defoliation by insects, or other events. For example, both Audubon and Wilson are reported to have commented on the rarity of Chestnut-sided Warbler, a species typical of successional shrublands that now is relatively common throughout its breeding range (Chapman 1917).

The wave of Western European settlement, beginning in the late 1600s, brought dramatic changes to the New York landscape, affecting large areas in a relatively short period of time. Between 1700 and 1900, approximately 75% of New York's land area was deforested, with deforestation reaching 85% or more for some counties, as land was cleared for settlement and agriculture (Caslick 1975). Dickerman (1987) concluded that, in the wake of

31

extensive cutting of eastern white pine and hemlock forests, a distinctive northeastern subspecies of Red Crossbill *(Loxia curvirostra neogaea)* also disappeared from the Northeast, although he cited some evidence of a return of the subspecies to its former range as forest regeneration has proceeded through the twentieth century. And, although Passenger Pigeon and Heath Hen were lost to settlement, other birds, such as Upland Sandpiper, Horned Lark, Chestnut-sided Warbler, and grassland sparrows may have moved into our region, and their populations most likely increased for a period of time following settlement.

During the twentieth century, a prevalent pattern of landscape change in New York and most of the Northeast has been one of increasing forested acreage following a decline in agricultural activities (Stanton and Bills 1996). The most recent information available and reported by the U.S. Forest Service (Alerich and Drake 1995) indicates that New York State in 1993 was 62% forested land, with 14% of the state land area of 30 million acres in cropland, 4% in pasture, and the balance (20%) assigned to other categories of land cover, including suburban and urban development. This has been a significant change in land cover in the twentieth century, perhaps comparable, with respect to land area affected and changes in habitat structure, to the clearing of land for settlement and agriculture occurring between the end of the Revolutionary War and the close of the nineteenth century. In 1880, an estimated 23.8 million acres, nearly 80% of the state land area, was in farms (Stanton and Bills 1996). The movement of at least one species, the Horned Lark, into New York in the wake of widespread agricultural development is well documented (see species account). Other grassland species most likely followed or accompanied the Horned Lark and may today still be more common in New York and the Northeast than they were in presettlement times.

Although generally poorly documented, the postsettlement changes in some distinctive habitat types have been estimated by Noss and colleagues (1996) largely on the basis of the work of Reschke (1993) and others. The plant communities most dramatically affected have been those that occupied relatively small land areas in the first place or that occurred in areas with the longest histories of settlement and development, such as Long Island. Although local reductions in numbers of specialist species, such as grassland birds, probably occurred with loss of patches of prairie grassland such as the Hempstead Plains, only one species, the Passenger Pigeon (Haney and Schaadt 1996), and two subspecies, the Heath Hen and the northeastern form of Red Crossbill described above, can be associated clearly with loss of grassland and forested habitats in New York. Statewide reductions in numbers for many species of forest birds, such as Pileated Woodpecker, Common Raven, and some raptors, probably occurred, but there also most likely were gains in numbers of species associated with agricultural open lands and successional shrublands that proliferated after some agricultural lands were abandoned.

The Significance of Succession

When agricultural lands are abandoned, or forest regeneration begins after clear-cutting, fire, disease, insect defoliations, severe wind storms, or other disturbances, a somewhat predictable series of changes in vegetation and associated species of animals occurs. This well-documented sequence of change is called ecological succession. In upstate New York a successional series of vegetation communities following abandonment of an upland farm might proceed from pasture to an old-field community, dominated by grasses, goldenrods, and asters; to a mixed shrubland community, including viburnums and dogwoods; to a deciduous sapling community, including ashes, maples, and possibly, white pines (depending upon seed sources); and eventually to a mature northern hardwoods forest. The time period required may be on the order of 50–80 years, depending on soil fertility, drainage, and other site conditions. Studies in second-growth Allegheny northern hardwoods forest communities of the central Southern Tier region of New York showed that a species composition qualitatively similar to that of the presettlement regional forest can be regained in less than 50 years (Fain et al. 1994). The studies followed a silvicultural treatment that reduced forest basal areas by one-third in 1935. A different assemblage of breeding birds can be associated with each type of vegetative community along the successional continuum, with some species gained and others lost, as a site progresses from one plant community to another over decades (Keller 1982). Indeed, within the first five years after clear-cutting of forest, both the highest densities of birds and the greatest varieties of birds can be observed as forest regeneration begins (Keller 1980). It is the process of ecological succession that has led to reforestation of significant acreages of New York State, in the wake of abandonment of farmland in the period following the Great Depression. And, because not all lands began to revert to forest at the same time, and not all sites proceed from abandonment to forest at the same rates, the result is a complex mosaic, a patchwork, of plant and animal communities across the landscape (Keller and Smith 1983).

Succession is a natural ecological process, not necessarily a "threat," as some have asserted in the context of the Important Bird Areas (IBA) project of the National Audubon Society. As plant communities change over large areas of the Northeast, some species, such as Golden-winged Warbler, Eastern Towhee, and grassland birds, can be expected to be lost or reduced in abundance; other species, such as forest songbirds, may increase. As already described, most of New York and the Northeast was forested prior to settlement. If not actively managed, most upland sites not committed to agricultural uses and urban or suburban development will proceed through a successional series back to forests. Forestalling succession on upland sites requires a substantial investment of time and energy to maintain open lands or shrublands instead of forests. A decision to manage for maintenance of early successional vegetation types and their associated species of birds is a long-term commitment to active management, based on ecological, economic, political, and philosophical considerations that are, it is hoped, in the context of an adaptive approach to management (Crowe 1983). Maintaining many bird species of successional habitats will require cutting of mature forests to encourage forest regeneration and ensure the presence of successional habitats on the landscape.

Creation of successional habitats for some species requiring them need not be on a grand scale. Species such as Chestnut-sided Warbler, Mourning Warbler, Common Yellowthroat, and Indigo Bunting can respond in one to two growing seasons to forest openings as small as five acres created in the midst of mature deciduous forest (pers. obs.) or to a forest opening created by loss of a single, large, dominant canopy tree due to a wind storm (J. Keller, pers. comm.). The prevalence of moderately shade-tolerant tree species, especially basswood and ash, across the presettlement landscape of the Finger Lakes region (Marks et al. 1992) suggests a regime of disturbance greater than that resulting from many modern forest management practices (Fain et al. 1994), probably creating adequate opportunities for nesting by many bird species requiring successional habitats, especially shrubby areas, in a largely forested landscape.

Vegetative Associations and New York Birds

In 1974, Bull identified broad categories of "forest habitats" and "open-country habitats" and described several general vegetation types related to the birds of New York within those categories. Included were southern hardwoods (oak-hickory), northern hardwoods (beech-birch-maple-hemlock), northern conifers (spruce-fir and larch–white cedar bogs), freshwater marshes and bogs, coastal salt marshes, and grassy fields and meadows (either cultivated or uncultivated). By comparison, from the perspective of a plant community ecologist, Reschke (1990) identified more than 200 ecological communities determined by the New York Natural Heritage Program to occur within the state. This tremendous growth in our capacity to identify and map plant communities on the landscape has resulted from the cooperative efforts of NYSDEC and TNC through the New York Natural Heritage Program and exemplifies the basis for a coarse-filter approach to conservation. Although the 200+ communities reported by Reschke are relevant to the aims and goals of plant ecologists, it is unlikely that birds are discriminating their habitats at such a level of detail. What we will do for the balance of this chapter is draw upon the work of Reschke and others to present an abbreviated list of habitat types that appear most relevant to the distributions of New York birds, especially breeding species, at this time. It is important also to be aware that this is very much a work in progress. As the gap analysis database for New York is refined and expanded in cooperation with our Natural Heritage Program and NYSDEC, additional information will become available and our insights and understanding will evolve, and the account of habitats that follows will have to be modified and updated.

The habitats described below are generally a combination of several ecological communities, as reported by Reschke (1990). These ecological communities can be distinguished botanically, but the various vegetative associations listed together are used by a common group of bird species. The list is ranked first by vegetative structure: forest, shrubland, herbaceous/open, and unvegetated. Within structure categories, the list is ranked by leaf form (deciduous, evergreen) and soil moisture (upland, wetland).

The bird species list for each habitat is not exhaustive but is intended to be somewhat representative. Similarly, only the most common or representative plant species and ecological communities are listed. Rare communities that typically lack characteristic bird assemblages (e.g., perched swamp, white oak swamp) or for which information about bird assemblages does not exist (e.g., fens) are not considered here. Ecological community names follow those described by the New York Natural Heritage Program (Reschke 1990); more-detailed descriptions of ecological communities, including extensive lists of plant species, may be found in that publication.

Forests

Mainly deciduous upland forests. Included here are a wide variety of forests predominantly with 60% deciduous tree cover and occasional inclusions of conifers. This is New York's most abundant habitat, covering almost half the state. Birds that may be found in this habitat include Sharp-shinned Hawk, Cooper's Hawk, Red-shouldered Hawk, Wild Turkey (most common with oaks), Red-bellied Woodpecker, Acadian Flycatcher, Least Flycatcher, Red-eyed Vireo, Wood Thrush, Black-throated Blue Warbler, American Redstart, Ovenbird, Scarlet Tanager, and Rose-breasted Grosbeak; where conifers are intermixed, Blue-headed Vireo and Black-throated Green Warbler may be added. Common tree species representative of this type include sugar maple, beech, green ash, white ash, basswood, white oak, red oak, black cherry, aspen, birch. The ecological communities (Reschke 1990) included in this type are maple-basswood–rich mesic forest, beech-maple mesic forest, rich mesophytic forest, pine–northern hardwoods forest, Appalachian oak-hickory forest, Allegheny oak forest, chestnut-oak forest, successional northern hardwoods, successional southern hardwoods, limestone woodlands.

Deciduous wetland and floodplain forests. These are rich forests found in low, wet areas and along the shores of lakes and rivers. Birds that may be found in this habitat include Black-crowned Night-Heron, Wood Duck, Red-bellied Woodpecker, Pileated Woodpecker, Yellow-throated Vireo, Warbling Vireo, Tufted Titmouse, and Cerulean Warbler. Common tree species included are silver maple, red maple, sycamore, cottonwood, black willow, black ash, swamp white oak, and basswood. The ecological communities (Reschke 1990) included in this type are floodplain forest, red maple–hardwood swamp, silver maple–ash swamp, and freshwater tidal swamp.

Mainly evergreen upland forests. These are predominantly conifer forests with some deciduous species included and are well distributed throughout the state. Hemlock forests are frequently in ravines or on north slopes, and forests dominated by fir and spruce occur mainly in the higher elevations of the Adirondacks and Catskills. Birds that may be found in this habitat include Wild Turkey, Pileated Woodpecker, Blue-headed Vireo, Gray Jay, Boreal Chickadee, Red-breasted Nuthatch, Golden-crowned Kinglet, Bicknell's Thrush, Swainson's Thrush, Hermit Thrush, Black-throated Green Warbler, Pine Warbler (in mature, well-spaced pines), Bay-breasted Warbler, Blackpoll Warbler, and White-throated Sparrow. Common tree species include hemlock, white pine, red pine, and paper birch. The ecological communities (Reschke 1990) included in this type are pine–northern hardwoods forest, hemlock–northern hardwoods forest, spruce–northern hardwoods forest, mountain spruce–fir forests, spruce flats, and balsam flats.

Conifer plantations. These are stands of conifers planted for cultivation and harvest, usually for timber resources. These plantations may be monocultures or mixed stands, with at least 50% of the forest canopy cover consisting of one or two of the tree species listed below. Birds that may be found in this habitat include Red-breasted Nuthatch, Golden-crowned Kinglet, Magnolia Warbler, and Yellow-rumped Warbler. Common tree species are white pine, red pine, Scotch pine, pitch pine, jack pine, Norway spruce, white spruce, balsam fir, Douglas-fir. The ecological communities (Reschke 1990) included in this type are pine plantation, spruce-fir plantation, and conifer plantation.

Pitch pine barrens. These are woodland or shrub-savanna communities on well-drained, sandy soils, dominated by tall or dwarf pitch pines. This habitat is restricted to the coastal lowlands of Long Island and lower portions of the Hudson Valley (including the Albany Pine Bush and Shawangunk Hills). Birds that may be found in this habitat include Brown Thrasher, Pine Warbler, Prairie Warbler, Ovenbird, and Eastern Towhee. Common tree species include pitch pine with black huckleberry, scrub oaks, and white oak. The ecological communities (Reschke 1990) included in this type are pitch pine–scrub oak barrens, dwarf pine plains/ridges, and pitch pine–oak–heath woodlands.

Evergreen wetland forests. This habitat includes seasonally flooded forests and permanently flooded or saturated swamps with at least 50% canopy cover of coniferous or mixed deciduous-coniferous trees, found mostly in the Adirondacks. Birds that may occur in this habitat include Olive-sided Flycatcher, Gray Jay, Boreal Chickadee, Winter Wren, Golden-crowned Kinglet, Swainson's Thrush, and White-throated Sparrow. Common tree species are red spruce, balsam fir, hemlock, green ash, black cherry, yellow birch, black spruce, and tamarack. The ecological communities (Reschke 1990) included in this type are spruce-fir swamp, black spruce–tamarack bog, hemlock-hardwoods swamp, northern white cedar swamp, and black spruce–tamarack bog.

Shrublands

Successional shrublands. This habitat includes sites that have been cleared for farming, logging, or other development and through time have revegetated to be dominated by shrubs (at least 50% cover). These habitats usually are transitional through ecological succession to forest types. Birds that may be found in this habitat include Brown Thrasher, Blue-winged Warbler, Golden-winged Warbler, Chestnut-sided Warbler, Yellow-breasted Chat, Eastern Towhee, Field Sparrow, Song Sparrow, and Indigo Bunting. Characteristic plant species are gray dogwood, eastern red cedar, hawthorn, choke cherry, arrowwood, silky dogwood, multiflora rose, serviceberry, sumac, and goldenrods. The ecological community (Reschke 1990) included in this type is successional shrubland.

Coastal shrublands. These are shrubland communities found near the sea on Long Island and exposed to salt spray. These habitats also occur in the transitional zone (ecotone) between salt-marsh and upland vegetation. Birds that may be found in this habitat include Black-crowned Night-Heron, Fish Crow, Yellow-breasted Chat, and migratory songbirds (especially in fall). Characteristic plant species are beach-plum, sand-rose, wild rose, bayberry, eastern red cedar, black cherry, shadbush, groundsel tree, saltmarsh-elder, and salt-meadow grass. The ecological communities (Reschke 1990) included in this type are maritime shrubland and salt shrub.

Shrub swamps. These shrub-dominated wetlands generally occur along lake shores, in wet depressions, or as a transitional zone (ecotone) between a marsh or bog and a swamp or upland. Birds that may be found in this habitat include American Bittern, Alder Flycatcher, Willow Flycatcher, and Lincoln's Sparrow. Characteristic plant species are smooth alder, speckled alder, red-osier dogwood, silky dogwood, willows, and buttonbush. The ecological community (Reschke 1990) included in this type is shrub swamp.

Herbaceous/Open

Grasslands, meadows, and old fields. These are meadow habitats dominated by forbs or grasses (with less than 50% shrub cover), frequently in areas that have been cleared or plowed. Some areas may be maintained by grazing, mowing, or planting, and other areas are abandoned farm fields in an early successional stage. Birds that may be found in this habitat include Northern Harrier, Killdeer, Upland Sandpiper, Sedge Wren, Grasshopper Sparrow, Henslow's Sparrow, Bobolink, Red-winged Blackbird, and Eastern Meadowlark. Characteristic plant species are timothy, orchard grass, bluegrasses, smooth brome, goldenrods, and multiflora rose. The ecological communities (Reschke 1990) included in this type are pastureland, successional old field, Hempstead Plains grassland, and sedge meadows.

Agricultural lands and croplands. These are lands that are maintained (or recently abandoned) as cropland, pastures, or hayfields. Birds that may be found in this habitat include Upland Sandpiper, Horned Lark, Vesper Sparrow, and Red-winged Blackbird. Characteristic plant species are alfalfa, corn, soybeans, potatoes, timothy, orchard grass, smooth brome, and goldenrods. The ecological communities (Reschke 1990) included in this type are pastureland, cropland/field crops, and cropland/row crops.

Urban parks and cemeteries. These are urban open areas dominated by short grass or lawn, often with some shrubs and trees. Birds that may be found in this habitat include Rock Dove, Mourning Dove, Blue Jay, American Robin, Northern Mockingbird, Northern Cardinal, House Finch, American Goldfinch, House Sparrow, and migratory songbirds (especially in spring.) Characteristic plant species are bluegrasses (lawns), maples, oaks, basswood, and willows. The ecological communities (Reschke 1990) included in this type are mowed lawn and mowed lawn with trees.

Golf courses and airports. These are expansive open areas dominated by short grass or lawn, often with some shrubs and trees. Birds that may be found in this habitat include Upland Sandpiper, gulls, American Crow, Horned Lark, Savannah Sparrow, and Grasshopper Sparrow. Characteristic plant species are bluegrasses and fescues. The ecological communities (Reschke 1990) included in this type are mowed lawn and mowed lawn with trees.

Sandy beaches and dunes along freshwater lakes. These are sparsely vegetated habitats on unstable and stable sandy shores of large freshwater lakes throughout the state. Dunes are found along the eastern shores of Lake Ontario. Birds that may be found in this habitat include Piping Plover (formerly), Spotted Sandpiper, and migratory shorebirds. Characteristic plant species are beach-pea, sea-rocket, tall wormwood, silverweed, sand dropseed, panic grass, beachgrass, red-osier dogwood, sand cherry, and cottonwood. The ecological communities (Reschke 1990) included in this type are Great Lakes dunes and sand beach.

Freshwater tidal marshes. These marsh communities occur in shallow bays, shoals, and at the mouths of tributaries of large tidal river systems (e.g., Hudson River), where the water usually is fresh and less than six feet deep at high tide. Birds that may be found in this habitat include Least Bittern, Virginia Rail, Willow Flycatcher, Marsh Wren, Yellow Warbler, Common Yellowthroat, Song Sparrow, Swamp Sparrow, Red-winged Blackbird, and American Goldfinch. Characteristic plant species include arrowleaf, blue flag, narrowleaf cattail, pickerel-weed, purple loosestrife, reedgrass, and spatterdock. The ecological community (Reschke 1990) included in this type is freshwater tidal marsh.

Freshwater lakeshores and marshes. These are seasonally inundated to permanently saturated marshes along lakes and streams. Birds that may be found in this habitat include Pied-billed Grebe, American Bittern, Least Bittern, King Rail, Virginia Rail, Marsh Wren, and Red-winged Blackbird. Characteristic plant species are bluejoint grass, reed canary grass, rice cut-grass, mannagrass, bulrushes, water plantain, sweetflag, water smartweed, smartweed, yellow pond-lily, white water-lily, cattails, bur-reed, and wild rice. The ecological communities (Reschke 1990) included in this type are shallow emergent marsh and deep emergent marsh.

Coastal shores and beaches. These are the maritime shorelines of Long Island, with sparsely vegetated sand, gravel, and cobble shores above mean high tide levels. Birds that may be found in this habitat include Piping Plover, Roseate Tern, Common Tern, and Least Tern. Characteristic plant species are beachgrass, sea-rocket, seaside atriplex, seabeach atriplex, and seaside spurge. The ecological community (Reschke 1990) included in this type is maritime beach.

Coastal dunes. These are seacoast dunes, both active and stabilized, with a mosaic of grasses, low shrubs, and unvegetated areas, reflecting past disturbances from dune migration. Birds that may be found in this habitat include Northern Harrier, Short-eared Owl, and Savannah Sparrow. Characteristic plant species are beachgrass, dusty-miller, beach pea, seaside goldenrod, and sand-rose. The ecological community (Reschke 1990) included in this type is maritime dunes.

Salt marshes. Included here are coastal marsh communities with regular or periodic flooding from tides. This habitat is found in sheltered areas along the seacoast, extending into the lower reaches of the Hudson River. Birds that may be found in this habitat include Least Bittern, American Black Duck, Black Rail, Clapper Rail, Willet, Willow Flycatcher, Marsh Wren, Yellow Warbler, Common Yellowthroat, Saltmarsh Sharp-tailed Sparrow, Seaside Sparrow, Song Sparrow, Swamp Sparrow, and Red-winged Blackbird. Characteristic plant species are salt-meadow grass, cordgrass, spikegrass, black-grass, and switchgrass. The ecological communities (Reschke 1990) included in this type are high salt marsh, low salt marsh, and brackish tidal marsh.

Sparsely Vegetated or Unvegetated Habitats

Shorelines of lakes and rivers. Included here are open freshwater lakes, ponds, rivers, and streams. Birds that may be found in this habitat include Common Loon, Pied-billed Grebe, Great Blue Heron, waterfowl, Osprey, Bald Eagle, and gulls. Characteristic plant species are spikerushes, marsh rush, bulrushes, smartweed, water lobelia, and cyperus. The ecological communities (Reschke 1990) included in this type are inland calcareous and noncalcareous lake shores, and various lake, pond, and riverine communities.

Calcareous pavement barrens. A community made up of a mosaic of shrub-savanna, grass-savanna, and rock outcrop vegetation, occurring on nearly level outcrops of calcareous bedrock (limestone and dolomite), at the eastern end of Lake Ontario (Limerick Cedars and Chaumont Barrens, both in Jefferson County). Characteristic birds include Upland Sandpiper, Loggerhead Shrike (formerly), Prairie Warbler, and Eastern Towhee. Characteristic vegetation includes eastern red cedar, northern white cedar, bur oak, gray dogwood, common juniper, poverty-grass, and a variety of foliose and fructicose lichens. The ecological community (Reschke 1990) included in this type is calcareous pavement barrens (also called "alvar" communities in other contexts.)

Cliffs. These are steep, nearly vertical rock faces with sparse to no vegetation. Birds that may be found in this habitat include Golden Eagle (formerly), Peregrine Falcon, Common Raven, Northern Rough-winged Swallow, and Cliff Swallow. Characteristic plant species are rock polypody, marginal wood fern, common hairgrass, mountain laurel, hemlock, purple cliff brake, bulblet fern, and eastern red cedar. The ecological communities (Reschke 1990) included in this type are cliff community, calcareous cliff community, and shale cliff and talus community.

Urban. These are developed areas dominated by buildings and pavement, with sparse vegetation. Birds that may be found in this habitat include Peregrine Falcon, gulls, Rock Dove, Common Nighthawk, Chimney Swift, American Robin, European Starling, House Finch, and House Sparrow. Characteristic plant species include sparsely distributed ornamental trees, lawn grasses, ornamental gardens, and invasive weeds. The ecological communities (Reschke 1990) included in this type are urban vacant lot, urban structure exterior, paved road, paved path, and landfill/dump.

Future Prospects

A century ago, a number of distinguished conservationists, with many New Yorkers among them, contributed significantly to the birth of the American conservation movement. Frank M. Chapman, George Bird Grinnell, William Hornaday, Clinton Hart Merriam, and Theodore

Roosevelt had seen dramatic declines of American bison, pronghorn *(Antilocapra americana)*, Passenger Pigeon, Heath Hen, and most shore-birds and wading birds in their lifetimes. Their work led to the creation of our system of national parks and to the passage of the Migratory Bird Treaty Act of 1918, followed by other significant legislation aimed at protection of wildlife species (Regier 1986; Mitchell 1987).

Now it is clear that similar consideration must also be extended to the habitats birds and other wildlife species require for survival and reproduction on both public and private lands. The fine-filter approach, with its focus on species, is being complemented by the coarse-filter approach of TNC to conservation of ecological communities. The work of the New York Gap Analysis Project aims to expand the coarse-filter approach to landscapes and to establishing and verifying unambiguous associations of birds and other wildlife with habitat types that can be identified and measured using satellite remote-sensing and computer technologies. Although much basic research remains to be done in this area, birders can make contributions by increasing their awareness of the kinds of habitats birds use and the terminology used to describe those habitats and by reporting associations of birds with clearly defined habitats at different times of the year. Using satellite remote sensing and a standardized taxonomy of habitats, we are likely to have a statewide system for mapping habitats and monitoring their change at the landscape scale, growing out of the New York Gap Analysis Project, by the year 2001. Such a system will set the stage for describing landscape changes over large areas and for long periods of time and will facilitate science-based bird conservation at the landscape scale across all of New York State.

ACKNOWLEDGMENTS

This summary and review has resulted from the New York Gap Analysis Project, funded by the U.S. Department of the Interior through the New York Cooperative Fish and Wildlife Research Unit in the Department of Natural Resources at Cornell University. The work of the senior author also has been supported through U.S. Department of Agriculture Hatch Project NYC-147406 and by the U.S. Forest Service. In particular, the kind cooperation of the New York Natural Heritage Program, NYSDEC, and the Cornell Institute for Resource Information Systems is gratefully acknowledged. Greg Edinger and David Hunt of the New York Natural Heritage Program read an earlier version of the manuscript and made numerous suggestions for its improvement. Ray T. Oglesby also reviewed the manuscript for historical accuracy. Most of this work would not have been possible without the generous and enthusiastic support provided by Daniel J. Decker, James P. Lassoie, and Milo E. Richmond of the Department of Natural Resources at Cornell University.

The Role of the Federation in Conservation of New York Birds: The Past Twenty Years

Charles R. Smith

Department of Natural Resources
Cornell University

To ensure understanding, perhaps we should begin with a definition of *conservation*. Throughout this chapter, the following definition will apply: "The management of human use of the biosphere so that it may yield the greatest sustainable benefit to present generations, while maintaining its potential to meet the needs and aspirations of future generations. Thus conservation is positive, embracing preservation, maintenance, sustainable utilization, restoration, and enhancement of the natural environment" (McNeely et al. 1990). Within this definition, conservation of birds includes a range of activities. Here in New York, the Federation of New York State Bird Clubs (FNYSBC) has been the leading nongovernmental organization for bird conservation efforts since 1948. No equivalent organization existed in New York before that date.

Bird conservation is not just a good idea, it is the law. The concept of legal protection for all species of migratory birds, considered "shared resources" among the United States and other countries, is embodied in the Migratory Bird Treaty Act of 1918, originally enacted between the United States and Great Britain (acting in behalf of Canada) as an implementation of the recommendations of the 1916 Convention with Great Britain for the Protection of Migratory Birds. There are now additional separate treaties including the United States, Canada, Mexico, Russia, and Japan among its signatories (Bean 1983). Russia and Japan are included because of migratory species that move among Alaska and Hawaii and those countries. All native (i.e., not introduced from other parts of the world) species of birds, even those we consider "residents" (e.g., Black-capped Chickadee), are protected under the Migratory Bird Treaty Act because some members of their populations do migrate annually, even if they just move short distances during dispersal from the territories of their parents. The lead federal agency for enforcement of the provisions of the Migratory Bird Treaty Act is the U.S. Fish and Wildlife Service (USFWS) of the Department of the Interior. Under provisions of the act, USFWS delegates certain of its management responsibilities to state agencies through cooperative agreements. In New

York, the lead agency for migratory bird conservation is the New York State Department of Environmental Conservation (NYSDEC) through its Bureau of Wildlife. A strong basis for cooperation between NYSDEC and the Federation really began to develop at the 1978 annual meeting of the Federation in Rochester, which was well attended by NYSDEC nongame and endangered species biologists, under the leadership of Eugene McCaffrey. From that beginning a number of productive partnerships between the Federation and NYSDEC have evolved.

At one end of a very long continuum are those species listed as Endangered or Threatened under state and federal statutes. We extend the greatest protection possible under our system of laws in efforts to preserve or restore those species. Over the past 20 years, the efforts of NYSDEC in behalf of Endangered and Threatened birds have been exemplary, especially with respect to birds of prey. As a result of the work of the Endangered Species Unit of NYSDEC, we all have been beneficiaries of successful efforts to reestablish Bald Eagle and Peregrine Falcon populations in New York (Nye 1996). As more and better information has become available, our state list of Endangered, Threatened, and Special Concern species has been revised and updated (see Table 1). Three species have been removed from the list entirely, and three have had their status changed for the better: one from Endangered to Threatened, two from Threatened to Special Concern. But the status of eight species has worsened—one from Threatened to Endangered, three from Special Concern to Endangered, and four from Special Concern to Threatened—and 13 species have been added. The status of the remaining 14 species has not changed.

NYSDEC, through its Nongame Species Unit, also has taken the lead in monitoring the population status of colonially nesting herons, egrets, gulls, and terns, especially on Long Island.

At the other end of the conservation continuum, state and federal laws allow the privilege of regulated "taking" of some species of migratory birds through a permit process and setting of legal seasons and bag limits for hunting of waterfowl or upland game birds such as Wild Turkey. Indeed, the Wild Turkey itself is a modern conservation success story. It had become an extirpated species in New York by the early 1900s. Now, after a statewide reintroduction effort, the Wild Turkey is seen often at bird feeders and in many rural backyards.

A Context of Increased Accountability for Wildlife Management and Conservation

The administrative context in which modern management and conservation must be done has changed dramatically over the past 20 years. There is a greater public demand for accountability, especially for state and federal

Table 1. A comparison of past and present (proposed) NYSDEC lists of species identified as either Endangered (E), Threatened (T), or of Special Concern (SC) in New York State

Species	1987 list	Proposed Revised
Common Loon	SC	SC
Pied-billed Grebe	Unlisted	T
American Bittern	Unlisted	SC
Least Bittern	SC	T
Osprey	T	SC
Bald Eagle	E*	E†
Northern Harrier	T	T
Sharp-shinned Hawk	Unlisted	SC
Cooper's Hawk	SC	SC
Northern Goshawk	Unlisted	SC
Red-shouldered Hawk	T	SC
Golden Eagle	E‡	E‡
Peregrine Falcon	E*	E*
Spruce Grouse	T	E
Black Rail	SC	E
King Rail	Unlisted	T
Piping Plover	E*†	E*†
Upland Sandpiper	SC	T
Eskimo Curlew	E*‡	E*‡
Roseate Tern	E*	E*
Common Tern	T	T
Least Tern	E	T
Black Tern	SC	E
Black Skimmer	Unlisted	SC
Barn Owl	SC	Unlisted
Short-eared Owl	SC	E
Common Nighthawk	SC	SC
Whip-poor-will	Unlisted	SC
Red-headed Woodpecker	Unlisted	SC
Loggerhead Shrike	E	E
Common Raven	SC	Unlisted
Horned Lark	Unlisted	SC
Sedge Wren	SC	T
Eastern Bluebird	SC	Unlisted
Golden-winged Warbler	Unlisted	SC
Cerulean Warbler	Unlisted	SC
Yellow-breasted Chat	Unlisted	SC
Vesper Sparrow	SC	SC
Grasshopper Sparrow	SC	SC
Henslow's Sparrow	SC	T
Seaside Sparrow	Unlisted	SC

Note: The revised list of species was not official policy as of the end of 1996. There is no federal equivalent to the Special Concern category. All but the Eskimo Curlew are listed by the Federation of New York State Bird Clubs as breeding birds in New York State.
* Species concurrently listed as Endangered by the U.S. Department of the Interior.
† Species concurrently listed as Threatened by the U.S. Department of the Interior. The Piping Plover is federally listed as Endangered for the Great Lakes region and as Threatened for the Atlantic coastal region.
‡ Species extirpated from New York State.

agencies and their employees, now than ever before. Measurable goals and objectives have to be set, reached, and assessed in order to demonstrate that progress has occurred, rather than proclaiming progress without proof. Successful conservation partnerships with state and federal agencies demand an understanding of and sensitivity to the context within which the daily activities of those agencies have to be performed.

Increasingly, modern wildlife management and bird conservation activities are taking place in the context of adaptive resource management and comprehensive planning for wildlife resources (Crowe 1983), especially for state and federal resource management agencies, in which accountability is expected for expenditures of public funds. According to Crowe (1983), such an approach characterizes the "management cycle" and requires that a series of straightforward questions be asked and associated activities performed in sequence. The first step is to determine where we are and to take stock through resource inventories and assessments of program status to answer the question "Where are we?" Next comes development of a strategic plan in which clearly measurable goals and objectives, strategies for reaching those goals and objectives, and amounts of time required are explicitly identified, answering the question "Where do we want to be?" The third step is to couple goals and objectives to priorities and budgets through development of an operational plan, addressing the question "How will we get there?" A fourth, critical step requires an evaluation of progress in the context of the strategic and operational plans—"Did we make it?" On the basis of the results of an assessment of progress at step four, the management cycle can be repeated, with modifications and development of new goals, objectives, strategies, priorities, and budgets. Unfortunately, there still are many conservation efforts, especially those of nongovernmental organizations, in which goals and objectives are not explicitly stated in measurable terms, and the evaluation step is ignored.

The Need to Monitor and Assess Distribution and Abundance of Birds

Information about geographical distributions and population status (trend or relative abundance or both) of birds during the breeding season is absolutely essential for making decisions and setting management priorities to achieve conservation of birds (C. R. Smith 1991b). Basically, one needs to answer two questions: (1) Where are birds found on the landscape during their breeding season? (2) How many of them are found there? In addition, information required to understand better the conservation needs of birds must be based on science not on supposition (C. R. Smith et al. 1993). With initiation of its Atlas project in 1979, the FNYSBC began a long-term program, in close cooperation with NYSDEC, to determine comprehensively the distributions and population status of the breeding birds of New York State. *The Atlas of Breeding Birds in New York State* (hereafter referred to as Atlas 1988) provides the geographical distribution component of the program. In 1985, in cooperation with NYSDEC, we also began to summarize and evaluate information about the population status of breeding birds, gained from the USFWS Breeding Bird Survey (BBS), to complement the distributional information provided by our Atlas project (C. R. Smith 1989).

The Atlas techniques that proved successful at the state level also have been applied at the local scale to assist the U.S. Forest Service with its monitoring and inventorying responsibilities on the Finger Lakes National Forest (C. R. Smith 1991a). Most recently, landscape imagery obtained through satellite remote-sensing techniques is being integrated with our information about distributions and abundances of breeding birds to assess bird-habitat relationships at the landscape scale across New York State's 30 million acres (Smith 1990). From the very beginning, the series of projects that make up our program in avian conservation and ecology for New York State have been based on cooperation among a variety of partners. Indeed, the success of these projects would not have been possible without such partnerships.

Breeding Bird Surveys

To answer the question How many of them are found there? and to provide the population status component of our bird conservation program, New York State has 112 U.S. Fish and Wildlife Breeding Bird Survey (BBS) Routes, covered each summer by nearly 100 volunteers, who contribute more than 500 total hours annually to the project. The BBS was begun nationally in 1965 with the purpose of obtaining annual information useful in assessing the population status of North American breeding birds. A detailed account of the history and procedures employed by the BBS can be found in Robbins et al. 1986. The BBS employs a modified transect sampling procedure along a specified 24.5 mile automobile route. Volunteer observers who are thoroughly familiar with the birds of their region travel assigned survey routes during the breeding season, beginning exactly one-half hour before local sunrise, stopping every one-half mile, observing for three minutes, and counting and recording every bird they see or hear during each three-minute period. The result is a representative sample of the breeding birds at 50 three-minute stops along the survey route, from which indices of abundance for breeding bird species can be derived. Because the BBS methodology samples an area of unknown size along each route, density estimates (i.e., estimates of the number of birds per unit of land area) cannot be derived from BBS counts.

Each volunteer observer is responsible for summarizing the observations for his or her assigned route and submitting the results to the U.S. Department of the Interior. In New York an individual observer may be responsible for one to seven survey routes, depending upon the person's expertise and enthusiasm. Each survey route requires from four to four and one-half hours in the field, followed by one to one and one-half hours to complete written reports for submission.

Since I became coordinator for the BBS in New York State in 1985, by involving our leading state bird conservation organization, the FNYSBC, fully, coverage of our BBS routes has climbed steadily, from a low of nearly 50% to recent highs of 85% or better. A key to this success has been full and explicit incorporation of the BBS into the research and monitoring agenda of the Federation, with frequent personal contact and feedback to participants, both through verbal reports of progress at annual meetings of the FNYSBC and through an annual printed newsletter to volunteers now prepared and distributed by the BBS coordinators at the Patuxent Wildlife Research Center in Laurel, Maryland.

A summary of the BBS data collected from 1966 through 1985 (C. R. Smith 1989) has been useful to NYSDEC, in combination with the Atlas data, in setting management goals and priorities for the breeding birds of the state. For example, in December 1993, Atlas information and BBS population status information figured prominently in a review and update of NYSDEC's list of species identified as Endangered, Threatened, or of Special Concern in New York State (Table 1). Several Federation members, including myself, were invited to participate in that review process. At a larger scale, BBS data from New York State also have contributed to our understanding of the population status of breeding birds in the northeastern United States (C. R. Smith et al. 1993). In October 1993, the BBS was transferred administratively to the newly formed National Biological Service (NBS). In October 1996, NBS became the Biological Resources Division of the U.S. Geological Survey, a branch of the Department of the Interior, charged by Secretary of the Interior Bruce Babbitt with the responsibility for monitoring status and trends of biological indicators of environmental health throughout the United States.

Breeding Bird Atlas

The Atlas was initiated in 1979 by FNYSBC in cooperation with NYSDEC. The Atlas project was modeled after the very successful British breeding bird atlas, first published in 1976 (Sharrock 1976) and again in 1993 (Gibbons et al. 1993). Originally conceived as a ten-year project, our Atlas concluded in 1988, with publication of *The Atlas of Breeding Birds in New York State*. With the careful leadership of Gordon M. Meade, Richard

Sloss, Robert Andrle, Janet Carroll, and a management team of additional Federation members, the project concluded six months ahead of schedule and approximately $5000 under budget.

Funding for the Atlas was provided primarily by NYSDEC's Return a Gift to Wildlife Program, with many Federation members included among the nearly 4000 volunteers who contributed some 200,000 hours of fieldwork to the project. The value of those in-kind services from our volunteers was nearly $1.5 million, with NYSDEC receiving returns of almost $20 worth of volunteer services for each dollar it invested in the project. The success of the project was due, in large part, to frequent personal contact and direct training of volunteers, coordinated with production of a newsletter distributed to volunteers three times a year to report the project's progress. Production of the published Atlas required the services of two full-time editors, four artists, and 19 contributing authors.

The Atlas achieved a 99.8% coverage of the land area of the state (30 million acres) using 5335 survey blocks, each 25 square kilometers (9 square miles) in area. To date, New York State is the largest land area in the world covered with the thoroughness and detail achieved by our breeding bird atlas. Today, our Atlas data are a significant component of the New York State Gap Analysis Project of the Department of the Interior (Scott et al. 1991), and planning already is under way for the second New York Atlas, scheduled to begin in 1999. As the British have demonstrated quite clearly, repetition of the breeding bird atlas at approximately 20–25 year intervals can provide valuable information and important insights into the changing distributions of the breeding birds of a region (Gibbons et al. 1993).

State Parks Checklists

In 1987 the New York State Office of Parks, Recreation, and Historic Preservation (OPRHP) formed a Birdlife Advisory Committee, composed largely of Federation members, to advise parks staff and administrators on conservation of birds in state parks and historic sites. A major initiative under the direction of the Birdlife Advisory Committee has been the State Parks Checklist Project. As of April 1994, bird checklists had been produced for 13 state parks and historic sites (Table 2). Local member clubs of the Federation have been instrumental in collecting and documenting information for production of state parks checklists.

The state parks checklists published so far provide documented occurrences for at least 353 species of birds, 78% of the 451 total species reported for New York State (FNYSBC 1996), on lands managed by OPRHP (Table 2). Among those 353 species reported from the state parks and historic sites listed in Table 2, there are 26 of the 38 species that were identified as Endangered, Threatened, or of Special Concern by NYSDEC

Table 2. The variety of species reported on state parks checklists as of April 1994

State Park or Historic Site	Total no. of species	Park size (acres)	Percentage of NYS total no. of species
Allegany State Park	245	63,000	54.3
Bear Mountain/Harriman State Parks	253	51,000	56.1
Caleb Smith State Park Preserve	153	543	33.9
Clay Pit Ponds State Park Preserve	173	250	38.4
Connetquot River State Park Preserve	193	3473	42.8
Crown Point State Historic Site	180	360	39.9
Hamlin Beach State Park	272	1200	60.3
Heckscher State Park	281	1657	62.3
Jones Beach State Park	329	2400	72.9
Letchworth State Park	225	14,340	49.9
Saratoga Spa State Park	156	2200	34.6
Sunken Meadow State Park	214	1200	47.5
Thousand Islands State Park	266	15,046	59.0

Note: Species numbers and acreages for state parks are from state parks checklists on lands managed by the Office of Parks, Recreation, and Historic Preservation. In some cases, parks with fewer species of birds might not have been studied as intensively as those with more species, so there may be sampling biases of an unknown nature in some of the species counts.

in 1993 (Table 1; Cobb 1993). If more checklists are created and published, a clearer picture will emerge of the potential long-term contribution of state parks and historic sites to maintaining the local and regional bird species diversity of New York State, since state parks and historic sites are among the most protected of public land areas in New York. Unfortunately, the Birdlife Advisory Committee and the state parks checklist project were temporarily suspended early in 1995. However, the Commissioner of OPRHP reactivated the committee early in 1997.

Finger Lakes National Forest Study

Lessons learned from our statewide survey and monitoring projects are being applied to a comprehensive model program of monitoring and inventorying breeding birds at a local scale for a smaller area (14,000 acres), the Finger Lakes National Forest (FLNF). The key partners in this effort are the U.S. Forest Service, FNYSBC, and the Department of Natural Resources at Cornell University. In 1992, we were joined by the U.S. Department of the Interior through the New York Cooperative Fish and Wildlife Research Unit at Cornell. At FLNF, we have used breeding bird atlas and habitat-specific point count methodologies to determine distributions and relative abundances for 120 species of breeding birds, 50% of the breeding bird species recorded from New York State (Atlas 1988) on a land area only 0.05% of the total land area of New York State. Volunteers have contributed significantly to our breeding bird atlas for FLNF, and under-graduate interns from Cornell's Department of Natural Resources have par-ticipated in summer research at FLNF since the project began in 1989 (C. R. Smith 1991a). The breeding bird atlas for FLNF is the first in North America to be conducted on a relatively small land area and the first to be completed for any forest in the National Forest System.

Information collected at FLNF already has provided managers with infor-mation needed to ensure conservation of rare grassland bird species such as Grasshopper Sparrow and Henslow's Sparrow that occur on public pasture-lands at FLNF (Smith 1992; Smith and Smith 1992; Smith, in press). In addition, our research team in the Department of Natural Resources is using landscape imagery from FLNF, in conjunction with Atlas data col-lected by Federation volunteers, to assess the relationships of breeding birds to habitat types that can be identified by sensors on satellites in space. Such information will be useful to managers by helping them determine what kinds of habitats, in what kinds of configurations, for a given area, con-tribute most to local breeding bird species variety.

Current Status of Breeding Birds in New York

With information from the BBS, we now have an unprecedented capacity to assess periodically the population status for 128 of the breeding bird species of New York (Tables 3–5). In general, most breeding bird species in New York that are monitored adequately by BBS procedures are doing well.

Based on a review of BBS data collected through 1994 and summarized in Tables 3 to 5, the following conclusions regarding the status of breeding birds in New York can be reached.

- Declines for all 128 breeding bird species surveyed adequately by BBS methods within New York State are less (31.2%, Table 4) than would be expected by chance alone (33%), when compared with increasing species (Table 3) and species for which no change can be detected.
- Most (68.8%) breeding bird species populations in New York State sampled by BBS either are not changing detectably or are increasing in abundance (Table 3).
- More of breeding bird species that use successional habitats (openlands and shrublands) are declining (45%) than are species that use mature forests and woodlands (32.5%; Table 5). This finding reflects national trends (Peterjohn et al. 1995).
- Among Neotropical migrants (56 species), most species either are showing no detectable changes in populations or are increasing (71.5%). This finding also reflects national trends (Peterjohn et al. 1995; Maurer and Villard 1996; Vohs n.d.).

Table 3. Statistically significant, long-term, increasing population trends for 34 of 128 breeding bird species in New York State

Species	Trend Period		
	1966–1994	1966–1979	1980–1994
American Bittern	**	NC	NC
Great Blue Heron	***	NC	NC
Turkey Vulture	**	NC	***
Canada Goose	***	***	*
Mallard	***	**	***
Sharp-shinned Hawk	*	NC	NC
Red-tailed Hawk	*	NC	NC
Wild Turkey	*	NC	***
Ring-billed Gull	***	***	NC
Rock Dove	*	***	NC
Mourning Dove	***	***	***
Ruby-throated Hummingbird	**	NC	***
Red-bellied Woodpecker	**	NC	*
Pileated Woodpecker	***	NC	*
Blue-headed Vireo	***	NC	***
Warbling Vireo	***	*	NC
Red-eyed Vireo	***	***	***
American Crow	***	NC	***
Common Raven	***	***	***
Black-capped Chickadee	***	**	NC
Tufted Titmouse	***	NC	***
Red-breasted Nuthatch	***	NC	*
Carolina Wren	**	NC	***
House Wren	**	***	*
Golden-crowned Kinglet	*	NC	NC
Hermit Thrush	***	*	***
Northern Mockingbird	***	***	NC
Yellow Warbler	**	NC	NC
Magnolia Warbler	***	NC	NC
Yellow-rumped Warbler	***	**	*
Ovenbird	***	NC	***
Northern Cardinal	***	***	***
House Finch	***	***	***
Evening Grosbeak	**	NC	***

Source: Data are from the Breeding Bird Surveys (Sauer et al. 1996).
Note: Asterisks indicate the statistical significance of the increase at three levels: *$P < 0.10$, **$P < 0.05$, ***$P < 0.01$. These probability levels indicate that the likelihood that an increase of the kind observed would occur because of chance alone is less than 10, 5, and 1 out of 100 trials, respectively. NC, no detectable population change that is statistically significant at $P \leq 0.10$.

Table 4. Statistically significant, long-term, decreasing population trends for 40 of 128 breeding bird species in New York State

Species	Trend Period		
	1966–1994	1966–1979	1980–1994
American Black Duck	*	***	NC
Ring-necked Pheasant	**	***	NC
Killdeer	***	** (increase)	***
Spotted Sandpiper	***	***	*
Chimney Swift	**	***	NC
Red-headed Woodpecker	***	NC	***
Downy Woodpecker	***	NC	***
Northern Flicker	***	***	***
Olive-sided Flycatcher	***	**	***
Eastern Wood-Pewee	***	**	*
Least Flycatcher	***	***	NC
Eastern Kingbird	***	*	***
Horned Lark	***	***	*
Purple Martin	*	** (increase)	*
Bank Swallow	*	NC	NC
Ruby-crowned Kinglet	*	NC	NC
Veery	**	NC	***
Wood Thrush	***	NC	***
American Robin	**	***	NC
Brown Thrasher	***	***	***
European Starling	***	***	NC
Golden-winged Warbler	***	NC	**
Black-and-white Warbler	**	NC	NC
Canada Warbler	***	***	***
Scarlet Tanager	***	NC	***
Eastern Towhee	***	***	***
Field Sparrow	***	***	***
Vesper Sparrow	***	***	NC
Savannah Sparrow	***	**	*
Grasshopper Sparrow	***	***	NC
Henslow's Sparrow	***	***	*
Song Sparrow	***	***	NC
White-throated Sparrow	*	***	NC
Red-winged Blackbird	***	***	***
Eastern Meadowlark	***	***	***
Common Grackle	***	NC	***
Brown-headed Cowbird	***	***	**
Purple Finch	*	NC	NC
American Goldfinch	***	***	NC
House Sparrow	***	*	***

Source: Data are from the Breeding Bird Surveys (Sauer et al. 1996).
Note: Asterisks indicate the statistical significance of the decrease at three levels: *P < 0.10, **P < 0.05, ***P < 0.01. These probability levels indicate that the likelihood that a decrease of the kind observed would occur because of chance alone is less than 10, 5, and 1 out of 100 trials, respectively. NC, no detectable population change that is statistically significant at P ≤ 0.10. Note that two species show both increasing and decreasing trends that are statistically significant for the shorter time periods.

Table 5. Grouping of 40 bird species in New York State with significantly decreasing, long-term population trends (Table 4) by general habitat type as a percentage of the total number of decreasing species

Forest/woodland (32.5%)	Shrubland (20.0%)	Openland (25.0%)	Edges/other (22.5%)
Red-headed Woodpecker	Eastern Kingbird	Ring-necked Pheasant	American Black Duck
Downy Woodpecker	Brown Thrasher	Killdeer	Spotted Sandpiper
Olive-sided Flycatcher	Golden-winged Warbler	Northern Flicker	Chimney Swift
Eastern Wood-Pewee	Eastern Towhee	Horned Lark	Purple Martin
Least Flycatcher	Field Sparrow	Vesper Sparrow	Bank Swallow
Ruby-crowned Kinglet	Song Sparrow	Savannah Sparrow	European Starling
Veery	White-throated Sparrow	Grasshopper Sparrow	Common Grackle
Wood Thrush	American Goldfinch	Henslow's Sparrow	Brown-headed Cowbird
American Robin		Red-winged Blackbird	House Sparrow
Black-and-white Warbler		Eastern Meadowlark	
Canada Warbler			
Scarlet Tanager			
Purple Finch			

Source: Species are from the Breeding Bird Surveys (Sauer et al. 1996).

Note: Woodland is defined as a tree-dominated habitat with a canopy cover of less than 60%. Openland habitats include grasslands, hayfields, meadows, pastures, and in some cases (e.g., Killdeer, Horned Lark) cultivated fields. Edge can be at the interface between any two of the other habitat types.

- The perception, promoted since 1990 by many nonscientific "environmental" groups, of widespread "catastrophic" declines of Neotropical migratory birds is not supported by the data. This lack of factual support raises important issues related to the responsibilities for truth telling in bird conservation efforts by any environmental organization in a position of leadership.

Remarks and Future Prospects

Our experiences in New York State make it clear that partnerships with state management agencies are essential to achieving the monitoring and inventorying work necessary in planning and setting priorities for bird conservation. Success with volunteers depends on personal contact and frequent tangible feedback through verbal presentations, training sessions, and printed materials. Efforts must be goal-oriented, must produce tangible products, and must be coordinated by competent, articulate professionals who are well known and respected by volunteers.

The scale at which our efforts have been mounted and their success in New York could not have been possible without the existence of a strong, well-managed, project-oriented, all-volunteer, state organization, the Federation of New York State Bird Clubs (FNYSBC). Our projects have been undertaken with the goal of finding out more about the birds of our state in order to provide better for their conservation through meeting the information needs of state and federal resource management agencies and professionals. Fund raising, increasing membership, and fostering support for the FNYSBC have been by-products of that effort but never its primary goal, a lesson to which other nongovernmental organizations might pay careful attention. We in New York State now are fortunate to have a wealth of information about the birds of our state. That information is of increasing value for developing comprehensive wildlife conservation and management strategies and has resulted from successful cooperation among a variety of partners, including state and federal agencies, nongovernmental organizations, and academic researchers and educators—a pattern of cooperation demonstrated clearly by the very successful New York State Breeding Bird Atlas Project. So far, the Federation has maintained its focus on birds and science-based conservation of birds and has worked closely with state agencies to develop monitoring, conservation, and management actions that are based in fact.

At its September 1991 annual meeting, the FNYSBC, representing some 20,000 members, adopted a resolution of recognition and support for the leadership demonstrated by the National Fish and Wildlife Foundation in initiating the Neotropical Migratory Bird Conservation Program ("Partners in Flight—Aves de las Americas"). During 1993, a state Partners in Flight Working Group was formed, under the leadership of NYSDEC, with many representatives from the Federation among its members. Similarly, in 1996 the National Audubon Society launched its Important Bird Areas (IBA) program for New York State, coordinated with Partners in Flight. The IBA is intended to identify and protect areas that are of demonstrable importance in conservation of migratory birds, with input from Federation member clubs and local Audubon chapters.

Partners in the Neotropical Migratory Bird Conservation Program and related causes continually have to be mindful that our goal is the conservation of a resource: migratory birds. Achieving objectives to reach that conservation goal must be undertaken in the context of a modern, comprehensive approach to wildlife conservation, embracing a wide range of wildlife values and species, while creatively identifying a diversity of funding sources to support wildlife conservation and management. Whether new causes like Partners in Flight or Important Bird Areas will have positive, measurable effects on migratory bird populations in New York State in the future remains to be seen.

It continues to be an exciting and challenging time to be working for conservation of birds in New York State. Like so many other challenges in the conservation of biological resources, long-term conservation of birds must be science-based, depending upon communication and cooperation, not upon conflict and competition, and having a shared, multidisciplinary vision of the needs of the resource foremost in the minds of the various partners. Exaggerated or unsubstantiated claims, designed to build or stir memberships, without a scientific basis in ecology, are unethical. Economics and sociology determine the political context within which conservation must be achieved. If the public does not want to buy conservation, we are not going to be able to sell it. And if we do not work hard to instill a sense of ethical conservation and an awareness of and appreciation for living nature in our youngsters through education, the foundations upon which we will build future conservation efforts will be weak or nonexistent.

ACKNOWLEDGMENTS

In addition to the extensive contributions made by volunteers, our program in New York State could not have been possible without funding support from NYSDEC, USFWS, and U.S. Forest Service. My recent research into applications of remote sensing to assess bird-habitat relationships has been funded by the U.S. Department of Agriculture (Hatch Project No. NYC-147406) and U.S. Department of the Interior (Gap Analysis Program). Robert Budliger read an earlier draft of this chapter and made suggestions for its improvement. Most of this work would not have been possible without the generous and enthusiastic support provided by Daniel J. Decker, James P. Lassoie, and Milo E. Richmond of the Department of Natural Resources at Cornell University.

From Glaciers to Global Warming: Long-Term Changes in the Birdlife of New York State

David W. Steadman

Florida Museum of Natural History

Anyone who studies birds for more than several years knows that the avifauna of a region is always changing. Within their lifetimes, ornithologists and birdwatchers document changes in the distribution and abundance of various species. Such changes often are analyzed on decadal time scales, such as the declines of the Osprey and Bald Eagle in the 1940s through 1960s, followed by their increases in the 1970s and 1980s. Because birds are relatively well studied compared with most other groups of organisms, one often can relate the observed changes in birdlife to some cause. For the Osprey and Bald Eagle, both the decreases and increases in population were due to human factors. Habitat loss and pesticides were the primary causes of the declines, whereas habitat protection, the banning of certain pesticides, and breeding manipulation led to the increases.

The purpose of this chapter is to provide a much longer perspective on the avifauna of New York State, one that covers both prehistoric time (before the arrival of Europeans and Africans) as well as historic time (the past four or five centuries). The species of birds that inhabit New York State today are the products of many millions of years of evolution. In this regard, the record of prehistoric birds in New York State is grossly inadequate, for no remains of birds have been found in the state that are more than about 11,000 years old. The prehistoric evidence that does exist, however, is of great value in understanding the processes that have influenced New York's avifauna in postglacial times.

The prehistory of New York State's birds has been reviewed only once before (Steadman 1988a). Parts of this chapter are an update of that effort. Bones excavated and identified from archaeological (cultural) and paleontological (noncultural) sites provide the evidence for prehistoric birdlife. Most of the sites (see the accompanying map) are archaeological in origin. Some sites, such as the Dutchess Quarry Caves (Orange County), Joralemon's Cave (Albany County), and the Hiscock Site (Genesee County), include bones deposited by humans as well as other predators and scavengers (Steadman and Funk 1987; Steadman 1988b; Steadman et al. 1993b; Funk and Steadman 1994).

The Pleistocene

Some explanations of geological time units are warranted. Geological time is divided into eras, which are divided into periods consisting of epochs. We are living today in the Holocene Epoch, a relatively warm (interglacial) time interval that comprises the past 10,000 years. The Pleistocene Epoch is a much longer interval that began about 1.7 million years ago and ended only 10,000 years ago. The Quaternary Period, which consists of the Pleistocene and Holocene epochs combined, is the final period of the Cenozoic Era, which began about 65 million years ago. Dinosaurs died out at the end of the Mesozoic Era, the era that preceded the Cenozoic.

The Pleistocene includes all of the earth's most recent ice ages. At the height of the last glaciation (18,000 years ago), all of New York State was covered with ice except Long Island and the part of Cattaraugus County south of the Allegheny River. Major changes in climate, hydrology, and habitat occurred in New York State as the continental ice masses retreated from the region 17,000 to 11,000 years ago (Miller 1973a, 1973b, 1988; Muller and Calkin 1988; Jackson 1989; Peteet et al. 1993). The newly deglaciated terrain was first occupied by a tundra-like community dominated by sedges, grasses, and other herbaceous plants that are characteristic today of high northern latitudes. Except perhaps for dwarf willows and birches, no trees or shrubs lived in this stark setting. At about 12,000 years ago, this plant community was colonized by boreal conifers (black spruce, white spruce, jack pine, larch) to form an open woodland that persisted until about 10,000 years ago. During this interval of about 2000 years, the density of trees increased, as did the relative abundance of jack pine. The overall climatic trend was one of warming, although this was an inconsistent progression interrupted by cold intervals.

About 10,000 years ago, various species of deciduous trees (oaks, maples, and others), temperate species of pines (white and red), and hemlocks arrived from the south and eventually (within about the next 1000 years) replaced most of the boreal conifers. This highly variable "mixed decidu-ous–coniferous forest" has persisted into modern times in most of New York State. Temporal fluctuations on this general theme have included a rapid, large reduction in hemlock about 5000 years ago (followed by a gradual increase) and a slight increase in boreal species during the past 2000 years.

Bones of at least nine species of extinct large mammals have been found in late Pleistocene sediments in New York State (Fisher 1955; Drumm 1963; Laub et al. 1988; Funk and Steadman 1994; Laub 1994). These spectacular species include a ground sloth *(Megalonyx* sp.*)*, giant beaver *(Castoroides ohioensis)*, American mastodon *(Mammut americanum)*, wooly mammoth *(Mammuthus primigenius)*, Jefferson's mammoth *(Mammuthus* *jeffersonii*), flat-headed peccary *(Platygonus compressus)*, moose-elk or stag-elk *(Cervalces scotti)*, vero tapir *(Tapirus veroensis)*, and a zebra-like horse *(Equus* sp.*)*. These large mammals became extinct in New York, as well as across North America, between 11,500 and 10,500 years ago. The cause of their extinction is controversial, with the major competing theories favoring either the changing climates and habitats (Graham and Lundelius 1984) or the arrival of North America's first people (Martin 1990). Three other species of large mammals recorded from late Pleistocene deposits are the wapiti or American elk *(Cervus canadensis)*, caribou *(Rangifer tarandus)*, and musk ox *(Ovibos moschatus)*. These species survive today only outside of New York State.

One can only imagine what a fascinatingly different place New York State was when these 12 species of large mammals (the "megafauna") were part of the biota. Unfortunately, only one site has yielded evidence of the birds that lived alongside New York's extinct megafauna. This is the 11,000 year old Hiscock Site (site 1 on the map), where three bones of the California Condor have been found associated with bones of the American mastodon, moose-elk, and caribou (Steadman and Miller 1987; Steadman 1988b; Laub 1994). The California Condor currently is an endangered species that has survived the past decade only because of an intensive captive breeding program. Historical records of the California Condor are confined to the West Coast of North America, mostly in California. Late Pleistocene bones of the California Condor have been found, however, across the southern United States and northern Mexico, from Florida to California (Lundelius et al. 1983). The condor bones from the Hiscock Site represent a north-ward range extension of about 1000 miles. The fossil plant record from the Hiscock Site indicates that the habitat 11,000 years ago in western New York was an open woodland of spruce and jack pine (Miller 1988). Herds of large mammals grazed and browsed on the late Pleistocene vegetation, not unlike in an African game park today (Steadman and Martin 1984). The California Condor was able to live in this boreal environment because food, in the form of carrion from the megafauna, was abundant. With the loss of most species of large mammals by 10,500 years ago, the range of the California Condor retreated across North America to the Pacific Coast (Emslie 1987; Steadman and Miller 1987). Although the California Condor barely survived the megafaunal extinction, it fared better than the many other species of scavenging birds that became extinct at that time, such as various eagles, "Old World" vultures, teratorns, storks, and other condors (Steadman and Martin 1984).

Complete and partial feathers have also been found in the late Pleistocene levels of the Hiscock Site. The feathers were discovered in sediment samples collected from a freshly exposed wall of the excavation in 1986 (Steadman 1988a, 1988b). Considering their ages, the feathers are marvelously preserved, retaining color as well as microstructure. The color and wear stage of the feathers can indicate seasonality. Three of the feathers have been identified microscopically and macroscopically by Roxie C. Laybourne and Carla J. Dove (USFWS). From sediments dated at 11,000 years old is a lower breast feather of a Pied-billed Grebe. This feather is fresh (unworn), suggesting deposition in September or October. From sediments dated at about 10,000 years old are two upper back or lower neck feathers of an adult male Baltimore Oriole. These two feathers, from a bird in breeding plumage, most likely were deposited during May to July.

The Holocene
Cultural Influences

The remainder of the prehistoric record of birds from New York State is confined to the Holocene rather than the Pleistocene. Most of the Holocene record is archaeological in origin. Humans have lived in New York State for about 11,000 years. Thus all except the first millennium of human occupation is within the Holocene. Archaeologists have divided the human residency in the state into a cultural sequence that in large part was based initially upon stylistic changes in artifacts, especially in stone projectile points and, during the Woodland periods (see below), ceramics (Ritchie 1971, 1980). Many stratified archaeological sites with radiocarbon-dated materials have been excavated in New York and adjacent states in the past two decades. This excavation has led to refinements of the cultural sequence that incorporate site location and configuration, faunal and botanical remains, and other information in addition to artifact typologies (see summaries in Funk 1988, 1991, 1993).

Briefly, the traditional cultural sequence for New York State is divided into nine periods as follows: Paleoindian (11,000 to 10,000 years ago), Early Archaic (10,000 to 7000 years ago), Middle Archaic (7000 to 5000 years ago), Late Archaic (5000 to 3500 years ago), Transition (3500 to 3000 years ago), Early Woodland (3000 to 1600 years ago), Middle Woodland (1600 to 1000 years ago), Late Woodland (1000 to 500 years ago), and Historic (500 years ago to today). The influence of non-North American peoples (primarily European and African) generally has increased during the Historic Period.

This cultural sequence is useful in understanding the relative chronology of the sites listed in the accompanying map, although one should keep in mind that (1) the chronology of each period is approximate; (2) the cultural attributes within each period vary temporally and geographically (see Funk 1993 for a current and thorough discussion); and (3) the transitions between periods may be abrupt or gradual. An alternative model to the traditional cultural sequence has been proposed (Funk 1993). This new model, with four primary stages and nine substages, is directly comparable to the traditional sequence (Funk 1993: table 15).

Several important biases influence New York's Holocene record of birds. By *bias* I mean that the species recorded in the prehistoric bone assemblages do not reflect the actual species composition of local bird communities at the time the site was being formed. One bias is the vast incompleteness of the record. Only at the Hiscock Site (Holocene levels) and at Dutchess Quarry Caves No. 1 and 8 does the number of identified bird bones exceed 100. For most sites, fewer than 10 birds bones have been identified. Such tiny samples cannot possibly represent an entire local avifauna.

Another bias involves the geographical distribution of sites, which are most frequent in the Hudson and Mohawk river valleys and the Finger Lakes region. The prehistoric record of birds is lacking or very limited for Long Island, the Adirondacks, Tug Hill Plateau, St. Lawrence lowlands, and Allegheny River drainage.

A third bias favors large rather than small species of birds, because the sediments of most archaeological sites have been sieved through screens with mesh sizes no smaller than 1/4 inch or even 1/2 inch. Such screens do not thoroughly sample the bones of small species, such as certain shorebirds, nightjars, swifts, hummingbirds, kingfishers, woodpeckers, and passerines. Abundant bones of small species have been recovered at sites such as the Dutchess Quarry Caves, Joralemon's Cave, and Hiscock, demonstrating the value of using screens with 1/8 inch or smaller mesh for obtaining more thorough faunal samples. Even when bones of small species are recovered, it is often difficult or impossible to identify the bones to species. Particularly difficult groups are, not surprisingly, small passerines such as *Empidonax* flycatchers or paruline warblers.

A fourth bias is that the species of birds recorded from archaeological sites are those that were of interest to prehistoric peoples. Thus, species that were preferred as food should be expected to dominate prehistoric bone assemblages. Indeed, that seems to be the case, with an apparent bias toward species still regarded today as game birds, especially the Ruffed Grouse, Wild Turkey, and Passenger Pigeon (Steadman 1988a; Funk 1993; also see Game Birds, below). Food was not, however, the only reason why prehistoric peoples hunted birds. With the onset of agriculture during the Woodland periods, birds undoubtedly were hunted to control crop damage (Starna et al. 1984). Bird bones were used as tools (awls, fishhooks) and ornaments (beads, pendants). The longest, straightest bones in the wing and leg (ulna, radius, tibiotarsus) of large birds were preferred for these purposes. The claws of hawks, eagles, and owls also provided ornamentation, as did feathers from many different species of birds.

Another use was related in part to ornamentation. Certain types of birds had ritualistic or spiritualistic value for prehistoric peoples. Bird effigies were carved on ornaments, pipes, ladles, and combs made of clay, stone, antler or bone, wood, and shell (Wray 1963; Kinsey 1989). The Passenger Pigeon, considered a harbinger of spring and abundant food, was celebrated in a special dance by the Seneca (Fenton 1955). A celestial Iroquoian legend associated with another bird dance involved the Turkey Vulture, Bald Eagle, and Golden Eagle (Converse 1908). Other birds of special significance included the Great Egret, Wild Turkey, Ruffed Grouse, various owls, Whip-poor-will, Common Raven, American Crow, Black-capped Chickadee, American Robin, and many others (Converse 1908; Wray 1964). Many of the Iroquoian names for particular species of birds were onomatopoetic: that is, an imitation of the bird's song or call (Mithun 1984).

Additional examples of nonculinary uses of birds include a Great Blue Heron that was buried with an Iroquois woman (perhaps Seneca) near Avon along the Genesee River (Wray 1964). Three of the eight clans of the Seneca were named after birds: heron, hawk, and snipe (Converse 1908; Wray 1964). Transformation legends involved a number of zoological subjects: the Dark-eyed Junco or Snow Bunting of winter turned into a Chipping Sparrow in the summer, and the Canada Goose arrived in the autumn but became a beaver during the winter, retaining only the webbed feet of the goose (Speck and Witthoft 1947).

Game Birds

In some ways, the concept of what constitutes a highly desired game bird in North America has not changed much from prehistoric to modern times. In both cases, gallinaceous birds (turkey, grouse, quail), anatid waterfowl (swans, geese, and ducks), woodcock, and columbids (pigeons and doves) have been the primary targets of hunters. Availability is an obvious and important factor; if Passenger Pigeons still existed, today's hunters undoubtedly would pursue them each autumn more vigorously than they pursue Mourning Doves. The Wild Turkey has been hunted avidly for millennia throughout its range in Mexico, the United States, and southernmost Canada (Steadman 1980). At the northern margin of the turkey's range in New York State, however, turkey hunting was not possible during the first half of the twentieth century because deforestation and unregulated hunting had eliminated the entire turkey population (Eaton 1910; Eaton 1953, 1981, 1992). New York's only indigenous quail, the Northern Bobwhite, has become so scarce and local that it is no longer hunted near the northern limits of its range in New York or southern New England.

There are, nevertheless, some fundamental differences between prehistoric and modern concepts of hunting birds in New York State. The first is type of weapon. Traditional hunters used nets, snares, slings, stones, spears, and arrows to kill birds. Use of those weapons has been replaced today nearly worldwide, including essentially all of temperate North America, by the use of firearms. The second is dietary preferences. Presumably, prehistoric New York State peoples included in their repertoire of game birds some of the same species that modern less-sophisticated peoples eat. The latter eat species of birds (such as grebes, coots, plovers, sandpipers, terns, parrots, woodpeckers, and passerines) that most New Yorkers would eat today only under conditions of duress. The third is use. The fact that birds were killed in prehistoric times not just for food or sport but also for feathers, bones, and claws used in tools, decoration, and ritual resulted in the hunting of herons, egrets, cranes, hawks, eagles, owls, and many other types of birds that often are not regarded as game birds today.

Paleoecology

Despite biases in New York State's prehistoric record of birds, it is clear that the most commonly recorded species (Tables 6 and 7) represent two major habitat types, forests and wetlands. Among the species that prefer forests, the Ruffed Grouse, Wild Turkey, and Passenger Pigeon are by far the most common, reflecting in part their status as game birds. The relative abundance of closely related species with different habitat preferences provides further evidence for the prevalence of forest species over those more characteristic of open habitats. This evidence includes the greater number of records of Red-shouldered Hawks than of Red-tailed Hawks, Passenger Pigeons versus Mourning Dove, and Barred Owls versus Great Horned

Table 6. Bird species recorded from prehistoric sites in New York State

Family	Species	Sites recorded*
Gaviidae: Loons	Common Loon *(Gavia immer)*	13
Podicipedidae: Grebes	Pied-billed Grebe *(Podilymbus podiceps)*	1
	Horned Grebe *(Podiceps auritus)*	7
Ardeidae: Herons	American Bittern *(Botaurus lentiginosus)*	2
	Great Blue Heron *(Ardea herodias)*	7, 13, 15, 31, 34
Cathartidae: Vultures and condors	Black Vulture *(Coragyps atratus)*	4
	Turkey Vulture *(Cathartes aura)*	2–4
	California Condor *(Gymnogyps californianus)*†	1
Anatidae: Geese, swans, and ducks	Snow (Blue) Goose *(Chen caerulescens)*	16
	Canada Goose *(Branta canadensis)*	2, 5, 7, 15, 17, 18, 21, 27, 35, 44
	Trumpeter Swan *(Olor buccinator)*†	4
	Wood Duck *(Aix sponsa)*	2, 4, 7, 18
	Gadwall *(Anas strepera)*	13
	American Black Duck/Mallard *(Anas rubripes/platyrhynchos)*	2, 13, 15, 18, 26, 45, 47
	Blue-winged Teal *(Anas discors)*	2, 25

Table 6. *Continued*

Family	Species	Sites recorded*
	Northern Pintail *(Anas acuta)*	4
	Green-winged Teal *(Anas crecca)*	18, 22?, 45
	Unidentified dabbling duck *(Anas sp.)*	13, 15, 22, 55
	Canvasback *(Aythya valisineria)*	15
	Ring-necked Duck *(Aythya collaris)*	2
	Unidentified pochard *(Aythya* sp.)	15, 35
	White-winged Scoter *(Melanitta fusca)*	4, 44
	Bufflehead *(Bucephala albeola)*	7
	Common Goldeneye *(Bucephala clangula)*	15
	Common Merganser *(Mergus merganser)*	15
	Red-breasted Merganser *(Mergus serrator)*	15
	Unidentified merganser *(Mergus* sp.)	17
	Unidentified duck (Anatidae sp.)	2, 8, 14–16, 24, 27, 35, 43, 44, 48, 49, 51, 52, 55
Accipitridae: Hawks and eagles	Bald Eagle *(Haliaeetus leucocephalus)*	8, 15
	Cooper's Hawk *(Accipiter cooperii)*	18
	Northern Goshawk *(Accipiter gentilis)*	7
	Red-shouldered Hawk *(Buteo lineatus)*	7, 18, 43
	Red-tailed Hawk *(Buteo jamaicensis)*	2, 37
	Unidentified hawk *(Buteo* sp.)	13, 35
	Golden Eagle *(Aquila chrysaetos)*	7
	Unidentified hawk (Accipitridae sp.)	6, 35, 54
Phasianidae: Partridges, grouse, and turkeys	Ruffed Grouse *(Bonasa umbellus)*	2–5, 7, 8, 10, 13, 15, 18, 20, 23, 26, 27, 29, 31, 35, 37, 43, 46, 47
	Wild Turkey *(Meleagris gallopavo)*	2, 4–9, 11–24, 27, 28, 30?, 32, 33, 35–40, 42, 43, 45, 47, 48, 52–55, 58
Odontophoridae: New World quail	Northern Bobwhite *(Colinus virginianus)*	2, 4, 5, 13
Rallidae: Rails	Virginia Rail *(Rallus limicola)*	4
	Virginia Rail/Sora *(Rallus limicola/ Porzana carolina)*	18
Gruidae: Cranes	Sandhill Crane *(Grus canadensis)*	35
	Whooping Crane *(Grus americana)*[†]	4
Scolopacidae: Sandpipers	Lesser Yellowlegs *(Tringa flavipes)*	4
	Solitary Sandpiper *(Tringa solitaria)*	18
	Eskimo Curlew *(Numenius borealis)*[†]	2
	Hudsonian Godwit *(Limosa haemastica)*	4
	American Woodcock *(Scolopax minor)*	2, 4, 43

63

Table 6. *Continued*

Family	Species	Sites recorded*
Columbidae: Pigeons and doves	Mourning Dove *(Zenaida macroura)*	13
	Passenger Pigeon *(Ectopistes migratorius)*†	2, 4–8, 10, 13, 18, 25–28, 35, 39 41, 43, 45–47, 49–51, 54, 57
Cuculidae: Cuckoos	Yellow-billed Cuckoo *(Coccyzus americanus)*	4
	Unidentified cuckoo *(Coccyzus sp.)*	18
Tytonidae: Barn Owls	Barn Owl *(Tyto alba)*	4
Strigidae: Typical owls	Eastern Screech-Owl *(Otus asio)*	4, 13
	Great Horned Owl *(Bubo virginianus)*	7, 13
	Barred Owl *(Strix varia)*	2, 5, 13, 18, 43, 47
	Unidentified owl (Strigidae sp.)	35, 49, 54
Caprimulgidae: Goatsuckers	Common Nighthawk *(Chordeiles minor)*	47
Picidae: Woodpeckers	Red-bellied Woodpecker *(Melanerpes carolinus)*	2
	Yellow-bellied Sapsucker *(Sphyrapicus varius)*	18
	Downy Woodpecker *(Picoides pubescens)*	18, 56
	Hairy Woodpecker *(Picoides villosus)*	2, 47
	Northern Flicker *(Colaptes auratus)*	2, 18
	Pileated Woodpecker *(Dryocopus pileatus)*	2, 4
	Unidentified woodpecker (Picidae sp.)	4
Tyrannidae: Flycatchers	Eastern Phoebe *(Sayornis phoebe)*	2, 4, 37
Corvidae: Jays and crows	Blue Jay *(Cyanocitta cristata)*	2–4, 6?, 18, 43
	American Crow *(Corvus brachyrhynchos)*	2, 5, 13, 43
	Common Raven *(Corvus corax)*	18
Turdidae: Thrushes	American Robin *(Turdus migratorius)*	2, 4, 13, 18
Mimidae: Mockingbirds, thrashers, and catbirds	Gray Catbird *(Dumetella carolinensis)*	18
Emberizidae: New World sparrows	Unidentified sparrow (Emberizinae sp.)	55
Icteridae: Blackbirds	Red-winged Blackbird *(Agelaius phoeniceus)*	4
	Rusty Blackbird *(Euphagus carolinus)*	4
	Common Grackle *(Quiscalus quiscula)*	18
	Baltimore Oriole *(Icterus galbula)*	1
Undetermined	Unidentified passerine (Passeriformes sp.)	2, 4, 18

* Sites located and described in the accompanying map, p. 70.
† Species no longer occurs regularly or at all in New York State.

Table 7. Summary by family of prehistoric records of birds from New York State

Family	Number of sites
Phasianidae	48
Anatidae	27
Columbidae	25
Accipitridae	11
Strigidae	11
Corvidae	8
Ardeidae	6
Picidae	5
Cathartidae	4
Odontophoridae	4
Scolopacidae	4
Turdidae	4
Tyrannidae	3
Icteridae	3
Podicipedidae	2
Gruidae	2
Rallidae	2
Cuculidae	2
Gaviidae	1
Tytonidae	1
Caprimulgidae	1
Mimidae	1
Emberizidae	1

Owls. The regular occurrence of woodpecker bones in carefully excavated sites is also suggestive of forests.

The wetland species are dominated by anatid waterfowl but also include loons, grebes, herons, rails, cranes, sandpipers, phoebes, and blackbirds. Because wetlands provide a great variety of exploitable biotic resources, humans in New York State have preferentially lived near wetlands for thousands of years (Funk 1992). The six archaeological sites in Table 6 that have the most species of birds (sites 2, 4, 18, 13, 15, and 7 on the map) are all located within less than a mile (1 km) of a major wetland.

Extinct Species

Six of North America's extinct species or subspecies of birds certainly or presumably once lived in New York State. At least five of these six taxa survived into historic times within the state. The quality and quantity of evidence to support these statements vary considerably. Just two of the species (Eskimo Curlew, Passenger Pigeon) are known both from skins (nineteenth-century specimens) and prehistoric bones. That no prehistoric bones of the Labrador Duck, Heath Hen, or Great Auk have been found in the state is probably only a reflection of how few bird bones have been recovered from archaeological sites on Long Island.

The Laborador Duck once wintered in New York State, almost exclusively along the Atlantic Coast. Its former breeding grounds, supposedly in Labrador, are not known with certainty (Greenway 1958; Palmer 1976). All specimens of Labrador Duck were taken (mostly by market hunters) within its nonbreeding range from Nova Scotia and New Brunswick to New Jersey (Palmer 1976; AOU 1983). The last specimen of Labrador Duck to be preserved was collected off Long Island in the fall of 1875 (Eaton 1910; Bull 1974). The inland record from Elmira is questionable (Palmer 1976). The Labrador Duck is a tragic example of a species that became extinct before much was learned about its biology.

The Heath Hen, usually regarded as a subspecies of the Greater Prairie-Chicken, became extinct in 1932 at Martha's Vineyard, Massachusetts (Greenway 1958). The Heath Hen inhabited grasslands (including scrub oaks and pine barrens) along the Atlantic seaboard from southern Maine to Virginia, including New York's Long Island and Hudson River Valley (Gross 1928; Greenway 1958). It declined throughout colonial times and was gone from most of its range in New York State and elsewhere by the late 1700s to early 1800s. The Heath Hen survived on Long Island into the 1840s (DeKay 1844; Dutcher 1893). Although the Heath Hen was a popular game bird until its demise, no specimens collected in New York State still exist.

The Eskimo Curlew nested on the Canadian and Alaskan tundra and wintered in southern South America. It was a fall migrant in New York State, occurring most regularly on Long Island but with at least six inland records scattered across the state (Eaton 1910). The five New York State specimens from other than Long Island are two birds taken at Otisco (Onondaga County) in 1873 (Eaton 1910), one at Lockport (Niagara County) on 2 October 1879, one at Manitou (Monroe County) on 23 September 1890, and a single bone (an ulna) that I identified from Dutchess Quarry Cave No. 1 in Orange County. The last certain records of the Eskimo Curlew in New York were in the early 1890s (Eaton 1910), although four birds were seen at Montauk (eastern Long Island) in September 1932 (Murphy 1933; Bull 1974). The Eskimo Curlew was a favorite target of nineteenth-century market hunters (Swenk 1916). As a result, the world population of Eskimo Curlews crashed in the late 1800s (Banks 1977). Despite intensive searches, there have been no unequivocal (specimen) records of the Eskimo Curlew anywhere since 1963 (Faanes and Senner 1991; Anonymous 1994, 1995; Castro et al. 1994). If this species is not genuinely extinct, it must be very nearly so.

The Great Auk became extinct when the last birds were killed on remote

Funk Island (off Newfoundland) in 1844 (Lucas 1890). Although not recorded with certainty in New York State from either historical or prehistoric contexts, bones of the Great Auk have been found in prehistoric sites (early to late Holocene) along the Atlantic Coast from Newfoundland and Nova Scotia to Florida (Greenway 1958; Brodkorb 1967). Thus New York's coastal waters once were part of the winter range of this large, flightless alcid. Whether this was true into historical times is undetermined.

The Passenger Pigeon was New York State's most abundant bird until its precipitous decline in the nineteenth century. After surviving millennia of hunting by Native Americans, the Passenger Pigeon was unable to withstand the large-scale logging and market hunting that characterized the westward commercial expansion of the United States. Within New York State, this expansion was stimulated and sustained by a new system of canals and railroads that allowed commercial access to remote regions of the state. Lumbermen and hunters combined to wipe out the Passenger Pigeon across its range.

The last truly huge (i.e., millions of birds, measured in square miles) nesting ground of Passenger Pigeons in New York State was in 1868 along Bell's Run, near Ceres, on the Pennsylvania line in southern Allegany County (Eaton 1910). Both the Seneca and white hunters camped there during the nesting season, killing adult and nestling birds by the tens or hundreds of thousands.

Passenger Pigeons continued to be observed and hunted, albeit locally and sporadically, over the next few decades. Most of these records were from the western or northern parts of the state (Eaton 1910; Beardslee and Mitchell 1965), although the two very last reports of Passenger Pigeons in New York State were from the mid-Hudson Valley region. In May 1907, writer and naturalist John Burroughs saw a large flock of Passenger Pigeons near Kingston (Ulster County). A single Passenger Pigeon was seen during the summer of 1907 in Rensselaerville (southwestern Albany County) by Edmund Niles Huyck, after whom the E. N. Huyck Preserve and Biological Field Station would be named three decades later (Steadman 1996a). The last individual Passenger Pigeon anywhere, a captive bird named Martha, died in the Cincinatti Zoological Garden in September 1914.

The hyperabundance of the Passenger Pigeon into the nineteenth century was not because of any conservation practices by Native Americans. In fact, as seen in the numerous prehistoric sites that have produced bones of the Passenger Pigeon, Native Americans hunted this tasty columbid just as avidly as they hunted the larger Ruffed Grouse and Wild Turkey. Even at the Hiscock Site, where humans probably were not involved in accumulating the bird bones, the Passenger Pigeon represents more than 80% of all bird bones recovered (Steadman 1988b). In the great deciduous and mixed deciduous–coniferous forests that stretched from southern New England through the Great Lakes states, Passenger Pigeons probably were more numerous than any other species of bird. Without the Passenger Pigeon, our forests will never be the same, nor will springtime ever be as exciting.

The Carolina Parakeet is an extinct species usually regarded as more characteristic of the southeastern United States than the Northeast. Before its demise in the early twentieth century, however, this colorful seed predator reached its northern limit here in New York State. A "large flock" of parakeets was observed 25 miles northwest of Albany during the winter of 1780 (McKinley 1959; the sighting was erroneously dated as 1795 by DeKay [1844] and various subsequent authors). A flock of 13 Carolina Parakeets was seen by David F. Day on 20 December 1889 in Buffalo (Bergtold 1927; Beardslee and Mitchell 1965). The same Mr. Day also "knew of a lot [of parakeets] being captured at West Seneca [Erie County] (N.Y.) many years ago" (Beardslee and Mitchell 1965). These few records would suggest that the Carolina Parakeet wandered north to New York State occasionally but did not breed here.

Although not extinct, two other species of birds recorded prehistorically have undergone huge range contractions in historical times and no longer occur in the Northeast. These are the Trumpeter Swan *(Cygnus buccinator)* and Whooping Crane *(Grus americana)*, each recorded from Dutchess Quarry Cave No. 8. It is likely that these large, tasty species once were regular migrants and perhaps even breeding species in New York State's wetlands, although both disappeared before being well documented.

The only historical evidence of a Trumpeter Swan from the state is a bird shot in April 1863 at Tifft Farm near Buffalo (specimen not preserved; Beardslee and Mitchell 1965) and a more equivocal record from Cayuga Lake (Eaton 1910). Historical New York State records of the Whooping Crane also are poorly substantiated, consisting of a bird killed in the 1890s at Cayuga Lake (specimen not preserved) and a seventeenth-century description from New York Bay (Eaton 1910). Whether or not one accepts these historical records from New York State, it is certain that both the Trumpeter Swan and the Whooping Crane were widespread in eastern North America until the nineteenth century (Ridgway 1895; AOU 1957; Schorger 1964; Palmer 1976). Both species were eliminated through unregulated hunting and wetland losses, leaving behind only bones and early written records as evidence of their former distribution (Goslin 1955; Brodkorb 1964, 1967; Guilday and Parmalee 1965; Parmalee 1967; Mayfield 1972).

Long-Term Changes

The data suggest that forest and wetland species dominated New York State's prehistoric avifauna. After the arrival of Europeans, forest and wetland species of birds (and many other groups of organisms) were decimated by unregulated hunting and habitat loss. These declines were especially intense in the nineteenth century. Some species, such as the Passenger Pigeon, did not survive the environmental bottleneck. During the twentieth century, populations of certain forest species of birds have increased once again as the state's patchwork of forests has begun to mature (Baird 1990). What a logger or typical landowner regards today as a "mature" forest, however, bears little resemblance to the truly mature forests that once covered most of New York and adjacent states (Hough 1936, 1965; Davis 1996).

The losses of the Labrador Duck, Heath Hen, Eskimo Curlew, Great Auk, Passenger Pigeon, and Carolina Parakeet are irrevocable, but the losses of the Trumpeter Swan and Whooping Crane are not inevitable. In fact, a pair or two of the former nested in 1995 and 1996 at the Perch River Wildlife Management Area in Jefferson County, possibly originating from birds translocated to Ontario (E. Levine, pers. comm.).

If anything is predictable about the future, it is that unexpected changes, both negative and positive, are likely to occur. With the information available at the time, James DeKay had little reason to suspect in 1844 that the Passenger Pigeon would be extinct only seven decades later. Similarly, E. Howard Eaton, writing in 1910, could describe the Wild Turkey in New York State only in the past tense, unaware that this magnificent bird would return within four decades and that his yet to be born son, Stephen W. Eaton, would document the recovery.

Losing at least six species over the past several centuries may seem, at first glance, like a rather low rate of extinction. From an evolutionary perspective, however, nothing could be further from the truth. If you extrapolate this extinction rate into the future, about 20 species per millennium will be lost (Steadman 1996b). In a mere 10,000 years (an incomprehensibly long period of time to an economist or politician but a rather short time to most geologists, paleontologists, and evolutionary biologists), New York State could lose roughly half of its species of birds. Not only would evolution cease for the birds themselves, the community ecology of all natural habitats would be altered in ways difficult to predict. In fact, such extinction of birds would be unlikely to occur unless accompanied by the losses of many other species of plants and animals.

Whether governments, private institutions, and the citizenry will be able to curtail much of this potential extinction is uncertain. Birds are important to the few who read this, but I would bet that most New Yorkers would find the extinction of only one or two species of birds a century to be an acceptable rate. My parting wish is that observing and studying birds in New York State will be as rich and rewarding in the year 2996 as it is in the year 1996.

7. Archaeological Sites

ACKNOWLEDGMENTS

Funding for this research was provided by the National Science Foundation (grant EAR-18683), National Geographic Society (grant 3359–86), and the New York State Biological Survey. I thank Emanuel Levine for inviting me to write this paper. For generously sharing their time and knowledge, I thank L. Anderson, C. C. Bodner, J. Bopp, H. R. Decker, C. J. Dove, the late W. F. Ehlers, Jr., L. Friday, R. E. Funk, R. Futyma, G. Hamell, R. C. Laybourne, R. S. Laub, R. Lerman, N. G. Miller, D. S. Pahlavan, S. E. Schubel, J. Schulenberg, L. Sullivan, B. Wellman, S. Wolfe, L. S. Wootan, and M. C. Zarriello. The manuscript was improved through comments by S. W. Eaton, R. E. Funk, R. S. Laub, E. Levine, N. G. Miller, and R. S. Palmer. Finally, I dedicate this paper to Stephen W. Eaton, Robert E. Funk, and Ralph S. Palmer—good friends, wise mentors, unselfish scholars, and productive scientists. Their encyclopedic knowledge of the natural and cultural history of New York State never ceases to inspire me.

Whither Taxonomy?

Carole S. Griffiths

American Museum of Natural History

The changes in the list of New York birds that have occurred since Bull's book was published in 1974 are described in other chapters. Those changes, which reflect, in part, the results of ongoing systematic research, highlight the current dynamic nature of bird classification. This dynamism is a direct result of the revolution in systematics that began in the mid-1970s. Systematics is the study of biodiversity, and avian systematists study variation in current species in an attempt to recover their evolutionary history. The revolution in the mid-1970s transformed systematics from a largely descriptive science to one based on quantitative analytical methods. In addition, new biochemical methods were developed that allowed scientists to use genetic data for systematics, increasing by orders of magnitude the information available for classifications.

The effects of this revolution on bird classification are just starting to become apparent. At a theoretical level, these effects range from new ideas for defining species concepts to new ideas about classifications. For example, the trend now is for classifications to directly reflect the evolutionary history of birds, although the most efficient method for accomplishing that goal is controversial.

The end goal of systematic research, the phylogenies, are hypotheses of evolutionary relationships that can provide information at many taxonomic levels. Are different populations of a species divergent enough to warrant splitting the species, as, for example, the Spotted Owl or the different types of Red Crossbills? Are the families of birds that currently constitute an order really related to each other? For example, are the New World vultures related to storks or to birds of prey? The New World vultures were traditionally considered to be a family within the order Falconiformes, the diurnal birds of prey, on the basis of several characteristics including bill morphology. The alternative suggestion that the New World vultures are related to storks was proposed by Sibley and Ahlquist, who used one kind of DNA data derived from DNA-DNA hybridization studies. On the other hand, recent morphological studies and DNA sequence data support the relatedness of New World vultures and birds of prey. For the moment, the AOU (1997) has formally settled this matter by removing the family Cathartidae (New World vultures) from the order Falconiformes (birds of prey) and placing it in the order Ciconiiformes (herons and allies).

Phylogenies also provide the necessary information for comparing the morphology and behavior of species of birds. Patterns of plumage color, differences in nest building, or differences in mating behavior can be interpreted only within a phylogenetic framework.

The new systematic methodology developed in the 1970s proposed that evolutionary relationships can be determined by finding shared, derived characters that related species have inherited from a common ancestor. To determine these relationships, systematists examine anatomical or genetic characteristics of species and produce detailed lists of the similarities or differences in each characteristic among species. The methodology then relies on computer procedures to derive the exact pattern of relationships of the species, that is, the branching diagram or phylogenetic tree, determined by the many different characters.

These characters were originally derived from the morphology of birds: the skeletons, the bill shape, and so on. However, the primary data now being used for systematics are biochemical. DNA-DNA hybridization data were among the first of the biochemical data collected. Although still used, these data have been largely supplanted by DNA gene sequences. The explosion in the use of sequence data that has occurred since the early 1990s has resulted from two developments. The polymerase chain reaction (PCR) provides an efficient method for amplifying the target gene of interest. New sequencing methodologies allow rapid, and relatively inexpensive, production of the exact sequences of the amplified gene.

These additional data provide hypotheses to compare with ideas based on morphological data. More important, DNA sequence data provide information on relationships for which morphological data are insufficient. This information may have the greatest effect on species-level problems. For example, two isolated populations of a species may not be different morphologically, but they may have accumulated enough differences in DNA sequences to warrant designating the populations as species.

Will these changes affect our enjoyment of birding? Not likely! There certainly will be more species recognized. However, many of these species will have been familiar to birders as subspecies. The most difficult problem may be that of morphologically similar but genetically distinct species. Knowledge of the distributions of these species will be needed to distinguish among them.

Historical Review of the New York State Checklist

Emanuel Levine

I n his two-volume monograph, Eaton (1910, 1914) acknowledged 411 species. Bull (1974), however, applied more-rigorous standards for acceptance of records as well as subsequent taxonomic changes, and he accepted only 366 of Eaton's 411 species. Until the creation of the New York State Avian Records Committee in 1977, Bull's work was regarded as the official New York list by the birding community, and we start with his baseline number of 366.

Bull (1974) gave cachet to an additional 44 species, bringing the total to 410. (He also created a Hypothetical category, to which 22 species were assigned. Of the 22 Hypothetical species, only eight have made it to official status, to date.) His 44 additions were:

Yellow-billed Loon	Rock Pigeon (now Rock Dove)
Eared Grebe	
Yellow-nosed Albatross	White-winged Dove
Northern Fulmar	Monk Parakeet
South Trinidad Petrel (now Herald Petrel)	Burrowing Owl
	Chuck-will's-widow
Manx Shearwater	Willow Flycatcher
Red-billed Tropicbird	Ash-throated Flycatcher
Cattle Egret	Scissor-tailed Flycatcher
Fulvous Tree Duck (now Fulvous Whistling-Duck)	Bell's Vireo
	Black-billed Magpie
Mute Swan	Bewick's Wren
Tufted Duck	Sage Thrasher
Smew	Black-throated Gray Warbler
Gray Partridge	Green-tailed Towhee
Bar-tailed Godwit	Bachman's Sparrow
Franklin's Gull	Clay-colored Sparrow
Black-headed Gull	Harris's Sparrow
Thayer's Gull	Black-headed Grosbeak
Lesser Black-backed Gull	Painted Bunting
Sandwich Tern	Western Meadowlark
Bridled Tern	Brewer's Blackbird
Thin-billed Murre (now Common Murre)	Boat-tailed Grackle
	House Finch

Although Bull listed the Monk Parakeet as part of the state's avifauna, the species was not recognized by NYSARC when they issued the official *Checklist of the Birds of New York State* in 1989. The species was finally added in 1996.

Bull's 1976 supplement added three species (one of which was from the Hypothetical list: marked with an asterisk), making the total 413:

Mountain Bluebird
Swainson's Warbler*
Smith's Longspur

In 1977, the Federation of New York State Bird Clubs (FNYSBC), recognizing the proliferation of sight reports in the state, the increasing dependence on such records because of the legal and ethical restrictions on collecting, and the need for documentation and evaluation of such reports, established the New York State Avian Records Committee (NYSARC). In 1989, this body issued its first official checklist of the birds of the state, which then stood at 435 species, or a gain of 23 since 1976. For readers who can add, please keep in mind that Bull recognized Monk Parakeet but NYSARC had not done so in 1989, accounting for the discrepancy of one. In the 23 additions, those that had been on Bull's Hypothetical list are indicated with an asterisk:

Western Grebe*
White-faced Storm-Petrel
Ross's Goose
White-tailed Kite
Mississippi Kite
Azure Gallinule
Wood Sandpiper
Red-necked Stint
Little Stint
Sharp-tailed Sandpiper
South Polar Skua
Mew Gull

California Gull
Ross's Gull
Vermilion Flycatcher
Fork-tailed Flycatcher*
Rock Wren
Fieldfare
Redwing*
Townsend's Warbler*
Painted Redstart
Golden-crowned Sparrow*
Brambling*

In 1991, when the checklist was reprinted, the total list became 438 with the addition of:

Reddish Egret
White-winged Tern
Cave Swallow

The most recent edition of the checklist was published in mid-1996, at which time the total list stood at 451 species. In the 13 additions, daggers (†) indicate those added by virtue of taxonomic splits (AOU 1995):

Anhinga	Ancient Murrelet
Roseate Spoonbill	Monk Parakeet
Eurasian Hobby	Rufous Hummingbird
Spotted Redshank	Bicknell's Thrush[t]
Slaty-backed Gull	Spotted Towhee[t]
Marbled Murrelet (now Long-billed Murrelet)	Nelson's Sharp-tailed Sparrow[t]
	Bullock's Oriole[t]

Subsequently, Lewis's Woodpecker, which had been on Bull's Hypothetical list, was also added to the checklist, bringing the official total to 452. Then early in 1997, in the basis of additional information, NYSARC reversed its decision on the one Eurasian Hobby record (of April 1996) and withdrew its approval. This change reduces the official total for New York State to 451 species.

Breeding Birds Added

According to Eaton (1914), there were 190 species of birds that either had bred or were still breeding in the state. Bull (1974) brought that total to 228. When the first official checklist was published by NYSARC in 1989, no attempt was made to indicate which of the 435 species on that list were, or had been, breeders. However, in 1991 the second printing of the official checklist indicated that 239 species bred or had bred in the state. This total was revised to 243 in the 1996 updating of the checklist.

The additions since Bull 1974 are:

Canvasback	Chuck-will's-widow
Merlin	Bewick's Wren
Wilson's Phalarope	Yellow-throated Warbler
Gull-billed Tern	Palm Warbler
Caspian Tern	Blue Grosbeak
Forster's Tern	Boat-tailed Grackle
White-winged Tern	White-winged Crossbill

Although it did not increase the number of breeders, a new name on the breeding list was Bicknell's Thrush, which took the place of Gray-cheeked Thrush owing to the split of *Catharus minimus* into two species, with *C. bicknelli*, rather than *C. minimus*, being the breeding bird in New York.

English Bird Name Changes

Since Bull (1974), there have been a number of changes in English names of birds. Many of these changes were made in an attempt to achieve uniformity of popular nomenclature in the English-speaking world. Changes for taxonomic reasons are followed by an asterisk.

Bull (1974) name	Current name
Arctic Loon	Pacific Loon*
Wilson's Storm Petrel	Wilson's Storm-Petrel
Leach's Storm Petrel	Leach's Storm-Petrel
Gannet	Northern Gannet
Black-crowned Night Heron	Black-crowned Night-Heron
Yellow-crowned Night Heron	Yellow-crowned Night-Heron
Fulvous Tree Duck	Fulvous Whistling-Duck
Whistling Swan	Tundra Swan
Common Pintail	Northern Pintail
Common Pheasant	Ring-necked Pheasant
American Spruce Grouse	Spruce Grouse
Greater Prairie Chicken	Greater Prairie-Chicken
Common Bobwhite	Northern Bobwhite
Sora Rail	Sora
Common Gallinule	Common Moorhen
Eurasian Lapwing	Northern Lapwing
Lesser Golden Plover	American Golden-Plover*
Northern Phalarope	Red-necked Phalarope
Skua	Great Skua*
	South Polar Skua*
Thin-billed Murre	Common Murre
Common Puffin	Atlantic Puffin
Rock Pigeon	Rock Dove
Common Barn Owl	Barn Owl
Common Screech Owl	Eastern Screech-Owl*
Saw-whet Owl	Northern Saw-whet Owl
Northern Three-toed Woodpecker	Three-toed Woodpecker
Black-backed Three-toed Woodpecker	Black-backed Woodpecker
Common Flicker	Northern Flicker
Eastern Wood Pewee	Eastern Wood-Pewee
Solitary Vireo	Blue-headed Vireo*
Skylark	Sky Lark
Rough-winged Swallow	Northern Rough-winged Swallow*
Short-billed Marsh Wren	Sedge Wren
Long-billed Marsh Wren	Marsh Wren
Common Mockingbird	Northern Mockingbird
Common Starling	European Starling
Water Pipit	American Pipit*
Parula Warbler	Northern Parula
Myrtle Warbler	Yellow-rumped Warbler*
Black and White Warbler	Black-and-white Warbler
Rufous-sided Towhee	Eastern Towhee*
Tree Sparrow	American Tree Sparrow
Sharp-tailed Sparrow	Saltmarsh Sharp-tailed Sparrow*
	Nelson's Sharp-tailed Sparrow*
Common Cardinal	Northern Cardinal
Eurasian Goldfinch	European Goldfinch

Scientific Bird Name Changes

In the present work, all scientific names derive from the sixth edition of *The AOU Check-List of North American Birds* (1983) and all subsequent Supplements to that publication, which appeared in *The Auk* through 1997 (AOU 1985, 1987, 1989, 1991, 1993, 1995, 1997).

Bull (1974, 1976) followed, for the most part, the fifth edition (1957) of that same publication. At times he departed from their taxonomy and nomenclature either because he disagreed with them or knew that a change was in the works for the forthcoming sixth edition.

In order to eliminate any confusion, we list below the current English name of the bird, the generic name as it appears in Bull (1974, 1976), and the generic name as specified in the sixth edition (1983) of the AOU Check-list and Supplements thereto through 1997. A binomial is shown if the scientific species name has been modified in any manner.

Current English name	Bull (1974, 1976)	AOU 6th ed. and supp.
Cory's Shearwater	*Puffinus*	*Calonectris*
Northern Gannet	*Sula bassana*	*Morus bassanus*
Great Egret	*Egretta*	*Ardea*
Yellow-crowned Night-Heron	*Nycticorax*	*Nyctanassa*
Snow Goose	*Anser*	*Chen*
Smew	*Mergus*	*Mergellus*
Hooded Merganser	*Mergus*	*Lophodytes*
Black-necked Stilt	*Himantopus himantopus*	*H. mexicanus*
Stilt Sandpiper	*Micropalama*	*Calidris*
Common Snipe	*Capella*	*Gallinago*
Red Phalarope	*Phalaropus fulicarius*	*P. fulicaria*
Skua	*Stercorarius*	*Catharacta*
Black-legged Kittiwake	*Larus tridactylus*	*Rissa tridactyla*
Sabine's Gull	*Larus*	*Xema*
Least Tern	*Sterna albifrons*	*S. antillarum*
Scissor-tailed Flycatcher	*Muscivora forficata*	*Tyrannus forficatus*
Fork-tailed Flycatcher	*Muscivora tyrannus*	*Tyrannus savana*
Northern Rough-winged Swallow	*Stelgidopteryx ruficollis*	*S. serripennis*
Brown Creeper	*Certhia familiaris*	*C. americana*
Bewick's Wren	*Thryothorus*	*Thryomanes*
Wood Thrush	*Catharus*	*Hylocichla*
Varied Thrush	*Zoothera*	*Ixoreus*
American Pipit	*Anthus spinoletta*	*A. rubescens*
Savannah Sparrow	*Ammodramus*	*Passerculus*
Song Sparrow	*Passerella*	*Melospiza*
Lincoln's Sparrow	*Passerella*	*Melospiza*
Swamp Sparrow	*Passerella*	*Melospiza*
Blue Grosbeak	*Passerina*	*Guiraca*
Common Redpoll	*Acanthis*	*Carduelis*
Hoary Redpoll	*Acanthis*	*Carduelis*
Pine Siskin	*Spinus*	*Carduelis*
American Goldfinch	*Spinus*	*Carduelis*

Checklist of the Birds of New York State

Published by the Federation of New York State Bird Clubs, Inc. © 1996

With updates through July 1997. The taxonomic order herein is in accordance with the Forty-first Supplement to the AOU Check-list (AOU 1997).

Notations

* Species known to breed, to have bred, or to have established breeding in New York State (243 species)

† Extinct (2 species)

I Introduced (8 species)

E Extirpated: no longer breeds in New York State but is not extinct (1 species)

IE Introduced population existed but no longer occurs in New York State (2 species)

Family Gaviidae—Loons
   Red-throated Loon   *Gavia stellata*
   Pacific Loon   *G. pacifica*
   Common Loon*   *G. immer*
   Yellow-billed Loon   *G. adamsii*

Family Podicipedidae—Grebes
   Pied-billed Grebe*   *Podilymbus podiceps*
   Horned Grebe   *Podiceps auritus*
   Red-necked Grebe   *P. grisegena*
   Eared Grebe   *P. nigricollis*
   Western Grebe   *Aechmophorus occidentalis*

Family Diomedeidae—Albatrosses
   Yellow-nosed Albatross   *Thalassarche chlororhynchos*

Family Procellariidae—Shearwaters and Petrels
   Northern Fulmar   *Fulmarus glacialis*
   Black-capped Petrel   *Pterodroma hasitata*
   Mottled Petrel   *P. inexpectata*
   Herald Petrel   *P. arminjoniana*
   Cory's Shearwater   *Calonectris diomedea*
   Greater Shearwater   *Puffinus gravis*
   Sooty Shearwater   *P. griseus*

Manx Shearwater   *Puffinus puffinus*
Audubon's Shearwater   *P. lherminieri*

Family Hydrobatidae—Storm-Petrels
Wilson's Storm-Petrel   *Oceanites oceanicus*
White-faced Storm-Petrel   *Pelagodroma marina*
Leach's Storm-Petrel   *Oceanodroma leucorhoa*

Family Phaethontidae—Tropicbirds
White-tailed Tropicbird   *Phaethon lepturus*
Red-billed Tropicbird   *P. aethereus*

Family Sulidae—Boobies and Gannets
Brown Booby   *Sula leucogaster*
Northern Gannet   *Morus bassanus*

Family Pelecanidae—Pelicans
American White Pelican   *Pelecanus erythrorhynchos*
Brown Pelican   *P. occidentalis*

Family Phalacrocoracidae—Cormorants
Great Cormorant   *Phalacrocorax carbo*
Double-crested Cormorant*   *P. auritus*

Family Anhingidae—Darters
Anhinga   *Anhinga anhinga*

Family Fregatidae—Frigatebirds
Magnificent Frigatebird   *Fregata magnificens*

Family Ardeidae—Bitterns, Herons, and Allies
American Bittern*   *Botaurus lentiginosus*
Least Bittern*   *Ixobrychus exilis*
Great Blue Heron*   *Ardea herodias*
Great Egret*   *A. alba*
Snowy Egret*   *Egretta thula*
Little Blue Heron*   *E. caerulea*
Tricolored Heron*   *E. tricolor*
Reddish Egret   *E. rufescens*
Cattle Egret*   *Bubulcus ibis*
Green Heron*   *Butorides virescens*
Black-crowned Night-Heron*   *Nycticorax nycticorax*
Yellow-crowned Night-Heron*   *Nyctanassa violacea*

Family Threskiornithidae—Ibises and Spoonbills
White Ibis   *Eudocimus albus*
Glossy Ibis*   *Plegadis falcinellus*
White-faced Ibis   *P. chihi*
Roseate Spoonbill   *Ajaia ajaja*

Family Ciconiidae—Storks
Wood Stork   *Mycteria americana*

Family Cathartidae—New World Vultures
Black Vulture *Coragyps atratus*
Turkey Vulture* *Cathartes aura*

Family Anatidae—Geese, Swans, and Ducks
Fulvous Whistling-Duck *Dendrocygna bicolor*
Greater White-fronted Goose *Anser albifrons*
Snow Goose *Chen caerulescens*
Ross's Goose *C. rossii*
Canada Goose* *Branta canadensis*
Brant *B. bernicla*
Barnacle Goose *B. leucopsis*
Mute Swan* *Cygnus olor*
Tundra Swan *C. columbianus*
Wood Duck* *Aix sponsa*
Gadwall* *Anas strepera*
Eurasian Wigeon *A. penelope*
American Wigeon* *A. americana*
American Black Duck* *A. rubripes*
Mallard* *A. platyrhynchos*
Blue-winged Teal* *A. discors*
Cinnamon Teal *A. cyanoptera*
Northern Shoveler* *A. clypeata*
Northern Pintail* *A. acuta*
Green-winged Teal* *A. crecca*
Canvasback* *Aythya valisneria*
Redhead* *A. americana*
Ring-necked Duck* *A. collaris*
Tufted Duck *A. fuligula*
Greater Scaup *A. marila*
Lesser Scaup* *A. affinis*
King Eider *Somateria spectabilis*
Common Eider *S. mollissima*
Harlequin Duck *Histrionicus histrionicus*
Labrador Duck† *Camptorhynchus labradorius*
Surf Scoter *Melanitta perspicillata*
White-winged Scoter *M. fusca*
Black Scoter *M. nigra*
Oldsquaw *Clangula hyemalis*
Bufflehead *Bucephala albeola*
Common Goldeneye* *B. clangula*
Barrow's Goldeneye *B. islandica*
Smew *Mergellus albellus*
Hooded Merganser* *Lophodytes cucullatus*

Common Merganser*   *Mergus merganser*
Red-breasted Merganser*   *M. serrator*
Ruddy Duck*   *Oxyura jamaicensis*

Family Accipitridae—Kites, Eagles, Hawks, and Allies
Osprey*   *Pandion haliaetus*
Swallow-tailed Kite   *Elanoides forficatus*
White-tailed Kite   *Elanus leucurus*
Mississippi Kite   *Ictinia mississippiensis*
Bald Eagle*   *Haliaeetus leucocephalus*
Northern Harrier*   *Circus cyaneus*
Sharp-shinned Hawk*   *Accipiter striatus*
Cooper's Hawk*   *A. cooperii*
Northern Goshawk*   *A. gentilis*
Red-shouldered Hawk*   *Buteo lineatus*
Broad-winged Hawk*   *B. platypterus*
Swainson's Hawk   *B. swainsoni*
Red-tailed Hawk*   *B. jamaicensis*
Rough-legged Hawk   *B. lagopus*
Golden Eagle*   *Aquila chrysaetos*

Family Falconidae—Caracaras and Falcons
American Kestrel*   *Falco sparverius*
Merlin*   *F. columbarius*
Peregrine Falcon*   *F. peregrinus*
Gyrfalcon   *F. rusticolus*

Family Phasianidae—Partridges, Grouse, and Turkeys
Gray Partridge (I)*   *Perdix perdix*
Ring-necked Pheasant (I)*   *Phasianus colchicus*
Spruce Grouse*   *Falcipennis canadensis*
Ruffed Grouse*   *Bonasa umbellus*
Greater Prairie-Chicken (E)   *Tympanuchus cupido*
Wild Turkey*   *Meleagris gallopavo*

Family Odontophoridae—New World Quail
Northern Bobwhite*   *Colinus virginianus*

Family Rallidae—Rails, Gallinules, and Coots
Yellow Rail   *Coturnicops noveboracensis*
Black Rail*   *Laterallus jamaicensis*
Corn Crake   *Crex crex*
Clapper Rail*   *Rallus longirostris*
King Rail*   *R. elegans*
Virginia Rail*   *R. limicola*
Sora*   *Porzana carolina*
Purple Gallinule   *Porphyrula martinica*

Azure Gallinule   *P. flavirostris*
Common Moorhen*   *Gallinula chloropus*
American Coot*   *Fulica americana*

Family Gruidae—Cranes
Sandhill Crane   *Grus canadensis*

Family Charadriidae—Plovers and Lapwings
Northern Lapwing   *Vanellus vanellus*
Black-bellied Plover   *Pluvialis squatarola*
American Golden-Plover   *P. dominica*
Wilson's Plover   *Charadrius wilsonia*
Semipalmated Plover   *C. semipalmatus*
Piping Plover*   *C. melodus*
Killdeer*   *C. vociferus*

Family Haematopodidae—Oystercatchers
American Oystercatcher*   *Haematopus palliatus*

Family Recurvirostridae—Stilts and Avocets
Black-necked Stilt   *Himantopus mexicanus*
American Avocet   *Recurvirostra americana*

Family Scolopacidae—Sandpipers, Phalaropes, and Allies
Greater Yellowlegs   *Tringa melanoleuca*
Lesser Yellowlegs   *T. flavipes*
Spotted Redshank   *T. erythropus*
Wood Sandpiper   *T. glareola*
Solitary Sandpiper   *T. solitaria*
Willet*   *Catoptrophorus semipalmatus*
Spotted Sandpiper*   *Actitis macularia*
Upland Sandpiper*   *Bartramia longicauda*
Eskimo Curlew   *Numenius borealis*
Whimbrel   *N. phaeopus*
Eurasian Curlew   *N. arquata*
Long-billed Curlew   *N. americanus*
Hudsonian Godwit   *Limosa haemastica*
Bar-tailed Godwit   *L. lapponica*
Marbled Godwit   *L. fedoa*
Ruddy Turnstone   *Arenaria interpres*
Red Knot   *Calidris canutus*
Sanderling   *C. alba*
Semipalmated Sandpiper   *C. pusilla*
Western Sandpiper   *C. mauri*
Red-necked Stint   *C. ruficollis*
Little Stint   *C. minuta*
Least Sandpiper   *C. minutilla*

White-rumped Sandpiper   *Calidris fusicollis*
Baird's Sandpiper   *C. bairdii*
Pectoral Sandpiper   *C. melanotos*
Sharp-tailed Sandpiper   *C. acuminata*
Purple Sandpiper   *C. maritima*
Dunlin   *C. alpina*
Curlew Sandpiper   *C. ferruginea*
Stilt Sandpiper   *C. himantopus*
Buff-breasted Sandpiper   *Tryngites subruficollis*
Ruff   *Philomachus pugnax*
Short-billed Dowitcher   *Limnodromus griseus*
Long-billed Dowitcher   *L. scolopaceus*
Common Snipe*   *Gallinago gallinago*
American Woodcock*   *Scolopax minor*
Wilson's Phalarope*   *Phalaropus tricolor*
Red-necked Phalarope   *P. lobatus*
Red Phalarope   *P. fulicaria*

Family Laridae—Skuas, Gulls, Terns, and Skimmers
Great Skua   *Catharacta skua*
South Polar Skua   *C. maccormicki*
Pomarine Jaeger   *Stercorarius pomarinus*
Parasitic Jaeger   *S. parasiticus*
Long-tailed Jaeger   *S. longicaudus*
Laughing Gull*   *Larus atricilla*
Franklin's Gull   *L. pipixcan*
Little Gull   *L. minutus*
Black-headed Gull   *L. ridibundus*
Bonaparte's Gull   *L. philadelphia*
Mew Gull   *L. canus*
Ring-billed Gull*   *L. delawarensis*
California Gull   *L. californicus*
Herring Gull*   *L. argentatus*
Thayer's Gull   *L. thayeri*
Iceland Gull   *L. glaucoides*
Lesser Black-backed Gull   *L. fuscus*
Slaty-backed Gull   *L. schistisagus*
Glaucous Gull   *L. hyperboreus*
Great Black-backed Gull*   *L. marinus*
Black-legged Kittiwake   *Rissa tridactyla*
Ross's Gull   *Rhodostethia rosea*
Sabine's Gull   *Xema sabini*
Ivory Gull   *Pagophila eburnea*
Gull-billed Tern*   *Sterna nilotica*

Caspian Tern*   *S. caspia*
Royal Tern   *S. maxima*
Sandwich Tern   *S. sandvicensis*
Roseate Tern*   *S. dougallii*
Common Tern*   *S. hirundo*
Arctic Tern   *S. paradisaea*
Forster's Tern*   *S. forsteri*
Least Tern*   *S. antillarum*
Bridled Tern   *S. anaethetus*
Sooty Tern   *S. fuscata*
White-winged Tern*   *Chlidonias leucopterus*
Black Tern*   *C. niger*
Black Skimmer*   *Rynchops niger*

Family Alcidae—Auks, Murres, and Puffins
Dovekie   *Alle alle*
Common Murre   *Uria aalge*
Thick-billed Murre   *U. lomvia*
Razorbill   *Alca torda*
Black Guillemot   *Cepphus grylle*
Long-billed Murrelet   *Brachyramphus perdix*
Ancient Murrelet   *Synthliboramphus antiquus*
Atlantic Puffin   *Fratercula arctica*

Family Columbidae—Pigeons and Doves
Rock Dove (I)*   *Columba livia*
White-winged Dove   *Zenaida asiatica*
Mourning Dove*   *Z. macroura*
Passenger Pigeon†*   *Ectopistes migratorius*

Family Psittacidae—Parrots
Monk Parakeet (I)*   *Myiopsitta monachus*

Family Cuculidae—Cuckoos, Roadrunners, and Anis
Black-billed Cuckoo*   *Coccyzus erythropthalmus*
Yellow-billed Cuckoo*   *C. americanus*

Family Tytonidae—Barn Owls
Barn Owl*   *Tyto alba*

Family Strigidae—Typical Owls
Eastern Screech-Owl*   *Otus asio*
Great Horned Owl*   *Bubo virginianus*
Snowy Owl   *Nyctea scandiaca*
Northern Hawk Owl   *Surnia ulula*
Burrowing Owl   *Athene cunicularia*
Barred Owl*   *Strix varia*
Great Gray Owl   *S. nebulosa*

Long-eared Owl*   *Asio otus*
Short-eared Owl*   *A. flammeus*
Boreal Owl   *Aegolius funereus*
Northern Saw-whet Owl*   *A. acadicus*

Family Caprimulgidae—Goatsuckers
Common Nighthawk*   *Chordeiles minor*
Chuck-will's-widow*   *Caprimulgus carolinensis*
Whip-poor-will*   *C. vociferus*

Family Apodidae—Swifts
Chimney Swift*   *Chaetura pelagica*

Family Trochilidae—Hummingbirds
Ruby-throated Hummingbird*   *Archilochus colubris*
Rufous Hummingbird   *Selasphorus rufus*

Family Alcedinidae—Kingfishers
Belted Kingfisher*   *Ceryle alcyon*

Family Picidae—Woodpeckers and Allies
Lewis's Woodpecker   *Melanerpes lewis*
Red-headed Woodpecker*   *M. erythrocephalus*
Red-bellied Woodpecker*   *M. carolinus*
Yellow-bellied Sapsucker*   *Sphyrapicus varius*
Downy Woodpecker*   *Picoides pubescens*
Hairy Woodpecker*   *P. villosus*
Three-toed Woodpecker*   *P. tridactylus*
Black-backed Woodpecker*   *P. arcticus*
Northern Flicker*   *Colaptes auratus*
Pileated Woodpecker*   *Dryocopus pileatus*

Family Tyrannidae—Tyrant Flycatchers
Olive-sided Flycatcher*   *Contopus cooperi*
Eastern Wood-Pewee*   *C. virens*
Yellow-bellied Flycatcher*   *Empidonax flaviventris*
Acadian Flycatcher*   *E. virescens*
Alder Flycatcher*   *E. alnorum*
Willow Flycatcher*   *E. traillii*
Least Flycatcher*   *E. minimus*
Eastern Phoebe*   *Sayornis phoebe*
Say's Phoebe   *S. saya*
Vermilion Flycatcher   *Pyrocephalus rubinus*
Ash-throated Flycatcher   *Myiarchus cinerascens*
Great Crested Flycatcher*   *M. crinitus*
Western Kingbird   *Tyrannus verticalis*
Eastern Kingbird*   *T. tyrannus*
Gray Kingbird   *T. dominicensis*

Scissor-tailed Flycatcher   *T. forficatus*
Fork-tailed Flycatcher   *T. savana*

Family Laniidae—Shrikes
Northern Shrike   *Lanius excubitor*
Loggerhead Shrike*   *L. ludovicianus*

Family Vireonidae—Vireos
White-eyed Vireo*   *Vireo griseus*
Bell's Vireo   *V. bellii*
Blue-headed Vireo*   *V. solitarius*
Yellow-throated Vireo*   *V. flavifrons*
Warbling Vireo*   *V. gilvus*
Philadelphia Vireo*   *V. philadelphicus*
Red-eyed Vireo*   *V. olivaceus*

Family Corvidae—Jays, Magpies, and Crows
Gray Jay*   *Perisoreus canadensis*
Blue Jay*   *Cyanocitta cristata*
Black-billed Magpie   *Pica pica*
American Crow*   *Corvus brachyrhynchos*
Fish Crow*   *C. ossifragus*
Common Raven*   *C. corax*

Family Alaudidae—Larks
Sky Lark (IE)*   *Alauda arvensis*
Horned Lark*   *Eremophila alpestris*

Family Hirundinidae—Swallows
Purple Martin*   *Progne subis*
Tree Swallow*   *Tachycineta bicolor*
Northern Rough-winged Swallow*   *Stelgidopteryx serripennis*
Bank Swallow*   *Riparia riparia*
Barn Swallow*   *Hirundo rustica*
Cliff Swallow*   *Petrochelidon pyrrhonota*
Cave Swallow   *P. fulva*

Family Paridae—Chickadees and Titmice
Black-capped Chickadee*   *Poecile atricapillus*
Boreal Chickadee*   *P. hudsonicus*
Tufted Titmouse*   *Baeolophus bicolor*

Family Sittidae—Nuthatches
Red-breasted Nuthatch*   *Sitta canadensis*
White-breasted Nuthatch*   *S. carolinensis*
Brown-headed Nuthatch   *S. pusilla*

Family Certhiidae—Creepers
Brown Creeper*   *Certhia americana*

Family Troglodytidae—Wrens
  Rock Wren   *Salpinctes obsoletus*
  Carolina Wren*   *Thryothorus ludovicianus*
  Bewick's Wren*   *Thryomanes bewickii*
  House Wren*   *Troglodytes aedon*
  Winter Wren*   *T. troglodytes*
  Sedge Wren*   *Cistothorus platensis*
  Marsh Wren*   *C. palustris*

Family Regulidae—Kinglets
  Golden-crowned Kinglet*   *Regulus satrapa*
  Ruby-crowned Kinglet*   *R. calendula*

Family Sylviidae—Old World Warblers and Gnatcatchers
  Blue-gray Gnatcatcher*   *Polioptila caerulea*

Family Turdidae—Thrushes
  Northern Wheatear   *Oenanthe oenanthe*
  Eastern Bluebird*   *Sialia sialis*
  Mountain Bluebird   *S. currucoides*
  Townsend's Solitaire   *Myadestes townsendi*
  Veery*   *Catharus fuscescens*
  Gray-cheeked Thrush   *C. minimus*
  Bicknell's Thrush*   *C. bicknelli*
  Swainson's Thrush*   *C. ustulatus*
  Hermit Thrush*   *C. guttatus*
  Wood Thrush*   *Hylocichla mustelina*
  Fieldfare   *Turdus pilaris*
  Redwing   *T. iliacus*
  American Robin*   *T. migratorius*
  Varied Thrush   *Ixoreus naevius*

Family Mimidae—Mockingbirds, Thrashers, and Allies
  Gray Catbird*   *Dumetella carolinensis*
  Northern Mockingbird*   *Mimus polyglottos*
  Sage Thrasher   *Oreoscoptes montanus*
  Brown Thrasher*   *Toxostoma rufum*

Family Sturnidae—Starlings and Allies
  European Starling (I)*   *Sturnus vulgaris*

Family Motacillidae—Wagtails and Pipits
  American Pipit   *Anthus rubescens*

Family Bombycillidae—Waxwings
  Bohemian Waxwing   *Bombycilla garrulus*
  Cedar Waxwing*   *B. cedrorum*

Family Parulidae—Wood Warblers
  Blue-winged Warbler*   *Vermivora pinus*

Golden-winged Warbler*   *V. chrysoptera*
Tennessee Warbler*   *V. peregrina*
Orange-crowned Warbler   *V. celata*
Nashville Warbler*   *V. ruficapilla*
Northern Parula*   *Parula americana*
Yellow Warbler*   *Dendroica petechia*
Chestnut-sided Warbler*   *D. pensylvanica*
Magnolia Warbler*   *D. magnolia*
Cape May Warbler*   *D. tigrina*
Black-throated Blue Warbler*   *D. caerulescens*
Yellow-rumped Warbler*   *D. coronata*
Black-throated Gray Warbler   *D. nigrescens*
Townsend's Warbler   *D. townsendi*
Black-throated Green Warbler*   *D. virens*
Blackburnian Warbler*   *D. fusca*
Yellow-throated Warbler*   *D. dominica*
Pine Warbler*   *D. pinus*
Prairie Warbler*   *D. discolor*
Palm Warbler*   *D. palmarum*
Bay-breasted Warbler*   *D. castanea*
Blackpoll Warbler*   *D. striata*
Cerulean Warbler*   *D. cerulea*
Black-and-white Warbler*   *Mniotilta varia*
American Redstart*   *Setophaga ruticilla*
Prothonotary Warbler*   *Protonotaria citrea*
Worm-eating Warbler*   *Helmitheros vermivorus*
Swainson's Warbler   *Limnothlypis swainsonii*
Ovenbird*   *Seiurus aurocapillus*
Northern Waterthrush*   *S. noveboracensis*
Louisiana Waterthrush*   *S. motacilla*
Kentucky Warbler*   *Oporornis formosus*
Connecticut Warbler   *O. agilis*
Mourning Warbler*   *O. philadelphia*
Common Yellowthroat*   *Geothlypis trichas*
Hooded Warbler*   *Wilsonia citrina*
Wilson's Warbler*   *W. pusilla*
Canada Warbler*   *W. canadensis*
Painted Redstart   *Myioborus pictus*
Yellow-breasted Chat*   *Icteria virens*

Family Thraupidae—Tanagers
Summer Tanager   *Piranga rubra*
Scarlet Tanager*   *P. olivacea*
Western Tanager   *P. ludoviciana*

Family Emberizidae—New World Sparrows
   Green-tailed Towhee *Pipilo chlorurus*
   Eastern Towhee* *P. erythrophthalmus*
   Spotted Towhee *P. maculatus*
   Bachman's Sparrow *Aimophila aestivalis*
   American Tree Sparrow *Spizella arborea*
   Chipping Sparrow* *S. passerina*
   Clay-colored Sparrow* *S. pallida*
   Field Sparrow* *S. pusilla*
   Vesper Sparrow* *Pooecetes gramineus*
   Lark Sparrow *Chondestes grammacus*
   Lark Bunting *Calamospiza melanocorys*
   Savannah Sparrow* *Passerculus sandwichensis*
   Baird's Sparrow *Ammodramus bairdii*
   Grasshopper Sparrow* *A. savannarum*
   Henslow's Sparrow* *A. henslowii*
   Le Conte's Sparrow *A. leconteii*
   Saltmarsh Sharp-tailed Sparrow* *A. caudacutus*
   Nelson's Sharp-tailed Sparrow *A. nelsoni*
   Seaside Sparrow* *A. maritimus*
   Fox Sparrow *Passerella iliaca*
   Song Sparrow* *Melospiza melodia*
   Lincoln's Sparrow* *M. lincolnii*
   Swamp Sparrow* *M. georgiana*
   White-throated Sparrow* *Zonotrichia albicollis*
   Harris's Sparrow *Z. querula*
   White-crowned Sparrow *Z. leucophrys*
   Golden-crowned Sparrow *Z. atricapilla*
   Dark-eyed Junco* *Junco hyemalis*
   Lapland Longspur *Calcarius lapponicus*
   Smith's Longspur *C. pictus*
   Chestnut-collared Longspur *C. ornatus*
   Snow Bunting *Plectrophenax nivalis*

Family Cardinalidae—Grosbeaks and Buntings
   Northern Cardinal* *Cardinalis cardinalis*
   Rose-breasted Grosbeak* *Pheucticus ludovicianus*
   Black-headed Grosbeak *P. melanocephalus*
   Blue Grosbeak* *Guiraca caerulea*
   Indigo Bunting* *Passerina cyanea*
   Painted Bunting *P. ciris*
   Dickcissel* *Spiza americana*

Family Icteridae—Blackbirds
   Bobolink* *Dolichonyx oryzivorus*

Red-winged Blackbird*   *Agelaius phoeniceus*
Eastern Meadowlark*   *Sturnella magna*
Western Meadowlark*   *S. neglecta*
Yellow-headed Blackbird   *Xanthocephalus xanthocephalus*
Rusty Blackbird*   *Euphagus carolinus*
Brewer's Blackbird   *E. cyanocephalus*
Common Grackle*   *Quiscalu quiscula*
Boat-tailed Grackle*   *Q. major*
Brown-headed Cowbird*   *Molothrus ater*
Orchard Oriole*   *Icterus spurius*
Baltimore Oriole*   *I. galbula*
Bullock's Oriole   *I. bullockii*

Family Fringillidae—Fringilline and Cardueline Finches
Brambling   *Fringilla montifringilla*
Pine Grosbeak   *Pinicola enucleator*
Purple Finch*   *Carpodacus purpureus*
House Finch*   *C. mexicanus*
Red Crossbill*   *Loxia curvirostra*
White-winged Crossbill*   *L. leucoptera*
Common Redpoll   *Carduelis flammea*
Hoary Redpoll   *C. hornemanni*
Pine Siskin*   *C. pinus*
American Goldfinch*   *C. tristis*
European Goldfinch (IE)*   *C. carduelis*
Evening Grosbeak*   *Coccothraustes vespertinus*

Family Passeridae—Old World Sparrows
House Sparrow (I)*   *Passer domesticus*

Part II

Species Accounts

The standard for Latin and English nomenclature, as well as taxonomic sequence, used in preparation of this volume was the Sixth Edition of the American Ornithologists' Union's *The Check-list of North American Birds* (1983) and its Supplements through the Forty-first Supplement in 1997. When the Seventh Edition appeared, it contained some sequential taxonomic changes of which your editor was unaware. Time constraints would not permit the inclusion of these in the text of this volume.

Listed below are new taxonomic sequences according to the Seventh Edition of *The A.O.U. Check-list of North American Birds* (1998). Other than these, all sequences in the text of this volume are correct.

Herald Petrel
Mottled Petrel
Black-Capped Petrel

Double-crested Cormorant
Great Cormorant

Gyrfalcon
Peregrine Falcon

Sabine's Gull
Black-legged Kittiwake
Ross's Gull

Loggerhead Shrike
Northern Shrike

Yellow-throated Vireo
Blue-headed Vireo

Cliff Swallow
Cave Swallow
Barn Swallow

Black-throated Green Warbler
Townsend's Warbler

Spotted Towhee
Eastern Towhee

Grasshopper Sparrow
Baird's Sparrow

Nelson's Sharp-tailed Sparrow
Saltmarsh Sharp-tailed Sparrow

LOONS—GAVIIDAE

Red-Throated Loon *Gavia stellata*

Range Holarctic, in North America breeding from Ellesmere Island south to northeastern Alberta, northern Manitoba, and to eastern Quebec and northern Newfoundland. In the east, winters on the Atlantic Coast from Maine to Florida and along the Gulf Coast.

Status Abundant to very abundant migrant and locally abundant winter visitant.

Occurrence A fall migrant, abundant to very abundant along L. Ontario, fairly common on the Finger Lakes, and abundant off Montauk. It is also very common to locally abundant off Montauk in winter. Highly variable in numbers, though scarce at times. Usually rare on smaller lakes. Fairly common in spring and very rare in summer.

    Coastal maxima: 686 Montauk CBC 17 Dec 1994; 480 East Hampton to Montauk, Suffolk Co. 28 Dec 1941. *Inland maxima:* 2000 Point Breeze, Orleans Co. 31 Oct 1989; 1413 Hamlin Beach SP, Monroe Co. 16 Nov 1993; unprecedented away from the Great Lakes were 150 Saratoga L., Saratoga Co. 18 Nov 1962.

Remarks This species sometimes outnumbers the Common Loon and is especially numerous along the south-central and southwestern shores of L. Ontario in fall. It apparently uses two migratory pathways through NY during fall migration. During early to mid-Nov it is a nearshore coastal migrant, with the majority of sightings less than 30 mi off Montauk (Powers and Cherry 1983). The other pathway follows the south shore of L. Ontario, heading west (D'Anna 1995). Presumably these birds then fly south over L. Erie and travel overland to wintering sites along the mid-Atlantic coast.
Steve Kelling

Pacific Loon *Gavia pacifica*

Range Holarctic, breeding from eastern Siberia east to northern Alaska and southern Baffin Island south, in North America to Hudson Bay. Winters mainly on the Pacific Coast, rarely to the Atlantic Coast.

Status Very rare vagrant.

Occurrence Bull (1974) gave one verified record for NY, a specimen of an adult male in alternate plumage, Sands Point, Nassau Co. 29 Apr 1893 AMNH 10980. He also accepted three sight reports of birds in alternate plumage: (1) Montauk, Suffolk Co. 30 Mar 1941 (Helmuth); (2) L. Ontario shore at Point Breeze, Orleans Co. 26 Apr 1959 (Axtell); (3) L. Ontario shore at Pultneyville, Wayne Co. 5 May 1963 (Kemnitzer).

    There have been two additional records of birds in alternate plumage:

(1) a sight report 5 May 1987, L. Ontario at Greece, Monroe Co. (Griffith) (KB 37:147) was accepted by NYSARC (1988); (2) one bird picked up in a field, photographed and released, 23 Apr 1992, Riverhead, Suffolk Co. (DeLuca) (KB 42:202).

Bull (1974) rejected all reports of birds in basic plumage because of the difficulties of separating "Arctic/Pacific" loons from Red-throated and small Common Loons. NYSARC (1993) has accepted one sight report of a basic plumaged bird: 12–14 Dec 1991, Dead Horse Inlet, Brooklyn (Machover and Saphir). Other reports, some perhaps correct, have not been reviewed by NYSARC.

Remarks The AOU, in its Thirty-fifth Supplement (AOU 1985), split Pacific Loon from Arctic Loon *(G. arctica),* creating yet another identification headache for birders. These two species are hard to distinguish in the field in alternate plumage and can be extremely difficult to separate from the other loons in basic plumage; Walsh (1988), Kaufman (1990), and McCaskie et al. (1990) summarized the identification problems.

In accepting the 1987 record, NYSARC (1988) stated, "Although the description of this individual did not rule out Arctic Loon, Pacific Loon is the only species known to occur in the eastern U.S. and no North American specimens of Arctic Loon are known east of Alaska and the Pacific Coast of Canada." Obviously, this situation could change if a specimen of Arctic Loon is found on the East Coast. Veit and Petersen (1993) reported about 20 records of Pacific Loon in MA, with reports almost annually in recent years, although no specimen exists for the state. Halliwell (1995) listed 23 in NJ, again almost annually, and RI more than matches that figure (Conway 1992). Since the dates of the publications listed above, sight records have continued on an annual basis in adjoining states but not in NY.

Joseph DiCostanzo

Common Loon *Gavia immer*

Range Holarctic, breeding in North America from Alaska to Newfoundland (and Greenland) and south; in the east to northern Michigan, New York, and New England. Winters from southern Canada southward, mainly along the coasts.

Status Fairly common breeder in the Adirondacks; very rare elsewhere. Common to abundant migrant on larger bodies of water, both on the coast and inland, especially numerous in the L. Ontario area; also numerous in winter on the ocean off eastern LI.

Breeding It is restricted to the Adirondacks, where it is still a common breeder, and the St. Lawrence Valley, where it is an uncommon breeder (Atlas 1988). The NYSDEC has listed it as a Species of Special Concern because of possible declines in breeding success due to lake acidification and human disturbance in the Adirondacks. Some NY studies (Blair 1990) have found no correlation between water quality and the breeding of Common Loon, although such a relationship has been seen elsewhere in the species' range. The loss of breeding lakes to increased human activity has long been a concern (Atlas 1988).

Nonbreeding During migration the Common Loon appears throughout the state, being most numerous in Apr and Nov. It is regularly seen flying overhead in May, sometimes giving its wonderful wailing call. Evans et al. (1994) documented an apparently important fall flyway over the Finger Lakes region, with 8374 birds counted in 1993 and 12,934 in 1995 (KB 46:49). In winter, especially after a severe interior freeze, large numbers may be seen on coastal salt waters. Summering nonbreeders are not uncommon in LI waters and larger inland lakes and reservoirs.

Coastal maxima: 600 off Mecox Bay, Suffolk Co. 26 May 1975—very late for large numbers; 300 Long Beach, Nassau Co. 11 Apr 1933. *Inland maxima:* 3365 Taughannock SP Loonwatch, Tompkins Co. 29 Nov 1995 and 3337 on 22 Nov 1995; 3000 Hamlin Beach SP, Monroe Co. 1 Nov 1986.

Remarks The frequent summering of nonbreeders on large inland lakes and reservoirs sometimes leads people to mistakenly suspect breeding. The presence of nonflying young birds would normally be considered proof positive of breeding, but Parker (1987) reported the case of a flightless juvenile found at MNWR, 13 Jul 1986, where there was no further evidence of local breeding. It was thought that some person had transported the bird there.

Joseph DiCostanzo

Yellow-billed Loon *Gavia adamsii*

Range Holarctic, breeding in North America east nearly to the northwestern shore of Hudson Bay. The North American breeding population apparently migrates west along the Arctic Coast to its chief wintering grounds off the Pacific coast of Alaska.

Status Accidental.

Occurrence The only known record in eastern North America south of Greenland, where it is also accidental, was the remains of a specimen picked up on the beach on eastern LI, "early" 1930. Only the mandible is preserved (Thayer) AMNH skeletal collection 4005. It was identified by Zimmer (Auk 64:145) and corroborated by Alexander Wetmore. It is not known whether this bird died near the recovery site or was carried there by currents. On 21 Dec 1997, a Yellow-billed Loon was identified by G. Phillips in Oswego harbor, Oswego Co. Also present were S. Boettger, B.

Gruenbaum and M. A. Koeneke. It remained until 6 Jan 1998 and was seen by dozens of birders (KB in press). Photos and details have been submitted to NYSARC.

Remarks The Yellow-billed Loon is closely related to the Common Loon. Together they constitute a superspecies and are considered conspecific by some authors.
Stanley R. Lincoln

GREBES—PODICIPEDIDAE

Pied-billed Grebe *Podilymbus podiceps*

Range Nearctic and Neotropical, breeding from British Columbia to Nova Scotia and south locally throughout the United States, the West Indies, Middle America, and South America to Chile and Argentina. Winters nearly throughout, withdrawing from more northern areas. Tropical populations are sedentary.

Status Rare to uncommon local breeder; fairly common migrant, more numerous in fall; rare but regular winter visitant.

Breeding Believed by many observers to have seriously declined in numbers, this species has been recommended for Threatened status by NYSDEC. The reasons for its decline are not fully understood, but loss of wetlands may be a factor.

The Atlas project found it to be a locally rare to uncommon breeder in relatively few, but widely distributed, blocks in all regions of the state. Except along the Hudson R., it was found primarily at state and federal wildlife refuges. It was absent from the Adirondack High Peaks, Catskill Peaks, and Allegany Hills.

Earlier, Bull (1964) reported it had increased in occurrence on the coast, despite reductions in marshland. At least 40 pairs with young were reported at JBWR in 1961. By 1980, however, the species was reported to have "all but disappeared as a resident bird on Long Island," with only one bird at JBWR that May (KB 30:193). Atlas workers Confirmed breeding there and in only two other coastal blocks.

Inland, the Pied-billed Grebe is generally found nesting in small numbers. Refuge officials interviewed in 1996 estimate that 75 pairs breed at the INWR-OOWMA-TWMA complex on a year-to-year basis.

It prefers open water with an abundance of emergent aquatic vegetation. The nest, built over water, usually floats and is anchored to, or built around, emergent dead or growing vegetation. Although it can be extremely secretive while nesting, its loud, cuckoo-like call betrays its presence.

Nonbreeding It usually arrives by early Mar on the coast and from mid-Mar to early Apr upstate. It is most numerous in the fall, when most maxima have occurred, including: 200 Oneida L., Oneida Co. 13 Nov 1955; 150 MNWR 12 Oct 1961; 65 Shinnecock Bay, Suffolk Co. 24 Sep 1952.

It is a rare but regular winter visitant, more common on the coast, but lingering fairly regularly on open waters in the Finger Lakes, on the Allegany and Oswego rivers, and at Dunkirk Harbor, Chautauqua Co., where an unusually high count of 17 was reported 26 Jan 1986.
Robert E. Marcotte

Horned Grebe

Podiceps auritus

Range Holarctic, in North America breeding from Alaska and northern Manitoba south, east to central Wisconsin and southeastern Ontario. In the east, winters on the Atlantic and Gulf coasts from Nova Scotia to Florida and west to southern Texas, less often on inland waters.

Status Common to abundant migrant and winter visitant along the coast. Common migrant and uncommon winter visitant on interior lakes. Rare in summer.

Occurrence Found in good numbers on inland bodies of water and along the coast during migration; concentrations seem to be greater on the larger bodies of water such as the Great Lakes, L. Champlain, Chautauqua L., and in some years the Finger Lakes. The largest concentrations are traditionally along the coast in late fall and winter. The peaks in migration occur during Apr, Oct, and Nov. Winter concentrations are most numerous in the warmer coastal regions.

  Coastal maxima: 2000+ Montauk 19 Feb 1984; 1000 Atlantic Beach to Point Lookout, Nassau Co. 8 Mar 1959. *Inland maxima:* 600 Bear and Cassadaga lakes, Chautauqua Co. 19 Apr 1962; 350 Oneida L. 24 Nov 1955; 350 mouth of the Niagara R. 18 Nov 1956; 350 Hamlin Beach, Monroe Co. 29 Oct 1967.

Bull (1974) remarked that fairly large numbers of Horned Grebes have been known to go over the falls at Niagara, noting two such large events. The first was on 21 Apr 1949, when 36 dead birds were recovered from an estimated 375 seen above and 75 below the falls. The second, on 8 Apr 1954, was larger, with 75 dead birds recovered from an estimated 600 that were near the falls.

It has also been known to have large put-downs on frozen bodies of water or even highways, mistaking the icy surfaces for water. One such occurrence was on 12 Jan 1978 at Quaker L., Chautauqua Co., when 75 birds landed on the ice; 53 of them survived and were released on open water (KB 28:102).

Remarks There were early references to Horned Grebe breeding in NY (Eaton 1910; Beardslee and Mitchell 1965; KB 16:234). None of these reports were substantiated (Bull 1974). Since Horned Grebes do nest as close as eastern ON, observers in the northern and western portions of NY should probably be on the alert for the possibility.
Kevin C. Griffith

Red-necked Grebe *Podiceps grisegena*

Range Holarctic, in North America breeding from northwestern Alaska to western Ontario, south to central Washington and east to southern Quebec. In the east, winters along the coast from Newfoundland to Florida, mostly in the northern portion.

Status Rare to uncommon, sometimes common, migrant and winter visitant in coastal areas and on the Great and Finger lakes and larger bodies of water and rivers inland.

Occurrence As a migrant and winter resident, Red-necked Grebe is almost never abundant. It is most numerous in severe winters when the Great Lakes freeze over or in migration when overland migrants are put down by adverse weather or fog. Major wintering areas for this species have never been discovered but are suspected by some to be in the central portions of the northerly Great Lakes (Granlund 1994).

It usually appears in very small numbers in Nov and early Dec and will sometimes show site fidelity for the entire winter season. It typically returns through NY in Mar and Apr, along with Red-throated Loon coastally and Common Loon on upstate lakes. Data from CBCs showed a few scattered singles on large lakes upstate and in the east in Dec (30 records, 1960–1989) and much larger numbers in Greater NYC and eastern LI (117 records). Only the Montauk CBC records the species routinely. It has been reported in every month but is typically very rare as a lingerer after Apr or as an early migrant before Oct. Two major irruptions, in Feb 1934 and Feb

1994, have been noted, with a large die-off of birds recorded in the 1934 event.

Coastal maxima: Spring: 115 East Hampton to Montauk, Suffolk Co. 7 Apr 1940; 64 Point Lookout, Nassau Co. 11 Apr 1939. *Winter:* 425 (225 dead) Montauk 22 Feb 1934; 60 Montauk to Shinnecock 26 Feb 1994.
Inland maxima: Spring: 130 Seneca L. 17 Mar 1994; 73 Sheldrake, Seneca Co. 10 Apr 1994. *Fall:* 30 Sandy Pond, Oswego Co. 6 Nov 1955. *Winter:* 105 Cayuga L. 20 Feb 1994; 45 Tompkins Co. 12 Feb–3 Mar 1912.

No noteworthy coastal late-fall high counts have been published.

Remarks More open lake surveys in midwinter on the Great Lakes might reveal Red-necked Grebe to be a common wintering species in the state. For more on the 1994 flight, see Lantz 1994; the 1934 flight is discussed in Hickey 1935. Beardslee and Mitchell (1965) noted the possibility of nesting in the Niagara Frontier region, inasmuch as nesting has occurred at Burlington, ON. Summering birds were noted in 1993 in the vicinity of MNWR (KB 42:424).
Edward S. Brinkley

Eared Grebe   *Podiceps nigricollis*

Range Holarctic and Ethiopian, breeding in North America from central British Columbia east to southern Manitoba and central Minnesota and south to Baja California and southern Texas. Winters from southern Canada to Guatemala; rarely, but regularly, along the Atlantic Coast from Massachusetts to Florida.

Status Rare but regular migrant and winter visitant on the Great Lakes; very rare migrant and winter visitant on the coast. Casual elsewhere.

Occurrence It was first reported in NY on the South Shore of LI in 1938 and on the Great Lakes in 1948. In recent years it has been recorded nearly annually on migration in the Niagara area and along the shores of the Great Lakes. On the coast it is most often reported at JBWR and the south shore of SI but has also been found all along the LI South Shore. One in Rye, Westchester Co. 30 Sep–8 Oct 1995 was the first downstate record away from LI (KB 46:87). Bull (1974) reported at least 70 occurences from the entire state; there are now well over 100. Most are from mid-Oct to late Apr.

Maxima: 3 JBWR 10 Sep 1994; 2 Big Tupper L., Franklin Co. 2 Apr 1984. The latter two, in alternate plumage, were a first county record and only the second record for the Adirondack region. *Extreme dates:* 6 Sep and 3 Jun.

There are two summer records: Kendall, Orleans Co. 28 Jul–12 Aug 1979; JBSP 4 Aug 1983.

Remarks This species is perhaps regularly overlooked in winter because of its similarity to Horned Grebe in basic plumage. Spring birds in changing plumage have to be identified with even greater caution because the two species can then be nearly indistinguishable.
Joseph DiCostanzo

Western Grebe   *Aechmophorus occidentalis*

Range Nearctic, breeding from southeastern Alaska, Alberta, and Manitoba south to California and New Mexico and east to western Minnesota. Winters mainly on the Pacific Coast south to Baja California; rare but regular visitant to the Atlantic Coast.

Status Casual vagrant.

Occurrence There are four records accepted by NYSARC (1979, 1987): (1) a summering individual, photographed, on Tupper L., St. Lawrence Co. 2 Jul–7 Oct 1978 (Delehanty 1978); (2) one photographed during its stay at Ditch Plains, Suffolk Co. 12 Jan–23 Mar 1985 (DiCostanzo, Morris) (KB 35:153); (3) again at Ditch Plains 5 Dec 1985–17 Feb 1986; (4) Greece, Monroe Co. 6 Dec 1986 (Spahn). The Ditch Plains records were probably the same individual returning to winter in the same location two years in a row.

These four are the only records accepted by NYSARC as definitely referring to this species. Other reports through the years could be assigned only to genus as details sufficient to distinguish the species (see Remarks) were not noted before they were "split."

A report of a bird seen 22 Oct 1995 at Hamlin Beach SP, Monroe Co. (Symonds) (KB 46:43) has not yet been reviewed by NYSARC.

Remarks Bull (1974) placed Western Grebe on the Hypothetical list because of the lack of a specimen or photograph. He reported more than a dozen sight reports, most upstate, at least some of which he believed to be correct. In 1985 the AOU complicated the matter when it gave species status, as Clark's Grebe (*A. clarkii*), to what had been considered the light morph of the Western Grebe, leaving what had been the dark morph as Western Grebe (AOU 1985). Kaufman (1990) and Eckert (1993, 1995) discussed the problems of separating these two sibling species in the field.

Reported status in CT (Zeranski and Baptist 1990) and PA (Santner et al. 1992) is approximately the same as that in NY. The Western Grebe has been recorded with much greater frequency in MA (Veit and Petersen 1993) and NJ (Halliwell 1995).
Joseph DiCostanzo

ALBATROSSES—DIOMEDEIDAE

Yellow-nosed Albatross · *Thalassarche chlororhynchos*

Range Southern Atlantic and Indian oceans, breeding on the Tristan da Cunha Islands and Gough Island in the Atlantic and on St. Paul Island in the Indian Ocean. Vagrant in the North Atlantic.

Status Casual vagrant.

Occurrence An adult was observed by 60 people, and photographed, 29 May 1960, about two miles off Jones Beach during a Linnaean Society of New York pelagic trip. Post (1968) documented the event and commented on seven other eastern North America observations. Remembrances, after 33 years, of this first record for NY were provided by Fisher (1993).

Weissman and Howe (1976) described their close observation of an adult driven 25 miles up the Hudson R. to the southern tip of Croton Point, Westchester Co. by Hurricane Belle on 10 Aug 1976. The bird passed within 30 ft of the astonished observers.

A bird reported as this species, flying over Crown Point peninsula on L. Champlain, Essex Co. on 8 May 1994, was accepted by NYSARC as an albatross of this genus, but the committee felt it could not be assigned to a species (NYSARC 1996). Whatever the species, the record is remarkable.

Remarks Sightings on pelagic trips to Cox's Ledge, RI include a subadult on 21 Aug 1976, likely also a result of Hurricane Belle, and another, photographed, on 21 Aug 1979 (Conway 1992). MA has two sight records, May 1971 and Jun 1976 (Veit and Peterson 1993).

Berna B. Lincoln

SHEARWATERS AND PETRELS—PROCELLARIIDAE

Northern Fulmar · *Fulmarus glacialis*

Range Northern Holarctic, breeding in North America from the Bering Sea and Aleutians east to Baffin Island, Greenland, and Iceland, south to Newfoundland (since 1973). Winters at sea south to the Grand Banks off Newfoundland and the fishing banks off Massachusetts; less commonly but regularly south to South Carolina.

Status Common to abundant offshore visitant. Casual inland.

Occurrence An offshore wintering population is present in most years but may be inexplicably absent in others. High counts include: 265 Block Canyon 12 Mar 1977; 100 Hudson Canyon 28 May 1983. Of the land-based sightings, the most notable was 24 seen in the Fire I. Inlet, Suffolk Co. 24 Sep 1977.

L. Ontario records include: 1 New Haven, Oswego Co. 3 Oct 1971; 1 just east of Oswego 19 Dec 1974; 1 Derby Hill, Oswego Co. 3 Dec 1992; 2 Moses-Saunders Power Dam, Massena, St. Lawrence Co. 15–19 Dec 1994.

Extreme dates: 10 Sep and 18 Jun, the latter established by two seen 20 mi south of Montauk in 1975.

Remarks The status of Northern Fulmar in NY has changed dramatically in the past 25 years. The species was once known as very rare to casual in the western Atlantic. Its fairly recent breeding range expansion into Newfoundland from northern Europe may be responsible for the large wintering population we know today.
John P. Askildsen

Black-capped Petrel   *Pterodroma hasitata*

Range Neotropical, breeding at high elevations on Hispaniola, Cuba, and other islands of the West Indies; ranges at sea north to Cape Hatteras, North Carolina, and south to Brazil; recorded principally after hurricanes north to Ontario, New Hampshire, Connecticut, and New York.

Status Very rare vagrant.

Occurrence Until 1996 there are seven records, the first five documented by specimens. (1) Quogue, Suffolk Co. Jul 1850 (Lawrence collection) AMNH 46145. (2) Verona Beach, Oneida L., Oneida Co. 28 Aug 1893 (Biederman) AMNH 458986. (3) labeled only as Cayuga Sep 1893 (Foster) AMNH 98754 (Murphy 1936:693). (4) New Paltz, Ulster Co. 26 Jan 1895 (Vradenburgh), a mounted specimen examined by Foster and formerly in a private collection (Auk 12:179). This individual was apparently found alive in the snow in an exhausted condition. (5) An adult male found near Owego, Tioga Co. 26 Aug 1933 (Loomis) CUM 5838. It was found alive but exhausted and was no doubt deposited there by the hurricane of 22 Aug. This same storm was responsible for the transportation of NY's first Herald Petrel.

The next record for the state came 56 years later, when an individual was found on a school lawn in Horseheads, Chemung Co., 25 Sep 1989, two days after Hurricane Hugo (KB 41:241). The seventh record was at Hudson Canyon 16 Sep 1991 (AB 46:67, ph 46:166). That bird's appearance may have been related to the passage of Hurricane Bob on 19 Aug.

Then, on 7 Sep 1996, Hurricane Fran swept across the state, moving west and north to L. Erie and depositing several Black-capped Petrels along the way. At least nine were reported. Seven of them occurred 12–21 Sep in Region 1, and one was seen at Hamlin Beach, Monroe Co. 23 Sep. One bird was picked up in Skaneateles, Onondaga Co. on 12 Sep and relocated to NC, where it died. This storm more than doubled all previous records for the species.

Remarks Three records exist for MA (Veit and Petersen 1993). Surprisingly, two are from Mar and Apr, and the third was seen from land during Hurricane Bob 19 Aug 1991. CT has one record from 7 Oct 1938, just after the great hurricane of that year (Zeranski and Baptist 1990). PA has five records, all related to Hurricane Hugo, 23 Sep 1989 (Santner et al. 1992), NJ three (Halliwell 1995), and RI two (Conway 1992).

In its normal range, it can be abundant at times even as far north as the Gulf Stream waters off NC. North of this boundary it is a great rarity but is not considered out of the question during the warm summer months. With the rise in popularity of pelagic birding, there will undoubtedly be more records established for NY, other than hurricane related.
John P. Askildsen

Mottled Petrel   *Pterodroma inexpectata*

Range Breeds in New Zealand and on nearby islands, in recent years in considerably reduced numbers; in the nonbreeding season ranges eastward and northward through the Pacific Ocean to at least the Aleutian Islands (rarely).

Status Accidental.

Occurrence There is one specimen record: Mt. Morris, Livingston Co. early April 1880 (Smith) MCZ 205224 (*fide* Paynter). "One of the laborers while ploughing an old cornfield, noticed it [the petrel] running in a freshly turned furrow and despatched it with a stick. It was apparently exhausted, for it made no attempt to escape." (Brewster, *Bulletin Nuttall Ornith. Club* 6[1881]:91). An illustration of the mounted specimen of this most unexpected occurrence is found in Eaton 1910.

Remarks This individual is the type specimen and remains the only record for North America outside of the Pacific basin (E. Brinkley, pers. comm.).
John P. Askildsen

Herald Petrel   *Pterodroma arminjoniana*

Range Pantropical, breeding on oceanic islands south of the equator in the Atlantic, Indian, and Pacific oceans; in the South Atlantic off the Brazilian coast on South Trinidad Island.

Status Accidental.

Occurrence There is one record: a light morph male found alive, but exhausted, near Caroline Center, Tompkins Co., after the hurricane of 22 Aug 1933. It died a few days later and is now specimen number 348070 in the USNM collection.

Remarks A heightened interest in pelagic birding off the NC coast in the last 10 years has revealed that this is a rare but regularly seen species, recorded several times a year 22 May–26 Sep (E. Brinkley, pers. comm.). It should be diligently looked for on pelagic trips in NY waters.
John P. Askildsen

Cory's Shearwater   *Calonectris diomedea*

Range Primarily Palearctic, breeding on islands in the warm temperate waters of the eastern Atlantic and the Mediterranean. Ranges at sea west to the North American coast and south to Brazil and South Africa.

Status Common to abundant late summer and fall visitant off eastern LI, usually much less numerous westward.

Occurrence After the breeding season, it disperses westward into the Atlantic in late summer and then may occur in large numbers in NY waters, when it may be seen from the outer beaches, especially after storms or prolonged east winds. Some typical numbers recorded in 1936 by Helmuth off Montauk were: 300, 27 Aug; 500, 8 Sep; 750, 11 Oct. A count of 435 at JBSP, 16 Oct 1966, is exceptional because of the western location. Even more extraordinary were 20 just outside of NY Harbor, 27 Aug 1962.

More-recent data show the species present in reasonable numbers even in early summer: 25 Montauk 10 Jun 1993; 90 off Fire I., Suffolk Co. 3 Jul 1993. Offshore, notable recent counts include: 440, 13 Aug 1981; 420, 15 mi south of Montauk, 17 Jul 1981. It is normally much less numerous before Jul and after mid-Nov.

Extreme dates: 29 May and 1 Dec.

Remarks The subspecies commonly found in our waters is *borealis*. The smaller nominate subspecies, *diomedea*, which breeds east of *borealis*, has been collected in NY on five occasions, with verification by R.C. Murphy; the skins are in the AMNH collection. Two were taken at Jones Beach, Nassau Co. 4 Oct 1902, and two at Montauk, 15 Aug 1907; one was found dead at Montauk 22 Sep 1938, after the great hurricane. The subspecies *diomedea* is considered accidental in North America and is known only from these five specimens. The two forms are not distinguishable in the field.
John P. Askildsen

Greater Shearwater *Puffinus gravis*

Range Pelagic in the nonbreeding season, breeding only in the South Atlantic Ocean on the Tristan da Cunha Islands and on Gough Island; also in 1961 in the Falkland Islands. Ranges north and west after breeding season through the western Atlantic to the northeastern coast of North America, then migrates eastward in fall toward the eastern Atlantic.

Status Regular visitant to offshore waters and occasionally inshore mid-spring through late fall. Casual inland.

Occurrence The most commonly seen shearwater in NY waters, this species, like many others in its genus, spends the austral winter in the North Atlantic, with usual occurrence 1 May–3 Dec. Common to very abundant during its peak period, its numbers are virtually unpredictable, as is true with many pelagic species. Record high counts include: 2500 Hudson Canyon 30 May 1981; 625 well south of Montauk 7 Sep 1991; 330 Hudson Canyon 16 Sep 1991.

It can linger into Dec, as was discovered on a pelagic trip 3 Dec 1994, when 14 were found at Hudson Canyon, establishing a new late date for NY. During the summer of 1993, impressive numbers were recorded from shore at Montauk, including 75 on 5 June and 1000 on 2 July.

Two inland reports include one seen at Alcove Reservoir, Albany Co., 23 Sep 1990 (KB 40:50), and another seen flying up the Hudson R. in Greene and Albany counties on 14 Jun 1976 (R. Guthrie). It was rescued, exhausted, from L. Champlain at Burlington, VT on 16 Jun, was photographed with Guthrie, and died on 19 Jun (Peterson 1976).

Remarks The species was formerly more abundant in the North Atlantic. The early 1980s saw a swift and steady decline in numbers offshore. It is generally theorized that when both ocean dumping and foreign fishing fleets were no longer allowed in U.S. waters, the pattern of postbreeding dispersal shifted elsewhere to "greener pastures." In past years, 20,000–200,000 birds have been found in richer waters to the east of NY on Georges Banks, MA during several one-day pelagic trips ranging from Jun to Nov (Veit and Petersen 1993).
John P. Askildsen

Sooty Shearwater *Puffinus griseus*

Range Southern oceans, breeding on islands off southeastern Australia and New Zealand and off the southern coast of South America. Ranges at sea, in the Pacific north to southern Bering Sea and in the western Atlantic north to Newfoundland; also in the Gulf of Mexico west to Texas. Casual inland, mostly after storms.

Status Very common to abundant offshore visitant. Accidental inland.

Occurrence Most commonly found in NY waters in spring, it is most abundant from late May through late Jun. It has been recorded just outside NY at Cox's Ledge, RI as early as 25 Apr. A single bird was observed from JBSP 9 May 1987. Land-based sightings typically occur during this period, when fog and east winds come into play, and usually come from inlets and bays from Fire I. east to Montauk. High counts from land include: 1000 Shinnecock Inlet to Montauk 26 May 1975; 250 Suffolk Co. south shore 24 May 1975. From the deep-water canyons, there is a high count of 800–900 Hudson Canyon 30 May 1981.

Numbers begin to thin out markedly by mid-Jul. There is an early record at Block Canyon 2 Feb 1978, which may be a wintering individual, and an extremely late bird, 30 Nov 1957, which followed a fishing boat into L. Montauk.

Away from the coast, there was a rare sighting in the Hudson R. from Dobbs Ferry, Westchester Co. 6 Sep 1980 just after Hurricane David. John P. Askildsen

Manx Shearwater *Puffinus puffinus*

Range Mainly western Palearctic, breeding in North America in Massachusetts (1973) and Newfoundland (since 1976); also in Iceland and the Faroe and Shetland islands, around the British Isles, and in western France to the Azores and around the Mediterranean Sea. Ranges at sea, in the western Atlantic, from Newfoundland to Maryland and Bermuda and off South America from Trinidad to Argentina.

Status Uncommon visitor in offshore waters of LI.

Occurrence Bull (1974) described it as "accidental." There are only two specimens, both from LI, both found dead on South Shore beaches. The first is Ocean Beach, Fire I., Suffolk Co. 20 Aug 1917, (Thurston) AMNH 349273. The second was found at Far Rockaway, Queens Co., 79 years later, 9 Dec 1996 (Gormley) AMNH 831714.

This cold-water species is probably present in NY waters every month of the year. Because pelagic trips are popular from May to Oct, most recorded observations fall into that time period. Recent trips in Dec and Mar have provided new data on its presence in winter. Unfortunately, because of the impracticality of scheduling pelagic trips in the harsh weather of Jan and Feb, data for those months will remain sketchy.

Maxima: 5, 30 mi south of Montauk 22 Aug 1982; 4 "off Montauk" 23 Aug 1980; 4 seen from land at Fire I. 4 Jul 1993.

Late dates include: 3 Dec 1994 (two at Hudson Canyon) and 11 Dec 1994 (one at Montauk). Close to 50 records exist of single birds observed from points on the South Shore of LI.

Remarks Manx Shearwater is much more common in the waters off Cape Cod, MA and north, especially from spring to fall. NY high counts pale in comparison. According to Veit and Petersen (1993), it has been recorded in such stunning single-day numbers as 200, 120, 50, and 25. Such numbers are not likely to ever be recorded in NY, because our waters are probably not cold enough.

A single record exists from western LI Sound, but not in NY. A bird was observed on 17 May 1980 at Greenwich Point, CT (Zeranski and Baptist 1990). The most significant discovery about this species in the New World was that of a first breeding record for North America at Penikese I., MA 6 Jun 1973 (Veit and Petersen 1993). This location is not far from NY as the shearwater flies, so it seems not out of the question for breeding to occur on one of NY's offshore islands such as Fishers, Plum, Great Gull, Robins, or Gardiners.

John P. Askildsen

Audubon's Shearwater *Puffinus lherminieri*

Range Pantropical, breeding chiefly on oceanic islands nearly throughout; in the western North Atlantic north to the Bahamas and Bermuda. Wanders north to Long Island and Massachusetts.

Status Fairly common visitant to offshore waters Jun–Sep.

Occurrence Treated by Bull (1974) as a casually occurring southern wanderer to NY waters, its status has changed considerably. Arriving as early as 28 Jun and remaining as late as 29 Sep, this species is probably most abundant during the periods when water temperatures are at their warmest. It has been recorded in 63°–73°F water offshore during the above months.

It is decidedly the least likely of all locally occurring species in the *Puffinus* genus to be seen from shore. Five specimen records exist of individuals picked up on beaches in four events: (1) One specimen was picked up at Great South Bay off Bellport, Suffolk Co. 1 Aug 1887 (Dutcher Collection) AMNH 64714. (2) The second specimen was found dead, Point Lookout, Nassau Co. 24 Jul 1938 AMNH 4110. (3) Two were found in 1951 in Suffolk Co.: one at Dix Hills 31 Jul AMNH 6590, the other at Cedar Beach 4 Sep. The latter was deposited in the Nassau County Museum. (4) Finally, a bird found alive but in a weakened condition on Fire I., opposite Blue Point, Suffolk Co. 28 Jul 1967 expired the same day, AMNH 788362. There was only one observation from land, a bird seen and photographed from Oakwood Beach, Richmond Co. 14 Aug 1955 just two days after Hurricane Connie. Bull (1964) treated this record as "probable" on the basis of comments by R. C. Murphy.

Today, a one-day pelagic trip during the summer might encounter 1–6 individuals. Trips during the peak period, combined with favorable, warm-water conditions, may expect to encounter 20–40 in a day, as supported by the following: 27 "off Long Island" 7 Aug 1980 at 200–300 fathoms (Rowlett) (KB 30:260); 5 at Hudson Canyon 1–2 Sep 1978 (Lorenzi) (KB 28:262); a remarkable record count of 225 tending a Russian research vessel slightly south of Hudson Canyon at 1000 fathoms, 19 Sep 1979 (Rowlett) (AB 34:144).

Remarks The dramatic change in this species' status in NY can probably be attributed to one of two possibilities or a combination thereof. Either the austral wintering range expanded northward in the last two decades, as has that of many formerly "southern" species during the same period, or the increase of interest in pelagic birding has been a factor. Regardless of the reason, this species should now be treated as an expected visitant.
John P. Askildsen

STORM-PETRELS—HYDROBATIDAE

Wilson's Storm-Petrel

Oceanites oceanicus

Range Antarctic and sub-Antarctic, breeding north to islands off southern South America. After the breeding season, ranges north in the Atlantic to Labrador, Iceland, and the British Isles and in the Gulf of Mexico to Texas and the Gulf Coast.

Status Common to very abundant visitant on open ocean. Very rare on eastern LI Sound; casual western LI Sound and inland.

Occurrence Perhaps the most abundant pelagic species in NY waters, it is regularly found by the hundreds and even low thousands during some one-day periods. The best way to observe Wilson's Storm-Petrel is by chumming from a boat. Offshore, high counts include 50,000–75,000 at Hudson Canyon, 28 May 1983 (KB 43:351). An impressive count from shore of 750 was recorded 5 Jun 1993 at Montauk.

Despite its incredible abundance at sea, this species is extremely rare inland, even after hurricanes. Only five inland records are recognized: (1) a specimen, found dead at Lockport, Niagara Co. Oct 1875 (Davison Collection) (BMS 6386), probably transported by the hurricane of 10–13 Oct; (2) another specimen, collected alive at L. Titus, Franklin Co. 26 Aug 1933 (Hale) (NYSM 5261), undoubtedly a result of the 22 Aug hurricane; (3) one at Irvington, Westchester Co. in 1933; (4) one observed on L. Ontario, Charlotte, Monroe Co. 25 Sep 1938 (Meade), after the great hurricane of 1938. (5) The fifth record, accepted by NYSARC, was observed 18 Aug 1986 off Piermont Pier, Rockland Co. as a result of Tropical Storm Charlie (Derven 1986).

A Nov 1882 specimen from Monroe Co., mentioned by Eaton (1910), was, according to Bull (1974), apparently not extant, and presumably Eaton did not examine it. A sight report from LI Sound off Bronx Co. 12 Jun 1986 was apparently not submitted to NYSARC (AB 40:1183).

This species arrives in numbers the last week in May. The bulk of the population departs by mid-Sep.

Extreme dates: 18 May and 22 Oct.
John P. Askildsen

White-faced Storm-Petrel *Pelagodroma marina*

Range Worldwide pelagic, breeding in the Atlantic on the Cape Verde and Tristan da Cunha islands, Gough Island, and possibly others including the Canary Islands. Ranges widely at sea; off the eastern North American coast, from Massachusetts to North Carolina.

Status Casual offshore vagrant.

Occurrence This warm-water species is known to occur in the western Atlantic from mid-Aug through early Oct. The six records in NY all occurred during that period except for one in May, which is a rare date in the western Atlantic. All were at Hudson Canyon. They are: a specimen collected 18 Aug 1953 (NYSARC 1979); and sight records 26 May 1976 (AB 30:818); 11 Sep 1979 (AB 35:162); 19 Sep 1979 (KB 30:60); 18 Sep 1987 (RNJB 14:15); 17 Sep 1988 (KB 38:282).

Remarks CT has one land-based record. MA has 10, all from well off-shore, and RI lists two. NJ claims several, many of them originating from trips to Hudson Canyon, which is within the pelagic boundaries of NY. For discussion of the status and distribution of this species in the Atlantic, see Watson et al. 1986.

John P. Askildsen

Leach's Storm-Petrel   *Oceanodroma leucorhoa*

Range North Atlantic and North Pacific, breeding on offshore islands; in the western Atlantic from southern Labrador south to Massachusetts. Atlantic birds winter south along both coasts to Florida, the West Indies, and Brazil; also off Africa, to South Africa.

Status Very rare visitant inshore, perhaps regular well offshore beyond the continental shelf. Very rare inland; seen there only after tropical storms.

Occurrence There are more than 75 reports, mostly after storms, some found dead. For instance, after the hurricane of 22 Aug 1933, many were reported, but oddly enough all were upstate. No fewer than 20 were picked up dead at Sylvan Beach, Oneida Co. 7–30 Sep 1933. Also after this storm, individuals were observed in Herkimer and Schenectady counties. Another inland record, after a storm, notable because it is the latest fall report, was of a bird seen flying over Otsego L., Otsego Co. 26 Nov 1950. More recent records include: 4 Block Canyon 7 Jun 1980 during a FNYSBC chartered trip; 7 Hudson Canyon 30 May 1986; 2 Montauk 19 Aug 1991. Last, one was observed flying above the surf off Cedar Beach, Suffolk Co. 26 Sep 1992 (KB 43:80). This record, accepted by NYSARC (1994), was apparently associated with a very weak tropical depression, which passed offshore south of LI just before the sighting.

These birds are active at night, as evidenced by the fact that they have hit lighthouses. Further proof of nocturnal activity is provided by two caught in mistnets at night and banded on Great Gull I., Suffolk Co. 4 and 6 Aug 1967.

For additional records from the NYC region, see Bull 1964. Six old occurrences from the upper Hudson Valley were summarized by Eaton (1910).

The maximum daily high count remains 12, observed from Montauk 1 Oct 1932.

Extreme dates: 4 May and 26 Nov.

Remarks Records in NJ and RI approximate those of NY, and even CT has recorded it in LI Sound, but the MA figures are truly astounding. There are many reports of flocks in the multihundreds, and one of 10,000+. These numbers are unrelated to the fact that there is a small breeding colony in Buzzards Bay on Penikese I., although that colony probably accounts for some inshore summer records in MA (Veit and Petersen 1993).

John P. Askildsen

TROPICBIRDS—PHAETHONTIDAE

White-tailed Tropicbird *Phaethon lepturus*

Range Pantropical, breeding in Bermuda, the Bahamas, and the Greater and Lesser Antilles. Ranges at sea northwest to the Atlantic Coast but rarely north of North Carolina. Recorded as a vagrant north to New York, Massachusetts, and Nova Scotia.

Status Casual vagrant.

Occurrence There are six documented records, five of them by specimen, all hurricane related. An immature, Knowlesville, Orleans Co. 19 Sep 1876, a mounted specimen in the NYSM exhibition collection, was the only record until 1938. The great hurricane of 21 Sep 1938 produced all of the LI records: one observed flying over Jones Beach on 25 Sep (Brennan, Tengwell, and Russell); three found dead and preserved: two in East Hampton 22 Sep and 3 Oct 1938; the remains of another at Montauk 1 Jan 1939 (all by Helmuth, formerly in his collection). An immature was found dead on the L. Ontario shore near Ellisburg, Jefferson Co. 26 Oct 1954 (Belknap) NYSM 17046, after the hurricane of 15 Oct.

Remarks Another "hurricane only" species in NY, in recent years it has become rare but regular as far north as the Gulf Stream waters off NC, with more than 30 seen there during the summer of 1995.

Bordering states have records similar in pattern of occurrence and even dates. MA has at least seven records (Veit and Petersen 1993), VT has three, all in the aftermath of the 1938 hurricane (Spear 1976), PA lists two (Santner et al. 1992), and NJ has one (RNJB 9:83).
John P. Askildsen

Red-billed Tropicbird *Phaethon aethereus*

Range Pantropical, breeding locally in the Caribbean region from Puerto Rico and the Virgin Islands south to Tobago and Panama. Ranges at sea north to the Bahamas and the Atlantic Coast of Florida and North Carolina.

Status Accidental.

Occurrence One record: an immature female found dead on the shore of Bergen Beach, Jamaica Bay, Kings Co. 10 Jun 1963 (Lynch) AMNH 776556. This vagrant was probably carried there by the tropical storm of 4 Jun 1963 that had originated south of the Bahamas two days previously (Auk 81:433).

Remarks This species is rare but regular as far north as the Gulf Stream off NC (B. Patteson, pers. comm.). North of there it becomes extremely rare,

undoubtedly because at the Outer Banks of NC the Gulf Stream veers farther out into the Atlantic, away from the northeastern states. There are a handful of records from neighboring states. NJ's only record was an oiled immature found May 1983 (RNJB 9:63). MA has documented three records, perhaps of the same individual. An adult was seen at Martha's Vineyard, 1986, 1987, and 1988, in each case lingering for several weeks (Veit and Petersen 1993). RI has two museum specimens: one found alive in 1973, one found dead in 1975 (Conway 1992).
John P. Askildsen

BOOBIES AND GANNETS—SULIDAE

Brown Booby *Sula leucogaster*

Range Pantropical, in the Atlantic and Caribbean regions breeding on islands from the Bahamas to northern South America and off Middle America. Ranges at sea to Florida's Dry Tortugas, the Gulf Coast (rarely), Bermuda, and along the Atlantic Coast to Massachusetts, casually to Nova Scotia.

Status Very rare summer and fall visitant to offshore waters of LI.

Occurrence The first record was a specimen examined by Dutcher, collected at Moriches Bay, Suffolk Co. "many years ago." Dutcher died in 1920, so we can assume it was collected in the nineteenth century or very early in the twentieth century. The second record was of two birds, 2 Sep 1936 at Mecox Bay, Suffolk Co. after a hurricane. One at Moriches Inlet, 3 Sep 1949, after another hurricane.

There was a 26-year hiatus until the fall of 1975, when there were an unprecedented six sightings, consisting of possibly 11 individuals, all on the South Shore of LI: an immature over Bellport Bay, 28 Sep; two adults at Tiana Beach, 30 Sep; two adults at Shinnecock Inlet, 2 Oct; one adult at Gilgo Beach, 6 Oct; two adults at JBSP, 12 Oct. As curious as this sudden spate of records is, it is made more so by the fact that they are not attributable to any weather event (Raynor 1976a).

Since then there have been four reports, all of adults: two, Jacob Riis Park, Queens Co. 29 Sep 1977 (Richards and Chevalier 1978); one, JBSP 4 Oct 1990 (KB 41:63); one, RMSP 14 Jul 1991 (KB 41:289); one, Amagansett, Suffolk Co. 18 Aug 1992 (KB 42:279).

Remarks Surprisingly, MA has only two records and RI three. NJ has a good number of sightings, mostly from its southern coast.
John P. Askildsen

Northern Gannet   *Morus bassanus*

Range Palearctic and Nearctic, breeding in Iceland and around the British Isles and in the western Atlantic from Newfoundland to islands off the Gaspe Peninsula, in the Gulf of St. Lawrence, Nova Scotia, and New Brunswick. North American birds range at sea from the breeding area along the Atlantic Coast to Florida and the Gulf Coast to Texas.

Status Common to very abundant migrant off LI, less numerous in winter, and rare but regular in summer. Rare to uncommon elsewhere.

Occurrence Northern Gannet is most numerous at Montauk mid-fall through early winter. During this peak period, 2000–5000 may be observed feeding off the point. They are undoubtedly working the rich waters between the point and Block Island, RI. Traveling in a somewhat circular fashion, they plunge-dive into baitfish schools in the strong currents before the group moves on en masse. Almost any beachfront location along the South Shore from Breezy Point, Queens Co. east to Montauk, Suffolk Co. is a suitable site in these seasons. Even the south shore of SI produces flights during peak migration.

    Maxima: 10,000 Montauk 9 Nov 1991; 4000 Montauk 5 Dec 1993; 3600 Block Canyon 12 Mar 1979.

    Previously considered uncommon to rare in LI Sound, beginning in 1985 this species staged remarkable late-Nov invasions as far west as Larchmont, Westchester Co. during periods with sustained east winds. On 28 Nov 1985, 18 were observed from Rye, Westchester Co., and 11 were at Hempstead Harbor, Nassau Co. 25 Nov 1991. These late-fall flights generally begin by 20 Nov and cease by 10 Dec. More recently, small numbers have been observed from both sides of LI Sound intermittently throughout the winter and into midspring, whenever east winds prevail. The original invasion in the fall of 1985 was probably weather-related. Today, this annual Nov influx is expected and appears to be tied into the Sound's being used as a food source.

    It is rare inland, with most records from the L. Ontario shore, where it is not unexpected. Spring and fall records, primarily of immature birds, do exist for many inland upstate locations, well away from the L. Ontario shoreline. Very rare on the Hudson R.; one bird was present at Poughkeepsie, Dutchess Co. for two days, 27–28 Nov 1986 (KB 37:241). John P. Askildsen

PELICANS—PELECANIDAE

American White Pelican   *Pelecanus erythrorhynchos*

Range Western Nearctic; breeding in southern Canada east to southwestern Ontario, south locally to northern California and southwestern

Minnesota; also in southeastern Texas. Winters east and south to the Gulf states and Florida and south to Guatemala.

Status Rare visitant; in recent years increasingly regular both inland and coastal.

Occurrence Bull (1974) reported at least 25 records, mostly from LI. In the ensuing two decades there have been an additional 36 reports, 27 upstate and only 9 downstate. This bird is a hard one to miss in the field, and there is no doubt duplication of records as these conspicuous creatures move through the state; the records noted above have been adjusted to correct for probable duplication. From 1988 to 1996 it was recorded every year at various locations, with reports from all Regions but Region 7. The majority were in Apr or May, with the balance Jun–Nov. Most records are of single individuals, but occasionally multiples have been recorded. A recent one was from North Sea Harbor, Suffolk Co., where four birds appeared on 1 Oct 1996 and stayed at least two weeks.

There is one winter record. Three birds were recorded on the Southern Nassau Co. CBC 2 Jan 1994. As they flew east through the 15-mi diameter count circle, five parties spotted them.

Remarks The preponderance of records in the last two decades shows a shift from LI to upstate, reversing the pattern recorded in Bull (1974). This reversal makes sense when one takes into account the proximity of the species' breeding range to western NY. Contiguous states show much the same occurrence, except perusal of NASFN records showed that half of those sightings took place in winter.
Anthony J. Lauro

Brown Pelican   *Pelecanus occidentalis*

Range Southern Nearctic and Neotropical, breeding locally on islands along the Pacific Coast from California to Chile and on the Gulf and Atlantic coasts from North Carolina to Venezuela; also in the West Indies. Vagrant north along the East Coast to Massachusetts.

Status Formerly rare, recently uncommon to regular summer visitant to LI. Casual away from the coast.

Occurrence Like the American White Pelican, this species' distribution pattern has undergone a remarkable change in recent years. Bull (1974) reported 11 occurrences, nine on LI and two upstate, covering the period 1902–1970. An upstate record in Sep 1982 (KB 32:39) on L. Ontario was presumed to be that of an escaped bird. The next record of note was of four birds flying along the barrier beach at Fire I., Suffolk Co. 2 Jul 1983 (KB 33:297). Then, between 1987 and 1995, some 50 citations can be found in *The Kingbird*, all from LI, ranging from single birds to a maximum of 87 on 12 Jul 1992 (KB 42:279), with flocks of 15–25 also reported. There were two records away from LI in that period: two at Croton Bay, Westchester Co. 30 Jul 1992 (KB 42:274); and one at Buffalo, Erie Co. 10 Jun 1992 (KB 42:232). However, 1996 produced only one report anywhere. Whether this change forecasts a return to previous status remains to be seen.

Remarks The perhaps ephemeral northward expansion has been strictly a seasonal littoral movement with no evidence of breeding. In 1993, 18 nests were built in Raritan Bay, NJ, but no eggs were laid and this activity was not repeated. R. Kane (pers. comm.) believes that the increased presence of the species off the NJ and LI coasts in summer coincided with an increase of menhaden in that same period. Examination of NASFN reports revealed no records in 1996 in New England or NJ, mirroring NY, following the spurt of the last decade.

Anthony J. Lauro

CORMORANTS— PHALACROCORACIDAE

Great Cormorant *Phalacrocorax carbo*

Range Cosmopolitan, breeding in North America in the Gulf of St. Lawrence area and along the coast in Nova Scotia and Maine. Winters in breeding range, south to North Carolina and inland to Lake Ontario.

Status A locally uncommon to very common winter visitant on the coast; increasing along the Hudson R.; very rare upstate.

Occurrence Writing in 1923, Griscom considered this species a rare visitant, with only one definite record for the South Shore of LI. By 1942, Cruickshank noted that it had become "much more regular" in occurrence, but he still considered it "one of our rare winter finds" and was reluctant to accept many reports because of the "delicate task" of separating it from Double-crested Cormorant. By 1964, Bull found it to be locally uncommon to very common in winter. The "great increase in recent years," he noted, was "probably due to its recent success on the northern breeding grounds."

Bull said this species was most frequently encountered in the Montauk area and on the rocky islands and jetties off both shores of LI Sound. Its numbers still appear to be increasing. By averaging the counts on the FWC one finds: 1976–1980, about 55 a year; 1981–1985, 121 a year; 1986–1990, 256; 1991–1995, 339. With the increase in coastal numbers has come an increase in sightings on the Hudson R. and nearby reservoirs.

The first confirmed inland record was an adult shot illegally at Cornwall,

Orange Co. 2 Nov 1969. By the winter of 1991–1992, no fewer than 30 were reported wintering on the Hudson between Croton Point, Westchester Co. and Bannermans I., Dutchess Co (KB 42:119). Farther up the Hudson, single birds are now reported almost annually, including two sightings on the Mohawk R. in the Cohoes-Colonie area, Albany Co. in 1993 and 1994 (KB 43:151; 45:52).

Elsewhere upstate, there have been three on L. Ontario and one on the St. Lawrence R., starting with an adult at Oswego Harbor, Oswego Co. 19–20 May 1973. Others include an adult, Webster, Monroe Co. 14 Apr 1980 (KB 31:206); an immature, Rochester, Monroe Co. 9 Jan 1983 (KB 33:118); an adult, Moses-Saunders Dam, St. Lawrence Co. 3 May 1991 (KB 41:202); and one bird, BBWMA 5 Sep 1995 (KB 46:43,46).

This species is seen regularly on the coast Oct–Apr. Bull listed extreme dates of 6 Sep and 9 Jun, but, as he predicted, there have been a handful of summer records, blurring departure and arrival dates.

Maxima: include 400+ in the Gardiners Bay area, Suffolk Co. during the winter of 1973–1974.

Robert E. Marcotte

Double-crested Cormorant   *Phalacrocorax auritus*

Range Nearctic, breeding from southern Alaska to southern Newfoundland south, in the east coastally in isolated colonies to Florida and very locally in interior areas. Winters, in the east, from southern New England south to Florida and the Greater Antilles.

Status Locally abundant breeder at several large colonies on LI, in the NYC area, and on Lakes Champlain and Erie, Oneida L., and eastern L. Ontario, where the largest nesting colony in NY, and possibly in North America, is located. Common migrant throughout, particularly near large, inland lakes and on LI.

Breeding Double-crested Cormorants were first reported breeding in NY in 1945 at Gull I., Jefferson Co. in eastern L. Ontario (Kutz and Allen 1947). Bull (1974) did not describe any other locations and reported that the Gull I. colony continued to support about 20 nests as late as the mid-1960s. The Atlas reported an increasing breeding distribution, which has continued to the present.

Cormorants are thought to have spread into the Canadian Great Lakes from the west, occurring initially at the far western end of L. Superior in 1913, then eastward to Lakes Michigan and Huron in the early 1930s, and finally to Lakes Ontario and Erie in the late 1930s. Populations increased steadily during the 1930s and 1940s, and by the early 1950s the cormorant was so common that control measures were authorized in some parts of

ON to reduce suspected competition with commercial and recreational interests. The Great Lakes population declined throughout the 1960s and early 1970s, from a peak of about 900 nests in 1950 to 114 in 1973 (Weseloh and Collier 1995; Weseloh et al. 1995). This decline, along with that of other fish-eating birds, was associated with high levels of toxic contaminants, particularly DDE and PCBs, found in the Great Lakes ecosystem.

After these contaminants had been reduced because of government antipollution programs and laws, cormorants made a remarkable recovery in the Great Lakes and elsewhere (Price and Weseloh 1986). Over the past two decades, breeding numbers and locations have increased dramatically throughout NY. In L. Ontario, the Gull I. colony probably died out in the 1960s, but nearby Little Galloo I. was occupied in 1974, when 22 nests were counted. Nest counts at the Little Galloo colony, the largest Double-crested Cormorant colony in NY and perhaps in all of North America, increased at the rate of 36% per year between 1974 and 1993 (Weseloh and Ewins 1994). A nest count of 8410 was recorded in Jun 1996 (NYSDEC 1996). Little Galloo, a 43-acre tilted limestone shelf 5½ mi due west of Henderson Harbor, Jefferson Co. also provides nesting habitat for Caspian Tern, Black-crowned Night-Heron, Great Black-backed Gull, Herring Gull, and upward of 80,000 pairs of Ring-billed Gulls.

Double-crested Cormorants have colonized new nesting sites at other upstate locations, presumably as a result of the expanding Great Lakes population. Colonies at L. Champlain (High Peaks Audubon Society 1984), Oneida L. (Claypoole 1988), and the Niagara Frontier (Watson 1995a) have been established. Reports of a few nests at other locations have been received by the author, prompting speculation that additional permanent nesting colonies may result.

The Atlantic Coast population has also increased, moving southward from breeding sites in the Maritime Provinces to ME to MA, and eventually to LI, at Fishers I. in 1977 (Bull 1981). Cormorant numbers have increased significantly in the LI-NYC region, from 585 breeding pairs in 1985 to 3528 pairs in 1995 (Sommers et al. 1996). Breeding locations include Fishers (three sites), Gardiners, and Plum islands in Suffolk Co., South Brother and Shooters islands in NYC, and Huckleberry I. in Westchester Co.

Nonbreeding Large flocks, typically flying in long single lines or V-formations, can be seen both spring and fall along the shores of LI and inland along the eastern shore of L. Ontario. Daily counts will sometimes top 10,000 in both seasons on heavy flight days along the coast, particularly in late Sep. Inland, up to 2000 birds have been reported in the fall at Oneida L.

Regions 9 and 10 also harbor a good number of wintering birds, as evidenced by the 400+ individuals that were accounted for on the 1995

CBCs. Suffice it to say that numbers are increasing along the coast, and the range is expanding each year.

Remarks Recent ecological changes in L. Ontario affecting fish populations may eventually affect Double-crested Cormorants there. Studies of L. Ontario suggest that the lake's productivity is declining because of reduced phosphorus levels, the result of successful antipollution programs throughout the Great Lakes basin. As the lake gets "cleaner," the production of microscopic plants and animals decreases and less food is available to support fish populations. The recent invasion of an exotic mollusk, the zebra mussel, is also cause for concern. Zebra mussels are filter-feeders with voracious appetites that can interfere with food-web dynamics and, when they become numerous enough, compete with forage fish for food. The long-range outlook for L. Ontario cormorants indicates a declining prey base.

Public concern for increasing cormorant populations and potential detrimental impacts on sport fishing and island habitats led the NYSDEC to form a citizen's task group in 1994 to develop a set of management objectives directed at L. Ontario and Oneida L. cormorant issues. The task group, made up of individuals representing environmental, tourism, commercial and recreational fishing, and other interest groups, reached a consensus after a series of meetings. As a result of this public process, the NYSDEC has altered its fish-stocking methods and has prevented cormorants from initiating nesting colonies on Gull and Bass islands, Jefferson Co.

Food studies of cormorants nesting at Little Galloo I. showed that this species feeds primarily on alewives, perch, and other forage fish. Game species make up only a small part of their diet (Karwowski 1994).
Robert L. Miller

DARTERS—ANHINGIDAE

Anhinga *Anhinga anhinga*

Range Nearctic and Neotropical, breeding from central and eastern Texas east through the Gulf states to Florida and north to coastal North Carolina; also in Cuba and in Middle and South America. Winters in the southeastern United States from central South Carolina southward throughout the breeding range.

Status Casual vagrant.

Occurrence There is one record accepted by NYSARC: an adult seen soaring over Central Park, Manhattan, 28 Apr 1992 (DiCostanzo 1993). There was one other recent sight report, 7 May 1994, Alley Pond Park, Queens Co. (Clinton) (NASFN 48:280).

Remarks A published report of an Anhinga in Nassau Co. (Davis and Lauro 1978), although regarded by many as correct, was subsequently not accepted by NYSARC (1985) because of disagreement between the observers. In neighboring states Zeranski and Baptist (1990) reported one in CT in 1987, and Veit and Petersen (1993) reported two in MA in 1987 and 1991. In NJ there have been many more since the 1971 report in Leck 1984. The only regional specimen appears to be one found dead in Dec 1988 at Ocean, NJ (AB 43:290). Following the recent increase in reports in the Northeast, in May 1996 an unprecedented flock of 33 was seen in MD (NASFN 50:262). Double-crested Cormorants have also increased greatly in the Northeast in recent years, and great care must be taken in distinguishing between a soaring cormorant and a soaring Anhinga.
Joseph DiCostanzo

FRIGATEBIRDS—FREGATIDAE

Magnificent Frigatebird *Fregata magnificens*

Range Pantropical, breeding in North America on scattered islets off the coast of Baja California and Central America in the west and in the Atlantic and Caribbean regions off Florida, Texas, and Mexico. Also in the West Indies north to the Bahamas. Ranges at sea, in the east, throughout the Gulf of Mexico and north to North Carolina, casually farther north.

Status Very rare vagrant.

Occurrence It has been reported 18 times, with 16 sight records and two specimens. Seventeen records were from Region 10, with 13 from Suffolk Co. The only upstate record was from Oswego Co. on L. Ontario. This species has been recorded every month but Dec; however, 83% of records are May–Sep.

Suffolk Co. reports (all singles) since Bull (1976) are: Three Mile Harbor 30 June 1979 (Ash) (KB 29:242); Orient Point 11 Aug 1979 (Hollander) (KB 29:242); Great Gull I. 25 Aug 1979 (DiCostanzo) (KB 29:242; NYSARC 1980); Cold Spring Harbor 28 Aug 1979 (Rupert) (KB 29:242); Great Gull I. 3 Jun 1985 (DiCostanzo) (KB 36:52). Elsewhere: Great Kills, Richmond Co. 12 Jan 1986 (Richard) (KB 37:100); Mexico, Oswego Co. 23 Sep 1990 (NYSARC 1992); 9 JBWR Aug 1992 (KB 42:281).

The specimens, both from Suffolk Co., are: adult female, Gardiners I. 4 Aug 1886 AMNH 11705; adult male, found alive after a storm, West Babylon 14 Mar 1993 AMNH skeleton 21469 (NYSARC 1995).

Remarks The pattern of occurrence in NY, usually in coastal locations from late spring to early fall, is matched in neighboring states. There are seven

121

records from NJ (Leck 1984), three from CT (Zeranski and Baptist 1990), seven from RI (Conway 1992), and 11 from MA (Veit and Petersen 1993). All were Mar–Dec, with 78% May–Sep.

Observers should note that any frigatebird observed in NY should be carefully scrutinized. The occurrence of a Lesser Frigatebird *(F. ariel)* in ME (Snyder 1961) means that one cannot automatically assume the identity. In fact, two records of frigatebirds in the state have been accepted by NYSARC only as *Fregata* sp.: South Beach, Richmond Co. 27 Sep 1985 (NYSARC 1988) and Rockland Co. 7 Apr 1982 (Deed 1982). Paul R. Sweet

BITTERNS, HERONS, AND ALLIES—ARDEIDAE

American Bittern   *Botaurus lentiginosus*

Range Nearctic, breeding in eastern North America from northern Manitoba to Newfoundland, south to central United States, rarely and locally to the Gulf states and Mexico. Winters from Massachusetts and New York southward, chiefly along the coast, and in the West Indies.

Status Uncommon and declining breeder throughout. In winter, uncommon but regular along the coast and rare elsewhere.

Breeding The Atlas project showed this species to be widely distributed in the state, except that it was missing from most blocks in the eastern Appalachian Plateau and was scarce west of the Finger Lakes owing to the lack of wetlands. It was found on the Great Lakes Plain, primarily in Orleans, Genesee, Monroe, and Wayne counties in protected wetlands, around Oneida L., and south of the five major Finger Lakes. It occurs in wetland areas along river systems in the northern and central Adirondacks. Also found in the wetlands bordering and near the St. Lawrence R., in the Champlain Valley, and in a few of the remaining large tidal marshes along the Hudson R. and on LI.

The preferred nesting habitat inland is cattail-bulrush marshes, but it has also been found in sedge meadows, beaver ponds and meadows, kettlehole bogs, alder thickets, and shrub swamps. Coastally, it breeds mainly in salt or freshwater tidal marshes. It apparently has a minimum size requirement of about 10 acres.

The Atlas noted that in 1910 this species was considered "a fairly common summer resident on eastern LI and on all the marshes of the interior." It has declined since the 1950s, both within the state and elsewhere, probably because of loss of habitat. A significant population decline, attributed to habitat loss, was documented between 1940 and 1970 in the Cayuga basin. Habitat loss is believed to be related to its decline in other parts of the state as well. Bull (1974) described it as a "widespread breeder," at a time when it was apparently already in decline. This species has been recommended for inclusion on the NYSDEC's list of Species of Special Concern.

Speiser (1982) surveyed breeding birds in the Hudson Highlands from 1976 to 1981 and found this species no longer present, whereas it had been present in a study of the same area 100 years earlier.

Nonbreeding Uncommon in spring, it generally arrives in mid-Apr, but early arrivals the last week of Mar have occasionally been reported. One was reported 9 Mar 1975 at Forest Lawn Cemetery, Erie Co. It is uncommon in fall.

In winter, this species is rare upstate and uncommon but regular along the coast. There are several winter records from Regions 2 and 3 in the early 1990s. Cumulative results of LI CBCs showed it was found annually in the 1970s and 1980s, with at least 5 and up to 30 reported. The Southern Nassau Co. CBC alone found 10 or more in nearly half of those years, with a high of 17 in 1974.

Maxima: There are few reports of more than six from any one location; seven were noted at TWMA 14 May 1994 and "10+" at Black Creek Marsh, Albany Co. 12 May 1991.
Scott J. Stoner

Least Bittern   *Ixobrychus exilis*

Range Nearctic and Neotropical, breeding in eastern North America from southern Manitoba to southern New Brunswick, south to Florida, the Gulf states, Texas, and the Greater Antilles; also in temperate South America. Winters from northern Florida and southern Texas south through Middle America and to the limits of its breeding range in South America.

Status Uncommon to rare breeder of spotty distribution. In winter, very rare along the coast and unknown upstate.

Breeding The Atlas reported its nesting abundance as only uncommon to rare but did find it more widely distributed than described earlier. Although it was known to have nested in the L. Champlain Valley, Atlas workers established a stronger presence than previously had been suspected. They also recorded breeding activity in parts of the Adirondacks where nesting had not been recorded earlier.

Other Atlas records, from the Black River Valley, highland regions of the Central Adirondacks, and the Appalachian and Tug Hill plateaus, indicated nesting in areas with few previous records. However, it was not found in most of the Appalachian Plateau or in the Catskills. Consistent with historical record, its stronghold is still the lower Hudson Valley, the Coastal Lowlands, and the Great Lakes Plain. This species has been recommended for inclusion on the NYSDEC's list of Species of Special Concern.

There is a distinct possibility that this species was underreported during the Atlas period because of the bird's secretive nature and the difficulty of exploring the interiors of some extensive marshlands.

The variety of wetland habitats utilized includes cattail and sedge marshes, salt marshes, and other places with emergent vegetation (Atlas 1988). Large marshes are important. The draining of wetlands has had an adverse impact on both the population and range of this small and inconspicuous species (Atlas 1988). NY is near the northern periphery of its range, but its spotty distribution is consistent with the scattered occurrence of the remaining wetland habitat.

Nonbreeding It is rarely reported in migration or anywhere away from its breeding grounds, and it is rare before May and after Sep.

Very rare in winter along the coast, it is not recorded upstate in that season. Bull (1974) reported three midwinter specimens from LI, along with single-individual sight reports from Regions 9 and 10. One was at Calverton, Suffolk Co. 27 Dec 1975 (KB 26:119). A review of CBC data 1960–1989 noted singles on the Lower Hudson count in 1975 and 1976 and one on the Central Suffolk Co. CBC in 1976.

Maxima: 11 Lakeview WMA, Jefferson Co. 2 Aug 1975; 9 at the same location 26 Jul 1976. *Extreme dates: Coastal:* 16 Apr and 19 Nov. *Inland:* 17 Apr and 17 Oct.

Remarks The rare melanistic morph, called "Cory's" Least Bittern, is known from two records: a specimen taken in the marshes near Ithaca, Tompkins Co. 17 May 1913; one observed at JBWR, 28 Aug 1992 (KB 43:349).
Scott J. Stoner

Great Blue Heron

Ardea herodias

Range Nearctic and Neotropical, breeding from southern Alaska across southern Canada to Nova Scotia and south, locally, throughout the United States to the Gulf Coast and southern Florida; also in the West Indies and much of Mexico. Winters in much of the breeding range; on the Atlantic Coast, from Massachusetts south to northern South America.

Status Resident and very common migrant.

Breeding Today there are wider distribution and more breeding sites in NY than during the 1960s. It continues to recover from persecution at the turn of the century and can be found breeding in most of the state.

The only Region in the state that did not have a Confirmed breeding site during Atlas work was Region 10. The last known site on LI was on Gardiners I. at the turn of the century.

There are more than 100 breeding sites in NY. A corridor containing the bulk of the heronries, about 40–50 mi wide, runs from Broome Co. north through Cortland and Onondaga counties into Jefferson Co. (Atlas 1988). The larger NWRs in the state, Montezuma and Iroquois, also contain fairly large heronries. The number of nests fluctuates from year to year, and sites also shift, as changes occur in habitat. The species prefers lowland swamp or upland hardwood forests; other habitats are used less frequently.

Some of the largest known heronries include: (1) historical sites: "several hundred" nests, Tonawanda Swamp, Genesee Co. 1896; 150 nests, West Barre, Orleans Co. 1906; 300 nests, north shore of Oneida L., Oswego Co. 1909. (2) recent sites: 1000 nests, Ironsides I. in the St. Lawrence R., Jefferson Co. 1991, with a steady increase from 240 in 1968; 666 nests, Valcour I. in L. Champlain, Clinton Co. 1986.

Nonbreeding Our largest member of the heron family can be seen at almost any time of the year, although most leave the state in winter. Spring arrivals vary from late Mar to early Apr. Fall departures are more difficult to assess owing to the tendency of some individuals to remain through the winter, but along the coast some depart by mid-Jul.

Upstate, birds may be seen late into the fall before they depart. They are more numerous in the winter along the coast but may be seen inland, particularly on the Great Lakes littoral, if open water exists.

Winter maxima: 116 Central Suffolk Co. CBC 27 Dec 1983; 72 Bronx-Westchester CBC 22 Dec 1991; 50 Niagara R. 19 Jan 1993.

Remarks A "Great White Heron," a color morph, was observed on LI after a FL hurricane in 1949. It was first seen on 3 Sep on Tobay Pond, Nassau Co., was reported again on 17 Sep at Mecox Bay, Suffolk Co., and stayed until 15 Oct.

Kevin C. Griffith

Great Egret   *Ardea alba*

Range Cosmopolitan, breeding in eastern North America along the Atlantic Coast from Maine to Florida, in the Mississippi drainage area from Minnesota south, and along the Gulf Coast. Winters on the Atlantic Coast from the Carolinas to Florida, rarely north to Massachusetts and Long Island, along the Gulf Coast to Texas, through Mexico and Middle America, and in the West Indies.

Status Local breeder on LI, rare elsewhere. Common to locally abundant summer visitant along the coast, much less common inland but occasionally numerous. Rare but regular in winter on the coast.

Breeding Great Egret breeds on the coastal islands and barrier beaches of LI. The first confirmed breeding was on Fishers I. in 1953. The number of colonies has fluctuated greatly since then. By the early 1960s there were four colonies, which had reached 13 in 1974, and 20 by 1991. The number of colonies varies on a yearly basis. A 10-year high of 707 pairs was reached in 1993, dropping to 514 in 1995, but over 11 years there was still a significantly increasing trend (Sommers et al. 1996).

In the summer of 1995, two pairs of Great Egrets built nests on Motor I. in the Niagara R., Niagara Co. (KB 45:284). Eggs were laid, and two young were hatched in each nest. The nests were then destroyed by vandals. Two young were found dead in one nest, apparently having been stoned to death, and the two in the other nest were not found. In 1996, three pairs built nests in the same place, but this time successfully fledged eight young, three each from two pairs, and two from the third pair (W. Watson, in litt.). These nestings in two consecutive years may be the forerunner of a range expansion, or they may be an anomaly.

The largest single colony to date had 200+ nests at JBSP in 1975. Some of the other larger colonies, all in Region 10, are at Canarsie Pol, Gardiners I., North and South Brother islands, Plum I., and Shooters I. The only colony in Region 9 is on Huckleberry I., Westchester Co.

Nonbreeding Although the Great Egret is best known in numbers along the coast, it has increased inland and has been observed in spring, summer, and fall. Postbreeding dispersal, movement of both adults and young out from the colonies, accounts for most of the upstate sightings.

Coastal maxima: 280 Tobay Pond, Nassau Co. 4 Sep 1949; 70 JBWR 23 Nov 1959. *Inland maxima:* 240 along 50 mi of Hudson R., Kingston to Albany, 12 Sep 1948; 50 near Buffalo, Erie Co. 21 Aug 1933; 50 MNWR 8 Sep 1961. *Winter maxima:* 15 Queens Co. CBC, Dec 1980; 4 HLSP 13 Feb 1954. *Extreme dates: Coastal:* 2 Mar. *Inland:* 23 Mar and 5 Dec.

Kevin C. Griffith

Snowy Egret *Egretta thula*

Range Nearctic and Neotropical, breeding in eastern North America on the Atlantic Coast from southern Maine to Florida, along the Gulf Coast, and north along the Mississippi River to southern Illinois. Winters mainly in the breeding range, north to New York and south to northern South America.

Status Locally common to abundant breeder and summer visitant on LI; rare there in winter. Rare but regular at any time inland.

Breeding The first recorded breeding was in 1885 on Fire I., Suffolk Co. It was not found breeding again until 1949 at Oak Beach, Suffolk Co.

In the late 1800s, the entire population of these birds was virtually destroyed by plume hunters who specifically killed breeding adults because, at that time, the Snowy develops those beautiful "aigrette" feathers sought by the millinery trade of that era.

With protection, the species made a dramatic recovery, and during the 1950s more sites on LI were colonized. By 1978, there were 21 active colonies and more than 1400 nesting pairs (Atlas 1988). Since then, there has been a steady decline in the number of colonies and nesting pairs. The lowest year was 1984, when only four colonies were found, but in 1995 there were 16 colonies and an estimated 686 pairs (Sommers et al. 1996). Although there has been fluctuation since 1985, the trend appears stable, and the species has continued to expand its range. With nestings in VT and Canada, it is quite possible there will be inland NY nestings in the future.

The number of colonies and estimated pairs found in Region 10 from 1989 to 1995 were: 1989: 14 colonies, 846 pairs; 1990: 11, 939; 1991: 21, 1163; 1992: 15, 789; 1993: 16, 788; 1995: 16, 686 (Sommers et al. 1996).

Nonbreeding The Snowy Egret is most numerous from Aug to Oct, during postbreeding dispersal, when young and adults move away from the breeding area to feeding sites even well north of LI, with numbers being augmented by an influx of birds dispersing from breeding areas out of state. Inland records have continued to increase, with reports from Apr to Dec. During the 1960s and 70s, there were few inland reports of multiple birds. Multiple sightings have become more common since then.

Coastal maxima: 300 JBWR 1 Sep 1964; 175 East Moriches, Suffolk Co. 17 Aug 1964; 160 Rye, Westchester Co. 11 Sep 1993. *Inland maxima:* 12 Vischers Ferry, Saratoga Co. 6 Aug 1992; 9 Cornwall, Orange Co. 31 May 1977; 6 Amawalk Reservoir, Westchester Co. 12 May 1985. *Winter maxima:* 25 Brooklyn CBC Dec 1984; 7 Southern Nassau Co. CBC 30 Dec 1967.

A few are regularly reported along the South Shore of LI in winter. They have shown up on coastal CBCs nearly every year since the 1960s.

Kevin C. Griffith

Little Blue Heron   *Egretta caerulea*

Range Nearctic and Neotropical, in the east breeding along the Atlantic Coast from southern Maine to Florida, south to the West Indies and northern South America; also from central Oklahoma to central Alabama and in the west from southern California and Texas south along both coasts of Mexico and Middle America. Winters, in the east, from South Carolina and the Gulf Coast south to South America.

Status Uncommon breeder on LI, as well as uncommon summer visitant. Uncommon spring and summer visitant elsewhere.

Breeding It has been recorded as a breeder only on LI, where it occurs in mixed-species heronries. It was first found breeding at Tobay Pond, Nassau Co, in 1958. Nesting was found over the next few years at scattered locations on LI. Further study proved continuous and successful breeding from 1974 to 1978, with a mean of 20 pairs at four sites on the South Shore (Buckley and Buckley 1980). In 1985, the Atlas reported 68 breeding pairs in eight colonies. Then, between 1985 and 1995, nesting pairs fluctuated between a high of 68 in 1985 to a low of 27 in 1995, with a mean of 51 (Sommers et al. 1996). Very few sites have consistently reported this species, with breeding scattered through some 20 or so mixed-species colonies over the years.

Nonbreeding Eaton (1910) considered the species an accidental summer visitant. Griscom (1923) deemed it a rare summer visitant, and Cruickshank (1942) spoke of it in the same vein. Bull (1964) upgraded its status to uncommon summer visitant but listed some truly extraordinary maxima: 120 Suffolk Co. 20 Aug 1930; 54 Iona I., Rockland Co. 9 Sep 1936; 50 Suffolk Co. 30 Aug 1948. These undoubtedly represented postbreeding dispersal, characteristic of the Ardeidae. These numbers have never been repeated, even with the establishment of breeding colonies. Rather, there has been a steady progression of relatively low numbers, with scattered but regular appearances away from nesting sites at all seasons of the year.

Since 1974, there have been about 100 records away from the main breeding locales on LI and SI. Westchester Co. and lower Hudson Valley: spring, 16; summer, 25; fall, 11. Elsewhere upstate: spring, 27; summer, 12; fall, 8.

These figures are consistent with the postbreeding dispersal phenomenon already discussed, as well as the tendency of the herons to wander widely on spring overshoots.

Remarks The species is unique in that during its first year the plumage is entirely white, making for some confusion between it and the Snowy Egret. In the first spring, the white plumage is replaced by dark feathers, giving it a mottled and piebald appearance until full adult plumage is achieved that spring.

Anthony J. Lauro

Tricolored Heron   *Egretta tricolor*

Range Nearctic and Neotropical, breeding along the Atlantic and Gulf coasts from southern Maine to Florida and Texas; also in the West Indies and along both coasts of Middle America to northern South America. Winters from New Jersey south through the remainder of the breeding range.

Status Uncommon breeder on LI as well as uncommon summer visitant. Rare spring and summer visitant elsewhere.

Breeding The first breeding was recorded on 17 May 1955 at JBWR. Another nest was discovered, again at JBWR, some 11 years later. In 1970, and again in 1971, successful nests were found in Nassau Co. on the South Shore of LI. A study (Buckley and Buckley 1980) established a mean of 13 nesting pairs at five heronries in southwestern LI between 1974 and 1978. Since then, the breeding population has increased slightly and seemingly stabilized. A regular survey, 1985–1996, demonstrated a mean of 22 pairs, rebounding from a ten-year low of eight in 1993 to 26 in 1995 (Sommers et al. 1996). Like the Little Blue Heron, this species nests in mixed-species heronries, and no one site has proved more successful than another.

Nonbreeding Giraud (1844), Eaton (1910), and Griscom (1923) all listed one specimen, the only one extant, taken in Patchogue, Suffolk Co. in 1836. Cruickshank (1942) reported 12 sight records in the NYC area. Bull (1964) called the species a rare but annual visitant to LI. In 1974 he upgraded the status to "rare to uncommon, but regular visitor on the south shore of western Long Island." Since then, its numbers have seemingly stabilized, and in recent years the bird can be found on LI in small numbers. Elsewhere it is rare, with some 35 sight records since 1974 distributed as follows. Westchester Co. and lower Hudson Valley: spring, 8; summer, 5; fall, 4. Elsewhere upstate: spring, 13; summer, 3; fall, 2.

Since 1974 there have been 15 winter records, all from LI.

Anthony J. Lauro

Reddish Egret   *Egretta rufescens*

Range Nearctic, breeding in coastal Texas, the Florida Keys, and in the Bahamas, Cuba, and Hispaniola. Disperses northward to Colorado, southern Illinois, and Massachusetts.

Status Accidental.

Occurrence There is one record, of a dark morph adult seen and photographed at JBWR. Discovered on 18 May 1991, the egret remained in the environs of Jamaica Bay at least to 26 May, although it was observed only very irregularly during that period (Walter, Kurtz et al.) (NYSARC 1993).

Remarks This species is a very scarce wanderer up the Atlantic seaboard, with at least seven records north of VA (three in MA); of these, four have appeared in May and the other three in Jul.
Thomas A. Burke

Cattle Egret   *Bubulcus ibis*

Range Cosmopolitan, now breeding in North America locally from California and southern Saskatchewan east to Nova Scotia and south, primarily in coastal lowlands and scattered inland sites, to Texas and Florida; also in the West Indies and Middle and South America. Winters in much of breeding range, from southern California to Florida and south to South America.

Status Currently breeds in NYC area and one upstate location.

Breeding It nested in ON, on Pigeon I. in eastern L. Ontario, about 5 mi from the NY border in 1968. It was not reported breeding in NY until 1970, when a nest with an adult and two eggs was found on Gardiners I., Suffolk Co. 7 June (Puleston) (KB 20:178). The second known nesting was discovered at Zachs Bay, JBSP in June 1973 (Buckley et al.) (AB 27:848). Five downy young were banded and photographed, and the photos were deposited in the AMNH.

The first upstate breeding record was of several pairs and one active nest in a Black-crowned Night-Heron colony on Four Brothers Islands in L. Champlain, Essex Co. in 1973. A second upstate location was also in a Black-crowned Night-Heron colony at Braddock Bay, Monroe Co. in 1974. That colony was viable for only the one year (O'Hara) (KB 24:189); the L. Champlain location had 20 nesting pairs in 1974 (Mack) (KB 24:204) and 30 in 1978 (KB 28:262). Coastal colonies increased from 16 pairs at three sites to 136 pairs at four sites in 1978 (Atlas 1988). In 1977 two nests were found on Little Galloo I. in eastern L. Ontario, Jefferson Co. by the Canadian Wildlife Service (Blokpoel and Weseloh 1982).

In the early 1980s the two upstate colonies showed a downward trend, and the coastal colonies continued to increase to about 351 pairs in four colonies on southwestern LI and SI in 1985 (Atlas 1988). Since that time those colonies have also decreased or in some cases disappeared. Sommers et al. (1996) recorded only 42 pairs in four colonies on LI in the latest survey year of 1995. This followed a decade of counts with a mean of 142 pairs.

The L. Champlain birds returned and nested on Four Brothers Islands B and D after a decade of absence as a breeder; 21 nests were located and 14 birds were banded between 12 Jun and 3 Aug 1994. These, the Little Galloo I. birds, and probably those at Braddock Bay, which were one-time nesters, were no doubt from the Canadian population and distinct from the NY coastal population.

Nonbreeding It first appeared in NY 17–27 May 1954 at East Moriches, Suffolk Co. and was recorded regularly after 1958. The first large invasion, about 100 birds, occurred in 1962. By 1970 it was a locally common visitant, chiefly in spring. For the next seven years, mostly single birds were seen, on LI. The first upstate bird was photographed at Niskayuna, Schenectady Co. 25 May 1957 (Tepper).

Coastal maxima: 60 JBWR 26 Sep 1973, the largest nonbreeding concentration ever reported; many birds summered there in that year, but no proof of breeding was found; 20 Baiting Hollow, Suffolk Co. 14 May 1983 (Raynor). *Inland maxima:* 13 Phelps, Ontario Co. 5 Jun 1976; 12 Valley Cottage, Rockland Co. 5 May 1977. *Extreme dates: Coastal:* 12 Dec; *Inland:* 21 Dec. They usually arrive mid-Mar to mid-Apr and depart mid-Oct to mid-Nov.

Remarks An Old World species, which came to North America via South America, it was first seen in the United States at Clewiston, FL in 1941 or 1942 and first nested at L. Okeechobee, FL on 5 May 1953. This heron fills a niche distinct from other herons, feeding on insects and vertebrates in fields and pastures, and it is the only one to breed in its first year. As expected with an invading species, the extension into new habitat initially takes off rapidly, then levels off or decreases as the environment offers resistance.

Lee B. Chamberlaine

Green Heron *Butorides virescens*

Range Nearctic, breeding in southern Canada from British Columbia to Nova Scotia and south throughout most of the United States east of the Great Plains; also in Middle America and the West Indies. Winters, in the east, from South Carolina, the Gulf states, and southern Texas to northern South America.

Status Widespread breeder at low elevations. Fairly common to common migrant, locally abundant at postbreeding roosts. Very rare in winter.

Breeding Recorded in 48% of the blocks during the Atlas survey, it breeds throughout the state in lowland areas wherever suitable nesting sites occur but is rare at elevations over 1000 ft. Unlike most herons, this species is usually a solitary nester and is able to use a wide range of wetland habitats; in 1994 it even bred successfully in Central Park, Manhattan (pers. obs.).

Nonbreeding Common during both spring and fall migration. Large congregations occur at postbreeding roosts in late summer. Some notable counts are: 400 MNWR 22 Aug 1967; 241 Clay Swamp, Onondaga Co. 19 Aug 1969; 143 Far Rockaway, Queens Co. 31 Jul 1949. These herons start to arrive in the state in mid-Apr and most leave by mid-Oct. Small numbers linger through Dec, particularly in coastal areas, from where there are more than 50 CBC records since 1960. There are only a handful of published records from later winter: Baldwin, Nassau Co. 2 Jan 1954; Quogue, Suffolk Co. all winter 1961–1962; Chatham, Columbia Co. 7 March 1963; East Quogue, Suffolk Co. 2 Jan 1965; JBWR 6 Jan 1979; Chatham, Columbia Co. 21 Jan 1979; Naples, Ontario Co. 1 Jan 1987. Extreme migration dates given by Bull (1974), ending with 21 Dec, are not separable from wintering records starting on 15 Dec.

Remarks Species limits in the genus *Butorides* are controversial. The birds in our area were traditionally assigned to *B. virescens* until 1983, when the AOU Check-list lumped this taxon with the Cosmopolitan *B. striatus,* giving it the English name Green-backed Heron (AOU 1983). This decision was reversed in 1993 (AOU 1993) when the *virescens* group of North and Middle America was returned to full species rank as *B. virescens,* the Green Heron.
Paul R. Sweet

Black-crowned Night-Heron *Nycticorax nycticorax*

Range Cosmopolitan, breeding in North America from southern Canada locally through the United States, the West Indies, and Middle America. Winters, in the east, from southern New England south throughout the breeding range.

Status Locally common to abundant resident and migrant on the coast; rare and local inland, but common at a few breeding locations.

Breeding Loss of wetlands and forcible removal of some colonies have greatly reduced this species' breeding population in NY. Cruickshank (1942) estimated the breeding population on LI at more than 3000 pairs in 18–20 colonies. By the mid-1970s, the breeding population had dropped to 430–760 pairs at 23 colonies (Buckley and Buckley 1980). DDT contamination, which caused losses elsewhere in the United States during the 1960s, may have contributed to this decline.

Numbers on LI have since rebounded but still average only about half what they were, ranging from 1105 pairs at 17 colonies in 1992 to 1887 pairs at 23 colonies in 1993 (Sommers et al. 1994). The latest survey in 1995 was nearly the same as 1992. The ten-year survey of this species has shown no significant trend (Sommers et al. 1996).

Upstate, the losses have been even more dramatic. Colonies that held

600 nests on Grand I., Erie Co. have all but disappeared. Bull (1974) listed about 10 locations where the species had been known to breed on the Hudson R. away from NYC, but Atlas workers confirmed none. Breeding was Confirmed in only eight blocks in western NY, where Bull had listed 22 nesting locations. There were no confirmations along the Niagara R., although concentrations of up to 100 birds are reported there in spring. About 12 pairs have since been reported nesting on Motor I., Niagara Co. (KB 45:284); others nest on islands just over the Canadian border.

Remaining colonies upstate are relatively small, mostly under 100 pairs. They include: Four Brothers Islands, Essex Co.; Little Galloo I. and Gull I., Jefferson Co.; and MNWR. As on LI, breeding numbers at these locations can be highly variable from year to year.

Nonbreeding Migrants usually arrive by mid-Mar on the coast, and by mid to late Apr upstate. In many inland parts of NY it is rarely seen, and then only during migration or in late summer, when adults and young disperse from breeding areas. During a mild winter, 179 were found on the Southern Nassau Co. CBC 2 Jan 1983 (KB 33:145). It is very rare inland in winter, although as many as nine at a time wintered in a large spruce in a Buffalo residential area for at least four years (KB 44:117).

Remarks The constant noise, foul odors, and whitewash associated with large heronries caused some to be forcibly removed. For a particularly illuminating account of how residents hired a marksman to eradicate one such colony in the Mohawk Valley in 1953, see George 1991.
Robert E. Marcotte

Yellow-crowned Night-Heron   *Nyctanassa violacea*

Range Nearctic and Neotropical, breeding in the east along the Atlantic Coast from Massachusetts to Florida, and in the West Indies; also, locally, from Minnesota and Wisconsin south to the Gulf Coast and along both coasts of Middle America to northern South America. Winters on the Gulf and Atlantic coasts north to South Carolina.

Status Uncommon breeder and summer visitant along the coast, rare in winter. Rare anytime inland.

Breeding The first state breeding took place in Massapequa, Nassau Co. in 1938. In subsequent years, as many as 18 breeding locations were found, all on LI, except for a single site in Westchester Co.

The latest data available show that over an 11-year period since the Atlas project (1985–1995 inclusive), the mean was only 22 pairs, with a high of 31 in 1995 (Sommers et al. 1996). In 1995, the Westchester site was no longer active. However, as P. A. Buckley (pers. comm.) pointed out, this species tends to nest in small numbers away from mixed species heronries and therefore tends to be missed if surveys are conducted from the air. Therefore, this apparent decrease in breeding in the past two decades may not reflect the true status.

Between 1925 and 1960 the species underwent a dramatic range expansion, establishing itself as a breeder in 11 new states (Watts 1995).

Nonbreeding Eaton (1910) considered this bird the rarest heron in the state, with only six records, and Griscom (1923) did not upgrade this assessment, nor did he add any new records. Cruickshank (1942), citing an annual spate of records, considered it to be "an uncommon and regular summer visitor." Bull (1974) advised that fewer than a dozen occurrences had been recorded "upstate" up to that year. Since then, there have been 40 records north of Westchester Co., 18 in spring, 21 in summer, and 1 in fall: 4 Region 1; 6 Region 2; 1 Region 3; 7 Region 5; 1 Region 7; 3 Region 8; 7 Region 9.

All winter records are from LI, where it is quite rare in that season. Anthony J. Lauro

IBISES AND SPOONBILLS— THRESKIORNITHIDAE

White Ibis *Eudocimus albus*

Range Nearctic and Neotropical, breeding (resident) along the Gulf and Atlantic coasts north to southern North Carolina. Vagrant north to Ontario and Newfoundland.

Status Very rare midsummer to fall visitant to the coast and nearby areas. Casual coastal spring visitant and at any season inland.

Occurrence It has occurred in NY mainly as a postbreeding wanderer from midsummer to late fall, with an additional four occurrences of probable spring migration overshoots, three in Mar and one in May. Nearly all records have been single birds, although a major dispersal in 1977 totaled about 11 immatures. This phenomenon occurred over nearly two months, with the first seen at Teatown L., Westchester Co. 13–16 Jul and the last at Montauk 11 Sep. From 16 Jul to 17 Aug, up to seven were to be found feeding at Mt. Sinai harbor and roosting several miles west at Stony Brook harbor, both in Suffolk Co. This unprecedented influx was well documented by Davis (1979a).

The vast majority of the approximately 26 total records, including three of the four specimens, are from LI. All of the recent records, including those in the 1977 irruption, have been sight records or photographs, most reported to and accepted by NYSARC. The inland records include: a specimen taken near Rochester in 1895, noted by Eaton (1910), but neither specimen nor the correspondence of David Bruce with the NYSM is extant; the first of the 1977 series of related reports; an immature near Braddock Bay, Monroe Co. 17–18 Jul 1980 (KB 30:228); an immature, Rye, Westchester Co. 5–30 Sep 1980 (KB 31:50); and one at North Collins, Erie Co. 6–7 Nov 1990 (KB 41:29).

Spring occurrences are: Moriches, Suffolk Co. early Mar 1843; an adult at Cedar Beach, Suffolk Co. 29 Mar to early Apr 1970; an adult in Brooklyn, 17 May 1980 (KB 30:193); an adult, East Moriches, Suffolk Co. 21–28 March 1993 (KB 43:270).

Remarks The first three specimen records were obtained in only eight years, 1836–1844. After that, there was only one record, the 1895 specimen, during the 125 years to 1969. Certainly, the expansion of breeding colonies in the southeast and into VA in 1977 is responsible for the increase in sightings in NY and the Northeast after 1970. Yet, since the great dispersal of 1977, which brought speculation of the possibility of further increases and even future breeding in NY (Davis 1979a), there has followed a simple continuation of sight records of single wanderers every two to five years and no further expansion of its breeding range northward.
Robert G. Spahn

Glossy Ibis   *Plegadis falcinellus*

Range Cosmopolitan, breeding in North America along the East Coast from southern Maine to Florida and west on the Gulf Coast to Louisiana; also locally in the Greater Antilles. Withdraws in winter to South Carolina, Florida, and southward.

Status In recent years a very common to abundant local breeder on LI and SI. Elsewhere it is an uncommon to fairly common visitant.

Breeding The first confirmed breeding in the state was at JBWR in 1961, with an increase to more than 100 pairs in 1967. In 1970 it extended its range eastward to Gardiners I., Suffolk Co. In 1973 Buckley (AB 27:848) estimated 500 pairs nested in the Jones Beach area and another 75 on Gardiners I. The increase continued to a peak of 883 pairs in 15 colonies on LI and SI in 1978 (Atlas 1988). Since that time, colonial waterbird censuses have tallied 548–746 pairs in 9–14 colonies, with a significant downward trend over the 11 years this species has been surveyed (Sommers et al. 1996).

Since the earliest discovery of nesting in the state, the center of breeding activity has remained in southwestern LI. Most nesting has occurred in mixed-species colonies, with the nests low in the vegetation and with old nests of Snowy Egret and Black-crowned Night-Heron sometimes used.

The number of pairs in specific colonies has abruptly dropped from as many as 100+ to zero in only a single or very few years, with comparable numbers appearing in nearby areas on the same time scale. Careful studies would probably show the local shifts due to a combination of human disturbance and natural events, such as storms.

Nonbreeding Through the early part of this century, it was considered a rare summer visitant, with many rumors of sightings but just eight specimens on record (Eaton 1910). Bull (1974) reported a change from this status to nearly annual occurrence between 1935 and 1959. With breeding beginning in 1961, the peak nonbreeding numbers recorded have increased somewhat, although actually remaining relatively constant over the past 30 years. Inland this species is recorded almost annually in small numbers, and the flock of 12 at OOWMA, 29 Apr–13 May 1939 has been surpassed only by a count of 15 at Braddock Bay, Monroe Co., 3 May 1970. Most occurrences have been in spring, late summer, or fall in marshes along the south shore of L. Ontario or in the remains of the swamp belt running from INWR to MNWR. Region 7 added the species to its list in the spring of 1978 at Plattsburg, Clinton Co. (KB 28:189), and Region 4 followed suit with three birds at Little York, Cortland Co. on 2 Apr 1981 (KB 31:170).

Before 1970, there were very few winter records, but 14 were found on the Brooklyn CBC in 1971, and NYC and LI area CBCs have tallied one to seven birds in 14 of the 23 years from 1972 to 1994. Upstate, the only winter records are: 1 Scio, Allegany Co. 21–28 Dec 1970; 1–3 Braddock Bay area, Monroe Co. Nov–16 Dec 1990 (KB 41:34,104). The only record later than Dec is a single on 1 Jan 1966 at JBWR.

Coastal maxima: 250 JBWR 12 Apr 1991; 225 JBWR 31 Aug 1969.
Extreme dates: Coastal: 2 Mar; *Inland:* 26 Mar.
Robert G. Spahn

White-faced Ibis *Plegadis chihi*

Range Nearctic and Neotropical, breeding in North America locally from central California, eastern Oregon and southern North Dakota south to the Gulf Coast, central and southern Texas, and south to central Mexico; also in South America, south to central Chile and central Argentina. In North America winters from the Gulf Coast south to Guatemala and El Salvador.

Status Very rare vagrant.

Occurrence There are nine records, including two old specimens, both adults from Grand I. in the Niagara R., Erie Co., dated Aug 1844 (Hurst) NYSM 205 and 18 Sep 1908 (Reynolds, specimen discarded). Seven recent records, all of adults and all on LI, include: one photographed by Darrow at Pearsalls Hassock, Nassau Co. 8 May 1979 (Davis 1980); one frequenting JBWR from 10 Jun 1979, joined by a second on 4 Aug, the last sighting on 7 Sep (Davis 1980); two following a pattern similar to the 1979 birds at JBWR 6 Apr–3 Sep 1980 (Davis) (KB 30:193); singles appearing at JBWR during the springs of 1981, 1991, 1992 (Dremeaux, Morris, Clinton) (KB 31:194, 41:217, 42:202); and two regularly visiting Pond X in Lawrence, Nassau Co. 6 Jun–6 Jul 1993 (Lauro) (KB 43:351).

Remarks Possible breeding was conjectured but not proved relative to the presence of two adults at JBWR in 1979 and 1980 and again at Lawrence in 1993. In each case, these birds presumably frequented nearby Glossy Ibis colonies for the season, and thus the possibility of attempted hybridization with that species is also a consideration. Records for this regional rarity diminish in a northeasterly progression, with about 15 records in NJ but only six combined in CT, MA, and NH.
Thomas A. Burke

Roseate Spoonbill   *Ajaia ajaja*

Range Nearctic and Neotropical, resident locally in southern Florida, southwestern Louisiana, and the Gulf Coast of Texas south through Middle America; also in the West Indies and in South America. Wanders north, in the east, to North Carolina, casually or accidently farther north.

Status Accidental.

Occurrence The sole record was of a juvenile, photographed during its stay, 20 Aug–5 Sep 1992, at Goethals Bridge Pond, Richmond Co. (Salzman and Salzman 1993; NYSARC 1994).

Remarks There appear to be no other records of this species in northeastern North America and only two or three poorly documented reports north of the Carolinas.
Eric Salzman

STORKS—CICONIIDAE

Wood Stork   *Mycteria americana*

Range Nearctic and Neotropical, resident coastally from South Carolina to southern Florida and the Gulf states to Texas. Also in Central and South America to Argentina and Peru. Wanders widely after breeding season, in the east, to the Great Lakes and New England.

Status Very rare vagrant.

Occurrence There are at least 20 records, starting with five collected in the nineteenth century. Of these, eight have been coastal. Most of them have summer dates, the birds presumed to be postbreeding wanderers, as is the pattern for this family and the closely related ibises and herons. Virtually all inland records have been single birds, except the small flock of up to five, 14 Jul–25 Aug 1978, Portville, Cattaraugus Co. (Forness 1979).

Coastally there have been four singles, but also flocks of 10, 13, 11, and 15 between 1958 and 1962. Uncharacteristically, one of these flocks flew in on 2 Apr 1962 in the company of 135 egrets that had just arrived on their breeding grounds in Nassau Co., undoubtedly accompanying the egrets from their mutual wintering quarters.

Remarks No flocks have been reported since 1962 in coastal NY, while single wanderers continue to be sighted inland. In MA the bird was unrecorded since 1963 (Veit and Petersen 1993), until one showed up in Dec 1994 and another in Dec 1995. PA, with virtually no coastline, has more than 10 records (Santner et al. 1992), while NJ has well over 30 sightings, 13 since 1975 (Halliwell 1995).
Robert E. Marcotte

NEW WORLD
VULTURES—CATHARTIDAE

Black Vulture *Coragyps atratus*

Range Nearctic and Neotropical, in eastern United States resident north to northern New Jersey, Pennsylvania, Ohio, Indiana, and Illinois; extending northward. Frequently wanders farther north.

Status Rare to fairly common visitant.

Occurrence Bull (1974) mentioned a total of nearly three dozen historical reports, mostly from LI. At least 10 of those were specimen records, of which three are known to be extant. This vulture continues to be sighted very rarely and irregularly upstate, mainly in the Finger Lakes Highlands and the Erie-Ontario Plain.

Since the early 1980s it has been reported more frequently and in increasing numbers in the southeast, particularly in the Hudson Valley and over the Hudson Highlands and Shawangunk Hills. From one to eight individuals in a day have been observed during Mar, Apr, Sep, and Oct at raptor watches, especially Mt. Peter and Bear Mtn., Orange Co.; Hook Mtn., Rockland Co.; and Mohonk, Ulster Co. It has also been recorded in small numbers in eight other downstate counties and has summered in Region 9. There have been fewer sightings on LI than previously. Breeding is likely but has not been discovered to date. Winter records have also been more frequent in the southeast, and it has now been seen in every month of the year.

Remarks The Black Vulture has been occurring with increasing frequency in eastern PA and also with multiple records annually in NJ since 1973 (Leck 1984). Recently, it has also been seen more often in CT (Zeranski and Baptist 1990) and nearly annually in MA (Veit and Petersen 1993). In 1989, breeding was confirmed northward to the Delaware Water Gap area in eastern PA (AB 43:1295) and to northwestern NJ (AB 42:413), where breeding was first confirmed in 1981.

The Black Vulture is essentially a lowland bird, has a tendency to wander, and makes local flights rather than true migrations. Reasons for its range expansion northward in eastern United States are not known for certain, but climate change, food availability, and its tendency to seek food in areas with increasing human activities may have a bearing.
Robert Andrle

Turkey Vulture *Cathartes aura*

Range Nearctic and Neotropical, widespread in temperate North America, breeding in northeastern United States north to northern Vermont and New Hampshire. Northern breeders winter in southeastern United States and Middle America with some overwintering in New York.

Status Widespread breeder. Variously common to abundant migrant throughout except for Coastal Lowlands, where it is rare at any season. In recent years has become resident locally.

Breeding The Atlas recorded Turkey Vulture in 40% of the blocks, but Confirmed nesting in only 12. This reflects both the large range used by individual birds as well as the difficulty in locating their nests. Both Atlas and BBS showed the species present in breeding season in most parts of the state except the Coastal Lowlands and the Adirondacks. Since the Atlas there have been summer reports in the center of the Adirondacks, although no specific breeding evidence is yet reported.

Nonbreeding Migrants generally arrive in the southeast in late Feb, most of the rest of the state in Mar, but not until Apr in the northern areas. Although sightings of small groups overhead are a regular occurrence throughout most of the state, a good road kill or other large source of food can lead to large, temporary aggregations of vultures. They also gather in large numbers at roosts for nighttime shelter. Freer (pers. comm.) monitored a spring-summer roost in Ellenville, Ulster Co. in a grove of Norway spruce. In 1989, the roost peaked at 60 in late Apr, declined to about 10 through the summer, increased again in the fall and was vacated by Oct.

Counts peaked at 80 on 16 Mar 1990, and the roost has continued. Many other roosts in other parts of the state have been noted.

Watchers at the major spring hawk migration sites, Braddock Bay, Monroe Co. and Derby Hill, Oswego Co. have witnessed phenomenal increases. At Derby Hill, the season total for 1976 was 233, which soared to 7385 in 1994. Braddock Bay saw increases in the same period from 87 to 8430. Other spring hawkwatches also have seen increases, if less dramatic.

The bulk of the population that moves north along L. Ontario in spring returns south past the western end of L. Erie in fall. Fall hawkwatches in the state see substantially lower counts than in spring. Butler Sanctuary, Westchester Co. had the highest fall season totals, with 867 in 1991 and 850 in 1995. Most of the other fall watches have seasonal totals in the 50–200 range. All show a gradual increase.

As far back as the 1930s and 1940s (Mohonk records) there had been a few records outside the usual date range of Mar–Oct. Since the 1970s, such records have become more frequent and more widespread. In the mid-1970s, the first Jan records occurred, and by the end of the decade Turkey Vulture was wintering in the lower Hudson Valley in small numbers. A winter roost of 53 was found at Pawling, Dutchess Co. on 18 Dec 1977. During the 1980s, most other parts of the state had winter sightings, including a report from Franklin Co. in Jan 1985 and one in Essex Co. 8 Jan 1996. A winter roost of 15–20 was documented at Letchworth SP, Wyoming/Livingston Co. in 1988 (Bassett 1989), and winter reports from that area have continued. In the 1990s the Pawling, Dutchess Co. CBC continued to include good numbers, and Turkey Vultures began showing up on the Rockland Co. CBC with a count of 59 in 1992. Not far to the south, CBCs in NJ report counts of more than 100.

Spring maxima: 1989 BOS Apr Count 4 Apr 1993; 1891 Braddock Bay 6 Apr 1985; 1853 Braddock Bay 20 Mar 1995. *Fall maxima:* 100 at a landfill, Orange Co., late Sep 1984; 97 BOS Count 11 Oct 1992; 78 Butler Sanctuary, Westchester Co. 20 Oct 1991. *Roosts:* 127 Fahnestock SP, Putnam Co. 30 Mar 1955; 115 Stony Point, Rockland Co. spring 1991; 100 OOWMA 14 Jul 1935, an unusually large number for the "early" years.

Remarks The increase in NY populations is part of a major range expansion into the Northeast after 1920. Possible factors include climate changes, increasing deer populations, and increased highway mortality of wildlife (Wilbur 1983). Wilbur also noted some evidence of declines in numbers in the southern and central part of its range. Outside of the spring migration numbers, the changes are principally in expansions in range and in seasonal occurrence.

Barbara A. Butler

GEESE, SWANS,
AND DUCKS—ANATIDAE

Fulvous Whistling-Duck   *Dendrocygna bicolor*

Range Cosmopolitan, breeding in widely disjunct areas; in North America in southern California, southwestern Arizona, central and eastern Texas, and southern Louisiana, south to Honduras; also locally in southern Florida and the West Indies. Disperses north widely and irregularly, in the east to southern Ontario and Quebec, Nova Scotia, and New England.

Status Very rare vagrant.

Occurrence Not recorded in NY until 22 Dec 1962, when three birds out of a flock of eight were shot by hunters on Sexton I., Great South Bay, Suffolk Co. One of those is now AMNH specimen 781279. There have been about 15 more records, all but six coastal. Five of the inland records were single birds, whereas the coastal sightings have been small flocks. The most spectacular was the 18 on 20 Nov 1977, HLSP (Dempsey, Dieterich, et al.) (KB 28:61, 127). Seven of the records were in Nov, three in May, two in Apr, and one each in Jun, Sep, and Dec.

Remarks It is difficult to find a pattern for this species, which breeds on four continents and has bred as close as NC. The occurrence picture is mirrored closely in MA; their first record was a small flock on the same day as NY's, 22 Dec 1962. They have had no records since 1989 (Veit and Petersen 1993), and the last in NY was in 1991. Although NJ (Halliwell 1995) has accounted for more than two dozen records starting in 1961, there seem to be no reports since 1985.
Robert E. Marcotte

Greater White-fronted Goose   *Anser albifrons*

Range Northern Holarctic, breeding from Alaska east to Hudson Bay, in western Greenland, and northern Eurasia. In North America, winters south to Mexico, along the Gulf Coast of Texas and Louisiana, and rarely in the lower Mississippi Valley. In migration seen primarily west of the Mississippi River, but casually in eastern areas from Labrador to the Gulf Coast.

Status Rare spring and winter visitant; very rare in fall.

Occurrence Those who patiently peruse NY's vast flocks of Canada Geese will, sooner or later, encounter this rare but now regular visitant.

Sightings through the 1960s were treated with skepticism because of the possibility that they had escaped from captivity. Bull (1964, 1974) mentioned only about nine coastal and about a dozen upstate records, including seven specimens. However, an adult male shot at Sagaponack, Suffolk Co. 23 Dec 1968 confirmed this species as a wild bird in NY. It had been banded as a juvenile at Mantario, SA on 28 Sep 1962.

Since then, this species has been reported with increased frequency. About 130 sightings were reported in *The Kingbird* from 1975 through 1995. These reports clearly suggest an increase in occurrence. Greater numbers of observers, increased familiarity with the species, and even closer scrutiny of flocks of geese for censuses and for neckband numbers may have contributed to the increase in sightings.

It is seen most often upstate, and most often in spring. Of the 130 sightings, nearly 90 were upstate, the rest downstate, including about 20 coastal. About 80 were in Mar and Apr. Usually single birds, or small groups of 2–4, are spotted, mixed with flocks of Canada Goose. *Maxima*: Thirteen were at Braddock Bay, Monroe Co. 6–13 Mar 1980; 11 at Miller Place, Suffolk Co. 5 Apr 1883; and 8 at Aurelius, Cayuga Co. 2 Apr 1982.

Extreme dates: 2 Oct and 27 May.

Remarks Of the four to five subspecies that are recognized, Bull (1974) reported that only *frontalis* (pink-billed, breeding in Canada) had been recorded in NY, but he suggested that *flavirostris* (orange-billed, breeding in Greenland) might also occur. Of 21 sightings since 1975 in which the subspecies was recorded, 16 were *flavirostris*, five were *frontalis*. Robert E. Marcotte

Snow Goose *Chen caerulescens*

Range Holarctic, in North America, breeding from northern Alaska across Arctic Canada to Ellesmere and Baffin islands and northwestern Greenland and south to Hudson Bay; also in Siberia. In eastern North America, winters along the Atlantic Coast from Massachusetts to Florida, primarily in the Chesapeake Bay area, and on the Gulf Coast.

Status Uncommon to very abundant migrant in some regions. In winter, uncommon to common along the coast, rare on larger inland bodies of water.

Occurrence Snow Goose has two color morphs: the light, which is the "Snow," and the dark, or "Blue." They can be seen in numbers during migration along the coast and in select locations inland. Winter reports have increased as larger numbers of other geese have remained for the winter.

Historically, the "Blues" predominated in the western portions of the state, and the "Snows" were dominant in the east. Numbers of "Blues" were reported in the east in the late 1970s, but they have not been readily apparent since. Few current reports are broken down into color morphs, except when individuals or small numbers are reported.

The largest flights are coastal in fall, with the birds arriving in late Sep. Inland, the largest concentrations are at MNWR in spring. Arrivals there are in mid to late Mar, with departure by late Apr. Fall flights can be good along L. Champlain, with numbers in the thousands in some years. A perusal of Jan FWC tables over the last two decades showed appreciable numbers in Region 10 each year, with just a few scattered around the rest of the state.

Spring maxima: 30,000 MNWR 18 Apr 1983; 17,000 MNWR 12 Apr 1989. *Fall maxima:* 12,000 Point au Roche, Clinton Co. 16 Dec 1990; 10,000 Stuyvesant, Columbia Co. 29 Oct 1990.

Remarks Two subspecies occur in the state: the nominate *caerulescens* and *atlanticus*. Separation is difficult in the field, as evidently the difference is one of measurements. The larger *atlanticus* winters on the Atlantic Coast from MD to NC and migrates to and from its breeding grounds via the St. Lawrence R., the Champlain-Hudson valley, and the coast. The smaller nominate subspecies uses the Mississippi Flyway as its route and shows up in western NY. The different routes would account for the greater number of the blue morph in the western part of the state, as the blue is common in *caerulescens* and very rare in *atlanticus* (G. Cooch, pers. comm.).

Specimens of *caerulescens* include a juvenile "Snow" taken on the south shore of Cayuga L. 22 Nov 1952 (Parkes) CUM 24066. Specimens of *atlanticus* include two adult "Snow" killed by flying into power lines during a heavy fog, between L. George and Glens Falls, Warren Co. 15 Apr 1962 NYSM 20569 and 20570.

The nominate *caerulescens*, sometimes also referred to as "Lesser" Snow Goose is increasing at a high rate in both the central Arctic and the Hudson Bay–Foxe Basin areas, making it likely that greater numbers will be seen wintering on the East Coast, with a higher percentage of the blue morph than previously noted (R. Rockwell, pers. comm.).
Kevin C. Griffith

Ross's Goose   *Chen rossii*

Range Nearctic, breeding in the high Arctic tundra area of northern Mackenzie and Keewatin and on southern Southampton Island and the west coast of Hudson Bay south to Cape Churchill. Winters to California, Texas, and the Gulf Coast. Casual in Ontario and Quebec and along the Atlantic Coast from New York to Florida.

Status Very rare vagrant.

Occurrence The first NY record was a bird seen on 13 Mar 1983 in Amenia, Dutchess Co. (Treacy 1983), resulting in the placement of the species on the NY checklist by NYSARC (1984). Since then, there have been over ten more records, most in spring, and all found in the company of Snow Goose. The first fall report was in Randolph, Cattaraugus Co. 7 Oct 1992 (KB 43:41), and the first winter bird was at Water Mill, Suffolk Co. 5 Jan 1991 (KB 41:133).

Remarks The pattern of occurrence in NY is fairly consistent with the NJ picture. Since 1990, Ross's Goose has been reported in PA four times, resulting in that state's first records. CT and MA have not yet recorded it. The population in central Arctic and Hudson Bay–Foxe Basin areas is increasing at a high rate, and it is likely there will be more reports in our area (R. Rockwell, pers. comm.).
Kevin C. Griffith

Canada Goose *Branta canadensis*

Range Nearctic, breeding from the Arctic Coast of Alaska and Canada east to Labrador and Greenland and south, in the east, to southern Canada; in the United States, irregularly along the Atlantic Coast and inland, where introduced stock may be of historical significance. Winters from the southern portion of the breeding range to the Gulf states and northern Mexico.

Status Breeds throughout; very common resident locally. Very abundant migrant, especially in west. Very abundant in winter on LI and the Finger Lakes.

Breeding As a breeder it was not present before the 1930s, when breeding stock from captive birds was introduced, although information on results of those introductions is not readily available. The first recorded nestings took place at MNWR in 1941 and at OOWMA in 1950. In the 1950s and 1960s the NYSDEC released more birds in those two places as well as other upstate locations.

In the last two decades the number of breeding birds has increased steadily. In 1995 the NYSDEC estimated the statewide breeding population at more than 25,000 pairs, with a postbreeding population in excess of 70,000 (B. Swift, pers. comm.). It is believed that the increase in nesting is due to dispersal and reproduction by descendants of the introductions, rather than wild migratory birds that have chosen to stay in the state and breed.

Major breeding concentrations occur in the lower Hudson Valley, on LI, and along the St. Lawrence R. near Massena. Local nesting or "resident" geese become a problem in many urban and suburban areas where parks, golf courses, and other lawn areas near water provide ideal habitat for feeding and molting.

Nonbreeding Large flocks of Canada Geese are a common sight during migration throughout much of NY, when thousands land to rest and feed for the trip to and from the northern breeding grounds. MNWR and INWR are two favorite stopover locations; large numbers also feed and rest on the L. Ontario littoral. Numbers and concentrations are larger during the spring migration but can be impressive in fall.

Spring maxima: 140,000 MNWR 10 Mar 1983; 100,000 Cayuga L. 15 Mar 1975; 100,000 Rochester to Point Breeze, Monroe and Orleans counties 18 Mar 1979. *Fall maxima:* 58,940 MNWR 19 Nov 1986; 46,000 MNWR 9 Oct 1978. *Winter maxima:* 105,835 Cayuga L. 29 Jan 1991 (NYSDEC aerial survey); 54,267 Seneca L. 12 Jan 1992.

Remarks Migratory geese in NY include a mix of the nominate subspecies *canadensis* and *interior*. *Canadensis* is believed to be the predominant form on LI, whereas *interior* probably accounts for many of the sightings elsewhere. Resident breeding geese probably include some of both and a large proportion of *maxima*, or "Giant" Canada Goose.

Interior is known as a more western breeder. There are seven specimens: three from Montauk, four from the east shore of Cayuga L. This subspecies is much darker on the underparts than *canadensis*, and the light area extends up around the back of the neck to the base of the black "stocking" (Parkes 1952). Under good viewing conditions it is separable in the field.

A fourth subspecies is the very small, subarctic *hutchinsi*, about half the size of the other three and with a small bill. There are two specimens of it: OOWMA Apr 1964 BMS 5081; Sayres Pond, Suffolk Co. 20 Nov 1968 AMNH 789787. Photographs exist of a third at Tobay Pond, Nassau Co. 15 Oct 1966.

Kevin C. Griffith

Brant   *Branta bernicla*

Range Northern Holarctic, breeding in North America in the high Arctic from Alaska to Ellesmere Island, south to Southampton and Baffin islands; also in Siberia, Greenland, Spitsbergen, and Franz Josef Land. Winters on the Atlantic Coast to North Carolina and on the Pacific Coast to Baja California.

Status Abundant to very abundant migrant and winter visitant on western LI. Less numerous elsewhere along the coast. Locally common to very abundant inland, particularly in the Great Lakes littoral and the Hudson Valley. Uncommon away from the larger bodies of water.

Occurrence As a wintering species it had been known primarily from the South Shore of LI, where it was considered uncommon before 1931. During the 1930s and 1940s the entire population declined dramatically due to a die-off of a primary food source, eel grass, which was attacked by a blight. During the mid-1940s the Brant recovered, having adapted its diet to sea lettuce and moving out of the water to feed on adjacent open land.

Then the eel grass recovered as well, and the Brant began occurring in unprecedented numbers, even to the extent of summering birds being recorded annually. The number of inland sightings increased, although few birds land unless adverse weather conditions force them down.

They are one of the latest migrant waterfowl. On mid-May evenings large flocks depart JBWR and other coastal locations and can be seen flying up the lower Hudson Valley. Spring flights as well as regular fall movements along the shores of L. Ontario and Cayuga L. have become more common.

Coastal maxima: 48,000 Southern Nassau Co. CBC 3 Jan 1988; 28,000 Southern Nassau CBC 2 Jan 1995. **Inland maxima:** 9000 Derby Hill, Oswego Co. 23 Oct 1965; 7500 Derby Hill 21 Oct 1987.

Remarks Two subspecies that occur in NY are separable in the field at close range. *Hrota*, the one commonly seen, and often referred to as Atlantic Brant, breeds in northern and western Greenland, northern Canadian islands, and the mainland coast west to about 100°W. *Nigricans*, known as Pacific or Black Brant, breeds in northern Canada from Perry R. and nearby islands westward to coastal Alaska (Johnsgard 1978). There have been acknowledged records of *nigricans* in NY, all singles, all on LI: Islip 1840; Babylon 1889; Babylon 1908; Merrick Bay 30 Mar 1946; Mattituck 25 Oct 1959; JBWR 14 Oct–29 Nov 1974; Riis Park, Queens Co. 3 Mar 1977.
Kevin C. Griffith

Barnacle Goose *Branta leucopsis*

Range Northwestern Palearctic, breeding west to eastern Greenland. Winters south to British Isles, northern Europe, and casually to northern Africa. Vagrant in eastern North America from Labrador to James Bay south to Quebec, the Maritime Provinces, and along the Atlantic Coast to South Carolina; also variously inland.

Status Very rare vagrant.

Occurrence Before 1974 there were about a dozen reports divided between western NY and LI. Since then, reports have increased, with some coming from the center of the state as well.

Because the species is commonly kept in wildfowl collections, there is no easy way to determine whether an individual is a wild bird or an escaped captive. Observers should carefully document behavior in their reports, and perhaps, over the years, some pattern will emerge that may help in determining the status of a particular individual.

The only specimen extant is a female collected on Jamaica Bay, Queens Co. 18 Oct 1876, USNM 80015.

Remarks Surrounding areas have experienced the same difficulty with this species. MA listed two records that were possibly wild, but others were determined to be escapes. CT records included two before 1970 and two in the mid-1980s. The origins again were in question, but it was suggested that records from northeastern Canada indicate that vagrants to New England and NY might be possible. Reports from NJ are thought to be of escaped birds.

Kevin C. Griffith

Mute Swan *Cygnus olor*

Range Palearctic; introduced to North America. Mainly resident along the East Coast from Massachusetts to Virginia and sporadically around the Great Lakes.

Status Abundant, increasing resident downstate; very local but increasing upstate.

Breeding The spread of this elegant, but aggressive and sometimes destructive, interloper has led NYSDEC to adopt a management plan that, in some instances, allows removal and even humane killing. A Eurasian species, it was first introduced in the late 1800s to beautify parks and private estates on the lower Hudson R. and LI. It did not become established in the wild until after the release of 216 at Rhinebeck, Dutchess Co. in 1910 and another 328 at Southampton and Oakdale in Suffolk Co. in 1912.

Bull (1964, 1974) reported that it had become established throughout the NYC area into Dutchess and Rockland counties but was most numerous on the eastern end of LI. The Oakdale population, for example, had grown to 700 by 1967. The Atlas also described its stronghold as the east end of the island and suggested that its numbers on LI were stabilizing. Instead, it has continued to increase. One at JBWR on western LI was considered to be in an "unusual location" in 1980 (KB 30:193). Yet 55 were reported there by 1988, increasing to 205 in 1994 (KB 44:341).

Along the Hudson, this species is steadily expanding northward, with numbers increasing in Greene and Columbia counties. NYSDEC workers captured a pair attempting to nest as far north as Round L., Saratoga Co. in 1992 (KB 43:71). Elsewhere upstate, Atlas workers found this species in only two blocks and Confirmed breeding only at PRWMA. Breeding populations are now firmly established not only there but also at Rochester, Monroe Co., where breeding was first confirmed at Braddock Bay WMA in 1990 (KB 40:245). By 1995, nesting occurred at four locations in Rochester, producing upwards of 20 offspring (KB 45:291).

Nonbreeding Although primarily a sedentary species, it will relocate short distances in search of open water during winter.

147

Remarks This species' aggressive behavior while breeding, and its willingness to nest in heavily populated areas, has inevitably brought it into
conflict with humans. It has been known to chase jet-skiers, canoeists, and
even small children who wander near its nests. According to NYSDEC
(1993), several areas on LI have had elevated levels of coliform bacteria in
water where it congregates, prompting concern about water quality.

NYSDEC also cited RI studies showing that Mute Swans reduce aquatic
vegetation in coastal ponds, leaving a pond bottom "barren and cratered in
appearance." Along with Canada Goose, it has interfered with attempts to
restore wetland vegetation along the lower Hudson R. (NYSDEC 1993).

The Atlas referred to a CT study (O'Brien and Askins 1985) that found
no competition between Mute Swan and native waterfowl, since they feed
on different vegetation and at different depths. Other studies, however,
have shown that it is often intolerant of other waterfowl and will sometimes
destroy their nests and young (NYSDEC 1993).

NYSDEC's management policy is, in part, to prevent the release or relo-
cation of Mute Swans in the wild, remove them from state-managed areas,
and issue permits to landowners and other agencies to remove or control
them.

Robert E. Marcotte

Tundra Swan   *Cygnus columbianus*

Range Nearctic, breeding from northwestern Alaska east along the Arctic
Coast to Baffin Island, and south to the Hudson Bay area. Winters, in the
east, along the Atlantic Coast from Maryland to North Carolina, casually
farther north and south, and in the Great Lakes region.

Status Common to abundant spring migrant in extreme western NY, less
numerous in fall; rare to uncommon east of the Finger Lakes.

Occurrence Western NY plays host to sizable flights of Tundra Swans. The
larger lakes, particularly Chautauqua L., L. Ontario, and the larger Finger
Lakes, attract good numbers in spring. INWR and MNWR also play host to
good numbers at this season. Historically, the Niagara R. was a major
stopover, but this seems to be less true at present. The fall migration is
much less spectacular and consists of much smaller numbers. The flight
from the arctic breeding grounds begins in Sep and includes a stop at the
Devils L. area of ND and on the Mississippi R. near Weaver, MN in early
Oct. From there, the eastern wintering population makes a nonstop migration to Chesapeake Bay and eastern NC. This would account for the considerably smaller fall totals in western NY. Individuals have also been known
to summer and winter in the state. They frequent bays and ponds along the
LI coast but are decidedly uncommon there at any season and are virtually
never seen in double digits. They are recorded each year on the FWC, con-

Montauk Point is exciting at any time of the year but most especially after easterly storms and during winter. During that season, huge numbers of Northern Gannets gather to fish in the waters surrounding the point.

ducted during early Jan. Historical data describe numbers of Tundra Swans swept over the falls at Niagara. This no longer seems to occur.

Spring maxima: all in Chautauqua Co.: 3000 Chautauqua L. 20 Mar 1950; 1000 Conewango L. 26 Mar 1968; 1000 Chautauqua L. 7 Mar 1987. *Fall maxima:* 1000 Burgeson Wildlife Sanctuary, Chautauqua Co. 10 Nov 1979; 700+ near Buffalo, Erie Co. 6 Nov 1966. *Winter maxima:* 500 Chautauqua L. 3 Dec 1978. *Extreme dates:* 15 Sep and 31 May.

It is rare before Oct and after Apr. There have been summer reports, all upstate and most at such places as OOWMA and MNWR.
Kevin C. Griffith

Wood Duck   *Aix sponsa*

Range Nearctic, in the east breeding from east central Saskatchewan to Nova Scotia, south to the Gulf states and Cuba. Winters mainly in the southern portions of the breeding range north to New England.

Status Common breeder throughout. Locally common to abundant fall migrant, particularly in the west. Less common in spring, rare in winter.

Breeding The Atlas Confirmed it in every county, with additional Probable sites scattered widely throughout the state. The greatest areas of concentration were in the western and central portions of the state and the Hudson Valley. A surprising number of sites were in heavily populated LI. Most of the Confirmed records were below 2000 ft.

This is the only dabbling duck that is a hole nester. It readily accepts the numerous boxes that have been placed during the last two decades. Add to this the increase in prime breeding habitat created by the resurgent beaver and the result is a burgeoning duck population. It is no accident that this species has been either the first or second most numerous in the hunter's bag during the 1980s and 1990s.

Nonbreeding It generally arrives in mid-Mar and departs by mid-Nov, with numbers decidedly lower in spring than in fall. The lower spring numbers could be the result of a successful breeding season counterbalanced by an equally successful hunting season. Bull (1974) showed a high fall count of no more than 900 at MNWR 12 Oct 1968, a number now easily exceeded each fall at that same location.

Fall maxima: 2230 Toad Harbor, Oswego Co. 27 Sep 1992; 2100 MNWR 30 Sep 1978; 2072 Toad Harbor, Oswego Co. 26 Sep 1988.

There is a scattering of wintering birds throughout the state as shown by CBC and FWC totals, with most records concentrated in Nassau Co., where double digits came up quite frequently on the Northern Nassau CBC during the last two decades.
Emanuel Levine

Gadwall   *Anas strepera*

Range Holarctic, but local in its distribution; in North America chiefly in the west, breeding from Alaska to California and Texas and east to Manitoba and Wisconsin; in the east, sporadically from southeastern Ontario, northwestern Pennsylvania, western New York, and along the Atlantic Coast from Long Island to South Carolina. Winters north to New York.

Status A rare to uncommon breeder at an increasing number of inland sites. Locally common to very common resident and migrant on LI while generally an uncommon to fairly common migrant and winter visitant inland, although abundant to very abundant at peak fall migration at MNWR.

Breeding DeKay (1844) reported breeding but Eaton (1910) noted no further confirmation through the turn of the century; verification of breeding was not obtained until 1947 at Tobay Pond, Nassau Co. By 1970, Bull (1974) noted increased breeding on the South Shore and east end of LI and at MNWR and INWR. The Atlas noted increased breeding at these earlier locales plus the addition of WHWMA and other sites along the St. Lawrence R.; Stony I. in eastern L. Ontario, Jefferson Co.; Chazy Landing, Clinton Co.; and a few other scattered blocks. In the years since the Atlas, breeding has been Confirmed at additional sites in Kendall, Orleans Co. (KB 40:248), the Braddock Bay area, Monroe Co. (KB 43:314), and Vischers Ferry, Saratoga Co. (KB 45:322).

Nonbreeding Another story of steady increases recently, mirroring increases in the heart of its mainly western range, although even there it is subject to large population swings (Bellrose 1976). At the turn of the century, Eaton (1910) noted Gadwall as not common, although frequently taken in migration upstate near the marshes along L. Ontario and the Finger Lakes, but accidental on LI. Bull noted substantial increases on LI, accompanied by breeding, and very large concentrations at MNWR in fall. At that time winter records were mainly from LI and the Buffalo, Erie Co. CBC. The migration pattern has continued in recent years, with the major concentration point still MNWR, with much smaller numbers in the areas noted by Eaton, and with only scattered records elsewhere. After 1971, the number of CBCs reporting Gadwall increased dramatically, the number of individuals per site trended upward, and the species became regular on many counts across the state. The coastal CBC total passed 1000 in 1972 and in most years since; 2000 was surpassed in 1987. The FWC tracked this increase through 1992 but since has shown a decrease of more than 30%. It would seem obvious from the large CBC and FWC counts of recent years that local sites on LI must see peaks at least as large as the coastal maxima below, but such counts have not been reported separately from the overall totals.

Inland maxima: Fall: all at MNWR: 35,000 Dec 1987; 10,000 12 Nov 1967; 8000 29 Oct 1981. Since 1984, maxima have generally been less than 2000. *Coastal maxima:* 150 Babylon, Suffolk Co. 28 Nov 1963; 130 Wantagh, Nassau Co., 11 Jan 1964.
Robert G. Spahn

Eurasian Wigeon   *Anas penelope*

Range Palearctic, breeding from Iceland east to Siberia and Kamchatka. Rare but regular winter visitant to North America; on the Atlantic and Gulf coasts, from Newfoundland to Florida and Texas. Irregular, primarily spring migrant in interior North America.

Status Rare but regular visitant coastally; rare to very rare inland.

Occurrence The handsome drake is conspicuous among the American Wigeon with which it usually associates. It was considered an accidental vagrant in NY before 1900 but was sighted more frequently in the early part of this century, especially on LI. Bull (1974) said it was most prevalent from the 1920s to the early 1950s and had since decreased in occurrence, despite an increase in the numbers of American Wigeon. However, there are indications that this species is again occurring more frequently. Spring flights were reported inland in 1992, with up to eight individuals across five Regions, and in 1995 when nine were sighted in five Regions.

At least six times since 1980, as many as eight to ten individuals have wintered on the coast. Another 14 were reported from Brooklyn to Mattituck, Suffolk Co. during the winter of 1991–1992. Other maxima include: 14 South Haven, Suffolk Co. 3 Nov 1935; 11 from Tobay Pond to Valley Stream, Nassau Co. 20 Dec 1952; 7 Rockville Center, Nassau Co. 7 Dec 1947. Usually, however, only scattered singles are observed. Inland, this species is seen more often in spring than in fall, with most reports in Mar and Apr. It is generally rare before Oct and after Apr. There are a handful of summer records, at MNWR (1970, 1982) and JBWR (1980, 1988, 1994). *Extreme dates:* 7 Aug and 1 Jun.

Remarks This species may be underreported because of the similarity of the female to the female American Wigeon. Bull's speculation that the widespread sightings in the United States might be due to a breeding population somewhere in the Canadian Arctic has not been supported by any evidence. Banding returns indicate European origins.
Robert E. Marcotte

American Wigeon

Anas americana

Range Chiefly western Nearctic, rare and local breeder in the east. Breeds regularly east and south to Manitoba and Wisconsin; since the 1950s spreading eastward and southward, but very locally, to eastern Canada and New York including Long Island. Winters in the southeastern United States north to Long Island and Massachusetts.

Status Uncommon, local breeder upstate, rare breeder on LI. Common to very abundant migrant, especially at MNWR. In winter primarily found on LI.

Breeding In the early 1900s it occurred only as a migrant (Eaton 1910), but in 1959 it was first found nesting at MNWR. There was a general increase in eastern populations beginning about 1950 (Palmer 1976). By the 1980s the Atlas found it in 42 blocks and Confirmed it in 10: along the Niagara R., at the TWMA, INWR, MNWR, PRWMA, WHWMA; along L. Champlain in Clinton Co., and Great Peconic Bay, Suffolk Co. It still nests along the Niagara R., where one adult with six young were seen at Buckhorn I. SP 21 June 1994. It continues to be reported as breeding, or present in Jun and Jul, in the other areas mentioned in the Atlas. Breeding at JBWR or nearby Flushing Meadows has not been noted since the original reports in 1961. Another single nesting occurred in the lower Hudson Valley at Piermont Pier, Rockland Co. 21 July 1974 (KB 24:209).

A first breeding record for Region 2 was established with an observation of a female with brood in Carlton, Orleans Co. in summer 1986 and again 6 Jul 1989 (KB 36:216, 39:228). At Webb Royce Swamp, Essex Co. a first summer record was on 11 Jul 1992, and it was suggested that the species may be extending its range from Clinton Co. south along L. Champlain (KB 42:264, 266).

Nonbreeding It occurs along the coast Sep–May; inland, Mar–May and Sep–Nov. Rare to uncommon upstate in winter, it is very abundant along the coast, where 90% of individuals reported on FWCs come from LI. In the period 1957–1960 counts were at all-time highs and averaged 4200 individuals. Since then they have gradually decreased; 1990–1995 counts averaged 1280, ranging from a low of 596, after a very cold Dec in 1990, to a high of 1919, after a very warm Dec in 1995. Fluctuations in number appear to be related to severity of weather in Dec and Jan when, with the freezing of open water, birds are forced farther south. Nesting success may also be involved.

Coastal maxima: 8000 JBWR 13 Nov 1959; 5000 JBWR 28 Sep 1960. *Inland maxima:* 27,000 MNWR 28 Sep 1965; 26,000 MNWR 23 Nov 1966.

Stephen W. Eaton

American Black Duck *Anas rubripes*

Range Eastern Nearctic, breeding from northeastern Saskatchewan east to Labrador and Newfoundland and south to the central United States; in the east, to North Carolina. Sedentary and migratory, wintering through much of the range and south to southern Texas, the Gulf Coast, and central Florida.

Status Widespread breeder, common to very abundant migrant and winter visitant.

Breeding Atlas work produced Confirmed breeding in every county with the exception of New York Co. The concentration of breeders is greatest in LI, the Hudson Valley, and in the Adirondacks at elevations up to 3000 ft. Populations are thinner in the western parts, where breeding is more local. Historically, it was the commonest breeding duck in the state, but the species suffered an almost 60% decline between the early 1950s and early 1980s (Atlas 1988). Correspondingly, the Mallard, in that same time period, became established as the predominant breeding duck in the state. It was recorded in three times as many blocks as the American Black Duck in the Atlas period.

There have been studies that seem to indicate that this species is being genetically swamped through interbreeding with its congener, the Mallard. This theory seems to be borne out by statistics (KB 40:218). The 16-year average for the two species as recorded on FWCs 1973–1989 were: American Black Duck 19,398; Mallard 23,374. Between 1990 and 1994, also on FWCs, the five-year averages were: American Black Duck 22,355; Mallard 47,284. It would seem that some biodynamic phenomenon is at work. Even so, the American Black Duck seems to be holding its own numerically.

Nonbreeding Burgeoning populations in the fall, particularly at places like MNWR and LI, are indicative of the migrant flow into the state. The numbers do not really give credence to the theory of "genetic swamping" discussed above. Although there has been a phenomenal increase in the Mallard population, there really has not been a corresponding decrease in American Black Duck.

Spring maxima: 5000 MNWR 31 Mar 1983. *Fall maxima:* 20,000 MNWR 15 Nov 1984; 15,000 MNWR Nov 1990. *Winter maxima:* Region 10 FWCs ranged from 15,000 to 23,000 every year since 1985, except 1988 (13,091) and 1994 (12,360).

Emanuel Levine

Mallard   *Anas platyrhynchos*

Range Holarctic, in North America widely distributed in the west, breeding from Alaska and northern Canada to Mexico; in the east only from southern Quebec and southern Maine south to northern Virginia. Sedentary and migratory, wintering in eastern North America south to the Gulf states and the northern West Indies.

Status Resident throughout and abundant migrant.

Breeding It nests virtually everywhere with minimal habitat requirements. The greatest concentrations are on the Great Lakes Plain and in the Hudson Valley and Coastal Lowlands. Nesting is minimal at elevations over 1000 ft (Atlas 1988). Notwithstanding the fact that it is today the best known breeding duck in the state, it was almost unknown as a breeder until the beginning of the twentieth century. Numbers increased steadily until the 1950s, when a virtual population explosion began, which is continuing today. The catalyst for this phenomenon was the combined actions by NYSDEC of creating new marsh habitat and the release of some 20,000 birds (Atlas 1988). For a discussion of the possible effect of the increase of this species on its congener, American Black Duck, see that account.

Nonbreeding Although there is a large resident population, the buildup of numbers in the fall is evidence of huge migratory influx as well. The maxima listed below far surpass any of those in Bull 1974.

Spring maxima: 7000 MNWR 31 Mar 1983; 5500 MNWR 22 Mar 1989. *Fall maxima:* 400,000 MNWR 15 Nov 1984; 180,000 Seneca L. 30 Nov 1982. *Winter maxima:* up to 50,000 overwintering on Seneca L. in 1995.

Emanuel Levine

Blue-winged Teal   *Anas discors*

Range Nearctic, breeding in the east from southern Quebec and Nova Scotia south to central Louisiana and eastern North Carolina. Winters along the Atlantic and Gulf coasts from North Carolina and Texas south to middle South America.

Status Local breeder in small numbers. Locally common fall migrant, very abundant at MNWR; much less numerous but common in spring throughout the state.

Breeding It was found in 9% of Atlas blocks and was Confirmed or Probable in 66% of those. Nesting was concentrated in several regions. The highest concentrations occur around L. Ontario, the Finger Lakes, the St. Lawrence Plains, and the Cattaraugus Highlands. It was also found in smaller numbers on LI and in the Mohawk, Hudson, and Champlain valleys (Atlas 1988). The highest recorded nesting population was in the INWR complex, where 111 nests were counted in 1988 and breeding success was measured at 21% (Estel 1989).

There is evidence that in the early 1980s there was a decline in the number nesting in their prime areas. Data from MNWR suggest a decrease in annual production from several hundred to about 25 per year over a short time period (Gingrich 1995). Declines were also noted at the same time at El Dorado Beach (KB 34:257) and in other marshes along L. Ontario (KB 32:272). The cause of this decline is unknown.

Nonbreeding In spring it is recorded throughout the state. Average arrival date is 28 Mar and earliest is 9 Mar. It is seen in small numbers in mixed flocks of dabbling ducks. Highest spring concentrations are at MNWR, where a peak daily count of over 1000 has been recorded in a single year.

Peak of fall migration occurs in the last two weeks of Sep, and few birds remain after the end of Oct. Highest counts of fall migrants are also from MNWR. It is occasionally found on CBCs in the LI region. One to four individuals are found on 50% of the FWCs (KB 30:210).

Coastal maxima: Fall: 250 Tobay Pond, Nassau Co. 7 Sep 1941; 150 Mastic, Suffolk Co. 20 Aug 1952. *Winter:* 14 Southern Nassau Co. CBC 30 Dec 1984; 7 Southern Nassan Co. CBC 30 Dec 1978. *Inland maxima: Spring:* 1200 MNWR 4 Apr 1975; 1100 MNWR 1995. *Fall:* 8000 MNWR 21 Sep 1970; 3200 MNWR 1995.

Dominic F. Sherony

Cinnamon Teal   *Anas cyanoptera*

Range Western Nearctic, breeding from southern Canada east to the western Dakotas, Nebraska, and Kansas south to central Texas and northern Mexico. Winters from central California east to central Texas and south through Middle America to northern South America. Vagrant to the Atlantic Coast.

Status Casual vagrant.

Occurrence Cinnamon Teal are sometimes bred in captivity, and escapes do occur. Tame birds should be treated as escapes. There are five to seven records for western NY thought to be wild; all were males. A specimen was taken on the shore of Seneca L., Yates Co. mid-Apr 1886. One was reported at Times Beach, Erie Co. 15 Aug 1973; one was photographed at MNWR 1 Apr 1974 (Haramis 1974), and possibly the same bird was seen there on 21 Jul (KB 25:38); one was at Tonawanda WMA, 26 June 1975 and, possibly the same bird, at INWR on 25 Aug (KB 26:36); two in eclipse plumage were reported at Prendergast Point, Chautauqua Co. 21 Aug 1977 (KB 28:38).

There are two recent records suggestive of Blue-winged × Cinnamon Teal hybrids (KB 30:204, 36:148). Bull (1974) listed three such occurrences on LI. One at JBWR 20 May–18 Jul 1964 was thought to be an escape.

Remarks In recent years, MA had two records regarded as wild birds (Veit and Petersen 1993), CT one, PA two, and NJ five (Halliwell 1995). Dominic F. Sherony

Northern Shoveler *Anas clypeata*

Range Holarctic, in North America widespread in the west but breeding locally in the east around the Great Lakes east to New Brunswick and Prince Edward Island and south to Massachusetts, New York, New Jersey, and Pennsylvania. Winters from South Carolina south to the Gulf Coast, through Middle America and the West Indies to northern South America; also rarely north to the Great Lakes, New England, and Nova Scotia.

Status Rare breeder. Abundant to very abundant migrant at MNWR, locally common to very common elsewhere. Common to abundant winter visitant in coastal areas.

Breeding A very local, rare breeder, preferring large, protected marshes such as those at wildlife management and refuge areas. Eaton (1910) reported it nesting at MNWR early in the century. As many as eight broods were raised there in 1962. During Atlas work, it was reported in fewer blocks than any other dabbling duck, and was Confirmed only at MNWR, at Lawrence Marsh, Nassau Co. and at JBWR, where there are also records from 1956 and 1978.

It is known to have nested at seven other locations: OOWMA; WHWMA; HIWMA; Tobay Pond, Nassau Co.; and, most recently, at Tifft Farm Nature Preserve, Erie Co. Jun 1988 (KB 38:257); in the Chazy–Little Chazy rivers area, Clinton Co. Jul 1994 (KB 44:328); and at Rockland L. SP, Rockland Co. May 1995 (KB 45:229).

Nonbreeding Bull (1974) reported a marked increase in the previous 20 years. Its numbers have since leveled off and, if anything, declined. USFWS surveys showed that the breeding population reached a record high in North America in 1994, perhaps signaling a resurgence in NY.

It migrates in spring Mar–May, generally peaking at MNWR anytime in late Mar through Apr. In fall, migration is primarily Sep–Nov. MNWR attracts the largest concentrations, with maximum spring counts generally 200–800 and higher counts in fall. The 9000 reported 30 Mar 1983 (KB 33:193) was a startlingly high spring count; a fall count of 7000 on 12 Nov 1967 was unprecedented. It can be locally common in traditional spots elsewhere during migration, but in many areas it is uncommon to rare.

Rarely reported inland in winter, it can be a very common winter visitant in coastal areas.

Robert E. Marcotte

Northern Pintail   *Anas acuta*

Range Holarctic, in eastern North America breeding from southern Hudson Bay to Newfoundland and Nova Scotia and south to the Great Lakes, the St. Lawrence River, and locally to northern portions of Ohio, Pennsylvania, and New York, very rarely to Long Island. Winters in the southeastern United States north to Massachusetts and in Middle America and Cuba.

Status Very local breeder. Locally common to very abundant migrant. Rare to common winter visitant inland, very common to abundant winter visitant in coastal areas.

Breeding Preferring open habitat with many scattered bodies of water, it is known to have nested at 12 locations, all but one upstate.

The first known breeding record was in 1945 at PRWMA. It has also been found nesting at Little Galloo I. in L. Ontario, Jefferson Co.; WHWMA; MNWR; HIWMA (where as many as 15–20 broods were raised in 1960 and 1961); OOWMA; Four Brothers Islands in L. Champlain, Essex Co.; BBWMA; and Clay Marsh WMA, Onondaga Co.

The Atlas Confirmed nesting in only three blocks: Chazy Landing, Clinton Co.; the St. Regis Lakes area, Franklin Co.; and MNWR. The report acknowledged that other sites might have been missed in large, inaccessible marshes. The only report of nesting in coastal areas came from JBWR in 1962. Nonbreeding individuals are rarely encountered in summer.

Nonbreeding Once rare in the Northeast, the species increased markedly after the early 1920s. Bull (1974) called them "at times our most numerous dabbling ducks."

That status is now in jeopardy. Long-term loss of nesting habitat to agriculture and losses to predators, combined with prolonged drought in the 1980s in key waterfowl nesting areas outside NY, appear to have taken a severe toll that is reflected in the numbers of migrants. For example: fall maxima at MNWR, a key staging area, dropped from 10,000 in 1983 to a mere 40 in 1986; average fall maxima for the six years prior to 1986 was 3366; for the next six years, 236. (Refuge officials caution that at least some of this decrease is because of changes in personnel taking the counts.)

Northen Pintails can still occasionally be found in abundance, as evidenced by the 7500 at MNWR on 22 Mar 1989; 1300 at BBWMA 14 Mar 1990; and 1023 at Sandy Pond, Oswego Co. 8 Oct 1987.

The average state arrival date is 12–15 Mar, with peak numbers at MNWR generally late Mar–Apr. In fall, peak numbers occur mid-Oct–Nov.

It remains a very common to abundant winter visitant in coastal areas. Inland it is generally rare in winter, although 41 were recorded in Region 8 during the 1992 FWC. An estimated 400 at MNWR on 18 Jan 1980 was an exceptional count during an unusually mild winter.

Robert E. Marcotte

Green-winged Teal *Anas crecca*

Range Holarctic, in North America breeding from Alaska to Newfoundland and south; in the west to Oregon, Colorado, and southern Minnesota; in the east to southern Canada and northern Maine, with sporadic local breeding farther south. Winters from the Aleutians and southern Canada south to Mexico, the Gulf Coast, southern Florida, Cuba, and the Bahamas.

Status Uncommon breeder in scattered localities. Locally common to abundant migrant and winter visitant.

Breeding It has never been more than an uncommon breeder in the state. Eaton (1910) reported only two breeding records, and it was not until the 1950s that breeding was documented upstate and not until the 1960s on LI. Today, most nesting is at MNWR and several LI sites. The Atlas Confirmed breeding in only 32 blocks. Many Possible records could have been summering birds not necessarily breeding.

Nonbreeding All high counts are from MNWR, and all are dated 1989 or earlier. Other records are mostly from upstate and are usually fewer than 100 birds. The exceptions are the CBCs and FWCs in Region 10. The highest CBC counts are from the Southern Nassau Co. CBC, with a high of 653 in 1994. In most years the totals are considerably lower.

Spring maxima: 4500 MNWR 30 Mar 1983; 1100 MNWR 24 Apr 1989. *Fall maxima:* 8000 MNWR 29 Oct 1980; 5000 MNWR 31 Oct

1982 and 13 Oct 1983. *Winter maxima:* combined Region 10 CBCs: 1222, 1984; 983, 1979; 911, 1987.

Remarks Two subspecies occur in the state, adult males of which are easily recognizable in the field. The breeding and common migrant bird is *carolinensis*. The nominate *crecca*, usually referred to as "Eurasian" Teal, shows a white stripe along the scapulars, instead of the white vertical "shoulder" bar of *carolinensis*. The Eurasian form has been recorded 19 times in *The Kingbird* since Bull 1974. Eleven of those records are from Region 10; seven came in 1992. Those records are from scattered localities, as are the eight upstate sightings. The paucity of records over that length of time makes it obvious that a sighting of a "Eurasian" Teal is indeed fortuitous. Emanuel Levine

Canvasback *Aythya valisineria*

Range Nearctic, breeding from central Alaska to southeastern Manitoba south to northern California and east to northern Minnesota. Winters on the west coast to Baja California and in the east from New England to Florida, the Gulf Coast, and to southern Mexico.

Status Common to locally very abundant winter visitant; less numerous in migration.

Breeding A pair with six young was reported at the Montezuma Marshes in 1962 (Morse). Breeding was reported there again in 1965. Since it breeds primarily in the west, the birds in those instances were believed to be introduced stock. On 3 Jul 1980, a brood of five, estimated at five weeks of age, was discovered at MNWR, and on 7 Jul 1981, another brood of nine one-week-old young was reported (Atlas 1988). In the summer of 1992, nestlings were reported at the same place and in the summer of 1993, 10–25 nestlings were there (KB 43:318). There is no information to determine if these broods were from wild or introduced birds. The closest documented breeding east of the normal range is at L. St. Clair, ON (Godfrey 1986). Since a release program was carried out at MNWR 1993–1995, any birds hatched after 1993 should be considered to be from introduced stock.

Nonbreeding Canvasback, often found associating with Redhead and scaup, are most numerous in winter in upstate waters, especially in the Niagara R. region and on the larger inland lakes, such as Cayuga and Oneida. On the latter, they are abundant during the migrations. These ducks are also found in large numbers on the bays of western LI. They have increased greatly since the late 1940s and have been recorded in every Region of the state. Although normally present Oct–Apr, they have been recorded in small numbers at scattered locations every month of the year.

Coastal maxima: 10,878 Lower Hudson CBC 1980; 6175 Queens Co. CBC 1979. *Inland maxima:* 30,000 Cayuga L. Jan 1958; 15,000 Niagara Falls 31 Oct 1981.

CBC statewide totals reached highs of 32,044 in 1985; 31,846 in 1982; and 24,487 in 1980. The FWC in 1976 recorded 33,984.

Robert W. Brock

Redhead *Aythya americana*

Range Western Nearctic, breeding mainly in northwestern North America east to eastern Michigan; rarely and sporadically to northwestern Pennsylvania, southeastern Ontario, southwestern Quebec, and New Brunswick. In the east winters north to southern Massachusetts and Lake Ontario.

Status Introduced locally as a breeder. Common winter visitant and migrant; very abundant in the Finger Lakes region.

Breeding In 1939, a nesting occurred at Montezuma, which might have been wild stock (Weller 1964). The NYSDEC began a release program in 1952, so all subsequent breeding at MNWR should be considered to be by introduced stock. In the 1950s and 1960s, nine other refuges and water-fowl preserves were stocked. Although ten breeding areas were noted by Bull (1974), the Atlas Confirmed breeding at only four sites: MNWR; JBWR; Upper Chateaugay L., Clinton Co.; and Saranac R., Franklin Co. After a peak of 20 nests at HIWMA in 1964 and nine at nearby MNWR in 1967, only one to two were reported in the mid-1980s. At JBWR, there were ten nests in 1965 but only single broods found in 1980 and 1983. In 1993, it was no longer considered a breeding site. In summer 1993, breeding occurred among stocked birds at INWR (AB 47:1092).

Nonbreeding Concentrations of diving ducks, including Redhead, can be seen on the deepwater lakes of central NY.

Maxima: all at Finger Lakes: 50,000 Seneca 28–30 Jan 1976; 7230 Cayuga 1 Jan 1976; 6811 Canandaigua 12–19 Jan 1992.

Before the late 1920s, it was also present in impressive numbers on the bays and ponds of eastern LI. High counts were recorded earlier in the century but are now in decline: 2000 Moriches Bay, Suffolk Co. 17 Nov 1905; 600 Montauk 5 Jan 1924. More recently, 414 on the Montauk CBC 15 Dec 1984. The extent to which wintering populations have declined is indicated by the 60 NY CBCs in 1993. Only 18 counts reported Redhead and only five recorded numbers above 20. On the coast, the Orient CBC, Suffolk Co. reported 77 and Ithaca, Tompkins Co., inland, had the high of 411. The Central Cayuga count, which had 7230 in 1976, reported 30.

Robert W. Brock

Ring-necked Duck   *Aythya collaris*

Range Nearctic, breeding south to the northern portions of New York and New England, very rarely to northwestern Pennsylvania and northeastern Massachusetts. In winter, withdraws from the more northern portions of the breeding range.

Status Fairly common, but local breeder in the Adirondacks. Locally common to very abundant migrant and winter visitant, most numerous in central NY.

Breeding A relatively new breeder in the state, the first recorded nesting was in 1946 at Jones Pond, Franklin Co. (Auk 64:626). Studies conducted by the NYSDEC indicated that breeding may have reached a peak in the 1960s and then declined. Seventeen broods were recorded in the Adirondacks in 1955, a high of 59 in 1966 and a drop to 29 by 1970 (Moser 1982). In 1974, it was reported breeding on 20 bodies of water in six northern counties: Clinton, Essex, Franklin, Hamilton, Jefferson, and St. Lawrence. The Atlas revealed a slight expansion of nesting range with Confirmed breeding in three additional counties: Herkimer, Warren, and Washington. No evidence of breeding was found in Jefferson Co., nor at several other former sites, but it was Confirmed in 23 Atlas blocks.

Nonbreeding Eaton (1910) described it as a rare migrant in eastern NY but plentiful in central marshes and the bays of L. Ontario, where it was common in the spring and rarely seen in fall. Recently on the Niagara Frontier, regional spring censuses produced counts of 1564 in Apr 1992 and 815 in Apr 1993; it remains less numerous in the fall. The opposite may be true on interior lakes and marshes, where it can be very abundant, leading to large fall counts at MNWR such as 8000, 30 Oct 1984; 4500, 23 Oct 1991; 2000, 21 Oct 1992. There was a count of 1000 at the Upper and Lower Lakes WMA, St. Lawrence Co. 4 Nov 1976.

Although formerly very scarce on the coast, it became much more widespread and in increasing numbers by the 1930s. Along the coast it frequents the deepwater lakes and reservoirs but is seldom recorded in shallow ponds and marshes. It has become common to abundant in counties on and adjacent to the coast. This is the only area that records numbers of wintering birds: 235 on the 1981 Central Suffolk Co. CBC; 143 on the 1985 Captree, Suffolk Co. CBC. In 1993, the Smithtown and Central Suffolk CBCs on north-central LI totaled 360; in the lower Hudson Valley the CBCs in Putnam and Dutchess counties recorded a combined 194.

It is locally common throughout the state with records in all Regions. Summering nonbreeders are infrequent, but it has been recorded in every month. Current numbers seem to be declining, but a review of *The Kingbird* and other records indicated that the mostly transient population rises and falls from year to year or over periods of several years. Even areas in which nesting has occurred show great variability.
Robert W. Brock

Tufted Duck *Aythya fuligula*

Range Palearctic, breeding from Iceland east through Scandinavia to Sakhalin and the Commander Islands and south through central Eurasia to Japan. Casual visitant in small numbers on both coasts of North America and around the Great Lakes.

Status Rare visitant, but almost regular.

Occurrence Ascertaining whether NY occurrences of this species are wandering European birds or escapes is impossible. It is common in captivity, and some sightings are known to be escapes, including a male found in East Aurora, Erie Co. 16–27 Jul 1993 (KB 44:297). Fall and winter sightings over several years lead to speculation that some are wild birds returning to the same locations each year.

Reports in the 1950s and 1960s were all from the Hudson-Harlem river drainage, Bronx Co.: one at Spuyten Duyvil 26 Dec 1955–1 Feb 1956; a male, Jerome Reservoir, 15 Mar 1962; a male at localities between the George Washington Bridge and Randalls I. each winter from February 1966 through 1968–1969. In the 1970s, the species started making almost regular appearances in additional areas of Regions 9 and 10. In 1974–1975, a pair wintered on the East R., Manhattan.

The most extensive set of records for one location is from Central Park, Manhattan. After a single female, 30 Dec 1979–13 Jan 1980; two females, 15 Dec 1981–10 Jan 1982; and a male, 5 Apr 1982, single males were reported every fall and winter through 1991, except 1987. A similar series of records from Rye, Westchester Co., included an immature male on 25 Dec 1991 and an adult male each winter through 9 Jan 1994. On 16 Feb 1995 a female was seen on Kensico Reservoir, Westchester Co. There are numerous records from LI as well, including several during the fall and winter of 1995–1996.

The first upstate record was of a male reported at Nine Mile Point, Oswego Co. 8–9 Apr 1971. Another male was at Saratoga L., Saratoga Co. 9 Nov and 7–15 Dec 1991. A Region 6 first, a male, was recorded at Long Point SP, Jefferson Co. 1 Apr 1995, and a Region 2 first, also a male, at Charlotte, Monroe Co. 24 Dec 1995.

Remarks Speculation that wild Tufted Ducks are wintering along the coast may be strengthened by five recent records from RI and two from MA. Up to seven birds wintered in MA the winter of 1994–1995.
Robert W. Brock

Greater Scaup *Aythya marila*

Range Holarctic, breeding in North America from central Alaska east to southeastern Newfoundland and south to northwestern British Columbia and east to the southern shores of Hudson Bay; rarely to southeastern Quebec. Winters, in the eastern portions, from the Great Lakes and Quebec to Florida.

Status Very abundant winter visitant on LI; much less numerous on the Great Lakes and in the Niagara R. region.

Occurrence On the coast Greater Scaup has been by far the most widespread of our winter ducks, especially abundant on the saltwater bays of LI: 250,000 Great South Bay, Suffolk Co. 3 Dec 1929; 60,000 Pelham Bay, Bronx Co. 31 Dec 1953. Recent records indicate a population decline. The FWC on LI recorded highs of 50,132 in Jan 1984 and 45,394 in Jan 1988. Data from adjacent states confirm the decline. Recorded every month of the year, 21 summered at JBWR in 1965.

Smaller numbers winter in all other areas, particularly in the Great Lakes area, with 7000 Oswego Bay 1958–1959; 6000 Niagara R. 17 Jan 1953. On eastern L. Ontario: 30,300 from Henderson Bay to the St. Lawrence R., Jefferson Co. 8 Nov 1979; 10,000–15,000 Black River Bay, Jefferson Co. 29 Oct 1978. Statewide CBC totals exceeded 85,000 in 1964, 1974, and 1975.
Robert W. Brock

Lesser Scaup   *Aythya affinis*

Range Western Nearctic, breeding from central Alaska south to Idaho, Colorado, and northwestern Minnesota, very rarely to the Lake Erie–western Lake Ontario region. Winters throughout the southern United States, north occasionally to southeastern Massachusetts and south through Middle America to northern South America.

Status A single breeding record. Locally very abundant migrant, less common in winter.

Breeding The only known breeding in NY was recorded by Mitchell, who observed a female with a brood of seven downy young at the Tifft Street Marsh in Buffalo, Erie Co. 1 Jun 1946 (Beardslee and Mitchell 1965). The Atlas noted that the species was not Confirmed during the survey, and no species account was published.

Nonbreeding Although it has been recorded in all Regions and during all months of the year, summer records are rare. The largest counts have been recorded in fall around L. Ontario: 10,000 Black R. Bay, Jefferson Co. 21 Nov 1982; 9500 Lewiston Reservoir, Niagara Co. 8 Nov 1989; and 7800 there 1–31 Oct 1988.

Winter reports illustrate the shift toward southern and eastern coastal waters as FWC counts from LI average more than twice as high as inland counts. As the return movement toward the breeding range begins in spring, interior lakes have had highs of: 2000 Oneida L. 12 Apr 1959; 1800 Celoron, Chautauqua Co. 1 Apr 1992.

Remarks Accurate counts are difficult if not impossible to obtain because of the great difficulty in differentiating between Greater and Lesser Scaup when seen at a distance and in mixed flocks. The two scaup are so similar in appearance that field marks can be accurately assessed only in good light conditions, when head shape is clearly viewable, and at relatively short distances. FWC reports did not differentiate between scaup species until 1979, and NYSDEC aerial surveys still cannot make the separation.
Robert W. Brock

King Eider *Somateria spectabilis*

Range Holarctic, breeding south in North America to southern Baffin Island and the southwestern shore of Hudson Bay. Winters along the coast from southern Labrador south to Chesapeake Bay and North Carolina and on the Great Lakes.

Status Rare to uncommon, occasionally fairly common, regular winter visitant along the coast of LI and on the Great Lakes.

Occurrence It is nearly annual off the shores of LI and at specific localities on the Great Lakes, particularly off Monroe Co. and the mouth of the Oswego R., with sporadic sightings on other inland bodies of water. Numbers off eastern LI are typically much lower than those of Common Eider, with which it often associates. Upstate this species is by far the more numerous of the two eiders. Since females and juveniles predominate, and identification of these under distant or difficult conditions is difficult, numerical counts lack some precision. Adult males are rare anywhere at this latitude. Eight birds, including three adult males, were reported at Ithaca, Tompkins Co. 26 Oct 1993 (KB 44:44).
   Coastal maxima: all Montauk: 30 (at least 10 males) 8 Apr 1887; 15–28, 14–15 Dec 1991; 27 FWC Jan 1991. Elsewhere: 9 Point Lookout, Nassau Co. 7 Dec 1991–19 Jan 1992. *Inland maxima:* 22 mouth of the Niagara R. 14 Jan 1967; 20 (3 collected) Cayuga L., Tompkins Co. 3 Nov 1908. *Extreme dates:* 5 Sep and 9 Jun.
   Summer stragglers have been reported off LI on several occasions (1924, 1960, 1961, 1968), but identification to species was questionable. A male in breeding plumage was at Montauk the entire summer of 1938.
Ordinarily rare before Nov and after Apr.
Robert G. Spahn

Common Eider *Somateria mollissima*

Range Holarctic, breeding in eastern North America from islands in Hudson and James bays to Ellesmere and Baffin islands and south along the coast to southern Maine. Winters on open waters in the breeding range and south on the coast to Maryland, rarely to Florida and inland to the Great Lakes.

Status Fairly common to occasionally abundant winter visitant to the Montauk area and rare to uncommon elsewhere on LI. Very rare inland.

Occurrence It may be seen on most late fall to early spring trips to Montauk and vicinity. Given the occurrence of King Eiders mixed with the Common Eiders and the difficulties in separating immatures and females, there is some margin of error in the counts to species, but the continued increases in recent years have led to the following representative maxima at Montauk: 7071 FWC Jan 1996; 2000–5000, 3 Dec 1995–29 Feb 1996; 3000, 18 Feb 1994. The winter of 1996–1997 witnessed unprecedented numbers at Montauk. For example, from a previous high count of 5493 on the Montauk CBC on 16 Dec 1995, that same CBC on 21 Dec 1996 tallied 12,000+. Earlier, on 30 Nov 1996, several observers advised that there were many, many thousands passing the point for some hours, with some estimates approaching six figures. The flood of eiders was not confined to Montauk. The East Hampton CBC on 22 Dec 1996 counted some 4000 at Sagaponack, roughly a dozen miles west of Montauk. The reasons for the steady annual increase in Common Eider numbers is not readily apparent.

Away from LI, this species has always been very rare, although the number of accepted records has more than tripled in the past 20 years to 22, five of them specimens. Nearly all have been of single birds, mostly females, and most have been from the coastal areas in Region 9 or from the Great Lakes, with a half dozen exceptions from smaller, inland bodies of water.

Extreme dates: 2 Sep and 14 May. Usually rare before mid-Nov and after Mar, there are four summer records 1974–1994 at JBWR and the Montauk-Orient area.

Bull (1974) commented on a notable increase since 1942. From FWC data of the past 20 years, the highest counts have set new records, but the numbers have been highly variable, ranging down to zero and one in 1985 and 1989. The number of inland sight records has increased dramatically, reflecting a real increase in vagrant individuals, increased birding activity, and increased willingness by birders to address difficult identification problems.

Remarks There are four subspecies of Common Eider recognized in North America; three have been recorded in NY. The southernmost eastern breeding subspecies *dresseri* (broad lobe at base of the bill), is presumed predominant in NY. Two specimens from LI are in the AMNH collection. A female collected at Ossining, Westchester Co. 14 Dec 1894 is MCZ 300372. Another female, taken on the Niagara R. 29 Sep 1960, is BMS 4522. The more northern coastal subspecies, *borealis* (distinguished by a very narrow lobe at the base of the bill), has been collected at least once. A female was shot at Montauk, 15 Dec 1945. It has also been collected several times in MA waters (Parkes 1952). The inland *sedentaria* (females and juveniles with paler, grayer plumage) breeds south to James Bay. Records of this subspecies include a specimen, a young male shot on the Niagara R. 21 Nov 1936 (Parkes 1952). Observers are encouraged to submit details of observations made under good conditions, which might allow the identification to subspecies and aid in better assessing the relative numbers of these subspecies visiting NY.

Robert G. Spahn

Harlequin Duck *Histrionicus histrionicus*

Range Holarctic, in eastern North America breeding from Baffin Island south to the Gaspe Peninsula; in the west from western Alaska and southern Alberta south to eastern Oregon and western Wyoming. Eastern population winters from Newfoundland south to Long Island; less commonly on the coast to Florida and Texas and inland to the Great Lakes.

Status Rare to fairly common winter visitant on LI. Rare winter visitant on the Great Lakes, Niagara Falls, along the St. Lawrence R., and Lakes George and Champlain.

Occurrence Rocky areas, whether natural or human-made jetties, on LI are the favored areas of this most beautiful of ducks. Probably the best spot is the west side of the Jones Inlet, Nassau Co., from Point Lookout, where there have been high counts of 25 in late Dec 1989 and 18 on 5 Nov 1992. Other favored locales are in Suffolk Co. at Shinnecock Inlet and Montauk, where single birds to a maximum of 10 occur regularly in the winter. Upstate, it can be found in most winters along the Niagara Gorge, the Great Lakes, and along the St. Lawrence R. to Massena. There are also records from L. George, Warren Co.; L. Champlain, Clinton Co.; Indian L., Hamilton Co.; and Phoenix, Oswego Co.

Thus far, it seems that Regions 3, 4, and 8 have not recorded the species. Sightings in the last two decades have increased dramatically, and birders in those Regions should take note.

Normal date parameters are late Nov and mid-Apr, with extremes of 20 Oct and 26 May, both quite exceptional.

Anthony J. Lauro

Labrador Duck   *Camptorhynchus labradorius*

Range An extinct species of very restricted range; breeding area unknown, supposedly in Labrador. Wintered on the Atlantic Coast south to Long Island, possibly farther south but evidence is lacking.

Status Extinct.

Occurrence The only NY specimens are from the South Shore of LI. At least 15 extant specimens were listed by Dutcher (Auk 8:201, 11:4), including five in the AMNH, the remainder scattered in other collections, most without detailed data. One male was shot as it landed among decoys in Great South Bay near Quoque, Suffolk Co. in 1858. The last recorded LI specimen was collected in the fall of 1875, USNM 77126. A duck, alleged to be this species, was shot near Elmira, Chemung Co. 12 Dec 1878. Because the specimen was not preserved and was never examined by an ornithologist, Eaton (1910) and Bull (1974), considering both the date and inland location, found the evidence insufficient for this record.

Remarks Very little is known of this extinct bird's habits. Greenway (1958) stated, "The mature male was always rare, even during the first half of the nineteenth century when the birds could sometimes be found in the markets of New York. In winter the birds were found in sandy bays and estuaries. The reasons for its extinction are not known." (See also From Glaciers to Global Warming: Extinct Species.)
Stanley R. Lincoln

Surf Scoter   *Melanitta perspicillata*

Range Nearctic, breeding from western Alaska to central Labrador, south to central British Columbia, and locally east to northern Ontario and eastern Quebec. Winters, in the east, on the Great Lakes, on the Atlantic Coast from southern Newfoundland to Florida, and on the Gulf Coast to Texas.

Status Common to very abundant migrant and winter visitant on the coast; much less numerous inland.

Occurrence This species is generally the second most numerous of the scoters in NY but occasionally outnumbers White-winged Scoter locally. Nonbreeders are recorded infrequently during summer months, with a maximum of 50 at Mt. Sinai, Suffolk Co. 28 Jun 1955. Inland, one was observed in the Niagara Gorge 13 Jul 1946.

In winter this species is abundant on the ocean and LI Sound, particularly at the eastern end. Coastal maxima were recorded at Montauk in 1930 with 25,000 on 1 Jan and 120,000 on 16 Mar. Recent CBC totals for LI waters are usually less than 3000. Inland this species is common on the

Great Lakes during migration, but winter numbers are low. In some years it is not recorded by upstate CBC observers.
Paul R. Sweet

White-winged Scoter *Melanitta fusca*

Range Holarctic, in North America breeding from Alaska and north-western Canada south to northeastern Washington east to northern Ontario; also from Hudson Bay east to Labrador and Newfoundland. Winters, in the east, on the Great Lakes and along the Atlantic Coast from Newfoundland to Florida.

Status Very abundant migrant and winter visitant on the coast; much less numerous inland.

Occurrence This species is generally the most numerous of the scoters in NY, although sometimes outnumbered locally by Surf Scoter. A few non-breeding birds regularly summer in coastal waters, and large flocks are present there during winter. Smaller numbers winter on the Great Lakes and occasionally on smaller lakes. On migration it could occur on any body of water throughout the state.

Fall migration starts in earnest in early Oct, and most birds have departed the state by mid-May. Summer maximum counts are 100 at Orient, Suffolk Co. in the summer of 1964 and 150 three miles off Mt. Sinai, Suffolk Co. 28 Jun 1955. The maximum winter count for the coast is 180,000 off Montauk 16 Mar 1930. Other counts of 75,000 at Montauk 1 Jan 1930 and 90,000 off JBSP 7 Dec 1952 are notable.

Recent CBC totals for LI waters are always in the thousands with the highest concentrations usually at Orient Point or Montauk Point. However, as pointed out with the other two scoter species, all high counts go back a number of decades. Inland this species winters annually on L. Ontario and less frequently on other lakes.

Bull (1974) noted a large migratory movement along L. Ontario on 23 Oct 1965, with 2000 at Hamlin Beach, Monroe Co. and 4700 at Derby Hill, Oswego Co. In 1985 the Rochester CBC recorded 2981. A count of 250 on Chautauqua L. off Mayville, Chautauqua Co. 1 May 1955 (Beardslee and Mitchell 1965) is the highest inland count away from the Great Lakes.
Paul R. Sweet

Black Scoter *Melanitta nigra*

Range Holarctic, breeding in North America in Alaska and locally in central and eastern Canada to Newfoundland. Winters, in the east, on the

Great Lakes and on the Atlantic Coast from Newfoundland to Florida and on the Gulf Coast.

Status Common to abundant migrant and winter visitant on the coast; much less numerous inland.

Occurrence This species is generally the least numerous of the scoters wintering in NY's coastal waters. It is, however, more numerous than Surf Scoter on fresh water and is the most likely scoter to be found on small bodies of water. It is much rarer in summer than the others.

The maximum winter count for the coast is 10,000 off Montauk on 3 Jan and 16 Mar 1930. A spring count of 18,000 off Jones Beach, Nassau Co. on 5 Apr 1936 is also notable, probably representing migrating birds.

Inland, the highest winter counts are from the Great Lakes, with 5200 on L. Erie at Dunkirk, Chautauqua Co. 7 Feb 1969 and 3300 on L. Ontario at Derby Hill, Oswego Co. 23 Oct 1965.

It should be noted that there are no high counts of recent vintage. Paul R. Sweet

Oldsquaw *Clangula hyemalis*

Range Holarctic, in eastern North America breeding from the Arctic region south to James Bay and the coast of Labrador. Winters on the Great Lakes and coastally from Newfoundland south to South Carolina. Casual to Florida, the Gulf Coast, and Texas.

Status Common to very abundant winter visitant along the coast and on the larger lakes.

Occurrence Most numerous in the Great Lakes area, the LI coast, and occasionally in large numbers on the Finger Lakes. If one uses maximum numbers as a yardstick, this species has more than held its own since Bull (1974). The largest recorded count was an unprecedented 15,000 at the mouth of the Niagara R. 20 Dec 1985. Coastally, an impressive 4500 were seen off JBSP 11 Mar 1988. A high Finger Lakes count was 1000 at the north end of Keuka L. 22 Apr 1965.

It has been recorded every month of the year but is generally not seen in any numbers before mid-Oct or after early May.

Remarks This species is unusual for the fact that the bird is much more attractive in basic than in alternate plumage. Also, it has an extensive vocal repertoire, which has given it various colloquial names such as Noisy Duck, Hound Duck, and Organ Duck. If one is close enough to a group, a constant cacophony of strange noises will be heard, especially if it is shortly before the flock is to return to the breeding grounds. Anthony J. Lauro

Bufflehead   *Bucephala albeola*

Range Chiefly western Nearctic, breeding from central Alaska south and east to southern Ontario and central Quebec. Winters, in the east, south to southern United States; also along the Atlantic Coast south from Newfoundland.

Status Locally common to abundant winter visitant and migrant.

Occurrence Buffleheads are a common sight in winter on sheltered bays on the coast and open lakes and rivers in western NY. On the coast it occurs chiefly from mid-Oct to mid-Apr, inland from mid-Nov to mid-May, but it has occurred in every month of the year. Although ordinarily very rare in midsummer, it has occurred in that season across the state, with records from Suffolk, Chautauqua, and Genesee counties in the past 20 years.

   Coastal maxima: 1000 JBWR 21 Nov 1965; 800+ JBWR 4 Nov 1980.
Inland maxima: 2200 Niagara R. 28 Dec 1970; 1500 Hamlin Beach SP, Monroe Co. 10 Nov 1979.
Joseph DiCostanzo

Common Goldeneye   *Bucephala clangula*

Range Holarctic, breeding in North America from Alaska to Newfoundland south to extreme northern United States. Winters, in the east, from southern portions of breeding range to Florida and the Gulf states.

Status Rare to uncommon breeder in the Adirondacks and the L. Champlain Valley. Common to very abundant winter visitant on the coast, L. Ontario, and the St. Lawrence R.; especially numerous on the ocean off eastern LI.

Breeding NY is at the southern limit of the breeding range. It breeds in the state in two disjunct areas: (1) the Champlain Valley from the north end of L. Champlain to the Canadian border; (2) in the Western Adirondack Foothills and less commonly the Central Adirondacks (Atlas 1988). A female with five young near Big Moose L., Herkimer Co. Jun 1994 was the first confirmed breeding for that area (Lee) (KB 44:317). A cavity nester, it has benefited from the erection of duck nest boxes.

Nonbreeding It is locally common on the larger inland lakes and rivers until a freeze-up forces it to the coast. Normally common on the coast, it can become abundant after being frozen out of inland waters. Rare before Nov and after Apr, but has been reported in every month of the year. A female summered at JBWR in 1963.

   Coastal maxima: 10,000 Gardiners Bay, Suffolk Co. 24 Mar 1910; 8000 Orient, Suffolk Co. 26 Dec 1924; 4000 Montauk 15 Mar 1945. No numbers even approaching these have been reported in the last 50 years.
Inland maxima: 4300 eastern L. Ontario, Jan 1992 FWC; 2500 Moses-

Saunders Dam, St. Lawrence Co. 9 Jan 1991; 2500 Manitou, Monroe Co. 26 Jan 1961.

Remarks See Barrow's Goldeneye for references on distinguishing between the two species in the field and identifying hybrids.
Joseph DiCostanzo

Barrow's Goldeneye *Bucephala islandica*

Range Chiefly Nearctic, breeding from Alaska to Greenland and south, in the east only to northeastern Quebec and northern Labrador; also in Iceland. In the Atlantic region winters primarily on the coast, from the Gulf of St. Lawrence to New York, rarely farther south.

Status Rare winter visitant.

Occurrence Bull (1974) reported that the Barrow's Goldeneye "is seldom recorded in New York State," but noted that since the mid-1950s it had been reported annually, twice in three separate years. Since the 1970s, it has continued to be found annually, often with more than one report per winter. On the coast it is most often found on eastern LI. Upstate it is most frequent on the St. Lawrence R. but is also regularly found on the Great Lakes.

Hybrids with Common Goldeneye have been reported on occasion: in 1988, 1992, 1994, and 1996 at Massena and the Moses-Saunders Dam, St. Lawrence Co. (Di Labio) (KB 42:109, 45:239, 46:168); in 1992 on LI Sound, Westchester Co. (Burke) (KB 42:121). Some of these records may refer to the one individual returning to winter in the same area again and again. It is probably possible to distinguish only hybrid adult males in the field and then only in some cases (Martin and Di Labio 1994).

Maxima: 6 Orient, Suffolk Co. 5 Jan 1909; 6 Moses-Saunders Dam, St. Lawrence Co. 21 Feb 1987; 6 there on 25 Feb 1988. *Extreme dates:* 8 Nov and 26 Apr.

Remarks The increase in records in recent years probably has more to do with the increase in birders and increased knowledge on how to separate Barrow's from Common Goldeneye than any actual increase in occurrence of the species. See Tobish 1986 for a discussion on distinguishing these two species in the field. Another possible factor in the increase in reports is the tendency for a bird to return to the same wintering location year after year. In NJ an adult male returned to Shark R. Inlet for 15 consecutive winters 1970–1984 (AB 39:151). In NY a female wintered under the Throgs Neck Bridge, Bronx Co. for three winters (AB 47:244). Thus, once a bird is located, birders check that spot in subsequent years.
Joseph DiCostanzo

Smew *Mergellus albellus*

Range Northern Paleartic, wintering in the western portion south to the British Isles and France, rarely to Spain and Portugal. Accidental in North America.

Status Accidental.

Occurrence The only known occurrence of this species in NY is that of one individual, believed to have been an immature, observed in the Buffalo, Erie Co. harbor and at various places in the Niagara R. region 17 Jan–30 Mar 1960 (Andrle, Coggeshall, Thill). Attempts to collect it were unsuccessful, but good color photographs were taken by Gunn (Beardslee and Mitchell 1965; Post 1966).

Remarks AOU (1983) mentioned, in addition to the Buffalo report, two other eastern North American records, one in RI and the other in southern ON. We cannot eliminate the possibility that the Buffalo and ON records are of the same individual. The AOU added, "some of the eastern North American reports may pertain to escaped individuals."
Stanley R. Lincoln

Hooded Merganser

Lophodytes cucullatus

Range Nearctic, in the east breeding from southern Canada locally to the Gulf states, having a much more southerly distribution than the other mergansers. Winters in southeastern United States and north through the Atlantic coastal states to New York and southeastern Massachusetts.

Status Fairly common breeder in the Central Adirondacks and Eastern Adirondack Transition. Widespread but uncommon breeder elsewhere. Common to very common migrant, to abundant and very abundant at large freshwater wetlands. Winters primarily in Regions 9 and 10.

Breeding It is now the fifth most common nesting duck in the state (Atlas 1988). Since the 1970s it has increased greatly as a breeder and migrant. A bird of freshwater, wooded wetlands, it requires clear and unpolluted streams or ponds for capturing small fish, crayfish, and aquatic insects, as well as suitable nesting holes. It can make use of Pileated Woodpecker holes and finds active beaver flowage excellent habitat for raising its brood (Brown and Parsons 1979). It readily accepts nest boxes more often intended for Wood Ducks and may lay along with the Wood Duck in the same box. It also lays eggs in the same box with Common Goldeneye and Common Merganser, other hole nesters in its range.

Scheider (1966) observed a hybrid Hooded Merganser × Common Goldeneye in Oswego Co. Another was reported in Black Rock Canal, Erie Co. (Chilton) (KB 43:120). A male hybrid Hooded Merganser × Common Merganser was observed in the Niagara R. (Axtell) (Beardslee and Mitchell 1965).

The Atlas added 17 counties to an earlier survey (Browne 1975). Browne surveyed NYSDEC personnel and the literature and catalogued 26 counties where Hooded Merganser was nesting. Schoharie Co. should be added to these (Riexinger et al. 1978), making a total of 44 counties reporting breeding. The use of beaver flowage as breeding habitat was studied in Fulton, Hamilton, Saratoga, Warren, and Washington counties (Brown and Parsons 1979) and was shown to be as productive as small human-made wildlife marshes.

It arrives at breeding sites as ice melts, which occurs upstate near the end of Mar on the Appalachian Plateau, two or more weeks later in the Central Adirondacks and Eastern Adirondack Transition.

Nonbreeding In FWCs from 1955 to 1980, only 41 were recorded in 1978, the lowest count, during one of the worst winters of that period. This number has since risen to 1183 in 1993. Regions 9 and 10 supply almost 90% of this total after much water upstate becomes ice covered.

After birds leave their brood-rearing areas in Sep they move to larger wetlands where food is available. Locally raised birds become mixed with migrants from the north at many upstate areas and become abundant to very abundant at several localities in Nov to mid-Dec.

The Hooded Merganser has increased along with many other species with the return of the forest to the Appalachian Plateau, a greater appreciation of our wetlands and their inhabitants, the increase in the Pileated Woodpecker, the return of the beaver, and the erection of nesting boxes by the NYSDEC and interested citizens.
Stephen W. Eaton

Common Merganser *Mergus merganser*

Range Holarctic, in North America breeding from southern Alaska and central Labrador south, in the west to the mountains of northern Mexico, but in the east only as far as southeastern Ontario and the northern portions of New York and New England; rarely or very rarely to the Berkshires, Catskills, and Poconos, and casually to northwestern Connecticut, southwestern New York, and northwestern Pennsylvania. Winters nearly throughout the breeding range, in the east to the Gulf states.

Status Common breeder in the Adirondacks, fairly common in the Delaware R. drainage, and rapidly becoming established in the Susquehanna, Genesee, and Allegheny river systems. Common to very abundant winter visitant on the Niagara R., the Great Lakes, and the Finger Lakes; less numerous on the lower Hudson R. and near the coast.

Breeding More generally distributed in the Adirondacks and in the Delaware R. watershed, but less so on the Appalachian Plateau, than the Hooded Merganser (Atlas 1988). The Common Merganser is three times as heavy as the Hooded and hence needs a much greater food source, available in the larger, clear-flowing, medium-gradient streams and rivers. The Common is less widespread than the Hooded on the Appalachian Plateau, where wetlands and beaver dams, which the Hooded like, are more generally distributed than are larger streams and rivers. Cattaraugus Co. can be added to the Common Merganser's expanding distribution (ph, Baird) (KB 39:225). The Common Merganser is essentially a tree-nesting duck using natural holes. Where such sites are not available it may nest on the ground, in an unused chimney, or in artificial nest boxes.

Nonbreeding It prefers to be in social groups of a few to about a score of individuals, which sometimes combine in assemblies of 50–75 birds (Palmer 1976). These can be seen in late summer on rivers, reservoirs, and lakes and in Oct and Nov in impressive numbers at dusk when they assemble to "roost" near the Moses-Saunders Dam on the St. Lawrence R. (KB 34:57) or on the Niagara R. when the emerald shiner *(Notropis atherinoides)* is unusually abundant (Beardslee and Mitchell 1965). A buildup at the Moses-Saunders Dam in the fall of 1988 went from 9 on 2 Aug to 80 on 30 Oct, 3500 on 11 Nov, and 10,000 on 27 Nov (KB 38:47). The FWC 1955–1980 documented statewide numbers in mid-Jan ranging from 4895 to 20,170 with an average of 10,700 (Jones 1980). From 1981 to 1993 this statewide census has varied from 7617 to 29,809, with a yearly average of 13,800. Greatest numbers are usually recorded on L. Erie and the Niagara R., but counts are sometimes highest in Regions 5, 6, or 9, depending mostly on the abundance and availability of food and probably annual productivity.

In areas along the Allegheny, Genesee, Susquehanna, and Delaware rivers, Common Merganser can be seen all year, and, immediately after ice-out, migrants increase the numbers in these areas and the larger lakes.

Remarks An interesting example of commensal feeding was described between American Crows and Common Mergansers on the Beaverkill R.,

Delaware Co.: "Rushing upstream in short spurts 13 mergansers drove their quarry into shallow pools between the rocks near shore. Simultaneously 4 Common Crows hopped from rock to rock alongside the mergansers, feeding on the prey flushed by the mergansers" (Bowman 1974).

Regular mortality was suggested by collisions with power lines near Moses-Saunders Dam (Van Riet) (KB 34:57). Dense fog over the Niagara Falls caused about 2000 ducks to be swept over and many were killed; most were Common Mergansers (Thill) (KB 34:106).
Stephen W. Eaton

Red-breasted Merganser   *Mergus serrator*

Range Holarctic, in eastern North America breeding south in the interior only as far as northern New York, but on the coast to Massachusetts and Long Island (rarely); casually farther south. Winters, in the east, in the Great Lakes and along the Atlantic and Gulf coasts from Newfoundland to Texas.

Status Very rare breeder along shores of the Great Lakes, L. Champlain, and LI. Common to very abundant migrant on the coast, Great Lakes, and Finger Lakes but casual in the Central Adirondacks.

Breeding Often confused with the Common Merganser as a breeder because of the similarities of the females and young, it is a ground nester and more restricted to shores of large bodies of water, marine and fresh. Marine nesting locations were documented by Bull (1964) along the South Shore and islands and bays at the eastern end of LI. Inland nestings were documented by Hyde (1939) and Bull (1974) on Little Galloo and Gull islands in eastern L. Ontario. The Atlas failed to Confirm nesting in all but one of the seven LI historical sites, and none were Confirmed in eastern L. Ontario, although there was one Probable record. On Four Brothers Islands in L. Champlain, the Atlas Confirmed breeding, and one nests there perhaps every other year (J. M. C. Peterson, pers. comm.).

The history of the confusion of the breeding merganser of the Adirondacks appears to have begun with DeKay (1844), for he says, under Red-breasted Sheldrake *(M. serrator)*, "It breeds in the interior of the State and generally throughout the Union." Roosevelt and Minot (1877; reprint 1923) listed it as a breeder in Franklin Co. These may be the sources of Eaton's (1910) statement, "a few are known to nest in the Adirondacks." This has been repeated over the years by many authors. Bagg (1911) called it a "common summer resident in West Canada Creek Valley. Breeds." Stoner (1932), repeating the error, found no nests but recorded many individuals in Jun and Jul. Reilly and Parkes (1959) said, "possibly breeds Adirondacks, common breeder Thousand Islands and eastern Lake Ontario;

local breeder Long Island." Brown and Parsons (1979) listed it as another duck nesting in the Adirondacks. These records illustrate how misinformation can be continued and the difficulties of field identification between female Common and Red-breasted mergansers with young. To sum up, during the Atlas fieldwork, Red-breasted Merganser was recorded in only 14 blocks, with breeding Confirmed in only two, one on LI and one on L. Champlain.

It is sometimes reported in summer off LI and on lakes and rivers at inland locations, but these are probably mostly nonbreeders or misidentifications. The Pennsylvania Atlas project (Brauning 1992) did not record this species breeding there, where the Common Merganser was found nesting widely across the northern half of the state. NY is at the southern limit of breeding of the Red-breasted Merganser.

Nonbreeding Normal dates are Oct–Apr (coastal), Apr–Jun and Oct–Dec (inland). It is an earlier migrant in fall than the other two mergansers and on spring migration is characteristically later than the Common Merganser (Phillips 1986). In spring it leaves the marine areas in Mar and Apr and is very abundant then along the shores of L. Ontario. By early Apr it is often the commonest duck on the Niagara R.; 6000 were there on 1 Apr 1981.

Coastal maxima: Fall: 25,000 from Montauk to East Hampton, Suffolk Co. 27 Nov 1941 and 40,000 on 30 Nov 1941. *Inland maxima: Spring:* 12,000 Braddock Bay, Monroe Co. 27 Apr 1952; 6000 Sandy Pond, Oswego Co. 8 May 1957. *Fall:* 10,000 Sandy Pond, Oswego Co. 28 Oct 1956; 10,000 Derby Hill, Oswego Co. 29 Oct 1966.

The FWCs 1955–1980 gave statewide totals averaging 3400 (range 1425–4453) and from 1981 to 1994 averaging 5035 (range 1655–7677). Over a short span, 1991–1994, the average was 6398 (range 4046–7677). About 90% of these were from Region 10 and the rest were usually reported from Regions l, 2, and 5, adjacent to the Great Lakes. There appears to be a gradual increase in winter numbers.
Stephen W. Eaton

Ruddy Duck *Oxyura jamaicensis*

Range Nearctic and Neotropical, breeding in North America mainly in the western regions east to the prairies; sporadically to the East Coast and south to Florida. Withdraws from northern portions of breeding range in winter to the Great Lakes and the Atlantic Coast from Massachusetts, south throughout southern United States.

Status Rare and local breeder. Uncommon fall migrant over most of state, but common to locally abundant in a few upstate locations; less numerous in spring. Locally numerous on LI in winter.

Breeding For 30 years, 1955–1985, it was a fairly common to common breeder at JBWR. It apparently peaked there as a nester in the early 1960s, with 40 broods reported in 1963. Over the last decade, however, as the West Pond at JBWR has become increasingly brackish, it has declined to the point that none bred there in 1995 (Riepe) (NASFN 49:912). The only other coastal breeding record was a brood found at Patchoque, Suffolk Co. in 1982 (Raynor) (AB 36:959). Inland, it has bred sporadically at MNWR and OOWMA, plus a single 1891 record at Sandy Creek, Monroe Co. (Atlas 1988).

Nonbreeding Increased numbers were reported starting in the 1940s, but numbers seem to be declining again in recent years.

   Coastal maxima: 2000 Water Mill and Mecox Bay, Suffolk Co. 13 Dec 1948; 2000 Hudson R., Rockland Co. 14 Dec 1965; 600+ Lawrence, Nassau Co., winter 1995–1996. *Inland maxima:* 2600 Chautauqua L., Chautauqua Co. 29 Oct 1950; 500 MNWR 16 Nov 1970.

Remarks As in NY, Ruddy Duck has undergone considerable fluctuation in abundance in both MA (Veit and Petersen 1993) and NJ (Leck 1984). Perhaps no other eastern state can rival the winter concentrations that were found on the Delaware R. in NJ in the 1950s, when counts of up to 40,000 or more were reported (Leck 1984). Nothing even remotely approaching those numbers has been seen there in recent decades. Joseph DiCostanzo

KITES, EAGLES, HAWKS, AND ALLIES—ACCIPITRIDAE

Osprey   *Pandion haliaetus*

Range Cosmopolitan, breeding in North America from Alaska and across much of Canada and, in the east, along the Atlantic Coast from Labrador and Newfoundland to Florida. Winters from Florida and Texas south through the West Indies and Central America to Argentina.

Status Common breeder on eastern LI, uncommon breeder in the Adirondacks and St. Lawrence Valley, with a few scattered nests in the central and southwestern parts of the state. Fairly common migrant along the coast, the Hudson R., and L. Ontario.

Breeding The piscivorous Osprey suffered precipitous declines, like many large raptors, due largely to DDT-induced eggshell thinning. Shooting, habitat destruction, and some nest robbing also played a role (Poole 1989). The LI breeding population's decline was noted during the 1950s, and a low point was reached in the mid-1970s. LI areas that had nearly 500 active nests in 1940 had fewer than 75 by 1970 (Spitzer 1980).

When DDT was banned by the early 1970s, people began to erect nesting platforms in many areas to help the population. By the late 1970s, the number of nests began to increase along with productivity, and many new nesters were using platforms. The population recovered sufficiently so that in 1983 it was downgraded to Threatened on the state list from its 1976 listing as Endangered, and a further downgrade to species of Special Concern has been recommended. In 1994 there were 313 breeding pairs statewide, at least 192 of which successfully produced a minimum of 363 young. Of the 313 pairs, 247 were on LI, 54 were in the Adirondacks and St. Lawrence R. area in the north, and the remaining 12 were scattered in central, western, and southern NY.

On LI, Ospreys return in mid-Mar. Egg laying, typically of three eggs, occurs during the latter part of Apr and May. Hatching takes place in Jun, with fledging by early to mid-Jul. In the Adirondacks, Clum (1986) reported that the birds arrive on the breeding ground 13–17 Apr and lay their first eggs 28 Apr–6 May. Incubation for this upstate population ranged between 34 and 39 days. The nestling period lasted from the hatching of the first egg, 1–14 Jun, to the flight of the first young, 28 Jul–21 Aug; average time in the nest was 61 days. Productivity is generally higher on LI than in the Adirondacks, where one study (Clum 1986) found that this upstate population appeared to be food stressed. Lake pH at foraging sites seemed to be correlated with breeding success, and aluminum contamination may be limiting productivity. Additional research is needed. Reproductive success in some areas, for example, Gardiners I. off eastern LI, may be limited by food availability (Spitzer 1978, 1980). Both the Adirondack and Gardiners I. populations could be negatively affected by bad weather but are, for the most part, reproducing well. On eastern LI, Osprey productivity has possibly been affected, since 1985, by the "brown tide," an algal bloom that may affect the bird's ability to hunt effectively (Scheibel, pers. comm.).

In 1994 at least 1.2 young per breeding pair were produced statewide. The NYSDEC has monitored the status and productivity of nearly all of NY's population for 25 years through aerial and ground surveys and maintains one of the most complete data sets in the United States. From 1980 to 1987, NYSDEC also participated in releasing 36 Ospreys from LI nests in Cattaraugus Co. in an attempt to establish some nesting pairs in western NY. This attempt was successful, and several active nests are now present in the Allegheny Reservoir. A second project involving the release of 31 LI Ospreys was conducted by NYSDEC in Genesee Co. 1992–1994 but has not yet resulted in any new nests.

Nonbreeding It can be seen almost anywhere during migration but is very rare in winter. In 1994 the total at Derby Hill, Oswego Co. during spring migration, 2 Apr–31 May, was 500, with a peak flight of 156 on 26 Apr.

The Braddock Bay Hawkwatch, Monroe Co. reported 313 on 2 Apr–6 Jun, with a peak flight of 52 on 14 Apr. During the fall of 1994, an impressive 690 were seen over Central Park, Manhattan. On 19 Sep 1993, a record day on the coast, there were counts of 129 at Ft. Tilden and 125 at Fire I., with a total of 321 for the season at the latter site.

The NYSDEC cooperated with the University of Minnesota in Jun 1996 in a National Science Foundation–funded study of migratory routes, critical stopover locations, and wintering areas. Birds are being captured in OR, MN, and NY to obtain a diverse sample. With the support of the Nature Conservancy's Mashomack Preserve staff, three adults were captured on LI in late Jun, fitted with satellite radio transmitters, and released. All three departed in mid to late Aug; one was tracked to Cuba, one to Venezuela, and one to Brazil.

Remarks This species has made a good comeback since the decline in DDT residues and the acceptance of nesting platforms. With continued protection and management, coupled with periodic productivity surveys, the Osprey should remain an interesting component of NY's avifauna.
Barbara Allen Loucks

Swallow-tailed Kite *Elanoides forficatus*

Range Southeastern Nearctic and Neotropical, breeding in North America locally from South Carolina south to Florida and west to Louisiana and through most of Middle America. Winters in South America. Vagrant north to New England and the Great Lakes.

Status Very rare vagrant.

Occurrence Of the 27 documented occurrences, 17 were after 1978. Eighteen were in spring, with 13 coastal and 5 along the hawk migration routes on the shores of the Great Lakes.

Of the summer records, seven were near water, a requirement of their preferred prey of dragonflies and other large insects. Three occurred in Aug, which is the normal migration period for this species.

The two fall records were coastal. One was in early Sep during the species' migration period. The other was on 2 Oct, which is well out of the migration period, as most individuals have completed migrating through TX by mid-Sep.

Remarks It is significant that the majority and greater frequency of documented records took place after 1977, which is the year that HMANA was formed, greatly increasing the number of hawkwatches in the state.
Although there has been no significant expansion for this species, there has been an increase in population levels coincidental with the increased frequency of sightings in NY and the Northeast (Palmer 1988). Veit and

Petersen (1993) acknowledged 18 records in MA. Since that publication, NASFN listed an additional six in the next three years there, plus two in CT, three in RI, and eight in NJ. The fact that the northernmost extension of its range is along the southeastern seaboard likely explains why the majority of sightings are coastal. Also, because most sightings occur during spring and summer, they are probably a result of the species' tendency to wander in a northerly and northeasterly direction in a postbreeding dispersal (Palmer 1988).
Jeff Dodge

White-tailed Kite   *Elanus leucurus*

Range: Cosmopolitan, in the Americas resident from Oregon to Baja California and from Oklahoma, western Louisiana, and Texas south through Middle and South America to Argentina and Chile. In the United States, a casual straggler farther north and east.

Status Accidental.

Occurrence One record, an adult seen on 26 and 27 Apr 1983 in Hopewell Junction, Dutchess Co. by Rota, J. Key, and M. Key and added to the NYS checklist (Key and Key 1983; NYSARC 1984).

Remarks The species was formerly known as Black-shouldered Kite and was lumped with that species under *Elanus caeruleus*. Then in 1993, in the Thirty-ninth Supplement to the AOU Check-list (Auk 110:675), it was returned to full species status as *E. leucurus*, and the English name was changed back to White-tailed Kite. There are scattered records in the eastern United States, including two in MA, one in VA, and one each in NC and SC.
Jeff Dodge

Mississippi Kite   *Ictinia mississippiensis*

Range Southern Nearctic, breeding from central Arizona generally east through southern Missouri and the northern portion of the Gulf states to South Carolina south to Texas, the Gulf Coast, and Florida. Range expanding northward in recent years. Winters primarily in central South America but also occasionally in Central America and north to southern Texas. Wanders north to New England and the Great Lakes.

Status Very rare vagrant.

Occurrence Mississippi Kite is a newcomer to NY. It first occurred 28 May–8 Jun 1979 on SI, where two feasted on the "plague" of 17-year cicadas (Clermont 1979; NYSARC 1980).
   Since then there have been 22 more documented occurrences. Most (13)

were in spring, with 11 being along the hawk migration routes on the Great Lakes shores. The other two were coastal. Of the seven summer sightings, only one was coastal, with the others at Braddock Bay, Monroe Co. There have been only two fall records, again upstate, both on 9 Sep, which is late in this species' migration period.

Remarks It has rapidly expanded its breeding range up the Mississippi R. basin and locally along the East Coast (Palmer 1988); occurrences in NY are coincidental with the range expansion. Most sightings were of immatures or subadults, which can be difficult to identify. The increase in hawkwatches and the expertise in hawk identification developed by many hawk specialists are important factors in the increased documentation of this species.

As is the case with Swallow-tailed Kite, most sightings were near water when large insects, particularly dragonflies, were abundant. The Braddock Bay Raptor Research team purposely increased hawkwatch coverage on days with heavy dragonfly movements. This action accounts for six of the seven summer sightings. The picture is much the same in PA and NJ, with multiple sightings in recent years. It was finally recorded for the first time in CT in 1995 but is as yet unrecorded in RI.

Jeff Dodge and Frank J. Nicoletti

Bald Eagle   *Haliaeetus leucocephalus*

Range Nearctic, breeding from Alaska and Canada to southern United States. Winters nearly throughout range.

Status Nearly extirpated as both a winter visitant and breeder 1950–1975; now locally common migrant and winter visitant and very local breeder.

Breeding Approximately 80 locations have been identified where Bald Eagles have nested in NY since the early nineteenth century. These sites were concentrated within the Adirondacks, the Great Lakes shorelines, and the Oneida L. wetlands. With the loss of suitable habitat, increased human disturbance, and the pressure of illegal shooting over the years, populations steadily declined. The final blow came after World War II, with the widespread introduction of DDT for agricultural pest control. Runoff from farms and forests sprayed with DDT found its way into the waters hunted by Bald Eagles for their staple food, fish. This poisonous pesticide worked its way into the aquatic ecosystem, becoming concentrated in tissues of fish and then to the top of the food chain in the Bald Eagle.

The effect of DDT and its breakdown products (DDE and DDD) on calcium production in birds results in eggs with shells so thin that they often break under the weight of an incubating adult before they hatch. In 1972, the use of DDT was banned, at least in this country. Although much has been made of the role of DDT in the demise of several well-known raptors (e.g., Bald Eagle, Peregrine Falcon, Osprey), it is important to understand, at least for the Bald Eagle in NY, that a significant decline had already occurred before the introduction of DDT in 1946. By that time, shooting, logging, habitat loss, and human disturbance had reduced our breeding population to fewer than 20 pairs. DDT then ensured the disappearance of all but one of those by 1970.

With new federal legislation for the protection of raptors, increased public awareness stimulated by a growing conservation movement, and an active reestablishment program initiated by the NYSDEC, a slow recovery began. Methods used by NYSDEC included egg transplants, fostering (of eaglets from other sources), and hacking (hand rearing and releasing older nestlings in the absence of parent birds). Of these techniques, hacking, pioneered by the NYSDEC in 1976, proved the most successful. Between 1976 and 1988, 198 nestlings were translocated to NY, raised, and released at four sites throughout the state. About 90% of those birds were collected from wild nesting pairs in Alaska. Of those 198 hacked eagles, at least 32 did not survive, with 50% of the deaths due to illegal shooting. Others survived, however, and in 1980 the first nest ever reestablished by hacking successfully fledged two young in Jefferson Co. As shown in Figure 1, by 1990 there were 13 nesting pairs confirmed in the state, of which 9 fledged 16 young. In 1996, 29 pairs nested and 37 young were fledged by 19 successful pairs. NY breeders are typically on territory by late Feb.

Egg dates since 1975 are 8 Mar–23 Apr, hatch dates are 16 Apr–30 May,

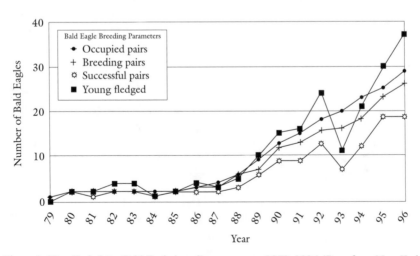

Figure 1. New York State Bald Eagle breeding summary, 1979–1996 (Data from New York State Department of Environmental Conservation)

and fledgling dates 15 Jul–31 Aug. Breeding habitat is in or very near wetlands, lakes, and rivers, most often in supercanopy white pines in areas of limited to no human disturbance. Of the current nesting population, approximately 50% are at historically used nesting sites. The goal of the NYSDEC is the reestablishment of 40–50 breeding pairs. Until such time, the status of Endangered will be maintained in NY even though the USFWS upgraded the Bald Eagle nationally to Threatened in Jul 1995.

Nonbreeding Recorded every month of the year, during migration it is observed at all hawkwatches in the state, whether on mountain ridges, the L. Ontario shoreline, or the coast. During winter, when breeding areas north of NY freeze over, the birds move south into NY to find open water and their primary prey, fish. Each year, a statewide, winter count of individuals is coordinated by the NYSDEC during the month of Jan. In 1994, for example, a total of 116 eagles was tallied statewide, with significant concentrations in four areas: the upper Delaware R. watershed, the St. Lawrence R., the lower Hudson R., and the Sacandaga R. The winter of 1993–1994 was a particularly brutal one in Canada, which no doubt accounts for the 27 Bald Eagles in one CBC circle in Jefferson Co. As with our nesting population, our wintering populations continue to grow. During 1996, 174 eagles were observed during the annual midwinter survey (Figure 2). Many of the fledglings produced from NY nests are verified annually on our wintering areas, primarily at the largest, the upper Delaware R. watershed.

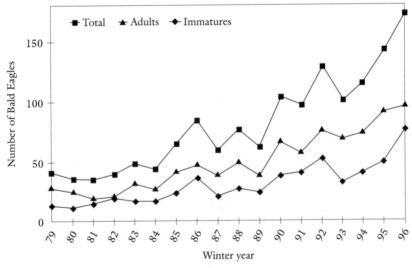

Figure 2. Number of Bald Eagles observed in New York State during annual national midwinter survey (Data from New York State Department of Environmental Conservation)

Migrants can occur within the state during almost any month, depending on their origin. Southern birds are known to move through and summer in NY (postbreeding) Apr–Oct. Northern breeding birds and fledglings from the northeastern United States and eastern Canada move through and into the state Sep–Mar. Northern Bald Eagles wintering in NY do so Nov–Mar, with peaks in Jan and Feb. Bald Eagles from throughout the eastern United States and Canada, as well as from MI and TX have been verified in NY.

Remarks Although previously two subspecies were recognized, the southern *leucocephalus* and the northern *alascanus*, the distinctions between these two were vague and largely based only on size, which was clinal. A very arbitrary demarcation between these two "subspecies" was the fortieth parallel (40° latitude). Subspecific designations are no longer recognized. Indeed, with widespread hacking projects throughout the eastern United States, eagles from AK, MB, NS, and the Great Lakes (to name just a few sources) have been released and are now mixing with birds from GA to ME, further obscuring any slight differences that might have existed.
Peter G. Nye

Northern Harrier   *Circus cyaneus*

Range Holarctic, in North America breeding from Alaska and Canada south to Baja California, Arizona, and Texas but in the east only as far as Ohio and Virginia. In winter withdraws from more-northern portions.

Status Widespread but rare breeder. Fairly common to common fall migrant; very common spring migrant and uncommon to rare in winter.

Breeding Until the mid-1950s the Northern Harrier was considered a common breeding bird throughout the state. A subsequent severe decline, paralleling, among other factors, the extensive use of toxic pesticides, caused it to be listed as Threatened in NY.

The Atlas documented Confirmed and Probable breeding sites in the western Great Lakes Plain's counties of Niagara, Orleans, and Monroe; west of the Finger Lakes; in the north from the St. Lawrence Plains through to and including the L. Champlain Valley; and on LI. Elsewhere, Confirmed breeding was sparse or not recorded at all.

Nonbreeding It migrates regularly in moderate numbers past the several hawkwatch sites in the state. It is more numerous in spring than in fall, probably owing to the forced concentration as the birds traveling north reach the L. Ontario barrier, compared with the freedom to disperse on the return flight south.

An analysis of the numbers at the Braddock Bay, Monroe Co. and Derby Hill, Oswego Co. hawkwatches each spring 1976–1995 showed a series of peaks, one approximately every five years, each peak higher than the last, with an all-time record in 1995. Between highs, however, are troughs sufficiently deep and wide to balance out the summits. Therefore, the most accurate conclusion we can come to is that the species is holding steady.

In fall migration, this hawk often follows the coast. Its long wings and relatively light body make it less dependent on rising thermals than are other hawks. These physical traits adapt it well to long periods of low, constant flight, often over salt marshes, where resting sites and food may easily be found.

Spring maxima: 402 Braddock Bay, Monroe Co. 14 Apr 1994; 235 Derby Hill, Oswego Co. 24 Mar 1994. *Season maxima:* 2094 Braddock Bay 1994; 1554 Derby Hill 1995. *Fall maxima:* 150+ Fire I., Suffolk Co. 23 Sep 1974, unusually high for the coast; 53 at the same site 16 Sep 1986; 40+ per day, Point Peninsula, Jefferson Co. late Nov 1987. *Season maxima:* 278 Butler Sanctuary, Westchester Co. 1987; 251 Fire I., Suffolk Co. 1986.

Wintering records present a fluctuating pattern. CBCs 1975–1989 in every part of the state except the coastal region showed most units reporting occasional harriers but only a few finding them regularly. Most counts are below ten, although 1988 produced exceptions. CBC data for the Coastal Lowlands, however, present consistently higher numbers. Most are double digit, up to about 40.

The great variability of winter records is undoubtedly related to the abundance of its chief food, small rodents found in open fields or marshes. In winter such habitats may change radically very suddenly. Deep snow, flooding, freezing, sudden thaws, and other extreme weather factors alter the availability of prey. Coastal areas, subject to the moderating influence of the ocean, are less subject to such sudden meteorological changes. Totals of winter records for all regions show a gradual but undeniable increase in numbers.

An interesting research project on wintering hawks on a 25 sq mi tract at Point Peninsula, Jefferson Co. in the winter of 1987–1988 noted on 18 Dec 1987 a "peak roadside survey count of Northern Harrier of 57 birds." In the four years previous to the study, one to four per day in Jan and occasional birds in Feb were observed in the same general area (G. A. Smith 1989). No followup to that study has been published.
Harriet T. Marsi and Gail M. Kirch

Sharp-shinned Hawk   *Accipiter striatus*

Range Nearctic and Neotropical, breeding from Alaska to southern Labrador and Newfoundland south to the central portions of the southwestern states, the northern portions of the Gulf states, and South Carolina; also in the highlands of Mexico and the Greater Antilles. Winters south to Panama, withdrawing from the more northern portions of the range.

Status A widespread but unevenly distributed secretive breeder in all Regions. Common to very common migrant but rare to uncommon resident, increasing in winter.

Breeding The Atlas showed Confirmed breeding in 93 (11%) out of the 859 blocks where it was found. Recorded in every county except the five that constitute NYC. It breeds in heavily forested areas throughout the state but most notably in the Adirondacks and the Appalachian Plateau. A secretive breeder, its nests in hemlocks are hard to find. An analysis of BBS data 1966–1994 showed that the NY Sharp-shinned Hawk population was increasing. In 1966–1979 the population was level, but in 1980–1994 there was an average increase of 9.1% per year (Peterjohn 1995).

Nonbreeding The increase in bird feeders has afforded increased opportunities for predation. The hawks exploit these "fleshpots," feasting until the prey birds become wise and go elsewhere, whereupon the "sharpies" likewise depart to seek out other feeders. Cooper's Hawks are similarly attracted to feeders, presenting formidable competition, especially in some rural areas. Analysis of CBC data 1975–1993 showed that the NY Sharp-shinned Hawk population had been increasing from a low in the late 1980s.

This raptor seems to exhibit a fluctuating population cycle. In the Cayuga basin, the population increased during 1935–1950, then underwent a precipitous decrease during 1950–1957, and a slighter decline in 1957–1971 (Temple and Temple 1976). Analysis of data from seven fall and eight spring hawkwatches reveals that the downtrend in migrants over the past decade may be leveling off. Data from Derby Hill, Oswego Co., a spring watch, reveal low counts in the mid-1970s; counts were higher in the late 1970s and into the 1980s. In 1984, an extraordinary 11,582 were reported. Lower counts prevailed afterward into the early 1990s but were back up again in the mid-1990s. Whether it is decreasing or increasing depends on the time span being analyzed. It may also depend on the geographical area being considered. Fall migrants declined in the NYC area 1978–1986 (Panko 1990) but then recovered somewhat.

Recent information remains mixed. In fall 1996, Fire I., Suffolk Co. had its worst year ever (Panko, pers. comm.), but Mt. Peter, Orange Co. had its highest count since 1990. Hawkwatch observations in spring 1995 were hampered by adverse weather, and counts from Derby Hill and Braddock Bay, Monroe Co. were lower than expected. Bad weather also contributed to a mediocre flight over Derby Hill in 1996. Data from these hawkwatches reveal no consistent theme. Instead, they are like investments in a well-diversified portfolio, in that when some go up, others go down. The species has been recommended for inclusiom on NYSDEC's list of Species of Special Concern.

Spring maxima: 3183 Braddock Bay, Monroe Co. 9 May 1988 and 2093 on 10 May, a two-day total of 5276; 3019 Derby Hill, Oswego Co. 28 Apr 1984. **Fall maxima:** 394 Hook Mtn., Rockland Co. 20 Sep 1993; 234 Fire I., Suffolk Co. 24 Sep 1989. **CBC maxima:** 17 Southern Nassau Co. CBC 2 Jan 1994.

Remarks The northeastern U.S. population as a whole may be changing, in numbers as well as in distribution. A 500% increase in "sharpies" wintering in New England has been reported by Duncan (1996). They may be exploiting the bird-feeder resource by not migrating or by changing their migration patterns. The increase reported on CBCs since 1988 bears out both scenarios. Whereas hawkwatches provide the most data, they record migrants passing through. CBCs are more apt to reveal winter visitants. If birds stay through the winter, there may be more in the spring to breed.

Autumn migrants have been stable at Holiday Beach, ON but have been decreasing since 1985 at Cape May, NJ (Chartier 1994). No consistent trends were found in 1972–1987 in an analysis of data from six widely dispersed northeastern hawkwatches (Titus and Fuller 1990). Some mechanisms possibly responsible for any recent decline in migrants have been postulated by Kerlinger (1993) to be acid rain and the spraying of insecticides for spruce budworm. Eggs collected from nests in south-central ON contained pesticide residues and had thin shells (Elliott and Martin 1994). Donald A. Windsor

Cooper's Hawk *Accipiter cooperii*

Range Nearctic, breeding from southern Canada to northern Mexico and the Gulf states. Winters nearly throughout the breeding range and south to Guatemala and Honduras.

Status Uncommon widespread breeder. Fairly common migrant, locally common in winter.

Breeding Found breeding in all parts of NY except NYC, LI, and Rockland and Niagara counties, where the lack of forest habitat is undoubtedly the restricting factor. Nests are often located in wooded bottomlands particularly in the south-central region of the state, an area that includes the Finger Lakes and the valleys of the larger rivers such as the Allegheny, Chemung, Genesee, and the east branch of the Susquehanna. Tributaries of the Delaware and Hudson rivers and in the Taconic Highlands also support nesting pairs. Nesting locations vary from deep within a forest to along its edges. The nest is often situated near a clearing where small birds can be hunted. Sometimes a nest may be found near a village with a dependable food base of pigeons and sparrows. There are no nests reported near large urban centers.

Nonbreeding Historically it has been reported only in moderate numbers. In the early decades of the twentieth century, farmers, protecting their loose barnyard chickens from this persistent predator, kept the Cooper's Hawk population in a gradual decline, which did not stop even after the passage of legislation protecting birds of prey. During the "DDT years" (1946–1972), however, there was such a serious drop in numbers that it was placed on the NYSDEC Species of Special Concern list. After the phaseout of DDT the numbers increased, almost imperceptibly at first, but eventually steadily. This recovery was maintained through the first half of the 1990s.

The fall migration is widespread and long. Data from hawkwatch stations indicate that it may begin as early as mid-Aug and last late into Nov. In between there is never any pronounced peak but, instead, a steady trickle of one, two, three birds per day augmented by small surges of sometimes low double-digit figures. These usually occur from mid-Sep through mid-Oct. There seems to be no noticeable preference for either inland or coastal flyways.

Spring migration is a different story, heavily influenced by the obvious pressure of an early start on breeding as well as by the forced concentration of species as they reach the L. Ontario water barrier. The Braddock Bay, Monroe Co. and Derby Hill, Oswego Co. hawkwatches commonly report daily flights of approximately 100, with peak periods from late Mar through mid-Apr. Braddock Bay reported an extraordinary high count of 213 for one day, 26 Mar 1988, and another of 210 on 14 Apr 1994. On the basis of such reports, we can assume that the Cooper's Hawk is holding its own if not slowly increasing.

Spring maxima: Season: 1176 Derby Hill, Oswego Co. 1995; 1031 Braddock Bay, Monroe Co. 1994. *Fall maxima:* 37 Butler Sanctuary, Westchester Co. 4 Oct 1991. *Season:* 308 Butler Sanctuary 1991.

Winter reports also indicate a rise in populations. This may reflect an actual population increase, but it may also be due partly to the growing interest in maintaining bird feeders in winter, which attract predators, including the Cooper's Hawk. This is a bird that might be overlooked in the woods but is relatively conspicuous in one's backyard. The increase may also be partly the product of the growing popularity of birding as a sport. Many more birders are correctly identifying hawks in flight.

Harriet T. Marsi and Gail M. Kirch

Northern Goshawk *Accipiter gentilis*

Range Holarctic, in North America breeding from Alaska to Newfoundland and south, in the east, to Michigan, Pennsylvania, New

York, and northwestern Connecticut. Winters nearly throughout the breeding range and south to Florida.

Status Formerly very rare breeder, now rare to uncommon and widely distributed. Regular fall migrant along inland ridges and a rare to fairly common spring migrant along the L. Ontario shore. Rare and irregular winter visitant.

Breeding Eaton (1914) described this species as a rare summer resident "even in the wildest portions of the Adirondack forest." Bull (1974) reported only four definite breeding records from that early time and no others until 1952. Bent (1937) noted common breeding in the Northeast before the final demise of the Passenger Pigeon about 1900 and suggested regular breeding in the Adirondacks into this century, although with no specific data referenced. Bull then documented a dramatic increase in breeding from 1952 to the early 1970s, with 52 additional sites specifically listed and mapped. This increase continued through the Atlas, with workers finding the goshawk in 445 blocks; breeding was Confirmed in 128 of them. That nearly half of these confirmations came from a single researcher studying the species in Chenango and Madison counties may indicate it was still underreported. During the 1990s, reports in *The Kingbird* noted about nine additional nesting sites and the abandonment of several old ones. Without serious field efforts on the scale of the Atlas, there are no data to indicate any significant change in the breeding distribution from that shown in the Atlas.

It is a species of boreal and mature northern upland mixed and deciduous forests. The surge in nesting in NY has accompanied the reforestation and maturing of the forests on large tracts of land since the 1930s. Atlas workers found the species in all but 11 counties and in all areas except the farmlands of the L. Ontario plain in the west and NYC and LI in the southeast, all of which lack the requisite extended areas of relatively undisturbed forest.

Nonbreeding Its status as a rare migrant and winter visitant over most of the state has not changed. For most birders, an encounter is by chance in the field or at the backyard feeder. Occurrence at most locales is irregular. Numbers moving south are highly variable from year to year, with peaks occurring at about ten-year intervals. The quarterly reports in *The Kingbird* document the rarity of encounters in most locales and show no clear trends over the past 20 years. CBCs probably provide the best data for tracking trends in the general winter population. Data compiled from CBCs since 1960 showed a jump from a statewide total of three to six for the first ten years to 15 in 1969, with no subsequent years totaling fewer than 13.

Regularly staffed hawkwatches, only begun in NY in the 1970s and increasing in number and level of attention to detail through the 1980s, have provided the most accurate monitoring of populations. There is a strong movement along the south shore of L. Ontario in the spring, monitored by several hawkwatches, particularly Braddock Bay, Monroe Co. and Derby Hill, Oswego Co. Peak daily counts have typically been fewer than ten since the early 1970s, with annual totals generally 20–50. Exceptional "flight" periods were documented in 1969, with 141 tallied at Derby Hill; in 1982–1984, with 76, 141, and 90 at Braddock Bay and 142, 162, and 174 at Derby Hill; in 1993–1995, with 46, 99, and 48 at Braddock Bay and 73, 125, and 79 at Derby Hill. This movement typically begins in mid-Feb, peaks in mid-Mar to early Apr, and sees the last birds counted in mid-May.

The fall migration is mainly along the inland ridges of the Appalachians, with only the recently activated Franklin Mtn. Hawkwatch, Otsego Co. seeing any significant numbers; totals there were 31, 34, and 62 in the 1992–1994 period. The more easterly mountain watches have typically tallied 5–15 birds annually and the beach watches one or none. It remains difficult to separate the various environmental and observer effects from even these detailed data.

Maxima: 88 Derby Hill, Oswego Co. 29 Mar 1973; 42 Braddock Bay, Monroe Co. 4 Apr 1983; 36 Derby Hill 22 Mar 1984.

Remarks This species has been recommended for inclusion on the NYSDEC's list of Species of Special Concern. It remains to be seen whether the breeding gains can be maintained as more people use some of these "remote" areas. The goshawk is often a very aggressive defender of its nesting territory. In Region 2, shotgun shells under the nest tree and the disappearance of the long-resident pair in a recreation area that had recently become more heavily used paint a clear picture. The birds nested at the intersection of two main trails very near the picnic area and interacted violently with any passersby. Speiser (1992) discussed similar issues in detail, relative to the small breeding population along the NY-NJ border.
Robert G. Spahn

Red-shouldered Hawk *Buteo lineatus*

Range Nearctic, breeding in eastern North America from the extreme southern portions of Ontario, Quebec, and New Brunswick south to Texas and Florida; also in California and northern Mexico. Winters north to southern Wisconsin and southeastern Massachusetts.

Status Uncommon, but increasing breeder throughout. Common to very common migrant. In spring, most numerous along shores of the Great Lakes; in fall, in the lower Hudson Valley. In winter, occurs casually everywhere except the Adirondacks.

Hook Mountain, Rockland Co., is one of many hawkwatch sites in the state, where raptor enthusiasts gather to record the migration data of species such as the Broad-winged Hawk.

Breeding It has disappeared as a breeder along the lake plains but is a not uncommon breeder in upland areas such as Appalachian Plateau, Eastern and Western Adirondack foothills, and Taconic Highlands when searched for. Habitat varies from bottomland hardwoods and flooded deciduous swamps to upland mixed deciduous-coniferous forest. It is officially listed as Threatened in NY. The Atlas confirmed Bull's (1974) opinion that it had all but disappeared as a breeder from the L. Ontario plain swamps. In fact, it was recorded in only 702 blocks and Confirmed in only 15% of those, which represents less than 2% of all the blocks. A reduction in contiguous wooded habitat has permitted the larger, more aggressive Red-tailed Hawk to usurp these woodlots (Bednarz and Dinsmore 1982; Bryant 1986). However, there appears to have been a decided increase in breeding in the more heavily wooded upland regions statewide (Crocoll and Parker 1989; Johnson and Chambers 1994). The reason for this change is not entirely clear but must in part be due to abandoned farmland reverting to forest (Peterson and Crocoll 1992). It has even become a regular, though rare breeder in Region 10.

Nonbreeding Migration numbers have fluctuated since Bull 1974, but no trend is apparent. Spring migration generally occurs from the second or third week of Mar to the last week of Apr, with an unusual record of 8 Feb 1995 at Dryden, Tompkins Co. Fall migration generally occurs from the first week of Oct to the first or second week of Nov.

    Spring maxima: 956 Braddock Bay, Monroe Co. 13 Mar 1990; 722 Derby Hill 5 Apr 1993. *Fall maxima:* 63 Hook Mtn., Rockland Co. 27 Oct 1990; 41 Butler Sanctuary, Westchester Co. 4 Nov 1989.

Remarks Although still rare in winter, its appearance is no longer confined to the coast. In any winter, it is reported somewhere in the state and has appeared in every area except the Adirondacks. In fact, during some years, it has been reported in up to half of the Regions, although usually only one or two individuals per Region. It most commonly occurs in Regions 1, 2, and 3, south of the L. Ontario plain, and in Regions 9 and 10. Its increasing occurrence may be due principally to more active observers and occasional mild winters.

Scott T. Crocoll

Broad-winged Hawk   *Buteo platypterus*

Range Nearctic, breeding in central Alberta and Saskatchewan and from southern Manitoba and New Brunswick south to eastern Texas, Florida, and the West Indies. Continental population winters from extreme southern Florida and Mexico to Brazil and Peru.

Status Statewide breeder. Abundant to very abundant migrant.

Breeding It is found breeding in most extensively forested areas. During the Atlas project it was recorded in 1944 blocks and was Confirmed in 20% of those. It is a rare breeder along the L. Ontario and St. Lawrence plains and in the Mohawk Valley. Nesting habitat is deciduous or deciduous-coniferous forests or conifer plantations (Crocoll and Parker 1989). The Atlas map indicated an expansion of its range south and west of the Mohawk Valley as well as in the Catskills and the Hudson Valley. The reasons for this range expansion may be twofold. First, as agriculture has declined in the state, many areas have reverted to forest, creating more suitable habitat. Second, because it does not vocalize much during the breeding season, it may have been overlooked before the Atlas project because experienced birders were not searching for it.

Nonbreeding Migration numbers from the various hawkwatches, although showing yearly variation, indicate no consistent trend in occurrence or numbers during spring or fall. The apparently larger numbers since 1974 may be due to increased observation effort and not to an increase in population. However, there has been a change in the early and late dates of migrants since 1974 when Bull stated that they were rare before Apr and after late Oct. They are now being reported almost annually both before and after those months, with an early date of 1 Mar and a late date of 2 Jan on a CBC.

    Spring maxima: 15,597 Braddock Bay, Monroe Co. 20 Apr 1992; 12,676 Braddock Bay 29 Apr 1991. *Fall maxima:* 15,459 Pelham Bay, Bronx Co. 17 Sep 1990; 8212 Bear Mtn., Rockland Co. 21 Sep 1987.

    Bull (1974, 1976) noted only two substantiated winter records for this species. Since then a minimum of 15 birds have been reported during winter, from the Hudson Valley, LI, and western NY. The normal winter range of this species is from southern Mexico south through Central America and parts of South America. The only place where it occurs regularly during winter in the United States is south of Miami (Tabb 1973). The increase in winter reports in NY could be due to a combination of mild winters, sick individuals, and misidentifications of immature Red-shouldered and other hawks (Goodrich et al., 1996).
Scott T. Crocoll

Swainson's Hawk   *Buteo swainsoni*

Range Nearctic, breeding locally in Alaska and in the Great Plains, east to Minnesota and western Illinois. Winters primarily on the pampas of southern South America and casually north to southwestern United States and Florida. Casual in northeastern North America.

Status Rare vagrant, but becoming increasingly regular.

Occurrence Bull (1974) accepted only two nineteenth-century specimen records and one sight record from 1970. Of all the hawks, this species' status has been most affected by the the proliferation of hawkwatch sites stimulated by the HMANA. There have been 53 documented occurrences of this gregarious raptor, 47 since 1979, two years after the formation of the organization. Of these 47 records, all but seven were at hawkwatches. Braddock Bay, Monroe Co. alone is responsible for 20 of them. NY is not alone in experiencing this phenomenon. Hawkwatching sites throughout the Northeast and Midwest have all experienced increased sightings.

Thirty-nine sightings took place in the spring, with dates ranging from 31 Mar to 30 May, all occurring inland and all but two along the hawk migration routes on the Great Lakes shores. The ages of 31 of these were determined. Adults (12) appeared during the first week of Apr, at the peak of the Turkey Vulture migration, and during the last week of Apr, at the peak of the adult Broad-winged Hawk migration. Both species migrate with Swainson's Hawk through South and Central America. Since all three species flock in large numbers, some Swainson's Hawks probably stay with the other two. Immatures (19) occur mainly in May with immature Broad-winged Hawks. Twice, two Swainson's were recorded.

There has been only one summer sighting, 22 Aug 1991, at Braddock Bay (pers. obs.). This should be considered a fall migrant, and as such is the earliest arrival date.

There have been 13 fall records, most in Sep and early Oct, but ranging from 5 Sep–1 Nov, the last an extremely late date (KB 38:282). All but two were near the coast. Of the six birds aged during the fall, two were adults and four immature.

Remarks Swainson's Hawks occur in three color morphs: light, dark, and rufous. Of the 33 that were identified as to color, four were dark and 29 light. No rufous morphs were noted, but until the publication of Wheeler and Clark 1995, this had been a difficult separation in the field.
Jeff Dodge and Frank J. Nicoletti

Red-tailed Hawk *Buteo jamaicensis*

Range Nearctic and northern Neotropical, breeding nearly throughout temperate North America, from Alaska to Nova Scotia south to Panama, and in the West Indies. Winters from southern Canada throughout the rest of the breeding range.

Status Widespread breeder and resident. Common to abundant migrant; winter visitant.

Breeding During the Atlas project it was recorded in 70% of all blocks, with breeding Confirmed in 28% of those. A glance at the Atlas map shows absence of breeding evidence only in heavily urbanized NYC and the densely forested areas of the Adirondacks. In 1995, however, an enterprising pair nested on an apartment ledge in Manhattan near the AMNH.

As a breeder, it prefers wood lots adjacent to open fields and occasionally wooded swamp and marsh habitat used by Red-shouldered Hawk. Along with American Kestrel, it has made great use of the habitat created along the medians and rights of way of the state's highways.

Nonbreeding Our population is both sedentary and migratory, with more individuals migrating through than resident, and some of those migrants remaining for all or part of the winter.

In spring, the first migrants appear in mid to late Feb. Adults peak in late Mar, and immatures during the last week in Apr. The migration continues into mid-May, with individuals still moving in Jun.

The spring migration is much more spectacular than the fall. This is true for many buteo species, since buteos will not cross L. Ontario and are therefore concentrated along the southern shore of the lake as they move north. In the fall, the same phenomenon occurs, but then they mass on the northern shore. Many then move west through ON before turning south or continuing west, completely bypassing NY. Some do, however, move along the north-south ridges in the southeastern part of the state.

The fall migration for this species is particularly interesting, beginning as a postbreeding dispersal in late Jul. These early migrants, all immatures, are concentrated along the southern shore of L. Ontario. A study of banded birds at Braddock Bay, Monroe Co. suggested that they are migrating north. On 17 Aug 1991, an estimated 5000 were observed there. Banding recoveries also suggest that these young birds continue to move north until late Sep and early Oct, at which time they join the southward migration, which peaks in mid to late Oct and continues into Nov.

Winter residents and visitants use the same habitat as breeders. They are widespread and solitary but can often be found in loose groups where food (especially *Microtus* sp.) is abundant.

Spring maxima: 4591 Derby Hill, Oswego Co. 10 Apr 1995; 1628 Braddock Bay, Monroe Co. 26 Mar 1987. *Season:* 19,531 Derby Hill 1995; 11,412 Braddock Bay 1986. *Fall maxima:* 2218 Braddock Bay 17 Aug 1991; 1075 Franklin Mtn., Otsego Co. 10 Nov 1994. *Season:* 2226 Franklin Mtn. 1994; 1884 Franklin Mtn. 1993.

Remarks Five subspecies, *borealis, kriderii, harlani, calurus,* and *albieticola,* have been identified as having occurred in the state, but only two by specimens. Our breeding bird is *borealis,* and *albieticola* is a rare migrant with numerous specimens collected. No specimen of *kriderii, harlani,* or *calurus* has ever been collected in NY (Dickerman and Parkes 1987). Positive inclu-

sion of these three forms in the state avifauna awaits a specimen or a photo of a bird that can be unequivocally identified.
Jeff Dodge and Frank J. Nicoletti

Rough-legged Hawk *Buteo lagopus*

Range Northern Holarctic, breeding in North America from northern Alaska across arctic Canada to Baffin Island and south, in the east to Newfoundland and the Gulf of St. Lawrence. Winters south to Virginia and Tennessee, rarely to the Gulf Coast.

Status A migrant and winter visitant, rare to uncommon coastally, more numerous and even occasionally common on the L. Ontario plain. Irruptive.

Occurrence Most Rough-legged Hawks migrate through NY, but some stay for the winter. As a winter visitant, it chiefly inhabits open fields and marshes and is most prevalent in years of meadow vole abundance. It is especially numerous along L. Ontario and in the rich agricultural country south and east of the lake.

The fall migration begins in mid to late Oct, peaks in late Nov, and continues well into the winter. Often, as is common with irruptive species, the largest influx of migrants occurs in the latter half of Dec or, more rarely, in Jan.

In spring, the migration often starts in mid-Feb but certainly by early Mar, and peaks during the last week in Apr. It then drops off quickly, with migrants becoming uncommon to rare. The spring migration is much more spectacular than the fall. See the discussion of the concentrating effect of L. Ontario on buteo migration under Red-tailed Hawk.

Spring maxima: 189 Braddock Bay, Monroe Co. 14 Mar 1996; 171 Braddock Bay 19 Apr 1996; 165 Derby Hill, Oswego Co. 22 Feb 1981. *Season:* 1815 Braddock Bay 1996; 661 Braddock Bay 1992; 585 Derby Hill 1981. *Fall maxima:* 32 east end of L. Ontario 7 Nov 1979; 4 Franklin Mtn., Otsego Co. 22 Oct 1990. *Season:* 115 Palatine Bridge, Montgomery Co. 1979; 100 east end of L. Ontario 1979. *Winter roosts:* 127 Point Peninsula, Jefferson Co. 1990.

Remarks Rough-legged Hawks occur in two color morphs, light and dark, although Wheeler and Clark (1995) stated that there is a continuous cline between them. In a five-year sample of 2410 migrants at Braddock Bay, 78.4% were light morphs and 21.6% were dark. The order of spring migration for the same sample was established: adult males (Feb–early Apr); adult females (Mar–late Apr); immatures (late Mar–early May).
Jeff Dodge

Golden Eagle   *Aquila chrysaetos*

Range Holarctic, breeding in eastern North America from northeastern Manitoba and northern Quebec south to southern Manitoba, the Gaspe Peninsula, and irregularly in northern New England and (formerly) northern new York. Winters at scattered locations in southeastern United States and rarely but regularly north to Massachusetts and New York.

Status Extirpated as a breeder. Uncommon migrant, mostly inland, and rare winter visitant.

Occurrence Seen most often during migration, especially in fall, when breeding birds and their young, believed to be largely from interior eastern Canada (Quebec and Labrador), move south through NY toward more southerly (unknown) wintering locations. Peak observations occur Oct–Nov and Mar–Apr, with the most in Nov and Apr. Increased observer effort, particularly at hawkwatches, has dramatically increased the number of reports, especially since 1990. The hawkwatch at Franklin Mtn., Otsego Co. has been reporting increasing numbers of Golden Eagles each fall since 1989, a trend not duplicated by other NY hawkwatches, spring or fall, although Hawk Mtn., immediately south in PA, has also witnessed increasing numbers over the past two decades. The maximum seasonal count of 139 at Franklin Mtn. during the fall of 1993 is an eastern U.S. record.

    Maxima: 19 Franklin Mtn. 27 Oct 1992; 12 Franklin Mtn. 8 Dec 1994; 7 Braddock Bay, Monroe Co. 9 Apr 1993.

    Visitants are recorded every month, although sightings from May to Sep are very rare; even rarer are observations of adult birds. Every Region is represented in observations, with Region 9 recording the most, followed by Region 6, then Regions 3 and 7; sightings within Region 1 are extremely rare. The occasional Golden Eagle is observed nearly every winter within Region 9, mostly at the same sites occupied by wintering Bald Eagles. They are frequently seen feeding on carrion or waterfowl. Nearly all of these are immature birds, and the author has captured, banded, and radio-tracked four within southeastern NY since 1980. Many of these tagged individuals spent a considerable part of the winter in this area.

    Our most regular visitants are the adult pair that have wintered annually since 1969 in the vicinity of Pine Plains, Dutchess Co.; one or both arrive each year as early as mid-Oct and depart by mid-Mar. Although this pair built a nest in a large white pine there during the winter of 1992–1993, this was likely simply pair bonding and they migrated north as usual in Mar.

    Golden Eagle is now considered extirpated as a breeder in NY and is listed by the NYSDEC as Endangered. The last known successful breeding was in Hamilton Co. in 1970. The last known nesting attempt (eggs laid) was at the same site in 1979, although no young were hatched. Summer (Jun–Jul) sightings are almost exclusively from Regions 6 and 7 of northern

NY. A significant sighting of a "pair" was made in Hamilton Co. during Jun 1992, although no nest was found (KB 42:263).

Remarks Although the Golden Eagle was not "definitively" confirmed breeding in NY until the successful banding and fledging of an eaglet from an eyrie in St. Lawrence Co. in 1957 (Spofford 1971b), it undoubtedly nested in NY since at least the 1800s, albeit probably never in great numbers. Numerous historical references to nests and birds in NY, the availability of large amounts of suitable open habitat, including breeding cliffs, and the likelihood that they would not be encountered by humans because of the remote nature of their territories are some of the reasons Golden Eagle surely bred historically in our state. During the 1900s, at least six nesting sites were confirmed within northern NY (W. R. Spofford, pers. comm.), as well as one confirmed site in the lower Hudson Highlands during the early 1800s. At least five additional sites in northern NY could be regarded as Probable nesting locations.

The recent twentieth-century sites, however, have not been very successful; only a few young were Confirmed between 1950 and 1970 (Spofford 1971b). The lack of breeding success, the intermittent nature of nesting activity, and the ultimate extirpation as a breeder can be ascribed to several factors. Trapping and shooting, especially around known breeding territories, claimed a considerable number of birds over the years. For a species with very few individuals in this part of its range to begin with, such losses are not readily overcome. Data from NYSDEC files on recoveries of 25 Golden Eagles in NY 1930–1996 revealed that 44% of all birds were trapped and another 16% were shot. They are also reportedly extremely sensitive to human disturbance during nesting, and in at least three of the confirmed NY breeding territories, human disturbances were observed and cited as a factor in their failure.

The Golden Eagle is well known to be a species of open areas such as those throughout much of the West, where it is common. It was never common in the East, but has the amount of suitable "open" Golden Eagle habitat diminished in NY? A habitat analysis, completed by NYSDEC, of areas surrounding the northern NY nesting sites, covering the period 1942–1968, revealed that open area had been reduced around six of seven sites evaluated. Active campaigns to suppress wildfires is one cause of reduced open areas. Natural succession is another. Finally, pesticides have been implicated in reproductive failure of Golden Eagles breeding in the eastern United States. As other types of open habitats have declined, remaining birds may have shifted their use to wetland bog or marsh habitats and their prey to wetland-dependent species such as herons and bitterns (Spofford 1971a). These prey species, as compared with those of uplands, often carry a significantly higher burden of contaminants accumulated through the aquatic food chain, which are passed along to the birds that consume them. These factors have weighed negatively on the success of Golden Eagle in NY since 1940. Only one factor, illegal killing of birds, may have been ameliorated since 1970.

Peter G. Nye

CARACARAS AND
FALCONS—FALCONIDAE

American Kestrel *Falco sparverius*

Range Nearctic, breeding from Alaska to Newfoundland and south to California and the Gulf Coast; also in much of Middle and South America. Winters nearly throughout, but with northern populations migrating as far as Panama.

Status Widespread breeder throughout. Common to occasionally very abundant fall coastal migrant and common to occasionally abundant spring migrant inland. Locally uncommon to fairly common in the winter.

Breeding Prevalent in open country, especially in agricultural districts, along roadsides, and wherever there are fields, meadows, and even swampy areas with standing dead trees. Equally at home in such places as airports, golf courses, and city parks. During the Atlas project it was found in 3450 blocks and Confirmed in 36% of those. It was located in all parts of the state except for the most extensively and heavily forested portions of the mountainous regions.

As a hole nester, it selects such diverse nest sites as tree cavities, old woodpecker holes in telephone poles or fence posts, bird boxes, and building crevices. Populations did not suffer the declines of most other raptor species, possibly owing to the predominance of insects in their prey base. However, competition for cavities and the increasing removal of dead trees for firewood may limit breeding populations. Their ready use of nest boxes could be useful in maintaining numbers.

Nonbreeding It is sometimes seen in very large numbers in fall passage along the outer beaches of LI, with numbers falling to one-third or less only a short distance inland. Counts are typically much lower at spring hawkwatches on the south shore of L. Ontario, although the Braddock Bay, Monroe Co. watch has topped or neared 1000 in nine of the past 14 years and Derby Hill, Oswego Co. approached that number in 1995.

Coastal maxima: Fall: Fire I., Suffolk Co.: 1386, 1 Oct 1987; 1314, 19 Sep 1993. Ft. Tilden, Queens Co.: 638, 19 Sep 1993; 545, 18 Oct 1993. *Season:* Fire I.: 3245 in 1987; 3271 in 1993. *Inland maxima: Spring:* Braddock Bay: 1166, 19 Apr 1983; 347, 25 Mar 1988. Typical daily highs there and at Derby Hill have ranged up to about 250 for many years.

In winter, CBC totals for the state rose steadily from 1960 to the mid-1970s, peaking at 1058 in 1975. Since that time, there has been a steady decline to the point where 1991–1994 produced the lowest cluster of totals since 1970. Winter banding studies upstate have shown good site fidelity to winter territories by single birds. Some summer residents remain on territory, and some move a short distance; some summer territories are taken by migrants not banded locally. It also appears that males and females show different site preferences, with females tending toward areas with taller grasses and males often found near shorter grass fields or orchards (Griffith, pers. comm.).

Remarks There is no clear evidence in NY data of any major change in the status of American Kestrel from early accounts, such as Eaton (1914), to the present. The Cape May, NJ fall migration count showed a continuing decline in totals since 1985, excepting 1987.
Robert G. Spahn

Merlin   *Falco columbarius*

Range Holarctic, in North America breeding from Alaska and northern Labrador south to eastern Oregon and east to southern Ontario and Quebec, less frequently to Nova Scotia and recently in northern New York. Winters to Middle America, northern South America, and the West Indies.

Status Very rare breeder in the Adirondacks. Rare to common migrant, most regular and very common to occasionally abundant along the coast in fall. Rare winter visitant.

Breeding Despite the lack of extant skins, eggs, surviving firsthand correspondence, or any other proof, there are several early reports suggestive of very rare breeding in the Adirondacks and even farther south and west in the state. Bull (1974) dismissed them all. In view of recent developments, one secondhand report with some credibility might be that related by Eaton (1914) of "young scarcely able to fly near Indian Lake, Hamilton Co."

Nicoletti reported young with limited flight capability on Cascade Mtn., Essex Co. in the summer of 1985 (J. M. C. Peterson, pers. comm.), but neither it nor other reports of midsummer sightings in the Adirondacks were reported to the Atlas project.

Breeding was finally confirmed to the satisfaction of all with a nesting pair initially noted on 3 or 4 May 1992 on Spitfire L., Franklin Co. Identification was confirmed by Montgomery on 14 Jun, nestlings were seen on 12 Jul, and fledging occurred on 20 Jul (Montgomery 1992). Additional breeding records have been confirmed in each year since: L.

Placid Golf Course, Essex Co. 4 Aug 1993 (KB 43:337); Blue Mtn. L., Hamilton Co. 19–24 Jul 1993 (KB 43:337); 2–3 fledglings daily, Mirror L., Essex Co., late Jul 1994 (KB 44:326); adults with 5 young Osgood Pond, Franklin Co. 26 Jul 1994 (KB 44:326); adults with juvenile, Racquette L., Hamilton Co. 25 Jul 1994 (KB 44:326); 4 young fledged 14 Jul 1995 at Mirror L. Golf Course (J. M. C. Peterson, pers. comm.); a pair feeding nestlings in a cavity nest on 14 Jul 1995, L. Placid (J. M. C. Peterson, pers. comm.); and an increasing number of nesting sites reported in Region 7 in the summer of 1996 (KB 46:360).

Other nearby sightings included a pair at Lows L., Town of Colton, St. Lawrence Co. in the summer of 1995 (KB 45:310) and a pair with two young in late Aug 1996 in Potsdam, St. Lawrence Co. (KB 46:354).

Merlins typically nest in coniferous or mixed forest near the edge of relatively large openings provided by lakes, burns, clearcuts, or other human activity, using available platforms, most often in coniferous trees, provided by old nests of other birds or squirrels, broken tree tops, or existing cavities. The adults are apparently not at all deterred by human presence or activity during the breeding season and have frequently located nests close to camps or other structures. They are often highly vocal near the nest site, yet the nests themselves can be very difficult to locate until both parents are feeding sizable nestlings.

Nonbreeding Historically, Eaton (1914) noted a considerable spring flight along the south shore of L. Ontario; Beardslee and Mitchell (1965) noted it as a rare spring transient. The examination of hawkwatch summaries showed a jump in totals about 1982 and a steady, slow upward trend since. Eaton suggested the species was common in fall passage along the coast, and Duncan (1993) suggested a decrease in those flights in the middle of the DDT period. The Fire I., Suffolk Co. hawkwatch provides the most complete recent data and appears to show a jump about 1985, increases to 1989, then possibly slight declines more recently. However, it is very hard to separate the changes conclusively from accompanying changes in hours of coverage. As noted in Duncan 1993 and other data since then, the numbers from Cape May, NJ are more clearly indicative of annual decreases since 1988, both in totals and totals per observer hour.

The winter picture appears to have remained fairly constant from Eaton's assessment of Merlin as an occasional winter visitant on LI, with only one record upstate at Canandaigua, Ontario Co., Jan 1906, to Beardslee and Mitchell, who noted four upstate winter records. Since the early 1970s, there have been more than 80 winter sightings away from the coast reported in *The Kingbird*, with reports now from all Regions. Sightings continue to be sporadic, except for some individuals showing high site fidelity over several years. CBC data echo this pattern; statewide totals were

0–6 in the 1960–1971 period, 2–15 in 1972–1978, and 10–26 after 1978. It must be noted that during all of those periods, CBC totals away from LI have typically been only 0–3, even when the overall totals have topped 20. Winter records are still predominantly coastal.

In spring migration, when it peaks in Apr, it is rare to occasionally common past inland hawkwatches, especially on the south shore of L. Ontario. In fall, its status is similar at inland sites, whereas it is very common to occasionally abundant in passage at coastal beaches, peaking from mid-Sep to mid, or recently, even late Oct.

Coastal maxima: Fall: Fire I., Suffolk Co.: 292, 1 Oct 1987; 227, 22 Oct 1989; 224, 2 Oct 1990. Ft. Tilden, Queens Co.: 202, 2 Oct 1990. ***Inland maxima: Spring season:*** 117 Braddock Bay, Monroe Co. 1996, more than double the record 53 set at Derby Hill, Oswego Co. in 1995. ***Inland maxima: Fall:*** Hook Mtn., Rockland Co., all in 1990: 16 on 26 Sep; 11 on 6 Oct; 18 on 10 Oct; 10 on 18 Oct. ***Extreme dates:*** 28 Feb and 6 Jun; 5 Aug and 27 Nov.

Remarks Duncan (1993) presented an excellent review of the status of the Merlin, looking at populations nationwide at various seasons in the pre-DDT, mid-DDT, and post-DDT periods. In the pre-DDT period, there is little doubt that some regions, including the Northeast and NY recorded the species as rare except during migration, when numbers we would term common were noted at barriers such as the Atlantic Coast or the Great Lakes. Numbers decreased somewhat during the peak DDT period, and there was a rebound since the late 1970s or early 1980s.
Robert G. Spahn

Peregrine Falcon

Falco peregrinus

Range Cosmopolitan, in North America breeding from northern Alaska across arctic Canada to Baffin Island and Labrador south to southwestern United States and northern Mexico, but absent in tropical and subtropical America. Since the 1950s has been absent as a breeder through much of continental North America, especially in the eastern part south of the Canadian Arctic. Recently reestablished through introductions in many areas, especially in northeastern United States.

Status Once extirpated as a breeder, now a local breeder. Resident in and around the southeast, including NYC. Fairly common fall migrant on the outer coast, rarer inland.

Breeding There were 40–50 historical nest sites in NY, mainly on cliffs affording good views of the surrounding area. There were also a few nests in abandoned stone quarries, one on the St. Regis Hotel in Manhattan, and one on the Bear Mtn. Bridge in the lower Hudson Valley. These eyries were mainly in the eastern half of the state except for a few in the Finger Lakes region, as reported in Bull (1974). Main population areas were in the Adirondacks and the lower Hudson Valley, the latter population well studied by Herbert and Herbert over a 30-year period (1965, 1969). These eyries became inactive mainly because of pesticide effects (primarily DDT) on the birds' productivity. Other factors negatively affecting NY's population included habitat loss and disturbance by humans (e.g., taking of young and eggs and shooting). By the early 1960s, the Peregrine had disappeared as a breeder from NY, as well as from other places in the eastern United States.

After DDT use was banned in this country in 1972, the NYSDEC decided to get involved with an experiment with restoration through the release of captive-bred birds obtained through the Peregrine Fund. A total of 168 young falcons was hacked at more than a dozen sites in the state from 1974 to 1988, with 123 (73%) dispersing normally. *Hacking* is a falconry term and involves the feeding of and caring for young raptors by people until they are capable of surviving on their own. Hack sites are generally staffed by two workers who feed the Peregrines using a food chute in such a manner that the birds remain wild and do not associate people with food. Most NY hack sites were at cliffs in the Adirondacks, but birds were also released in the Shawangunks, and on buildings in New Paltz, Albany, and Manhattan. An additional 12 birds were hacked in 1994 in Rochester by Rochester Gas and Electric Corporation.

After an absence of more than 20 years, the Peregrine finally returned as a nesting bird to NY in 1983 at two NYC bridge sites, the Throgs Neck and the Verrazano Narrows bridges. Three of the four breeding birds had been hacked elsewhere (NY, NJ, unknown), and one adult had been produced naturally at a cliff site in NH. In 1985, the species returned to two historical eyries in the Adirondacks in Essex Co. One of those breeding birds had been hacked in VT two years earlier. The origin of the other three breeders is unknown, as is the case with many of our nesting falcons, because of the difficulty in reading their leg bands. As shown in Figure 3, the population has increased steadily, from two pairs in 1983 to 32 territorial pairs in 1996, 26 of which bred; 24 were successful in producing a record 48 young. From one to five young have been produced at successful eyries, with eggs generally present Mar–May, young Apr–Jun, and most fledging in Jun or Jul. In the NYC area, mortality during the first months after fledging is fairly high.

The current nesting population is in two main areas. The downstate pairs, more than half of the state total, are in the NYC area on bridges and buildings and along the lower Hudson R. on four bridges and one cliff. The upstate pairs are mainly cliff nesters in the High Peaks, L. George, and L. Champlain areas, with the first urban nest sites occupied in Buffalo and Rochester in 1996. Some of the cliff sites are historical eyries, but the majority are new and the proliferation of nests in NYC was a surprise to many. NYC probably now has the largest urban population in the world, with some nesting pairs only about a kilometer apart. The mainstay of the city diet is Rock Dove and other year-round resident avians such as Blue Jay, Northern Flicker, Red-winged Blackbird, and European Starling. More than 60 prey species were recorded at one NYC eyrie during a two-year study (Nadareski 1992). Nonbreeding pairs have also been reported in Albany and Syracuse.

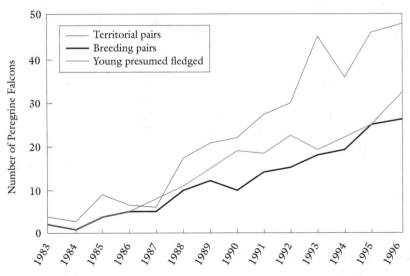

Figure 3. New York State Peregrine Falcon breeding summary, 1983–1996 (Data from New York State Department of Environmental Conservation)

Although the USFWS has published an intent to propose federal delisting of the Peregrine Falcon as an Endangered species, the NYSDEC recommended against that move at this time. The population has made a remarkable recovery due to restoration efforts and the continued intensive protection and management currently afforded all our nesting sites. This involves many individuals and agencies, especially the NYC Department of Environmental Protection. The future of the species in NY is not yet assured, and the present population is not believed to be self-sustaining; it is still quite vulnerable, and concerns remain. Delisting on the state level will not take place for some time yet, as state recovery goals call for 30 occupied nesting territories to be present for three or more consecutive years with at least 15 of them under protective management.

Nonbreeding Recorded every month of the year. During fall, Peregrines (mainly immatures) are seen along the beaches of LI, and in the spring in smaller numbers at hawkwatches along L. Ontario. Recent (1990–1994) reports at two major spring hawkwatches reveal that birds are observed 13 Apr–31 May (Braddock Bay, Monroe Co.) and 15 Apr–22 May (Derby Hill, Oswego Co.), with seasonal totals 7–22 at Braddock Bay and 1–12 at Derby Hill. A single-day Derby Hill record was set on 10 May 1996 with five observed. In fall, the watch at Fire I., Suffolk Co. reported a season high of 249 in 1990, and a single-day record of 49 on 2 Oct 1989. Ft. Tilden, Queens Co. reported a season high of 92 in 1991, and a one-day maximum of 21 on 5 Oct 1991. NYC area and some Hudson Valley birds are present year-round.

Remarks Of the roughly 19 subspecies, two, *anatum* and *tundrius*, occurred historically in the state. Our breeder was *anatum*, and *tundrius* was seen moving through on fall migration. After *anatum* disappeared from the eastern United States, releases of captive-raised young in that area were readily identifiable as Peregrine Falcons but not easily identifiable as to subspecies or genetic background. The young released were from a variety of wild stocks, including both endangered and more common nonlisted subspecies and combinations thereof, including European subspecies. To ensure protection of all free-flying Peregrines, the USFWS gave protection to all such birds found within the lower 48 states because of their similarity in appearance. However, this protection could be withdrawn if the federal government decides to delist the species.
Barbara Allen Loucks

Gyrfalcon   *Falco rusticolus*

Range Holarctic, breeding in North America in arctic Canada south to the Mackenzie River Delta and northern portions of Manitoba, Quebec, and

Labrador. Winters mainly in the breeding range, south irregularly to southern Canada and the extreme northern United States; also casually to northern California and, in the east, to Delaware, Pennsylvania, New York, and Massachusetts.

Status A rare winter visitant.

Occurrence This is one of the rarest of our winter visitants, and Bull (1974) cited only about 50 reliable reports. It is easily misidentified because of the various color morphs. Gradations between them further confuse identification in the field. Free-flying birds wearing jesses occasionally have been seen in NY, and identification is further complicated by various falcon hybrids deliberately produced by falconers and found in NY on at least two occasions. One of these birds was traced back to a Missouri falconer (NYSARC, KB 35:230). On 28 Feb 1993, after a gray Gyrfalcon had been reported at JBSP on 15 Feb, Schiff, Wollin, and Levine closely studied a pair of very large pale gray falcons flying about and roosting on the water tower. These birds were not the known resident pair of Peregrines. Although the dark black hood and moustache contrasting with the pale body indicated some kind of Peregrine, a thorough study of all the Peregrine and Gyrfalcon skins in the AMNH collection did not reveal a match. It was finally concluded that the birds were probably Peregrine × Gyrfalcon crosses (KB 43:161).

Bull (1974) accounted for ten extant specimens from 20 collected, six from upstate and four from Fishers I., Suffolk Co. Nine of the ten were dark or intermediate, and one was light. Since Bull 1974, more than 70 birds have been observed, most being described as gray or dark morphs and only about 10% as white morphs or light-colored birds. There was one specimen collected in this period, a dark morph killed in a collision with a plane at the Buffalo Airport, Erie Co. 17 Nov 1982 (Clark) specimen at BMS (KB 33:48).

Most of the observations are from lakeshores, large rivers, and ocean beach habitats where waterfowl and gulls are abundant or at open grasslands in active farm country where voles *(Microtus* sp.*)* and Rock Doves provide a good prey base for the wintering birds. L. Champlain and much of the Great Lakes shoreline, as well as the Hudson R. corridor and LI, provide these habitats. It is not surprising that many of the sight records were in Clinton Co. (third highest) and Essex Co. (fourth highest) along L. Champlain; Monroe Co. (second highest), Oswego Co., and Jefferson Co. (highest) along L. Ontario; Erie Co. along L. Erie; Dutchess Co. along the Hudson R. and Nassau Co. at JBSP and vicinity (fifth highest.) Numbers varied from year to year and no doubt depended on the severity of the winters and available food in the north. The big years were the winters of 1978–1979, 1979–1980, 1981–1982, 1987–1988, 1989–1990, 1990–1991, and 1991–1992 with three to five birds reported in each.

Winter 1992–1993 was outstanding with at least 20 reports, and 1993–1994 had another very high count with 22 sightings of at least 15 birds, all in the north. The only winter since 1974 with no birds reported was 1976–1977. The highest concentration was at least five (two dark and three gray) at Cape Vincent, Jefferson Co. 6–17 Feb 1994.

Extreme dates: 9 Sep and 5 Apr, both in Monroe Co. The highest number of sightings occurred in Feb (17), Dec (15), and Mar (14).

Remarks Winter 1993–1994 was a big invasion year throughout the Northeast. PQ had a higher than normal count of 15+ individuals along the St. Lawrence R., ON reported 19, PA had 2, VT had 1 on the Burlington CBC, and MD recorded its first ever. A late bird was in MA on 1 May. Lee B. Chamberlaine

PARTRIDGES, GROUSE, AND TURKEYS—PHASIANIDAE

Gray Partridge   *Perdix perdix*

Range Western Palearctic; introduced into North America and established locally, chiefly in southern Canada from British Columbia to Nova Scotia and northern United States from California to New York and Vermont.

Status An introduced resident, now uncommon in its past range in Jefferson, St. Lawrence, Franklin, and Clinton counties. Nearly 28,000 birds were introduced 1927–1932, chiefly from Czechoslovakia, and no known supplemental restocking has been made since.

Breeding Bull (1974) described a limited distribution along the L. Ontario plain and the St. Lawrence and L. Champlain valleys. Changes in land use from 1950 to 1959, with a decline in croplands of hay, small grains, and grasses and the loss of grain stubble and associated weed species resulted in a decrease in habitat. The Atlas confirmed this continuing decrease in population and distribution. The NY range is marginal (Austin, pers. comm.), and any change in farming activity or loss of habitat from development or farm abandonment will have a negative impact. Earlier mowing of hay fields (Carroll 1993) and increased use of pesticides may have resulted in increased mortality as they did in Great Britain (Potts 1980, 1986). Since the Atlas the number of observations of the species has decreased greatly. The last stronghold appears to be the area along the St. Lawrence R. at Cape Vincent, Jefferson Co., where 52 in four coveys were reported in summer 1992 (Wood) (KB 42:259). It is periodically reported around Massena, St. Lawrence Co.

Nonbreeding Recent reports include: 12 Moses-Saunders Dam, St. Lawrence Co. 11 Feb 1988; 24 there spring 1988; 15 Ingraham, Clinton

Co. 9 Dec 1993. Some out-of-range observations have been reported. They were probably released birds from private sources. Six birds were at Westport, Essex Co. 23 Jan 1981, down from 14 seen in Nov 1980 (Will 1981).

Remarks This partridge has a high mortality rate, short life span, and high reproductive capability (Carroll 1993).
Lee B. Chamberlaine

Ring-necked Pheasant   *Phasianus colchicus*

Range Originally central and eastern Palearctic, widely introduced into various parts of the world. In eastern North America, resident from Minnesota and Missouri to the East Coast and from Nova Scotia to New Jersey and Pennsylvania.

Status Common resident in its range, but numbers have dropped sharply.

Breeding After rebounding from severe declines in the 1940s, this introduced game bird now faces a new combination of threats. In the late 1960s it reached record high numbers: nearly 200 birds per square mile in its primary range (Penrod and Hill 1983). Since then, plant succession and the end of federal set-aside programs such as the Soil Bank have eliminated many of the fallow grasslands in which this species thrives. In addition, there is loss of protective cover, including low, dense hedgerows, and increased losses to predation. According to NYSDEC, most successful reproduction occurs in areas dominated by residual grasses (Penrod and Hill 1983).

Data from seven BBS routes in the Great Lakes Plain (the species' primary range in NY) clearly illustrate these losses. Average number of birds per run dropped from 40.0 during 1966–1975 to 23.4 and 25.6 during 1976–1985 and 1986–1994, respectively. Not coincidentally, some of the smallest counts came on the heels of one or more winters featuring both severe cold and extended snow cover.

In addition to the Great Lakes Plain, it is found primarily in the Hudson R. Valley and on LI (Atlas 1988).

Nonbreeding During winter, pheasants retreat to areas of brush and cattail marshes when snow is on the ground. The proximity of this habitat to suitable nesting areas is crucial when hens disperse in the spring. The farther they must travel, the less likely they are to survive (Penrod and Hill n.d.).

Remarks Since about 1980 the state has annually released about 30,000 adult pheasants for hunting and distributed 60,000 day-old chicks to cooperators to raise and release; others are released by private reserves and breeders. However, their impact on "wild" populations is negligible, as

fewer than 5% survive to the following spring (Penrod and Hill 1983). Clearly, maintenance of fallow grasslands close to suitable cover is key to maintaining "wild" populations. Bull (1974) noted that several strains have been introduced in NY since the 1890s, leading to a mixed stock, with males ranging from those with complete white collars to those with none.
Robert E. Marcotte

Spruce Grouse *Falcipennis canadensis*

Range Northern Nearctic, resident from Alaska, across northern Canada to Nova Scotia, and south, in the east, to extreme northern United States.

Status Very local, rare to uncommon resident and breeder in the Adirondacks.

Breeding Considered a common resident of the North Country (Adirondacks) in the late nineteenth century, it is now listed as Threatened by NYSDEC and recommended for Endangered status.

It is most abundant in early to middle-age spruce-fir forest. Its decline has been attributed to the loss of this forest type to logging, to the progressive maturation of spruce-fir forest in forever-wild areas, and to this species' unwariness around humans.

Its remaining stronghold is in relatively inaccessible, remnant spruce-fir patches in the Western Adirondack Foothills, primarily in southwest Franklin and southeast St. Lawrence counties. Bull (1974) listed 16 historical breeding locations in six counties; Atlas workers Confirmed breeding in 12 blocks in four counties. Bouta and Chambers (1990) found that its range had decreased to half its former size, and they estimated the entire Adirondack breeding population at only 175–315 birds. However, because of this species' secretive nature, and the extent of available habitat, more study is needed to determine the full extent of its breeding range.

Nonbreeding It is unobtrusive and seldom seen, unless searched for diligently and often. It does not flush when discovered, relying on natural camouflage.

Remarks Eaton warned as early as 1910 of "extermination in our state." Isolated as they are in scattered islands of suitable habitat, separate breeding groups risk losing their viability and disappearing without continued immigration of birds from other areas (Fritz 1979). Chambers (pers. comm.) emphasized the need to inform landowners how to protect, maintain, and improve habitat through judicious timber management and to educate hunters to avoid accidental shootings. The creation of the Nature Conservancy's projected 75,000-acre Boreal Heritage Preserve in Franklin

Co.—in the heart of this species' range—may help ensure a foothold in NY (KB 36:233).
Robert E. Marcotte

Ruffed Grouse *Bonasa umbellus*

Range Nearctic, breeding from Alaska to Newfoundland south, in the east to Minnesota and Virginia, and in the mountains to northern Georgia. Sedentary.

Status Uncommon to fairly common resident throughout except near metropolitan areas and in agricultural regions such as the Great Lakes Plain.

Breeding Found in forested areas of the state from pine-oak on eastern LI to timberline on Mt. Marcy. It is particularly attracted to second-growth hardwoods and conifers, forest clearings and edges, but it seeks conifers for cover. Grouse nest on the ground at the base of a tree or some upright object with protection on one side. They rely on camouflage, clear views of approaching danger, and sudden disarming takeoffs. The Atlas Confirmed breeding in 1753 blocks (56% of those in which they were recorded) across the Appalachian Plateau, the Catskills, the Adirondacks, eastern half of LI, and in forested areas of the lake plains.

Populations at the time of the Atlas had stabilized at levels very near historical highs, but during the late 1880s it was feared that the Ruffed Grouse would follow the Heath Hen (a subspecies of the Greater Prairie-Chicken) to extinction. Land clearing, logging, and fire had reduced the forest in the state to 25%, but changes in agriculture and industrialization reversed the trend. A century later, more than 60% of the state was forested (Considine 1984). This increase in forested area brought back the Ruffed Grouse.

The species is well known to show approximately ten-year cycles. The most complete discussion for NY and neighboring areas can be found in Bump et al. 1947. More recently Temple and Temple (1976) described these cycles from 1935 to 1972 from records obtained at weekly seminars at Cornell University. These show 1944–1945, 1954–1955, 1963–1964 to be years of scarcity in the Cayuga L. basin. Scarcities do not occur statewide but seem to be localized in different ecological regions.

Major avian predators of adult Ruffed Grouse are Great Horned Owl, Northen Goshawk, and Cooper's Hawk. With the return of the goshawk to the Appalachian Plateau (Atlas 1988), it can now be considered a major predator.

Remarks (By K. C. Parkes) There are three subspecies and a probable fourth represented in NY. The nominate race, *umbellus*, is the grouse of the

deciduous forest of much of the state; *umbellus* of the Adirondacks is inseparable from *togata*, the subspecies of southern ON, southern PQ, New
England, and the Maritimes. In many parts of the state, *umbellus* and *togata*
intergrade; in the Catskills and the eastern Mohawk Valley, many individuals
are closest to *togata*, and others are intermediate. In the Hudson
Highlands, intermediates are found alongside *umbellus*-like birds. A third
subspecies, *monticola*, is the grouse of the southern Appalachians, and its
range enters NY at the southwestern corner; a specimen from the mountainous portion of Cattaraugus Co. is typical of *monticola*. The influence of
this subspecies can be seen in specimens from farther east in the
Appalachian Plateau, where those examined have been *umbellus-monticola*
intergrades. The many birds examined from the southern Finger Lakes
region are *umbellus*, with some specimens showing intergradation with *monticola* and others, from Ithaca, Tompkins Co. northeast at least to Pharsalia,
Chenango Co. being intergrades with *togata*. No specimens were examined
from the western part of the state from Keuka L. to Buffalo; these can be
expected to be referable to *umbellus*.

Bailey (1941) described a subspecies *helmei* based on a series of 40 old
specimens from Miller Place, Suffolk Co. The native Ruffed Grouse of LI
are rumored to have suffered near or total extinction, but grouse from
other populations have been introduced from time to time. Most authors
have either ignored *helmei* or have written it off as *umbellus-togata* intergrades. Zoogeographically, this intergradation seems unlikely on the face
of it. Bailey's series is remarkably uniform for supposed intergrades.
Specimens examined by Parkes strongly suggest that *helmei* was not a LI
endemic but also inhabited the Hudson Valley, between the highlands on
either side. A specimen from Dutchess Co. and two of three from
Schenectady Co. look just like the Miller Place *helmei*, the third being referable to *umbellus*. A detailed study of NY Ruffed Grouse is clearly called for
(Parkes, in litt.).

A color plate of the color morphs of the Ruffed Grouse can be seen in
Bump et al. 1947. In gray morph birds the tail shows a prominence of gray
with black subterminal bands; red morphs show a dominance of red in the
tail with black subterminal bands and black ruffs. Another variation, which
shows a brown or coppery subterminal band and a brown ruff, occurs in
the red morph. Gray morphs can also have brown ruffs and brown subterminal tail bands. As one goes from coniferous and aspen-birch in the north
to the hardwoods toward the south, and as snow becomes less of a permanent element in the winter ecology, the prevalence of red morph over gray
morph increases, as in MN.

Guillion and Marshall (1968) showed that during years when snow cover
was deficient in their study area west of Duluth, red morph birds sustained
proportionally greater loss than gray morphs, but when conditions for
burrow-roosting in snow occurred, red morphs survived as well as the gray.

Gray morphs are essentially birds of the coniferous forests, and red morphs of the southern hardwoods. Color of substrate and snow depth in winter appear to be strong selective agents.
Stephen W. Eaton and Kenneth C. Parkes

Greater Prairie-Chicken *Tympanuchus cupido cupido*

Range Nearctic, locally, in much reduced numbers, in central United States and the coastal plains of Texas. Formerly ranged widely from southern Canada east to Massachusetts and south to eastern Texas, southwestern Louisiana and the central sections of the eastern United States. In the east, after 1835 confined to the island of Martha's Vineyard, Massachusetts, where last reported in 1932.

Status Extirpated (eastern subspecies *cupido* only); formerly a local resident.

Occurrence The nominate subspecies, *cupido*, known as the Heath Hen, was found along the coastal plain from MA to VA and locally inland to eastern PA (Pocono Plateau). It occurred also on Martha's Vineyard, where it was last reported in 1932. In NY this bird was common in the more open scrub oak and pine barrens of eastern and central LI, locally west to the Hempstead Plains. It possibly occurred in similar habitat on the scrub sand plains west of Albany, but definite evidence is lacking. The Heath Hen *(T. c. cupido)* apparently was last reported on LI about 1835, but no known NY specimen exists with data.

Remarks Very little is known of this bird's disappearance within our area; its ultimate extirpation was perhaps due to extensive shooting and fire. Although it undoubtedly bred in the state, there are no nests or eggs in any museum collection, nor does the literature make any mention of nesting. (See also From Glaciers to Global Warming: Extinct Species.)
Stanley R. Lincoln

Wild Turkey *Meleagris gallopavo*

Range Southern Nearctic and northern Neotropical, the subspecies *silvestris* resident in the eastern United States from New York and New England generally south and west to Florida, the Gulf states, and central Texas.

Status An American original and game bird of extraordinary tenacity. Common to very common resident across the Appalachian Plateau, fairly common elsewhere except in highly agricultural or urbanized areas, and in the Central Adirondacks, where rare or uncommon.

Breeding Found in forested areas of the state, the strongest populations are where forest cover is over 50%, in northern hardwoods, oak–northern hardwoods, hemlock–northern hardwoods, and where human populations are thinly distributed. Birds can use open areas for brood range, where poults can find abundant insects, and areas where the forest is invading open areas with shrubs, which supply fruits such as hawthorn. To supply the energy for continued growth in the fall and to fatten up for the winter, they need the mast produced by the hardwoods, such as acorns and beechnuts. These conditions are best met on the Appalachian Plateau, where mast is abundant and snow in winter is not too deep for travel. The Central Adirondacks and Tug Hill will probably never develop sustainable populations because of the lack of sufficient mast and long winters with deep snows.

Wild Turkeys nest on the ground, often at the base of a tree or in a brush pile adjacent to a woods road or small opening. The hens remain with the poults through the summer and fall. In late fall to early winter, when toms become heavier than hens, they usually leave the flock and unite with other young toms to form a tom flock. The hen and female poults remain together through the winter and in Mar disband to start new social groups. At this time young hens may travel up to 30 mi or more, seeking a new social group (Eaton et al. 1976). This establishment of new social groups has led to movement into unoccupied range.

Near extirpation by the mid-1800s, it was found only in the counties of Sullivan, Rockland, Orange, Allegany, and Cattaraugus (DeKay 1844). Not long after 1844, it disappeared from NY (Eaton 1910) but persisted in south-central PA. From this residual stock, it began to spread north about 1938 without the benefit of game farm stocking. By the late 1940s it became established in the hemlock hardwoods of the high plateau of Potter and McKean counties in PA (Wunz 1973). What started the resurgence is not completely understood, but the reversion of farmland to forest was probably the most important factor, in addition to the recovery of the forests from excessive lumbering and a lessening of hunting during World War II. From north-central PA it spilled over into Allegany and Cattaraugus counties (Eaton 1953; Evans 1983). Although game-farm releases were attempted in the 1950s, none of these added to the increasing population. A new technique, not unlike hacking, was established whereby a hen and her hen poults, and a yearling or older tom, were cannon-netted during the winter and transplanted to suitable unoccupied range. From 1959 to the mid-1980s this management effort helped reestablish the bird throughout the state. NYSDEC also sent this stock to all New England states, NJ, and ON, where they have also been reestablished.

Populations in 1974 and at the time of the Atlas project were still expanding into new range, on their own and by NYSDEC transplants. Found in 1567 Atlas blocks and Confirmed in 46% of those, they have continued to expand their range. By the mid-1990s they had bred within sight of LI Sound in Westchester Co., were wandering through suburban back-yards, and were even being seen in the Bronx (B. Lincoln, pers. comm.). From virtual extirpation to game bird in 1959 they have continued to prosper, as evidenced by relaxed hunting regulations. In 1995 two bearded turkeys (one a day) could be taken 1–31 May in all of NY north of the Bronx-Westchester county boundary. In fall season two turkeys of either sex may be taken in eastern NY and one on the western and east-central Appalachian Plateau, St. Lawrence Plains, and Adirondack foothills (NYSDEC 1994–1995).

Remarks The Spanish first introduced the turkey from America into Europe in the early 1500s. From Spain it spread rapidly as a domestic fowl throughout Europe, but knowledge of its place of origin did not. In the Middle Ages nearly everything exotic was obtained in or through Turkish, or Arabian, territories. Even our corn is still known in the Near East and India as Turkey wheat. There is little doubt that our bird derived its name from the country Turkey (Schorger 1966).
Stephen W. Eaton

NEW WORLD QUAIL—ODONTOPHORIDAE

Northern Bobwhite   *Colinus virginianus*

Range Southern Nearctic and northern Neotropical east of the Rocky Mountains, resident from Wyoming, the Dakotas, and extreme southern Canada south through eastern and central United States, and through Middle America to Guatemala. Also introduced and established in western states.

Status Uncommon and declining resident on LI; rare to very rare elsewhere.

Breeding The twentieth-century history of this well-known bird has been characterized by an almost continuous concern over its disappearance from NY. In 1910, Eaton considered it to be well distributed as far north as Jefferson, Oneida, Saratoga, and Washington counties. In the 1940s, Bronx-Westchester CBCs were still listing one to four dozen birds, but fewer were being found from upper Westchester Co. north (Cruickshank 1942). Bull (1964 and 1974) described it as "greatly decreased in recent years," and the Atlas suggested that the relatively few records north of LI were "probably traceable to the releases of quail raised in captivity." Hunting, changes in farming practices, the decline of agriculture, loss of habitat, severe winters, and the introduction of poorly adapted non-native stock are some of the commonly listed causes for the decline of a species that is at or near the northern edge of its range in NY. The LI population, always the most substantial in the state, has also decreased, due to the loss of woodland, oldfield, and hedgerows, which provide suitable feeding and nesting habitat.

It should be noted that the NYSDEC raised bobwhites on LI for release locally and throughout the state until the 1960s and that subsequent releases have been made by hunters and game clubs in many areas, including the CBC circles on LI. It is thought that few of these birds survive to the spring.

Nonbreeding This entirely sedentary species is found year-round in suitable territory. A few birds are reported annually from Westchester Co., the Hudson Valley, and along the Appalachian Plateau, but the only remaining viable population in the state is on LI, where the species has been in decline since the 1970s. The highest numbers have been regularly recorded on the Central Suffolk Co. CBCs from their initiation in 1953 to the present. These show both the typical population cycles and the overall downward trend of the past two decades. The same count circle has been used since 1975 for a mid-May census, which shows similar trends but with less-steep declines. Because CBCs depend on observers' being able to find winter coveys, the results may be more erratic than in the spring, when singing birds can be heard over long distances. Both May and Dec population surveys may be inflated by the release of game-farm birds.

Remarks (By K. C. Parkes) Aldrich (1946, Auk 63:493) reviewed the U.S. subspecies. Within the range traditionally attributed to *virginianus* (type locality Charleston, SC), he recognized three forms: an interior subspecies, *mexicanus* (type locality Louisiana), a southeastern (the nominate) subspecies, and the "Old New England Bobwhite," *marilandicus* (type locality "New England"). Two of these are ascribed to NY, *mexicanus* coming in from the west along the Great Lakes and *marilandicus* up the Hudson Valley, a pattern with precedent in other species. A series of nineteenth-century specimens from LI in the CMNH matches equally old specimens from MA and CT, and there is no doubt that the "Old New England Bobwhite" was valid. The characters supposedly distinguishing *mexicanus* from *virginianus* are subtler, and the two might well be lumped. In any case, there have been so many introductions and translocations over the years that the populations within the original ranges are now heterogeneous. While recognizing that two subspecies originally inhabited NY, it would be best now to list the species as a binomial, *Colinus virginianus* subsp.

Eric Salzman and Kenneth C. Parkes

RAILS, GALLINULES,
AND COOTS—RALLIDAE

Yellow Rail *Coturnicops noveboracensis*

Range Nearctic, breeding very locally in eastern Alberta and Mackenzie, sporadically east to New Brunswick and Maine, rarely and very locally to northeastern Ohio. Winters mainly in the Gulf states and Florida, exceptionally north along the coast to Long Island and Rhode Island (specimens).

Status Rare but probably regular fall migrant, undoubtedly overlooked, and very rare spring migrant. Casual winter visitant.

Occurrence A very elusive and secretive creature skulking in grassy meadows and marshes, occasionally in upland fields. Most observers have never seen one alive, and the vast majority of NY records are based on specimens taken primarily during the fall hunting season, usually with the aid of trained "rail" dogs. For details of sightings in coastal marshes see Bull 1964. With the decrease in the hunting of shorebirds and rails, this source of specimens and observations has declined. Tower kills accounted for three of the four specimens added in the past 20 years, and luck for the bulk of the eight sightings. More than half of the 50 or so specimens taken are extant. The majority of these are in the AMNH collection and are from LI. At least half were taken in Sep and Oct, the period of principal occurrence. In contrast, there are only eight spring specimens, fewer yet preserved.

During their nocturnal migrations, rails sometimes become stranded in cities, and the Yellow Rail is no exception. The two most recent instances were: a bird found in an alley by window shoppers in New Rochelle, Westchester Co., 14 Oct 1984, released later that day at Marshlands Conservancy in Rye (KB 35:67), and one found dead in a driveway in Lisbon, St. Lawrence Co. 30 Sep 1985, specimen at St. Lawrence University (KB 36:37). Bull (1974) cited two other instances.

On the basis of specimens, the usual migration dates seem to be Apr–mid-May and late Aug–Dec.

The only spring record, accepted by NYSARC, of the past 20 years was a bird flushed in Knox, Albany Co. 15 May 1984 (NYSARC 1985). A specimen taken at Braddock Bay, Monroe Co. "June" 1880 is NYSM specimen 283. An exceptionally early individual was flushed from the marshes at the mouth of Crooked Creek, St. Lawrence Co. 11 Aug 1936.

There are four winter specimens, all from LI. In the AMNH collection: Sayville 17 Jan 1894; Seaford 10 Jan 1909; Islip 22 Feb 1929. In the NYSM collection: Orient 1 Jan 1956. An early winter sight record was added on 17 Dec 1995 by K. Feustel and S. Feustel at Oak Beach Marsh, Suffolk Co. (KB 46:186).

Remarks It is significant that breeding bird atlas work in nearby MI (Walkinshaw 1991) and ON (Prescott 1987), within the prime breeding range for this species, produced relatively few records, fewer yet of confirmed breeding. It is truly an elusive species whose real status remains very little known in NY and elsewhere. No proof of breeding in NY exists. The most tantalizing hints are the citation from *The Auk* (79:698) mentioned by Bull, referring to a possible nest found by Dr. Allen in the Cayuga L. marshes near Ithaca, Tompkins Co. in the 1950s, although no evidence was ever presented. Very recently there was a report of a bird heard calling in appropriate habitat in the Town of Lisbon, St. Lawrence Co. on 2 Jul 1995 by Buckley (KB 45:309). The latter is of particular interest owing to recent breeding records from the Ottawa, ON area less than 100 miles to the north, but NY awaits something more substantial. Robert G. Spahn

Black Rail *Laterallus jamaicensis*

Range Nearctic and Neotropical, breeding locally in California, in midwestern United States from Kansas to northwestern Ohio, and along the Atlantic Coast from Long Island to Florida; also in western South America. Winters along the Gulf Coast from southeastern Texas to Florida.

Status Very rare and local breeder, known only along the South Shore of LI and in coastal Westchester Co. Casual on the coast in winter. Accidental in the Cayuga L. basin.

Breeding Breeding has been documented only three times. A nest with eight eggs was found at Oak Beach, Suffolk Co. 20 Jun 1937, and fledged young were observed on 27 Jun. On 30 Jun 1937, four young were banded at Long Beach, Nassau Co. A nest with nine eggs at Lido Beach, Nassau Co. was found on 12 Jul 1940. In the years since the species was "rediscovered" at Oak Beach in 1968 (Post and Enders 1969), birds have been reported during about half the breeding seasons. The unditched *Spartina alterniflora* marsh there remains the most consistent locality, but summer birds have been reported from Middle Line I., Nassau Co. (KB 40:278), marshes on the south shore of Suffolk Co. (KB 42:203), Oceanside Preserve, Nassau Co., and Cedar Beach, Suffolk Co. (KB 42:281). From three to five pairs were believed breeding at Oak Beach, 1968–1971, and four individuals were reported calling at Cupsoque County Park (Moriches Inlet), Suffolk Co. 28 Jul 1991 (KB 41:289).

The only accepted record off LI is of one bird in salt marsh at Marshlands Conservancy, Rye, Westchester Co. 9 Jun 1986, which remained for several days (Burke) (NYSARC 1987).

The largest numbers ever seen were at Moriches Inlet, Suffolk Co., where ten were flushed in less than an hour 9 Sep 1939, and six were seen on 12 Sep 1953 (Bull 1964). Breeding birds are vulnerable to disturbance by birders, especially by the playing of taped calls.

Nonbreeding The very few records outside the breeding season are almost all from LI. Since 1974 there have been only four coastal records outside the period May–Sep: one, JBMR 16 Oct 1990 (KB 41:66); the others were at John F. Kennedy Wildlife Sanctuary, Tobay, Nassau Co., one on 2 Dec 1991 (KB 41:133), two on 11 Dec 1983 (KB 34:141), and one on 6 Jan 1985 (KB 35:154). The winter records, which are remarkable given the difficulty of detecting the species when it is not calling, suggest that at least some individuals may be resident.

Also remarkable are two sight records from Tompkins Co.: one, 27 Apr 1971 near Ithaca Airport (Mai et al.) (KB 21:154); one, 6 Oct 1996, Dryden (Howard, submitted to NYSARC).

Nineteenth-century specimens from Yates, Schuyler, and Monroe counties are no longer extant. These and a number of unsubstantiated sight records away from LI were rejected by Bull (1974).

This is currently listed by the NYSDEC as a Species of Special Concern but has been recommended for upgrading to an Endangered species.

Extreme dates: 19 Apr and 6 Jan.

Kenneth P. Able

Corn Crake   *Crex crex*

Range Palearctic. Winters south to central and southern Africa. Vagrant in Greenland. Has wandered to Bermuda and along the east coast of North America south to Maryland.

Status Formerly casual vagrant, accidental in twentieth century.

Occurrence There are six specimen records, five from the late nineteenth century, and all but one from LI: (1) LI, no locality or date, AMNH 12537; (2) Oakdale, Suffolk Co. 2 Nov 1880, AMNH 64959, "shot in heavy cover at the foot of the uplands where they join the meadows"; (3) near Cohoes, Albany Co. 5 Nov 1883, NYSM 463, "collected in a cabbage field along the Mohawk River"; (4) Amagansett, Suffolk Co. 18 Aug 1885, AMNH 64858, "shot on dry uplands with Meadowlarks"; (5) Montauk, 1 Nov 1888, AMNH 64860, "secured about three miles west of the Point in the meadow while shooting quail"; (6) Orient, Suffolk Co. 2 Nov 1963, NYSM 24890, "shot in a field of young rye 200 yards from salt marsh." Note that four of the specimens were taken during the first week of Nov and that four were taken within a nine-year period (1880–1888). The 1963 record was the first in 75 years. No sight report has been confirmed.

Remarks The Corn Crake is primarily a bird of grasslands. In Europe it has decreased markedly in the past 70 years, particularly in the British Isles and to a lesser extent on the continent. According to Witherby et al. (1941) and

Norris (1947), this decrease is due chiefly to present-day methods of mowing by machine and mowing earlier in the season, when the birds are nesting. In the few areas where mowing is still done by hand, the species is reported as flourishing. Leck (1984) mentioned two old (1854 and 1905) NJ records and a 1965 single-observer sight record from Brigantine NWR. Zeranski and Baptist (1990) mentioned specimens from CT in 1887, 1925, and 1943.
Stanley R. Lincoln

Clapper Rail *Rallus longirostris*

Range Nearctic and Neotropical, breeding on the Pacific Coast from California to Peru, and on the Atlantic and Gulf coasts from Massachusetts to southern Florida and southern Texas; also in the West Indies, Mexico, and south to Brazil. Sedentary and migratory, winters regularly north to New York and Massachusetts.

Status Fairly common breeder restricted to coastal marshes. Rare and local on LI, SI, and Bronx and Westchester counties. Uncommon winter resident.

Breeding Most numerous in salt marshes along the South Shore of LI west of Great South Bay. Numbers declined during the 1970s and have not recovered to former levels. In 1965, nearly 200 nests were found in Town of Hempstead wetlands, southern Nassau Co. (MacNamara and Udell 1970). In 1979, Zarudsky (KB 29:240) recorded only nine pairs breeding on three islands in Hempstead Bay. The decline in numbers and contraction of range may be due to continued loss of salt marsh, effects of Hurricane Belle in 1976, and mortality during successive hard winters in the late 1970s (Atlas 1988).

In Westchester Co., from one to five have been present during the breeding season in recent years at Marshlands Conservancy, Rye. Three adults and 10 young were seen there 20 Jul 1992 (KB 42:276). On SI, where the species was thought extirpated (Atlas 1988), three nesting pairs with fledglings were observed at Saw Mill Creek during summer 1992 (KB 42:278). A pair breeding along the Hudson R. at Piermont, Rockland Co. in 1959 constitutes the farthest known inland breeding report.

Nonbreeding Regularly recorded in small numbers on LI CBCs, where the highest counts were 18 on the Smithtown CBC in 1974 and 12 on the Southern Nassau Co. CBC in 1975. Totals for all LI CBCs have reached 45 (1974), but since 1978 have been much lower. Very rarely recorded away from salt water. There are reports from Central Park, Manhattan (including a specimen, 17 Oct 1888), Prospect Park, Brooklyn, and along the Hudson

R. at Ossining, Westchester Co. (specimen no longer extant). A reported record from central NY (AOU 1983) is apparently in error.

Remarks See remarks under King Rail.
Kenneth P. Able

King Rail *Rallus elegans*

Range Nearctic and northern Neotropical, breeding in North America in lowlands from the Great Lakes, New York, and Massachusetts south to Texas and Florida; also in Mexico and Cuba. Winters nearly throughout, but rare in the northern portions. Sedentary and migratory.

Status Very rare and local breeder in fresh and brackish marshes south of the Adirondacks. Very rare in winter, perhaps resident.

Breeding During the past 30 years, the King Rail has declined alarmingly, especially in the northern part of its range (Meanley 1992). NY, at the northern periphery of its breeding range, has witnessed this decline. In recent years, the species has been reported two to three times a year during the breeding season from a very few scattered localities across the state south of the Adirondacks. Although surely nesting annually, its breeding has not been confirmed in many years. It is most frequently reported from extensive marshes in western NY (e.g., INWR, the Rochester area), and from southeastern NY (Putnam, Dutchess, and Westchester counties). It formerly bred at several localities on LI, but the only coastal records in recent years are from Rye, Westchester Co. (KB 42:274, 43:265). It is probably overlooked.

Nonbreeding For so rare and secretive a species, it is reported with surprising frequency in winter. Most records are from coastal areas, where specimens are taken in muskrat traps set in salt marsh. One to two individuals were reported from CBCs in the lower Hudson Valley and LI in 11 of 30 years, 1960–1989. Much less frequently reported upstate in winter. Bull (1974) listed three winter specimens from central and western NY, and one was reported from MNWR, 31 Dec 1979 (KB 30:111).

Remarks This species has been recommended for inclusion on the NYSDEC's list of Threatened species. It is very closely related to the Clapper Rail and is considered by some to be conspecific (Ripley 1977). Mixed pairs have been observed along the Atlantic and Gulf coasts (Meanley 1992). They are similar in appearance, and their vocalizations are virtually identical, rendering field identification, especially by voice, difficult. Clapper Rails are casual at inland localities (AOU 1983). Thus, records away from coastal areas cannot arbitrarily be assumed to be King Rails.

Confusion with calls of other species (e.g., Virginia Rail) is also possible, and all records should be carefully documented.
Kenneth P. Able

Virginia Rail *Rallus limicola*

Range Nearctic and Neotropical, breeding locally from southern British Columbia and Nova Scotia south to California and North Carolina; also in central Mexico and northwestern South America. In eastern United States winters on the Gulf Coast and from Florida north to Massachusetts (rarely).

Status Fairly common breeder and migrant throughout, except at higher elevations. Rare but regular in winter on the coast, very rare inland.

Breeding The most widespread and numerous rail in NY, it can be found nesting in freshwater and coastal salt marshes in all parts of the state except the higher mountains. Although it is believed to have decreased in abundance since the 1940s (Zimmerman 1977), the Atlas project found it in 9% of all blocks. Centers of abundance are in the vast marshes of the OOWMA-INWR complex, MNWR, where refuge personnel counted 150 in 1973 (KB 24:20), and the St. Lawrence Valley, but it can be found nesting in even quite small wetlands. On LI it seems largely confined to unditched salt marshes of *Spartina alterniflora* (Post and Enders 1970). The last known concentration there was at Oak Beach, Suffolk Co., where 9–11 pairs were found in 1974 (KB 25:61).

Nonbreeding Its average spring arrival date is 20 Apr, but it may arrive as early as mid-Mar in southern, central, and western NY. In northern areas, it may not arrive until early to mid-May.

 Spring maxima: 8 Round Pond, Monroe Co. 17 May 1959. *Fall maxima:* 9 Skaneateles, Onondaga Co. 8 Sep 1957; 7 Mecox and Shinnecock bays, Suffolk Co. 7 Sep 1929.

 It is regular in winter in the lower Hudson Valley and along the coast, with CBC maxima of 13 at Montauk (1988), and 8 on the Central Suffolk (1977) and Lower Hudson (1972) CBCs. Elsewhere, single birds are recorded on an upstate CBC in about 40% of years, most frequently in the Rochester area. Records in late winter through early spring indicate that overwintering may be successful upstate (e.g., Mendon Ponds, Monroe Co., a regular wintering locale) in some years (KB 29:91; 30:108; 41:107). Winter mortality has been recorded on several occasions, however. Latham found six dead or dying in Orient, Suffolk Co. 21 Dec 1919–1 Feb 1920. On 8 Jan 1972 near Phoenix, Oswego Co., one live and five dead rails were found huddled together (KB 22:96).

Remarks Good estimates of populations of rails and other marsh birds are badly needed. The Virginia Rail is currently classified as a game bird with an open season from 1 Sep to 9 Nov, and a bag limit of 25 birds per day. (Rail hunting is not permitted on LI or in coastal Westchester Co.) Accurate harvest figures for the state are not available. In the face of continuing habitat losses and uncertain population figures, the status of Virginia Rail as a game species should probably be reassessed.
Kenneth P. Able

Sora

Porzana carolina

Range Nearctic, breeding from British Columbia east to Nova Scotia and south to California and southwestern United States, but in the east only as far south as Maryland. Winters from southeastern United States to northern South America, rarely north to New York and New England.

Status Uncommon migrant and breeder except on LI, where very rare and irregular. Very rare in winter. Formerly more numerous.

Breeding Although Eaton (1910) described the Sora as the most abundant rail in NY, it is now much less widespread and numerous than the Virginia Rail. During this century, it has declined dramatically throughout the Northeast (Odom 1977), apparently because of the progressive loss of the extensive cattail marshes that it favors. The Atlas recorded it in 5% of all blocks. It is most numerous in the OOWMA-INWR complex and on wildlife management areas on the St. Lawrence Plains (Atlas 1988). A rail census at MNWR in 1973 recorded 40 Soras (versus 150 Virginia Rails.) On LI, Soras nest very locally and irregularly in salt marsh. Bull (1974) listed six historical breeding sites, but the species had not been documented breeding since 1935. The Atlas Confirmed breeding at Oak Beach, Suffolk Co. and recorded Possible breeding at another location on the South Shore;

Possible breeding was noted on SI. At Oak Beach, three nests were found in 1980 (Greenlaw and Miller 1982). At least one was also present in 1979, but almost daily work in the marsh did not reveal the species in 1977, 1978, or 1981.

Nonbreeding Average spring arrival date is 26 Apr, ranging from 11 Apr in the west to 9 May in the north. In fall, Soras stage in very large numbers before migration. An estimated 1000 were on the Storage Pool at MNWR in Oct 1971 (KB 22:34). Such numbers are extraordinary today, but in the nineteenth century hundreds might be shot in a day during autumn.

Fall maxima: 1000 (estimated) MNWR, Oct 1971; 7 shot, 20 more flushed in salt marsh near Lattingtown, Nassau Co. 14 Sep 1953; 12 Buck Pond, Monroe Co. 24 Oct 1953.

In winter they are recorded most regularly in the lower Hudson Valley and coastal sections. Usually one or two individuals are noted on CBCs in about half the years. It is much less frequent upstate but has successfully overwintered at Mendon Ponds, Monroe Co., where it is fairly regular (KB 30:108, 42:96, 43:125). Near Phoenix, Oswego Co., one was found dead and one alive on 8 Jan 1972 (KB 22:96).

Remarks See remarks under Virginia Rail. The status, except for the known declining populations of the Sora, and situation are identical for the two species.
Kenneth P. Able

Purple Gallinule   *Porphyrula martinica*

Range Nearctic and Neotropical, breeding in eastern North America primarily in lowlands from Maryland and Delaware south to Florida, the Gulf states, and Texas; also locally in interior areas. Winters from southern Florida, the Gulf states, and southern Texas south through Middle America.

Status Very rare vagrant.

Occurrence Bull (1974) reported more than two dozen records, at least ten of them specimens, and Bull (1976) recorded an additional specimen of an adult found dead 15 Jun 1967 at Orient, Suffolk Co. (Latham). Spencer (1982) summarized 30 NY records through 1980; only five were away from LI (Broome, Monroe, Westchester, and Wyoming counties and the "Montezuma Marshes"), and only three were immatures. Since 1980 there have been five additional records, including the first two winter occurrences: (1) adult, Montauk 17 Jul 1981 (Spencer) (KB 31:266); (2) adult, Prospect Park, Kings Co. 6–9 May 1983 (KB 33:226); (3) adult, Prospect Park 11 May 1985 (Wade) (KB 35:216); (4) age not reported, Greenpoint, Kings Co. 26–27 Jan 1987 (KB 37:98); (5) immature, "Chinatown" Manhattan 31 Dec 1991 AMNH 827877 (Cormons 1992).

Extreme dates: 4 Apr and 27 Jan. Most records are in Apr and May.
Joseph DiCostanzo

Azure Gallinule   *Porphyrula flavirostris*

Range   Neotropical lowlands of South America east of the Andes.

Status   Accidental.

Occurrence   One record of an adult male, found dead in a backyard adjacent to a marsh in Ft. Salonga, Suffolk Co. on 14 Dec 1986 (Wright). The bird was identified as this species at the Theodore Roosevelt Sanctuary (Spencer and Kolodnicki) (AB 42:25) and confirmed as such at the AMNH, where the skin is deposited as AMNH 817820. The specimen was noted by Dickerman as being "in good flesh—very little fat" and appeared to have none of the typical marks of a caged bird such as abnormal feather wear or overgrown nails. On the strength of this and other evidence the record was accepted by NYSARC (1988) and the AOU (1991).

Remarks   This record will be revisited by the AOU and ABA checklist committees. If withdrawn by the AOU because of doubtful origin, it will also be deleted from the New York State checklist.

   This is the only record for this species north of Trinidad and northern South America. A comprehensive discussion of patterns of vagrancy in the rallids, and this species in particular, by Remsen and Parker (1990) concluded that "the New York specimen should be regarded as a valid record of a wild bird until proven otherwise." Several small puncture marks in the bird's breast indicated that it may have been killed by a cat, a catastrophe perhaps as disastrous as habitat loss everywhere.
Thomas A. Burke

Common Moorhen   *Gallinula chloropus*

Range   Cosmopolitan, breeding in eastern North America from extreme southern Canada and northern New England south to Texas and Florida. Sedentary and migratory, wintering north to New York and southern New England.

Status   Local, but declining, breeder, at lower elevations. Fairly common but local migrant; rare but regular in winter on the coast.

Breeding   It breeds in lower elevation freshwater marshes throughout the state but is virtually absent above 1000 ft in elevation. It prefers marshes with an abundance of cattail and other emergent vegetation but requires some nearby open water. Less abundant and widespread than formerly because of habitat loss due to draining of marshes or other local changes.

At MNWR, one of its upstate strongholds, from the 1950s to the mid-1970s up to 100 pairs nested, but by the early 1980s numbers were "down drastically" (KB 33:54), and by 1986 none nested (Atlas 1988). MNWR staff considered the replacement of cattails by purple loosestrife and the destruction of nearby habitat possible factors. Apparently owing to the increasing brackishness of the ponds, by 1995 it no longer bred at JBWR, formerly one of its coastal strongholds (Riepe) (NASFN 49:912).

Nonbreeding Usually arrives in mid-Apr and departs by mid-Nov. Because of its fondness for thick marsh vegetation, it may be more common than the number of sightings indicates. Rare in winter but reported almost annually on the South Shore of LI. Even rarer upstate in winter, but there are a few records: 5 on the Genesee R., near Rochester, Monroe Co. 31 Dec 1967; 2 Buffalo, Erie Co. 5–21 Jan 1947; 1 Pleasant Valley, Dutchess Co. 1 Dec 1974–29 Jan 1975 (KB 25:111) was a first winter record for that county; singles at Irondequoit Bay 2 Jan 1993 and Mendon Ponds 10 Jan 1993, both Monroe Co. (KB 43:125).

Remarks Also declining as a breeder in MA (Veit and Petersen 1993). Listed as Threatened in CT (Bevier 1994).
Joseph DiCostanzo

American Coot   *Fulica americana*

Range Nearctic and Neotropical, breeding locally throughout much of North America from Alaska and southern Canada south to the Gulf Coast, southern Florida, the West Indies, and Middle America. Winters north to the Canadian border.

Status Rare to common, but local, breeder in the central and western portions, rare on the coast. Common to locally abundant fall migrant, occasionally very abundant; less numerous in winter along the coast, rare inland.

Breeding Nesting in freshwater habitats at elevations below 1000 ft throughout the state, but absent from the Hudson Valley, it is less widespread than Common Moorhen, which occurs in the same habitat. The two main breeding locations upstate are the TWMA-INWR-OOWMA complex and MNWR (Atlas 1988). There was no Confirmed breeding at Chautauqua L., Chautauqua Co. despite the large numbers that sometimes appear there in the fall. On the coast, it was formerly a common breeder at JBWR but was gone from there by 1986, apparently because of the increasing brackishness of the ponds (Atlas 1988).

Nonbreeding Much more aquatic than other members of the Rallidae, coots are often observed on open water with various species of ducks.

Coastal maxima: 2300 Water Mill, Suffolk Co. 8 Nov 1948; 750 Mecox Bay, Suffolk Co. 12 Jan 1957. *Inland maxima:* 6500 MNWR 15 Oct 1967; 4900 Chautauqua L. 16 Dec 1975. Numbers such as these have not been recorded in recent years.

Remarks Coot has declined as a breeder in NJ (Leck 1984), is a rare breeder in MA (Veit and Petersen 1993), and has not nested in CT in decades (Zeranski and Baptist 1990).
Joseph DiCostanzo

CRANES—GRUIDAE

Sandhill Crane *Grus canadensis*

Range Holarctic, breeding from northeastern Siberia east to Baffin Island and south, locally, in western North America to southern Colorado, and in the east to southeastern Michigan; also resident in extreme southeastern United States and Cuba. Winters north to the southern portions of California and Texas, occasionally farther. Wanders east to the Atlantic Coast from Prince Edward Island to South Carolina.

Status A rare but increasingly regular visitant.

Occurrence Bull (1974, 1976) listed only 15 occurrences, all single birds, 13 upstate and two downstate. They occurred in six months of the year: three in Apr, four in May, two in Jun, two in Jul, one in Oct, three in Nov. Of four specimens, only one was extant: a male illegally shot at MNWR 13 Nov 1968 CUM 33179. Sightings were sparse in the 1970s. In the 1980s, NYSARC submissions with good photographic evidence became available. The locations of many of those observations were at hawkwatches and other sites where observers were present many days of the year, such as along the Great Lakes shorelines and large inland wetland units managed for waterfowl in the western part of the state. Others were associated with major river systems such as the Susquehanna, Allegheny, Hudson, Black, and St. Lawrence. A few were at rather unexpected locations such as Blue Mtn. L., Hamilton Co. 21 Jun 1986, for a first record for that county and the Adirondack Park (KB 36:232), and Mt. Sinai, Suffolk Co. where an adult and immature were seen 17–30 Nov 1985 (KB 36:49).

There are now more than 15 new NYSARC records, along with many other sightings. Most of those were in Mar–Apr or Oct–Nov, the peak migration periods. Summer and winter records are: two adults courtship dancing in a corn field near Frewsburg, Chautauqua Co. 15–18 Jun 1982 (Leichner, MacIssac) (KB 32:267); one, MNWR 25 Aug 1982 (Dewey) (KB 32:276); two, INWR 15–22 Dec 1988 (KB 39:108); one, King Ferry,

Cayuga Co. 19–22 Jan 1993 (KB 43:128). One, presumably wild, was with a Common Crane *(G. grus)*, a known escape, 2 Jul–5 Aug 1993 near Lowville, Lewis Co. (KB 43:330), dancing and bugling (R. Henrickson and B. Hughes, pers. comm.).

Maxima: 6 flying in formation Braddock Bay, Monroe Co. 30 Mar 1994.

Remarks The MNWR specimen of 1968 was identified by Archibald as *tabida*, the "Greater" Sandhill Crane, which winters in central FL and southern GA. It is assumed that the nominate form *canadensis* represents the balance of the records. Reports in adjacent states and provinces indicate an increase in sightings, with many recent reports in MA, VT, CT, NJ, PA, ON, and PQ. In extreme western PA, the first breeding in the state produced one young 3 Aug 1993; the birds remained until Nov (AB 48:109). Adults were in the same vicinity in the summer of 1994, with no indication of nesting or young (NASFN 48:943).
Lee B. Chamberlaine

PLOVERS AND LAPWINGS—CHARADRIIDAE

Northern Lapwing *Vanellus vanellus*

Range Palearctic, wintering in the western portion of its range from the British Isles to northern Africa. Wanders to Greenland and Baffin Island, south to the Bahamas and Barbados.

Status Casual vagrant.

Occurrence Bull's (1974) details of the previous records were: (1) a specimen taken at Merrick, Nassau Co. 27 Dec 1883 is apparently not extant; (2) another specimen collected on Mecox Bay, Suffolk Co. late fall 1905 is a mount in a private collection; (3) one seen near Montauk, Suffolk Co. 3–18 Dec 1966, photos on file, AMNH collection (Davis and Trimble 1967).

There are two additional occurrences, the first upstate record and an additional LI record. One was found on a residential lawn with Killdeer in the Town of New Scotland, Albany Co. 22 Mar 1991 (Boehm, Beale). A photo of this individual appeared in AB 45:510. One was observed in fields east of Mecox Bay, Southhampton, Suffolk Co. 28 Jan–25 Mar 1995 (Buhl, Ednie, ph) (AB 49:132; KB 45:145).

Remarks An examination of the literature of bordering states revealed only one additional record, a specimen collected 20 Nov 1932 on Block I., RI (Conway 1992).
Ken Feustel

Black-bellied Plover *Pluvialis squatarola*

Range Nearctic and eastern Palearctic, breeding in the high Arctic south to the Yukon River and islands in northern Hudson Bay. Winters, in eastern North America, along the Gulf and Atlantic coasts north to Long Island, more rarely to Massachusetts, and south to Argentina and Chile.

Status Very common to abundant coastal migrant, occasionally more numerous; much less numerous inland in fall, even rarer in spring. Regular and locally common in winter on the outer coast, where it is also a regular summering nonbreeder.

Occurrence It occurs in large numbers on the extensive mudflats along the South Shore of LI, especially at the western end. It is most numerous in spring, when the flight is concentrated in May, and occurs in smaller flocks in fall, when migration is more protracted, Aug–Nov. Inland this species is reported most frequently on the beaches and flats of L. Ontario, May–Nov but especially during Oct. It is apparently much less common in spring in the interior.

Coastal maxima: Spring: 6000 Hewlett-Oceanside marshes, Nassau Co. 30 May 1954; 1200 JBWR 17 May 1939. *Fall:* all JBWR: 1203, 18 Aug 1983; 1193, 31 Aug 1988; 1159, 4 Sep 1987. *Winter:* all Southern Nassau Co. CBC: 547, 29 Dec 1991; 304, 30 Dec 1985; 290, 4 Jan 1987. *Inland maxima: Spring:* 22 Sandy Pond, Oswego Co. 4 Jun 1961. *Fall:* all Monroe Co.: 100 Summerville 27 Aug 1955; 75 Shore Acres 2 Oct 1966; 50 Salmon Creek 10 Oct 1959.
Ken Feustel

American Golden-Plover *Pluvialis dominica*

Range Nearctic, breeding across northern Alaska and arctic Canada east to northern Baffin Island and south to northwestern British Columbia, northern Ontario, and southern Baffin Island. Winters on the pampas of temperate South America.

Status Uncommon to fairly common fall migrant throughout the state, much less numerous in spring in most areas, with the occasional exception of the L. Ontario area; decidedly rare downstate in spring.

Occurrence Historically, it was an abundant migrant in northeastern North America, particularly in the fall, when gunners took thousands from NY's coastal meadows and fields. By the 1890s it had become quite rare, and only in the past five decades has it been seen in healthy numbers in the Northeast. It prefers short grass areas to the mudflats favored by its close relative, the Black-bellied Plover. Plowed fields, airports, golf courses, salt meadows, and dry dredge-spoil areas are most attractive to fall migrants, which sometimes number in the hundreds, particularly after strong winds from the east and southeast, in typical stopover locations such as the eastern end of LI or on the Great Lakes Plain.

Coastal maxima: Spring: 9 JBWR 23 Apr 1957; 6 Sagaponack, Suffolk Co. 17 May 1948. *Fall:* both Suffolk Co.: 300 Sagaponack 16 Sep 1973; 200 East Hampton 16 Sep 1944 (after a hurricane). *Inland maxima: Spring:* all Monroe Co.: 210 L. Ontario shore 1 May 1954; 100 Braddock Bay 21 Apr 1954. *Fall:* 500 Batavia, Genesee Co. 11 Oct 1970; 500 Hamptonburgh, Orange Co. 17 Oct 1970; 360 Syracuse Airport, Onondaga Co. 15 Oct 1964. *Extreme dates:* 21 Mar and 9 Jun; 9 Jul and 4 Dec.

Remarks When surveying golden-plovers at any season, observers should be aware of recent winter records in Bermuda and Barbados of Pacific Golden-Plover *(P. fulva)*, formerly considered conspecific with *P. dominica* and now recognized as a full species (AOU 1995), and also of regular spring records of Greater Golden-Plover *(P. apricaria)* in Newfoundland.

American Golden-Plover is a powerful flier, and many more probably overfly the state and adjacent lakes and ocean than are detected in migration. As with other shorebird species, adults arrive ahead of the young of the year. Of 76 at the Syracuse Airport 6 Sep 1964, all but about 10% were adults; of the 300 there 18 Oct 1964, more than 75% were juveniles (D. Crumb, pers. comm.).
Edward S. Brinkley

Wilson's Plover   *Charadrius wilsonia*

Range Chiefly Nearctic, breeding along the Gulf and Atlantic coasts of the United States regularly northward to Virginia (formerly New Jersey); rarely wanders north to Nova Scotia. Winters on the Gulf Coast and south to northern South America.

Status Very rare vagrant.

Occurrence Since 1968, seven additional records have been added to the more than 25 in Bull 1974. All have occurred on the coast, with five in May, one in Jun, and one in Sep. (1) Great Kills Park, Richmond Co. 20–21 May 1978 (Claremont et al.) (Davis 1979b; NYSARC 1979; KB 28:199); (2) Shinnecock Inlet, Suffolk Co. 28 May 1978 (Keith) (Davis 1979b); (3) JBWR 2 Sep 1978 (Hemmerick) (KB 29:58); (4) Great Kills Park 27 Jun 1984 (Morris) (KB 34:271); (5) Tobay Beach, Nassau Co. 3 May 1988 (Hines) (KB 38:283); (6) JBWR 19 May 1989 (LeBaron et al.) (KB 39:190); (7) Napeague Inlet, Suffolk Co. 28 May 1993 (Vezo, Lindsay, Lauro) (KB 43:271). There are no accepted inland records.

Extreme Dates: 24 Apr (specimen) and 2 Oct.

Remarks Considering that this species bred in southern NJ until the late 1950s, it is surprising that so few have been recorded in our bordering states, with a mere handful from PA and CT. In MA, however, although described as "rare," it is also called "almost annual" (Veit and Petersen 1993).

Ken Feustel

Semipalmated Plover   *Charadrius semipalmatus*

Range Nearctic, breeding from the southern Arctic tundra south to Nova Scotia. On the East Coast, winters north to South Carolina, rarely to Long Island, and south to Argentina.

Status Abundant to very abundant coastal migrant, common to very common inland migrant. Rare in winter on the coast.

Occurrence It is among our most numerous shorebirds on the extensive tidal mudflats along the South Shore of LI. Inland it occurs in some numbers, especially on the shore of L. Ontario.

Coastal maxima: Spring: 6000 JBWR 17 May 1939; 700 JBWR 1 Jun 1948. *Fall:* 4000 JBWR 24 Aug 1951; 1203 JBWR 18 Aug 1983. *Winter:* 12 Northern Nassau Co. CBC 26 Dec 1991, an unusually high number. *Inland maxima: Spring:* 120 Groveland, Livingston Co. 23 May 1948; 100 MNWR 30 May 1967. *Fall:* 100 El Dorado Beach, Jefferson Co. 2 Sep 1961; 65 MNWR 14 Sep 1965; 60 Delta L., Oneida Co. 28 Sep 1969. *Extreme dates: Coastal:* 18 Mar; *Inland:* 5 Mar and 29 Nov.

It is rare before late Apr (inland and coastal) and after Oct (inland) and Nov (coastal). No late fall dates are given for coastal locations because of the increase in winter reports. Since 1974 there have been four Dec–Feb reports of two to four birds, all on LI, and at least nine additional reports from coastal CBCs of single individuals in Dec. Inland late spring and early fall dates nearly overlap. On the coast, it is regular in small numbers throughout the summer.

Remarks Birders should be aware of the possibility of the very similar-appearing Common Ringed Plover *(C. hiaticula)* occurring in NY. One in juvenal plumage was observed and photographed at North Monomoy, MA on 5 Sep 1990, representing a first state record (Veit and Petersen 1993). The first RI sighting was 15 Sep 1991 (Conway 1992).

Ken Feustel

Piping Plover

Charadrius melodus

Range Nearctic, breeding in two separate areas, coastal beaches from southeastern Quebec and southwestern Newfoundland south to Virginia, and inland beaches from eastern Alberta and Nebraska east to the shores of Lake Ontario. Winters in the Greater Antilles and on the Atlantic and Gulf coasts from South Carolina to Florida and west to eastern Texas.

Status Fairly common breeder and migrant on sandy beaches and spoil banks of coastal LI. Casual breeder and very rare transient on L. Ontario; casual transient MNWR, L. Oneida, and L. Champlain.

Breeding In 1986 the Piping Plover was federally designated as Endangered on the Great Lakes and Threatened on the Atlantic Coast. It has been listed as Endangered by the NYSDEC. The breeding population on LI has increased from 114 pairs in 1985 to a fairly stable level of around 190 pairs between 1989 and 1995. Some of this increase may be due to closer coverage since federal and state listing (Sommers et al. 1996). These figures are far below the approximately 500 pairs estimated on LI in 1939 (Wilcox 1959). They are probably higher, however, than in the early twentieth century before Piping Plover was protected from hunting in 1913. The main limiting factor today is human and vehicular traffic on the beaches to which they are restricted for nesting. Additional pressure comes from predators, such as gulls, foxes, crows, rats, and cats, many of which have become more numerous because of human development. The posting of tern colonies has helped this species, since it often nests in their vicinity, most often near Least Terns. Installing wire cages over Piping Plover nests has also increased productivity by deterring predators.

The only recent breeding location on the NY shore of the Great Lakes is Sandy Pond, Oswego Co., where a pair nested in 1984 after a hiatus of 29 years (KB 35:226). Nesting has not been verified in NY away from LI since then.

Nonbreeding Migrants swell the LI population in Mar and late Aug. Maximum counts reached 100 birds at those seasons 30–50 years ago. The last count that high was 100 at Moriches Inlet, Suffolk Co. 22 Aug 1970. More recently, a third of that would be a very good spring or fall count.

They usually arrive on LI in late Mar, exceptionally as early as 3 Mar, and leave LI in early Sep. Only stragglers are found after mid-Sep. In the last 20 years one fall straggler, 21 Nov 1982 (KB 32:70) and one winter bird, 8 Jan 1977 (KB 27:116) have been recorded on LI.

Upstate transient records are less than annual and concentrated on L. Ontario. Of 10 upstate observations published in *The Kingbird* in the last 20 years, 7 were on L. Ontario: four in Apr–May, two in Aug–Sep, plus another extraordinarily late one at Braddock Bay, Monroe Co. 21 Nov–15 Dec 1991 (KB 42:96). Other recent upstate records include two fall reports, one at Oneida L. 3–13 Oct 1978 (KB 29:122) and the second ever for the NY shore of L. Champlain at Westport, Essex Co. 26–28 Aug 1993 (KB 43:339). There were two spring records at MNWR in the early 1970s (KB 30:69). All upstate records presumably are related to the now much diminished breeding population farther west on the Great Lakes, rather than to Atlantic coastal populations. This presumption would seem to explain the absence of records from the St. Lawrence R. and their great rarity anywhere inland. The lack of recent records from the NY shore of L. Erie, however, is puzzling.
Robert O. Paxton

Killdeer   *Charadrius vociferus*

Range Nearctic, breeding throughout temperate North America; in the east, north to northern Ontario, central Quebec, and western Newfoundland. Winters from southern New England and Ohio south to Florida and the Gulf Coast and in the West Indies and northern South America.

Status Widespread breeder, common to abundant migrant. In winter locally common along the coast but rare to uncommon inland.

Breeding It breeds throughout most of the state wherever suitable open habitat occurs; absent only in heavily forested upland areas.

Nonbreeding Common on both spring and fall migration. Flocks of 300 have been recorded several times in the fall: MNWR 4 Jul 1967; Delta L., Oneida Co. 28 Sep 1969; Lima, Livingston Co. 15 Sep 1970. A spring count of 250 from Derby Hill, Oswego Co. 13 Apr 1972 is impressive. Migrants arrive in numbers in Mar and depart by late Nov, although many birds remain during winter, when the species is uncommon upstate but locally common in coastal areas. In 1976 the Southern Nassau Co. CBC recorded 105 birds, part of a Region 10 total of more than 500.
Paul R. Sweet

OYSTERCATCHERS—HAEMATOPODIDAE

American Oystercatcher *Haematopus palliatus*

Range Nearctic and Neotropical, breeding locally along the Atlantic and Gulf coasts from Massachusetts to Louisiana and Texas and south through the Caribbean to northern South America. North American breeders winter mainly from southern Virginia to the Gulf Coast.

Status Breeds on LI. In fall migration, locally abundant there and rare but regular in winter. Accidental elsewhere.

Breeding American Oystercatcher has colonized coastal LI with spectacular success. Previously known to nest only on southeastern U.S. beaches, it first nested in NY in 1957 on Gardiners I., Suffolk Co. (Post and Raynor 1964). Learning to substitute spoil banks and sand hummocks in salt marshes for their traditional outer beach habitat (Zarudsky 1985), it colonized the bays and estuaries of the entire South Shore of LI and the eastern end of the North Fork on LI Sound. Censused at 46–48 pairs by aerial survey in 1975 (AB 29:951), the LI breeding population exploded in the late 1970s and early 1980s, leveling off between 1986 and 1992 at around 130 pairs. It grew again in 1993 to 213 pairs and dropped in 1995 to 178, but the overall trend was significantly increasing over the nine years since the species was added to the colonial waterbird survey (Sommers et al. 1996).

In 1994 the first mainland nest was found at Rye, Westchester Co. (NASFN 48:928), and a few have summered on SI since 1991. American Oystercatcher is pressing at the limits of available habitat. Reasonably tolerant of boat traffic, it could nest wherever suitable sand hummocks protrude in coastal estuaries and salt marshes.

Nonbreeding It usually arrives in early Mar. After the breeding season, adults and young concentrate in late summer in favored spots, such as North Line I., Nassau Co. (250 birds on 22 Aug 1992) (KB 43:351), and JBWR (153 on 18 Aug 1986) (KB 39:90). Some remain quite late in fall (25 JBWR 31 Dec 1985) (KB 36:59). Occasional midwinter observations began in the late 1970s, and since the mid-1980s a few individuals have overwintered.

The only record away from the coast is of a single bird at Barcelona Harbor, Chautauqua Co. on L. Erie, 22 May 1986, a date when coastal birds may have downy young.

Robert O. Paxton

STILTS AND AVOCETS—
RECURVIROSTRIDAE

Black-necked Stilt *Himantopus mexicanus*

Range Nearctic and Neotropical, breeding locally along the southeast Atlantic Coast north to Delaware and in 1993 to southern New Jersey; also widely in the western United States and south through Central and South America to southern Chile and Argentina. Winters from southern Florida, the West Indies, the Gulf Coast, and southern California south to the limits of the breeding range.

Status Rare vagrant. Before the 1970s very rare, now nearly annual in spring.

Occurrence Bull (1974, 1976) listed ten records of this species in the 133-year period 1843–1976. With the exception of one report of two birds in 1953, all were of single individuals. Since 1976, there have been at least 18 additional reports involving 26 birds, including the second upstate record. The increase in sightings of this species can be attributed to an increase in the number of observers and a northward extension of the species' nesting range. It is most often found in late spring near coastal salt ponds and fields with standing water.

Seven specimens, six of them extant, were collected, presumably on the South Shore of LI many years ago. Five of these in the AMNH collection are without data, except one taken on Great South Bay in 1843, AMNH 436941. The only known specimen taken in the twentieth century is one from Georgica, Suffolk Co. 4 Jun 1924, NYSM 24963. Of the 18 sight reports since 1976, one has was in Apr, 11 in May, four in Jun, and two in Jul. The second inland record was an individual seen 20–22 May 1989 at Beaver Lake, Onondaga Co. (Adair et al.) and photographed (DeBenedictis 1989).

Maxima: 4 Oak Beach, Suffolk Co. 24–28 May 1978; 4 Cold Spring Harbor, Suffolk Co. 14–19 Apr 1980. *Extreme dates:* 14 Apr and 19 Jul.

Remarks A pair nested in Cape May Co., NJ in 1993, the first evidence of breeding in that state since the nineteenth century (AB 47:399), and nesting was recorded at Philadelphia, PA in 1991 (AB 46:1124). The first MD nesting was in 1987 (AB 41:1418), and it has been nesting in DE since 1964. DeBenedictis (1989) noted that this species is increasing in numbers along the Atlantic Coast and "is a potential future addition to the breeding avifauna of New York State."
Ken Feustel

American Avocet *Recurvirostra americana*

Range Western Nearctic, breeding east to southern Manitoba and western Minnesota south to southern California and Texas. Winters from south-western United States to Guatemala and also locally on the Atlantic Coast to southern Florida. Nonbreeding individuals may summer in the wintering range. Migrates primarily in western United States but also rarely in the east from southern Canada to Florida and the Gulf Coast.

Status Rare vagrant, increasingly regular.

Occurrence This species favors salt and brackish ponds along the coast and lake shores, fields with standing water, and freshwater impoundments inland. Bull (1974) described it as "apparently always a very rare bird on Long Island and an even rarer visitant upstate." The American Avocet now occurs nearly annually. Since 1976 there have been 32 records; 20 of the reports are from the coast, and 12 from upstate. Of the 20 coastal observations, two were in spring (Jun) and 18 in fall, with seven in Aug and 6 in Oct. This species is more common inland in spring than along the coast, with six upstate records, of which five were in May. Increased sightings are thought to be related to both the greater number of field observers and the increase of this species as a fall migrant on the Atlantic Coast.

   Coastal maxima: 3 JBWR 4 Oct 1984. *Inland maxima:* 5, photographed, Buffalo, Erie Co. 22 Aug 1972; 4 El Dorado Beach, Jefferson Co. 20 Aug 1971. *Extreme dates:* 3 May and 15 Nov.

   In spring, it is rare before mid-May (inland) and early Jun (coastal); in fall, rare after late Oct. Late fall observations of single birds include: JBSP 8 Nov 1990; Fair Haven Beach SP, Cayuga Co. 3 Nov 1992, photographed. Ken Feustel

SANDPIPERS, PHALAROPES, AND ALLIES—SCOLOPACIDAE

Greater Yellowlegs   *Tringa melanoleuca*

Range Nearctic, in the east breeding south to the central portions of Ontario and Quebec, Newfoundland, and Cape Breton Island, Nova Scotia. Winters on the Atlantic Coast from Massachusetts (sporadically) and Long Island south to southern South America.

Status Very common to abundant coastal migrant, common to very common inland. Uncommon but regular in winter on the coast.

Occurrence It occurs in a variety of habitats, including coastal flats, tidal pools, marshes, inland lake and river shores, ponds, flooded fields, and golf courses. This species is much more numerous in spring than the Lesser Yellowlegs but is often outnumbered by the latter, particularly in Jul and Aug, during the protracted fall migration; usually rare before late Mar (inland and coastal) and after mid-Nov (inland). Inland, the species has been recorded as late as 2 Dec. Individuals are present throughout the winter on the coast.

Coastal maxima: Spring: 400 East Hampton, Suffolk Co. 23 May 1927. *Fall:* 1000 JBWR 27 Sep 1965; 350 JBWR 27 Aug 1950; 150 JBWR 23 Oct 1955. *Winter:* 45 Southern Nassau Co. CBC 30 Dec 1984; 40 HLSP 1 Jan 1979. *Inland maxima: Spring:* 150 Hanover Center, Chautauqua Co. 25 Apr 1965. *Fall:* 123 OOWMA 4 Sep 1988; 120 MNWR 14 Oct 1964; 100 El Dorado Beach, Jefferson Co. 30 Jul 1964.

Ken Feustel

Lesser Yellowlegs   *Tringa flavipes*

Range Nearctic, breeding from central Alaska and northern Canada south and east to west-central Quebec, near James Bay. Winters from the Gulf states north to Maryland and southern New Jersey, more rarely to Long Island; south to Chile and Argentina. Migrates in spring chiefly through the Mississippi Valley.

Status Common to abundant fall migrant; in spring fairly common inland but uncommon, although regular, along the coast. Rare in winter on the coast.

Occurrence During migration the Lesser Yellowlegs favors grassy pools and ponds inland and salt meadows along the coast where shortgrass pools have been exposed by the receding tide. It is less likely than its larger relative, the Greater Yellowlegs, to occur on open beaches and mudflats. In spring, rare before Apr on the coast and inland. In fall, it arrives as early as the last week in Jun or the first week of Jul and is rare after Sep inland and Oct along the coast. Inland dates range from 20 Mar to 30 Nov.

Coastal maxima: Fall: 500 Napeague, Suffolk Co. 24 Aug 1924; 500 Oak Beach, Suffolk Co. 2 Aug 1974. *Winter:* 12 Southern Nassau Co. CBC 2 Jan 1988; 11 SI CBC 22 Dec 1974. Both winter observations represent unusually high concentrations, one or two individuals are more typically seen. *Inland maxima: Spring:* 520 Braddock Bay, Monroe Co. 3 May 1986, an unprecedented number; 80 Wolcottsville, Niagara Co. 4 May 1962. *Fall:* 280 Onondaga L., Onondaga Co. 18 Jul 1969; 260 MNWR 30 Jul 1967.

Remarks Reports of Lesser Yellowlegs in winter, particularly on CBCs, should be closely scrutinized owing to confusion with Greater Yellowlegs, which is the more likely species at that season. Reports of single individuals or small flocks of Lesser Yellowlegs in winter, where no size comparison with Greater Yellowlegs or other shorebirds can be made, are particularly problematic.

Ken Feustel

Spotted Redshank   *Tringa erythropus*

Range Palearctic, breeding on the tundra of northern Eurasia. Winters south from the Mediterranean basin, Persian Gulf, India, and eastern China.

Regular in migration in western Alaska; accidental elsewhere in North America.

Status Casual vagrant.

Occurrence The first record for NY was by J. Yrizarry and M. Yrizarry, 6 Dec 1992, in Brooklyn. This bird lingered at the place it was originally found until 18 Mar 1993 (Yrizarry 1993). What was undoubtedly the same individual turned up again at the identical location 30 Nov 1993 (Giunta) (NASFN 48:93) and stayed until 19 Jan 1994 (NASFN 48:188). Another individual was recorded at JBWR 3 Oct 1993 (R. Gochfeld) (NASFN 48:93).

Remarks Surrounding states all had their first records decades before NY, with RI and CT having one each, MA two, and NJ six. The most recent contiguous state record was at Brigantine, NJ 22–23 Oct 1993 (NASFN 48:93).
Emanuel Levine

Wood Sandpiper *Tringa glareola*

Range Northern Palearctic, breeding from Scandinavia east across northern Russia and northern Siberia south to southern Europe and central Russia, Kamchatka, and the Chukotski Peninsula; also, at least rarely in the western and central Aleutian Islands. Winters from the Mediterranean region and southern Asia south to southern Africa and Australia.

Status Casual vagrant.

Occurrence There are two records. A specimen from Gaines, Orleans Co., in the Milton S. Ray collection, dated 10 Oct 1907 and labeled as a Solitary Sandpiper was correctly identified at the MVZ (106848), University of California, Berkeley in 1979 as a winter adult of this species (AB 34:231).

A juvenile was photographed, tape recorded, and seen by many during its stay at Marshlands Conservancy, Rye, Westchester Co. 31 Oct–5 Nov 1990 (Burke 1991; NYSARC 1992).

Remarks These represent the only documented records for this Eurasian species in eastern North America.
Thomas A. Burke

Solitary Sandpiper *Tringa solitaria*

Range Nearctic, breeding in boreal forests from Alaska to central Labrador and south, in the east to the central portions of Ontario and Quebec. Winters primarily in Middle and South America south to Argentina and Peru but with stragglers along the Gulf Coast of North America.

Status Fairly common migrant.

Occurrence The Solitary Sandpiper frequents freshwater pools, woodland ponds and streams, and, to a lesser extent, creeks and marshes, both inland and along the coast. Contrary to its name, this species is sometimes observed in small flocks. A fairly common migrant in spring and fall inland, along the coast it is an uncommon migrant in spring and fall.

   Spring maxima: 51 Braddock Bay, Monroe Co. 3 May 1986; 50 Montezuma, Cayuga Co. 5 May 1973. *Fall maxima:* 20 near Texas, Oswego Co. 9 Aug 1956; 17 Otisco L., Onondaga Co. 8 Sep 1963. *Extreme dates:* 27 Mar and 18 Nov. Rare before late Apr and after mid-Oct.

Ken Feustel

Willet   *Catoptrophorus semipalmatus*

Range Nearctic, breeding very locally, in the east from southern Canada along the Atlantic and Gulf coasts to southern Florida and west to southern Texas, and in the West Indies. In the east winters in the West Indies and from Virginia and the Gulf Coast south to northern Brazil.

Status Common breeder in salt marshes on the South Shore of LI. Common migrant on the coast, rare migrant on the Great Lakes, very rare inland. Casual in winter on LI.

Breeding Willet was not proved to breed in NY until 1966, when three nests were discovered in the salt marshes of Great South Bay, Nassau Co. (Davis 1968). The breeding population spread to cover the South Shore of LI from Shinnecock Inlet to JBWR. By 1983, an estimated 150 pairs bred in the Jones Island salt marshes between the Wantagh Causeway and Robert Moses Causeway (B. Lauro) (KB 33:298). Postbreeding flocks grew rapidly in the mid-1980s. Fall shorebird surveys at JBWR found a daily maximum of two in 1981, increasing to 59 on 21 Jul 1988 (Davis 1984; Morris 1988, 1989). The postbreeding assemblage on the Line Islands, Nassau Co. reached 300 on 3 Jul 1993 (A. Lauro) (KB 43:51).

   Although the breeding population has leveled off on the South Shore since the late 1980s, apparent prospectors appeared in Jun in the 1990s at Marshlands Conservancy, Rye, Westchester Co. (KB 41:284, 44:338). Further expansion of breeding into the remaining coastal salt marshes appears likely.

Nonbreeding Migrants from other populations swell the coastal flocks after mid or late Jul, for flocks up to 80 occurred on LI before breeding began there. Shorebird surveys at JBWR in the 1980s showed that fall populations peak from late Jul through early Sep, becoming uncommon after late Oct. Spring arrivals are rare before mid-Apr. The earliest known arrival date on the coast was 24 Mar 1991 (KB 41:221), and a few have lingered on LI to late Dec. One at Acabonack, Suffolk Co. 15 Dec 1979–17 Feb 1980 was the first known to overwinter (KB 30:130).

The Great Lakes account for most migrant records away from the coast. It is not quite annual there, occurring more often in fall than in spring. There are occasional stopovers at smaller lakes and marshes inland, slightly more often in spring than in fall. There are only four recent records from MNWR, three in spring (KB 25:156, 41:187; NASFN 49:232) and one in fall (KB 35:46), although the area is closely scrutinized for shorebirds (Benning 1980). There are a handful of records from Onondaga and Oneida lakes, a May 1980 record from the Bashakill, Sullivan Co. (KB 30:190), four records from L. Champlain (KB 32:291, 43:339), and four from Dutchess Co. (KB 41:61).

Most inland observations are of single birds, but small groups are possible, particularly in fall. Multiple observations are more likely under grounding conditions; five, for example, were in central and northwestern NY after Hurricane Hugo, 23–30 Sep 1989 (KB 40:31). The largest group recorded inland was 22 at Fish Gulf, near Otisco L., Onondaga Co. 26 Aug 1968.

Remarks There are two subspecies recognized, the nominate *semipalmatus*, sometimes known as "Eastern" Willet, and *inornatus*, referred to as "Western" Willet. *Semipalmatus* is our breeding bird. Probably all migrants recorded other than coastally belong to *inornatus*. However, an examination of 30 specimens in the AMNH collection, collected on the South Shore of LI during the fall, all proved to be *inornatus*. This seeming contradiction mirrors the path of the fall migration of *inornatus*. The one upstate specimen was also of that subspecies, whereas the two spring specimens were *semipalmatus* (Bull 1974). It is difficult to separate the two subspecies in the field, but it is not impossible in mixed flocks. "Western" Willet is visibly larger and paler than "Eastern" Willet.
Robert O. Paxton

Spotted Sandpiper *Actitis macularia*

Range Nearctic, breeding from Alaska and Canada to the southwestern United States, on the east coast south to Virginia, and in the mountains to northern Alabama. Winters, in the east, north to South Carolina and from the Gulf states south through Central and South America to Chile.

Status Widespread breeder and common to occasionally very common migrant inland; less numerous along the coast.

Breeding The Spotted Sandpiper is a common breeder throughout the state, nesting on the ground in open grassy fields or occasionally in cultivation planted to grain and vegetable crops, also along ponds and streams, and in coastal sand dunes amidst beach grass. This species exhibits a tolerance for human activities near its nest site and will occupy newly created habitat, both human-made and natural. Its distribution is closely correlated with lakes, rivers, and shorelines. Of the nine species of shorebirds that breed in NY, only the Killdeer was recorded in more blocks by Atlas field-workers. This species was missing, however, from several rivers in the western Adirondacks, where forests grow to the river edge, and in the western Appalachians, where elevations exceed 1500 ft and there is a scarcity of lakes and ponds. Atlas workers found that the nest of this species was extremely hard to locate; an observed nest constituted only 10% of the Confirmed records. Some LI breeding maxima are: 20+ pairs at JBSP in 1951, 20 pairs on Fishers I. in 1965, and 15 nests on Great Gull I. in 1968 and 1969. The last named location, 17 acres in extent, had a breeding density of one nest per acre.

Nonbreeding On LI this species can be found in tidal and freshwater marshes, where it favors mudflats, ponds, and streams that have sufficient tidal influence to expose sandbars and edges. Away from the coast, it can be found in all freshwater habitats. It is usually rare before mid-Apr and after mid-Oct. An early spring inland report was 3 Apr 1977 at Castleton, Rensselaer Co.

   Inland maxima: Spring: 60 El Dorado Beach, Jefferson Co. 22 May 1965. *Fall:* 80 MNWR 4 Jul 1965; 70 Onondaga L., Onondaga Co. 14 Aug 1960. These numbers are exceptional, as groups of up to a half dozen are the norm.

   Since Bull (1974, 1976) there have been at least ten additional winter reports of single birds from both inland and coastal localities including: East Corning, Steuben Co. 3 Dec 1984 (KB 35:129); Rockland Co. CBC 23 Dec 1984 (AB 39:399); Rye, Westchester Co. 11–18 Jan 1992 (KB 42:122) and 26 Jan 1991 (Stanley) (AB 45:255); Southern Nassau Co. CBC 2 Jan 1993 (NASFN 48:372); Massapequa Preserve, Nassau Co. 18 Jan 1993 (Fritz) (KB 43:163).

Remarks Unique among NY's breeding birds, the female of this species will take more than one mate whenever there is a surplus of males. The female initiates courtship, leaving the male to incubate the eggs and care for the young (Atlas 1988).
Ken Feustel

Upland Sandpiper   *Bartramia longicauda*

Range Nearctic, breeding locally from Alaska and the Yukon southeast to southern Ontario, Quebec, and New Brunswick and south, in the east, to northern Kentucky and Virginia. Winters in South America south to central Argentina.

Status Widespread but generally uncommon breeder in open and agricultural areas; rare to fairly common migrant, especially inland in the fall. Declining both as a breeding species and migrant in recent years.

Breeding Only the Henslow's Sparrow is less widespread as a breeding grassland species than the Upland Sandpiper, which was reported from only 9% of all Atlas blocks. The apparent requirement of this species for large tracts of relatively flat, uninterrupted grassland limits its distribution significantly in NY (White 1983; Brauning 1992). At Finger Lakes National Forest, they have been observed in summer only in areas with 300–600 contiguous acres of pastureland, although smaller areas are acceptable.

From 1966 to 1994, BBS data show a general, but not significant, pattern of decline of 4.5% per year. However, a steep and significant decline of 13.6% per year occurred in the period 1966–1979, with the decline slowing and becoming statistically nonsignificant from 1980 to 1994. When calling or displaying it is conspicuous but is otherwise unobtrusive and is likely to go undetected where populations are small or where single pairs or small groups of pairs are widely scattered (Cadman et al. 1987). Although its population is low in NY, it may have stabilized in recent years, and populations in nearby ON appear to have increased between 1965 and 1979 (Cadman et al. 1987).

The Atlas map for this species shows a pattern of concentration and more widespread distribution in regions to the southwest and northwest of the Adirondacks, where there are few birders. A careful, intensive, statewide survey for this species could reveal that it is more common than suspected.

Nonbreeding There are no winter records for NY. Migrants usually arrive by mid-Apr and depart by mid-Sep. Fall concentrations are generally larger than in spring, with a maximum of 94 on 25 Aug 1965, at the Syracuse Airport, and a spring maximum of 20 at Manitou, Monroe Co. 28 Apr 1956.

Remarks With this species of the Midwestern prairies and agricultural regions, we see the typical pattern of long-term population decline and shrinking breeding range typical of most of those species in NY that require some form of open lands or grasslands for breeding. Its future in NY and the Northeast may depend exclusively upon human activities, especially agriculture and the maintenance of grassy cover types around airports and on closed landfills. For the Upland Sandpiper, however, an apparent additional requirement of large areas of habitat for nesting further limits its distribution.

All grassland species nesting in agricultural hayfields in NY face the same challenge. The first cutting of hay, the most nutritious and best quality from the farmer's perspective, occurs when grassland birds are incubating and vulnerable to nest loss from mowing equipment or exposure. Bollinger and

Gavin (1992) pointed out that conservation measures beneficial to Bobolink would benefit other grassland species, as well. Among their recommendations were: (1) maintain patches of relatively sparse, grass-dominated vegetation resembling old hay fields; (2) maintain larger patches of grassland habitat, at least 25–40 acres in size, whenever possible; and (3) cut hay from the patches every two to three years, preferably in Aug, to prevent encroachment of woody vegetation and reduce the likelihood of nest lost due to earlier mowing. It should be noted that subsequent studies (Smith and Smith 1992) have shown that larger hayfields of 75–80 acres, or larger, are desirable for maintaining populations of Henslow's Sparrow and probably Upland Sandpiper as well. A conservation strategy aimed at maintaining habitats of suitable size and quality for the larger or rarer grassland species will accommodate the needs of other, smaller grassland birds, too. Such a practice is currently in place on Finger Lakes National Forest in central NY (Smith, in press).

Because of its limited breeding distribution and pattern of population decline, Upland Sandpiper is identified as a Species of Special Concern by NYSDEC. It has been recommended that its conservation status be changed to Threatened, but no action had been taken on that recommendation as of July 1996. There appears to be no substantive research focused on this species in NY; further study clearly is needed, given its potentially threatened status and apparent need for conservation.
Charles R. Smith

Eskimo Curlew   *Numenius borealis*

Range Nearctic, formerly bred on the tundra of northern Canada and possibly Alaska and wintered on the pampas of southern South America. Reported in fall migration from Hudson Bay, from southern Labrador and the Gulf of St. Lawrence to New England, and south to South Carolina and the West Indies. Return migration was generally through interior North America.

Status Extirpated. Formerly local fall migrant, mostly on LI, but with several upstate records as well. Last reported in the state in the early 1890s.

Occurrence Bull reported (1964, 1974) that Eskimo Curlew had been observed "occasionally in the hundreds" on fields adjacent to the coast on eastern LI, especially after severe easterly storms, he could locate only eight NY specimens. Of the five presumably taken on LI, the only ones with specific dates and locations are two from Hampton Bays in 1880, now in the Princeton University Museum; one shot near Amityville 11 Sep 1880, University of Michigan 1818212; and the last known specimen, from Montauk, taken 16 Sep 1891. Others, including three at the AMNH, are without details.

From interior areas Bull found one specimen from Onondaga L., near Syracuse, NYSM 19177 but with collection date unknown; one taken 2 Oct 1879 at Lockport, Niagara Co., BMS 5040. One from Manitou, Monroe Co., taken 23 Sep 1890 was reported by Beardsley and Mitchell (1965) as BMS 785, but the specimen "cannot now be found." Eaton (1910) listed several other inland occurrences, but details are lacking.

Remarks Zeranski and Baptist (1990) gave the last CT record as a specimen taken 12 Sept 1889. Veit and Petersen (1993) stated that there have been no specimens collected and only one sight record in MA since 1913, on Martha's Vineyard (by Daniels) 6–7 Aug 1972.

The AOU (1983) considered the species nearly extinct. It had last been reported from its wintering grounds in Argentina in 1939. The AOU Check-list then detailed a number of "mostly sight" records since the mid-1950s, starting with one in Charleston, SC in 1956, followed by several from the TX coast starting in 1959, including one with photographs from Galveston in Mar–Apr 1962, as well as others continuing through 1980 from NJ to James Bay, Canada. It reported that the last recorded specimen was from Barbados 4 Sep 1963.

Nearer the NY area, Leck (1984) cited the last two NJ reports from the Cape May area in Sep 1959 and Sep 1960. In addition, T. Halliwell (pers. comm.) indicated that the most recent NJ record was 24 Aug 1992 at Brigantine NWR (Hyett).

Veit and Petersen commented that, "In evaluating reports . . . it has become apparent that the Upland Sandpiper, particularly when seen out of the context of its nesting habitat, can be confused with the Eskimo Curlew." (See also From Glaciers to Global Warming: Extinct Species.) Stanley R. Lincoln

Whimbrel *Numenius phaeopus*

Range Holarctic, breeding in northern Eurasia from Iceland to Siberia and in northern North America from Alaska and Yukon southeast to the Hudson Bay area. North American birds winter in coastal areas from central California, the Gulf Coast, and South Carolina south through Middle and South America, and in the West Indies. Nonbreeding birds may also summer in the winter range.

Status Variously rare to uncommon coastal migrant in spring, occasionally more numerous; usually common to very common in fall, but most flocks fly by without stopping. Inland this species is locally fairly common to common in spring, much less numerous in fall. Casual in winter on the South Shore of LI.

Occurrence Whimbrels, frequent coastal salt marshes, mudflats, shortgrass habitats such as sod farms, plowed agricultural fields, and at inland locations, lake shores. In late May flocks of up to several hundred may be seen along the Canadian shore of L. Erie (Beardslee and Mitchell 1965). In fall, the flight is primarily offshore, and after easterly gales large numbers are sometimes reported from eastern LI.

Coastal maxima: Spring: 250 East Hampton 5 May 1947. *Fall:* 200 East Hampton, Suffolk Co. 30 Jul 1922; 101 various South Shore LI localities 2 Aug 1992. *Inland maxima: Spring:* 120 Webster, Monroe Co. 27 May 1962; 47 Braddock Bay, Monroe Co. 28 May 1963. *Fall:* 212 Derby Hill, Oswego Co. 27 Aug 1986.

Three winter records have been added to the two in Bull (1974). The first Jan record was one observed on the Southern Nassau Co. CBC 2 Jan 1978 (Pembleton). A bird present at JBWR 19 Jan–10 Feb 1980 (Cook et al.) was the first midwinter record. Another was photographed on the Captree, Suffolk Co. CBC 15 Dec 1990 (AB 46:528).

Remarks In addition to our New World *hudsonicus*, one Old World subspecies, the nominate *phaeopus*, has been recorded in eastern North America. It breeds in northern Europe and western Siberia and winters in Africa, India, and the islands of the Indian Ocean and is separable in the field because it has an unbarred white rump and a paler belly and underwings. The first North American specimen of *phaeopus* was collected at Gilgo Inlet, south of Amityville, Suffolk Co. 4 Sep 1912, AMNH 11883. A more recent observation of a Whimbrel with a white rump, presumably the nominate, was made by Puleston et al. at Brookhaven, Suffolk Co. 27 Dec 1976 (KB 27:116).
Ken Feustel

Eurasian Curlew   *Numenius arquata*

Range Palearctic, breeding from northern Eurasia south to southern Europe. Winters south to southern Africa and southeast Asia. Vagrants have been recorded in Greenland, Iceland, Nova Scotia, Massachusetts, New York, and Bermuda.

Status Accidental.

Occurrence The only known occurrence in NY is a LI specimen, collected in 1853 (exact locality and collector unknown), NYSM 324. The question of whether this specimen was actually collected in NY, while historically debated, was reviewed, and the record was accepted as valid by Marshall and Dutcher (1892) and later by Eaton (1910) and Bull (1974).

Remarks Other North American records include one at Crescent Beach, ON (AOU 1983), one at Monomoy, MA 19 Sep–16 Oct 1976, one on

Martha's Vineyard, MA 18 Feb–18 Mar 1978, and another at Monomoy, MA 5 Sep–23 Nov 1984. A record from near Halifax, NS in May 1978 has also been noted. The MA and NS records are from Veit and Petersen 1993.
Stanley R. Lincoln

Long-billed Curlew *Numenius americanus*

Range West-central Nearctic, breeding east to southern Manitoba, formerly to southern Wisconsin, south to Utah and Texas. Winters chiefly from Louisiana west to California and south to Guatemala, but locally in small numbers on the coasts of South Carolina and Florida.

Status Now a casual vagrant. Before the 1860s a regular spring and fall migrant on the coast of LI.

Occurrence There are only two records since 1938. An individual, seen by many and color photographed, was on newly dredged sand fill on North Line I., Nassau Co., north of JBSP, 4–30 Jul 1975 (Dempsey et al. 1975; AB 29:952). A bird was seen on the ground with Whimbrel at Gilgo Beach, Suffolk Co. 18 Sep 1994 (Levine) (AB 49:27), details submitted to NYSARC.
   The disappearance of this species as a migrant from the Northeast is thought to be the result of destruction of most of its former breeding grounds in the Midwest and a corresponding shift in migratory pattern farther west. In the 1840s it was a regular spring and fall migrant on the LI coast, but its numbers had started to decline by the 1860s. By the turn of the century the species was decidedly rare, with only five records from 1889 to 1923. Between 1923 and 1938 there were an additional six sightings. After 1938 there were no confirmed records until the 1975 event.

Remarks An examination of records from bordering states revealed approximately a dozen documented occurrences in this century.
Ken Feustel

Hudsonian Godwit *Limosa haemastica*

Range Nearctic, breeding in Alaska, northwestern Mackenzie, and along the western shores of Hudson and James bays. Spring migration chiefly through the Great Plains; in fall mainly over the Atlantic Ocean. Winters primarily in coastal Argentina.

Status Rare to uncommon but regular fall migrant both on the coast and inland; sometimes more numerous. Very rare in spring anywhere.

Occurrence Much like other former game species, Hudsonian Godwit was markedly more common before the turn of the century than during the first half of the twentieth century. With legal protection, numbers have reverted to double-digit fall counts on the coast and occasionally upstate. Significant fluctuations in annual tallies may reflect the role of weather patterns in keeping migrants grounded, rather than population dynamics. The species' preference for mudflats or the muddy margins of freshwater impoundments largely determines where migrants will occur. Away from traditional stopover sites, such as those cited below, the species is considered very rare in most parts of NY.

Coastal maxima: Fall: 17 Moriches Inlet, Suffolk Co. 18 Aug 1962; 11 Moriches Inlet 24 Jul 1965; 9 JBWR 24 Oct 1992. *Inland maxima: Fall:* 50 Point Breeze, Monroe Co. 3 Sep 1995; 37 Buffalo, Erie Co. 17 Aug 1974; 25–40 MNWR 28–30 Sep 1967. *Extreme dates: Inland:* 14 Apr and 13 Jun. *Coastal:* 4 Jul and 26 Nov.

Remarks Creation of more reliable and stable staging areas in the form of mudflats, both coastally and inland, is desirable for this and other transient shorebirds. Although afforded legal protection from hunting pressure, shorebirds have never been provided the necessary stopover habitat that has been so lavishly furnished in the case of most Anatidae and other current game species.
Edward S. Brinkley

Bar-tailed Godwit *Limosa lapponica*

Range Chiefly Palearctic, breeding in northern Eurasia from northern Scandinavia to eastern Siberia and in Alaska east to Point Barrow south to the Yukon River Delta. Winters in western Europe from the British Isles to the Mediterranean region. Casual along both coasts of North America south to California and Florida.

Status Casual vagrant.

Occurrence There are five records. The first was a specimen collected at Moriches Inlet, Suffolk Co. 15 Nov 1946, AMNH 308880. The next two, sight records, were also at Moriches Inlet, 10 May 1971 (Conolly 1971) and 17 Aug 1974 (Davis 1975). Another was at Oak Beach Marsh, Suffolk Co. 23 Aug 1977. The most recent was photographed by Lindauer 5 Jun 1985 at Bay Park, East Rockaway, Nassau Co. (KB 36:52; NYSARC 1987).

Remarks NJ has five records as well (Halliwell 1995) but, like NY, none since 1985. MA has 14 records, three since 1985 (Veit and Petersen 1993). Of the 24 records in three states cited here, only three were before 1970, and only three were after 1985.
Emanuel Levine

Marbled Godwit   *Limosa fedoa*

Range Nearctic, breeding in southern Alaska, on the Great Plains south to the Dakotas and western Minnesota, and on James Bay. Winters primarily along the southern coasts in the United States and through Middle America to Colombia and northern Chile; on the Atlantic Coast regularly north to South Carolina. Migrates primarily through western North America but also casually in the eastern interior areas and along the Atlantic Coast.

Status Rare fall migrant on outer coast; very rare fall migrant inland. Very rare anywhere in spring.

Occurrence It prefers broad coastal mudflats and muddy shorelines in the interior and can be solitary or in the company of other large shorebirds including yellowlegs, Willet, and Hudsonian Godwit. In the nineteenth century it had a much more extensive breeding range than presently, and, as a result, was a regular migrant on the East Coast in spring and fall. After 1890 it became very rare because of hunting and habitat loss. By the early 1940s, it had recovered somewhat and was reported occasionally in flocks of up to ten. The maximum numbers seen have decreased since that time.

It is now seen annually in fall on the South Shore of LI and rarely in the interior on mudflats around large lakes or ponds. Most interior records are from the Great Lakes shorelines or lakes and ponds south of them. Eighty percent of all fall records are 21 Jul–22 Sep. The seven winter records are all coastal. There are 11 spring records for the past 20 years: six from LI, three from Monroe Co., and one each from Amenia, Dutchess Co. and Coles Creek Marina, St. Lawrence Co. Eighty percent of all occurrences in the past 20 years were of single individuals.

Coastal maxima: 10 Moriches Inlet, Suffolk Co. 14 Sep 1944; 8 JBWR 14 Aug 1951. *Extreme dates:* 8 May and 16 Jun; 4 Jul and 23 Feb.

Bull (1964) cited one very early spring record of 27 Mar 1950.

Remarks There are three distinct populations. The main one occupies the central plains. A small population on James Bay consists of birds averaging slightly smaller than those of the plains but otherwise identical. NY migrants from these two populations would be inseparable without banding records. A smaller subspecies was described by Gibson and Kessel (1989), from a population occupying a limited range on the Alaskan Peninsula. These birds winter in California and should not be expected in NY.
Dominic F. Sherony

Ruddy Turnstone   *Arenaria interpres*

Range Northern Holarctic, breeding in North America from northern Alaska and the Canadian Arctic islands east to Ellesmere Island and south to Southampton Island. Winters in the east from Massachusetts south to Tierra del Fuego.

A winter scene at Niagara Falls, sometimes called "the gull capital of the world." Sometimes as many as 14 species are recorded in one day. Bonaparte's Gulls, depicted here, occur in the tens of thousands, with the occasional Little Gull mixed in.

Status Common to abundant coastal migrant in spring and fall. Regular summering nonbreeder in small numbers and common in winter. Inland, generally uncommon in spring but fairly common in fall at selected locations on and near the Great Lakes.

Occurrence The primary spring migration route is along the coast, where it has a strong preference for beaches, rocky islands, and jetties; occasionally found on mudflats in small numbers. As are most high Arctic tundra nesters, it is a later migrant. Spring arrival averages 19 May; rare before 14 May and after 2 Jun. It is seen on the coast in flocks and inland in small numbers.

In fall, it is common on the coast in numbers from 20 to 100 or more, with adults arriving by 21 Jul and, as with most shorebirds, juveniles arriving about a month later, with an average date of 23 Aug (KB 40:148). The coastal peak of fall migration is 1 Aug–9 Sep. It is a fairly common wintering bird on the South Shore of LI, its numbers having increased in the past 20 years.

In the interior, it is a fairly common fall migrant on the Great Lakes, but later than on the coast, with an average arrival date of 31 Jul, and it is a regular migrant until 15 Sep, when numbers diminish, becoming very rare after Oct.

Coastal maxima: Spring: 1601 JBWR May 1990; 542 JBWR 16 May 1985. *Fall:* 412 JBWR 17 Aug 1987; 400 JBWR 4 Aug 1964. *Winter:* 193 Montauk, Suffolk Co. CBC 18 Dec 1993; 115 Orient, Suffolk Co. CBC 28 Dec 1991. *Inland maxima: Spring:* 135 Sandy Pond, Oswego Co. 29 May 1961; 100 Charlotte, Monroe Co. 4 Jun 1984. *Fall:* 55 El Dorado Beach, Jefferson Co. 19 Aug 1965; 43 same place 24 Aug 1985. *Extreme dates inland:* 15 Apr and 12 Jun; 21 Jul and 12 Nov.
Dominic F. Sherony

Red Knot   *Calidris canutus*

Range Northern Holarctic, breeding in North America from northern Alaska east to Ellesmere Island and south to Victoria and Southampton islands. Winters from Massachusetts south along the Atlantic and Gulf coasts to Tierra del Fuego.

Status Very common to abundant coastal migrant in spring and fall. Uncommon to fairly common and local on LI in winter. Inland, rare in spring, regular but uncommon in fall along the Great Lakes and some inland lakes.

Occurrence In the east, the main migration route in spring is along the Atlantic Coast. It tends to be a late migrant, because it is a high Arctic nester. Before 1890 it was reported to occur by the thousands, but its numbers decreased because of overhunting. It is seen regularly in spring in selected locations on the South Shore of LI along broad coastal salt meadows and mudflats, with the peak period of migration on the coast the last week of May; almost all inland spring records are 14–30 May.

In fall, more than 1000 can be seen at one time at certain coastal locations, with adults arriving by 19 Jul and juveniles by 21 Aug. Coastal concentrations are highest 24 Jul–26 Aug, with numbers decreasing after Aug. It is found annually on CBCs, numbers ranging from a few to 100, and it will winter on LI if conditions remain mild. It has been recorded in every month on the coast.

Inland, it is an uncommon fall migrant. From 1950 to at least the 1970s it was common on the shores of L. Ontario but is now seen in very small numbers. Data over the past two decades show that 75% of all fall records occur 18 Aug–8 Oct.

Coastal maxima: Spring: 2500 JBWR 30 May 1945; 450 JBWR 23 May 1985. **Fall:** 1685 JBWR 31 Jul 1985; 1225 JBWR 10 Aug 1987; 500 JBSP 6 Nov 1983. **Winter:** 110 Queens Co. CBC 20 Dec 1986; 103 Southern Nassau Co. CBC 5 Jan 1986. **Inland maxima: Spring:** 250 MNWR 1 Jun 1992; 250 Geneva, Ontario Co. 31 May 1993. **Fall:** 59 Hamlin Beach, Monroe Co. 15 Sep 1982; 7 El Dorado Beach, Jefferson Co. 27 Aug 1985; 7 Charlotte, Monroe Co. 15 Sep 1986. **Extreme dates inland:** 14 May and 22 Jun; 24 Jul and 23 Nov.

Dominic F. Sherony

Sanderling *Calidris alba*

Range Northern Holarctic, breeding in North America in northern Alaska and across the Canadian Arctic islands to Ellesmere Island and south to Hudson Bay. Winters along both coasts to Tierra del Fuego; on the Atlantic and Gulf coasts from Massachusetts south.

Status Common to abundant migrant on the outer coast; fairly common in winter and present as a summering nonbreeder. Fairly common fall migrant along the Great Lakes and certain inland lakes.

Occurrence Sanderlings collect in small flocks on long sandy beaches, usually feeding on the advancing and receding waves and roosting on the upper beach. They are rare visitants to small ponds, and then usually as individuals or possibly a few. As high Arctic breeders they are generally a late migrant. Spring arrival ranges from 7 to 31 May and average first arrival is 21 May (KB 37:19).

In fall, it usually arrives by late Jul in small groups mixed with other shorebirds. A few adults will appear in worn alternate plumage, but most will be molting. The average coastal arrival date is 20 Jul for adults and 27 Aug for juveniles (KB 40:148). It is common on the Great Lakes shorelines in fall, with migration most intense 21 Jul–20 Sep and numbers declining rapidly after that. Late records occur in Oct and sometimes into Nov. In winter, it is common on coastal LI, where flocks as high as 400–500 may be found. It has been recorded in every month on the coast.

Coastal maxima: Spring: 1500 East Hampton, Suffolk Co. 20 May 1927. **Fall:** 4000 JBWR 23 Aug 1991; 2000 Mecox Bay, Suffolk Co. 18 Sep 1924. **Winter:** 540 Southern Nassau Co. CBC 2 Jan 1994; 510 Quogue-Watermill, Suffolk Co. CBC 20 Dec 1986. **Inland maxima: Spring:** 26 Irondequoit Bay, Monroe Co. 30 May 1958; 20 Ontario Beach, Monroe Co. 4 Jun 1989. **Fall:** 230 Onondaga L. 1 Aug 1976; 179 El Dorado Beach, Jefferson Co. 21 Jul 1988. **Extreme dates inland:** 21 Apr and 11 Jun; 13 Jul and 27 Nov, exceptionally 18 Dec and 6 Jan. Dominic F. Sherony

Semipalmated Sandpiper   *Calidris pusilla*

Range Nearctic, breeding from northern Alaska east through Arctic Canada to northern Labrador and south to Hudson and James bays. Winters from southern Florida through the West Indies to southern Brazil.

Status Very abundant migrant on the coast, where it is also a regular summering nonbreeder in small numbers. Inland, common in spring and very common in fall.

Occurrence It is the most abundant migrant shorebird in the state and is usually found on tidal estuaries and mudflats, often associated with other small shorebirds. In spring, it is one of the later arrivals. Migrants first appear on the coast one to two weeks earlier than in the interior. Peak inland migration is in the last week of May; it is unusual before 10 May and has rarely occurred in Apr. Semipalmated Sandpiper migrates in three distinct groups (Paulson 1993). The disparity between the coastal and inland spring migration could be due to population differences.

In fall, the central and eastern Canadian populations migrate along the East Coast. They can be seen in the thousands on coastal mudflats and in the hundreds on the Great Lakes shorelines. Adults appear on the coast by 1 Jul; juveniles normally arrive 19 Aug (KB 40:148). A broad migration peak ranges from late Jul to the first week of Sep, with numbers dropping off rapidly after that. A few linger until Oct or even Nov. An unusually late 500 were seen at JBSP 6 Nov 1977 (Dremeaux, pers. comm.). Inland fall migration follows the same pattern as that on the coast.

Coastal maxima: Spring: 25,000 East Hampton to Mecox Bay, Suffolk

Co. 19 May 1924; 3342 JBWR 25 May 1985. *Fall:* 6000 JBWR 24 Aug 1951; 2291 JBWR 3 Aug 1985. *Inland maxima: Spring:* 2012 El Dorado Beach, Jefferson Co. 30 May 1979; 1000 Braddock Bay, Monroe Co. 1 Jun 1961. *Fall:* 1200 MNWR 14 Aug 1975; 1100 El Dorado Beach, Jefferson Co. 4 Aug 1966. *Extreme dates: Coastal:* 3 Apr and 20 Nov. *Inland:* 17 Apr and 16 Jun; 29 Jun and 10 Nov.

Remarks Semipalmated and Western sandpipers require some care in identification, especially when they are in basic plumage. Consult Veit and Jonsson 1984 or Hayman et al. 1986. Western is found in winter on the coast. Phillips (1975) established that there were no valid winter specimens of Semipalmated taken in the eastern United States except in FL, and late records are most probably Western. Winter birds identified as Semipalmated should be collected or photographed.
Dominic F. Sherony

Western Sandpiper   *Calidris mauri*

Range Eastern Palearctic, breeding only from northeastern Siberia east to northern and western coastal Alaska. In the Americas, winters along both coasts to South America, primarily in the west, but also in the east from Virginia south. Regular in migration on the East Coast north to Maine.

Status Uncommon to rare spring migrant throughout. In fall, a fairly common coastal migrant, uncommon but regular on L. Ontario.

Occurrence Only a small fraction of the population migrates southeast to the eastern seaboard before continuing on to wintering quarters. In fall, it is usually found in small numbers mixed with Semipalmated Sandpiper, which is closely related, but is sometimes observed in small flocks, primarily on the coast. The timing of its fall migration overlaps that of Semipalmated, but earliest arrivals and peak are both about three weeks behind its relative. Adults arrive in mid-Jul, and juveniles average about mid-Aug, with juveniles being more numerous than adults. Peak of migration is the last week of Aug to the first week of Sep. The inland fall migration is composed of individuals or small numbers in mixed flocks.

Almost all spring reports occur 2 May–4 Jun and consist of one to three individuals. There are two exceptional records for spring flocks, both inland: 60 studied and photographed at Northrup Creek, Monroe Co. 27 May 1977 (KB 27:152) and 25 at Point Breeze, Orleans Co. 26 May 1989 (KB 39:171).

Rare in winter on the coast, in recent years it has been found on LI CBCs in small numbers.

Coastal maxima: 250 Mecox Bay, Suffolk Co. 18 Sep 1944; 250 Cedar

Beach, Suffolk Co. 8 Aug 1990; 150 Line Islands, Nassau Co. 24 Jul 1993. *Inland maxima:* 39 MNWR 13 Oct 1993; 24 Point au Fer, Clinton Co. 25 Sep 1982. *Extreme dates: Coastal:* 25 Apr and 18 Jun; 2 Jul. *Inland:* 2 May and 17 Jun; 28 Jun and 13 Nov.

Remarks Separation of Western and Semipalmated sandpipers is always difficult but by no means impossible. See remarks and references under Semipalmated Sandpiper. Also see notes in Davis 1982, 1984.
Dominic F. Sherony

Red-necked Stint   *Calidris ruficollis*

Range Chiefly eastern Palearctic, breeding in northeastern Siberia and western Alaska. Winters from China to Australia and New Zealand, occasionally on the Pacific Coast of North America. Vagrant on the Atlantic Coast.

Status Casual vagrant.

Occurrence There are at least five records, all of adults in breeding plumage and all since 1985: one at JBWR 27 Jul–11 Aug 1985 (Cech, Dremeaux) (Morris 1986a; NYSARC 1987); two birds at Cedar Beach, Suffolk Co. 9 Aug 1992 (NYSARC 1995); what was presumed to be one of the same birds was also there 23–29 Aug 1992 (Lauro, Baldelli, ph) (KB 42:281); one at JBWR 8 Jul 1994 and, what may have been the same individual, 30 Jul–5 Aug 1994 (Quinlan, Fritz, Baldelli) (KB 44:342; NYSARC 1996); and the only report off LI, one in fading alternate plumage, briefly at Marshlands Conservancy, Rye, Westchester Co. 18 Aug 1995, submitted to NYSARC (Usai) (KB 45:327).

Remarks Although adults in basic plumage and juveniles probably pass through our region on occasion, the difficulties in separating them from various other *Calidris* species would make positive identification almost impossible. It was unreported in the Northeast before 1975, but there have been approximately 14 sightings since of breeding-plumaged adults from DE to ME, with the large majority occurring in Jul and Aug.
Thomas A. Burke

Little Stint   *Calidris minuta*

Range Palearctic, breeding from northern Scandinavia to western Siberia. Winters primarily in Africa and India. Vagrant to North America.

Status Casual vagrant.

Occurrence There are two records and an additional report, all from JBWR: an adult photographed during its stay on the East Pond 17–22 Jul

1983 (Davis) (NYSARC 1984); an adult visiting the West Pond only briefly 5 Jun 1984 (Buckley) (KB 34:271); and a carefully described juvenile at the East Pond 2 Sep 1987 (Downing, Howell) (NYSARC 1988).

Remarks With the increasing number of sightings of both this species and Red-necked Stint in the Northeast in recent years, the difficulties in some-times distinguishing the two in varying stages of alternate plumage are also becoming more apparent. There have been approximately 13 reports of Little Stint along the Atlantic Coast from DE to NS, commencing in 1979; this total is comparable to the number of Red-necked Stint reports, although the distribution differs somewhat, with MA recording the highest number of Little, and DE the most of Red-necked.
Thomas A. Burke

Least Sandpiper   *Calidris minutilla*

Range Nearctic, breeding across boreal Canada from western Alaska to northern Labrador south, in the east from northern Manitoba to the Gulf of St. Lawrence and Nova Scotia. Winters along the coast from Virginia to the Gulf states and Texas, south through Middle America, the West Indies, and central South America.

Status Common, occasionally abundant, migrant. Very rare in winter on the coast.

Occurrence This species, the smallest of our shorebirds, is common on grassy shores, flats, and pools, both coastal and inland, and after rains it may be seen on flooded golf courses, airports, and fields. As with other sand-pipers, fall adults generally arrive a month or more before juveniles. At JBWR adults have a fall mean arrival date of 3 Jul, and juveniles have a mean arrival date of 3 Aug (KB 36:70).

Coastal maxima: Spring: 5000 JBWR 19 May 1939; 500 eastern LI 9 May 1981. *Fall:* 1600 Moriches Inlet, Suffolk Co. 28 Sep 1936; 1200 Oak Beach, Suffolk Co. 18 Jul 1948. *Inland maxima: Spring:* 1000 Hamlin, Monroe Co. 21 May 1967, in flooded fields—an unprecedented number inland; 400 Tonawanda WMA, Niagara Co. 15 May 1995. *Fall:* 200 Oneida L. 3 Sep 1961; 180 Basic Creek, Albany Co. 21 Jul 1984. *Extreme dates:* 29 Mar and 2 Jun; 26 Jun and 24 Nov.

It is usually rare before May and after mid-Oct. Stragglers occur regularly on the coast in summer; there are only four mid-Jun records inland.

The Least Sandpiper has been recorded in winter on LI on eight occasions, mostly on CBCs. Seven of the reports were of one or two birds on the South Shore, with dates in mid to late Dec, except one on 10 Mar; the last was in 1977. Most unusual were five observed at JBWR 2 Jan 1955.

Remarks Its apparent decline, as evidenced by lower maxima in recent years, may be due to human population encroachment and the removal of migratory habitat, especially along the Atlantic Coast. On the Great Lakes shore, clean-water laws that have reduced the amount of nutrients, such as phosphates, have also reduced the algal mats, which contain the shorebird's invertebrate food source (G. Smith, pers. comm.).
William Watson

White-rumped Sandpiper   *Calidris fuscicollis*

Range Central Nearctic, breeding in the Arctic from northern Alaska and Bathurst Island south to southern Baffin Island and northwestern Hudson Bay. Winters in southern South America to Tierra del Fuego.

Status Uncommon to abundant fall coastal migrant, much less numerous in spring. Less common inland in both seasons.

Occurrence The White-rumped Sandpiper is one of the many species of shorebirds whose spring passage is chiefly by way of the center of the continent and in fall mainly along the Atlantic Coast. As a consequence, it is relatively rare in spring in NY and numerous in fall. This species, like some of its congeners, Pectoral, Baird's, and Least, prefers grassy meadows, pools, and pond edges to the more exposed flats that are frequented by many other waders. It is also found on lake and river shores upstate and sometimes on coastal estuaries and mudflats. This species is a notably late spring migrant, with flocks occurring well into Jun. It is rare before mid-May and after early Nov. At JBWR adults arrive in fall 18–31 Jul, with a mean arrival date of 25 Jul; juveniles arrive much later, 13 Sep–2 Oct, with a mean arrival date of 21 Sep (KB 36:70). Summer stragglers are not infrequent.

   Coastal maxima: Spring: 75 JBWR 5 Jun 1949; 60 East Hampton, Suffolk Co. 29 May 1927. *Fall:* (both covering multiple locations) 1000 East Hampton to Shinnecock Bay, Suffolk Co. 23 Aug 1930; 1000+ on the South Shore in the JBSP general area 26 Aug 1990. *Inland maxima: Spring:* 97 MNWR 30 May 1971; 38 Hamlin, Monroe Co. 1 Jun 1993. *Fall:* 35 Tonawanda, Erie Co. 8 Oct 1945; 33 Delta L., Oneida Co. 1 Sep 1985. *Extreme dates:* 23 Apr and 26 Jun; 9 Jul and 21 Dec.
William Watson

Baird's Sandpiper   *Calidris bairdii*

Range Holarctic, breeding in northeastern Siberia and from arctic Alaska and Canada south to Southampton and Baffin islands; also in Greenland. Winters in southern South America to Tierra del Fuego.

Status Uncommon but regular fall migrant. Casual in spring.

Occurrence Baird's Sandpiper prefers grassy areas either dry or moist and is found in fields and on turf farms and golf courses, especially after rain. It also frequents shores of grassy pools and coastal lagoons.

It migrates from far northern breeding grounds to its South American wintering grounds mainly through the middle of the continent, and the few birds we see are mostly first-year birds in fall. It is uncommon to occasionally fairly common in the Great Lakes Plain and Coastal Lowlands to very rare in the Appalachian Plateau and Adirondacks. Of the 533 birds reported 1975–1994, 13% were in Region 1, 11% in Region 2, 12% in Region 3, 23% in Region 5, 10% in Region 6, 3% in Region 7, 7% in Region 9, and 20% in Region 10. Upland, landlocked Regions 4 and 8 each had only 1% (KB 25:44).

There are only two spring records accepted by NYSARC: three birds photographed at Sharon Station, Dutchess Co. 31 May 1979 (Strauss, Manson, Pink) (KB 29:169; NYSARC 1980); one at Shinnecock Inlet, Suffolk Co. 5 Jun 1981 (Buckley) (KB 31:267; NYSARC 1982). Spring records should be carefully documented with details and photographs and submitted to NYSARC.

Coastal maxima: 18 East Hampton, Suffolk Co. 16 Sep 1933 (14 together and four others nearby—an exceptional concentration); 14 Cedar Beach, Suffolk Co. 3 Sep 1989. *Inland maxima:* 12 El Dorado Beach, Jefferson Co. 24 Aug 1988; 12 MNWR 3 Sep 1989. *Extreme dates:* 20 May and 13 Jun; 14 Jul and 20 Nov (inland specimen). December dates lack confirmation. Rare before Aug and after mid-Oct (only 5.4% of reports are before Aug, and only 3.6% are after Oct 15).
William Watson

Pectoral Sandpiper *Calidris melanotos*

Range Northern Palearctic and Nearctic, breeding along the Arctic Coast of Siberia east through arctic Canada to Southampton Island and south, in the east, to southern Hudson Bay. Winters to southern South America, casually north to the Gulf Coast and Florida.

Status On the coast, uncommon to common fall migrant; uncommon to fairly common spring migrant. Inland, just the reverse, common in fall but very common to abundant in spring. Most numerous upstate in the west, much less numerous in the east.

Occurrence Favors grassy pools and ponds and shortgrass meadows and, especially after heavy rains, fields, golf courses, and airports. Reports suggest that it is decreasing in numbers on the coast and increasing in the interior.

Unlike many of the common migrant shorebirds, this species is not known to summer in the state, nor is there a winter record authenticated by a specimen, photograph, or NYSARC acceptance. There are two CBC sightings, made by respected observers, which should be mentioned: Brooklyn 22 Dec 1962 by Davis and Heath (AB 17:102) and Montauk 2 Jan 1971 by Greenlaw and McKeever (AB 25:191).

Fall adults arrive six weeks before juveniles, with adults having a mean arrival date of 16 Jul and juveniles 27 Aug at JBWR (KB 36:70).

Coastal maxima: Spring: 72 JBWR 12 May 1970; 46 Goethals Bridge Pond, Richmond Co. 31 Mar 1987. *Fall:* 1200 Montauk to East Hampton, Suffolk Co. 25 Aug 1924; 350 Mecox Bay, Suffolk Co. 15 Sep 1935. *Inland maxima: Spring:* 1000+ Braddock Bay, Monroe Co. 12 Apr 1986; 508 Newstead and Clarence, Erie Co. 16 Apr 1977. There was a broad exceptional flight 5–19 Apr 1981: 450 Cattaraugus Co.; 400 Genesee Co.; 500 and 305 Monroe Co.; 300+ Livingston Co.; 550 Oswego Co. (KB 31:159,164,175). *Fall:* 400 MNWR early Sep 1976; 300 MNWR Aug 1989; 105 Hamlin, Monroe Co. 7 Aug 1992. *Extreme dates:* 2 Mar and 18 Jun; 1 Jul (inland) and 11 Dec. Usually rare before Apr and after Oct.

Remarks After wintering in South America, the majority migrate up the Mississippi Valley in spring, and western NY is favored by higher counts. In fall most migrate south over the Atlantic Ocean, which is why the coast gets large numbers after easterly storms in the fall.
William Watson

Sharp-tailed Sandpiper   *Calidris acuminata*

Range Eastern Palearctic, breeding in northeastern Siberia. Winters in the southwest Pacific from New Guinea and the Tonga Islands south to Australia. Regular in fall along the western coast of North America.

Status Accidental.

Occurrence There is one record. An adult was found by Davis and photographed during its stay on the East Pond at JBWR 18–24 Jul 1981 (Davis 1981b; NYSARC 1982). A published report of another (KB 33:298) was not accepted by NYSARC (1984).

Remarks This rare fall visitor to the East Coast has been reported at least ten times from VA to MA; dates of arrival were 30 Jun–3 Nov, with adults on the earlier dates and juveniles later.
Thomas A. Burke

Purple Sandpiper   *Calidiris maritima*

Range Holarctic except for Pacific quadrant, breeding in North America on islands in the Canadian Arctic south to the east shore of Hudson Bay.

Winters along rocky coasts from Newfoundland to Virginia, casually inland to the Great Lakes and along the Gulf Coast to southeastern Texas.

Status Locally a sometimes very common winter visitant on the coast. Uncommon at Niagara Falls and usually rare on the Great Lakes.

Occurrence It is mostly confined to rocky shores, and it is unusual to find it elsewhere. It is present in largest numbers on the wave-washed rock jetties along the South Shore of LI, the rocky promontories at Montauk, and on rocky islands and breakwaters in LI Sound. It lingers late in spring on the coast and in recent years at Niagara Falls.

Of 2650 birds reported 1976–1995, 6.2% were in Region 1, 2.3% in Region 2, 0.1% in Region 3, 2.3% in Region 5, 5.2% in Region 6, 0.1% in Region 7, 37.3% in Region 9, and 51.5% in Region 10. Landlocked Regions 4 and 8 do not have any records (KB 26:45). The totals for combined CBCs along the coast 1960–1989 range from 92 to 690 birds.

Coastal maxima: 200–300 JBSP 2 Mar 1984; 200 JBSP 17 May 1966; 150 Rye, Westchester Co. 1 Feb 1981. *Inland maxima:* A big flight along eastern L. Ontario shore, Jefferson Co. fall 1966: 27 on 11 Nov, 40 on 11 Dec, 23 on 17 Dec. Unprecedented away from the Great Lakes were 24 Oneida L. 14 Nov 1970. *Extreme dates:* 7 Sep and 7 Jun.

Eaton (1910) gave Sep dates for the Keuka L. area, but these dates were not supported by specimens. There are two specimens taken inland along the shore of Cayuga L. in Tompkins Co.: one near Ithaca 5 Nov 1921 (McNeil) CUM 2344 and one at Myers Point 27 Nov 1949 (Allen) CUM 23702. There is also a report of a bird seen by numerous observers on the shore of Seneca L. at Dresden, Yates Co. 4 Feb–19 Mar 1951 and a report of two birds at Geneva, Seneca Co. 27 May 1976 (KB 26:50). It is very rare in summer and reported lingering at Great Gull I., Suffolk Co. until mid-Jul as recently as 1988 (AB 43:1296). As for extreme dates inland, Niagara Falls should be treated differently from the rest of the Great Lakes basin. At Niagara Falls it is more likely to overwinter and stay later. Most of the other Great Lakes shoreline birds are migrants, and there is only one record beyond 23 Apr. In contrast, at Niagara Falls there have been six May records in the past ten years.

William Watson

Dunlin   *Calidris alpina*

Range Holarctic, breeding in arctic North America south to Hudson Bay. Winters along the Pacific and Gulf coasts and on the Atlantic Coast from Massachusetts to Florida.

Status Common to locally very abundant migrant on coast; only slightly less numerous inland. Common to locally very abundant in winter on coast; very rare inland. In summer very rare anywhere.

Occurrence One of the earliest of the common migrant shorebirds and also the latest. Its preferred feeding ground is a mudflat, where it probes for small mollusks, crustaceans, amphipods, insects, and such, often in flocks of 100 or more. Arrivals are regularly recorded in the first two weeks of Apr, although a very early single bird was reported at Greece, Monroe Co. 13 Mar 1982 (KB 32:191). Peak dates are generally around mid-May. By the end of May all but a few stragglers have departed.

Maxima vary greatly from year to year in part because of the impermanence of mudflats as a geographical feature. Some areas, such as the muddy edges of the bays and inlets of the large lakes and the coastal tidelands of LI, are large enough to compensate for the vagaries of nature. Some locales also benefit from regulation of water flow by manipulation of floodgates; MNWR and JBWR are two such places. Both areas are important stopovers for the species.

In the fall, although adults leave the breeding grounds four to eight weeks before the juveniles, no such large gap is apparent at the time of their arrival. In a nine-year study at JBWR, average arrival dates for adults were 7 Sep–24 Sep, with the mean date 17 Sep. For juveniles, average arrival dates were 5 Sep–20 Sep, with a mean date 13 Sep (KB 40:148). Peak dates for the state range from mid to late Oct. Departures spread out into Nov.

The coastal regions are the only places where Dunlins overwinter. The highest numbers have regularly been reported on the southern Nassau Co. CBCs, where there appears to have been a noticeable increase over the years. Before 1971, the count never reached 1000. In the 25 years since, on only five occasions has it been below 1100. The 1990–1995 average was 2075.

The few individuals reported inland during the winter months usually are not observed more than once or twice and are generally considered to be very late migrants. This is particularly true for reports from the Niagara Falls area and Braddock Bay, Monroe Co. One record of one or two birds at Charlotte, Monroe Co. 1–31 Jan 1993 (KB 43:125) is unusual and should be treated as a winter record.

Coastal maxima: Fall: 15,000 North Line Islands, Nassau Co. 9 Nov 1975; 4379 JBWR 27 Oct 1984. *Winter:* 4212 Southern Nassau Co. CBC Dec 1987. *Inland maxima: Spring:* 2125 Geneva lakefront, Ontario Co. 31 May 1993; 2000 MNWR 21 May 1995. *Fall:* 720 Sandy Pond, Oswego Co. 7 Oct 1976; 325 Derby Hill, Oswego Co. 19 Oct 1981.

Harriet T. Marsi and Gail M. Kirch

Curlew Sandpiper   *Calidris ferruginea*

Range Palearctic, breeding in northern Siberia, rarely to extreme northern Alaska. Winters over a wide range from the Mediterranean region to South

Africa and Madagascar and from tropical Asia to Australia and New Zealand. Wanders, almost regularly, to eastern North America (New Brunswick to New Jersey, but chiefly Long Island) and the Lesser Antilles.

Status Rare but regular coastal migrant. Casual away from the coast.

Occurrence One of the most sought-after shorebirds, it is very local and usually rare. The only reasonably certain locality where it might be seen is on the South Shore mudflats of LI. JBWR has accounted for more than two-thirds of all state records over the past 25 years. The only records away from the coast are one near Seneca Falls, Seneca Co. 16 and 18 May 1982 (Confer, Gray, Rybczynski) (KB 32:195; NYSARC 1983) and one at INWR 30–31 Jul 1990 (D'Anna, Potter) (KB 40:241; NYSARC 1992). Many records involve adults in at least partial breeding plumage. Most often found in fall migration, Jul–Sep; there is a smaller peak of occurrence in late May.

Maxima: All in the JBWR area: four, 14 May 1949; three, 21 May 1951; seasonal total of four, fall 1979 and fall 1980. *Extreme dates:* 2 May and 25 Nov, exceptionally to 19 Dec (specimen). One found at JBWR 23 and 27 Jan 1955 is the only midwinter record (P. A. Buckley et al., in litt.).

Remarks Bull (1974) advanced three theories that may explain its presence in North America. (1) Direct east-west crossing from Europe to North America during migration. According to Cramp (1983), many individuals follow a major migration route from their Siberian breeding grounds west through northern Europe, then south into Africa. It is possible that some may continue west to the coast of North America.

(2) Disruption of the southbound migration to Africa by tropical storms, with birds being carried to tropical America in the fall. These birds may account for the following spring's sightings along the coast. Veit and Petersen (1993) leaned toward this theory on the basis of the large number of spring records and the rarity of juveniles in New England. In MA and on LI, however, fall records actually outnumber spring records. The status of juveniles south of New England is unclear, because many reports do not include age details. Hayman et al. (1986) listed a record of a bird banded in Belgium and recovered 14 days later in Barbados. That bird probably followed either the direct east-west or the disrupted African route.

(3) Eastward migration through Siberia, with a few birds continuing on to North America. It is possible that some of these may move on to the East Coast. West Coast and inland occurrences, although less frequent than Atlantic Coast records, may represent birds that followed this path.

In addition, it has bred sporadically in Alaska. It is possible that the Alaskan birds may account for some East Coast records. Morris found a fresh juvenile at JBWR 25 Sep 1985 (AB 40:89). As is the case with Ruff, it seems likely that Curlew Sandpipers may arrive here by more than one route.

Michael F. Cooper

Stilt Sandpiper *Calidris himantopus*

Range Nearctic, breeding from northern Alaska and Victoria Island south and east to the Hudson Bay area. Winters chiefly in South America from central Brazil south to the northern parts of Argentina and Chile.

Status In fall, an annual, locally common migrant on the coast and at MNWR; uncommon along L. Ontario, and rare elsewhere. In spring, very rare throughout.

Occurrence Stilt Sandpipers frequently associate with Lesser Yellowlegs and dowitchers and, like them, wade and feed in shallow pools and marshes, where they can be found in fresh or brackish water 1–3 inches deep. Since their main spring migration route is through the Midwest, they are very rare then; there have been about 15 spring records for the past 25 years. Most are of single individuals, but four were seen at Oak Beach, Suffolk Co. 14 May 1983 (KB 33:226). Most have occurred 2 May–23 May, with several records in Apr.

In fall, it is regular at MNWR and selected coastal locations. Average dates for first arrival of adults and juveniles are 13 Jul and 17 Aug, respectively (KB 39:95). Ninety percent of their fall migration occurs 28 Jul–20 Oct, with the peak period 1 Sep–22 Sep; they are very rare after 28 Oct.

Coastal maxima: 200 Mastic, Suffolk Co. 12 Aug 1912; 80 JBWR 13 Sep 1984. *Inland maxima:* 125 MNWR 7 Sep 1986; 69 MNWR 8 Aug 1968. *Extreme dates:* 2 Apr and 10 Jun; 1 Jul and 17 Nov.

Dominic F. Sherony

Buff-breasted Sandpiper *Tryngites subruficollis*

Range Nearctic, breeding in Alaska and northwestern Canada. Migrates through the Central Flyway, almost exclusively in spring but with some Atlantic Coast return flight. Winters in Patagonia.

Status Rare but regular fall migrant, both on the coast and inland.

Occurrence Recorded only in its fall migration, except for one sighting, this sandpiper frequents areas of short dry grass, airports, meadows, and open fields, and occasionally the uppermost reaches of tidal flats. In recent years sod farms across upstate NY and on LI have been the most productive places to observe them. A sighting on 28 May 1977 at Sandy Pond, Oswego Co. (DeBenedictis 1977) is the only detailed spring record. There are no spring specimens.

Maxima: Two flocks of more than 40 on plowed fields near Mecox Bay, Suffolk Co. during late August 1973 and 70 near Sagaponack, Suffolk Co. on 9 Sep 1977 represent the largest concentrations recorded. Reports of this species have increased during the last 20 years, but groups of more than one or two individuals are still very rare. *Extreme dates:* A bird killed by a plane on 3 Aug 1963 at JFK Airport, Queens Co. (specimen USNM) is the earliest record. There are several reliable reports 10–15 Oct published in *The Kingbird*, the latter being the latest verified date. Rare before late Aug and after early Oct.

Remarks This species' spring migration is exclusively along the Central Flyway, primarily west of the Mississippi R. and east of the Rockies, and it is virtually unknown in the state during that season. Any spring sighting should be carefully documented and, if possible, substantiated by photographs. There are two spring sight records in MA, May 1971 and Apr 1984 (Viet and Petersen 1993), none in RI or NJ, and a few in PA (Santner et al. 1992).
Michael Lolya

Ruff *Philomachus pugnax*

Range Palearctic, breeding from Great Britain and Scandinavia east to northeastern Siberia and, occasionally, western Alaska. Winters to South Africa and Australasia. Rare but regular migrant throughout North America, also Barbados.

Status Formerly very rare; in recent years a rare but regular migrant.

Occurrence Before 1949 this species was known only from LI. Since 1960 it has appeared upstate with some regularity. It is most frequently observed at JBWR and in the JBSP area. It prefers muddy edges and grassy pools to open mudflats and occasionally appears on farm fields on eastern LI. Upstate it has been reported most often at MNWR and in the Braddock Bay, Monroe Co. area.

The number of reports has decreased significantly since the 1970s. In 1975–1980, *The Kingbird* listed approximately 40 records (16 upstate, 24 on LI). From 1987 to 1992, however, the number fell to about 13 (3 upstate, 10 on LI). The reason for this decline is unclear. Although many previously favored haunts may have been altered or destroyed, the decrease in records holds true for locations that still attract large numbers of other shorebirds, such as JBWR. The bulk of East Coast records now come from south of our area, with coastal DE being a current hot spot.

Coastal maxima: 3 JBWR 21 Apr–27 May 1956; 3 North Line I., Nassau Co. 4–11 Jul 1975. *Inland maxima:* 6 Onondaga L. 1 Jul–12 Sep 1964; 5 at the same location 1 Jul–20 Aug 1965. These counts have not been repeated in recent times. Apparently no more than two have been seen together anywhere in NY since 1975. *Extreme dates:* 7 Mar and 6 Nov. One at HLSP 16 Dec 1978–28 Jan 1979 provided the only winter record (Levine) (KB 29:115). Rarely recorded on LI before May or after Sep. Nearly all upstate records were May–Aug.

Remarks Bull (1974) favored a Siberian origin, on the basis of the frequency of occurrences away from the coast. It seems possible, if not likely, that migrants may be arriving from more than one source. Another possibility is direct passage from Europe or Africa to the Americas during fall migration as discussed under Curlew Sandpiper. More recently, it has been found breeding in Alaska (Hayman et al. 1986), and the presence of juvenal plumaged birds in fall on the East Coast has fueled speculation about the possibility of North American origins (AB 38:905). One seen by Morris at JBWR on 25 Sep 1985 was described as being in "exceptionally fresh" juvenal plumage (AB 40:89). This, surprisingly, was the first record of a juvenile at JBWR, a location that has accounted for more than 25% of all state records over the past 20 years. The Refuge's second juvenile appeared there the following fall, on 28 Sep 1986 (ph, KB 37:106).
Michael F. Cooper

Short-billed Dowitcher *Limnodromus griseus*

Range Nearctic, breeding in three widely separated areas: southern Alaska, west-central Canada east to western Hudson Bay, and the Ungava Peninsula in northern Quebec. Winters from California, the Gulf Coast, and South Carolina south through the West Indies and Middle America to Peru and Brazil. Migrates along both coasts and through interior North America.

Status Common to very abundant coastal migrant in spring and fall. Uncommon inland in spring.

Occurrence In May, Short-billed Dowitchers move through rapidly, migrating to their breeding habitats in the wet tundra of the Arctic. They appear at selected locations on the coast, where flocks of 100–200 are regularly seen, with the peak period being the first two weeks of May. In the interior they are uncommon and, on many occasions, are seen only after inclement weather, occurring as a few individuals or in flocks of 10–30. Eighty percent of inland spring records are 13–27 May.

In the fall, they concentrate on the coastal mudflats, with the mean date of first arrival 30 Jun for adults and 10 Aug for juveniles (KB 40:148). The coastal migration has a long peak period, ranging, on average, from 15 Jul to 15 Aug. Numbers then drop rapidly, but a few individuals will linger until the end of Oct.

In the interior, they are fairly common in fall where habitat is adequate. They are seen annually along the Great Lakes, INWR, and MNWR in numbers up to about 40, but 5–20 is more common. Data show two peaks: 3–24 Jul and 19 Aug–6 Sep, which would correspond to adults and juveniles. They can be seen through Sep and sometimes into Oct. In cases of late occurrence, identification needs to be carefully checked because of possible confusion with Long-billed Dowitcher.

Coastal maxima: Spring: 8000 JBWR 12 May 1939; 4000 Far Rockaway, Queens Co. 7 May 1950. *Fall:* 3800 JBWR 22 Jul 1978; 3500 Line Islands, Nassau Co. 24 Jul 1992. *Inland maxima: Spring:* 600 West Lake Shore, Monroe Co. 18 May 1980; 127 Cuba L., Allegany Co. 16 May 1979. *Fall:* 220 MNWR 13 Oct 1965; 175 Manitou, Monroe Co. 20 Aug 1960. *Extreme dates:* 20 Mar and 5 Jun; 25 Jun and 7 Nov. There is one winter record, 26 Dec 1979, Central Suffolk Co. CBC (AB 34:408), verified by call note.

Remarks There are three subspecies of Short-billed Dowitcher. The adults are separable in alternate plumage; juveniles are not separable in the field. The Pacific Coast subspecies, *caurinus*, has not been recorded in the East. The East Coast subspecies, *griseus*, is the common coastal migrant from FL to MA. The subspecies common in the Midwest is *hendersoni*, which breeds in central Canada. Although *hendersoni* is uncommon along the East Coast, it is observed in small numbers in fall on LI. There were four fall specimens of this form taken on LI (Pitelka 1950). It arrives on the coast in Jul, before *griseus* (Wilds and Newlon 1983). In the upstate region, *hendersoni* is the predominant spring migrant, on the basis of sight observations and specimens. Jaramillo et al. (1991) indicated that this subspecies is the predominant migrant in ON both spring and fall. Bull (1974) mentioned two inland specimens of *hendersoni*: Tonowanda, Erie Co. 5 Aug 1949 and Cayuga L. 9 Sep 1910. Another specimen was collected in Rochester, Monroe Co. 28 Jul 1946 and is in the RMAS. Beardslee and Mitchell (1965) noted six specimens of *hendersoni* taken in the Buffalo area and held by the BMS. Readers should consult Wilds and Newlon 1983, Paulson 1993, and Jaramillo et al. 1991 to study and understand the plumage differences.
Dominic F. Sherony

Long-billed Dowitcher   *Limnodromus scolopaceus*

Range Holarctic, breeding from northeastern Siberia east to Alaska and extreme northwestern Canada. Winters from California, Texas, the Gulf Coast, and Florida south through Middle America to Panama. Migrates primarily west of the Rockies; less frequently in the east, primarily in fall, from southern Canada to Florida.

Status Fairly common fall migrant on the coast, uncommon in winter. Uncommon in fall on the L. Ontario plain; rare elsewhere inland. Casual throughout in spring.

Occurrence It prefers freshwater ponds and marshes but also occurs on coastal shores and estuaries. Adults are observed primarily on the coast, with a mean first arrival of 22 Jul and a peak 5–30 Aug. In the interior, fall adults are rare and usually occur with mixed shorebird flocks. The migration of juveniles is later, but it does overlap that of adults. On the coast, the mean first arrival of juveniles is 27 Sep, and peak numbers occur 1–28 Oct. On the L. Ontario plain, juveniles are seen annually in small numbers in locations that attract large numbers of shorebirds. Data are sparse but show a peak 2 Sep–21 Oct (Sherony 1994). Juveniles can linger up to a month, if conditions permit, before continuing on to the Gulf Coast.

On average, it is recorded every other year on LI CBCs, being seen in small numbers in Dec and Jan. It can be very difficult to separate the two dowitcher species at this time, but juvenile Long-billed will retain some juvenal plumage. Late dowitchers are most likely Long-billed, but Short-billed is possible and cannot be ruled out by timing alone.

As a spring migrant, Long-billed Dowitcher is casual in NY. There have been three reports, none with details, published since 1976 (KB 26:179, 27:174, 38:196), with a range in dates from 30 Apr to 15 May, and one late spring report, without details, at Shinnecock Inlet, Suffolk Co. 23 Jun 1982 (KB 32:302). It is rare and irregular anywhere on the East Coast in spring (AB 46:400). Any spring bird should be carefully studied and, prefer-ably, photographed.

Coastal maxima: Fall: 34 JBWR 18 Oct 1987; 33 JBWR 9 Oct 1990. **Winter:** both on Southern Nassau Co. CBC: 7 on 29 Dec 1991; 7 on 3 Jan 1993. **Inland maxima: Fall:** 35 MNWR 17 Sep 1976; 25 MNWR 13 Oct 1967. **Extreme dates:** 17 Jul and 3 Jan, exceptionally to 27 Feb.

Remarks Recent advances in identification permit more reliable separation of the two dowitchers (Wilds and Newlon 1983; Hayman et al. 1986; Morris 1990; Paulson 1993). Juveniles and adults in alternate plumage are separable under close observation; adults in basic plumage are best separated by call.

Dominic F. Sherony

Common Snipe *Gallinago gallinago*

Range Holarctic, breeding in North America from Alaska to Labrador and south, in the east, to New England, northern New Jersey, Pennsylvania, Ohio, and Illinois. Winters in the east north to Massachusetts and south to northern South America.

Status Locally common breeder. Fairly common to very common migrant, less numerous on the coast; locally uncommon winter visitant on the coast, rarer inland.

Breeding This species is at the southern edge of its breeding range in NY, where it prefers bogs, marshes, wet meadows, and wet areas along streams. Atlas workers Confirmed breeding in 73 blocks, primarily in the Cattaraugus Highlands, Great Lakes and St. Lawrence plains, and L. Champlain Valley regions of western, central, and northern NY. Bull (1974) said it appeared to be quite rare in the Mohawk Valley, but Atlas workers found it well represented there and in the Black R. Valley. It was more scattered in the Adirondacks and Appalachian Plateau, where there are fewer suitable wetlands. In the southeast it was Confirmed in only one block, in the Hudson Valley in Orange Co.

Nonbreeding Fall migrants arrive as early as Jul in areas where it does not breed. Scattered single birds or occasionally small groups overwinter in wet areas. In spring, it is usually rare before mid-Mar.

  Spring maxima: 100 Watkins-Montour Airport marsh, Schuyler Co. 8 Apr 1962; 100 Eden, Erie Co. 11 Apr 1992. *Fall maxima:* 150 OOWMA 3 Nov 1968. *Winter maxima:* During the winter of 1975–1976, 35 were at Clove L. Park, Richmond Co.; 19 at Water Mill, Suffolk Co.; and 12 at Sagaponack, Suffolk Co.

Remarks The male, which arrives 10–14 days ahead of the female on breeding grounds, performs a remarkable courtship flight. During dives, the outer tail feathers vibrate, producing rapid hollow sounds. This sound is called winnowing.

Robert E. Marcotte

American Woodcock *Scolopax minor*

Range Eastern Nearctic, breeding from southern Manitoba and Minnesota to southern Newfoundland and south throughout eastern North America to Florida, the Gulf states, and Texas. Winters in the southern portion of the range, north rarely to New York and Massachusetts.

Status Widespread, locally common breeder, numerous and widespread migrant, more common inland in spring and on the coast in fall. Uncommon along the coast in winter, very rare elsewhere. Populations appear to be stable after many years of decline.

Breeding In 1839, in three days, Frank Forester bagged 234 birds with a muzzle-loading shotgun; in 1840, in the same locality, he downed 125 in one day. This extraordinary abundance, due to extensive clearing of the aboriginal forest, began to decline with the improvement of firearms and the advent of market hunting (Sheldon 1971). Sportsmen and writers in the late nineteenth century agreed that woodcock was in drastic decline. Eaton (1910) said that it "formerly nested commonly in every county of the State, but is now fast disappearing from the more inhabited districts on account of the incessant slaughter by gunners in the open season, and by telegraph wires at all seasons, the killing of its young by cats and other predatory animals, the draining of swamps and the destruction of its favorite coverts." He estimated a 98% reduction in population since the mid-nineteenth century! Since then, it has made a substantial recovery due to decreased hunting pressure, abandonment of farmland, and wetlands protection, although these gains have been partly offset by increases in pesticide residues (now somewhat but not entirely abated), extensive forest regrowth, and development.

Atlas workers found widespread breeding throughout the state, with major population clusters on the Great Lakes and St. Lawrence plains, upper Finger Lakes area, Champlain and Hudson valleys, SI, and LI from Brooklyn to within sight of the Montauk Lighthouse. It is likely to have been underreported away from population centers because it is most often detected by its aerial courtship flights, which take place, beginning in late Feb, at dawn and dusk. Breeding birds in remote blocks, surveyed late in the season, or on daylight visits from other areas, may have been overlooked.

It is among our earliest breeders, with males reported in display as early as the last week in Jan and, commonly, by the last week of Feb. Courtship flights often continue into May, and breeding activity is reported into Jun. A bird incubating three eggs 11–23 Jul 1982 in Oswego Co. was unusually late.

Males may occupy adjacent singing grounds, and, when contiguous habitat is available, a number appear to form a loose or "exploded" lek, such as 24 singing males at Wertheim NWR, Suffolk Co. 1993 (R. Parris, pers. comm.). Excess males, possibly young birds, remain in the vicinity of good singing territory, looking for a chance to flight-sing and mate (Sheldon 1971). Many of the details of this mating system are, surprisingly, still not well known.

Semi-open fields are required for the birds' breeding strategy, and relatively undisturbed wet areas with adjacent cover for nesting and feeding. Woodcock have thus benefited from wetlands protection, but forest regrowth has closed down singing fields in many undeveloped areas. On balance, populations appear to have stabilized, but at a level much below their former abundance.

Nonbreeding It regularly arrives in late Feb or early Mar in most regions and departs in late Nov or early Dec. The maxima reported by Bull (1974) have not been surpassed: 30 Monroe Co. 26 Mar 1963; 25 near Rochester, Monroe Co. 7 Apr 1954; 18 East Hampton, Suffolk Co. 31 Oct 1944.

A flock of 20 birds that landed on a second-story porch and took suet from a feeder in Callicoon Center, Sullivan Co. after a 26 Feb 1992 snowstorm suggests that, unless revealed by chance or unusual circumstances, migrant flocks generally pass through unnoticed.

It is not clear whether birds reported between mid-Dec and mid-Feb are stragglers, true overwinterers, or birds that have returned north during warm periods from nearby wintering grounds.
Eric Salzman

Wilson's Phalarope

Phalaropus tricolor

Range Nearctic, breeding from British Columbia and southern Ontario south to California and Texas; also to northern Indiana, southern Ontario, southwestern Quebec, and recently in New York and Massachusetts. Winters in western South America.

Status Has nested twice at a single locality. Uncommon fall migrant, rare spring migrant. Casual in summer.

Breeding Although this phalarope bred in adjacent ON as long ago as 1879 and 1959 (Beardslee and Mitchell 1965), and in southwestern PQ by the mid-1970s, it was not confirmed as a nester in NY until 1993 (Krueger 1993; NYSARC 1995). On the Gravelle Farm, on L. Champlain, Clinton Co., where one had been observed in Jun during the Atlas project (KB 31:182), a pair was present 18–31 May 1993. The male and three chicks were observed on 18 June and remained in the area until at least 19 Jul (KB 43:256, 337). In 1994, a pair returned to the adjacent Laurin Farm. The female was seen on 10 May and was last seen with the male on 15 May. The male remained and was observed with a nearly grown chick on 29 Jun and with two juveniles on 15 Jul (KB 44:327). A male was present in the same field 7 Jun 1995, but breeding was not confirmed (KB 45:314).

Nonbreeding Spring migration occurs primarily during May. Wilson's is the phalarope most frequently seen, but it never occurs in the occasional large numbers characteristic of the other two species. Spring migrants have typically departed by the first week of Jun, but summer stragglers occur. Two females spent the summer of 1977 in Greece, Monroe Co. (KB 27:218). It may be observed in fall throughout the state. Migrants may arrive by late Jun, and the migration is quite protracted.

Spring maxima: 3 MNWR 8 May 1955; 3 females, JBWR, most of May 1958. *Fall maxima:* 15 JBWR 13 Aug 1977; 10 Oak Beach, Suffolk Co. 10 Aug 1973. *Extreme dates:* 24 April; 19 Jun and 9 Nov, exceptionally to 20 Nov (specimen.)

Kenneth P. Able

Red-necked Phalarope *Phalaropus lobatus*

Range Holarctic, breeding in North America from northern Alaska and southern Baffin Island south to northwestern British Columbia and east to James Bay and Labrador. Winters at sea, primarily off Peru and West Africa.

Status Uncommon to occasionally abundant migrant offshore, especially in spring; more frequent inshore than Red Phalarope, but in smaller flocks. Rare to uncommon fall migrant inland, very rare in spring. Accidental in winter.

Occurrence Both on the coast of LI and on inland lakes, the Red-necked Phalarope occurs more frequently than the Red Phalarope. Although the two occur together, the Red-necked is more likely to be seen on mudflats, where it has been observed hawking insects with Wilson's Phalaropes (KB 21:11).

Coastal maxima: Spring: 900 Westhampton Beach to Shinnecock Inlet, Suffolk Co. 2 May 1958; 500 Shinnecock Bay, Suffolk Co. 29 Apr 1937. *Fall:* 165 off Montauk, Suffolk Co. 13 Sep 1916. *Inland maxima: Spring:* 6 Parma, Monroe Co. 30 May 1964; 3 collected near Albany 19 May 1882. *Fall:* 39 Derby Hill, Oswego Co. 19 Oct 1967; 17 MNWR 1 Sep 1975. *Extreme dates:* 29 Mar (specimen) and 7 Jun; 4 Jul (AMNH specimen collected at sea about 7 mi off East Hampton, Suffolk Co.) and 9 Dec.

Summer stragglers are seen offshore, and a female in alternate plumage was on the St. Lawrence R., off Grenadier I., Jefferson Co. 23 Jun 1955. The only winter record was of one bird at Irondequoit Bay, Monroe Co. 31 Dec 1982–5 Jan 1983 (KB 33:118).

Kenneth P. Able

Red Phalarope   *Phalaropus fulicaria*

Range Holarctic, breeding in North America from western Alaska to northern Baffin Islands, south to northern Quebec and northern Labrador. Winters at sea off West Africa and both coasts of South America. Migrates off both North American coasts and irregularly throughout the interior.

Status Regular pelagic and offshore migrant, occasionally very abundant in spring. Rare but regular fall migrant and winter visitant inland; casual in spring. Recorded in every month of the year.

Occurrence Occurs most commonly at the eastern end of LI in spring and at times may be seen in large numbers offshore or when forced inshore after storms or prolonged periods of fog. Nineteen birds that struck the Montauk Lighthouse in fog on the night of 30 Apr 1898 are in the AMNH. Numbers in fall are much smaller, perhaps because it migrates farther offshore then.

Inland it is most numerous during fall migration. Spring migrants are much rarer, and some early spring records may actually be of overwintering birds: for example, L. Ontario west of Rochester, 14 Mar 1982 (KB 32:191). There are only two other inland spring records: two, Buffalo Harbor, Erie Co. 6–9 Jun 1941; one in alternate plumage on a small pond in Ghent, Columbia Co. 20 May 1979 (KB 29:165). Single individuals or very small numbers may be found on open water in winter, both on the coast and inland. Inland, it is most frequent in the Rochester area (maximum of three on the 1971 CBC) and at Dunkirk Harbor, Chautauqua Co., where it has overwintered (KB 30:104). It is present off-shore in small numbers during summer.

Coastal maxima: A tremendous movement off Suffolk Co. in 1969 produced 12,000 in the Montauk area on 9 May and thousands from Westhampton to East Hampton on 11 May. *Inland maxima:* 13 L. Ontario at Derby Hill, Oswego Co. 22 Oct 1969; 7 at the same place 22 Oct 1976. *Extreme dates:* 14 Mar and 12 Jun (specimen); 24 Aug and 12 Dec. Kenneth P. Able

SKUAS, GULLS, TERNS, AND SKIMMERS—LARIDAE

Great Skua   *Catharacta skua*

Range Palearctic, breeding in Iceland and the Faroe, Shetland, and Orkney islands. Disperses widely over the North Atlantic in winter.

Status Very rare late fall and winter visitant to offshore waters of LI.

Occurrence The fifth edition of the AOU Check-list (1957) treated *C. skua* as a species consisting of five subspecies, under the English name Skua. In 1977, the five forms were put into two species, Great Skua *(C. skua)* and South Polar Skua *(C. maccormicki)*, and the sixth edition of the AOU Check-List (1983) listed them as such. The taxonomy of this genus seems still to be in flux.

There are nine records for Great Skua, all from offshore waters. The first was found on 17 Mar 1886 at Amagansett, Suffolk Co. AMNH 6463327. The next two were from Montauk, 11 Nov 1937 and 14 Dec 1937, but these may have been the same individual. The next record came on 20 Nov 1970 off Point O'Woods, Fire I., and another was seen on 20 Nov 1977 20 mi south of Montauk (KB 27:60). Given the dates of these records, it is likely that the four sightings are correctly assigned to this species, but one cannot be certain.

The next records took place after the 1977 split and have been assigned to *C. skua,* on the basis of both date and field identification, the latter being an admittedly difficult task. On 2 Feb 1978, three to five birds were seen 75 mi south of LI (KB 28:126). On 20 May 1978, another was spotted 95 mi southeast of Montauk just south of Block Canyon (KB 28:198), and the most recent was just north of Block Canyon 4 Mar 1995 (KB 45:233).

Remarks For further discussion of this genus, consult Devillers 1977 and Veit and Petersen 1993.

John P. Askildsen

South Polar Skua *Catharacta maccormicki*

Range Antarctic, breeding on the South Shetland Islands and along the Antarctic Coast. In southern winter, ranges at sea in the North Pacific to the Gulf of Alaska and Japan and in the North Atlantic to Georges Bank and Hudson Canyon, off Massachusetts and New York.

Status Very rare summer visitant to offshore LI waters.

Occurrence Please refer to the opening paragraph of Occurrence section under Great Skua. Birds of the species *maccormicki* seen in offshore LI waters May–Sep are Southern Hemisphere breeders spending their austral winters here. There are some seven records of 16 individuals dated earlier than 1977 and assigned to this species because of the summer date. One struck the Montauk Point Lighthouse 10 Aug 1896, and only the wing was preserved, AMNH 67894. Sight reports were: one 8 Jun 1974 Fire I. (KB 25:62); three 5 Jul 1975, 30 mi south of Fire I. Inlet (KB 25:235); three 18 Jun 1975, 20 miles south of Montauk (KB 25:234); one 25 May 1976, Hudson Canyon (AB 30:820); six 26 May 1976 (AB 30:820) Hudson Canyon; and one at RMSP 1 Oct 1977 (KB 28:62).

Since 1977, there were six sight records involving eight birds assigned to this species. One 26 May 1979, Hudson Canyon (KB 29:172); three 2 Jun 1979, Block Canyon (KB 29:172); one 18 Jul 1980, one 28 May 1987, one 9 Jun 1987, all off Montauk (KB 37:241); and one 20 Aug 1993, off Montauk (KB 43:350).

Remarks See the Remarks section under Great Skua.
John P. Askildsen

Pomarine Jaeger *Stercorarius pomarinus*

Range Northern Holarctic, breeding in North America from western and northern Alaska throughout the Canadian Arctic islands south to Hudson Bay. Winters at sea off both coasts, in the western Atlantic from North Carolina to northern South America. Casual in interior North America in migration.

Status Regular pelagic migrant off LI, uncommon in spring, fairly common in fall, occasional in summer and a few in winter. Rare on L. Ontario in fall and very rare inland throughout the state.

Occurrence Pomarine Jaegers are extremely powerful fliers, predators of the sea, able to chase down and catch a phalarope on the wing. Well known for their habit of harassing gulls, terns, and shearwaters, they collect in areas where small fish are abundant at the surface and seabirds are concentrated. They are annual on spring pelagic trips off LI, with sightings of one to four from late May to the end of Jun; a few are seen on summer trips. In fall they are the most common jaeger coastally and can occur in large numbers. Most fall observations occur 18 Aug–30 Sep, with a peak occurring 16–30 Sep (KB 28:139) when 5–30 are recorded. They may continue into Dec. Sightings from land are unusual on the coast.

Jaegers have a regular inland migration in fall and are seen annually on L. Ontario (see discussion under Parasitic Jaeger), but Pomarine is rare inland, usually occurring as single birds. Ninety percent of all sightings occur 22 Sep–1 Dec; most are juveniles, which leave the Arctic later than the adults (Harrison 1983). Data are insufficient to make a judgment on when juveniles arrive. They are accidental away from L. Ontario but have occurred on L. Erie, the Niagara R., and in a few other locations.

Coastal maxima: Spring: 30 off JBSP 13 Jun 1955; 12 Hudson Canyon 30 May 1992 and 24 May 1985. *Fall:* 35 off Montauk, Suffolk Co. 16 Sep 1973; 30 Block Canyon 20 Sep 1980. *Inland maxima: Fall:* 6 Hamlin Beach, Monroe Co. 16 Sep 1982; 3 same location 14 Oct 1979. *Extreme dates: Coastal:* 21 May and 13 Dec. *Inland:* 14 Sep and 10 Jan.

Sep records are rare inland. There are three Jan records from Monroe Co.: 1 Jan 1977, 9–10 Jan 1983, 1 Jan 1992. A single out-of-season adult spent a week at Manitou, Monroe Co. 19–25 June 1978 (KB 28:239).

Remarks Separation of jaeger species in flight requires some knowledge and practice. Those interested should consult Jonsson 1993, Stallcup 1990, or Harrison 1983.
Dominic F. Sherony

Parasitic Jaeger   *Stercorarius parasiticus*

Range Holarctic, breeding in North America from Alaska to Ellesmere Island and south, in the east to Hudson Bay and northern Labrador. Winters at sea off both coasts of South America and of the coast of West Africa, locally north to Maine. Migrates along the coasts and casually in interior North America, where recorded most frequently around the Great Lakes.

Status Uncommon spring and fall pelagic migrant off LI. Fairly common to uncommon on L. Ontario in fall. Rare elsewhere.

Occurrence On the coast, Parasitic Jaegers are seen more often from shore than any other jaeger, with 75% of LI sightings being from Montauk during spring and fall, most in Oct and Nov. On pelagic trips they are regularly seen in low numbers, usually from one to three, from late May to mid-Jun and from mid-Aug to early Oct.

Parasitic is the most frequent inland migrant jaeger in fall. It is known that jaegers migrate overland (Dean et al. 1976), and they are seen annually over L. Ontario (Crumb and Smith 1980), including several times when they have been observed heading inland from the southeastern corner of the lake. The belief is that these birds originate in James Bay and generally travel at high altitude, appearing over L. Ontario when there are northwest winds preceded by a cold front. If weather conditions permit, most probably bypass the lake. They had been a fairly common migrant from the 1960s through the 1980s but became uncommon after 1989. The reason for this change is not known, but their annual numbers can be cyclic. In general, there are higher numbers of Parasitic Jaegers on the eastern end of the lake and lower numbers on the western end, with a normal season producing 25–60 at Derby Hill and 15–30 at Hamlin Beach, occurring as individuals or twos. They begin to appear the last week of Aug, with the peak 22 Sep–27 Oct, continuing through Nov. They are rare on L. Erie and very rare throughout other inland areas of the state.

They are accidental anywhere inland in spring. Unprecedented was the observation of a total of 21 in three groups at Keuka L., Yates Co. 13 May 1945 (KB 32:21). This is the only inland spring record of migrant flocks. There is one spring record from a boat on L. Ontario 14 May 1986 and a single record for Monroe Co. 20 May 1947. The only inland summer report is from the Niagara R., Erie Co. 9 Jul 1992.

Coastal maxima: 30 off Moriches Inlet, Suffolk Co. 3 Sep 1949; 12 off

JBSP 13 Jun 1955. *Inland maxima:* 202 off Derby Hill, Oswego Co. 7 Oct 1979; 184 same location 5 Oct 1973. *Extreme dates: Coastal:* 28 Apr and 8 Jun; 3 Aug and 15 Jan. *Inland:* 10 Aug and 4 Dec. Dominic F. Sherony

Long-tailed Jaeger   *Stercorarius longicaudus*

Range Northern Holarctic, breeding in North America from western and northern Alaska throughout the Canadian Arctic islands and south to Hudson Bay and northern Quebec. Winters at sea, in the Atlantic off the coasts of Argentina and southwestern Africa. Pelagic in migration but also casually through the interior of North America, particularly on the Great Lakes.

Status Rare pelagic migrant spring and fall. Very rare inland.

Occurrence In the past 20 years there are records from four spring and four fall pelagic trips. Bull (1974) mentioned nine fall and three spring pelagic records. All spring occurrences were 26 May–19 Jun, and fall records were 25 Aug–6 Oct, with most occurring in early Sep. The maximum count was 10, 19 Jun 1992, seen 45 mi south of Montauk. Four juveniles were seen 90 mi from Montauk on 11 Sep 1993.

There are five sight records from land, all after 1977. The first was on 7 Jun 1977 on L. Champlain, seen from a research vessel (KB 27:232). Two were coastal fall records: one after Hurricane David at Shinnecock Inlet, Suffolk Co. 6 Sep 1979 (KB 30:62) and one at JBSP 23 Sep 1989 (KB 40:56). The two fall records from L. Ontario were an adult at Derby Hill, Oswego Co. 10 Sept 1977 (KB 27:206) and one from Hamlin Beach, Monroe Co. 30 Aug 1984 (KB 34:243).

Bull described three confirmed inland records of Long-tailed Jaegers found dead: Owasco L., Cayuga Co. 14 Sep 1908; Cayuga L., Tompkins Co. 8 Mar 1942; and Sandy Pond, Oswego Co. 31 Oct 1971. A fourth, a juvenile, was found dead at Sylvan Beach, Oneida Co. 3 Sep 1985 (KB 36:33). Three of these occurrences appear to be part of the inland fall jaeger migration over L. Ontario.
Dominic F. Sherony

Laughing Gull   *Larus atricilla*

Range Nearctic, breeding locally from Nova Scotia south on the Atlantic and Gulf coasts of the United States, in the Caribbean and along both coasts of Mexico; formerly on the Salton Sea of southern California. Atlantic birds winter from North Carolina and the Gulf Coast south to Panama.

Status Very local breeder on western LI. Abundant postbreeding visitant and common fall migrant on LI and lower Hudson R.; casual in winter. Inland, rare visitant spring, summer, and fall.

Breeding It was extirpated as a breeding bird in NY by 1900. After 1921 it was an increasingly common migrant and summer visitant to NY Harbor and LI Sound. As many as 1000, mostly immatures, were at Setauket, Suffolk Co. on 27 Jun 1934. Griscom (1923) already expected nesting "in the near future." Only in June 1978, however, were a nest and eggs discovered on the Line Islands, Nassau Co. (Buckley et al. 1978). Since 1979, a colony has flourished in JoCo Marsh, JBWR (Post and Riepe 1980), growing to 2741 pairs by 1985 (Atlas 1988) and to about 7600 pairs by 1990 (AB 44:1118). The NY Port Authority then began taking measures against this colony, because it is located near the end of a runway at Kennedy Airport, causing increasing collisions with aircraft. In the summer of 1990 Laughing Gull eggs were suffocated with mineral oil. By summer 1991, airport authorities estimated about 20,000 Laughing Gulls, both breeding and nonbreeding, present in the vicinity and began a program of shooting gulls that ventured onto the airport (AB 45:1099, 46:1125, 47:1094). By summer 1994, an estimated 37,000 had been shot, and fewer gulls gathered on the runway (*New York Times*, 15 Mar 1995, p. B6). Even so, the size of the JoCo Marsh colony was only slightly reduced, to about 5000 pairs (AB 48:929). In 1995, the Port Authority turned to habitat modification as well as shooting to make the runways less attractive, but the colony maintained itself at roughly the same size.

Surprisingly, additional Laughing Gull colonies are not known to have formed in other extensive marshes on the South Shore of LI. At the original Line I. site, one or two pairs nested in 1990 (AB 44:1118), but no other sites were known until 1995, when two pairs were found breeding on Young I., Suffolk Co. (Sommers et al. 1996).

Nonbreeding The postbreeding buildup on LI, supplemented by migrants from the New England population and wanderers from farther south, can be abundant. Numbers may be even higher after hurricanes, e.g., 5000–10,000 after Hurricane Belle in Aug–Sep 1976 (KB 27:59).

It wanders inland in spring, summer, and fall, increasingly frequently in recent years. It was "very rare" in the Niagara Frontier Region (Andrle 1977a, 1977b) and elsewhere on the Great Lakes but has become annual since the late 1980s. Most inland records are of single birds, but three lingered at Braddock Bay, Monroe Co. into Jun 1989, along with thousands of other gulls held there by a "sawbelly" (a type of alewife) die-off (AB 43:1296), and six were at Dunkirk Harbor, Chautauqua Co. in Oct 1977 (KB 27:37).

It can occur inland in any month, but most records are from mid-Apr to late May, and again in Aug and Sep. It is more frequent on the Great Lakes and inland after hurricanes.

Unknown in winter before 1925, it is now occasionally fairly common on LI into Dec, with 85 at Montauk 16 Dec 1978. Three midwinter records on the Great Lakes since 1985 were two at Dunkirk Harbor, Chautauqua Co. and one at Oswego.
Robert O. Paxton

Franklin's Gull   *Larus pipixcan*

Range Nearctic, breeding from southeastern Alberta and southwestern Manitoba south to eastern Oregon and northwestern Iowa. Winters primarily along the Pacific Coast of South America to southern Chile. Migrates chiefly through the Great Plains and regularly in small numbers east to the Great Lakes. Vagrant to the East Coast of North America.

Status Rare to uncommon vagrant but regular in fall in the vicinity of the Great Lakes; irregular, very rare in other regions.

Occurrence Franklin's Gull was not recorded by Eaton (1910, 1914). It was first reported in the state in 1939. A bird of the prairies, it infrequently winters in the eastern United States and on the Atlantic Coast. It is during these eastward wanderings that they appear with some regularity around the Great Lakes and infrequently in the interior and on the coast. From the early 1940s the species was reported at least once each fall in the Buffalo area. After 1964, small flocks were seen from time to time on the Niagara R. during Oct and Nov. It has now been recorded in every month of the year but is most likely to be seen in the fall. Sightings, mostly of single birds, are primarily in the vicinity of the Great Lakes, from Dunkirk on L. Erie in the west, through Buffalo and the Niagara R. and eastward to the end of L. Ontario. Inland, it has been reported several times, including exceptional spring and summer records of a flock of six in breeding plumage at MNWR Apr 1964 (Ives, Farnham) (KB 14:153) and four at Ithaca, Tompkins Co. Jul 1980 (Sibley) (KB 30:233). LI has had eight since 1975, after earlier observations in 1948, 1954, 1971, and 1974.

Sightings peaked in the late 1960s and the 1970s. Large numbers were recorded in the Buffalo area, with seven on 2 Oct 1968; 11 were on the Niagara R. 1 Nov 1967. In 1976, 17 birds were reported statewide, including four in the Buffalo area 26 Nov and six at Sandy Pond Inlet, Oswego Co. 23 Sep–2 Oct. In the fall of 1978 nine were reported along the Niagara R. between Buffalo and the falls, and 1979 produced the largest annual total, of 20 individuals, with a count of 14 for the second half of the year in the Buffalo vicinity and six in the Rochester area. After a relative

wealth of sightings, eight birds statewide in 1990, there have been only one or two records a year since.
Robert W. Brock

Little Gull   *Larus minutus*

Range Mainly Palearctic, but in North America breeding locally around the Great Lakes and, in 1981, at Churchill, Manitoba. Winters around the Great Lakes and on the Atlantic Coast from Massachusetts to Virginia.

Status Rare to uncommon visitant on the coast; rare to fairly common visitant in western NY.

Occurrence It is often found in association with Bonaparte's Gull. Usually only one to three individuals are found on the coast, in bays and inlets, wherever Bonaparte's occurs in numbers. Upstate it is most often found in the Buffalo–Niagara Falls and Rochester areas, where large flocks have occurred, although in most years only small numbers are reported, and it is regularly found on the St. Lawrence R. It could turn up on any large body of water, as did two adults on L. Champlain, Essex Co. 20 Dec 1977 (Carleton) (KB 28:119). It has occurred in every month of the year but is most often found Sep–Apr, upstate, and Nov–Apr on the coast.

    Coastal maxima: 8 Jones Inlet, Nassau Co. 16 Mar 1975; 6 Point Lookout, Nassau Co. 31 Mar 1994, near a dredging operation. *Inland maxima:* 78 Durand-Eastman Park, Rochester, Monroe Co. 29 Nov 1981 (KB 32:41), perhaps the largest single concentration ever recorded in North America; 61 Irondequoit Bay, Monroe Co. 28 Dec 1979.

Remarks The large numbers reported in western NY in the late 1970s and early 1980s occurred at a time when the species extended its known Canadian breeding range eastward into PQ (Bannon 1983).
Joseph DiCostanzo

Black-headed Gull   *Larus ridibundus*

Range Chiefly Palearctic, rare breeder and uncommon migrant in North America. Also breeds in Iceland. In North America, winters on the Great Lakes and along the Atlantic Coast from Newfoundland to Long Island; casually to Florida.

Status A rare to uncommon, but regular, winter visitant along the coast and very rare in fall and winter on the Niagara R. and Great Lakes.

Occurrence This species was first reported in the state in 1937, when Helmuth saw two adults at Montauk, Suffolk Co. 27 Dec 1937–4 Jan 1938. It was next observed during the winter of 1943–1944 in NY Harbor.

Since then it has been reported regularly from coastal areas and is usually seen near ocean inlets at Jones Beach, Fire I., and Moriches and Shinnecock inlets. It is almost invariably seen associating with Bonaparte's Gull, which it closely resembles. It is most numerous during the colder months, especially from late Nov to Mar. In 1961, six, possibly as many as nine, were seen in NY Harbor, and in 1964 six were at Moriches Inlet, Suffolk Co. Eleven reports from Richmond and Queens counties to Shinnecock Inlet, Suffolk Co., including an unusual summer record at JBWR on 14 Jun, made 1985 exceptional. The early 1990s had four to six reports each year, including two more in summer from JBWR, on 5 Jul 1992 and 27 Jun 1994. Only Aug has produced no coastal record.

First recorded in western New York in 1953, it has occurred frequently but not annually since. It is usually seen at Niagara Falls, Lewiston, or at the mouth of the Niagara R. at L. Ontario in association with large numbers of Bonaparte's Gulls. In January 1971, two were found at Dunkirk Harbor, Chautauqua Co. In 1994, two adults at the mouth of the Niagara R. were the latest spring records and first in Apr for the area. On eastern L. Ontario it is seen infrequently in Sep and Oct, but there is a late record at Oswego on 29 Dec 1985. Although it tends to be a fall and winter visitant, it has been seen every month of the year, including records at Kendall, Orleans Co. 9–21 Jul 1975; Irondequoit Bay, Monroe Co. 29 Jul 1981; and Niagara Falls 19 Aug 1983 and 31 Aug 1984.

Remarks In North America, this gull has established breeding in NF and NS. After an unsuccessful breeding attempt on North Monomoy I., MA in 1984, a nest with two eggs was discovered there 21 May 1986, representing the first successful breeding in the United States. The chicks died during heavy rains, and no further attempts have been documented (Veit and Petersen 1993).
Robert W. Brock

Bonaparte's Gull *Larus philadelphia*

Range Nearctic, breeding from western Alaska and northern Manitoba south to southern British Columbia and central Ontario. Winters along both coasts; in the east from Massachusetts to Florida.

Status Common to very abundant migrant and winter visitant; regular summering nonbreeder in small numbers.

Occurrence About the attractive Bonaparte's Gull, Eaton (1914) stated, "Next to Herring Gull this is the best known and most generally distributed gull in the State, especially in the interior." It has been recorded in every month of the year and has occurred in all Regions. It frequents LI waters, the lower Hudson R., and the Great Lakes region, where the largest numbers occur in the Niagara Falls and Buffalo area, especially in fall and winter. It is unusual on inland lakes and ponds.

Coastal maxima: Winter: 10,000 Gravesend Bay, Kings Co., early Jan 1962; 4500 Montauk, Suffolk Co. 5 Jan 1936. *Summer:* 88 North Line I., Nassau Co. 6 Jul 1977.

Around the Great Lakes the pace of its fall movement seems to be controlled by winter's intensity. Thousands are recorded in the Niagara region until the ice-clogged waters of Jan cause them to diminish or disappear.

Inland maxima: Fall: 100,000 along the Niagara R. and nearby reservoirs, 25 Nov 1959; 60,000 along the Niagara R. 28 Oct 1979. *Winter:* 40,000 at the mouth of the Niagara R. 8 Dec 1990, with 2800 remaining through 28 Mar 1991. *Spring:* 5000 Dunkirk, Chautauqua Co. 23 Apr 1967; 4500 Barcelona Harbor, Chautauqua Co. 30 Apr 1992.

Single or small groups of nonbreeding Bonaparte's Gulls are regularly recorded during the summer. Exceptional were 200 at Ontario Beach, Monroe Co. 27 Jul 1969.

Remarks Flocks of Bonaparte's Gull should always be carefully scrutinized because rarities such as Black-headed, Little, and Ross's gulls are often found in this way.
Robert W. Brock

Mew Gull   *Larus canus*

Range Holarctic, breeding in North America from Alaska and southern Yukon south to Vancouver Island, central Saskatchewan, and Manitoba (Churchill); also widely in northern Eurasia. In North America, winters south along the Pacific Coast to Baja California, casually inland and to the Atlantic Coast from Newfoundland to Maryland.

Status Casual vagrant.

Occurrence There are three records accepted by NYSARC: (1) an adult on the St. Lawrence R. at the Moses-Saunders Dam, near Massena, St. Lawrence Co. 4 Oct 1986 (Jones 1989); (2) one on the Niagara R., near the Robert Moses Power Plant, Lewiston, Niagara Co. 29 Nov and 4 Dec 1992 (Knapton, Wormington) (NYSARC 1994); (3) one at the Moses-Saunders Dam 27–29 Dec 1992 (Sibley) (KB 43:143; NYSARC 1994).

Another report of an individual at Dunkirk Harbor, Chautauqua Co. 3 Dec 1992 was apparently not submitted to NYSARC and may be the same bird as the Niagara R. bird mentioned above (AB 47:245).

Remarks The separation of Mew Gull from Ring-billed Gull in the field, particularly of immature birds, can be very difficult and is further complicated by differences between the three subspecies of Mew Gull. The three subspecies, considered by some authors to be full species are: (1) *canus*,

"Common Gull," which breeds in Iceland and northern Europe and winters in southern Europe and North Africa; (2) *brachyrhynchus*, "Mew Gull," also referred to as Short-billed Gull in the older literature, breeds in northwestern North America and winters on the West Coast from Alaska to southern California; (3) *kamtschatschensis*, "Kamchatka Gull," breeds in Siberia and winters south to Japan. For an extensive discussion on the separation of these forms see Lauro and Spencer 1980, Harrison 1985, Grant 1986, and Tove 1993. Of the three accepted NY records, the first two were attributed to *brachyrhynchus*; the third was identified as *canus*. As an example of the difficulty inherent in the identification of this species, see Lauro 1977. The observer, a competent and respected field person withdrew his report after extensive research (NYSARC 1979).

Veit and Petersen (1993) reported more than 20 records for MA; Zeranski and Baptist (1990) placed it on the hypothetical list in CT; and Leck (1984) listed fewer than five in NJ.
Joseph DiCostanzo

Ring-billed Gull *Larus delawarensis*

Range Nearctic, breeding locally with fairly separate western and eastern populations; in the east, from southern James Bay and the Great Lakes northeast mostly along the St. Lawrence Valley, extending into both Labrador and Newfoundland, and south to central New York, New Hampshire, and Maine. Steadily increasing its range. Winters around the Great Lakes, on the Atlantic Coast primarily from Massachusetts to Florida, and along the Gulf Coast to Texas.

Status Abundant to very abundant in the Great Lakes region and on the coast, less numerous in the interior. Local but very common to abundant breeder.

Breeding Eaton (1910) spoke of the Ring-billed Gull as a rare to uncommon visitant in upstate NY, chiefly occurring during migrations. An extension of the eastern breeding range through the eastern Great Lakes to the Atlantic has produced a population explosion in NY matched by few species. Although breeding took place in adjacent Canadian territory in 1927 (Quilliam 1965), the first reported NY breeding was in 1936 in L. Ontario on Gull I., Jefferson Co. (Hyde 1939). In 1938 nesting was observed on nearby Little Galloo I.

Forty-three acre Little Galloo was studied in depth by Belknap (1955, 1968), who witnessed a phenomenal population increase over the years. He estimated the buildup in the number of nests or pairs to be from about 1000 in 1945 to 19,000 in 1950, 45,000 in 1955, 63,000 in 1961, and 75,000–85,000 in 1965–1967. More-recent studies indicate that because of habitat limitations, the numbers have leveled off. In 1981, a census found 73,780 nests (Blokpoel and Weseloh 1982).

The Atlas Confirmed breeding in four other localities. Several colonies were located at Buffalo, Erie Co. and on the upper Niagara R. to the falls. In 1986 the area was estimated to contain 24,000 nests (Hotopp 1986). In the St. Lawrence R., nests were reported on several islands, with 135 on the Eagle Wing Group in 1984. Inland, a large colony was located on Island C of the Four Brothers Islands in L. Champlain, Essex Co. in 1949 (Belknap 1955). After counts of 2000 adults in 1955, it had grown to 16,329 nests in 1985. A colony was discovered in Oneida L., Oswego Co. in 1952, and by 1985 three islands held 2269 nests (Bollinger 1985). In 1984, the nesting population of the entire Great Lakes–St. Lawrence R. region was estimated at 700,000 nesting pairs (Blokpoel and Tessier 1986).

For the most part, breeding colonies are located on isolated islands, but as suitable locations have become saturated new ones have developed inland. In 1989 it established small colonies in such varied habitats as Watkins Glen Creek, Schuyler Co. (KB 39:229, 43:224) and on a building roof (100 nests) in Rochester, Monroe Co. (KB 39:227, 40:246). This phenomenon continued in 1994, with nesting on a small island in a shopping mall pond in Henrietta, Monroe Co. (KB 44:301) and on a Cortland Co. landfill (Toner) (KB 44:217.) As the population explosion continues, there are clashes with humans over such concerns as sanitation and safety, especially near airports.

Nonbreeding The Ring-billed Gull is recorded in all areas. It congregates in large numbers to feed and rest in open fields and around bodies of water of all sizes. It takes advantage of human activities, as scores of individuals follow the farmer's plow, consuming grubs. It frequents urban shopping mall parking lots, where it scavenges and where its vocalizations are as common as the sounds of automobiles.

Reports document the increase of this species. In the Great Lakes region: 156,000 along west lake shore, Monroe Co. 10 Dec 1979 and 61,256 on the Rochester CBC, 16 Dec 1979; 20,000 Dunkirk Harbor, Chautauqua Co. 26 Dec 1976; 15,000 Henderson, Jefferson Co. 10 Mar 1992. In the interior away from the Great Lakes: 6070 Ithaca, Tompkins Co. 9 Feb 1991; 3900 MNWR Jan 1989.

On the coast, there is a substantial population of mostly adult birds all year. The large numbers in winter are illustrated by some CBC records in that region: 23,063 Lower Hudson 1984; 7190 Northern Nassau 6500 Queens Co. 1985; 1985; 6069 Smithtown 1986; 3690 Central Suffolk 1986. Combined totals for all CBCs in that area were 56,977 in 1984 and 58,178 in 1985.

Robert W. Brock

California Gull   *Larus californicus*

Range   Nearctic, breeding from southern Mackenzie generally southeast to the Dakotas and south to northeastern California, northern Utah, and north-central Colorado. Winters from southern Washington and eastern Idaho south to Mexico. Casual or accidental to the Great Lakes, Mississippi Valley, and East Coast.

Status   Casual vagrant.

Occurrence   The state's, and the Northeast's, first documented California Gull was discovered on 4 Oct 1978 at Rockland L. SP, Rockland Co. by Weissman. This bird, an adult in basic plumage, was seen by hundreds until at least late Dec (NYSARC 1979; Weissman 1980).

Showing great site fidelity, the bird reappeared every Oct through 1981, staying for varying lengths of time but never through an entire winter. In 1980 and 1981 it reappeared in Mar, in full alternate plumage. When absent from Rockland L., it was searched for at other gull congregation spots in the lower Hudson Valley but was never located elsewhere (B. Lincoln, pers. obs.) and was last reported 12 Feb 1982.

The second record accepted by NYSARC (1994) was an adult found on the Niagara R. at Lewiston, Niagara Co. 29 Nov 1992 by M. Planck and R. Planck. Also seen on 1, 2, and 6 Dec, it was just one of three rare gulls in the gorge during that period. (The others were Mew and Slaty-backed.) California Gulls were reported at the same site each Nov from 1993 to 1996, with three different individuals identified in 1996 (KB 47:32). NYSARC has not yet evaluated those reports.

There were several other published reports of this species between the two accepted records, but they were either rejected by NYSARC or never submitted. In the latter category was a subadult photographed by P. Buckley at JBSP 31 Jul 1985 (AB 39:893).
Berna B. Lincoln

Herring Gull   *Larus argentatus*

Range   Holarctic, in North America breeding from northern Canada locally south to central British Columbia, the Great Lakes, and on the Atlantic Coast to northern South Carolina. Winters throughout much of the breeding range and south to the Caribbean and Mexico.

Status   Common breeder on LI and in the north, especially in the Adirondack and northeastern L. Ontario regions. Very abundant resident coastally and near large bodies of water and landfills inland. Most numerous in winter and late fall.

Breeding The breeding population is divided among upstate islands in eastern L. Ontario, the St. Lawrence R., L. Champlain, Oneida L., and many of the Adirondack lakes, and downstate, chiefly on LI and offshore islets, with more than 60 sites and 30–37 colonies. Since the LI Colonial Waterbird Survey began in 1985, the species has shown strong signs of population decline in downstate areas, from a high of 24,281 estimated pairs in 1985 to a low of 9558 pairs in 1993 (Sommers et al. 1994). However, the 1995 survey showed an increase to 11,065 pairs (Sommers et al. 1996).

In the Central Adirondacks and Sable Highlands, Herring Gulls nest in pairs rather than colonies and are rather uncommon, although there is no evidence of a declining population.

Nesting areas on the coast consist of sandy areas with scattered vegetation, dredge spoil sites, abandoned docks and buildings, and offshore rocks and islands. On the interior lakes, rocks and islands, or even buoys, are used, and in the Niagara R., talus slopes and cliff ledges provide nest sites.

Nonbreeding It is occasionally seen in the thousands passing raptor-monitoring stations upstate as well as on the coast, typically in Nov or Dec, although later flights can occur during periods of severe weather. The Common Loonwatch at Taughannock Falls SP, near Ithaca, Tompkins Co. records such flights annually. In winter, Herring Gulls can be found near larger bodies of fresh water, which provide both prey, chiefly small fish, and clean water for bathing and night roosting. They account for the majority of gulls at all landfills in winter, where they take all manner of offal and garbage. W. R. Evans (in litt.) has documented flights of more than 70 air miles per day from landfill to roosting and bathing sites on the Finger Lakes. They also scavenge along coastal areas, where they are found in their greatest numbers, typically not far from active landfills. Since the capacity of NY landfills has declined to the point that many have been closed, it is unsurprising that the LI colonies have been reduced in number. *Coastal maxima:* 135,600 Brooklyn CBC 26 Dec 1971; 75,302 SI CBC 19 Dec 1987; 68,000 Brooklyn CBC 15 Dec 1984. *Inland maxima:* 32,000 Buffalo, Erie Co. CBC 26 Dec 1965; 20,054 Rochester, Monroe Co. CBC 16 Dec 1979.

In 1970, all NY CBCs combined totaled more than 265,000 Herring Gulls.

Remarks Only the North American subspecies, *smithsonianus*, has been noted in NY. The massive expansion of the adaptable and predatory Herring and Great Black-backed gulls as nesters in the downstate portions of NY has spelled trouble for all manner of colonially nesting waterbirds, shorebirds, rails, and other species.
Edward S. Brinkley

Thayer's Gull *Larus thayeri*

Range Nearctic, breeding in Arctic Canada south to Southampton and Coats islands and northern Hudson Bay. Winters mainly on the Pacific Coast south to California. Vagrant on the East Coast in winter in recent years.

Status A rare winter visitant away from the Niagara and St. Lawrence rivers, where it occurs in most winters Dec–Feb. Very rare in the east and southeast.

Occurrence The status of Thayer's Gull in eastern North America has been clouded by a great deal of uncertainty over its taxonomy and its identification (see Remarks). This uncertainty persisted to the time of this writing, despite numerous photographically documented records and at least six specimens (Bull 1974) from the state. Those specimens were all taken in the Niagara Frontier region, 1945–1968 (Andrle 1969, 1977a, 1977b) and are all currently in the BMS.

Observers have a good chance of finding Thayer's among large aggregations of Herring Gulls in winter, especially inland at large landfills or along the Niagara R., particularly at the (Canadian) Sir Adam Beck Generating Station, or at Massena, St. Lawrence Co. at Moses-Saunders Dam, where Thayer's can be found annually in small numbers.

Most are reported as single birds. Two birds at a time have been reported on the following CBCs: Buffalo 22 Dec 1974; Oswego 23 Dec 1974; Herkimer 19 Dec 1987; Niagara 27 Dec 1987; Massena 28 Dec 1992. Highest counts come from border rivers: 4 Niagara Falls 5 Dec 1993; 5 Niagara Falls Dec 1992 (Cayuga Bird Club).

Remarks First described in 1917 as a subspecies of Herring Gull (Dwight 1917), *thayeri* was reclassified as a separate species first by Macpherson (1961) and N. G. Smith (1966b). In that the findings of Smith (1963, 1966a, 1966b, 1967) have been questioned by other researchers (Gaston and Decker 1985; Snell 1989), observers should continue to exercise caution in the identification of this taxon, which a minority of researchers believe to be conspecific with Iceland Gull, although conclusive fieldwork to demonstrate this relation has yet to be conducted. Excellent references, such as Zimmer 1991, exist for distinguishing members of this taxon from dark "Kumlien's" Iceland Gull.

Observers should also take precaution against identifying adult Herring Gulls with coppery irides as Thayer's Gull, as a few retain this eye color from subadult years. "Kumlien's" Gulls also often show medium-brown irides, and the small minority of Kumlien's types that are both dark-eyed and darker-mantled than Herring Gull probably represent intergrades with Thayer's. Such hybrids have been reported throughout the Northeast (Gosselin and David 1975; Lehman 1980). Various hybrids between Glaucous and Herring gulls are reported annually upstate, and these bear superficial resemblance to large male Thayer's but are larger than Herring Gull. Intergrades between Iceland and Herring gulls have not been reported but would approach Thayer's Gull in both proportion and plumage. Observers should continue to document Thayer's and Thayer's-like gulls in NY as thoroughly as is possible.

Veit and Petersen (1993) gave credence to six records for MA, including one specimen. It does not appear on the NJ checklist. RI has six sightings (Conway 1992), and CT one (Zeranski and Baptist 1990).
Edward S. Brinkley

Iceland Gull   *Larus glaucoides*

Range Northeastern Nearctic, with a limited breeding distribution on the southern coasts of Greenland, eastern and southern Baffin Island, and in extreme northwestern Quebec. Winters south to the Great Lakes and the New York coast; rarely farther south.

Status A rare to uncommon winter visitant in the southeast, and a variably uncommon to fairly common winter visitant near major rivers and lakes upstate.

Occurrence This species frequents much the same habitats as Herring Gull: landfills, large river systems, sewage outlets, and seafood- and chicken-processing plants. They may also be found on coastal shores, agricultural fields (where Herring Gulls are present), or on inland lakes, especially at the ice edge in winter. They are most numerous on the northern and western frontier rivers, Niagara and St. Lawrence, particularly at hydroelectric facilities, where small fish are brought to the surface. Severe winters usually yield the most records. It is rare after Apr or before Oct but has been recorded in every month.

Coastal maxima: 11 Lower Hudson CBC 21 Dec 1975; 10 Montauk 26 Dec 1937; 9 Lower Hudson CBC 21 Dec 1980. *Inland maxima:* all from Moses-Saunders Dam complex, St. Lawrence Co.: 67, 19 Jan 1991; 32, 7 Feb 1991; 27, 3 Feb 1992.

Remarks Although Bull (1974) noted that both subspecies of Iceland Gull, the nominate *glaucoides* and the "Kumlien's" Gull, *kumlieni*, occur in NY, there is no hard evidence, such as a specimen, to support the inclusion of *glaucoides* in our avifauna. In recent years there has been an increase in sight reports of adult Icelands, with apparently pure white primaries, no doubt fueled by the increased interest in gulls and knowledge of the observers. Perhaps the time has come to examine all of the extant specimens carefully and to think about the collecting of individuals with no visible gray in the primaries, such as the one that spent the winters 1987–1994 at

Shinnecock Inlet, Suffolk Co. Identification of darker subadult and first-winter individuals is treated in Zimmer 1991.
Edward S. Brinkley

Lesser Black-backed Gull *Larus fuscus*

Range Western Palearctic, breeding in Iceland, the Faroe Islands, northern Scandinavia, and northern Russia south to the British Isles and France. Regular visitor to the New World, primarily along the Atlantic Coast from Cape Cod to Florida and the Caribbean, but also north to northern Canada and southwest to central California and the Pacific Coast of Panama and Costa Rica.

Status Rare to uncommon winter visitant, steadily increasing in numbers, and a rare but increasing summer visitant.

Occurrence The first state record was collected at Buffalo, Erie Co. 14 Mar 1949 and is BMS 4084. From 1954 on it became rare but regular on the coast.

Almost never seen apart from the company of the abundant Herring Gulls, it has been recorded in all months from all corners of the state, but most regularly where Herring Gulls are most concentrated, especially along the Niagara Frontier and in coastal areas near landfills. It has proved to be a regular visitant in small numbers to smaller landfills throughout central NY as well. CBC data 1960–1989 revealed 19 upstate and 40 downstate records.

Coastal maxima: 6 Montauk, Suffolk Co. 15 Oct 1995. *Inland maxima:* 12 Niagara R., Erie Co. 26 Nov 1994.

Remarks There are three subspecies generally recognized. The nominate, *fuscus*, breeds in northern Scandinavia and disperses southward to Africa. The subspecies *graellsii*, which breeds in Iceland, the British Isles, and the Netherlands, is the taxon usually seen in NY.

The third, *intermedius*, breeds in southern Scandinavia, and individuals resembling this taxon have been reported every few years. Some such reports undoubtedly may be *graellsii* seen in poor light. However, some other birds have so clearly differed from *graellsii* in general proportions, amount of white in the primaries, and coloration of the dorsal wing surface and back, that suspicion of *intermedius* in NY is warranted (Post and Lewis 1995a, 1995b). One such bird was photographed by Post at Point Lookout, Nassau Co. 28 Sep 1985, immediately after Hurricane Gloria.

Complicating the identification of subspecies is the swamping of the *intermedius* gene pool by *graellsii* in western Europe, where separation of the two forms is no longer possible in many areas (Post and Lewis 1995b). Another difficulty is presented by the probable occurrence in NY of hybrids of Lesser Black-backed and Herring gulls (e.g., one adult, Spencer Landfill, Tioga Co. 1–22 Nov 1992; KB 42:35). Such hybrids are seen in North America and in Europe (Tinbergen 1929; Voous 1946, 1962; Harris et al. 1978) and variously resemble very large, paler-mantled *L. fuscus* or *L. cachinnans*, the Yellow-legged Gull of Europe, as the hybrids usually have some yellow pigment in their legs and feet. The latter species' massive expansion into northwestern Europe in the 1990s very much resembles that of *L. fuscus* 40 years prior, and its presence in North America has been substantiated by specimen and photographs (Wilds and Czaplak 1993). Careful study of the pigmentation pattern of the primaries may be sufficient to separate hybrids from the several *L. cachinnans* subspecies, but the backcrosses of fertile hybrids with Herring Gulls (Hansen 1960) may present field and museum ornithologists alike with utterly unidentifiable individuals.

The presence of several dozen juvenile (first-summer) Lesser Black-backed Gulls on the East Coast of North America each summer suggests that the species may nest on this continent, possibly in the far north. Nesting in Greenland is probably annual now (Post and Lewis 1995a). Edward S. Brinkley

Slaty-backed Gull   *Larus schistisagus*

Range Eastern Palearctic, breeding from the western Bering Sea south through Kamchatka and the Kurile Islands to Sakhalin and Japan. Winters throughout much of the breeding range and south to the coast of eastern China. Wanders rarely in nonbreeding season to western Alaska and the Pribilof and Aleutian islands. Casual in south-coastal Alaska. Accidental in British Columbia, inland United States, and the Hawaiian Islands.

Status Accidental.

Occurrence A Slaty-backed Gull was first positively identified in the Niagara region of ON by R. Planck and M. Planck on 24 Nov 1992 (AB 47:72). It was seen by many in the following days, and, while being observed from the ON shore of the upper rapids at Niagara Falls on 4 Dec 1992 (Brock 1994), it was seen to fly out over the river and across the International Boundary into NY. This first state record was submitted to NYSARC by R. van Twest and M. van Twest and was accepted (NYSARC 1994). It was seen again on 16 Dec 1992 near the Robert Moses Power Plant at Lewiston, Niagara Co. and on 20 Dec 1992 on the Buffalo CBC, when the gull was seen to fly over the Three Sisters and Goat islands, Niagara Falls, Niagara Co. It was last seen on 29 Dec 1992.

Remarks This was the first record of a Slaty-backed Gull east of the Mississippi R. (AB 47:72). It was closely followed by sightings of another at

Eastlake, OH 28–29 Dec 1992 and at Lorain, OH on 8 Feb 1993 (AB 47:263).
Robert W. Brock

Glaucous Gull   *Larus hyperboreus*

Range Northern Holarctic, in North America breeding in the Arctic from Alaska to Ellesmere Island south to Labrador and Hudson Bay. Winters, in the east, on the Atlantic Coast from Labrador to Virginia and inland to the Great Lakes.

Status Rare to uncommon winter visitant; occasionally fairly common in the vicinity of the Great Lakes and along the St. Lawrence R.

Occurrence Glaucous and Iceland gulls are the "white-winged" gulls of winter. Previously, they were most often looked for in the vicinity of garbage dumps in winter, but with the closing of landfills in recent years those gull congregation points are fast becoming a thing of the past. It may be found wherever gulls assemble at open water in winter: inlets, fishing piers, power dams, Niagara R., and Niagara Falls. Some of the less usual locations have been: one on L. Champlain, Essex Co. 17 Dec 1977; adult at a dump near Saranac L., Franklin Co. 12 Dec 1984; an immature at L. Flower, Franklin Co. 17 Dec 1984; five at Whitney Point Reservoir, Broome Co. 22 Nov 1987; three at Wanasink L., Sullivan Co. 28 Nov 1984.

   Coastal maxima: 6 Montauk, Suffolk Co. 26 Dec 1937; 5 Pelham Bay, Bronx Co. 17 Feb 1935. *Inland maxima:* 51 Hawkins Point on the St. Lawrence R., St. Lawrence Co. mid-Feb 1983; 43 Niagara Falls 10 Jan 1975; 35 Moses-Saunders Dam, St. Lawrence Co. 23 Feb 1980. These numbers are all exceptional, 5–10 would ordinarily be a very good count. *Extreme inland dates:* 18 Sep and 29 Jun.

   It is rare before Nov and after Apr but has been recorded on the coast in every month. Very rare in summer; an immature summered at Oakwood Beach, Richmond Co. 1932.
Joseph DiCostanzo

Great Black-backed Gull   *Larus marinus*

Range Holarctic but restricted to the North Atlantic. In North America breeds along the coast from southern Greenland to North Carolina; also, in increasing numbers at Lake Ontario and Lake Huron. In North America winters from Newfoundland to southern United States.

Status Regular breeder on the coast, local inland. Common to very abundant winter visitant on the coast; common to abundant on Great Lakes.

Breeding This species was formerly common only in winter along the outer coast, but, with breeding territory expanding southward through New England, it nested in NY for the first time in 1942 on Cartwright I., Suffolk Co. It nests in sandy areas of scattered vegetation, invariably in or near Herring Gull colonies. In 1948, a colony was established on Gardiners I., Suffolk Co.

In an 11-year study on LI, 1985–1995, nesting was recorded at 52 locations, with a mean of 7158 pairs per year. In 1995, 34 colonies were active, with Gardiners I. (3420 pairs) and Plum I. (1691 pairs) being the largest (Sommers et al. 1996). Over that period there was no significant trend.

Nesting was discovered inland in 1975 on Four Brothers Islands in L. Champlain, Essex Co. and has continued; there were nine nests in 1994. Four nests were found on Little Galloo I. in L. Ontario, Jefferson Co. in 1981 (Blokpoel and Weseloh 1982). Nesting has been unsuccessfully attempted in other locations: St. Lawrence R., Jefferson Co. and Oneida L., Oswego Co. 1983 (Atlas 1988), and Niagara R., Erie Co. 1994 (Leuchner and Roblee 1996). A successful nesting in a new inland location took place in 1996. A downy young with an adult in attendance was seen on 16 Jun and again on 28 Jun; the nest was located on 6 Aug on Garden I. in L. Champlain, Clinton Co. 1.3 m from the mainland (H. Klein, in litt.). All viable inland colonies have remained small, probably because of their location within other gull colonies.

Nonbreeding It has become more numerous on the coast at all times of the year and has increased steadily on the Great Lakes and smaller interior lakes. By 1970 it had been recorded in summer at many inland localities, including one bird that summered on Cayuga L., Tompkins Co. in 1964. It has been recorded in all Regions of the state.

Coastal maxima: all on CBCs: 15,865 SI 1976; 13,500 Brooklyn 1984; 4361 Queens 1984; 1981 Central Suffolk Co. 1988. *Inland maxima:* Increasingly large numbers are reported on or near the Great Lakes: 772 Braddock Bay, Monroe Co. 10 Dec 1979; 2500 Moses-Saunders Dam, St. Lawrence Co. 21 Nov 1989; 1086 Oswego R., Oswego Co. 7 Feb 1987 and 1379 there 21 Dec 1991. Elsewhere: 798 Ithaca, Tompkins Co. 9 Feb 1991; 89 Tioughnioga R., Cortland Co. 21 Jan 1994. It has also become very common in the Niagara-Buffalo area, but shared water space and count territories with Canada make accurate NY numbers difficult to ascertain. Robert W. Brock

Black-legged Kittiwake   *Rissa tridactyla*

Range Holarctic, breeding in North America from Baffin Island and northern Labrador south to islands in the Gulf of St. Lawrence, Newfoundland,

and off Cape Breton, Nova Scotia. Winters at sea in the western North Atlantic from Newfoundland to North Carolina.

Status Uncommon to very abundant late fall and winter pelagic visitant. Rare visitor to the Great Lakes.

Occurrence This pelagic gull wanders the Atlantic as far south as Bermuda and sometimes winters along the U.S. coast. It is seen at coastal areas, often after severe easterly gales, and especially off Montauk, Suffolk Co. Offshore trips during the colder months increase an observer's chances for studying this species. Off Montauk it is recorded Aug–May, with the largest numbers Nov and Dec. Over the years there have been numerous records of smaller numbers from beaches and inlets along the South Shore of LI.

It also occurs annually on the Niagara R. and the Great Lakes to the St. Lawrence R. Sep–Apr. Observers might see one or more individuals, usually accompanying flocks of Bonaparte's Gulls. Since it appears there regularly, records are no longer reviewed by NYSARC. Inland, away from the Great Lakes, sightings are rare. One was at Seneca L., Geneva, Ontario Co. 31 Dec 1968 and one at INWR 21 Feb 1981.

Coastal maxima: all Montauk: 7500, 26 Nov 1977 in a gale; 1750, 29 Dec 1956; 1380, 1983 CBC. *Inland maxima:* 132 Derby Hill, Oswego Co. 10–23 Oct 1982; 16 Derby Hill 6 Nov 1983, with 39 for the season; 11 Hamlin Beach, Monroe Co. 29 Oct 1983.

Remarks In a phenomenon not recorded before 1955, numbers of first-summer birds have spent parts of the summer at outer Cape Cod, MA, including 630 at Provincetown 23 Jun 1980 (Veit and Petersen 1993). Robert W. Brock

Ross's Gull   *Rhodostethia rosea*

Range Holarctic, breeding in northern Siberia and, in North America, near Bathurst Island, at Churchill, Manitoba, and at Disko Bay, Greenland. Probably winters at sea in open arctic waters. It is recorded as a vagrant at widely separated localities in North America and in the British Isles.

Status Casual vagrant.

Occurrence There are five records, two accepted by NYSARC thus far. The first, 11 Dec 1986, watched by a single observer as it fed in the entrance to the harbor at Montauk, Suffolk Co., was minutely described and added to the NYS Checklist (NYSARC 1987; Reddall 1988). The second was discovered by Levine, Feldman, and Wollin 17 Mar 1994 off Point Lookout, Nassau Co. and was seen by scores of observers during its periodic appearances through 30 Mar (Levine 1995; NYSARC 1996).

Three 1995 reports were submitted to NYSARC but have not yet been reviewed by the committee. The first was reported from Point Peninsula, Jefferson Co. 4 Jan 1995 (Dudones) (KB 45:240). The next was back at Point Lookout, Nassau Co. 12 Mar 1995, and that individual was seen by many on and off until 13 Apr (Kurtz) (KB 45:236). The last came, fittingly, from the "gull capital," Region 1's Niagara Falls and environs 12 Nov 1995 (Coady) (KB 46:40). Birds seen on 19 Nov and again on 25 Nov might have been different individuals.

Remarks A review of records in neighboring states showed three MA birds (1981, 1984, 1990) to add to the legendary "Lower 48" U.S. first of 1974 (Veit and Petersen 1993): one in CT in 1984 (Zeranski and Baptist 1990), one in NJ in 1993 (AB 48:93), and two in ON winter 1994–1995 (NASFN 49:144).
Emanuel Levine

Sabine's Gull   *Xema sabini*

Range Holarctic, breeding in high latitudes, in North America south locally to Hudson Bay and Baffin Island. Winters at sea off both coasts, primarily off South America, rarely in the North Atlantic. Casual through interior North America.

Status Rare vagrant.

Occurrence Bull (1974) considered the Sabine's Gull to be a great rarity in the state, although he mentioned nearly 30 records. There have been at least that many in the years since, and the species should be considered a rare but regular fall migrant throughout, although it is more commonly reported upstate than on the coast. NYSARC stopped reviewing fall records in 1981.

It is extremely rare for more than one individual to be seen at a time. Bull listed three occasions when two individuals were seen at once. Since that time there have been four records involving two individuals at once: two immatures, Derby Hill, Oswego Co. 15 Sep and 7 Oct 1979 (KB 30:42); two immatures, Niagara Falls 17–18 Nov 1979 (Axtell) (KB 30:29); two adults, Sodus Bay, Wayne Co. 30 Nov 1980 (M. Tetlow and T. Tetlow) (KB 31:27); two immatures, near Peace Bridge, Erie Co. 7 Oct 1987 (Andrle) (KB 38:231).

Extreme dates: 28 Jul and 23 Dec. Most records are in Sep and Oct. Bull listed a very old specimen from Freeport, Nassau Co. Jul 1837 but did not give an exact date.

Remarks The three NJ records listed by Leck (1984) were all in fall. Conway (1992) listed 13 in RI: 10 were between 8 Jul and 16 Sep, the remaining three in winter. Compared with the complete lack of spring records in NY, NJ, and RI, Veit and Petersen (1993) reported 11 in that

season in MA. Perhaps more spring pelagic trips off LI will produce a spring record in NY.
Joseph DiCostanzo

Ivory Gull   *Pagophila eburnea*

Range Northern Holarctic, breeding in eastern North America in the high Arctic south to northern Baffin Island. Winters on the Arctic Ocean pack ice and the Atlantic Coast from Newfoundland to New Jersey.

Status Very rare vagrant.

Occurrence There are at least 14 records. Bull (1974) listed six, including two specimens from Suffolk Co. The first, an adult collected near Sayville 3 Jan 1893, is not extant. An immature, found dead at Orient 17 Feb 1845 is NYSM 24989. The other four were sight records through 1964.

Other records have been: (1) immature photographed at Niagara Falls 29–31 Dec 1972 by Vaughan. Amazingly, the same observer saw the only previous inland record at the same place 39 years earlier on 10 Feb 1934; (2) an emaciated female immature, Southold, Suffolk Co. 8 Feb 1976 (Stoutenburgh) was found dead 10 Feb, AMNH 812041 (KB 26:119); (3) immature, Massena, St. Lawrence Co. 8 Dec 1977 and 13 Jan 1978 (VanRiet) (KB 28:118); (4) immature, Niagara R. Gorge 1 Jan 1981 (Andrle, Axtell) (KB 31:88); (5) immature, Newburgh, Orange Co. 11–20 Jan 1981 (Schieffer, Seguin, Treacy) (Treacy 1981); (6) immature, Charlotte, Monroe Co. 21 Jan 1981 (Davids, Griffiths, Kemnitzer, Reister) (Treacy 1981); (7) easily the most incredible, an adult visited a backyard bird feeder at the Coleman home in Saratoga Springs, Saratoga Co. 14–15 Jan 1982 (Able 1982) and was photographed, banded, and released; (8) immature, Sodus Point, Wayne Co. 2–3 Jan 1994 (Traver, Spahn, Gruenbaum, Lown) (NYSARC 1996).

An adult was reported at Newburgh, Orange Co. 11 Jan 1981 (Seguin) the same day and place as the immature cited above (KB 31:113), but no details were submitted to NYSARC. An adult seen in Dec 1924 in the Niagara Gorge was on the Canadian side of the border (Beardslee and Mitchell 1965).

Remarks The records are nearly evenly divided between upstate and the coast, with upstate having a slight edge, but records for immatures outnumber adults by three to one. A similar preponderance of immatures is found in nine records from MA (Veit and Petersen 1993). There was one immature in RI (Conway 1992). Leck (1984) did not indicate the ages for two records from NJ. There are no accepted records from CT (Zeranski and Baptist 1990).
Joseph DiCostanzo

Gull-billed Tern   *Sterna nilotica*

Range Cosmopolitan in tropical and warmer temperate regions but very local in distribution; in eastern North America breeding along the Atlantic and Gulf coasts from Long Island to Florida and southern Texas, also in the Caribbean. Winters from northern Florida, the Caribbean, and the Gulf Coast south through Middle America to northern Argentina and Peru.

Status Rare local breeder on LI.

Breeding On 11 Jun 1975 two adults, a nest, and two eggs were found on South Line I., Nassau Co. On 14 Jun another nest with eggs was discovered, and on 5 Jul one downy young was observed (Buckley et al. 1975). There were additional sight reports from nearby Cedar Beach, Suffolk Co. and JBWR in 1975 as well, but no evidence of breeding. After 1975, it nested sporadically at the original site and has been found nesting in Common Tern colonies along the barrier beaches nearby, although in very low numbers of usually only one to three pairs (Atlas 1988). The latest data again recorded only two pairs (Sommers et al. 1996). These nestings mark the extreme northern edge of the species' breeding range, and there has been no significant increase in the number of nesting pairs since the first one, 20 years ago.

Nonbreeding Before 1975, it was a very rare visitant to the outer coast of LI and was unreported elsewhere in the state. Two specimens existed from South Oyster Bay, Nassau Co., and it was sometimes reported after hurricanes. The only record away from the immediate coast was one at Marshland Conservancy, Rye, Westchester Co. 26 Jul 1993 (KB 43:347).

   Maxima: 28 Jones Inlet, Nassau Co. to Sagaponack, Suffolk Co. 12 Sep 1960 after Hurricane Donna; 27 Tobay, Nassau Co. 15 Sep 1975. *Extreme dates:* 2 May and 17 Sep.
Sharon M. Skelly

Caspian Tern   *Sterna caspia*

Range Cosmopolitan, in eastern North America breeding locally on islands and in marshes around inland lakes, along the Gulf of St. Lawrence, and on the Atlantic and Gulf coasts from Virginia to Texas. Winters north to North Carolina, casually to Long Island.

Status Very common to abundant breeder at one site in eastern L. Ontario. Rare to uncommon migrant elsewhere.

Breeding In Bull 1974, the closest nesting birds to NY were on Pigeon I., ON in eastern L. Ontario about 5 m from the International Boundary. Suspected as nesters in NY during the Atlas project, they were not Confirmed until a year after Atlas fieldwork ended, when Weseloh of the

Canadian Wildlife Service discovered 100+ nesting on Little Galloo I. in L. Ontario, Jefferson Co. on 21 Jun 1986. It was included in the Atlas since it was a new breeding species for the state. On a return trip on 7 Jul 1986, Weseloh counted 112 nests with 180 eggs and 2 young. Little Galloo I. at that time was also occupied by an estimated 70,000 pairs of nesting Ring-billed Gulls as well as other colonial nesters such as Black-crowned Night-Heron, Herring Gull, Double-crested Cormorant, Great Black-backed Gull, and Cattle Egret (Weseloh and Blokpoel 1993). It was surprising that the terns could find room to nest on this already "saturated" 43-acre island. Nesters since then have gradually increased: in 1990, 640 adults and 240 chicks, double the 1989 levels; 1991, 576 adults; 1992, 400 pairs; 1993, 896 nests; 1994, 682 nests.

Nesting of this species is limited to island situations with other colonial nesters, although courtship display, copulation, and food carrying have been observed at inland areas. As the Little Galloo I. population increases, a new nesting location would seem inevitable. Further nesting in eastern L. Ontario on the NY side may be limited because there are only 13 islands and undeveloped peninsulas are rare. Calf I., an unoccupied, undeveloped island not far from Little Galloo is a possibility, as is Galloo, the largest but somewhat developed island to the northwest. Stony I., a part of this archipelago of four, has too much development and human activity. Perhaps the next nesting location in NY will be on the St. Lawrence R. or L. Champlain.

Nonbreeding Migrants have been seen in increasing numbers as both the U.S. and Canadian breeding populations have increased and new colonies have been found in ON.

Great Lakes maxima: Ontario: 250 Sandy Pond, Oswego Co. 9 May 1992; 106 Sodus Bay, Wayne Co. 29 Apr 1992. *Erie:* 55 Dunkirk Harbor, Chautauqua Co. 18 Apr 1989; 40 Barcelona Harbor, Chautauqua Co. 24 Apr 1993. *Coastal maxima:* 5 Mecox Bay, Suffolk Co. 17 Apr 1985; 5 Moriches Inlet, Suffolk Co. 18 Apr 1990. *Inland maxima:* 40 Onondaga L., Onondaga Co. 7 Sep 1981; 35 Myers Point, Cayuga L., Tompkins Co. 23 Aug 1992. *Extreme dates:* 1 Apr (coastal) and 5 Dec (L. Ontario).

Lee B. Chamberlaine

Royal Tern *Sterna maxima*

Range Primarily southern Nearctic, breeding locally along the Atlantic Coast from Maryland to Georgia, also along the Gulf Coast of Texas and Louisiana, in Baja California, and in the West Indies. Atlantic birds winter from North Carolina south to central Argentina. Vagrant north to Nova Scotia.

Status Variously uncommon to fairly common coastal visitant, sometimes very common after tropical storms. Casual elsewhere.

Occurrence Before the 1950s, this species was considered a casual vagrant, and its occurrence was closely tied to hurricanes. Since then it has occurred regularly on the South Shore and east end of LI in late summer and fall, even in years when tropical storms do not reach our shores. The most reliable locations are Shinnecock Inlet and the Mecox-Sagaponack area, but it is found regularly in the JBSP area, irregularly to SI, and in the Peconic Bay to Riverhead, Suffolk Co. Peak numbers are present in Aug and Sep, but since the 1970s it has also been found in most years from May to Jul.

Away from the coast it has been found four times: L. De Forest, Rockland Co. 18 Jun 1960 (specimen); Croton Point, Westchester Co. 10 Aug 1976 after Hurricane Belle (KB 26:233); two near Coxsackie, Greene Co. 8 Sep 1979 after Hurricane David (KB 30:51); Braddock Bay, Monroe Co. 31 Jul–2 Aug 1983 (KB 33:267).

Maxima: 300 Jones Inlet, Nassau Co. to Sagaponack, Suffolk Co. 14 Sep 1960 after Hurricane Donna; 114 Shinnecock to Georgica Pond, Suffolk Co. 29 Sep 1982; 57 Great Kills, Richmond Co. 20 Aug 1991 after Hurricane Bob. *Extreme dates:* 29 Apr and 24 Nov.

Remarks As its breeding range has crept northward in recent decades, local observers eagerly await the first NY nesting. Adults are often seen feeding flying juveniles, but terns are notorious wanderers and continue to feed their young even in winter quarters, far in time and place from breeding sites. These sightings are not proof of breeding in our area.
Michael F. Cooper

Sandwich Tern   *Sterna sandvicensis*

Range Western Palearctic and warm temperate portions of the Nearctic, breeding locally and sporadically in the Caribbean, Gulf of Mexico, and on the Atlantic Coast of North and South Carolina, rarely to southern Virginia, and the Gulf Coast of Louisiana and Texas. Winters from Louisiana and Florida south to Colombia and on the Pacific Coast from southern Mexico to Panama.

Status Formerly very rare and irregular vagrant after tropical storms. In recent years has occurred with increasing regularity, at times independent of storms.

Occurrence It has been recorded only from the South Shore of LI, most frequently from JBSP to Mecox. Bull (1974) listed one record for the 1950s and two occurrences totaling at least 10 birds for the 1960s. There are records for most years through the 1970s and 1980s, and through the 1990s it has been recorded nearly every year.

The largest numbers were all hurricane related. At least nine individuals were found at six localities from JBSP, Nassau Co. to Sagaponack, Suffolk Co. 13–16 Sep 1960 after Hurricane Donna; 25+ from Fire I. Inlet to Montauk, Suffolk Co. 27 Sep 1985 after Hurricane Gloria; about 12 from JBSP to Georgica Pond, Suffolk Co., two at Montauk, and five at Great Gull I. 19–25 Aug 1991 after Hurricane Bob.

Extreme dates: 24 May and 22 Oct. Most come during the summer and early fall hurricane season, from late Jul through late Sep.

Remarks The increase of this species over the past several decades echoes a similar increase in the more common Royal Tern. Birders in NJ, and to a lesser degree in MA, are finding it more frequently as well. CT's first was photographed in Aug 1991. As the breeding ranges of these terns inch northward we should expect them to occur with greater regularity. Michael F. Cooper

Roseate Tern

Sterna dougallii

Range Cosmopolitan with local distribution, chiefly in warmer regions of the Old World. In North America, restricted to the North Atlantic coast, breeding locally on coastal islands and ocean beaches from Nova Scotia to Virginia, the Dry Tortugas, and the West Indies. The American population apparently winters in the West Indies and along the coast of South America as far as Bahia, Brazil.

Status Variously uncommon to locally abundant breeder and fall migrant on LI, chiefly at the east end. Rare and local elsewhere on the coast. For interior status, see Remarks.

Breeding Most nest on Great Gull I., Suffolk Co. at the eastern end of LI Sound. From 1985 to 1995 estimates of pairs there ranged from 700 to 1500. The figures for 1985, 1986, and 1987 are low because there was no regular check of Roseates in those years. From 1988 to 1996 a team dedicated to working only with Roseate Terns marked nests daily throughout the season, and the estimated numbers of pairs on Great Gull I. increased from 1200 to 1500. Nesting, ranging from two to 100 pairs, was recorded at about a dozen other LI sites 1985–1995 (Sommers et al. 1994; Meskill et al. 1995; Sommers et al. 1996).

Throughout the period, Cedar Beach, Suffolk Co. was the only site other than Great Gull I., that was occupied each year. Numbers at Cedar Beach decreased from an estimated 100 pairs in 1985 (Sommers et al. 1994) to 37 in 1995 (Burger and Gochfeld 1995). Between 17 and 23 Jun 1995 the colony suffered heavy predation by American Crows (NASFN 49:913). By 28 Jun there were no Roseate Tern nests left and only three active Common Tern nests. Subsequently the birds abandoned the colony site, and in Jul some terns and skimmers tried to nest on the outer beach (Burger and Gochfeld 1995). In 1996 there were an estimated 59 pairs of Roseate Terns and 585 pairs of Common Terns at Cedar Beach on 7 Jun, but by 27 Jun there were no Roseate and only 225 pairs of Common (Burger 1996). Burger noted that there had been heavy fox predation in the colony (Sommers and Alfieri 1997).

In 1995, Male, under contract with the NYSDEC, attracted 100 pairs of Roseates as well as about the same number of Commons (Hays 1995) to nest on Fort Tyler, an island just north of Gardiners I., Suffolk Co. Male set out decoys on the island in 1993 and 1994, attracting first one pair, then two. The birds nesting in 1995 fledged few young due to predation and disturbance. In 1996 four pairs of Roseates and 48 pairs of Commons nested on Fort Tyler (Sommers and Alfieri 1997).

Nonbreeding An uncommon migrant away from breeding colonies, its numbers fluctuate from year to year even in the Montauk and Orient areas. Flocks of more than a dozen are the exception rather than the rule. Rare before May and after Sep.

Spring maxima: 20 Rockaway Beach, Queens Co. 19 May 1956. *Fall maxima:* 500 Montauk, Suffolk Co. 21 Aug 1950; 300 Jones Inlet, Nassau Co. 15 Sep 1966 (Cooper et al. 1970). *Extreme dates:* 29 Apr and 5 Nov.

Remarks Coastal surveys of colonial waterbirds made in the late 1970s (Erwin 1979; Erwin and Korschgen 1979; Buckley and Buckley 1980) showed a population decline in the northeastern United States. In addition, the birds that remained were concentrated in a few large colonies, making them particularly vulnerable (Nisbet 1980; Buckley and Buckley 1981). Buckley and Buckley (1979) suggested that the Roseate Tern qualified as a Threatened species. Nisbet (1980), in a review of the status and population trends of the species throughout its range, agreed. Buckley and Buckley (1981) summarized declines in populations nesting along the East Coast as well as those documented in their aerial surveys of LI in 1974–1978. They argued convincingly that the Roseate Tern population in the Northeast was in danger of extinction and recommended that action be taken to begin procedures to list it as an Endangered species. On 30 Dec 1982 the USFWS published a notice of review in the Federal Register identifying vertebrate taxa, including the Roseate Tern, for addition to the list of endangered and threatened wildlife under the Endangered Species Act of 1973. On 2 Dec 1987 the Roseate Tern was officially listed as an Endangered species.

Eaton (1910) considered the Roseate Tern "accidental" in the interior of NY. Bull (1974) did not accept this status, as he considered that there were no satisfactory records from the interior. Although there are no known specimens, Davison did report collecting a Roseate Tern 31 May 1886 at Youngstown at the western end of L. Ontario (Davison 1889). He added this specimen to his own collection. Eaton listed the Davison record as well as two others from western NY, one from Keuka L. from the Auburn List and one from L. Erie from the Buffalo List. Subsequently, three sightings of single Roseates were reported on the Niagara R. at the falls: 22 Aug 1935 (Beardsley), 29 Jun 1937 (Mitchell), and 6 May 1938 (Bourne). A description of the third bird includes the diagnostic features that characterize Roseate Terns (Ulrich 1938).

In addition to these inland NY records there are two IN records. On 14 Aug 1916 Stoddard collected a male in breeding plumage, now Field Museum (Chicago) number 347766, on the shore of L. Michigan near Millers, IN (Stoddard 1917). The second record for that state was the recovery report of an adult on 1 Aug 1957 near Aurora, IN (Nisbet 1980). It had been originally banded, 533-90431, as a young bird on Bird I., MA. The latter record is unusual in that it is far inland, away from any of the Great Lakes.

The Stoddard specimen provides incontrovertible evidence that it is possible for Roseate Terns to wander inland. After reviewing the above records the author would agree with Eaton (1910) in describing the Roseate Tern's inland status in NY as "accidental."

Helen Hays

Common Tern   *Sterna hirundo*

Range Holarctic, breeding in North America from Canada south; inland locally to northern United States, and on the Atlantic Coast to North Carolina; absent as a breeder on the Pacific Coast. Eastern populations winter along the South American coast to northern Argentina.

Status Locally abundant breeder and migrant on LI, less numerous in the interior, breeding locally in the northwestern, central, and western portions.

Breeding It nests on inland lakes as well as along the coast. The inland population is part of the lower Great Lakes population, which reached peak levels in the early 1960s and had declined sharply by the late 1970s (Courtney and Blokpoel 1983). The authors listed a number of factors responsible for the decline, including displacement by Ring-billed and Herring gulls, increasing vegetation, flooding, predation, and human disturbance. They also pointed out that by 1980, 70% of the population nested on human-made structures. In 1983 the NYSDEC listed the Common Tern as Threatened because of the decline in the inland population, and from the mid-1980s to the present it has supported monitoring and habitat management programs throughout the state.

On the Niagara Frontier it nests on human-made structures. Three breakwaters a mile or more outside Buffalo harbor provide nest sites, as do cribs forming the bases of three power transmission towers in the Niagara R. It also nests on the North Tonawanda water intake structure. Nests were counted on these structures each year 1987–1995 (Horning et al. 1995). With slight variation, the number remained at about 800 throughout the count period and corresponds to the 1983 estimate of the population made by Hotopp (Atlas 1988). Watson (1995a) reported seeing fledglings 30 Jun 1995 one and a half miles from two colony sites on the Niagara Frontier. He also noted that on 6 Jun 1993, researchers picked up young, which they judged to be three weeks old on the basis of plumage, at the Short Breakwater colony. In the same year 106 nests were marked on the Short Breakwater, and 332 on the North Breakwater by 8 May (McBrayer et al. 1995). The early Jun estimates of the age of the juveniles as well as the numbers of nests found by 8 May suggest that Common Terns in these colonies may be laying eggs by the last week in Apr, two to three weeks earlier than the coastal population.

Navigational cribs were built in the St. Lawrence R. between 1973 and 1979. Terns were first observed nesting on them in 1976 by Van Riet, who put vegetation on the platforms to encourage them (KB 39:235). By 1982 many of the natural islands used by the terns either were taken over by Ring-billed Gulls or were rendered unsuitable because they had become covered with vegetation. By 1989, 70% of the terns in the area were nesting on navigational cribs. Nesting on human-made sites was more successful than was nesting on natural islands (Harper 1993; Karwowski et al. 1995). Between 1982 and 1995 counts of nests were made along 90 mi of river during the first week in Jun. Fieldworkers counted from 550 to a little over 600 nests at 18 sites each year.

In two instances droppings from roosting cormorants have limited reproductive success. On Reef Light outside Buffalo Harbor the nesting terns deserted after the area was covered with droppings, and they have not returned (Horning et al. 1995). In the St. Lawrence, reproductive success was lower in the section of the navigational crib where droppings from roosting cormorants fell on the eggs and, massing on the ground, hardened with the gravel into a relatively smooth surface (Harper 1993).

On Oneida L. in 1992 Common Terns nested on three islands. Most nests were on Little I., and there were a few on Long and Grassy islands (Kllnowski and Richmond 1992). The authors estimated the population to be 300–400 pairs on the basis of nests marked, a figure similar to the estimate, 300 pairs, by Courtney and Blokpoel (1983) for the Oneida L. population 1960–1980. The habitat on all islands is managed, and records on that population have been kept since 1979.

At MNWR in 1995 Gingrich (pers. comm.) reported that his assistant had observed two fledglings being fed by adults, strongly suggesting local nesting. Although it is present throughout the nesting season at MNWR and at the north end of Cayuga L. (S. Kelling, pers. comm.), this is the only record indicating nesting in many years.

The coastal colonies lie along the North and South shores of LI as well as on a few islands at the eastern end of LI Sound. Estimates of pairs for this area made 1985–1995 show a decline. There were an estimated 18,550 pairs in 1985, a high of 27,270 pairs in 1987, and subsequently decreasing numbers, with a low of 17,442 in 1995 (Sommers et al. 1994; Meskill et al. 1995; Sommers et al. 1996). In 1996, 9000 pairs nested on Great Gull I. at the eastern end of LI Sound, making it the largest colony in the Western Hemisphere. The island is owned by the AMNH, and researchers have monitored reproductive success in the colony each summer since 1969. Here again the terns have adapted to and succeeded in a human-made environment by nesting on the exfoliating concrete structures of an old army fort. The population more than doubled after researchers reintroduced meadow voles *(Microtus pennsylvanicus)* to the island in 1981 (Hays 1984) to reduce the vegetation that covered many areas where terns formerly had nested.

Bull (1974) and the Atlas mapped locations of LI colonies. In 1967 Common Tern was found nesting in salt marsh, and by 1985 more than half of the coastal colonies were found in salt marsh (Atlas 1988). In 1995 a pair nested on an offshore rock in North Milton Harbor, Rye, Westchester Co., a first county record (Usai, Farnsworth) (NASFN 49:913).

Nonbreeding: On the coast it is rare before May and after mid-Oct. In 1976 a number lingered late at Montauk, Suffolk Co., with 150+ on 8 Nov and six until 29 Nov. Inland it is rare before mid-Apr and after mid-Nov, arriving much earlier and departing later than on the coast. For most species, the reverse is true. It is extremely rare in winter, but there are at least three occurrences: Montauk 27 Dec 1957; Buffalo 27 Dec 1964–2 Jan 1965; Buffalo 16 Dec 1965–5 Jan 1966.

Coastal maxima: Spring: 1500 Oak Beach, Suffolk Co. 10 May 1936. *Fall:* 5000 Moriches Inlet, Suffolk Co. 3 Sep 1949 after a hurricane; 500+ Montauk, Suffolk Co. 26 Oct 1976. *Inland maxima: Spring:* 450 Buffalo, Erie Co. 18 Apr 1958, early for so many. *Fall:* 7800 Sandy Pond inlet and 3000 Derby Hill 15 Sep 1979, both Oswego Co. counts following

Hurricane Frederic. **Extreme dates:** 2 Apr and 7 Dec, exceptionally on the coast as early as 20 Mar.
Helen Hays

Arctic Tern   *Sterna paradisaea*

Range Circumpolar, breeding in North America throughout arctic Canada and south on the Atlantic Coast to Maine and Massachusetts. Migrates to the eastern Atlantic and then south to wintering grounds at the edge of the Antarctic pack ice. This species is virtually unrecorded in North America south of Long Island. After the breeding season the birds presumably migrate well offshore and do not visit coastal areas.

Status Very rare vagrant.

Occurrence There are more than a dozen published reports including the following six fully documented records: (1) 18 Jul 1884 Cartwright I., eastern LI; (2) 7 Oct 1897 LI; (3) 20 May 1916 Cayuga L., Tompkins Co.; (4) 23–26 Nov 1975 Montauk, Suffolk Co., photographed (Buckley et al.) (AB 30:43); (5) 13 and 23 Aug 1980 6–10 m south-southwest of Montauk (Crumb, Spencer) (KB 30:262); (6) 12–19 Nov 1989 Peace Bridge, Niagara R. (Galas et al.) (KB 40:30). The first three are specimen records, and the last two have been accepted by NYSARC (1981, 1991). The Nov record at Montauk is the latest in eastern North America.

An additional half dozen or so records involve birds seen by observers intimately familiar with the species and are undoubtedly correct. These range in date from 14 May to 23 Jun and from 21 Sep to 5 Oct and include several sightings of small groups. Five were reported at Shinnecock, Suffolk Co. 13 Jun 1984 (KB 34:272), four at the same location 23 Jun 1982 (KB 32:303), and two at Sagaponack, Suffolk Co. 21 Sep 1984 (KB 35:71).

Remarks This species presents great difficulty, both in terms of its identification and in the assessment of its status. Misidentifications and uncertain identifications happen to even the most careful observers, especially those without extensive comparative experience. On the other hand, the proximity of NY to its breeding grounds seems to make it a good candidate for vagrancy. At first blush it seems remarkable that a long-distance migrant that breeds in colonies just to our north could be so scarce on our shores. However, according to Veit and Petersen (1993), adults leave the colonies in early Aug and move north or east to Europe before heading south to Antarctica. They list just a handful of records for MA after mid-Aug. Spring migration routes are also far offshore. The upstate records may represent birds en route to and from inland breeding grounds in the Arctic.
Michael F. Cooper

Forster's Tern   *Sterna forsteri*

Range Nearctic, breeding from southeastern British Columbia and central Saskatchewan south to southern California and along the Gulf Coast from central Mexico to Louisiana, and, locally, along the Atlantic Coast from Long Island to North Carolina. Winters from Virginia south to Guatemala.

Status Recently established as a breeder in salt marshes on the South Shore of LI, where it is now locally common. Still rare in spring on LI away from breeding areas; rare to uncommon spring migrant on the Great Lakes; locally common fall migrant on the coast, and locally uncommon to fairly common fall migrant on the Great Lakes and lower Hudson R.; rare on other upstate lakes; casual in winter.

Breeding It was first found breeding in NY among Common Terns in Jun 1981 in salt marsh in Great South Bay, Hempstead, Nassau Co. (Zarudsky 1981), where a pair or two has usually been present since. One pair bred in JoCo Marsh, JBWR in 1991. A colony of 40–60 pairs has been established there since 1992 (Riepe 1994). That colony increased to 77 pairs in 1995 and represented the entire NY breeding population at that time. In 1996, this colong decreased to 38 pairs, with a few additional pairs nesting at two other sites (Sommers et al. 1996).

Nonbreeding Rare on the coast in spring migration until the last few years. Annual in fall on LI in numbers varying from a few individuals up to 80, Mecox Bay, Suffolk Co. 12 Oct 1983 (Raynor) (KB 33:71). Banding records (Veit and Petersen 1993) show that some, and possibly most, summer and fall birds along the coast are postbreeding wanderers from the south. Larger numbers occur after hurricanes.

   Uncommon to fairly common fall migrant along the lower Hudson R., rarely north to Dutchess Co. These birds may originate on the Great Lakes, since 1978 was a record year in both places. The maximum was 46 at Piermont, Rockland Co. 31 Oct 1978 (KB 30:55).

   Most upstate records come from bays and estuaries on the Great Lakes. They were more frequent in spring 1978, with seven individuals, 16 Apr–31 May. Rare in spring in the 1980s, only singles in 1984 and 1986, it has been nearly annual in Apr–May since 1991. Annual in late summer and fall in numbers varying from a few to several dozen. The maximum on L. Erie was 34 Dunkirk Harbor, Chautauqua Co. 30 Aug 1987; maxima on L. Ontario: 48 Alexandria Bay, Jefferson Co. 12 Aug 1977 (KB 27:48); 42 Braddock Bay, Monroe Co. 25 Aug 1978.

   Away from the Great Lakes upstate, since 1991, there are three fall records from Oneida L. and one spring and two fall records from MNWR. There are also two midsummer records upstate, both 1993: one early Jun, Seneca L., and two, Braddock Bay Jun 15. All upstate birds presumably come from the interior continental breeding populations.

Although Bull (1974) reported only one Dec record, from NYC, and no midwinter records, there have been three Dec records since 1983 on LI and two midwinter records: Fire I. Inlet, Suffolk Co. 23 Feb 1976 (KB 26:120) and Dunkirk Harbor, Chautauqua Co. 3–6 Jan 1991 (KB 41:101).

Remarks (Subspecies comments by K. C. Parkes) Local and irregular increases in NY over the past 20 years accord with developments in neighboring states and provinces. It has increased as a breeder in NJ since the middle 1950s (Leck 1984). In ON it has bred on L. Erie, but not, in recent years, on L. Ontario (Peck and James 1983). It became more common in southwestern ON in the 1960s and 1970s, but the current trend is not clear (R. Ridout, pers. comm.). MA had one confirmed nesting in 1990, representing the northernmost breeding on the Atlantic Coast (Veit and Petersen 1993).

Although the fifth edition of the AOU Check-List treated Forster's Tern as monotypic, Parkes agrees with Hellmayr and Conover (*Field Museum of Natural History Publications, Zoological Series* 13, p. 1, no. 3 [1948]:311) that *litoricola* Oberholser is a valid form. Furthermore, Parkes (1952) found that both *litoricola* and *forsteri* occur in NY. LI specimens are, as expected, of the coastal subspecies *litoricola*. The Forster's Terns seen increasingly in the Great Lakes region would be expected to be of the nominate subspecies, which breeds in the interior of the continent. The only inland specimen seen by Parkes was one from Cayuga L., 15 May 1914 CUM 3954, which is, indeed *forsteri*. The paler mantle of *forsteri* is obvious with specimens in the hand, but it would not be noticeable in the field except in the unlikely event of examples of *forsteri* and *litoricola* seen side by side. Robert O. Paxton and Kenneth C. Parkes

Least Tern   *Sterna antillarum*

Range Nearctic, breeding on the Pacific Coast, in the Mississippi Valley, and along the Atlantic and Gulf coasts from southern Maine to Florida and west to Texas; also in the West Indies. Winters along the Pacific Coast to southern Mexico and probably to northwestern South America and, in the east, from the coast of Colombia to Brazil.

Status Common local breeder and common to abundant migrant on LI, rare visitant anywhere else.

Breeding The smallest of the North American terns, it nests on sand beaches, dredges, and similar open shorelines along both the North Shore and South Shore of LI. Colonies tend to be small and free of vegetation; 64% of the colonies surveyed in 1985 had fewer than 50 adults, and vegetation covered less than 10% of the site in the majority of them. From 1974 to 1978, surveys indicated 1719–2628 pairs in 29–47 colonies. Surveys done 1982–1985 found that the numbers had increased to a maximum of 3114 pairs in up to 59 colonies (Atlas 1988). From 1985 to 1995, the mean number of nesting pairs was 3015, with a mean of 59 colonies. A ten-year low occurred in 1992, then average numbers in 1993, and another low year, with 2550, in 1994 (Sommers et al. 1996). This species is normally present from May through early Sep, with rare appearances in Apr and Oct. It is currently listed by the NYSDEC as Endangered and has been recommended for reclassification as Threatened.

Nonbreeding On 22 May 1988 a single Least Tern was reported at MNWR, which was the fourth Regional record and the first since 1965 (KB 38:198). A single individual was seen on 14 Aug 1955 on Keuka L. near Branchport, Yates Co. That sighting was probably related to Hurricane Connie, which pushed 13 Least Terns to West Point, Orange Co. and six to Piermont, Rockland Co. Hurricane Hugo, in the fall of 1989, is the likely cause of the three individuals that were reported from the Catskills 23 Sep 1989 (KB 40:50). The species has also been reported near the Buffalo area, including an immature on the extraordinary date of 5 Nov 1995 in Dunkirk Harbor, Chautauqua Co. On that same date, another was observed some 40 m west on the north shore of L. Erie in ON (KB 46:36,40). Closer to the breeding area, Least Terns have wandered inland to the Marshlands Conservancy, Rye, and Croton Bay, both Westchester Co.
Sharon M. Skelly

Bridled Tern *Sterna anaethetus*

Range Pantropical, in the western Atlantic-Caribbean region breeding in the Antilles and north to the Bahamas. Nonbreeders wander widely in the Gulf Stream at least to Cape Hatteras, North Carolina. In winter apparently disperses at sea, primarily between the West Indies and western Africa.

Status Very rare vagrant.

Occurrence All records of this species are from coastal waters. Bull (1974) listed two specimen records. The first was an immature found alive at Quogue, Suffolk Co. 11 Dec 1950. The second is a tern wing found along the stone jetty at Short Beach (JBSP), Nassau Co. 22 Jan 1967. This wing was identified by Bull and Parkes and is AMNH 786360.

The majority of records are in the fall as expected, given the relationship between tropical storms and this species' occurrence in NY. During the fall of 1979, five individuals were observed after Hurricane David, and a week later, after tropical storm Frederic, there were two reports of single birds (KB 30:62). There is one spring record, 29 May 1985, Shinnecock Inlet, Suffolk Co. (KB 35:216). Corresponding to an increased interest in pelagic birding, sightings are being reported from boat trips rather than just from storm passage. These pelagic sightings include: a single bird seen on a trip to Cox's Ledge on 23 Aug 1986 (KB 37:100); a single bird during a three-day trip 17–20 Sep 1987 (KB 38:282); and one on a one-day trip 90 m south of Montauk 11 Sep 1993 (KB 44:77). There is a fairly even split between adult and immature birds seen after storms.

Remarks As would be expected, the number of records for Bridled Tern increases to the south in NJ waters. There are about 20 records from NJ 1951–1992, all but two in fall. MA has about a dozen records, all in fall, a figure roughly comparable to NY's. No records exist for CT. There are six records for RI after hurricanes (Conway 1992).
Sharon M. Skelly

Sooty Tern *Sterna fuscata*

Range Pantropical, breeding, in the Atlantic-Gulf-Caribbean region, in the Greater and Lesser Antilles, on islands off the Yucatan Peninsula, Texas, and Louisiana, and on the Dry Tortugas and elsewhere in the tropical Atlantic. Ranges widely, principally after storms, to eastern North America north to Nova Scotia. Disperses eastward in winter to tropical Africa.

Status Very rare vagrant along the outer coast of LI after tropical storms; casual elsewhere.

Occurrence Bull (1974) reviewed storm records from 1878, 1928, 1955, and 1960, with all sightings from LI or along or near the Hudson R. Then, in 1979, Hurricane David hit on 6 Sep and produced the amazing total of more than 110 in eastern NY and LI. Of that total, approximately 20 were reported on the Hudson R. in Greene, Columbia, Albany, Dutchess, and Westchester counties. The balance were from Nassau, Suffolk, and Queens counties (KB 30:23, 49–64; AB 34:133–138, 143–144). There appear to be only three true "upstate" records. Eaton (1910) listed one 6 Sep 1876 at L. Champlain, Clinton Co. and another that same year at Owasco L., Cayuga Co.; both were storm related. The third, however, was an adult found dead at Irondequoit Bay, Monroe Co. 5 June 1963 (KB 13:209), although the first hurricane of that year did not occur until 3 Aug. The mounted specimen is in the RMAS, Accession 543.504.17.

Other than that specimen, there is only one spring record. On 20 May 1975, an adult was observed for three hours in a mixed Common and Roseate tern colony at Shinnecock Bay, Suffolk Co. (KB 25:236). Other records, seemingly unrelated to any tropical storm, are one at Piermont, Rockland Co. 26 Jul 1974 (KB 24:210) and one 26 Jun 1984 seen standing on a float 14 mi southeast of Montauk (KB 34:272).
Neil S. Moon and Laura W. Moon

White-winged Tern   *Chlidonias leucopterus*

Range Palearctic, breeding from eastern Europe to southern Siberia, Manchuria, and Sakhalin Island. Winters from tropical Africa and Southeast Asia south to southern Africa, the East Indies, and Australia. Casual or accidental in the British Isles, Scandinavia, and North America.

Status Casual vagrant and one breeding record.

Breeding On 17 Jun 1992, a White-winged Tern was found tending a nest with a Black Tern at PRWMA (Mazzocchi and Muller 1992). Two unfledged chicks were in the nest, and the observers banded one. On a subsequent visit to the nest 21 Jul, no chicks were observed, and no other evidence of their presence was ever found. It is uncertain whether a predator or the heavy rainstorm the previous evening was responsible for the disappearance of the young. The presumed parent White-winged Tern was last seen on 22 Jul.

Nonbreeding The first sight record for this Eurasian species occurred at Cedar Beach, adjacent to Fire I. Inlet, Suffolk Co. (A. Lauro) (KB 41:217) on 12 May 1991. This record established the species on the NYS checklist (NYSARC 1993) The next record was on 19 Jun 1991 at Salmon Creek, Monroe Co. (Skelly 1992); then came the unsuccessful nest in 1992 described above. The species was observed again at PRWMA 8 May 1994 (Worona) (KB 44:229).

Remarks There have been some 20+ records in the Northeast, and since 1975 the occurrences have been virtually annual, ranging from DE to NB. Anthony J. Lauro

Black Tern   *Chlidonias niger*

Range Holarctic, breeding in North America from British Columbia and California east to Maine and south to central California and northern New York. Winters chiefly in northern South America.

Status Very local breeder, nearly all extant colonies located on the Great Lakes Plain. Currently listed as a Species of Special Concern in NY, it has been recommended for reclassification as Endangered. Uncommon to fairly common migrant on the Great Lakes Plain and LI; rare elsewhere.

Breeding Bull (1974) described the Black Tern as "most plentiful" as a breeder in the freshwater marshes of Jefferson Co., along the L. Ontario shore in Oswego and Monroe counties, in the region south and west of Oneida L., and in the MNWR and OOWMA; he also cited two Adirondack localities. The Atlas found this distribution to be somewhat reduced. The loss of colonies south and west of Oneida L., in an area of expanding suburban development, was of major significance.

With the completion of the Atlas, concerns were expressed anew over the true status of the Black Tern in NY. On the basis of a review of the literature, contacts with knowledgeable individuals, and Atlas records, Carroll (1988) identified a total of 52 colony locations with at least 22 reported as no longer extant. Carroll also documented a significant long-term reduction in the number of breeding pairs at several well-known sites and recommended a field survey of active and historical colonies to reassess the species' status in the state. An initial statewide survey was conducted in 1989 and followup surveys were conducted in 1990, 1991, and again in 1994. The number of breeding pairs estimated during those surveys was 235, 215, 284, and 244, respectively. The 1989 and 1990 estimates were based primarily on the number of individual birds observed at each site surveyed, whereas intensive nest searches augmented adult counts in 1991 and 1994, making estimates from those years somewhat more accurate (Mazzocchi and Muller 1995). During the course of the work, more than 100 historical and potential colony sites were surveyed, with Black Terns counted at just 35 sites (with TWMA, INWR, and OOWMA counted as one "site"). Virtually all of the sites are located on the Great Lakes Plain, and, although terns did return to nest on the NY side of L. Champlain in 1993 for the first nesting in Region 7 in over a decade (KB 43:340), the Tupper L. location in the Adirondacks, and other former sites where suitable habitat still appears to be present, remained vacant. A "core" of 10 sites were occupied during each survey year and collectively harbored more than 75% of NY's nesting population. Many of these colonies are on state WMAs including Dexter Marsh, Lakeview, and Perch River, Jefferson Co.; Upper and Lower Lakes, St. Lawrence Co.; Braddock Bay, Monroe Co.; and the TWMA-INWR-OOWMA complex.

Nonbreeding Until 1970, migration along the upper Niagara R. in the fall numbered in the thousands (Carroll 1988), and large numbers were recorded at that season on the South Shore of LI as well. Through the 1970s and early 1980s, fall counts along the upper Niagara dropped dramatically, with numbers in the range of several hundred birds becoming the norm (Carroll 1988). LI counts experienced a concurrent drop.

The only substantial fall counts recorded since 1985 have come from a premigratory staging area in eastern L. Ontario, off Point Peninsula, Jefferson Co. (Mazzocchi and Muller 1991, 1995) and from LI during a coastal influx in early Sep 1994. The tremendous drop in fall migration counts reflects a decline in the breeding population throughout the Northeast.

Coastal maxima: Historical: 1500 JBWR 6 Sep 1955; 1000 East Hampton, Suffolk Co. 25 Aug 1933. *Recent:* 121 off Ft. Tilden, Queens Co. and 82 Wainscott Pond, Suffolk Co. both 5 Sep 1993. *Inland maxima: Historical:* all Niagara R.: 5500, 28 Aug 1965; 5000, 9 Sep

1953, 26 Jul 1958, 23 Aug 1961. *Recent:* Point Peninsula shoal: 479, 15 Aug 1991; 281, 19 Aug 1994. *Extreme dates:* 22 Apr and 27 Oct, exceptionally 1 Dec (inland). Rare before May and after Sep, but inland it usually arrives earlier in spring and lingers later in fall.

Remarks The BBS indicated a continual, significant decrease in Black Tern populations since 1967, with declines less steep in the 1980s (Dunn and Agro 1995). Migration counts on the Niagara R. and counts of nesting pairs at several well-known NY sites concurred with the timing of that decline (Carroll 1988). At MNWR, as many as 1000 pairs nested in the late 1950s, with numbers dropping into the hundreds in the 1960s, then down to 50–100 in the 1970s, and finally to no successful breeding pairs in the early 1990s (Carroll 1988; Novak 1990).

The loss and degradation of wetlands on the breeding grounds, in migratory stopover areas, and on the wintering range have probably been major contributing factors in the decline (Dunn and Agro 1995; Novak 1992). Since European settlement, an estimated 54% of all wetlands in the United States has been lost. This includes 4.75 million acres of palustrine emergent wetlands during the mid-1950s to mid-1970s (Tiner 1984), a period that corresponds well with documented Black Tern population declines. The quality of some remaining wetlands may be reduced because of pollution and runoff associated with increased development in their vicinity (Novak 1992). In NY, successional changes, the invasion by purple loosestrife *(Lythrum salicaria)*, and altered water levels in L. Ontario and the St. Lawrence R. have also undoubtedly contributed to a reduction in the number and extent of wetlands with the preferred mix of open water and emergent vegetation.

Organochlorines, including PCBs, DDT, DDE, and Dieldrin, and other contaminants have been detected in Black Tern eggs and may be involved in the decline by either contributing to reduced reproductive success or depressing favored prey populations or by both (Dunn and Agro 1995; Novak 1992).

Paul G. Novak

Black Skimmer *Rhynchops niger*

Range Primarily eastern Nearctic, breeding on the Atlantic and Gulf coasts from Massachusetts to Florida and Texas; also in Mexico and South America. Winters from North Carolina south to the Gulf of Mexico.

Status Locally common to abundant breeder only on the South Shore of LI; virtually unknown elsewhere.

Breeding The very distinctive Black Skimmer breeds commonly along the South Shore of LI, where it is found nesting in association with Common and Least terns. An unsuccessful nesting attempt was made in 1984 on

Great Gull I, and it does occasionally nest on the North Shore. Colonial waterbird surveys on LI 1974–1985 found 339–495 pairs in 9–13 colonies (Atlas 1988). From 1985 to 1995, the number of nesting skimmers ranged from 374–599 pairs, with a mean of 463 (Sommers et al. 1996). Despite sporadic nesting in CT and MA, LI is considered the northern limit of its range. It has been recommended for inclusion on the NYSDEC's list as a Species of Special Concern.

Nonbreeding Primarily a coastal species, it has nonetheless been seen on very rare occasions away from LI. Reports exist for Playland in Rye, Westchester Co., a site that had an annual visit from 1975 to 1978 (KB 28:258); the Marshlands Conservancy in Rye; an immature at Croton Bay, Westchester Co. 30 Aug 1987 (KB 37:239); and a 23 Nov 1992 sighting at Piermont Pier, Rockland Co., the latter the first record for that county (KB 43:109). Bull (1974) listed four historical upstate records; one collected near Utica, Oneida Co. in the fall of 1893; a bird collected on Braddock Bay, Monroe Co. 15 Sep 1924; one observed on the Mohawk R. at Niskayuna, Schenectady Co. 27 Aug 1933; and a single bird seen by several observers near Norwich, Chenango Co. 17 Oct 1954.

After hurricanes, large congregations may be found, such as 800 from Mecox Bay to Shinnecock Bay, Suffolk Co. 9 Sep 1954. Without hurricane help, 2000 were at JBWR 29 Sep 1965, but late-season numbers are more likely to be in the hundreds: e.g., 350 Flushing Bay, Queens Co. 3 Nov 1968; 466 JBWR 8 Oct 1988 (KB 39:71). Normally present from May to early Oct, it has been recorded in early Mar and on the Brooklyn CBC, when two were observed on 19 Dec 1992 at Canarsie Pier. The Southern Nassau Co. CBC 30 Dec 1995 was highlighted by eight skimmers at JBSP. Sharon M. Skelly

AUKS, MURRES, AND PUFFINS—ALCIDAE

Dovekie *Alle alle*

Range Northern Holarctic at high latitudes, breeding from extreme north-eastern Canada (Ellesmere Island) east to islands off north-central Siberia and south to Iceland and central Greenland. Winters at sea from the breeding range south; in the western Atlantic, to Long Island and, irregularly, along the continental slope to Maryland.

Status Rare to uncommon winter visitant to the outer coast; casual vagrant inland.

Occurrence Most recent records are from Montauk to Shinnecock Inlet, Suffolk Co., with reports as far west as Brooklyn and the Bronx Zoo (KB 34:71). Inland there are approximately two dozen reports, with the most recent being one at Charlotte-Ontario Beach, Wayne Co. 22 Sept 83 (KB 34:43). In winter, Dovekies are more pelagic than most other alcids and are not often seen from shore. They may be very common to abundant well offshore in mid to late winter. In the winter of 1994–1995, two pelagic trips were conducted to Block Canyon. The first was on 3 Dec 1994 and the other on 4 Mar 1995. The Dec trip encountered only one Dovekie, but the Mar trip tallied 300+, with flocks of up to 45–50 birds. A 10 Mar 1996 trip to Block Canyon recorded 220, with the first birds encountered at 35–40 mi off Montauk. More winter pelagic trips are needed to establish whether this is an annual phenomenon in NY waters. Most of those flocks were concentrated along thermoclines in the water. These temperature gradients serve to create upcurrents in the water column, which concentrate plankton, upon which Dovekies feed, at a depth that is accessible.

Almost all observations from shore occur Nov and Dec, coinciding with storms and easterly winds. Dovekies have been recorded every year. During one such storm on 19 Nov 1932, 3000 were seen between Moriches and Shinnecock inlets, Suffolk Co. On the same day 1000 were counted in the Jones Beach area. Reports such as these may be a small indication of the number of birds that winter offshore.

Oil spills are another disaster driving birds to shore. Bull (1974) reported," In late December 1928, over 50 oiled birds—all dead—were found between Montauk and Westhampton. Again during late December 1940, between Montauk and East Hampton, Helmuth found over 150 alive and dead, many badly oil-soaked."
Michael L. Usai

Common Murre   *Uria aalge*

Range Holarctic, breeding in the western North Atlantic from southern Greenland to the Gulf of St. Lawrence, with the larger population in eastern Newfoundland. Winters at sea primarily from the Grand Banks off Newfoundland to Georges Bank and Block Canyon off New England.

Status Very rare off LI. Unreported anywhere else.

Occurrence The Common Murre has been reliably reported only about two dozen times. It was first recorded in 1936, when several individuals were picked up in an oiled condition over a four-month period during the winter of 1936–1937 from Fishers I. and Montauk to Jones Beach. Dates ranged from 12 Dec to 4 Apr, the latter being the latest occurrence for this species in our area. Since then it has occurred irregularly, with most reports coming from Montauk, Suffolk Co. and generally involving one or two individuals a year, with several periods of two or three years without a sighting.

On 2 Jan 1993 a major oil spill in the Atlantic off Suffolk Co. produced many sightings and recoveries of oiled birds. The Okeanos Foundation treated and released many seabirds during the week after the spill, including eight Common Murres.

By far the most remarkable sighting took place on 4 Mar 1995 during a pelagic trip from Montauk to Block Canyon. During this trip record numbers for several alcid species were set, including a record total of 13 Common Murres (KB 45:233).

Remarks Although the name suggests otherwise, Common Murre is the rarer of the two murres; reports of Thick-billed Murre outnumber those of this species.
Michael Lolya

Thick-billed Murre   *Uria lomvia*

Range Holarctic, breeding in the western North Atlantic from Ellesmere Island and northern Greenland south to the Gulf of St. Lawrence. Winters at sea within the breeding range and south to New England, occasionally farther.

Status Rare and irregular winter visitant.

Occurrence Generally reported once or twice each winter, usually from Montauk, Suffolk Co., this species is sometimes picked up on shore after oil spills or major winter storms. It is also subject to occasional irruptions. Most notable were the winters of 1883–1884 and 1890–1891, when it was reported as far inland as Carmel, Putnam Co. and Croton Point, Westchester Co. As many as 14 specimens were picked up on the South Shore of LI during the winter of 1883–1884. A major storm on 25 Nov 1950 brought numerous reports from many upstate locations, where more than 50 specimens were collected. Surprisingly, none were reported from LI after that storm. More recently, a single bird was seen at Derby Hill, Oswego Co. 21 Oct 1982 (KB 33:61), unusual in both its upstate appearance and its representation as the earliest fall report. Rare before late Nov and after mid-Mar.

Remarks Great care must be taken in separating this species from immature Razorbills, which have relatively thin bills and are often mistaken for murres by inexperienced observers.
Michael Lolya

Razorbill

Alca torda

Range Northeastern Nearctic and northwestern Palearctic, in the former breeding south to islands in the Gulf of St. Lawrence and to northern Nova Scotia; very exceptionally to southern New Brunswick. Winters south to Long Island, rarely to New Jersey, and casually farther south.

Status Formerly rare and irregular, now uncommon to occasionally very common winter visitant to Montauk and offshore waters. Casual vagrant inland.

Occurrence Most records are from Montauk, Suffolk Co. and the South Shore of LI to Brooklyn and Queens. The few data available indicate that Razorbill is sometimes numerous offshore. It is uncommon before mid-Dec and after late Mar. Historically, there have been three summer records, the last an individual at Cox's Ledge, 30 mi southeast of Montauk on 2 Jul 1966.

There are three documented inland records. The first was an immature male near MNWR 5 Nov 1972, found dead on 10 Nov, probably of starvation (KB 23:138). The second was at Ft. Niagara, Niagara Co. 2 Jan 1985 (KB 35:122), and the third an individual at the Moses-Saunders Dam, St. Lawrence Co. 27 Nov 1987 (KB 38:47).

Maxima: 250+ flying northeast past Montauk toward Block I., RI Dec 1992; 125 Montauk 7 Mar 1993, 60 still present 11 Mar; 100 Montauk CBC 15 Dec 1994; 71 offshore trip to Block Canyon 4 Mar 1995; 25 between Montauk and JBSP 19–20 Jan 1991. *Extreme dates:* 2 Nov and 18 May.

Remarks The number reported from shore has jumped dramatically since the winter of 1990. With the exception of 38 at Montauk on 23 Jan 1977, it was rare before 1990 and not reported every year. After that year, winter reports of individuals became almost daily, and sightings of 20–30+ at a single time and place were not uncommon. The reasons for the escalation of reports are not clear. It may simply be an artifact of the increased number and skill of observers, but the abruptness of the increase suggests a true rise in the number wintering off LI.

Michael L. Usai

Black Guillemot   *Cepphus grylle*

Range Holarctic, breeding in North America in northern Alaska and from northern Hudson Bay, northern Labrador, and northern Greenland south to the Isles of Shoals off New Hampshire. Winters within the breeding range and south to Massachusetts; rarely to New York and New Jersey.

Status Very rare winter vagrant.

Occurrence This is one of our rarest alcids, with only about three dozen reports. A sighting from Rye, Westchester Co. 30 Jan 1932 is one of only two reliable reports away from LI. The second was of a single bird discovered on L. Champlain at Westport, Essex Co. on 7 Jan 1978 by the Hudson-Mohawk Bird Club and subsequently carefully studied and color photographed (Yunick 1978). During the past 20 years there have been about a dozen reports of up to three individuals, all from Suffolk Co., most from Montauk and Shinnecock Inlet. Several other reports of this species from upstate lakes are unconfirmed, and any sighting away from LI should be substantiated with photographs.
   Extreme dates: 26 Oct and 2 Apr.

Remarks Veit and Petersen (1993) called this species "common winter resident" in MA, with numbers sometimes reaching triple digits. The status in CT and RI is roughly as in NY; NJ has, predictably, fewer records.
Michael Lolya

Long-billed Murrelet   *Brachyramphus perdix*

Range Eastern Palearctic, breeding from northeastern Siberia south to Japan and wintering south to Japan. Accidental in several interior and northeastern North American sites.

Status Accidental.

Occurrence There is one record (NYSARC 1995; AB 48:94). This bird, found by DiLabio and Traynor at the Moses-Saunders Dam, Massena, St. Lawrence Co. 11 Oct 1993, was determined to be on the NY side on 24 Oct, making it eligible for the NYS checklist. It was last seen 26 Oct.

Remarks This record was originally accepted by NYSARC as Marbled Murrelet *(B. marmoratus)*. However, the Forty-first Supplement to the AOU Check-list raised what had been considered two subspecies, the nominate *marmoratus*, breeding from the Aleutians to the West Coast of North America, and *perdix*, the Asiatic form, to full species status.
   The accounts submitted to NYSARC did not permit a subspecific identification. However, this was the same individual that was well photographed (AB 48:105) and observed at close range by many observers on the Canadian side. From their descriptions, the Ontario Bird Records

Committee determined that it belonged to subspecies *perdix* (Bain 1994), which has now been elevated to full species status as Long-billed Murrelet.

With the added knowledge that all records in North America away from the Pacific Coast have been reported as *perdix*, and the specimen taken in MA in 1982 was also *perdix*, it behooves your editor to accept Long-billed Murrelet for this volume.

It is rather curious that it is the Asiatic species that shows up and not the North American one, but this is just another riddle about two truly enigmatic species.

Emanuel Levine

Ancient Murrelet   *Synthliboramphus antiquus*

Range Holarctic, breeding in North America from the Aleutian and Kodiak islands south to British Columbia, casually to northwestern Washington; also in eastern Asia south to Korea. In North America winters primarily offshore south to California. Casual in western interior areas and to the Great Lakes.

Status Accidental.

Occurrence There is one record, a bird discovered by Marcotte 31 Oct 1994 at the mouth of the Genesee R., Rochester, Monroe Co. and seen and photographed by many during its stay until 4 Nov. (Marcotte 1995; NYSARC 1996).

A flyby on 8 Nov off Hamlin Beach SP, Monroe Co., and one seen 13 Nov near St. Catharines, ON were presumably this same individual.

Remarks There are records in seven states east of the Mississippi and in two eastern Canadian provinces. Two were farther east than this sighting: Montreal, PQ 13 Apr 1913 and Rockport, MA 29 Nov 1992.

Robert E. Marcotte

Atlantic Puffin   *Fratercula arctica*

Range Holarctic, breeding in North America from Iceland and western Greenland to Newfoundland, Nova Scotia, and Maine. Disperses widely at sea in winter, with concentration along the continental slope south to the Chesapeake Bight.

Status Very rare and irregular winter vagrant along the shorelines of eastern LI. Perhaps more common farther offshore.

Occurrence There have been only about a dozen reliable reports, all from eastern LI between early Dec and late Apr, except for a 27 Sep 1963 live capture of an immature at Rhinebeck, Dutchess Co. That report represents the earliest sighting and the only specimen or sighting away from LI. Both the early date and the inland location suggest that this bird may have been a captive. The half-dozen or so reports of one or two individuals during the last 20 years, all from Suffolk Co., make the following report all the more remarkable. An unprecedented sighting of 58—54 immatures and 4 adults—carefully studied on 4 Mar 1995 during a Block Canyon pelagic trip from Montauk represents the largest recorded concentration for the western Atlantic away from the breeding grounds (KB 45:233).

Remarks The possibility that this species occurs offshore in larger numbers than previously believed possible merits further investigation by more off-shore studies during the late winter months.
Michael Lolya

PIGEONS AND DOVES—COLUMBIDAE

Rock Dove   *Columba livia*

Range Originally Palearctic, now introduced and resident, mainly in urban areas, throughout the world.

Status Introduced; abundant resident, except in forested areas and mountains.

Breeding The Atlas showed Confirmed breeding in 2003 blocks (53%) out of 3771 in which it was recorded. Breeding does not occur in heavily forested regions or in the higher elevations of the Adirondacks, Allegany Hills, Catskills, or Tug Hill (Atlas 1988). An analysis of BBS data 1966–1994 showed that the NY population was declining from a previous increase. From 1966 to 1979 the population was increasing by an average of 5.8% per year. From 1980 to 1994 it declined by 1.5% (Peterjohn 1995).

Nonbreeding Analysis of CBC data 1976–1994 showed that the population rebounded from a low in 1976 to a high in 1983 and had since been in a slight overall decline, which appeared to be leveling. Thus, the recent slight decline of populations in NY is corroborated by both CBC and BBS data. Burtt's monthly (Oct–May) feeder surveys in the *Syracuse Herald American* showed a slight progressive decline of Rock Dove from its 1983–1985 height to a rather stable lower level, where it has held since about 1988.

Although it is commonly regarded as an urban bird, many upstate farms have resident flocks, often seen standing on silos. These flocks can range from a dozen to several dozen, and the numbers tend to remain rather stable year after year. Those roosting in small cities, villages, and hamlets tend to fly out to the surrounding farmlands to feed, returning in the evening.

Maxima: 13,123 Lower Hudson CBC, Manhattan 16 Dec 1984; 300–400 Elmira, Chemung Co., Fall 1985.

Remarks The Rock Dove is now finally being recognized as a member of our avian fauna. In retrospect, it is difficult to imagine how it could not have been, since its collective biomass, its impact on the environment, and its competitive presence have all been quite substantial. Nevertheless, it was not officially included in CBCs before 1974. Even today it is still ignored by many birders, which is not easy to do since it is so numerous. It is an amazing bird, with an uncanny "street smart" ability to survive hostile conditions. That it can adapt from the wretchedness of the inner city to the bucolic idyll of upstate NY is even more cause for admiration. That it manages to survive relentless persecution (Coghlan 1990) confers upon it a heroic dimension. The Rock Dove was the first bird to be domesticated, in about 4500 B.C. (Zeuner 1963). It was first introduced to the New World from Europe by the French in the early 1600s (Schorger 1952). As a feral bird, its lineage has been contaminated and even invigorated with a considerable amount of human-induced specialized breeding. Yet its ancestral coloration (blue-gray with a white rump, iridescent head and neck, two black bars across each wing, and a dark band at the end of the tail) somehow persists, even in motley flocks richly endowed with various hues of brown and white. If ever there were a "melting pot" bird, the Rock Dove would be it.

Donald A. Windsor

White-winged Dove *Zenaida asiatica*

Range Primarily Neotropical, breeding in North America from southern Texas west to southern California and south through most of Middle America and locally to Panama; also in the Bahamas and Greater Antilles and recently introduced and established in southern Florida. Winters generally in the breeding range, but some northern birds move south to Central America.

Status Casual vagrant.

Occurrence There are five records of single birds: Water Mill, Suffolk Co. 14 Nov 1929; Riis Park, Queens Co. 8 Dec 1973; East Hampton, Suffolk Co. 24 Aug 1991 (KB 41:287; NYSARC 1993); Cedar Beach, Suffolk Co. 19 Dec 1993 (KB 44:159); Long Beach, Nassau Co. 20–26 May 1995 (KB 45:236, NASFN 49:233).

Remarks White-winged Dove has been recorded as far north as Ontario (AB 48:106), Quebec (NASFN 48:927, 49:18; AB 43:69, 47:61), New

Brunswick (AB 40:257, 42:235), and Nova Scotia (AB 40:257, 43:446). At least 15 sightings have been reported in MA from 1961 through 1994 (Veit and Petersen 1993; AB 47:1090). Only one of those was inland, at Holyoke; the rest were along the coast. Since these birds usually occur in summer and fall, Veit and Petersen suggest that they are young of the year, probably coming from a recently established and thriving population in southern Florida. However, several reports have been in the spring (NASFN 48:282, 49:28; AB 43:446), and even one in winter in NJ (AB 45:256). There are at least seven reports from NJ (Leck 1984) (NASFN 48:282, 49:28; AB 40:89, 45:256). Only a single (coastal) report exists for CT (Zeranski and Baptist 1990), and none for RI (Conway 1992).

The pace of White-winged Dove sightings in the Northeast has recently accelerated. Although there were four reports in 1985, there had been only one per year between 1986 and 1993, when two were reported. In 1994 a total of seven was recorded. It seems safe to say that White-winged Dove sightings are now an annual event in the Northeast, and, although NY may not yet have one every year, the probability that it will has certainly increased.

Donald A. Windsor

Mourning Dove *Zenaida macroura*

Range Nearctic and northern Neotropical, breeding throughout most of the United States and southern Canada south to Panama. Winters nearly throughout, but with movement south from the more northern parts of the breeding range.

Status Common to abundant resident in open and agricultural areas, but rare to absent in heavily forested areas or mountains. Sedentary and migratory.

Breeding The Atlas showed Confirmed breeding in 2115 blocks out of 4402 in which it was recorded (48%). Breeding does not occur in heavily forested regions or in the higher elevations of the Adirondacks, Allegany Hills, Catskills, or Tug Hill. It breeds in great numbers on LI, in the lower Hudson area, and on the L. Ontario plain; these regions are strongholds of breeding doves (Atlas 1988). An analysis of BBS data from 1966 to 1994 shows that the NY population is increasing, although this increase has abated somewhat. From 1966 to 1979 the population was increasing by an average of 4% per year. From 1980 to 1994 the rate of increase dropped to 3% (Peterjohn 1995). Populations are holding steady, but birds seem to be moving into new locations. A continuous breeder from Mar right into Sep, it often rears two or three broods.

Nonbreeding Analysis of CBC data from 1976 through 1994 showed that the NY winter population has remained steady, with some ups and downs. The level populations on the CBC and the increase on the BBS can be explained by some birds migrating south for the winter. Burtt's monthly (Oct–May) feeder surveys in the *Syracuse Herald American* showed something of an increase, which peaked from 1989 through 1992 and is now stabilizing at a slightly lower level.

So common that it is often ignored, the Mourning Dove has prospered because of human activities, from the cutting down of forests for agriculture to the division of farms for housing developments. Because it feeds almost entirely on seeds and nests in dense shrubs and small trees, it thrives in both rural and suburban settings. Those that migrate leave in irregular waves from August through October (Griscom 1923) for the southern states, where it is considered a game bird and is hunted. Birds that do not migrate tend to form winter flocks, which can number in the hundreds, and feed in fields or at bird feeders. When deep snow buries the fields, they exploit the bare areas on shoulders along roads and take advantage of barnyards and manure spreads. Along with starlings, Mourning Doves are common fixtures perched on electric wires.

It was originally abundant is southern New England before 1850, but extensive hunting pared its numbers by the late 1800s. Government regulation of hunting, coupled with deforestation, enabled the population to rebound and expand (Zeranski and Baptist 1990). The expansion is still occurring as the Mourning Dove follows human development. A northward expansion into Ontario, Quebec, and the Maritime Provinces is currently under way, and its progress is being chronicled in AB and NASFN. Key to this expansion is overcoming the severe cold, which can result in losing toes to frostbite (AB 40:279) or even iced-up bills (Chamberlaine 1994).

Maxima: 3695 East Orange Co. CBC 20 Dec 1986; a flock of more than 500 in Farmingdale, Nassau Co. 12 Aug 1989; 56 at a feeder, Ogdensburg, St. Lawrence Co. 20 Mar 1993 (KB 43:65, 248).

Remarks The Mourning Dove is a game bird in 39 states but not in NY, where this controversial issue arises repeatedly. Although the last attempt to make it a game bird was quelled, the issue will certainly come up again. The arguments favoring hunting are its high population level and prolific breeding (DeGraff 1974). The argument against concentrates on the danger of shooting other birds, such as American Kestrel or Killdeer by hunters who cannot (or will not) positively identify the doves before they shoot (Verhovek 1994).
Donald A. Windsor

Passenger Pigeon *Ectopistes migratorius*

Range Nearctic, mostly midwestern and eastern North America, formerly breeding from east-central Saskatchewan east to Nova Scotia and south to eastern Kansas, Oklahoma, Mississippi, and the mountains of northern Georgia and at lower elevations in the east to southeastern New York. Wintered south to northern Florida, the Gulf Coast, and Texas.

Status Extinct. Formerly a very abundant breeder and migrant.

Breeding Eaton (1910) reported that the last "great pigeon nesting" in NY was in 1868, when "millions of birds occupied the timber along Bell's Run, near Ceres, Allegany, on the Pennsylvania line." In this 14 mile long nesting tract the birds began laying in April, and nesting reached its peak about 10 May. Eaton added that nesting continued in the area until 1872 and also described a large roost near Painted Post, Steuben Co. in 1875, for which he could find no evidence of actual nesting.

Schorger (1955) described an enormous 1823 nesting that began near the Allegheny River, in Cattaraugus Co., and extended 30 miles north to Collins, Erie Co., and had an average width of 6 miles. He also described a nesting in about 1847, again 30 miles in length by 3 miles in width, from the vicinity of Annsville, Oneida Co. nearly to Watertown, Jefferson Co.

According to Eaton there is but scant surviving data giving exact breeding details in NY. He could find only seven specific reports, three of them from 1878.

Nonbreeding Migration was apparently mainly along the Appalachian Mountains and to the west of them.

Early maxima: Bull (1974) gives the following: "thousands" near Albany 25 Mar 1830 (Munsell); "millions arriving to feed at the salt springs" near Montezuma between 1 Apr and 15 Jun 1854 (Mershon). *Later maxima:* 200 Lowville, Lewis Co. 12 Apr 1884 (Miller); 300 Constableville, Lewis Co. 22 May 1896 (Felshaw). *Extreme dates:* 3 Mar, (earliest specimen), 23 Mar, and 6 Nov (specimen).

Remarks The last known extant specimen from NY was a male taken at Canandaigua, Ontario Co. 14 Sep 1898 (Wilbur), a mount in the CUM collection. The last known NY specimen was collected at Bolivar, Allegany Co. 10 Aug 1899 (Mealy). Bull (1974) commented that destruction of forests plus wholesale slaughter of adults and young for the market, and the taking of eggs as well, were too much for what must have been one of the most numerous birds of all time. He added that the species was highly gregarious during the breeding season and when the large colonial nestings were broken up the Passenger Pigeon was apparently unsuccessful in small aggregations. He concluded by stating that the fact that the species was not only single-brooded but also laid only one egg helped speed its ultimate extinction. (See also From Glaciers to Global Warming: Extinct Species.) Stanley R. Lincoln

PARROTS—PSITTACIDAE

Monk Parakeet *Myiopsitta monachus*

Range Neotropical, resident in central South America. Introduced and established in northeastern United States.

Status Introduced through escape from captivity. Local resident in NYC and western LI; formerly in widely scattered areas of western, central, and northern NY, but few recent reports in those areas.

Breeding This South American parakeet has been present in the NYC area and western LI since at least 1968 and has resisted all efforts at extermination. Between 1968 and 1971, its large communal stick nests were prominent in locations from SI, Central Park, Manhattan, Pelham Bay and City Island, Bronx Co., east to Babylon, Suffolk Co. The first breeding observed was in 1971 at Valley Stream, Nassau Co. and on SI. Beginning in 1973, a control program was initiated by state and federal agencies on the grounds that this species posed a theat to NY agricultural crops, that it was a carrier of psittacosis, and that it competed with native wildlife. By 1975, the birds were considered to be "largely" eliminated from the wild. There were very few reports during Atlas work, and in 1982 NYSARC deleted the bird from the state list (KB 32:233) with the remark that "data from the Breeding Bird Atlas indicates [*sic*] that this species was exterminated as a nesting species by the Department of Environmental Conservation before it had time to become established unquestionably within the State." However, this decision, which caused a sharp falloff in the reporting of the species, was premature. Although little noticed, Monk Parakeets continued to breed on SI and LI (Atlas 1988), in Brooklyn (KB 31:267), and probably elsewhere, but were not recorded in the Atlas. A large active stick nest in the gateway of Greenwood Cemetery, Brooklyn has been present there at least since the 1980s (pers. obs.). Numbers of birds in several locations in the winter and spring also suggest the continuing presence and increase of this species.

The species was restored to the NYS checklist in 1996.

Nonbreeding Reports in the 1970s from widely scattered upstate localities include Eden, Erie Co.; Elmira, Chemung Co.; Schenectady, Schenectady Co.; and Watertown, Jefferson Co., but no upstate breeding is known (Atlas 1988). Twenty-three birds on the 1991 Brooklyn CBC, 14 at Rockville Center, Nassau Co. 17 May 1991, 6 at Alley Pond, Queens Co. 27 May 1996, and single birds or pairs from other sites from SI to Montauk at various times of the year all suggest its continuing presence.

Remarks Black-hooded, or Nanday, Conures *(Nandayus nenday)*, also native to South America, apparently fledged young in Westchester Co. in 1984 (Atlas 1988). Escaped cage birds, including several species of psittacids, are common in the NYC area, often survive the winter, and occasionally fledge young. The Rose-ringed, or Ring-necked, Parakeet (*Psittacula krameri*), a species native to Africa and Asia, is now well established in parts of northwestern Europe, but other than Monk Parakeet, no escaped species are established or considered likely to become established here.

Eric Salzman

CUCKOOS, ROADRUNNERS, AND ANIS—CUCULIDAE

Black-billed Cuckoo   *Coccyzus erythropthalmus*

Range Chiefly eastern Nearctic, breeding from central Alberta across southern Canada to Nova Scotia and south to Wyoming, Nebraska, central Texas, northern Alabama, and South Carolina. Winters in northwestern South America, south to northern Peru.

Status Fairly common breeder; uncommon migrant.

Breeding More widespread than its more southern relative, the Yellow-billed Cuckoo. Like the Yellow-billed, its numbers can increase sharply during irruptions of gypsy moth and tent caterpillars.

Atlas workers recorded it in 1963 blocks, compared with 1281 for Yellow-billed. It was confirmed it in 267 blocks, compared with 186 for the Yellow-billed. It is far more likely to be found in northern NY and in highlands. During Atlas work, it was decidedly more prevalent in the hills of the Tug Hill Transition, the Cattaraugus Highlands, and the Taconic and Adirondack foothills than was the Yellow-billed. It was also recorded in significantly more blocks in the Appalachian Plateau, in much of the Great Lakes Plain, and in the western Mohawk Valley.

It tends to avoid heavy forests and areas near large urban centers but seems to prefer more-wooded areas than the Yellow-billed. Its nesting habitat includes brushy pastures, shrubby hedgerows at edges of fields, and dry, open upland woods and groves.

Robbins et al. (1986) reported that BBS data for 1965–1979 indicated a significant increase in numbers in the eastern United States. However, NY BBS data suggested that it had, if anything, declined in this state. Along routes on which this species was recorded, it averaged 0.79, 0.76, and 0.62 birds per run for 1966–1975, 1976–1985, and 1986–1994, respectively. Away from caterpillar infestations, it can be scarce and hard to find.

Nonbreeding Rarely if ever seen in large numbers, even during migration. Average arrival dates range from early May downstate to late May in the north. It is generally rare after mid-October.

Extreme dates: 17 Mar and 15 Nov in Monroe Co. and 8 Nov 1984 at

Croton Point, Westchester Co. (KB 35:67). An early coastal record is 11 Apr 1993 (KB 43:268) on LI, after overnight passage of a front with strong winds, and 13 Nov is the late record for coastal areas.

Remarks Both species of cuckoo, though not known to be parasitic, do lay eggs in other birds' nests, including each other's, on rare occasions.
Robert E. Marcotte

Yellow-billed Cuckoo *Coccyzus americanus*

Range Nearctic and Neotropical, breeding from southern Canada south throughout the United States and into Mexico and the West Indies. Winters in South America to Peru and Argentina.

Status Local breeder at lower elevations; uncommon migrant.

Breeding A secretive, uncommon to fairly common breeder that is not as widespread or, in most areas, as numerous as its more northerly relative, the Black-billed Cuckoo. Like the Black-billed, however, its numbers can increase sharply during irruptions of gypsy moth and tent caterpillars.

Statewide, it has been reported only half as often as Black-billed on BBS routes, and Atlas workers found only half as many nests. However, on parts of LI, in the lower Hudson Valley, and in part of the Great Lakes Plain, it has been more numerous on BBS runs.

During the summer of 1980, a year of extremely heavy gypsy moth infestation, Yellow-billed was reported to outnumber Black-billed in Rockland Co. 5:1 (KB 30:254).

Elsewhere, according to the Atlas, it is fairly local in distribution in such areas as the Finger Lakes Highlands and the central Appalachian Plateau. Although Bull (1974) reported that the Black-billed was the only cuckoo known to nest in and around the valleys of the Catskills and Adirondacks, Atlas workers managed to confirm Yellow-billed in isolated blocks in both regions.

It is found at elevations below 1000 ft, where it nests in open second-growth woods, overgrown orchards, and abandoned fields that have scattered bushes and small trees.

Robbins et al. (1986) said that BBS data showed it had increased significantly in the eastern and central United States during 1965–1979. However, BBS data for routes in NY suggest only static or declining populations for those years. For 1980–1994, BBS data for 42 NY routes showed an average annual decline of 10.4%. Away from caterpillar infestations, it continues to be scarce and often hard to find.

Nonbreeding Migrants are usually rare before mid-May and after mid-October. Extreme dates range from 11 Apr 1973 after a southerly storm at Commack, Suffolk Co. and 13 Apr 1986 at Rockland L., Rockland Co. to the extremely late 27 Dec 1982, when an apparently unhealthy bird was photographed at Moriches Inlet, Suffolk Co. (KB 33:103 ph). This eclipsed by nearly a month the previous late record of 29 Nov 1965, when an albino bird was captured at Arverne, Queens Co.

Remarks Cuckoos are almost never encountered in large numbers. Thus, it was remarkable when more than 1000 of both species passed along eastern LI in late Sep and Oct 1954. This astounding flight, which included many emaciated birds, was apparently related to Hurricane Edna of 11 Sep. Robert E. Marcotte

BARN OWLS—TYTONIDAE

Barn Owl   *Tyto alba*

Range Cosmopolitan in temperate and tropical regions, breeding in North America from southern Canada and northern United States south to the West Indies and Middle America. Mainly sedentary, but northernmost populations are partially migratory, wintering south to southern Mexico and the West Indies.

Status Resident and migratory. Very rare upstate to fairly common along the coast.

Breeding It is found only in areas with extensive meadowlands, and nowhere does it occur in forested or mountainous regions. Moving south from Albany, where it is rare, down the Hudson Valley, its status rises to fairly common in Richmond, Kings, and Queens counties and where nest boxes have been erected in LI tidal marshes.

Even with this downstate population, it was found in only 2% of Atlas blocks. The Atlas responded to its "extremely spotty distribution for a species seemingly well adapted for coexistence with humans" by suggesting that, as in Ohio, it increased "with the spread of agriculture and the clearing of forests in the 1800s and then began to decrease after the 1950s" because of farms' being abandoned and changing agricultural practices. Rosenburg (1992) added these factors: loss of nest sites due, for example, to screening of barn entrances to prevent Rock Dove access; increased predation; cyclical downturns in rodent populations; secondary poisoning from rodenticides and insecticides, and car collisions.

Half of the Atlas blocks where it was found are in Orange Co., metropolitan NYC, and LI; the rest are distributed very thinly across the rest of the state. Even that small upstate population may have been supplemented by the 182 young raised in Canada and released between 1974 and 1986 in southern ON. Despite that release, on the 1981–1985 Ontario Atlas Project only six blocks in the entire province produced nesting evidence (Cadman et al. 1987).

Resident Barn Owls nest in all seasons and are occasionally double-brooded when prey is abundant. In 1938, for example, a banded female at Hunts Point, Bronx Co. laid six eggs in Mar and another five in Nov. In 1939 the same female had five nestlings on 27 Jul and three more on 5 Dec. Tree cavities are the principal nest sites for this species in the Northeast, although human-made "cavities," especially within barns and silos, are also important. Opportunistic nesters, especially in metropolitan areas, these owls took up residence on the Bayonne Bridge, Richmond Co. in 1983 and in Yankee Stadium, Bronx Co. in 1984. Of the former, DiCostanzo noted, "New York City bridges . . . have a potentially useful future as the biggest and most expensive bird nest sites ever built by man" (KB 33:298).

Nonbreeding A North American distribution map for this species (Rosenburg 1992) showed NY at the northern edge of its range. Upstate is designated "Breeding," and only NYC and LI were within the area indicated as "Year-round." He summarized NJ banding data that indicated both dispersal of young and migration of adults southward in Oct and Nov, but he added CBC evidence that some birds remain on territory. NY CBC data for 1960–1989 gave partial support to this distinction, with an average of only one each year recorded upstate against 13 per year downstate (Salzman 1994).

Seen another way, however, these data merely reflect abundance in the two regions. Over the 20 years from 1975 to 1995, an annual average of only four adults and one nest was reported north of Orange and Putnam counties in KB accounts. Meanwhile, in 1983 alone 44 nests were observed in boxes on marsh islands in Kings, Queens, and Nassau counties.

Remarks The NYSDEC has listed the Barn Owl as a Species of Special Concern, but Rosenburg noted that these birds "have a high recovery and management potential." He called for preservation and expansion of dense grass foraging habitats and erection of nest boxes in appropriate areas, pointing out that each owl pair needs a secure nesting site near at least 1/4 square mile of these meadows. Responding to his own solicitation, he has mounted more than 50 nest boxes in western NY barns and silos. Two have already been occupied.

Gerry Rising and Charles Rosenburg

TYPICAL OWLS—STRIGIDAE

Eastern Screech-Owl *Otus asio*

Range Eastern Nearctic, resident from southern Manitoba east to southwestern Maine, south to southern Texas, the Gulf Coast, and southern Florida.

Status Fairly common resident in fragmented habitat throughout most of the state, uncommon in forested regions, rare or absent at higher elevations.

Breeding Important habitat characteristics include mature trees, with holes for nesting and roosting, open areas such as fields or lawns, and water features often associated with slopes. The presence of streams, ponds, or swamps near farms or homes and adjacent to mature woodland all but guarantees the presence of this owl throughout the state at low elevations. These observations are supported by Smith and Gilbert (1984), who determined that screech-owls prefer red maple woodlands and edge habitats, and Ellison (1980), who found them associated with running water, wet woodlands, and open weedy areas. Within these habitats, an average of 2.3 owls/km^2 (ranging from one to seven) seems to be a reasonable density estimate (Lynch and Smith 1984).

The Atlas documented screech-owls as Possible breeders in 466 blocks, Probable in 457, and Confirmed in 202. Their presence in only 21% of all blocks was undoubtedly an underestimate of their true frequency. They were undercounted because nocturnal surveys using imitation calls were not consistently used. Likewise, the techniques employed by other traditional bird counts, such as the BBS (Robbins et al. 1986), are designed to detect most species of birds, but they underestimate Eastern Screech-Owl. The mean number detected in NY on 103 BBS routes 1965–1979 was zero, and the Breeding Bird Census covered only 12 NY sites, finding one nest on LI. Lacking coverage during darkness with imitation calls, these counts do not indicate population levels of this species.

Nonbreeding A better estimate of populations might be gained from CBC data than from breeding surveys, because nocturnal surveys using imitation calls are more consistently used. But CBC data must be used cautiously. Figures 4 and 5 show data from the Greenwich-Stamford CT CBC, which illustrates some of the problems and potentials. Although most of this CBC is in CT, a substantial part of it is in Westchester Co. Panko and the compiler, G. Palmer, believe that this CBC's counts of screech-owls would be similar if its area were entirely in southeastern NY, outside of NYC. The counts from 1928 to 1994 reveal an explosive increase detected in the early 1970s (Figure 4), but they does not reflect a real population increase. They reflect instead, a sharp increase in observer effort and efficiency. At that time observers began to call in screech-owls using portable tape recorders (G. Palmer, pers. comm.). With participants of this count strongly encouraged to use taped calls at night, numbers increased dramatically.

The amount of annual effort can be corrected for by dividing the number of owls by party-hours owling or miles owling. In the data (Figure 5) for the Greenwich-Stamford CBC, however, those two measures of effort give different results when analyzed. Owls per mile shows no statistically significant trend over 14 years, but owls per hour shows a statistically

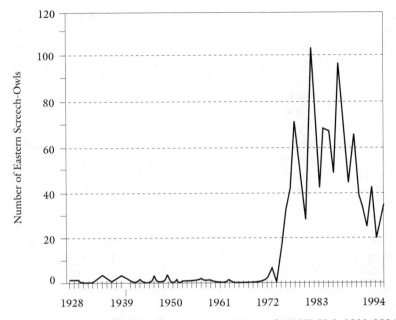

Figure 4. Number of Eastern Screech-Owls, Greenwich-Stamford CT CBC, 1928–1994

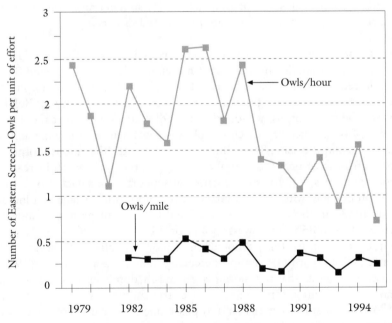

Figure 5. Number of Eastern Screech-Owls per unit effort (party-hours and miles), Greenwich-Stamford CT CBC, 1979–1994

significant decreasing trend, suggesting a decreasing population. Hours owling is probably more reliable than miles owling, so this decrease is likely to be real. Yet, it could also be a result of changes in how the owling was done. Neither owls per hour nor owls per mile accounts for an important parameter in owl detection: the number, duration, and location of stops. By collecting such information, CBCs could increase the ability of their data to reflect population trends.

Although the population has undoubtedly decreased in some areas because of urbanization and human activities, it has increased in others where low-density suburban development provides good habitat. It is very reasonable to believe that its population is well above what it was when the state was largely unbroken forest. Thus, the changes in habitat brought about by human settlement are likely a mixed blessing. The openings created in the forest greatly increased its population but introduced new hazards such as pesticides and automobiles as well as reduced nesting and roosting sites. This species will use artificial nest boxes and could significantly benefit from them in specific areas. It does not seem to be adversely affected by the noise pollution that accompanies human habitations.

Thought to be essentially nonmigratory, this species does disperse in the late summer and fall, but there are no documented long-range movements or concentrations (Johnsgard 1988). Personal experience has shown maximal response rates to imitation calls in late summer and early fall, presumably while young of the year are present and dispersing.

Remarks Screech-owls occur in two morphs: red and gray. Bull (1974) studied 144 NY specimens from eight museum collections and found 84 gray, 56 red, and 4 intermediate. His data indicate that the two morphs occur in the same regions but with different frequencies. Analyzing Bull's data for the two morphs, we found, with 99.5% confidence, that the frequency of occurrence of a given morph was dependent on the geographical location within the state. Thus, Bull's statement that "the rufous morph is predominant in or near the coastal districts . . . ; the gray morph increases in the interior areas . . ." has strong statistical support. Bull's data also reveal an apparent cline, with the percentage of red morphs in each region increasing from 13% in the west to 72% on LI and the percentage of gray morphs decreasing from 85% in the west to 23% on LI.

An explanation for this phenomenon of morph frequency by region is offered by Johnsgard (1988). In referencing Van Camp and Henny (1975), Johnsgard suggests that red morph is genetically dominant to gray, but that "gray birds evidently were able to survive stressful periods of heavy snowfall and low temperatures better than red-phase ones." In Westchester Co., we have seen both morphs in the same clutch.
Drew Panko and Gertrude R. Battaly

Great Horned Owl   *Bubo virginianus*

Range Nearctic and Neotropical, breeding from the tree limit in Alaska and across northern Canada, south throughout the Americas to Tierra del Fuego. Winters nearly throughout the breeding range.

Status Uncommon and local as a breeder but increasing and expanding. Uncommon to fairly common resident and winter visitant.

Breeding Eaton (1914) called the Great Horned Owl "no longer common . . . except in the wooded districts," and Griscom (1923) stated that the bird "prefers deep swamps or big areas of unlumbered woodland" and further added that it was "fierce, wild and untamable" and "cannot or will not tolerate civilization and retreats before it." Atlas work in the early 1980s, however, showed its densest populations in open settled areas such as lake plains, river valleys, bottomlands, farmland, and even suburban areas including the Great Lakes Plain, Cattaraugus Highlands, Finger Lakes, eastern half of the Appalachian Plateau, the L. Champlain Valley, Mohawk and Hudson valleys, and much of LI. It was least common in the wilder regions of the Adirondacks and Catskills and the western Appalachian Plateau. This new evidence suggests that its reputation as a denizen of wildlands was due to persecution from farmers, hunters, and game managers. The consequent reduction of its population in settled areas gave it the reputation of a rare wilderness bird when, in fact, it was barely surviving in marginal habitat. The species has benefited greatly from protective legislation since 1948 and from a change in public sentiment and has continued to increase its activities, numbers, and range, expanding particularly into suburban and even urban areas. It has nested on SI at least since 1978 (Siebenheller 1981), and a pair in residence at Forest Park, Queens Co. were likely breeders (KB 43:161). It has also nested next to the Syracuse Post Office employees' parking lot near the Syracuse Airport, Onondaga Co. (Minor and Minor 1981) and had bred for many years in Stewart Park, Ithaca, Tompkins Co. (Parkes 1952).

Nonbreeding Although this species is usually regarded as a permanent resident, there is often a good deal of movement during the fall and winter as many birds appear in areas where they do not breed, often in suburban or urban areas. Upwards of two dozen birds have been trapped at game farms in Tompkins and Cortland counties. A bird banded near Chatham, Columbia Co. on 1 Aug 1947, was found dead in October 1956 near Springfield, MA, a distance of about 50 mi. Great Horned Owls have been noted for many years as winter visitants from Rochester to NYC near landfills and in city parks that have evergreen groves, and they are often seen perching along highways in summer in many parts of their U.S. range, including NY (Bosakowski and Speiser 1984). Only an extensive banding program would show whether this species is at all migratory or, as is the case with other owls, irruptive in its movements.

Remarks Three subspecies have occurred within the state: (1) *virginianus* is the resident NY form and the most rufescent of all the subspecies of this widely distributed bird. (2) *subarcticus (= wapacuthu)*, the whitest of the genus, breeds in central Canada from the tree limit south to Alberta and northern Ontario and is represented by three NY specimens: Bronx Park, Bronx Co. 15 Feb 1910 AMNH 144845 (regarded by Parkes [1952] as intermediate with *occidentalis*); Orient, Suffolk Co. 20 Feb 1929 (Latham) NYSM 25034; Forest Lawn Cemetery, Buffalo, Erie Co. 1 Jan 1947 (Thorpe), collected 8 Jan by Mitchell, BMS 2157. There are also AMNH specimens from NJ and CT (Dickerman 1991). (3) *heterocnemis*, a large dark subspecies breeding along the eastern coast of Quebec, Labrador, and Newfoundland, also with three specimens: Fishers I., Suffolk Co. 15 Dec 1933 (Ferguson; examined by Bull); Connecticut Hill, Tompkins Co. 5 Dec 1933 (Cameron) CUM 3562; Ithaca, Tompkins Co., captured alive, died in captivity, Apr 1941 (Parkes 1952; Dickerman 1991). Several specimens that appear to be from intergrade *heterocnemis-virginianus* populations have been collected in NY (Parkes 1952).
Eric Salzman

Snowy Owl *Nyctea scandiaca*

Range Holarctic, in North America breeding from western Alaska east to Ellesmere Island and south, in the east, to Hudson Bay (at Churchill) and northern Labrador; also in Greenland. Winters irregularly south to southern Canada, Minnesota, New York, and New England; less frequently farther south to the Gulf states and Texas.

Status A winter visitant, rare to uncommon coastally, more numerous on the L. Ontario and St. Lawrence plains. Irruptive.

Occurrence Snowy Owls are found in open country, where they may be seen on the ground, on a hillock, or on some other low perch such as a tree stump, fence post, or rock. Also frequently observed at the mouths of rivers or at water edges, particularly when those are frozen. In cities, they may even perch on buildings, attracted by the resident pigeons or rats. Large winter irruptions have been reported, but there does not seem to be a regular cycle to the invasion years, as is the case with Northern Goshawk. It is believed that irruptions are coincidental with Arctic lemming population crashes.

Before this species became protected by law in 1960, great numbers of these owls were shot, and the pre-1960 maxima far exceed maxima after protection. This change does not suggest a population decline but rather points out the difficulty in determining the number of birds visiting the state. Individuals are very difficult to tell apart and, to complicate matters even more, different individuals use the same habitat in the same location, as revealed by banding studies. Many such birds were thought to be the same individual on subsequent visits, but after capture were found to be different. Since the start of extensive banding activities by Snowy Watch and Braddock Bay Raptor Research in 1990, accuracy of maxima counts is now approaching accuracy of counts before protection.

Maxima: One Rochester taxidermist received 40+ specimens in 1876–1877. Many of these birds had been feeding primarily on fish stranded along the L. Ontario shore. In 1926–1927 three Rochester taxidermists received 235 specimens, and another in Gloversville, Fulton Co. received 35. The same winter saw the greatest LI flight on record: 40 killed on Fishers I. during Nov and Dec; a single taxidermist received 36 additional birds from eastern LI. At Long Beach, Nassau Co., 8 were shot the morning of 5 Dec, and at least 75 more were shot elsewhere in the NYC region. In 1990–1991, 87 were captured and banded along the L. Ontario Plain between late Oct and mid-Mar. **Extreme dates:** 6 Jun and 7 Oct.

Remarks During irruptions, immature females are the first to arrive. Immature males follow, with adults generally the latest. Many of these owls pass through NY and return in the spring. Many received by rehabilitators or captured by banders are emaciated.
Jeff Dodge

Northern Hawk Owl *Surnia ulula*

Range Holarctic, breeding in North America from Alaska to Newfoundland and south, in the east, to southern Ontario and Quebec. Winters irregularly south to New York and New England, rarely farther south.

Status Very rare winter visitant.

Occurrence This long-tailed predator from northern boreal forests, although rarely found, is easily observed when once discovered. It prefers open, semiwooded areas, perching prominently on treetops. It has been found next to roads, and individual birds have stayed at the same spot for weeks, even months, at a time, enabling scores of eager birders to add this highly sought species to their lifelists. For example, birds at Millersport, Niagara Co. 28 Dec 1962–10 Feb 1963 and at Vernon, Oneida Co. 15 Dec 1974–15 Mar 1975 were seen and photographed by hundreds. Another lingered near Lake Placid, Essex Co. 18 Nov 1992–4 Apr 1993.

Only about 52 sightings have been reported in NY, many of them during three irruption years. Up to six were reported during the winter of 1991–1992; up to four in 1981–1982; and at least four during 1962–1963, when eight were also observed in Ontario.

Extreme dates: 24 Oct and 4 Apr.

Remarks Other than two old LI specimens, none have been found south of Ulster Co. This rarity may help explain the relatively small number of sightings in contiguous states that lie entirely or at least partly to the south of that line. These include four in PA, two in NJ, five in CT, and one in RI. MA has also reported only five.

Robert E. Marcotte

Burrowing Owl   *Athene cunicularia*

Range Nearctic and Neotropical, breeding on the Great Plains from southern British Columbia and southern Manitoba east to Minnesota and south to central Texas, Louisiana, and Baja California. Winters south to Panama. Vagrant east to Ontario, New Hampshire, Massachusetts, New York, and Virginia (all specimens) and Maryland (photograph.) Also resident in central Florida and the Bahamas.

Status Casual vagrant.

Occurrence There are six records, with four to add to the two in Bull (1974). (1) one caught alive in NYC 8 Aug 1875 was thought to be an escaped cage bird (Griscom 1923); (2) one collected at Westhampton, Suffolk Co. 27 Oct 1950 (Cooley); (3) a bird observed at Cedar Beach, Suffolk Co. 27–28 Dec 1976 (Gardner) (KB 27:116); (4) JFK Airport, Queens Co. 3 Dec 1978–1 Feb 1979 (Chevalier) (KB 29:115); (5) JFK Airport, Queens Co. 29 Mar 1982 (Richard 1988); (6) Shinnecock Inlet, Suffolk Co. 17–23 Oct 1985 (Elliott) (KB 36:49).

For a discussion of the Cedar Beach occurrence and the status of Burrowing Owl in NY, see Davis 1977 and Richard 1988.

Remarks Two subspecies have occurred in NY: the theoretically migratory western *hypugaea*, ranging from southwestern Canada to Mexico, and the supposedly sedentary FL subspecies *floridana*, occurring there and in the Bahamas. Most Burrowing Owls found in the Northeast either have been identified as *hypugaea* or have not been categorized subspecifically (Veit and Petersen 1993). The individual collected at Westhampton in 1950 was identified by Zimmer as belonging to *hypugaea*. The bird found in 1976 at Cedar Beach was examined by Bull and Farrand and determined to be *floridana*, whereas one of the individuals observed at Kennedy Airport was identified by the observers in the field as also belonging to the FL subspecies. The identification of two of the six NY records as the supposedly nonmigratory *floridana* raises the question of whether these birds benefited from assisted transport or possibly were escaped pets. Davis listed specimen records in Sykes 1974 of *floridana* from NC, AL, and Cuba and two sight reports at coastal locations in VA and SC. In addition, Davis discussed two instances of offshore sight reports involving boat-assisted transport off VA and FL. Sykes stated that since the coastal shipping lane is within 1–2 km of the southeastern coast of FL, boat-assisted transport is possible. Richard cited the two airport observations as a possible indication of plane-assisted passage.

Ken Feustel

Barred Owl *Strix varia*

Range Nearctic and Neotropical, resident from eastern Washington and southern British Columbia, east through wooded southern Canada to Nova Scotia, and south throughout the United States east of the Great Plains; also south into Mexico.

Status Locally uncommon to fairly common resident and breeder throughout but declining in developing areas; very rare on LI.

Breeding The breeding range in most of the state appears largely unchanged since the early 1900s, with the heaviest concentrations found in the densely forested areas of the Adirondacks, the L. Champlain Valley, and on the Tug Hill Plateau. Other areas of heavy forest cover, such as the Cattaraugus Highlands, Central Appalachians, Catskill Peaks, and Hudson Valley also support populations. The range, if not the habitat, closely resembles that of Northern Goshawk and Broad-winged Hawk (Atlas 1988).

Habitat preference is for low, wet tracts of coniferous, deciduous, or mixed forest and the higher, drier areas adjacent to them; thus it is similar to that of Cooper's and Red-shouldered hawks. While conducting studies on Cooper's Hawk, Meng (1951) found six occupied Barred Owl nests within a 17-mi radius in the Ithaca, Tompkins Co. area.

Size and contiguity of forest are apparently equally important habitat considerations. Peterson (Atlas 1988) noted that deforestation in the 1800s and reforestation in the 1900s probably had considerable impact on the range. Today, in areas where suburban development reduces or fragments large tracts of forest, the Barred Owl is declining. For example, it is retreating from many locations in lower Westchester Co. (KB 42:61), although numbers remain strong in the northern, more forested, sections of the county (KB 42:273, 119, 199).

Loss of habitat undoubtedly accounts for the absence of recent records on SI as well. Chapin and Cleaves (Bull 1964:273) found 11 nests there from 1905 to 1908, and Griscom (1923) stated that the species was "formerly common and probably still surviving here," but there are apparently no subsequent records from that area. Atlas observers during the early 1980s found no sign of the species on SI, by now densely urbanized.

It has always been considered rare on LI. Five breeding locations were noted before 1942: one in Nassau Co., near Jericho, and four in Suffolk Co., at HSP, East Patchogue, Sag Harbor, and Shelter I. No further evidence was recorded for more than 40 years, until Atlas observers Confirmed breeding on Fishers I. in 1983 and 1984 and recorded Possible breeding near Setauket in 1983, both in Suffolk Co.

Nonbreeding Essentially a sedentary species, it wanders during late fall and winter, and unusual locations and high counts are often reported during those seasons. A maximum of five from Bronx Park, Bronx Co. in 1943 may represent an unusual invasion event for the coastal section of the state. An "unusually high" CBC total of 10 was reported from the Niagara Frontier section of the state in the winter of 1991–1992 (KB 42:93), and Tioga Co. reported a high count of 10, Sep–Nov 1990 (KB 41:41). Maximum counts of four have been recorded on Ithaca, Elizabethtown (Essex Co.), and Dutchess Co. CBCs, and five were found on the Peekskill (Westchester Co.) CBC in 1961. Also of interest are reports from LI CBCs, all single birds: Smithtown 1975; Captree 1978; heard calling on the Southern Nassau CBC 3 Jan 1982, only the second such record in the 65-year history of that count.
Patricia J. Lindsay

Great Gray Owl *Strix nebulosa*

Range Holarctic, in North America breeding from Alaska and northwestern Canada southeast to northern Ontario and south, in the east, to northern Minnesota and Wisconsin and south-central Ontario. Sedentary except for irregular winter wandering and irruptions eastward to Nova Scotia and southward to southern New England, New York, New Jersey, and Pennsylvania.

Status Casual visitant.

Occurrence A total of nearly two dozen historical reports before 1974 was mentioned by Bull. Of these, 18 were specimens, but only two are known to still exist. This owl has occurred chiefly at low elevations in northern parts of the state, with records from November to May. A very late date was a bird seen in the Town of Yates, Orleans Co. 17–19 May 1996 (KB 46:227). Reports are usually of single individuals, but occasional irruptions of greater numbers take place; the two largest were in 1978–1979 and 1983–1984. Yunick (1980) reviewed the species' historical occurrence in the state and the largest irruption of the century in 1978–1979. His map of locations where 27 were reported from 1873 to early 1978 shows that 14 were in the northern part of the state, with the remainder scattered from east to west except for two on the North Shore of LI. His data also reveal that, from 1870 through 1969, the number of reports varied from one to four birds per decade, mostly in Franklin and St. Lawrence counties.

The numbers and distribution in the 1978–1979 irruption contrast greatly with those earlier records. There were 64 reports in 90 days, most of which (28) were clustered in St. Lawrence and Jefferson counties and in Saratoga, Albany, and Rensselaer counties (20). In Jefferson's major concentration, four were seen in one area in one day, a state maximum. Interestingly, except for two reports in Region 5 at Oswego, the southern shore of L. Ontario and Regions 1, 2, and 3 had no sightings, perhaps reflecting the blocking action that the lake has to the species' southward movement. Two were seen as far south as LI, one being present in a locality for at least 12 weeks. About one-third of those reported were seen on only one day. Vickery and Yunick (1979) reported that more than 334 were recorded in eight states and three Canadian provinces during this event, which lasted from Dec to Apr, and that 42 of the NY sightings were between 23 Jan and 22 Feb. At least six were reported to have been deposited as scientific specimens in collections.

In the 1983–1984 irruption, about 30 were seen in the Massena-Potsdam area of St. Lawrence Co., with 15 others reported from four other northern counties. At least one was on the North Shore of LI. In the years since this last irruption, there have been occasional reports of single individuals, mostly in the northern counties.

Remarks MA had very few reports in this century before the 1978–1979 irruption, when 17 were sighted (Veit and Petersen 1993). CT had only two vague reports during the flight (Zeranski and Baptist 1990). These authors mention that, in view of the species' not being recorded west of Michigan in this irruption, at least some of the birds sighted may have originated in Quebec, where the species is expected but has never been proved to breed. Yunick remarked on the difficulty of verifying reports and avoiding duplication during the 1978–1979 event. He said that more than half of 17 reports originally reported as Great Gray Owls proved to be Barred Owls. Total numbers of Great Gray Owls reported in these irruptions may be inflated because of such inaccuracies, but numbers actually involved are probably significantly greater than the numbers reported because some birds remain undiscovered. There is evidence from specimens that some are malnourished, and many in this condition probably do not survive. Shooting and collisions with vehicles also contribute to mortality. In some areas, concentrations have been noted where prey populations are high.

The same theory advanced to explain the cause of Snowy Owl irruptions into southern Canada and the United States from the breeding range is also mentioned for Great Gray Owl movements: high prey populations and the

resultant increase in production of young, followed by an abrupt decrease in prey populations and then an exodus of owls seeking food.
Robert Andrle

Long-eared Owl   *Asio otus*

Range Holarctic, breeding in North America from eastern British Columbia east to Nova Scotia and south to Oklahoma and Virginia. Winters from southern Canada south to the Gulf Coast and casually to Florida. Sedentary and migratory.

Status Rare and local breeder, undoubtedly overlooked, especially in more remote regions. Uncommon to locally fairly common winter visitant, most numerous in southeastern NY. Uncommon transient, or at least rarely detected on migration.

Breeding Although fairly widely distributed as a breeder in central and western portions and locally downstate, it is one of the state's least known nesters, especially away from regions with large urban centers. Breeding habitat consists of wooded swamps, plantations of conifers, and open wood-land. The species nests in conifers (pine, hemlock, and cedar in particular), frequently in abandoned crow or raptor nests, although one nest was found in an apple tree, another in a hollow in a maple. Data gathered for the Atlas suggest widely scattered breeding localities throughout upstate, with a disjunct population in the Coastal Lowlands but no records elsewhere in southeastern NY. Recent nesting records are lacking from the Catskills, the Allegany Hills, and all sites east of the lower Hudson Valley. The first recorded nesting on LI since the 1940s was at Muttontown Preserve, Suffolk Co. in April 1977 (Lindberg 1978).

Nonbreeding The species is typically found roosting communally in dense stands of conifers away from roosting areas of local Great Horned Owls, its chief predator. Such roosts, which can usually be found Nov–Mar, are often first detected by the presence of pellets under a tree or "whitewash" on the roost tree. Site fidelity is very strong, often over several decades. Typically only three or four birds are found, but occasionally there may be many more, when prey resources (passerines and especially rodents) are abundant. Northern Saw-whet Owl can often be found near such large roosts.

CBC data show Long-eared Owl to be most numerous as a wintering species in the southeastern portions of the state, although more fieldwork in private plantations of conifers in central NY may prove them to be more numerous there than previously was suspected. CBC data show 72 records in upstate areas during 1960–1989 and 467 such records in southeastern NY.

Maxima: 36 Pelham Bay Park, Bronx Co. 18 Jan 1968; 21 Bronx-Westchester CBC 26 Dec 1960; 20 Blooming Grove, Orange Co. winter 1968–1969; 12 Buffalo CBC 16 Dec 1984 and 18 Dec 1989.

Remarks Although the Long-eared Owl is not now considered by NYSDEC to be a candidate for listing as Endangered, Threatened, or of Special Concern, observers should treat this apparently rare nester with the same caution afforded the more easily censused species so listed.
Edward S. Brinkley

Short-eared Owl

Asio flammeus

Range Cosmopolitan, except for Australia; breeding in North America from Alaska to Newfoundland south to California and, in the east, to southern Illinois and northern Virginia. Winters south to Florida, the Gulf Coast, and Mexico; withdrawing from the northern portions of the breeding range.

Status Local breeder, greatly decreased in recent years. Generally uncommon migrant and winter visitant, but very irregular in occurrence, occasionally locally common.

Breeding Bull (1974) described breeding as limited to LI and scattered areas in the western parts of the state. The Atlas revealed additional Probable and Possible sites scattered across northern counties, with a Confirmed in St. Lawrence Co. Some of these northern locations are near the areas that Eaton (1914) described as "its commonest breeding grounds." The Atlas also graphically illustrated the tenuous hold this species has on viability as a breeder. It was reported in only 36 blocks, or about 1% of the total, and was actually Confirmed in only five blocks!

Its decrease as a breeder in NY has caused this owl to be listed as a Species of Special Concern by the NYSDEC, and it has been recommended for upgrade to Endangered. The Atlas mentions habitat loss and contamination from herbicides and pesticides as possible reasons for this decrease.

Nests are located on the ground, usually in open country along the coast, in marshes, or in agricultural or old-field habitats.

Nonbreeding Although this species is often the most visible of our owls and can at times occur in great concentrations, it is quite erratic in its visitations. Greatest numbers have been found in winter around Cayuga and Seneca lakes; the Point Peninsula area of Jefferson Co.; around Avon, Livingston Co.; and at Point Breeze, Orleans Co. Lower concentrations can be found downstate and on LI.

Inland maxima: 50–100 between Cayuga and Seneca lakes, winter 1991; 81 around Cayuga L. 22 Feb 1992; 75 Alden, Erie Co. 30 Dec 1969. *Coastal maxima:* 40 Canarsie Pol, Jamaica Bay, late Dec 1959; 10 Shinnecock, Suffolk Co., late Nov 1989.

Birds arrive at wintering locations from late Oct through Nov and may remain into early Apr.

Remarks This largely diurnal owl is most often seen over marshes, meadows, old fields, airports, and other open terrain. It relies heavily on voles *(Microtus* sp.) as a food source and may invade an area and remain there as long as the vole population is plentiful. The decrease in breeding birds noted above has been observed in neighboring states as well (Tate 1992).
Michael F. Cooper

Boreal Owl *Aegolius funereus*

Range Holarctic, in North America breeding in Alaska and boreal Canada from the tree limit south to northern British Columbia, east to northern Minnesota, western and central Ontario, and southern Quebec; casually on Grand Manan Island, New Brunswick. During irregular winter irruptions in the east, occurs south to southern New England, northern New York, New Jersey, and Pennsylvania.

Status Very rare vagrant.

Occurrence Of more than two dozen records, more than 12 were collected or found dead; several others were photographed (Yunick 1979). Most of the 10 records before 1960 are from the Adirondacks and vicinity. Since then there have been several near L. Ontario in Monroe and Oswego counties and a few in the eastern half of the state away from the Adirondacks. There is even one record from LI at Cedar Beach, Suffolk Co.: a bird found dead 15 Jan 1975. Except for the L. Ontario sightings, it has not been found in the western half of the state.

The Boreal seems to be less irruptive than the other northern owls, since the maximum in one winter is only three in 1978–1979 (Yunick 1979). Its secretive nature, however, makes locating it very difficult. It occurs in areas with dense cover, usually roosting in a conifer tree. The longest period over which a bird has been reported is only seven days, making the Boreal Owl one of the most sought-after of the owl species. More than half the sightings are in Feb and Mar.

Extreme dates: 14 Nov and 1 Apr.

Remarks Although three is the most found in NY in one winter, it has shown its irruptive tendencies elsewhere. In winter 1922–1923, 26 specimens were received by a single taxidermist in NH, 30 by another in ME, and 30 were taken in MA (Veit and Petersen 1993). In winter 1991–1992 there was a great irruption of all three of the rare northern owls in the Northeast; the numbers for Boreal Owl were: 15 in PQ, 26 in ON, 6 in MA, 1 in CT, and 1 in NY (AB 46:225).

William C. D'Anna

Northern Saw-whet Owl *Aegolius acadicus*

Range Nearctic, breeding from southern Alaska and central Saskatchewan east to Nova Scotia and south, in the east, to central Missouri, central Ohio, in the mountains of West Virginia and western Maryland, and on the Atlantic Coastal Plain to Cape Cod and Long Island. Winters south to the Gulf Coast and through the Atlantic states to central Florida.

Status Rare and local breeder. Variously rare to fairly common migrant and winter visitant, occasionally more numerous. Locally abundant spring migrant along the south shore of L. Ontario.

Breeding The known and suspected breeding sites are widely but sparsely scattered over the state, with heaviest concentrations found in the Adirondack region. Bull (1974) listed only 29 historical breeding locations, and the Atlas recorded only 17 Confirmed sites, with 112 Possible or Probable locations. Large portions of NY are completely unrepresented.

Despite the relative scarcity of breeding records, ornithologists have long suspected that it is actually much more common than it appears, perhaps because of the significant numbers observed during late fall and winter (Atlas 1988). The considerable number of reported road kills and large numbers banded during spring migration at Braddock Bay, Monroe Co. further substantiate this suspicion. A new area record was established in Clinton Co. when a juvenile was found dead in the summer of 1995 (NASFN 49:914).

Although lack of observation may account for the paucity of breeding records, the difficulty of locating nests is undoubtedly a factor as well. Largely nocturnal and generally silent during incubation, this hole nester may easily escape detection. It tends to sit tight even when closely approached.

This smallest of NY's breeding owls nests in abandoned woodpecker holes, natural tree cavities, and even nest boxes. It uses material left by former occupants, adding no new material. This relative inactivity at the nest site may also make it difficult to locate.

Nesting habitat varies, but the birds seem to prefer wooded swamps and often make use of forest edges. Atlas observers reported finding them in alder, northern white cedar, and tamarack swamps, mature conifers, deciduous woods, and along pond and lake shores. Other, more unusual nest sites include a spruce-sphagnum bog, an old apple orchard, and a box adjacent to a salt marsh in open country on LI. Full details of this last record, one of only four documented for LI, have been published by Schaeffer (1968). The banded female, last seen alive on 15 Jun 1968, was found shot 12 Jan 1969 almost 300 mi to the northeast at South Portland, ME.

Nonbreeding Both migratory and sedentary, it winters throughout its breeding range but is found most frequently in the dense conifer groves along the South Shore of LI and in city parks, where trees are concentrated and observers are numerous. Numbers fluctuate, with some years being more productive than others. In 1967 Ward and others estimated 26 within a distance of only a few miles in the pine groves between Oak and Cedar beaches, Suffolk Co. Up to 17 were reported 19 Nov 1995 from the west end of JBSP alone; other reports reflecting the extent of the 1995 incursion included one sleeping in a Christmas tree for sale in Manhattan and a pair feeding on mice in a warehouse in Syracuse for two weeks (NASFN 50:29).

The increased use of mistnets in recent years has produced records more illustrative of the species' occurrence, such as these from Nassau and Suffolk counties: 55 Atlantic Beach and Tobay (Nassau) and Huntington (Suffolk) 30 Sep–10 Nov 1965; 45 RMSP Oct–Dec 1974; 31 Atlantic Beach 30 Sep–30 Nov 1966; 23 Fire I. 1–24 Nov 1971; 12 Fire I. (Suffolk) 11 Nov 1972; 10 Fire I. 26 Oct. 1972; 7 Fire I. 27 Nov 1969.

Elsewhere, they are reported irregularly and in low numbers from nearly all upstate regions in fall and winter. However, banding efforts in spring in two areas along the south shore of L. Ontario have produced noteworthy numbers. The Braddock Bay Owl Banding Project, started in 1984, mistnets hundreds each spring. In 1992 an astounding 291 were banded there.

At Noyes Sanctuary in Scriba, Oswego Co. 33 were banded through 7 May in 1983, this date noted as "record late," with a maximum 6 on 30 Apr (KB 33:204); 18 were banded there in Mar–Apr 1986 (KB 36:228) and 28 between 25 Mar and 26 Apr 1987 (KB 37:153).

Remarks The irruption of the fall of 1995 was noted all across the Northeast, with the Cape May, NJ banding program netting 637, 24 Oct–14 Nov, over three times the previous record. Highest nightly count was 108 on 9 Nov (NASFN 50:29).
Patricia J. Lindsay

GOATSUCKERS—CAPRIMULGIDAE

Common Nighthawk *Chordeiles minor*

Range Nearctic and Neotropical, breeding nearly throughout North America from the tree limit in Alaska and Canada, south to the West Indies and Central America. Winters in South America, south to Argentina.

Status Widespread but localized breeder. Common to abundant fall migrant, less numerous in spring.

Breeding The decline of this species has been well documented (Bull 1964, 1974; Atlas 1988), and it is now listed by NYSDEC as a Species of Special Concern. Breeding is recorded throughout the state but appears to be highly localized. It is likely, however, that this species was underreported by Atlas workers because of its crepuscular nature. It is most common around towns and cities, where it utilizes flat gravel roofs. Contra Carleton (1958), it can still be found as a breeder in Brooklyn (pers. obs.) and Manhattan (KB 31:268). Reasons for the decline in natural, open-country breeding sites are unclear but may include intensive land use for agriculture, reforestation, and longevity of forested areas due to prevention of forest fires. Predation by crows may be a significant cause of decline in urban areas (KB 37:232; J. F. Thill, pers. comm.).

Nonbreeding A common to abundant fall migrant; peak numbers occur in late Aug and early Sep, with high counts of 1500 Port Chester, Westchester Co. 4 Sep 1936, 23 Aug 1949, and 7 Sep 1968; 1000 Somers, Westchester Co. 26 Aug 1951; 1000 Bayside, Queens Co. 20 Aug 1969; 1000 Elmira, Chemung Co. 6 Sep 1981. In spring it is less numerous; high counts of 350 Croton Point, Westchester Co. 21 May 1975; 300 Greece, Monroe Co. 30 May 1984; 200 Buffalo, Erie Co. 20 May 1959 are notable. This species is rare before May and after Sep. Extreme migration dates are 6 Apr and 11 Nov.
Paul R. Sweet

Chuck-will's-widow *Caprimulgus carolinensis*

Range Chiefly southeastern Nearctic, breeding from eastern Kansas to Long Island and south to Texas, the Gulf Coast, and Florida. Sporadically reported in summer farther north. Winters from northern Florida to the West Indies and from the Gulf states and Texas through Middle America to northern South America.

Status Rare and local breeder on LI and SI since the 1970s. Vagrant elsewhere.

Breeding Chuck-will's-widow colonized southern NJ in the 1950s and has been noted on LI since 1969, when a singing bird was heard at Islip, Suffolk Co. 27–30 May. It was taped, and the resulting sonogram is on file at the AMNH (KB 19:148). Nesting was confirmed six years later at Oak Beach, Suffolk Co. (Bull 1976; KB 25:132) and again in 1981 during Atlas work. Atlas workers on LI recorded Probable breeding (singing birds at stable locations) at a variety of South Shore and South Fork locations as far east as Amagansett and Montauk and in the central pine barrens. Populations are thought to have peaked in the mid-1980s, fallen somewhat in the late 1980s, and leveled off since. Calling birds have continued to be recorded at most of the above locations and have also been noted regularly since 1974 on SI (Siebenheller 1981; Atlas 1988).

Chuck-will's-widows are generally found in dry, open pine and oak woods, a habitat preference shared with the declining Whip-poor-will, and the southern species is often said to be replacing its northern congener. However, there is little evidence of direct interaction. Most Chuck-will's-widow records are from areas long vacated by Whip-poor-will, and there is only limited overlap on SI and in a few places in the central LI pine barrens.

Nonbreeding Aside from a specimen taken by Latham at Riverhead, Suffolk Co. in 1933, the first Chuck-will's-widows seen in NY were in Monroe Co., at Rochester in 1959 and Braddock Bay in 1961. More recently, this species was reported from Irondequoit, Monroe Co. on 13 Jun 1992. These birds may have had Midwestern origins as this species has bred north to Michigan and Ontario. It has also been noted since 1972 in May in Central Park, Manhattan and occasionally in other NYC parks, where they do not breed. The first sight record in several decades in Prospect Park, Kings Co. was on 6 May 1995 (R. Gochfeld, in litt.). NY is at or near the northern edge of the breeding range of this nocturnal and cryptic species, so it is perhaps not surprising that there are only a relatively few records of spring migrants and none at all for the fall. The earliest recorded arrival dates are 29 and 30 Apr at a Suffolk Co. breeding site; the latest published date is 22 Jul at Montauk.

Remarks Despite the intermittent presence of summering birds on Nantucket and Martha's Vineyard, MA since 1971, no confirmed breeding has yet been recorded (Veit and Petersen 1993).
Eric Salzman

Whip-poor-will   *Caprimulgus vociferus*

Range Primarily eastern Nearctic, breeding from central Saskatchewan to Nova Scotia and south, east of the Great Plains, to northern portions of the Gulf states and to the Carolinas; also breeds in the Southwest. Winters on the Gulf Coast and in Central America south to Honduras.

Status Locally common breeder, most numerous on the Coastal Lowlands, rare to absent in western and central NY and in the higher parts of the Adirondack, Catskill, and Tug Hill regions. Regular nocturnal migrant.

Breeding Its presence as a breeding bird is largely detected by the persistent and well-known nocturnal song and therefore best documented near areas likely to be visited at night during breeding season. Even assuming it is somewhat underdocumented, the species has clearly disappeared from large areas of NY, and populations have declined in the remaining strongholds. During Atlas work, it was absent throughout most of western and central NY and has shown few signs of recovery since. In one well-documented case, 10 pairs were estimated to be nesting on the L. Erie plain east of Buffalo in 1930 and 1931 (Saunders 1936); the same survey was repeated during Atlas work in the early 1980s, and no birds were found. Five calling birds were noted in the area in the spring of 1987 (KB 37:217), raising hopes for recovery, but reports from this region in the 1990s continue to emphasize its scarcity. It has also declined in favorite areas such as the Oneida L. region and in many parts of LI, apparently because of development, large-scale cutting of forests, and decreases in saturnid moths due to industrial pollution, pesticides, or other causes (Robbins et al. 1986).

If some populations are in a long-term decline, others may merely be subject to cyclical oscillations, common among insectivorous species. Where good habitat remains, they have remained relatively stable over long periods. BBS data 1965–1979 showed few changes in many areas throughout the state (Robbins et al. 1986). Declines on LI are clearly linked to loss or degradation of pine and oak barrens. Where suitable forests have remained relatively undisturbed, the species has continued to be fairly common, and the recent establishment of a pine barrens preserve in Suffolk Co. has raised hopes for its survival in that habitat.

Atlas workers also found that substantial populations still remained in hardwood forests in the Hudson and Champlain valleys and in a ring of low-elevation hardwood and aspen-birch forests surrounding the Adirondacks, with smaller populations on SI, in wet woods on the St. Lawrence and Great Lakes plains, in the Tug Hill and Oneida L. regions, and in highland areas adjacent to the Hudson Valley. In addition, a substantial and previously unknown population was discovered in forested river valleys south of the Finger Lakes.

Formerly, large numbers of calling birds were recorded in early spring in favorable areas on LI: up to 100 in Connetquot River SP in the pine barrens in 1974; 50 birds on the South Fork in 1942; at least 30 in Nassau Co. in 1945. Counts in recent years have tended to be much smaller: 15 on the 1988 mid-Jun Central Suffolk BBC; 12 at Connetquot in 1993. It has been recommended for inclusion on the NYSDEC's list of Species of Special Concern.

Nonbreeding Birds arrive in most locations in late Apr or early May. There is a record of a calling bird in Vestal, Broome Co. on the early date of 25 Mar and another report of one at New Russia, Essex Co. on 30 Mar (KB 32:196; 41:206); early coastal migrants have been reported on 2 and 8 Apr. Calling birds on LI in Jul and Aug often appear in areas where they do not usually breed; these may represent late breeding attempts, wandering males, or early migrants. Whip-poor-wills are difficult to detect in the fall, when they do not sing; the relatively small number of reports are concentrated in Sep, with a few in Oct. The latest records, both from Suffolk Co., are 6 Nov at Northport and a recently expired bird (AMNH 812033) found in Brookhaven on 24 Dec 1975 (KB 36:28).

Remarks The recent range expansion of the Chuck-will's-widow has been offered as an explanation for the decline of the Whip-poor-will on LI. However, there are only relatively small areas of overlap, and, in many cases, the disappearance of the latter clearly preceded the appearance of the former. Because of the nocturnal and cryptic nature of the Whip-poor-will, much still remains to be discovered about its breeding biology and true status in NY.
Eric Salzman

SWIFTS—APODIDAE

Chimney Swift *Chaetura pelagica*

Range Eastern Nearctic, breeding throughout eastern North America from southern Canada to Texas and Florida. Known to winter in Amazonian Peru and western Brazil; locally on the Pacific coast of Peru.

Status Widespread breeder. Common to abundant migrant, especially inland, occasionally very abundant.

Breeding Before the arrival of the Europeans in NY it nested mainly in caves and hollow trees. With the numerous dwellings of settlers available, the swift population probably soared. It has totally adapted to the presence of humans and now nests almost exclusively in chimneys and on the inside walls of buildings. It breeds in every county, and during the Atlas was even found throughout the Adirondacks, although no natural nesting sites were found there. Specific habitat requirements are difficult to determine, but it is often seen near water. It is, perhaps, least frequent in areas of extensive agriculture. The population appears to have changed little during this century, although BBS data have shown a 1.8% yearly decrease during the period 1966–1994.

Nonbreeding It usually arrives in the last half of Apr and departs early to mid Oct. Postbreeding flocks begin to form in late Jul and early Aug. Large numbers are often seen into Oct at Buffalo, Erie Co., when it is rare elsewhere at that time. This occurs when strong winds align with the axis of L. Erie and concentrate swifts at the northeastern end of the lake.

Spring maxima: 1000 Derby Hill, Oswego Co. 6 May 1961; 1000 Rochester, Monroe Co. 12 May 1956. At a spring roost in a chimney in Ithaca, Tompkins Co. in 1948, 4000+ were banded during the entire season, 2500+ of them on 19 May. *Fall maxima:* 1500 Ft. Tryon Park, Manhattan 30 Aug 1947; 1200 Middletown, Orange Co. 23 Sep 1979; "1000s" Buffalo, Erie Co. 2 Oct 1977. *Extreme dates: Inland:* 30 Mar and 24 Oct. *Coastal:* 1 Apr and 4 Nov.
William C. D'Anna

HUMMINGBIRDS—TROCHILIDAE

Ruby-throated Hummingbird *Archilochus colubris*

Range Eastern Nearctic, breeding from central Alberta east to Nova Scotia and south to Texas and Florida. Winters from Florida and the Gulf Coast south, through Mexico to Costa Rica.

Status Widespread breeder but rare or absent in densely populated areas. Fairly common to occasionally common migrant, especially inland.

Breeding It occurs in a wide variety of habitats but prefers rural areas. It is found in gardens, orchards, roadside thickets and trees, and forest clearings, often near streams. Eaton (1914) found it at up to 1067 m (3500 ft) on Mt. Marcy, Essex Co. Sugarwater feeders and showy nectar-producing flowers will attract this hummingbird to nest in or near people's yards. It is widely distributed throughout the state but rare or absent in large urban areas and less forested regions such as the western half of LI, the NYC area, the eastern L. Ontario and St. Lawrence plains, and the Mohawk Valley (Atlas 1988). The population has increased quietly, yet markedly. According to BBS data, in the period 1980–1994 it grew nearly 10% a year.

Nonbreeding It is greatly attracted to flowers such as jewelweed, bee balm, trumpet creeper, salvia, and, during late fall, petunias; it is also frequently found at sugarwater feeders. Usually rare before May and after Sep.

Spring maxima: 43 Derby Hill, Oswego Co. 16 May 1970; 42 there 19 May 1978; 25 Buffalo, Erie Co. 12 May 1956. *Fall maxima:* 30

Jamestown, Chautauqua Co. 2 Sep 1947; 25 Crugers, Westchester Co. 2 Sep 1991; 24 mistnetted, Vischers Ferry, Saratoga Co. 5 Sep 1970 and 23 more there 19 Sep. The following are fall season totals at Butler Sanctuary, Mt. Kisco, Westchester Co.: 52, 1983; 40, 1984; 75, 1985; 40, 1991. An unprecedented concentration of 50–60 at a feeding station in Bone Run, Cattaraugus Co. 31 Jul 1991 may have been caused by a lack of natural nectar sources due to drought (KB 41:258). *Extreme dates:* 14 Apr (coastal and inland) and 21 Nov (inland) and 23 Nov (coastal). Also, one was at Riis Park, Queens Co. 26 Nov–13 Dec 1961 and one at a feeder, Jamestown, Chautauqua Co. early Nov to 10 Dec 1988 (KB 39:107).
William C. D'Anna

Rufous Hummingbird   *Selasphorus rufus*

Range Western Nearctic, breeding from southern Alaska south through British Columbia and Alberta to northern California and east to western Montana. Winters to southern Texas and the Gulf Coast and in Mexico. Casual east to the Great Lakes region and along the Atlantic Coast from Nova Scotia to Florida.

Status Casual vagrant.

Occurrence Only two state records have been accepted by NYSARC. The first (NYSARC 1995) was an adult male found in the Town of Chester, Orange Co. on 9 Aug 1993. "The host family reported the bird to the local Audubon chapter. . . . Fortunately, J. Tramontano, a transplanted birder from California, was able to see the bird and also rule out Allen's Hummingbird" (KB 43:346). The second, an adult male, stayed at a feeder in Cambridge, Washington Co. from Oct to 3 Dec 1994, when it was captured by R. Guthrie and Yunick, photographed, and taken into captivity, where it died on 9 Dec (NYSARC 1996).

Since Carleton's report of a Rufous Hummingbird in Elizabethtown, Essex Co. 3–13 Sep 1980 (KB 31:2), there have been 11 other reports in NY. Unfortunately, only the two individuals cited have been acceptable to NYSARC because this species is very difficult to distinguish from Allen's Hummingbird (*S. sasin*) in some plumages. Thus the Elizabethtown record, and individuals reported from Ulysses, Tompkins Co. 21 Jul 1988 (S. Sibley); Riverdale, Bronx Co. 16 Nov 1993 (Loeb); and Queens 22–24 Nov 1993 (Lauro) were accepted only as *Selasphorus* species (NYSARC 1981, 1990; KB 44:79).

Remarks Despite NYSARC's reasonable rejection of these birds because identification is not conclusive, circumstantial evidence supports each as very probably Rufous Hummingbird. The breeding and winter ranges of Allen's Hummingbird are largely restricted to the west coast of central and north-

ern California, and Allen's is reported as accidental only east to Texas (Terres 1980). Rufous Hummingbird, on the other hand, has increasing numbers of extralimital individuals recorded (Terres 1980). A popular field guide calls this species "rare in the east, accidental in the spring" (National Geographic Society 1987).
Gerry Rising

KINGFISHERS—ALCEDINIDAE
Belted Kingfisher   *Ceryle alcyon*

Range Nearctic, breeding from Alaska to Newfoundland and south to the southern limits of the United States. In the east, winters from the southern Great Lakes and New England south to Florida and the Gulf Coast and in Bermuda, the West Indies, and northern South America.

Status Widespread breeder and fairly common migrant. Rare to common in winter.

Breeding This species seems to be unique in the sense that Eaton's (1914) assessment, "common summer resident and breeds in every county in New York State," basically need not be modified. In addition, it is one of the few species found breeding in all ecozones, from the Adirondack High Peaks to the Coastal Lowlands.

Although fish is a very important component of the kingfisher diet, the species apparently suffered no reproductive losses during the DDT years, such as were suffered by the Osprey. This resistance to the effects of DDT may reflect the fact that, whereas the Osprey diet is almost exclusively fish, and also good-sized ones at that, the Belted Kingfisher diet is not restricted only to small fish but also includes crayfish, mollusks, and insects.

Nonbreeding Fairly common on both spring and fall migration but never seen in any large numbers, it ordinarily arrives in mid-Mar and departs by late Nov. Widespread in winter where open water is available, it can be quite common in coastal areas at that time, less so upstate. Combined CBC totals for Region 10 often exceed 200.
Paul R. Sweet

WOODPECKERS AND ALLIES—PICIDAE
Lewis's Woodpecker   *Melanerpes lewis*

Range Western Nearctic, breeding from southern British Columbia to southwestern South Dakota, south to south-central California, southern

New Mexico and eastern Colorado. Winters south irregularly to northern Mexico and western Texas.

Status Casual.

Occurrence Bull (1974) listed this species as Hypothetical, even though there was one very well documented sight record, but no specimen or photograph. Fortunately, the observation made by the Swopes at their home feeder in Ossining, Westchester Co. on 27 Oct 1954, and verified by numerous persons through 6 Nov 1954, was finally submitted to NYSARC in 1995, accepted by that body, and officially placed on the NYS checklist (NYSARC 1996).

A second individual was recorded and this time well photographed by Cesari (ph to NYSARC). The bird showed up in Richfield Springs, Otsego Co. 10 Jun 1997 at a feeder maintained by Kurkowski, who, although not a birder, was able to identify it from his field guide. On 20 Jun, Hall, an active birder, was notified. He confirmed the identification and alerted the birding community. Unfortunately, the bird disappeared the next day.

Remarks There are two records from MA, in 1966 and 1969 (Veit and Petersen 1993), and a specimen from RI in 1928 (Conway 1992).
Emanuel Levine

Red-headed Woodpecker *Melanerpes erythrocephalus*

Range Eastern Nearctic, breeding from southern Saskatchewan east to New Brunswick and south to Texas, the Gulf Coast, and Florida. Winters within the southern parts of breeding range but occasionally north to the limits of the range.

Status Locally uncommon resident and breeder. It is both sedentary and migratory.

Breeding Formerly more numerous and widespread in suitable habitat. It was especially found in farm country with open grasslands, pastures, and woodlots. Population decrease in the last decade has averaged 5.6% a year across its total range (Friederici 1994). Suspected reasons for this decrease include mortality from vehicles due to the habit of hunting roadside and "flycatching" insects, and losing in competition for nesting holes with the European Starling. Other possible causes are the loss of woodlands and conversion to younger age stands without mast production and the old snags for nesting, loss of farms in the Northeast, and conversion of woodlots to agriculture in the Southeast, where many birds winter. Reduction of mast-producing trees from disease such as the chestnut blight early in the century and American beech decline and oak wilt in recent times may also be important factors in the decline of this species.

Numbers in the Northeast increased significantly on BBS routes during the period 1965–1979 (Robbins et al. 1986). A possible explanation was that the time frame coincided with the Dutch elm disease outbreak and spread in the northeast, which killed hundreds of thousands of elm trees, affording the birds both more nesting sites and an abundance of insect larvae as food. Small increases in the southeastern part of NY in the mid-1980s may be a result of there being more observers, doing Atlas fieldwork, at that time.

Breeding habitat consists of two distinct types: (1) stream courses with or without beaver ponds and (2) open country with extensive grasslands and scattered trees, or small woodlots.

The center of our population is in the Great Lakes Plains, adjacent Cattaraugus and Finger Lakes highlands, St. Lawrence Plains, and Mohawk Valley. This distribution generally cuts off sharply at the edge of the Appalachian Plateau, where elevations increase, except in an area southeast of Oneida L. (Atlas 1988). Other concentrations are from river valleys, especially in areas north and west of the central Hudson Valley. Adirondack locations are in the Western Adirondack Foothills near Bay Pond, Franklin Co.; a first breeding record, Westport, Essex Co. 14 May 1977 (KB 27:167); and a first breeding record for Clinton Co. Aug 1981 (Gretch et al. 1982).

Nonbreeding Nothing today even closely resembles the numbers once seen in fall flights along the coast. Helme reported "several hundred," principally immatures, before 10 A.M. 24 Sep 1881 at Miller Place, Suffolk Co. (Bull 1964). Today in that same area if more than six birds are reported in spring or fall it is a cause for rejoicing. This species has been recommended for inclusion on the NYSDEC's list of Species of Special Concern.

Spring maxima: Inland: 35 Avon, Livingston Co. 12 Mar 1977. A count on 16 May 1993 recorded a maximum of 12 individuals in Region 1. *Winter maxima: Coastal:* 22 on LI CBCs 17 Dec 1983, 9 of them on the Queens Co. count.

This woodpecker can be found anywhere in the state, including the Tug Hill and Adirondack regions, at any time of year. Locations are determined by the available food supply. It readily comes to feeders for sunflower seeds, peanuts, and suet.

Lee B. Chamberlaine

Red-bellied Woodpecker   *Melanerpes carolinus*

Range Southeastern Nearctic, resident from Minnesota and Massachusetts south to Texas and Florida. Casual north to southern Canada and west to eastern New Mexico.

Status Common to uncommon or rare local resident, increasing.

Breeding The first nesting recorded in the state was in Erie Co. in 1890. The breeding range is still in the process of expanding as the species moves eastward and northward. Bull (1974) found it uncommon in western NY and rare and local in the southeast. He considered it very rare elsewhere. Atlas work still showed the two distinct and disjunct areas Bull had described: (1) the southeastern counties and North Shore of LI; (2) the Genesee Valley and the Finger Lakes regions. The southeastern population surely came via expansion up the coast and into NJ, but the origins of the western group are much more obscure, with numerous but no totally satisfactory scenarios postulated. That mystery is enhanced by the fact that the species was known in that area since at least the late nineteenth century (Eaton 1914).

The Atlas found that the LI population had continued to expand and the southeastern population had moved up the Hudson R. to Columbia and Greene counties, while the Genesee Valley population had moved outward within that area. This expansion is still going on and will continue with advances and drawbacks. The bird may be filling the niche formerly occupied by the decreasing Red-headed Woodpecker. In many ways the two species are similar in preferred habitat and feeding behavior, the Red-bellied being more aggressive toward the European Starling and other competing species.

Of the 37 breeding locations listed by Bull, 27 were established from 1961 to 1971. The die-off of many elms from Dutch elm disease may partially explain this expansion. Breeding habitat and expansion routes follow watercourses, including forested stream bottoms, creeks, and wooded wetlands. Other habitats used include openings in mature forests, roadside sugar maples, and shagbark hickories in open pasture situations. Dry upland hard maple–beech woodlands may also be used (Atlas 1988).

Nonbreeding The first Catskill Park record was at Ashokan, Ulster Co. in fall 1982. Movement into the North Country was noted in 1984 with the first record for Region 7, a feeder bird at Ticonderoga, Essex Co. 20 Jan, and the first record for Region 6 near Canton, St. Lawrence Co. 14 Nov. Until 1990, all reports were in winter, usually at feeders. After that, birds were also reported in spring and summer; a maximum of seven were in Clinton Co. the spring of 1992.

Maxima: 95 Northern Nassau Co. CBC 26 Dec 1993; 92 Rochester, Monroe Co. CBC 19 Dec 1993: 73 Bronx-Westchester CBC 26 Dec 1993.

Remarks Adjacent states and provinces have experienced the same pattern of range and population expansion in the past 40 years. By 1996 this woodpecker had moved northward in ON as far as Thunder Bay and Moosonee; it was also north of Montreal in PQ.

Lee B. Chamberlaine

Yellow-bellied Sapsucker

Sphyrapicus varius

Range Nearctic, breeding across southern Canada to southern Newfoundland and south to southwestern United States; in the east, to the Berkshires, Catskills, Poconos, and the higher mountains to northern Georgia. Winters in southern United States, south to the West Indies and through Middle America to Panama, occasionally north to Massachusetts.

Status Local breeder in the Adirondacks and the Tug Hill and Appalachian plateaus. Uncommon to common migrant inland; fairly common to common fall coastal migrant, uncommon there in spring.

Breeding Although breeding evidence was recorded in 2205 (41%) of Atlas blocks, almost all of them (93%) include areas over 1000 ft elevation. Less than 4% of the blocks were below 500 ft. Sapsuckers prefer forested areas; less than 3% of their occupied blocks were identified as less than a third forested. It is a very rare breeder along the Great Lakes Plain and in the Mohawk, St. Lawrence, and Hudson river valleys, and no breeding has ever been recorded in or southeast of the Shawangunk Hills in Ulster and Orange counties or on the east side of the Hudson south of Columbia Co.

The Atlas suggested two distribution changes since earlier accounts: (1) retreat from areas formerly occupied in Niagara, Orleans, and Wayne counties along L. Ontario; (2) expansion locally into altitudes of 500–1000 ft, particularly noted in forested areas attached to the Tug Hill Plateau and the Adirondacks and in the central Finger Lakes region.

Evidence that breeding numbers are increasing is provided by western NY BBS records. Average total annual counts for this species on 18 BBSs by decade were: 1960s, 1.3; 1970s, 2.1; 1980s, 5.7; 1990–1994, 14.0 (Rising 1994c).

Nonbreeding Normally returning in early Apr, spring arrivals in central and western NY average only a few days later than those of downstate, but arrival times in the Adirondacks average 10 days to two weeks later. The paucity of fall data makes similar comparisons difficult, but it appears that the movement out of northeastern NY (average 4 Oct) is earlier by a similar number of days.

Bull (1974) recorded the fall migration as "mainly coastal," partly substantiated by his highest fall count of 28 in Bronx Co. 4 Oct 1925. BOS count data contradict this. Sapsucker is regularly recorded in Oct on the Niagara Frontier, with highs of 71 in 1970, 39 in 1937, 38 in 1990, and 37 in 1971. Those numbers compare with springtime maxima on corresponding counts of 71 May 1995; 55 Apr 1994; 43 May 1971; 41 May 1966.

Bull cited other maximum counts: 150 Dunkirk, Chautauqua Co. 2 May 1965; 75 near Binghamton, Broome Co. 11 Apr 1959; 25 netted and banded, Fire I. Lighthouse, Suffolk Co. 29 Sep 1969.

Each year a few overwinter, mostly downstate. Average total counts on 45 upstate CBCs were: 1960s, 1; 1970s, 6; 1980s, 5. Corresponding averages for 21 downstate CBCs were: 1960s, 6; 1970s, 12; 1980s, 25. Maximum total CBC counts were 20 upstate in 1981, 37 downstate in 1984 (Salzman 1994). The higher numbers in the 1980s may reflect a series of mild winters.

Gerry Rising

Downy Woodpecker   *Picoides pubescens*

Range Nearctic, resident throughout much of the wooded portions of North America from Alaska and central Canada to extreme southern United States.

Status Widespread breeder, fairly common to common throughout. Sedentary and migratory, it is a common migrant along the coast.

Breeding Found breeding at all elevations in most all habitats where deciduous trees occur, from mature forests to orchards, suburban backyards, and city parks. A cavity nester, it usually uses a dead tree, rarely a living one. It is more likely to nest around populated areas than is the Hairy Woodpecker (Atlas 1988). It was recorded in 86% of all Atlas blocks.

The Atlas reported the current population as probably the highest of the century. However, an analysis of BBS data for 1966–1994 indicated an average annual decrease of 1.7%, and a feeder survey in Sullivan Co., Dec–Mar 1981–1994, showed no significant changes in that county's population (Freer and Visconti 1996).

Nonbreeding It is considered ubiquitous owing to its widespread distribution, wide range of habitats, and tolerance of human populations. It has been reported to outnumber Hairy Woodpecker 3.35:1 on CBCs (KB 38:147). It is a regular visitant at feeders. Northern populations are reported to be mostly migratory, with irregular southward movements (KB

38:147). Banding has indicated that considerable migration also takes place along the Atlantic Coast. A study in central NY indicated that, in the study area, most Downy Woodpeckers did not abandon their breeding territory in winter. Instead, they commuted long distances (over 200 m) to a reliable abundant food source (Gordon and Confer 1996). Yunick (1988a) found a 27.5% decline in reported abundance on CBCs in the state, 1960–1985, and an erratic variation in annual reported abundance, which appeared to be correlated with irruptive migratory activity.

CBC maxima: 345 Ithaca, Tompkins Co. 1996; 316 Ithaca 1981; 286 Bronx-Westchester 1987.

Chad E. Covey

Hairy Woodpecker   *Picoides villosus*

Range Nearctic and northern Neotropical, resident throughout the forested portions of North America and in the mountains to Panama; also in the Bahamas.

Status Common resident in wooded areas throughout. Both sedentary and migratory.

Breeding It was recorded in 71% of all blocks during the Atlas period, absent only in the NYC area and the heavy agricultural sections of the eastern Ontario and St. Lawrence plains. It prefers to nest in extensive tracts of forest with plenty of large trees, snags, and fallen logs. With this habitat preference, it is curious that there is no record of changes in abundance during the deforestation of the 1800s and the early 1900s or the reforestation since then. What may account for its apparent adaptability is the fact that it nests not only in heavily forested tracts but also to a lesser degree in nearly all sylvan habitats (Atlas 1988).

Nonbreeding Although more common in extensive woodlands, it is found in most habitats where trees occur, such as suburban areas and the edges of fields and clearcuts. During winter, it is found mostly in less forested country and also in city parks and at backyard feeders. It is extremely difficult to quantify the extent of fall migratory movements, which evidently occur to some extent periodically and may be tied to irruptive movements of finches, nuthatches, and chickadees. The record of 35 moving south along Anthonys Nose, Westchester Co. 23 Oct 1954 still has not been surpassed.

An analysis of BBS data for 1966–1994 indicates no significant change in overall abundance. A feeder survey in Sullivan Co., Dec–Mar 1981–1994, showed no significant changes in that county's population (Freer and Visconti 1996). An assessment of NY CBCs for 1960–1985 showed a statewide decline of 54.5% in reports. Annual variations in abundance were observed that appeared to be attributable to irruptive migratory behavior. Data indicated that overall, Hairy Woodpeckers are outnumbered by Downy Woodpeckers by a ratio of 3.35:1 (Yunick 1988a).

CBC maxima: 290 Elizabethtown, Essex Co. 1982; 142 Bronx-Westchester 1962; 122 Ithaca, Tompkins Co. 1981.

Remarks There is a definite winter influx of the larger subspecies, *septentrionalis*, from the north. The extremes among them are visibly larger and whiter than the resident nominate subspecies, *villosus*. The size in the East is clinal, and Adirondack specimens are at the upper limit of *villosus*, with most of the winter visitants being intermediate between *villosus* and *septentrionalis*. Three undoubted *septentrionalis* can be found in the Cornell collection: Axton, Franklin Co. 22 Feb 1901; Ithaca, Tompkins Co. 11 Jan 1935; Danby, Tompkins Co. 8 Jan 1949 (K. C. Parkes, in litt.).
Chad E. Covey

Three-toed Woodpecker *Picoides tridactylus*

Range Holarctic, in North America breeding from northern Alaska across northern Canada to Newfoundland and south, in the west to the mountains of Arizona and New Mexico, but in the east only to northern New England and the Adirondack Mountains of New York. Essentially sedentary and non-migratory, but has wandered casually or irregularly south to Rhode Island and Delaware.

Status Rare local resident in the Adirondacks and on the Tug Hill Plateau and very rare winter visitant elsewhere.

Breeding Observers since the time of Merriam (1878–1879) have reported this species as even rarer than the related Black-backed Woodpecker. Eaton (1914), for example, described it as "evidently about one-half as common as that species." Atlas workers found Three-toed Woodpeckers in only 22 blocks as compared with 114 for the Black-backed. Although both were found at multiple locales within blocks, these data suggest that the population ratio is even less than Eaton's estimate. Only one Atlas block where the species was found was outside the Adirondack SP; it was on the central Tug Hill Plateau. Although this range description is almost a duplicate of that for Black-backed Woodpecker, the species were found together in only seven blocks.

Nonbreeding The species was not recorded on any CBCs 1960–1989 (Salzman 1994). Eaton (1914) grouped it with the Spruce Grouse, Gray Jay, and Boreal Chickadee as "our perfectly nonmigratory species," citing only one record, in Oneida Co., outside its breeding area. A few individuals have ventured beyond their residential areas. Bull (1974) cited three western NY records between 1956 and 1966. Since Bull, three other such reports, between 1975 and 1983, were published, but, when reviewed by NYSARC, were rejected.

The only record accepted by NYSARC was a female at Irvington, Westchester Co. 17 Dec 1984 (Stevenson) (NYSARC 1984).

Remarks The two three-toed species have very similar habitat requirements and are often found together, as in Ferd's Bog, Hamilton-Herkimer Co. The diet of each is three-fourths bark-boring insects (Bent 1939). Thus, they need the dying or recently dead trees that are often found in recent burns, new beaver marshes, and blowdown areas. The Three-toed Woodpecker is said to prefer spruce forests and the Black-backed pine and larch, but both accept mixed forests including deciduous trees (Winkler et al. 1995). Nor does elevation provide separation, although Eaton (1914) found a Three-toed Woodpecker higher than its congener, at 4000 ft between the peaks of Skylight and Marcy. Bull suggested that the necessary species separation is maintained by bill size, which leads to feeding differences; the Black-backed probes for deeper-burrowing insects than the smaller-billed Three-toed. But note that in the case of Downy and Hairy woodpeckers, the species with the smaller bill is more populous, whereas in this case the species with the larger bill is more numerous.
Gerry Rising

Black-backed Woodpecker   *Picoides arcticus*

Range Nearctic, breeding from Alaska east across boreal Canada to Labrador and Newfoundland and south, in the west, to the mountains of California and Nevada; in the east, to southern Ontario, the Adirondack Mountains, and northern New England. Wanders south irregularly in winter as far as Delaware.

Status Uncommon local resident in the Adirondacks and very rare on the Tug Hill Plateau. Very rare to rare winter visitant elsewhere.

Breeding The Adirondack locales in which this species and occasionally its congener, the Three-toed Woodpecker, reside, read like a Baedeker of wild places: Ferd's Bog, Duck Hole, Helldiver and Brown's Tract ponds, Old Forge, Killkare, Mohegan Lake, Baxter and Hurricane mountains. All of these locations are above 1500 ft.

It was found in 114 (2%) Atlas blocks; all but two were within the Adirondack SP border. The others were in the central Tug Hill Plateau. Only one block, near L. Champlain, was below 1000 ft. Despite differences in descriptive terms used historically, the Atlas concluded that there is no evidence that the population has actually changed since at least the turn of the century.

Nonbreeding Bull recorded southward irruptions of the two three-toed species in the winters of 1960–1961 and 1965–1966. Between 1975 and 1995 *The Kingbird* records not only fail to demonstrate widespread irruptions, but they also show little correlation between outward movements of the two species. During that period there were 14 Black-backed Woodpecker and three Three-toed Woodpecker reports outside the Adirondack Mountains and Tug Hill Plateau. In only one winter, 1984–1985, were both noted and then only one each. The maximum number of wandering Black-backed Woodpeckers between 1975 and 1995 was recorded in the fall and winter of 1981–1982, when there were two in Hamlin Beach SP, Monroe Co. and one in Phelps, Ontario Co. This falls far short of the nine found in the Buffalo and Syracuse areas during the 1960–1961 irruption. Four of the 14 recent records were downstate, but none on LI, where it has not been seen for many years. There were at least three recorded there earlier: in 1887, 1936, and 1963.

A review of NY CBCs (Salzman 1994) found that, outside their normal breeding range, a total of 15 individuals were recorded 1960–1989. Only one of those was downstate, on the 1962 Peekskill, Westchester Co. count. The 1960–1961 irruption produced five on CBCs: Geneva, Oneida, and three in Syracuse. The 1965–1966 irruption led to four: Conesus, Syracuse, and two in Rochester. The remaining five were: Schenectady 1962, Ithaca 1968, Watertown 1972, Buffalo 1975, and Geneva 1981.

Remarks The irruptions of the 1960s have often been associated with the outbreak of Dutch elm disease, and indeed both three-toed woodpeckers were observed peeling bark from American elms to get at the smaller European elm bark beetle *(Scolytus multistriatus)* vectors, but it is difficult to believe that the die-off of this tree somehow "pulled" these birds out of their breeding area, where few elms are found. Also, records show that individuals that do stray from their breeding area often find a locale and stay for weeks or even months. This too suggests that the birds were not following the beetles. More likely scenarios for these and other irruptive events are a very successful breeding season or a lack of food in residence ranges, or both, the effect of which is that individuals, especially younger birds, are forced out of their normal range.
Gerry Rising

Northern Flicker   *Colaptes auratus*

Range Nearctic and northern Neotropical, breeding from Alaska and Canada to Cuba and in the mountains to northern Nicaragua. Withdraws in winter from the northern portions.

Status Widespread breeder. Common to very abundant migrant. Regular in winter, most numerous along the coast.

Breeding Found breeding throughout the entire state wherever the opportunity for cavity nesting exists, in habitats ranging from city parks to remote heavily forested areas. It was recorded in 92% of all blocks during the Atlas period. It is most commonly found in woods or wood edges close to open areas used for foraging for food. A cavity nester, it usually excavates a new cavity but often uses an old one or a nest box. Dead trees are generally used, but it commonly uses live trees more often than other woodpeckers. It has been known to excavate holes in telephone poles, buildings, haystacks, and other cavity opportunities (Atlas 1988).

Although still widespread and common, significant declines in flicker numbers have been reported in recent years (Atlas 1988). An analysis of NY BBS data 1966–1994 indicated an average annual decrease of 6%. This decline has been attributed largely to the European Starling, which competes for nest cavities.

Nonbreeding Migrants usually arrive in early Mar and depart in late Nov. They are more numerous inland in spring and on the coast in fall. Great flights occur during both seasons. For example, on 6 Apr 1947, 1200 were observed migrating at Derby Hill, Oswego Co., and on 28 Sep 1976, observers estimated up to 12,000 at RMSP, Suffolk Co. (KB 26:59). Although migratory, they are frequently fairly common during mild winters.

CBC maxima: 323 Montauk, Suffolk Co. 1984; 310 Orient, Suffolk Co. 1988 and 298 there 1989. Upstate: 104 Troy, Rensselaer Co. 1989; 86 Syracuse, Onondaga Co. 1975; 72 Rochester, Monroe Co. 1984.

Remarks In 1982, Northern Flicker *(C. auratus)* was designated as the standard name for two formerly recognized species of flicker, the Red-shafted *(C. cafer)* and the Yellow-shafted *(C. auratus)* (AOU 1982). Where English name changes are a result of lumping, common practice usually allows for the continued use of the former species or subspecies name to refer to those populations where they remain distinct (KB 33:37). The two forms hybridize extensively in a wide zone of sympatry along the western border of the Great Plains, and intermediates are numerous. An apparent Yellow-shafted × Red-shafted intermediate was found dead in the Town of Canton, St. Lawrence Co. 31 May 1983 (KB 33:207). Chad E. Covey

Pileated Woodpecker *Dryocopus pileatus*

Range Nearctic, resident from British Columbia to Nova Scotia and south throughout nearly all the United States.

Status Fairly common and widespread resident except for the Coastal Lowlands, where it is a rare visitant.

Breeding Atlas workers found evidence of breeding in 2714 blocks, 51% of the total. Given the species' shyness, even this distribution report may be conservative. Away from the Coastal Lowlands, distribution is nearly comprehensive; only a few areas in western NY, in particular the Great Lakes Plain west of Rochester, have few breeding blocks. During the Atlas period only one Probable record came from LI.

Nonbreeding There is occasional good news in birdland. This handsome woodpecker is making a striking comeback across NY. It was evidently widespread and fairly common at the time of DeKay's 1844 report. Then, after woodlands were cleared statewide at the turn of the century, Eaton (1914) recorded the species as "confined to the evergreen forests of the Adirondacks and Catskills" with only a few in "the highlands along the Pennsylvania border and in various localities throughout central and western New York where there are mixed forests of unusual extent." But Bull (1974) reported recovery as "phenomenal and its present status is in startling contrast—for the better."

Happily, evidence suggests that this recovery continues. Table 8, for example, shows decade averages for censuses on the Niagara Frontier as compiled from May and Oct BOS counts and 18 BBS reports (Rising 1994b, 1994c, 1995). Note how the numbers in each column increased since Bull's positive report. In addition, statewide CBC annual totals rose from an average of 55 in the 1960s, to 69 in the 1970s, and 132 in the 1980s (Salzman 1994).

Bull related Apr appearances in four NYC parks in the Bronx and the northern tip of Manhattan. These likely represented exploratory forays for new breeding territories, unsuccessful in such small and heavily populated areas. Its clear preferences are for "mature, tall and extensive stands . . . of rather open deciduous to dense coniferous" forests, especially those with trees 40 to "over 70 years old, and often close to water" (Winkler et al. 1995).

The first report on LI this century was at Sag Harbor in 1947; 34 years later a female was located in Forest Park, Queens Co. on 11 Dec 1981 by Bernarth. It remained there until 1 May 1982 and may have been the bird

Table 8. Decade averages for Pileated Woodpecker censuses on the Niagara Frontier

	May BOS count	June BBS	Oct. BOS count
1960s	12.9	2.0	6.2
1970s	19.3	2.1	6.8
1980s	20.3	3.3	11.2
1990s	25.2	3.8	40.8

Sources: Rising 1994b, 1994c, 1995.

seen at Mill Neck, Nassau Co. on 8 May (KB 32:143, 223). Another was found the next year at Garvies Point, Nassau Co. by Cioffi on 14 May. It may have been the same bird that was present that summer, again at Mill Neck (KB 33:227, 299). Those reports were the source of the Probable Atlas record.

Remarks The reason for the Pileated Woodpecker's expansion is almost certainly straightforward. As the forests were cleared for farmland, its population declined and then, as cultivated land reduced and woodlands again spread across the state, its population has soared, providing a near perfect correlation between trees and birds. Given the continuing trend of reforestation, it is reasonable to predict ongoing good fortune for this species. Gerry Rising

TYRANT FLYCATCHERS—TYRANNIDAE

Olive-sided Flycatcher *Contopus cooperi*

Range Nearctic, breeding from Alaska to Newfoundland and south; in the east, to northern Michigan and New York, western Massachusetts, and locally in the Appalachian Mountains to Tennessee and North Carolina. Winters in Middle and South America to southeastern Peru.

Status Uncommon to rare breeder across the Adirondacks and Tug Hill Plateau, rare and local in the Catskills and the Rensselaer Hills; numbers decreasing sharply statewide. Rare to uncommon migrant.

Breeding Within its confined range this handsome bird has very specific habitat requirements. It is almost always found at 1000–3000 ft elevation, atop an isolated snag near standing water, often a beaver meadow. Atlas workers found it in 479 (9%) of all blocks, but only the three in the Rensselaer Hills were outside the Adirondack, Tug Hill, and Catskill preserves. All but 6% of the blocks where it was found fit the elevation requirements; 75% were in spruce–fir–northern hardwood forests, and almost all of the individual birds were in appropriate surroundings.

Only 33 (7%) of the Atlas records were Confirmed, and the late spring migration of this species, which often extends well into June, overlapped with much of the Atlas fieldwork. This result calls into question some of the Possible and even Probable records.

In any case, this species is very thinly distributed and seriously threatened. In 1974 Bull said, "This species is a fairly common breeder in the Adirondacks and is not rare in the Tug Hill district," but BBS data 1966–1994 indicated a highly significant 92% drop in numbers. Even worse, since 1980 the decline has steepened to over 13% each year (Peterjohn 1995).

Nonbreeding In spring seasons 1976–1995 this species was not recorded in about half of the Kingbird Regions and was missed only slightly less often in fall. (Those data, however, are especially subject to the vagaries of reporting.) The BOS Niagara Frontier May counts 1965–1995, recorded an average of two per year, with six in 1974 and a quite remarkable high of 11 on 20 May 1990 (Rising 1995).

Extreme dates: 4 May and 26 Sep. Usually rare before late May and after mid-Sep.

Remarks As the NY beaver population rebounded to the point where some consider it a pest, additional habitat was created that should be ready-made for Olive-sided Flycatcher occupation. However, numbers have been declining precipitously. Friedmann (1963) said, "The Olive-sided Flycatcher is a rarely reported victim of the Brown-headed Cowbird." He listed only three occurrences of parasitism. It is possible, however, that this level of parasitism may have changed since we have reports of increasing forest penetration by cowbirds. Sadly, we may not sort out the reasons for the decline of this lovely boreal flycatcher before it is lost to us.

Failure of the NYSDEC to list Olive-sided Flycatcher as at least a Species of Special Concern is lamentable.

Gerry Rising

Eastern Wood-Pewee   *Contopus virens*

Range Eastern Nearctic, breeding from southeastern Saskatchewan to Nova Scotia, south to Florida, the Gulf states, and Texas. Winters primarily in South America, south to Peru and western Brazil.

Status Common and widespread breeder in open deciduous and mixed woodlands and woodland edges but thought to be declining in certain areas. Fairly common to common spring and fall migrant. Occasional in winter in recent years.

Breeding Found as a breeder in all parts of NY except high-elevation spruce-fir forests, open agricultural areas, and the heavily urbanized portions of larger cities and towns. It is essentially a species of light, semi-open deciduous forests and forest edges and, as such, has undoubtedly benefited from the increase in second-growth forest in many parts of the state. It is also now well adapted to orchards, parks, gardens, and shade trees in suburban gardens and village streets.

Although Atlas workers reported that it was as widespread in the early 1980s as in the early part of the century, there is evidence that population levels have dropped in the late 1980s and 1990s. This decline, parallel to those of other Neotropical migrants, may be due to habitat, alteration on both breeding and wintering grounds. However, this species is fairly well adapted to edge habitat, and it has probably suffered less in this respect than species of unbroken forest, which are more severely affected by such changes. Like many other insectivorous birds, it may undergo long-term population oscillations in response to the cyclical outbreaks and die-offs of its flying insect prey.

It is a relatively late breeder, and, although a published egg date of 8 Sep has been thought to be an error, several reports of late fledglings up to 18 Sep are most likely correct (Bull 1974, 1976).

Nonbreeding It generally arrives in early to mid May, occasionally in late Apr, and normally departs in late Sep or early Oct. A bird near Ithaca, Tompkins Co. 13 Apr 1985 was extremely early (KB 35:189). In recent years, unprecedented numbers have lingered to the end of the year and beyond. In 1969, a specimen (AMNH 793548) was collected at Fire I. Lighthouse on 15 Nov, and unusual numbers of pewees were noted on coastal CBCs in 1981 and 1984. In 1993, they were reported on seven different counts on SI and LI.
Eric Salzman

Yellow-bellied Flycatcher *Empidonax flaviventris*

Range Chiefly central and eastern Nearctic, breeding from central Canada south to the northern portions of New York and New England; rarely to the Catskills and Poconos. Winters from Mexico to Panama.

Status Fairly common breeder locally in the Adirondacks, uncommon in the high Catskills, and very rare in the Tug Hill Plateau. Uncommon migrant.

Breeding It was recorded in 192 Atlas blocks, or 4% of the total. With only seven exceptions, these blocks fall within the Adirondack or Catskill forest preserves. Two are just outside the Adirondack boundary, and four are on the Tug Hill Plateau in Lewis Co. The other, with a Probable record, is a central Madison Co. location near Tully where this species was recorded as nesting by Eaton (1914) but not by Bull (1974).

Two factors complicate these observations. One is the difficulty of differentiating this *Empidonax* flycatcher from its more common congeners. This is not simply a matter of look-alikes: the song of the Yellow-bellied Flycatcher is similar to that of the Eastern Wood-Pewee and its call to that of the Least Flycatcher. The similarities suggest that the figures above may be conservative. On the other hand, this species is, like another relative, the Olive-sided Flycatcher, a very late migrant, often recorded in June when much of the Atlas fieldwork was in progress. This timing might have caused observers to misidentify migrants as Possible or Probable breeders. Note in this regard that breeding was Confirmed in only 16 blocks, a mere 8% of those where it was located.

Nonbreeding Because of the identification problems already noted, it is difficult to estimate the number of migrants. However, some data suggest that the species is more common than many fieldworkers believe. Although BOS annual May counts on the Niagara Frontier 1965–1995 average only 2.6 individuals per year, there were 12 in 1947, 15 in 1956, and 10 in 1985 (Rising 1995). Other high counts include: 12 banded 6 Jun 1965 Manitou, Monroe Co. (Leubner); 9 banded 20 May 1970 Fire I. Lighthouse, Suffolk Co. (Buckley); 4 picked up at the Elmira, Chemung Co. TV Tower 20 Sep 1966 (CUM collection); 11 banded 24 Aug 1968 Vischers Ferry, Saratoga Co. (Yunick).

Changes in decade averages for BOS May counts are not statistically significant.
Gerry Rising

Acadian Flycatcher   *Empidonax virescens*

Range Southeastern Nearctic, breeding from southern South Dakota, southern Ontario, and Massachusetts south to the Gulf Coast and central Florida. Winters from southern Mexico to Panama and Ecuador.

Status Formerly a local breeder, disappearing as such early in the century, it is now in the process of reoccupying and expanding its former range. As a migrant, it needs careful documentation.

Breeding Bull (1974) stated there had been "no definite breeding for over 45 years" save for an abortive attempt in Rockland Co. in 1957, and none proven "in extreme western NY in more than 60 years." There were some summer records in central NY up to the 1940s (Allen 1947), in Orleans Co. in western NY up to 1934 (Beardslee and Mitchell 1965), and in the NYC area up to 1915 (Griscom 1923). The reasons for its long retreat and later return are unknown.

Eaton (1914) described it as a common inhabitant of the lower Hudson Valley, fairly common on western LI, and rare to uncommon elsewhere. Bull, in his review of its breeding distribution, pointed out that the LI population inhabited the North Shore, north of the terminal moraine, and another population occurred in the lowlands of Westchester and Rockland counties, within a few miles of the Hudson R. To the west, he recorded a population in the Finger Lakes region in Tompkins, Schuyler, and Chemung counties. On the Great Lakes Plain he cited nesting in Cayuga, Ontario, Monroe, Orleans, and Niagara counties, mostly old records from Eaton and Beardslee and Mitchell.

Nearly all these areas have been repopulated and, in addition, the species has spread up the Delaware R. and its tributaries and has nested in many areas in Ulster Co. away from the Hudson R. In the west it has populated the ravines entering L. Erie and the tributaries of the Allegheny R. It is essentially a forest bird, and deforestation and urbanization seem to have reduced its range for a time, but it has returned to areas now reforested and not urbanized in southern and western areas of the state. Hints of this relatively recent recolonization were first recorded in the late 1950s and 1960s in southeastern NY and LI (KB 7:70, 102; KB 19:242) and upstate in the 1970s.

It is local, at present, in Suffolk Co. in wet maple woods along the Peconic R. and Great Peconic Bay; also Captree SP (KB 44:342). In Nassau Co. it was Confirmed near Oyster Bay (Atlas 1988). In the southeast, it has recolonized and is now local in Region 9 but not Confirmed in the Hudson Valley above Ulster and Dutchess counties (Atlas 1988). Most of the Region 9 sites are in hemlock ravines, a habitat under serious attack in the 1990s by wooly adelgids (B. Lincoln, pers. obs.). There are occasional summer records from Delaware and Broome counties (KB 36:222) but no confirmed breeding in Region 4. The gap between the western and southeastern populations reaches from the East Branch of the Susquehanna R. at Waverly, Tioga Co. to the Delaware R. in Sullivan Co.

Recolonization was first recorded in the Finger Lakes Highlands and Central Appalachians in 1979, when nesting was Confirmed on Cayuta L. outlet, Schuyler Co. (KB 29:219). On Connecticut Hill, Tompkins Co. a small population has recently become established in ravines bordering tributaries to Cayuta Creek, which flows south into the Susquehanna R. at Waverly (KB 44:251) and also in additional areas near Ithaca (KB 44:309). Probable breeding occurred in Chemung, Tompkins, Tioga, Cayuga, and Seneca counties during the 1980s (Atlas 1988).

In the southwest, first nesting was recorded in 1975 at Sheridan, Chautauqua Co. in mixed beech-maple forest (Bull 1976). It was reported in Cattaraugus Co. along tributaries of the Allegheny R. several times from 1971 to 1979, but first nesting was recorded 15 Jun 1980 (Eaton 1981). There it nested along small streams shaded by small to medium-sized hemlocks. Many nestings are now known in small ravines entering the L. Erie plain (KB 37:220, 40:243).

The Ontario plain is being recolonized in fairly extensive, mature, maple-beech woods. A nest with two young was found at Chestnut Ridge Park, Erie Co. 23 Jun 1991 (KB 41:258); it is also breeding in Hamburg and Cheektowaga (KB 42:234). The first recent nesting at Bergen Swamp, Genesee Co. was recorded 16 Jun 1979 (KB 29:215), followed by several records since in Region 2.

The first recent nesting in Region 5 occurred near Minetto, Oswego Co. 22 Jun 1985 (KB 35:277), with additional reports since in Onondaga Co.

at Whiskey Hollow, of a pair with three young (KB 43:326), and at Van Buren (KB 44:316).

Nonbreeding It occurs as a spring migrant along the coast and near breeding sites inland. It is difficult to identify unless calling, singing, or in hand. In fall the bird seldom calls or sings and has a yellower wash on the breast, making identification problematic. There are no fall specimens at BMS, *fide* A. Clark, nor at Cornell University, *fide* K. McGowan 3 Nov 1995. Fall migrant records should be documented by specimen or recognizable photo. In the fall of 1970, a rather remarkable total of 13 was mistnetted and banded, 11 at Fire I. Lighthouse, Suffolk Co. and 2 at Atlantic Beach, Nassau Co. Bull (1974) speculated that these birds "might represent a northern incursion." He may indeed have been correct, as evidenced by the breeding range expansion detailed in this account.

Extreme dates: 8 May and 30 Sep.

Stephen W. Eaton

"Traill's" Flycatcher   *Empidonax alnorum* and *E. traillii*

(See also Alder Flycatcher and Willow Flycatcher accounts, which follow.)

Alder and Willow flycatchers constitute a good example of a species pair or sibling species, collectively described by the term *superspecies*. Until 1973, they were regarded as the subspecies of "Traill's" flycatcher *(E. traillii)*. These taxa were discovered to be reproductively distinct, differing in vocalizations (songs and calls), habitat, range, and certain aspects of their breeding biology. They are most easily distinguished by their songs, generally transliterated as "fee-BEE-o" (Alder) and "FITZ-bew" (Willow). The two songs are more alike than the phonetic rendering would suggest, but note that the accents fall on different syllables. In addition to differences in song, the birds have noticeably different calls, but consistent plumage differences have never been demonstrated and noncalling birds cannot be separated, even in the hand.

The two populations appear to have been geographically isolated until relatively recently, when the Alder expanded to the South, shortly followed by the Willow moving north and east from its Midwest strongholds, sometimes coexisting with its sibling, sometimes replacing it. This zone of sympatry in NY played a major role in the studies that resulted in the separation of the two species.

Territorial songs permit an accurate assessment of breeding populations but, owing to the lack of historical record and of tools for distinguishing silent birds, little accurate information on migration paths and dates and on the relative abundance of the two is available. Collectively, they are uncommon migrants in the spring, fairly common in the fall. "Traill's" flycatcher in general, and Alder in particular, have been consistently noted as among the latest of all the spring migrants, with arrival dates on NY breeding grounds averaging 14–29 May. Mistnetting along the coast has shown that the spring migration of "Traill's" flycatcher peaks at the end of the first week in June and continues until the middle of the month; 10 birds netted and banded on Great Gull I., Suffolk Co. on 6 Jun 1970 and one netted on 15 Jun 1968 in the same locality illustrate the lateness of the migration (Bull 1964, 1970, 1974). These may have been Alder Flycatchers en route to northern breeding destinations, but this possibility cannot be verified because, even today, the two forms cannot be distinguished in the hand.

The return flight of "Traill's" flycatcher takes place in late Aug and early Sep. Sixteen individuals were mistnetted between 23 Aug and 1 Sep 1961, 12 of them between 28 Aug and 1 Sep; 9 were netted and banded at Tobay, Nassau Co. 28 Aug 1966, and 11 on 1 Sep 1970 at Fire I., Suffolk Co. (Bull 1970, 1974). Fall dates range from 11 Aug to 9 Sep, and there are scattered later records to 14 Oct.

For background on the separation of the two species, see Aldrich 1951, 1953; Stein 1958, 1963; Bull 1964, 1970, 1974; and Atlas 1988. For the difficulties in separating them in the field or in the hand, see Phillips et al. 1966; Whitney and Kaufman 1985, 1986; and Kaufman 1990.

Eric Salzman

Alder Flycatcher   *Empidonax alnorum*

Range Nearctic, breeding from Alaska to Newfoundland and south, in the east to Minnesota, southern New York, and southern New England, and in the mountains to northern Georgia. Winters, "traillii complex," in South America to northern Argentina and Peru.

Status Locally common breeder in damp thickets and marsh edges, primarily in northern and western NY. Migrant status is unclear because of confusion with Willow Flycatcher.

Breeding It breeds in marshes, bogs, and stream and pond edges over wide areas. According to the Atlas, this species is most common in the northern portions of the state and at higher elevations, including the Tug Hill Plateau and the Cattaraugus, Allegany, and Finger Lakes highlands in the west. More isolated reports of breeding or breeding clusters occur almost throughout the state, including the Great Lakes Plain, much of the Adirondack region, the entire eastern border from the L. Champlain region to the Taconic and Hudson highlands, and in the southeast in both the highlands and Hudson Valley, particularly the more northerly counties of Region 9. There are relatively few breeding sites in

Westchester Co. and only a handful of records of singing birds for NYC and LI (KB 28:261; Atlas 1988). In these areas, Alder is largely replaced by its sibling, Willow Flycatcher. Elsewhere, the two species are sympatric; that is, populations overlap without interbreeding. The relationship between these two taxa in NY is dynamic, and, as in the very similar case of Blue-winged and Golden-winged warblers, the midwestern species appears to be slowly pushing forward at the expense of its more northerly relative.

"Traill's" flycatcher, the superspecies from which Alder and Willow were split in 1973, was rare or absent as a breeder throughout much of the nineteenth century. Alder Flycatcher, then regarded as a subspecies of the nominate *E. t. traillii*, appears to have colonized most of its present NY breeding range in the early years of this century (DeKay 1844; Eaton 1910). It was subsequently replaced in many areas by the later invasion of its sibling.

Nonbreeding This species and the Willow Flycatcher form a species pair, or superspecies, and noncalling birds are virtually impossible to distinguish (Phillips et al. 1966; Kaufman 1990). See the discussion about migration under "Traill's" flycatcher. Singing Alder Flycatchers have been noted as early as 3 May, but the majority of birds are found in late May and early Jun.
Eric Salzman

Willow Flycatcher *Empidonax traillii*

Range Nearctic, breeding from central British Columbia across southern Canada to Nova Scotia and south, in the east, to Virginia, western North Carolina, and northern Georgia. Winters in Middle America south to Panama and perhaps to northern South America.

Status Uncommon to fairly common local breeder at lower elevations; apparently increasing within its known range and extending its range northward. Migrant status is unclear because of confusion with Alder Flycatcher.

Breeding Until 1973, Willow and Alder flycatchers were regarded, respectively, as the western and northern subspecies of "Traill's" flycatcher. To further complicate the picture, both appear to have invaded NY in this century, the Alder from the north and the Willow, somewhat later and possibly in two waves, from the Ohio and Mississippi basins to the west and southwest.

The Willow Flycatcher is most common in western NY, on the Great Lakes Plain and in portions of the Appalachian Plateau, as well as in the Mohawk and upper Hudson valleys, nesting mostly in upland thickets adjacent to grasslands, pastures, and small bodies of water. Occasionally it is also found in swampy areas, but, in general, it prefers drier habitat than the Alder. It also breeds widely in the lower Hudson Valley and on LI in coastal thickets; this population is expanding.

"Traill's" flycatcher was little noticed by early writers on the NY avifauna. The Alder Flycatcher spread south from a distinctly northern range in the early 1900s. The Willow, a species of the upper Midwest, expanded eastward into Alder range in the 1930s and 1940s, colonizing the western portion of the state through the lowlands and river valleys and spreading east to the Mohawk and upper Hudson valleys. In the process of overlapping with its sibling, it sometimes coexisted with it, sometimes displaced it. Song reports suggest that only Alders were present in the Ithaca, Tompkins Co. area before 1940, but these were largely replaced by Willows after 1950 (Stein 1958, 1963). Willow Flycatcher has continued to extend its range north and east, spreading into VT in the 1960s and colonizing much of southern New England and ON; it has also been increasingly reported in areas of northern NY where it was previously absent (Atlas 1988; KB vols. 40–45).

A secondary invasion seems to have taken place in the 1950s and 1960s, when it entered the lower Hudson Valley, SI, and LI from areas to the west and southwest (NJ and PA), which had already been colonized. It has continued to expand and increase in those areas as well. On LI, singing males are now commonly found in Jun and early Jul in suitable South Shore habitat from Brooklyn to Montauk, including many locations (Quogue, Amagansett) where this species was not noted during Atlas work.

Nonbreeding Owing to the difficulties of distinguishing this species from the Alder Flycatcher, with which it was lumped until 1973, it is very little known as a migrant. NY birds and the relatively small population breeding beyond the state's borders to the north and east appear to retrace their inland colonization routes, and few downstate coastal migrants have ever been identified outside the immediate breeding grounds. Considered collectively, the sibling species are among the latest of spring migrants, arriving on breeding grounds in late May to mid-Jun. A singing male on SI on 2 May 1991 is the earliest published date.
Eric Salzman

Least Flycatcher *Empidonax minimus*

Range Chiefly eastern Nearctic, breeding from southern British Columbia and south-central Canada to Nova Scotia, south to New York and, in the mountains, to Georgia. Winters from central Mexico south to Nicaragua, casually to Panama.

Status Widespread and common breeder except very rare on LI. Fairly common migrant.

Breeding Nests in a variety of deciduous or mixed-forest habitats but prefers successional to mature woods. Chooses open or semi-open situations within or on the edge of woodlands, including pond or stream borders, orchards, and parks. Less numerous in highly agricultural regions where woodlots are few and small. Has all but disappeared from LI, where it was once a local breeder on the North Shore. During and since the Atlas, only a few sites have been found in central Suffolk Co., none of which were classified as Confirmed. Observers have also noted a decline in southeastern mainland NY (Atlas 1988). Similarly, 1966–1994 BBS data showed a 1.3% annual decrease statewide.

Nonbreeding It usually arrives in late Apr or early May and departs before Oct. Silent individuals are difficult to distinguish from others of its genus. Unsubstantiated fall sightings should be regarded with caution.

Spring maxima: a phenomenal 100 Sandy Pond, Oswego Co. 19 May 1977; 38 Tug Hill Plateau 28 May 1979. *Fall maxima:* 13 banded, RMSP 1 Sep 1970; 23 banded, Binghamton, Broome Co. fall 1977, and 37 banded there fall 1981 (KB 32:46). *Extreme dates: Inland:* 18 Apr and 9 Oct. *Coastal:* 20 Apr and 9 Oct (banded) and 8 Nov (specimen) and an extraordinary report of a bird believed to be this species East Hampton Suffolk Co. 28 Nov–14 Dec 1991 (KB 42:66; AB 46:242).
William C. D'Anna

Eastern Phoebe *Sayornis phoebe*

Range Chiefly eastern North America, breeding from southern Canada south, in the east to the mountains of northern Georgia. Winters mainly in southeastern United States and Mexico, north on the East Coast to Maryland; rarely to Long Island and southern coastal New England.

Status Common breeder throughout the state except in the Adirondacks at higher elevations and in continuous forest; also absent from highly urbanized areas. A common to uncommon early and late migrant, rare in winter.

Breeding Adaptable in breeding, often nesting on structures built by humans, usually near water. Third after American Robin and Barn Swallow in active nests located during the Atlas, actually being Confirmed in more than 50% of the total blocks. It originally nested on sheltered cliffs or upturned roots of felled trees. Many nested under bridges where steel stringers formed flat nesting surfaces, but since large circular culverts are supplanting the older bridges there seem to be fewer bridge-nesting phoebes. The loss of small farms and the increase in urban areas have also hurt it. It is a favorite host of the Brown-headed Cowbird in open country (Jones 1975), but in more-forested areas it is relatively free of parasitism (Clark and Eaton 1977). Populations can rapidly spring back from poor breeding seasons because they are double brooded, often raising 9–10 offspring per season (Irving 1953; S. Eaton, pers. obs.). BBS trends in populations 1966–1979 showed an annual decrease of 4.1% and in 1980–1994 an increase of 4.6% (Peterjohn 1995).

There was a flurry of concern by Kingbird Regional editors after a blizzard, 3–5 April 1975 (KB 25:155; KB 28:184, 187), and the severe winter of 1976–1977 reportedly destroyed the population in the northern part of its winter range (Robbins et al. 1986). Populations in Regions 5 and 6 were apparently reduced the most. The Allegany Co. BBSs showed dramatic decreases between 1970 and 1985 (Klingensmith and Hoover 1986). By 1983, however, little concern over its status appeared in the Regional reports as numbers apparently returned to normal.

Nonbreeding Statewide average arrival and departure dates 1961–1986 were 24 Mar and 24 Oct (DeBenedictis 1987). It is difficult to separate late Feb arrivals from possible wintering birds.

Spring maxima: 35 Atlantic Beach, Nassau Co. 27 Mar 1949; 30 Derby Hill, Oswego Co. 22 Apr 1962 and 4 Apr 1969. *Fall maxima:* 85 JBSP 5 Oct 1963; 65 Idlewild, Queens Co. 25 Sep 1949.

Virtually every Region has Dec, Jan, and Feb records in mild winters; these birds switch to berry and backyard feeder diets in the insect-free months, but they most probably become victims of late winter storms. A record of particular note took place on LI, with a total of five birds recorded on three CBCs 16–29 Dec 1980.

Stephen W. Eaton

Say's Phoebe   *Sayornis saya*

Range Western Nearctic, breeding from central Alaska and Alberta and southwestern Manitoba south to southern California and east to central Dakotas and Kansas and northern Texas; also in Mexico. Winters from California southeast to Texas and south to Mexico. Vagrant east to Massachusetts, Connecticut, and New York (specimens).

Status Very rare vagrant.

Occurrence There are 13 records. Five, including one specimen (NYSM 25522), are cited in Bull 1974, with dates between 16 Sep and 19 Dec. One was photographed (Dignan) at RMSP on 23 Oct 1977 (KB 28:62). One was picked up alive near Ithaca, Tompkins Co. on 13 Dec 1977 and subsequently died at the Cornell Laboratory of Ornithology, where the specimen resides (KB 28:108). One remained in Baltimore Woods,

Marcellus, Onondaga Co. 8 Nov–19 Dec 1981 before succumbing to the elements (specimen AMNH 824924) (Crumb 1982). The last five were: one at RMSP on 6 Oct 1985 (Panko) (KB 36:49); one at Sandy Pond, Oswego Co. on 23 Oct 1986 (NYSARC 1987); one photographed during its stay at Delmar, Albany Co. 7–9 Feb 1987 (Mapes) (KB 37:73); one in Montgomery, Orange Co. 17 Dec 1988–8 Jan 1989 (Borko, Tramontano) (KB 39:125); and one photographed while in Menans, Albany Co. 23–30 Dec 1995 (Graves et al.) (KB 46:180).

Remarks Similar to the occurrences in NY, all of the approximately 35 records from surrounding states (NJ, CT, MA, and VT) have come between early Sep and Jan, with most arrivals in Sep and Oct. Two exceptions are one that wintered in VT, with a last date 28 Apr 1995 (NASFN 49:229) and two at Plum Island, MA 22 May 1996 (NASFN 50:256). Thomas A. Burke

Vermilion Flycatcher   *Pyrocephalus rubinus*

Range Neotropical and southern Nearctic, breeding from southern Nevada and central Arizona east to western Oklahoma, and south through Texas and Mexico to northern Guatemala; also widely in South America. Winters in the United States in the southern portions of the breeding range and east to the Gulf Coast and Florida; widely casual north and east of its breeding range.

Status Accidental.

Occurrence There is a single record, an immature male found by Gorson and photographed at the JBSP West End Coast Guard Station on 24 Sep 1987 (Bull 1988b).

Remarks The very rare appearances of this species in the Northeast, with approximately 13 records from NS to VA, have occurred in both spring and, more often, fall. The origin of these is birds unknown, but it is conceivable that some records, especially those in spring, might involve migrants from South American populations, as opposed to wanderers from the southwestern United States. Very detailed descriptions or other evidence should accompany any report to assist in this determination. Thomas A. Burke

Ash-throated Flycatcher   *Myiarchus cinerascens*

Range Western Nearctic, breeding from Washington and Idaho to northern Mexico, east to the Rocky Mountains of Colorado. Winters from Arizona and California to El Salvador. Vagrant east to Rhode Island, New York, and Maryland.

Status Very rare vagrant.

Occurrence This species is being seen along the East Coast with increasing frequency. The question arises as to whether this increase is due to the greater number of birders afield or to some natural factor as yet unknown. The first record was 21 Nov 1970 at Larchmont, Westchester Co., color photograph on file in AMNH collection. The second, an adult female, was at Ridge, Suffolk Co. 1 Dec 1973 (Ruscica). This bird was mistnetted and placed in an aviary, but it died 12 hours later (specimen AMNH 819464). Five years later there was an unusual spring sighting in Riis Park, Queens Co. 10 May 1978 (Buckley) (KB 28:199).

In November of 1985 and 1986 this species was again observed in fall near the coast. Another spring record was 21 May 1989 RMSP (Lauro) (KB 39:190). Since 1992 there have been six sightings, all in the fall, and five have occurred along the barrier beach: 24 Oct 1992 Riis Park, Queens Co. (Walter) (KB 43:83); one, photographed (Vezo) and also heard calling, 2–7 Nov 1993 JBSP (Quinlan) (KB 44:79); one 18 Nov 1993 Wave Hill, Bronx Co. (Burke) (KB 44:80).

After a three-year hiatus, an unprecedented three sightings in one day were recorded along the South Shore of LI. Shortly after daylight on 10 Nov 1996 one was observed at the eastern boundary of RMSP (P. Lindsay, pers. comm.). At about noon, approximately 15 m west, possibly the same bird was found at JBSP (J. Berube, pers. comm.). Late in the afternoon, the third was discovered a mile west of Shinnecock Inlet, Suffolk Co. (Ash, pers. comm.).

Remarks A review of records in neighboring states since 1989 shows 12 documented sightings: two in CT, five in MA, and five in NJ. All but one have occurred during fall migration. The lone spring record was on the CT coast 25 May 1989.

John J. Fritz and Joan L. Quinlan

Great Crested Flycatcher *Myiarchus crinitus*

Range Eastern Nearctic, breeding from east-central Alberta to southern Nova Scotia and south to Florida, the Gulf Coast, and Texas. Winters in Florida, Cuba, eastern Mexico, Central America, and northern South America.

Status Common and widespread breeder, increasing throughout, with the exception of high elevations, open agricultural regions, and built-up areas. Fairly common migrant.

Breeding It was originally restricted to mature, unbroken forest, where it nested in large knotholes, woodpecker excavations, and other tree cavities. Extensive deforestation in the nineteenth century reduced populations, but

371

in recent decades, with the maturation of second-growth forests and adaptation to more-open, disturbed habitats (suburbs, parks, orchards), population densities have increased and the species' local range has expanded in many parts of NY. Bull (1974) called it an "uncommon or local" breeder on the South Shore of LI, where it is now common. Kerlinger and Doremus (1981) did not include it in their survey of the LI pine barrens, although Atlas workers found it in every LI block with deciduous or mixed deciduous-conifer habitat. Raynor (1979) described it in central Suffolk Co. as "largely restricted to relatively undisturbed wooded areas with trees large enough for nest holes," but it is common today in wooded suburban areas and even disturbed edges, often nesting in boxes. Similar increases have been reported in many parts of the state; Atlas workers found breeding evidence in all wooded areas except the higher elevations of the Adirondacks and Catskills and in every county of the state except three in NYC: New York (Manhattan), Kings (Brooklyn), and Bronx.

In addition to the long-range changes described above, this species exhibits short-term or local population cycles. Klingensmith and Hoover (1986) found two full cycles in their 15-year survey of 18 12-m routes in Allegany Co. 1970–1984. Bull described this species as subject to "marked fluctuations." Like other insectivorous birds, it has benefited from cutbacks in pesticide use, but it remains to be seen if the present population growth represents stable increases over a wide area or is merely part of a long-range population oscillation.

Nonbreeding As breeding populations have increased, this species has also become more common as a migrant, especially in the southern portions of the state. This increase is particularly noticeable in places where it does not breed, such as the NYC parks. Formerly rare before May, it is now regularly reported in late Apr, and it has arrived on the coast as early as 13 Apr and inland on 16 Apr. It generally departs in mid to late Sep, occasionally early Oct, with a scattering of coastal records to late Oct and 2 Nov.

Remarks Fall and winter *Myiarchus* flycatchers should be studied carefully because late records of Great Crested Flycatcher now overlap the appearance dates of vagrant Ash-throated Flycatcher.
Eric Salzman

Western Kingbird *Tyrannus verticalis*

Range Chiefly western Nearctic, breeding from southern British Columbia to western Minnesota and south to northern Mexico and Texas; rarely to southern Ontario, southern Michigan and northwestern Ohio. Regular fall migrant along the East Coast from Nova Scotia to Florida. Winters chiefly in Central America to Costa Rica but also along the Atlantic Coast from South Carolina to Florida.

Status Regular, rare to uncommon fall visitant in coastal areas, very rare inland and in winter; casual in spring.

Occurrence Active birders regularly find this conspicuous fall straggler along the South Shore of LI, where as many as three to four birds at a time have been observed in places such as Fire I., Montauk, RMSP, JBSP, and Riis Park, Queens Co. As many as 23 were reported in fall 1954. Some birds have lingered into Dec and even Jan. It is much rarer inland, where about 30 sightings have occurred.

There have been only six spring sightings, all single birds: Orient, Suffolk Co. (specimen) 23 May 1930; East Hampton, Suffolk Co. 3 Jun 1950; Pleasant Plains, Richmond Co. 16 Jun 1958; Somerset, Niagara Co. 11 May 1988 (KB 38:193); Varna, Tompkins Co. 13 Apr 1992 (KB 42:168, 44:5); and Tiffany Creek Preserve, Suffolk Co. 21 Jun 1995 (KB 45:332).

Extreme dates: Inland: 6 Aug and 26 Dec. *Coastal:* 14 Aug and 24 Jan. Robert E. Marcotte

Eastern Kingbird

Tyrannus tyrannus

Range Nearctic, breeding from central British Columbia, northern Saskatchewan, southern Quebec, and Nova Scotia south to southwestern Washington and Florida. Winters in tropical South America.

Status Widespread and common breeder. Common to very common migrant, occasionally abundant in fall on outer coast.

Breeding It breeds in open country, especially in farms, orchards, rural roadsides, along lake and river shores, and in open woodlands, swamp edges, and clearings throughout the state, with the exception of urban areas and the heavily forested parts of the Adirondacks, Tug Hill Plateau, and the Allegany Hills. It was recorded in 4805 Atlas blocks (90%) and was Confirmed in 2627. It may have increased in the nineteenth century with clearing of agricultural land, but the population may now be decreasing as open land is lost to both succession and development; foraging behavior makes kingbirds vulnerable to being killed by cars. A Neotropical migrant, the species may also be losing wintering areas. The BBS shows no consistent population trends. In recent years some reports of low summer and fall numbers in central and northern NY suggest a declining breeding population (KB 43:324; 44:62; 45:213; but see also 43:289; 45:184).

Nonbreeding Spectacular fall flights of several hundred used to occur on the South Shore of LI, but large flights have not been reported there for 30 years. The spring flight is heaviest inland. The mean date for spring arrivals is 30 Apr but varies from 18 Apr on the coast to 10 May in the Adirondacks (KB 37:12). The mean fall departure date is 18 Sep; it ranges from 7 Sep in the Adirondacks to 8 Oct downstate (KB 37:18) and may be as late as 28 Sep in western NY (KB 30:29).

    Coastal maxima: Fall: 900 Riis Park, Queens Co. 29 Aug 1965 "observed between sunrise and late morning, mostly loose flocks of 5 to 20 birds"; 250 Far Rockaway, Queens Co. 10 Sep 1969. *Inland maxima: Spring:* 85 Pinehurst, Erie Co. 17 May 1980; 60 Lake View, Erie Co. 12 May 1962. *Fall:* 60 near Cayuga L., Cayuga Co. 20 Aug 1994. *Extreme dates: Coastal:* 4 Apr, after a strong southerly storm, and 30 Dec. *Inland:* 14 Apr and 16 Oct. Ordinarily rare before mid-Apr and after mid-Sep.
Kenneth L. Crowell

Gray Kingbird   *Tyrannus dominicensis*

Range Neotropical and southeastern Nearctic, breeding in West Indies, Florida, and north and west along the Atlantic and Gulf coasts, rarely to South Carolina and Mississippi. Winters from the West Indies to northern South America. Vagrant north to Massachusetts, often after tropical storms.

Status Very rare vagrant.

Occurrence There are nine records. In addition to the five LI records cited in Bull (1974), their dates ranging from 29 Apr to 19 Sep, including two specimens, one extant (NYSM 25091), four subsequent sightings have occurred. Two more LI records were: one at John F. Kennedy Wildlife Sanctuary, Tobay, Nassau Co. 11–12 Sep 1976 (Bull) (KB 26:204); one staying for a few days at Montauk, from 25 Sep 1989 (Purcell) (KB 40:56). Much more unusual were two occurring well inland: one photographed while present in the Town of Tyre, Seneca Co. 31 Oct–4 Nov 1987 (Crumb, Scheider) (NYSARC 1988); one near Tomhannock Reservoir, Rensselaer Co. 28 Oct–4 Nov 1992 (R. Guthrie) (KB 43:72).

Remarks Most regional appearances of this rare wanderer from the south, as corroborated by the approximately 11 records from surrounding states

(NJ, CT, and MA), occur along the coast in fall, with Sep the most frequent month of arrival.
Thomas A. Burke

Scissor-tailed Flycatcher *Tyrannus forficatus*

Range Nearctic and Neotropical, breeding in south-central United States, north to South Dakota and east to western Arkansas and Louisiana. Winters mainly in southern Central America, but also along the Gulf Coast and in Florida.

Status Very rare vagrant but becoming increasingly regular.

Occurrence A specimen collected at Sag Harbor, Suffolk Co. 11 Jun 1939 (Latham) NYSM 25087 is the first known record for the state. Since then there have been 38 additional occurrences, 29 of them on LI. The remainder were geographically diverse and included Monroe, Rensselaer, Herkimer, Chenango, Erie, Dutchess, and Oswego counties (Koeneke 1994). Seasonally, 23 records occurred in May–Jul and 13 in Sep–Nov. Most were of one day's duration, although fall sightings occasionally lasted longer, including one bird that stayed for 46 days at Sandy Creek, Oswego Co.

Remarks Records for MA show it to be a rare but regular spring and an irregular fall visitant. More than 25 records were in Apr–Jun, with the majority (18) in eastern MA; two summer and eight fall records were also noted (Veit and Petersen 1993). It is an accidental vagrant in CT, substantiated by one fall and two spring records, including one specimen (Zeranski and Baptist 1990). NJ had eight spring and four fall records (Leck 1984), but it has been virtually regular there since 1984. RI has one spring and one fall record (Conway 1992).
Mary Alice Koeneke

Fork-tailed Flycatcher *Tyrannus savana*

Range Neotropical, breeding in northern South America and from central Brazil to Argentina and Uruguay and locally in Middle America. Winters irregularly through the breeding range and casually in the southern Lesser Antilles. Casual vagrant in eastern North America, primarily along the Atlantic Coast to Nova Scotia but also inland to the Great Lakes.

Status Very rare vagrant.

Occurrence Bull (1974) considered this species Hypothetical, but he listed three records he believed reliable, the last in 1954. NYSARC (1987) added the species to the NY checklist with a 17 Jul 1986 sighting in Greenpoint, Kings Co. (Flack) (KB 37:103). Since then, there have been six more records: 7 May 1989 Oak Beach, Suffolk Co. (Cartwright) (KB 39:190); 26 Sep 1990 Ledyard, Cayuga Co. (Hess) (KB 42:6); 7–15 Oct 1990 Hamlin, Monroe Co. (Marcotte) (KB 41:3 ph); 13 Oct 1992 RMSP (Lauro) (KB 43:83); 8 Sep 1993 Ellisburg, Jefferson Co. (G. Smith et al.) (KB 44:62); and 3 Nov 1994 RMSP (Levine) (KB 45:61).

Remarks The almost yearly records after a gap of 32 years is similar to the picture in MA, where there were almost yearly occurrences after a 45-year hiatus (Veit and Petersen 1993). Curiously, RI had only one record (Conway 1992) until 20 Oct 1994, when one was seen at Charlestown. Robert E. Marcotte

SHRIKES—LANIIDAE

Northern Shrike *Lanius excubitor*

Range Holarctic, in North America breeding south to southern Alaska and east to northern Quebec and southern Labrador. Winters from the southern portions of the breeding range south to central California and east to New York and southern New England and, in major irruption years, in the east, to Maryland and Virginia.

Status Rare to uncommon late fall and winter visitant; more numerous in years of major irruptions but never common.

Occurrence Much more numerous in upstate areas than downstate, particularly just south of L. Ontario. The species frequents open country, particularly farm fields and pastures, and uses telephone wires, trees, and bushes for hunting perches. It appears to spend more time hunting from concealed perches than does Loggerhead Shrike, now a very rare bird in NY. In severe winters, Northern Shrike may frequent bird feeding stations to prey upon passerines and rodents attracted there. The species' occurrence in NY appears to be tied to prey availability (small birds and rodents, especially *Microtus* sp.) in areas to the north and northwest of NY, and significant irruptions occur irregularly. The 1970s (especially 1977) produced more records inland than had ever been observed until the winter of 1995–1996, when all previous state maxima, inland or coastal, were eclipsed by the largest irruption thus far observed.

A review of Regional Reports covering the winter season of 1995–1996 (KB 46:141) revealed the following maxima where specifics were given: Region 1, 47 on area CBCs; Region 3, 21 on area CBCs; Region 4, 13 on area CBCs; Region 5, 21 on Syracuse CBC; Region 7, 21 on area CBCs; Region 8, 55 separate records; Region 9, 80 separate records; Region 10, 42 on area CBCs.

Compare those figures with the maxima below, all prior to the winter of 1995–1996, and one gets an idea of the scope of this irruption.

Inland maxima: 17 Oneida Co. CBC 2 Jan 1977; 16 Syracuse CBC 18 Dec 1976; 15 Syracuse CBC 26 Dec 1970. *Coastal maxima:* 12 Montauk to East Hampton, Suffolk Co. 1 Jan 1950; 8 Montauk 11 Dec 1949. *Extreme dates: Inland:* 6 Oct. *Coastal:* 28 Apr.

Remarks This species is occasionally observed in diurnal migration passing raptor watches, such as the Mt. Pleasant Observatory in Varna, Tompkins Co. Northern Shrike is not currently treated as a raptor by most wildlife organizations (such as NYSDEC or HMANA) although its predatory habits, and the worldwide decline of shrikes, suggest that appropriate organizations should consider some form of data collection on all shrikes as raptors. Edward S. Brinkley

Loggerhead Shrike

Lanius ludovicianus

Range Nearctic, breeding widely in Canada and the United States from central Saskatchewan and southern Manitoba south to the Gulf states and Mexico, but increasingly rare and local in the Northeast in recent years. Winters in southern portions of breeding range and very rarely north to Long Island and southern New England.

Status Very rare or casual as a breeder, with all the most recent breeding records from the St. Lawrence Plains and no confirmed breeding records since 1988. Must now be considered as rare to very rare anywhere or at any season; but more likely to be seen in the Great Lakes Plain as a spring migrant and in the lower Hudson Valley and LI as a fall migrant.

Breeding It was once a widespread breeder in NY. In an extensive review of published and unpublished sources, Novak (1989) documented 168 records of confirmed breeding from 38 counties. The majority came from the Great Lakes Plain and the Mohawk Valley area of Oneida Co. Just 11

records of Confirmed or Probable breeding were reported during the Atlas, and all of those except the one in a Franklin Co. block were from areas considered historical strongholds.

An in-depth study of several nesting pairs was conducted in northern Franklin Co. during 1986–1988, but extensive searches elsewhere in the state during that time failed to turn up additional nesting pairs (Novak 1989). There are no records of attempted or confirmed nesting in NY since 1988. The only report since that time that even suggests attempted breeding was in 1992, when a bird was observed with a stick in its bill within a few miles of the northern Franklin Co. nest sites (KB 42:267). However, this observation should not have been characterized as "attempted nesting" as the bird was not seen again and it is unknown if nesting was really being attempted in this case (H. White, pers. comm.). Despite the lack of recent records, the Loggerhead Shrike may yet persist as a breeding species in the state. It seems likely that the bird is indeed gone as a breeder from historical breeding areas along the south shore of L. Ontario, areas that are well surveyed by legions of active birders, but extensive areas of Franklin, St. Lawrence, and Jefferson counties are infrequently birded and still retain areas of suitable habitat. The proximity of these counties to a few remaining "pockets" of occupied shrike habitat in southern ON increases the possibility that an isolated pair may occasionally breed in this northernmost region during at least some years.

Nonbreeding As this species has declined as a breeder in both NY and ON, so too has it declined as a migrant, to the point that it must be considered very rare anywhere in the state. Although it is still reported annually in both spring and fall, the Region 2 Great Lakes Plain area is the only one with more than one report in any season since 1988, and there is a strong possibility that, in at least some years, multiple reports from that Region in the same season represent separate sightings of the same individual. Most spring records still come from the Great Lakes Plain as most birds apparently follow the lake shoreline on their northward migration. There are a few late summer observations from various parts of the state, but virtually all recent fall records come from the lower Hudson Valley and LI.

Extreme dates: A coastal record of 26 Feb 1993 (KB 43:156) probably represents a "spring" migrant. Rare before mid-Mar and after Apr. At nests studied in northern Franklin Co., breeding birds were on territory by late Apr (Novak 1989). Dates of 19 and 26 Jul 1992 (KB 42:243, 254) probably represent very early fall migrants that moved south after failed breeding attempts as no suitable breeding habitat was available in the vicinity of these sightings. Most records are from late Aug through Sep. *Winter:* The only recent winter observations were from Sullivan Co. 5 Dec 1992 (KB 42:120); Chautauqua Co. 8 Dec 1993 (KB 43:121); and Chenango Co. 17 Dec 1994 (KB 45:124).

Bull (1974) remarked that some winter reports, particularly those from upstate, are highly questionable, and indeed the difficulty in separating this species from the Northern Shrike cannot be understated. Nevertheless, many winter sightings, particularly those from LI and those from other parts of the state during winters with little or no snow, are probably correct.

Remarks The Loggerhead Shrike is listed by NYSDEC as an Endangered species. Despite increased attention being given to the Loggerhead Shrike throughout its range, the reasons for the species' decline since the turn of the century remain poorly understood. Several recent studies have shown that in the eastern states and provinces the preferred habitat is grazed pastureland (Brooks and Temple 1986; Luukkonen 1987; Novak 1989; Grubb and Yosef 1994). Land use changes associated with the decline of agriculture, which result in a reduction in the amount of grazed pasture, have taken place throughout the eastern portion of the range (Novak 1989; Lymn and Temple 1991; Laporte and Robert 1995). The corresponding reduction in the amount of preferred habitat on both the breeding and wintering grounds has no doubt played a major role in the decline, but it is difficult to say whether changes on the breeding or wintering range have been more important. Furthermore, there is some indication that the fragmentation of habitat may also be involved (Yosef 1994).

Collisions with vehicles, blamed for declining shrike populations as early as 1930, continue to be an important source of mortality, as evidenced by the finding of road-killed birds in ON, northern NY, VA, and TX (Novak 1989; Blumton et al. 1990; Flickinger 1995). Although it is unclear how important this factor has been to the overall rangewide decline, recent observations in several areas of NY and ON (Novak 1989) indicated that it can be a serious problem once this species has been reduced to small isolated populations.

The role of pesticides in the rangewide decline has not been thoroughly investigated, but some studies and the food habits of the species lend support to the theory that pesticides have been involved and may continue to play a role (Busbee 1977; Anderson and Duzan 1978; Blumton et al. 1990; Lymn and Temple 1991; Grubb and Yosef 1994).
Paul G. Novak

VIREOS—VIREONIDAE

White-eyed Vireo *Vireo griseus*

Range Southeastern Nearctic, breeding from central Iowa and southern Wisconsin to eastern Massachusetts and south to Texas, the Gulf Coast, and Florida. Winters from the Gulf states to the West Indies, eastern Mexico, Belize, and Guatemala.

Status Local breeder on LI and SI, fairly common in Westchester Co. and expanding northward in the Hudson Valley and now becoming established in the west and north. Uncommon but increasing migrant in the southeast.

Breeding Long at or near its northern limits in the NYC area, it has expanded its range up the Hudson Valley and in western and northern NY and into New England, even as it has become more localized on LI and SI.

It was considered to be a common breeder on LI during the nineteenth century (DeKay 1844) but apparently decreased in the early years of the twentieth (Eaton 1914); by the time of Griscom (1923) and Cruickshank (1942) it was said to be rare in eastern LI. On the other hand, Bull (1974) mapped it as "generally distributed" and described it as locally common throughout LI, with high breeding densities. Even during periods of peak population expansion, it was always absent from the drier parts of the pine barrens, being largely confined to wet thickets in areas characterized by rich, moist soils, often near coasts, shores, or wetlands. More recently, its LI distribution has been erratic, remaining common in some areas but missing from other, apparently equally suitable, habitat.

It was reported as locally common in the NYC area until at least 1950, when breeding populations reportedly fell for unknown reasons (Siebenheller 1981). There has been recovery since, but breeding is now largely confined to the Nassau Co. North Shore, JBWR environs, and parts of SI. It was widely reported by Atlas workers in Westchester Co. but not found to be well established in Rockland Co., as Bull had indicated. There were Confirmed and Probable Atlas records for Orange, Putnam, Dutchess, and Columbia counties, all in the Hudson Valley, plus Probables from Cattaraugus, Monroe, and Franklin counties in three widely separated parts of the state.

Reports in *The Kingbird* since then indicate breeding localities in the Great Lakes Plain near Buffalo and Rochester, several sites in western NY (notably Letchworth and Allegany state parks), and areas of the Adirondack and St. Lawrence regions where it was previously unknown. A distribution of this kind indicates a species at the edge of its range with a history of advances, contractions, and reexpansions. The source of the birds in western and northern NY is probably the Midwestern population that colonized the L. Erie region in recent decades.

Nonbreeding All observers from the earlier part of the century up to and including Bull (1974) described the White-eyed Vireo as "rare to uncommon" as a migrant and largely confined to LI. In recent years it has been increasingly reported in the NYC parks and the Hudson Valley. It is also now being reported from upstate areas, where it is still quite rare; the small breeding populations most likely use the Central Flyway.

The earliest record is 28 Mar 1996 Miller Place, Suffolk Co. (Quinlan)

(KB 46:286). White-eyed Vireos have occasionally lingered to record late dates in recent years. They appeared on the 1983 SI and 1992 Montauk CBCs, and there is an upstate record for 18 Dec 1983 at Fulton, Oswego Co. and several in Nov, including one collected in Buffalo in 1955. It is rare before May and after early Oct.

Eric Salzman

Bell's Vireo   *Vireo bellii*

Range Chiefly southwestern Nearctic in United States and northern Mexico, breeding east to central Indiana and southwestern Ohio (1968). Winters from Mexico to Nicaragua. Vagrant in New Hampshire, New York (Long Island), and New Jersey.

Status Casual vagrant.

Occurrence Two documented records for this dull-colored species are: (1) One caught in a mistnet, banded, color photographed, and released by Wilcox 25 Sep 1959 Tiana Beach, Suffolk Co. (Buckley and Post 1970). Corroboration was made by Eisenmann and Bull by comparing the color slide with museum skins; ph on file AMNH collection. (2) One collected on 26 Sep 1970 RMSP (Ford) USNM 566493.

Remarks There are no recent records of this species for NY or adjoining states except for one photographed at Cape May, NJ 30 Oct–3 Nov 1994 (Halliwell 1995) and another at the same place 3–11 Dec 1996 (E. Salzman, pers. comm.) Field identification can be difficult. For an excellent overall discussion of this species, including several other "probables," see Buckley and Post 1970 and Buckley 1979a.

Joan L. Quinlan and John J. Fritz

Blue-headed Vireo   *Vireo solitarius*

Range Nearctic, breeding from northeastern British Columbia east in Canada to Newfoundland and south, in the west, through the higher mountains to El Salvador, and in the east to northern New Jersey and in the mountains to northern Georgia. Winters from the Gulf Coast states south to Guatemala.

Status Fairly common breeder at higher elevations in the Adirondacks, Catskills, and the Tug Hill Plateau. Local at higher elevations in the hill country elsewhere. Rare breeder in "cold" swamps at lower elevations. Uncommon to fairly common migrant across the state.

Breeding Blue-headed Vireo is a fairly common breeder in mixed evergreen-deciduous forests at considerable elevation. In the Adirondacks,

Eaton (1914) found it breeding on Mt. Marcy up to 3000 ft. In the Tug Hill region of southern Lewis Co., Scheider (1959) counted approximately 28 birds in 14 mi on 10 Jun 1957. It is also a known breeder in Allegany SP, at the higher elevations in Allegany and Cattaraugus counties, in the Finger Lakes hill country, and at higher elevations farther east. There is no breeding evidence for NYC and LI and little for the Great Lakes Plain. BBS data 1979–1994 showed some increase in population. Atlas workers found it to be widespread, with some breeding evidence in 35% of the blocks and some range expansion, presumably due to reforestation of higher elevation agricultural lands.

Nonbreeding With the exception of the Red-eyed Vireo, it is the most common member of the genus during migration. It is the earliest vireo to arrive in the spring and the latest to depart in fall. Statewide spring arrival dates range from 18 Apr to 28 Apr. Spring arrival is usually somewhat earlier downstate than upstate, and fall departure is often later. Statewide fall departure dates range from 8 Oct to 15 Oct. In 30 years of CBC data there are only two records of this species, both in the southern part of the state. There are two early Dec reports: 6 Dec 1992 Pelham Bay, Bronx Co. (KB 43:163) and 3 Dec 1988 RMSP (AB 43:292).

Spring maxima: 39 Buffalo area, Erie Co. 21 May 1993; 15 De Witt, Onondaga Co. 2 May 1992; 13 banded, Fire I., Suffolk Co. 9 May 1970. *Fall maxima:* 20 Prospect Park, Kings Co. 15 Oct 1947; 12 Jamestown, Chautauqua Co. 14 Sep 1957. *Extreme dates: Coastal:* 8 Apr, 2 Jun, and 6 Dec. *Inland:* 15 Apr.

Remarks The Forty-first supplement to the AOU Check-list (1997) split *V. solitarius* into three species: *V. solitarius*, Blue-headed Vireo; *V. cassinii*, Cassin's Vireo; and *V. plumbeus*, Plumbeous Vireo. There is no evidence that *cassinii* and *plumbeus* have occurred in NY.
Robert G. McKinney

Yellow-throated Vireo *Vireo flavifrons*

Range Eastern Nearctic, breeding from southern Manitoba across southern Canada and northern New England, south to Texas and central Florida. Winters chiefly from southern Mexico to northern South America.

Status Locally common breeder at lower elevations in western and central NY and the Hudson Valley; uncommon and local in the north and on LI. Uncommon to fairly common migrant upstate; uncommon near the coast.

Breeding During the nineteenth century, this species was rarer in the state than the White-eyed Vireo (DeKay 1844), but today it is much the more common and widespread bird. Originally a species of riparian woodlands, it has a primarily Midwestern and Piedmont range, preferring open, mature stands of trees with spreading crowns, conditions associated with riverine forests but which can also be found in mature woodlots next to open meadows, orchards, suburban gardens, and even village streets.

It spread to NY from its Midwestern strongholds at the end of the nineteenth century (Eaton 1914) and reached high population levels in western NY, on the shore of the Great Lakes, in the Finger Lakes region and along the Southern Tier (Eaton 1914; Axtell 1947; Benton 1949; Rosche 1967; Bull 1974). By the mid-twentieth century it had decreased in many areas (Temple and Temple 1976), but in the last two decades it recovered much of its former territory and even extended its range in the St. Lawrence region (Robbins et al. 1986; Atlas 1988). Bull (1976) described it as more numerous in the Finger Lakes region than in the southeast, but Atlas workers found it in a broad band running from north-west to southeast, mostly east of the Genesee R. and south of the Mohawk R., with the highest density of Confirmed blocks in the lower Hudson Valley. It is also found on the edges of the LI moraine, where it appears to be increasing. There is a single breeding record from SI in 1913 (Siebenheller 1981).

It is particularly susceptible to environmental change, including alterations to its habitat and fluctuations in its principal prey, various species of Lepidoptera, which are known for their periodic population cycles (McAtee 1926). Other population shifts have been attributed to the disappearance of its preferred nest tree, the American elm (Temple and Temple 1976), and to the effects of an increased and then decreased use of pesticides. It is also affected by forest fragmentation, with resulting high levels of brood parasitism by the Brown-headed Cowbird (Whitcomb et al. 1981). These explanations, by no means mutually exclusive, may shed light on this species' decline from historical population levels, but they are less useful in explaining its apparent, if partial and erratic, recovery.

Nonbreeding According to Bull (1974), this species decreased as a migrant after 1900, becoming uncommon upstate, rare and erratic near the coast. Since 1974 it has increased both on the coast and upstate. It appears to migrate mostly west of the Appalachians and is most common today in western and central NY. There are several late Sep and early Oct records for the northern part of the state. It is now an uncommon migrant near the coast, most often seen in spring, when it appears regularly in the NYC parks and across LI.

Maxima: 22 Onondaga Co. 14 May 1970; 8 Boonville, Oneida Co. 20 Sep 1964. *Extreme dates: Coastal:* 4 Apr and 12 Nov. *Upstate:* 27 Apr and 9 Oct. Regularly arrives in late Apr and generally departs in early Oct.

Eric Salzman

Warbling Vireo   *Vireo gilvus*

Range Nearctic and Neotropical, breeding from southeastern Alaska and across central and southern Canada south, in the west to southern California and western Texas, and east of the Rockies to the northern and central portions of the Gulf states, the highlands of Tennessee and North Carolina, and the coastal plain of Virginia (rare); also in Mexico. Winters from Mexico to Guatemala and El Salvador.

Status Common breeder and migrant throughout the state but uncommon on the Coastal Lowlands and absent at high altitudes.

Breeding Widespread breeder, favoring open deciduous woods, whether it be in rural areas or suburbia. In general, this vireo's breeding range extends statewide, except at high elevations. It is essentially absent from the Adirondack High Peaks, the Central Adirondacks, the Eastern and Western Adirondack foothills, the Central Tug Hill, much of the Catskill Peaks, the Delaware Hills, and the Allegany Hills (Atlas 1988). During the Atlas period it was found to be of limited distribution on the Coastal Lowlands for reasons not understood, being found only on the North Shore of LI. From 1991 to at least 1996, however, it did breed in HLSP (E. Levine, pers. comm.).

It seems to be holding its own in rural areas but elsewhere is declining owing to development and pesticide use. Because it is essentially an edge nester, preferring tall trees bordering streams, lakes, and golf courses, it is particularly vulnerable to cowbird parasitism.

Nonbreeding Most authors consider the Warbling Vireo an uncommon migrant, but given its widespread distribution this concept may have to be reevaluated. This perception may be attributed to its dull coloration and retiring habits. By late Apr the first arrivals can be found in the southern portions of the state, and in the fall most birds depart in Sep for their wintering grounds in Central America. An unusual observation of a bird in Region 8 on 3 Apr 1976 is the earliest arrival date. The latest departure dates are 30 Oct (coastal) and 7 Nov (inland).

Remarks In fall when it is not singing, and given its propensity for foraging in the upper foliage, it is certainly overlooked, making migration data unreliable. In the spring however, this drabbest of our vireos makes up for its lack of beauty by its melodious finchlike song.
John J. Fritz and Joan L. Quinlan

Philadelphia Vireo   *Vireo philadelphicus*

Range Nearctic, breeding from northeastern British Columbia and North Dakota east to central Quebec, New Brunswick, and southwestern Newfoundland, and in the northern mountains of New York, Vermont,

New Hampshire, and central Maine. Winters from Mexico to northwestern Colombia. Migrates in spring chiefly through the Mississippi Valley; in fall east of the Appalachians.

Status Very rare breeder in the Adirondacks. Rare to uncommon migrant, more common in the western portion of the state.

Breeding NY is at the southern edge of the Philadelphia Vireo's breeding range. Even in its restricted breeding ground of second-growth hardwoods of the Tug Hill Plateau and Adirondacks, where nesting usually occurs at elevations of 1500–2600 ft, it is uncommon. Suitable habitat was created around the turn of the century by extensive clear-cutting and severe forest fires. These factors led to increased breeding in a state that previously held scant evidence of this activity. Before 1980 there were only 12 documented records of breeding in the three northern counties of Franklin, Essex, and Hamilton. Six years of Atlas fieldwork produced only 11 Confirmed records, in those and St. Lawrence counties. Curtailment of massive logging operations in the Adirondacks and more-effective fire control procedures have allowed much of the forest to reach climax, a factor that alters the landscape preferred by breeding Philadelphia Vireos. With the gradual abandonment of farmland, however, suitable nesting habitat is being created outside of the Adirondacks once again.

Nonbreeding The sighting of Philadelphia Vireo during migration is not an everyday occurrence. Especially rare are spring encounters in the southeastern portion of the state. Therefore, seven sightings on Fire I. on 19 May 1996 (KB 46:286) were extraordinary. This unusual occurrence coincided with one of two outstanding passerine fallouts that took place during the 1996 spring migration.

The four-week period from mid-May to mid-Jun is when the major spring migration takes place. The earliest known arrival date is 20 Apr 1993, with a bird recorded at the Kestrel Haven Farm banding station in Region 3 (KB 43:227). Return migration begins in the latter part of Aug and continues into Oct along the coast, when it is unusual to encounter more than one bird a day. An outstanding late record was of a bird found lingering at Riis Park, Queens Co. on 7 Nov 1971. It is rarely seen in multiples, so the record of 10 banded at the Fire I. Lighthouse, Suffolk Co. 20 Sep 1970 is unique.

Remarks This vireo, slightly more colorful than the Warbling Vireo, is not readily identified by casual birders. Its song is similar to the Red-eyed Vireo's, and when seen it is occasionally mistaken for a fall Tennessee Warbler. These factors could lead to many birds' passing through the state undetected.

Joan L. Quinlan and John J. Fritz

Red-eyed Vireo *Vireo olivaceus*

Range Nearctic, breeding from northern British Columbia to southern Newfoundland and south, in the east, to eastern Texas, the Gulf Coast, and Florida. Winters in South America in the Amazon basin.

Status Very widespread breeder. Common to very common migrant.

Breeding The most widespread and numerous woodland breeding bird in NY, its distribution is limited only by the lack of deciduous trees. It has been recorded at above 4000 ft in the Adirondacks, at sea level on LI, in orchards, city parks, large gardens and shady streets, and in virtually all deciduous and mixed woodlands. It is absent only from dense conifer forests and treeless urban and agricultural areas.

The early status of this species is difficult to determine from the historical record. There is every indication that it underwent vast population increases after the eastern forest was logged in the nineteenth century and subsequently regenerated. The distribution of this bird—as described by Eaton in 1914, by Bull in 1974, in the Atlas of 1988, in the BBS (Robbins et al. 1986), and in reports in *The Kingbird* 1954–1995—is fundamentally unchanged, confirming the continuing dominance of this species in the deciduous forests of NY.

Atlas workers found it to be a widespread Confirmed or Probable breeder even in NYC and on LI, where decreases due to habitat destruction had previously been reported (Cruickshank 1942; Siebenheller 1981). It is a common breeder in all deciduous and mixed forests in the pine barrens, in North Shore wooded areas from Queens to Plum and Fishers islands, along the South Shore to Montauk and in four of the five city boroughs.

Local fluctuations have also been attributed to outbreaks and declines in insect populations as well as to cowbird parasitism; this is the second most victimized species in the state after Yellow Warbler.

Nonbreeding It is a common spring migrant from late Apr to early Jun, generally peaking in the latter part of May. Its return flight is more extended, with movements recorded from the end of Aug to mid-Oct or later. As is the case with a number of insectivorous Neotropical migrants, this species is being seen both earlier and later than in past years. Bull described the bird as casual before May and rare before mid-May and after mid-Oct, but reports from Apr and late Oct are now relatively common downstate and increasing upstate. The earliest published arrival dates are 11 Apr (coastal) and 27 Apr (inland). There is an extraordinary report of a bird at a feeder in New City, Rockland Co. on 23 Jan 1985, following a very warm early winter season, and another on 27 Nov 1952 in Rochester, Monroe Co.

Spring maxima: 60 Syracuse, Onondaga Co. 6 Jun 1956, illustrating the lateness of the spring flight; 50 Prospect Park, Kings Co. 17 May 1945.

Fall maxima: 91 struck the Fire I. Lighthouse, Suffolk Co. 23 Sep 1887; 59 banded, Fire I. Lighthouse 1 Sep 1970; 50 Selkirk Shores SP, Oswego Co. 30 Aug 1966.

Eric Salzman

JAYS, MAGPIES, AND CROWS—CORVIDAE

Gray Jay *Perisoreus canadensis*

Range Northern Nearctic, breeding from Alaska to Newfoundland and south, in the west, to the mountains of California, Arizona, and New Mexico, but in the east only to extreme northern portions of the United States from the Dakotas to New England. Winters throughout the breeding range and irregularly south to northwestern Nebraska and east to southern New England.

Status A fairly common sedentary Adirondack resident, rarely found elsewhere, even during so-called flight years.

Breeding Restricted to the black spruce–balsam fir–northern hardwoods of the Central Adirondacks and Western Adirondack Foothills, it is rare in the High Peaks section of Essex Co. (Atlas 1988). Bull (1974) listed 18 locations in six Adirondack counties, including Clinton, where no Gray Jays were found during Atlas work. Warren (1979) said it was once fairly common there, but today it is an accidental winter visitant. It probably breeds in many more locations than found in the Atlas, whose map suggests there are several disjunct populations, a suggestion which may not be entirely accurate. The species tends to favor boreal spruce forest and is replaced by the Blue Jay where balsam fir dominates (Erskine 1977). The Atlas concluded that the distribution today was determined by the loss of habitat from railroad fires in the late 1890s and early 1900s and the replanting of those large burned-over areas to red and Scotch pines in southern Franklin Co. and further suggested that the continued removal of softwoods by later logging may explain the separation of the High Peaks population. The reason for the low numbers in the High Peaks, however, is still unclear.

Adults travel in pairs, sometimes in family groups, until they nest in Mar and early Apr; pairs mate for life. They cache food or inedibles in tree crotches, on tree branches between twigs, and under bark, using a sticky saliva they produce (Strickland and Ouellet 1993). They are excellent mimics, particularly of their predators, and can be very raucous or very stealthy and quiet. They regularly feed on carrion, and adults and young cast pellets of insect chitin or seeds and can carry food in their feet after transfer from the bill. A dominant juvenile expels brood members from the natal territory at about 55–65 days of age (Strickland and Ouellet 1993). NY birds are warier than those in ON and PQ and do not readily come to people for food handouts since this is a learned behavior. They do come to camps after encouragement (J. M. C. Peterson, pers. comm.). Peterson states that they will find you before you see them and advises that, when looking for them, it pays to look behind you quite often and even to walk backward at times since they will quietly follow (KB 38:273).

The first recorded NY nest, a used one, was found during Atlas work at Long Pond outlet, St. Lawrence Co. 26 Jul 1983 by Medd and Mulligan (Atlas 1988; J. Ozard, pers. comm.).

Maxima: 15 Keese Mill Road, Franklin Co. 3 Sep 1988; 12+ Madawaska, Franklin Co. 11 Jun 1988; 7 (1 adult and 4 begging young plus a second adult with 1 young) Sabattis Road Bog, Hamilton Co. 21 Jun 1986; 5 Ferd's Bog, Hamilton Co. 2 May 1987; 5 (2 adults and 3 juveniles) Streeter L. Bog, St. Lawrence Co. 29 May 1994.

Nonbreeding Bull (1974) listed only a few records away from the breeding range, but since then there have been many more, probably reflecting an increase in observers. Counties with records, some documented, out of the normal range include: Dutchess (two), Oneida (two), Otsego, Schenectady, Seneca, Sullivan, St. Lawrence (four), Warren, and Westchester.

Maxima: 7 at hunting camps Halfway Brook, Franklin Co. 6 Dec 1982; 7 Saranac L. CBC 28 Dec 1991; 5 Spring Pond Bog, Franklin Co. 15 Nov 1983.

Remarks Flight years occur about once every 20 years, when the birds make irregular east-to-west flights along the north coast of the Gulf of St. Lawrence from mid-Aug to late Oct (Todd 1963; Campbell 1965). The last flight, in winter 1965–1966, consisted, in NY, of Canadian birds from ON and PQ and not the resident Adirondack population (G. Smith and J. M. C. Peterson, pers. comm.).
Lee B. Chamberlaine

Blue Jay *Cyanocitta cristata*

Range Nearctic, breeding throughout eastern and central North America from central Alberta east to southern Quebec and Newfoundland and south to Texas and Florida. Winters within North America, with northern populations regularly migratory, others irregularly so.

Status Resident and migratory. Common to very abundant migrant. Locally common in winter.

Breeding The breeding range has increased significantly during the past century. Whereas before 1900 it was limited primarily to forested areas of the state, the Atlas showed that only three species were reported in more blocks, with the most populous part of the state, the southeastern portion, showing breeding evidence in every block. In a ten-year breeding bird study on LI (1967–1976) Blue Jays were found "in almost all habitats except large fields" (Raynor 1979). In less populated areas, they prefer oak forests but can be found in all types and sizes of woods.

BBS data 1966–1994 showed them maintaining their population during the early period, but experiencing a decrease of 1.4% for the years 1980–1994 (Peterjohn 1995).

Nonbreeding Significant accounts of Blue Jay migrations are reported during the spring, with less dramatic numbers in the fall. Migration dates are difficult to determine because a large population overwinters. At Braddock Bay, Monroe Co. spring counts include 15,000 on 16 May 1986; 10,800 passed Derby Hill, Oswego Co. 25 Apr–31 May 1982.

Representative fall migration numbers include up to 100 a day along the L. Ontario shore Sep 1993; 280 near Ithaca, Tompkins Co. 20 Sep 1994; 2000 Riis Park, Queens Co. 28 Sep 1975.

The winter population in the state is closely linked to the mast crop, showing a significant increase if the acorn crop is not adequate to the north. CBC data show that the Blue Jay is most numerous in the southeast, with consistently highest numbers on the Bronx-Westchester CBC, followed by Central Suffolk. In 1965 and again in 1972 Bronx-Westchester reported 1300 individuals. Central Suffolk reported 1400 in 1966. The East Orange Co. CBC reported more than 500 on counts from 1985 to 1989; the highest was 804 in 1985. To the north and west, numbers rarely reach 500, with the exception of Ithaca, Tompkins Co., which reported more than 500 for four years, the high being 954 in 1981.

Remarks Bull observed on a number of occasions during fall passage that Blue Jays, perhaps more than any other species, become temporarily "confused" at coastal points, hesitating to make a water crossing when they reach the last bit of land. The flocks circle around, mount higher and higher in the air, and fly in the opposite direction from whence they were headed, only to reapproach that water barrier and finally, after one or more attempts, "reluctantly" make the crossing.
Phyllis R. Jones

Black-billed Magpie *Pica pica*

Range Holarctic, in North America breeding, and primarily resident, from southern Alaska to western Ontario and south to central California, western Oklahoma, and western Kansas. Casual or accidental farther east.

Status Very rare vagrant, although difficult to evaluate because of the incidence of released or escaped cage birds.

Occurrence NY records fall into three categories: (1) Suspected escapes such as the one found dead at JFK Airport, Queens Co. on 6 Nov 1990 (KB 41:65) and the individual that wintered at Montauk, Suffolk Co. 17 Nov 1990–3 Mar 1991 (KB 41:132, 218). (2) Possibly wild, uncaged birds (fresh, unworn plumage), all specimens: a female, Orient, Suffolk Co. 20 Dec 1927 (NYSM 25159); a male caught in a mink trap, Island Pond, Orange Co. 14 Nov 1935 (AMNH 300598); a female, Islip, Suffolk Co. 28 Mar 1951 (NYSM 25160). (3) Magpies observed in sustained flight during migration seasons, because well-defined migrations do occur outside the normal range of this species during some years.

Remarks There have been too many observations of this species for them all to have been escapes. A gradual extension of their range eastward is a possibility (Beardslee and Mitchell 1965), and a cluster of records from OH, TN, and NC as well as NY from 1959 to 1961 may well have been examples of this extension (Veit and Petersen 1993). In addition, a few escapes became established and bred in WV and western PA in the 1960s (Leck 1984).
Elizabeth W. Brooks

American Crow *Corvus brachyrhynchos*

Range Nearctic, breeding from north-central British Columbia to southern Newfoundland, south to central Arizona and east to southern Florida. Sedentary and migratory, with northern populations withdrawing southward in winter.

Status Widespread breeder. Common to very abundant migrant and locally abundant to very abundant in winter roosts.

Breeding It was recorded in 93% of Atlas blocks, with Confirmed breeding in half of those. There is virtually no place in the state where the species does not nest. It is most numerous in agricultural areas but is becoming increasingly frequent in suburban and urban locations, reflecting the adaptability of this species to human activities. Small woodlands surrounded by agricultural lands and mature suburban areas with large trees provide nesting opportunities. BBS data showed a significant increase in the abundance of crows 1966–1994, with much of it occurring 1980–1994. Because of their habit of eating eggs and nestlings of songbirds that build open cup nests in tree canopies (e.g., Red-eyed Vireo), the increase in number of crows may contribute to apparent declines in abundance of some songbird species.

Nonbreeding A noticeable spring and fall migration of crows occurs along the south shore of L. Ontario, and large numbers may be observed at winter roosts throughout the state. Bull (1974) reported daily counts of as many as 15,000 in spring along L. Ontario. At least three studies of winter roosting have been done in NY. The first was in the winter of 1932–1933 (Emlen 1938); another was conducted in 1963–1964 (Chamberlain 1964); and a third was completed by C. R. Smith in 1982–1983 (unpublished). The totals reported from these three surveys are: 1932–1933, 215,100; 1963–1964, 46,307; 1982–1983, 52,110. Emlen (1938) reported that the largest roost in his study contained an estimated 60,000, while the largest roost reported for the 1982–1983 survey was 9000.

In general, as compared with roosts in the 1930s, in recent times, it appears that winter roosts are smaller but there are more of them. However, CBC data showed an increasing trend since at least 1974, with the greatest numbers and largest roosts found in the southeastern part of NY during midwinter.

Changing land use patterns since 1932 (Caslick 1975; Nicholson 1985; Marks et al. 1992; B. E. Smith et al. 1993), with more small woodlots today than 50 years ago, may have provided increased roosting opportunities in winter, leading to more widely dispersed roosts. In addition, the pattern of reversion of agricultural land to shrubland and small woodlots may have reduced winter foraging opportunities for crows. Today's pattern is one of fewer American Crows, more widely dispersed throughout the state in winter, and occurring in smaller winter roosts today than 60 years ago, although they appear to have been increasing since the early 1970s.

Remarks The American Crow has not always been numerous and widespread. Describing a summer trip along the east side of Seneca L. in 1810, traveling from Ithaca to near Geneva, De Witt Clinton noted, "On our way we saw an eagle, cranes, and several ravens, as black, and at least twice as large as crows, of which latter there are none in this country" (Campbell 1849). Clinton was a keen observer and student of natural history, as reflected in other written accounts of his careful observations in NY (Webster 1980). In 1810, the westward expansion of development for agriculture in NY was just beginning and continued through the nineteenth century (Hedrick 1966), providing opportunities for crows to expand their range into NY, with the retreat of the Common Raven into the remoter regions of the state.

It is likely that the number of crows reported by Emlen (1938) was near the peak of the species' abundance in NY, just before the widespread decline of agriculture began in earnest, in the wake of the Great Depression. Now, in the Finger Lakes Region, we are witnessing the return of the raven, and crows still are numerous. Crows have been observed mobbing ravens in winter, in much the same manner they would mob a Red-tailed Hawk or a Great Horned Owl. However, when feeding on the ground at a deer carcass in winter, ravens clearly are able to hold their own against harassment by crows (pers. obs.). Future observations of interactions of ravens and crows would be of interest as the raven begins to reclaim parts of its former range, now occupied by the crow.

Though they once were widely persecuted at all times of the year as a nuisance species, largely because of their damage to agricultural crops, crows now benefit from a degree of federal protection and a "closed season" from mid-Apr until mid-Sep each year in NY. This policy resulted from amendment of the Federal Migratory Bird Treaty between the United States and Mexico in 1972, when Mexico insisted on extending protection to the Corvidae in order to protect rare species of Mexican jays. The recent increases in numbers and expansion into suburbia may have resulted in part from the crow's protected status in NY since 1972.
Charles R. Smith

Fish Crow   *Corvus ossifragus*

Range Southeastern Nearctic, resident along the Atlantic Coast from Massachusetts to Florida, along the Gulf Coast to Texas, and along the major eastern river valleys.

Status Common and increasing resident on LI, in NYC, and in the tidal portions of the Hudson Valley. Uncommon local resident, but increasing in central NY.

Breeding The Fish Crow, a predominantly southern coastal species, has been slowly colonizing NY for at least a century, a process that appears to be continuing through the 1990s. Unmentioned by Giraud in the mid-nineteenth century, it appeared in the NYC area late in that century and, by the early twentieth, was breeding on the edges of LI Sound, north in the Hudson Valley to Orange and, occasionally, Dutchess counties (Eaton 1914; Griscom 1923, 1933). By the 1920s, it was breeding at "scattered locations along the South Shore" (Cruickshank 1942). In 1964, Bull described it as "fairly common" around LI Sound, NYC waterways, and in the lower Hudson. In 1974 he was still calling it "very local and decidedly uncommon" on the South Shore of LI during breeding season but "frequent as a breeder" on SI, on the North Shore of LI, on the mainland opposite in Westchester Co., and in the Hudson Valley to Dutchess and Ulster counties. Atlas workers in the first half of the 1980s found this species to be very widespread in those areas, with significant concentrations and Confirmed nesting in all coastal and estuarine locations, including the South Shore and well inland along pine-barrens rivers on LI, in NYC, and in Westchester Co. In general it was breeding in pines and other conifers, often in isolated pairs away from the immediate coast. Breeding was also Confirmed in a narrow band up the Hudson Valley, now reaching north to Castleton and East Greenbush, Rensselaer Co.

It was long thought that the limits of tidewater in Rensselaer and Albany counties would prevent the further expansion inland and northward of a species associated with southern coastal estuaries, but, remarkably, breeding was also Confirmed by Atlas workers in Ithaca, Tompkins Co., where the birds have occurred regularly since 1974. Nesting was also suspected near the Susquehanna R. in Vestal, Broome Co. All these birds were thought to have entered the state through the Susquehanna R. valley (Bull 1976; Atlas 1988).

Throughout the 1980s and 1990s, Fish Crows continued to increase on the South Shore and East End of LI, where, however, they often continue to nest in isolated pairs rather than in the small colonies reported elsewhere (Atlas 1988; pers. obs.). A pair fledged two young in Central Park, Manhattan in 1986 and is believed to have nested there in subsequent years (KB 37:170). Since 1985, this species has also continued to increase in Regions 3 and 4, and possible nesting has now been reported in the Oneida L. area near Syracuse in Region 5, as well as in the following localities in Region 8: near the Mohawk R. in Schenectady Co.; in Saratoga Springs, Saratoga Co.; and near Sacandaga Reservoir, Mayfield, Fulton Co. (KB 45:208, 225, 320). It is possible that these records, mostly outside the Hudson Valley proper, represent a continuing influx from the Delaware-Susquehanna system, where the birds have followed fresh rather than salt waterways.

Nonbreeding Although Bull treated this species as a "partial migrant," it is resident throughout its southern range, and evidence for a migratory population in NY is lacking. The notable expansion of this species as a breeding bird in coastal areas, up the Hudson Valley, and in central NY, has produced corresponding increases in fall, winter, and early spring reports in these same general locations.

Maxima: The vast Fresh Kill, Richmond Co. garbage dump and landfill has accounted for unprecedented numbers on recent CBCs. There were 5121 on 17 Dec 1994, 8063 on 16 Dec 1995, and a mere 3500 on this same CBC Dec 1996 (P. Buckley, in litt.). Previously, the largest assemblage noted in the state was 500–600 at Belmont L., Suffolk Co. 29 Nov 1983 (KB 34:71). Compare the Fresh Kill numbers with such historical maxima as 175 East Hampton, Suffolk Co. 31 Mar 1914; 299 East Hampton 30 Aug 1922. Upstate highs include: 20 Colonie, Albany Co. 4 Nov 1994; 11 Ithaca, Tompkins Co. 14 Nov 1994. Upstate winter records are mostly recent: 20 Simmons I.–Peebles I. SP, Saratoga Co. 19 Feb 1995; 8 Ithaca CBC 1 Jan 1995. The smaller numbers reported in early spring, 6 in Chenango Valley SP, Broome Co. 13 Mar 1995 being a typical report, probably represent local breeding populations. Note that virtually all reports of this species are confined to those areas in the Susquehanna and Chenango river valleys, Cayuga and Oneida lake basins, Mohawk and

Hudson river valleys, and coastal regions where these birds are known or believed to breed.

Remarks Fish Crow has been expanding for some time in the Mississippi R. system north to IL and IN and west to OK; it has also colonized southeastern river systems for considerable distances inland.

For the difficulties in separating Fish Crow from American Crow in the field, see Bull 1974 and Madge 1994. Essentially, the two species cannot be told apart except by voice, and confusion with the calls of young American Crows is possible in the late spring and early summer.
Eric Salzman

Common Raven *Corvus corax*

Range Holarctic, widespread resident in western North America, but in the east more restricted to the boreal forests from Greenland and arctic Canada south to Maine and northern New England, New York, and in the Appalachians, to northern Georgia. Formerly also along the coast from southern New Jersey to Virginia.

Status Common resident in the Adirondacks, uncommon to rare elsewhere but increasing. Sedentary and migratory.

Breeding The raven is thought to have been widely distributed over the state before the virgin forest was eliminated, but it had become very scarce in the nineteenth century, and Eaton (1914) reported it restricted, in constantly diminishing numbers, to the western Adirondack region. No further documented breeding was observed until 1 Jun 1968, when Carleton and Chase found a nest with three young on a cliff opposite Chapel Pond, Essex Co. In the early 1970s three nests were found, two in Essex Co. and one in Hamilton Co. It is on the NYSDEC's list as a Species of Special Concern but has been recommended for delisting.

The Atlas described the raven as fairly common in the Adirondacks and uncommon to local in other parts of the state; reestablishment began in the 1970s, with about 500 sightings 1970–1979 (Bishop 1980). Further range expansion could be expected as forest cover increased and matured. The Atlas located the species in 313 blocks and Confirmed breeding in 14 blocks in the Adirondacks and L. Champlain Valley and in two blocks in the Catskill Peaks. Probable breeding was listed in the Taconic Highlands, Tug Hill Transition, and Appalachian Plateau.

Since the Atlas, the species has expanded its range suddenly and dramatically and may be found almost anywhere in the state. Most nesting sites are on cliff faces, some are in mature red pine plantations (KB 38:190), and they frequently are found on large tracts of public lands such as WMAs,

SPs, state forests, and forest preserves. It has attempted to nest on human-made structures such as a light tower at a stadium in Elmira, Chemung Co. (KB 41:163). No longer a wilderness species, it has nested just outside of Albany (KB 37:165), as far south as near the Hudson R. in Ulster Co., and east of the river in Dutchess Co. in 1992 (KB 42:196). It is resident and increasing in Putnam Co., with suspected nesting (KB 43:344), and just over the county line in Westchester.

The reasons for the rapid recovery of the species statewide are probably the reforestation of much cleared land; maturation of existing forests; an increasing deer herd and associated increase in road kills; increased coyote numbers, with coyote predation as a food source; and changes in public attitude (Bishop 1980). Further range expansion and filling in of unoccupied areas is expected to continue as forest cover increases and matures. Suitable nesting locations will be a limiting factor.

Nonbreeding It is quite often seen at all inland fall and spring hawkwatch sites in the state. It is also associated with garbage landfills, particularly in the winter (KB 42:35, 43:146, 44:151); closure of the Old Forge dump, Herkimer Co. reduced the numbers visiting this site in 1993 (KB 43:329). Often spotted feeding on deer innards or carcasses from hunting, road kill, or winter starvation, it is also occasionally seen at feeders (KB 40:122, 41:206, 44:58). It is rarely reported in Region 10, but two at Cold Spring Harbor, Nassau Co. 16 Apr 1994 (A. Wilson, in litt.) may foreshadow things to come. In winters of heavy finch invasions it has been seen patrolling highways to pick up road-killed crossbills and siskins (KB 40:116).

Maxima: In the Central Adirondacks, 150 at well-supplied suet feeders at Six Nation Indian Museum, Onchiota, Franklin Co. winter 1991–1992; 75–150 pairs in display flight Rattlesnake Mtn.–Mt. Discovery, Essex Co. 27 Sep 1992. In the Champlain Valley, 55 at Essex landfill, Essex Co. 26 Dec 1992. In the Tug Hill, 12 Osceola, Lewis Co. 1 Nov 1992. In the Catskills, 14 in a kettle, Sullivan Co. 4 Jan 1991. In the lower Hudson Valley, 4 Putnam Co. CBC 1 Jan 1994. On the Appalachian Plateau, 5 (2 adults and 3 young) Ward, Allegany Co. summer 1992.

Remarks The raven's changing status in adjacent states resembles its status in NY. It first nested in CT in 1987, with six nest sites in summer 1991 (AB 45:1096); 18 birds were in Canaan, in the northwestern part of the state, winter 1993–1994 (NASFN 48:183). Twenty nest sites had been located in MA by summer 1991 (AB 45:1096). Two different nests were found in NJ in 1993 and 1994 (NASFN 48:282), with two young from the 1994 nest successfully fledged (NASFN 48:929).
Lee B. Chamberlaine

LARKS—ALAUDIDAE

Sky Lark *Alauda arvensis*

Range Palearctic, breeding across northern Eurasia south to northwestern Africa and east to Japan. Winters in the southern portion of breeding range. Introduced into New York, Vancouver Island, Hawaii, Australia, and New Zealand.

Status Introduced but extirpated by 1913.

Occurrence A bird of open grassland, it was introduced in Brooklyn in 1887, especially the sections of Flatbush and Flatlands. It was well established by 1898 and was still present in numbers in 1907. Destruction of open land throughout this area caused it to disappear by 1913. Three specimens, all extant, were taken in Flatbush. Two fledglings in 1887, one on 13 Jun, the other on 1 Jul, and an adult on 22 Feb 1888 (all by Marshall) are AMNH 68248, 68249, and 65319, respectively. In addition, a nest and eggs were collected on 28 Jul 1895 (Proctor) AMNH collection. On 14 Jul 1887, Marshall found a nest in Flatbush that contained five half-grown young being fed by an adult. The nest was situated in a tuft of grass in a "long-grass field." The introduction of the species in the lower Hudson Valley was also unsuccessful.

Stanley R. Lincoln

Horned Lark *Eremophila alpestris*

Range Holarctic, breeding, in North America, from northern Alaska to Newfoundland and south nearly throughout except absent from the Gulf Coast and Florida regions. Winters throughout the breeding range, except for the northernmost areas, and south to the Gulf Coast and southern Florida.

Status Locally common breeder, especially in agricultural areas, throughout the state, but rare to absent at higher elevations. Very common to abundant migrant and winter visitant.

Breeding It is the earliest nester of any native NY songbird, with breeding concentrated on LI and in western NY, west and south of Oneida L. The Atlas showed distribution over 21% of the state. BBS data 1966–1994 exhibit an annual decline of 5.7%.

Its establishment as a breeding species in the northeastern states in the wake of settlement and clearing of land for agriculture is documented by Bull (1974) and well described by Eaton (1914) and Bent (1942). The species has adapted well to modern agriculture, often nesting and fledging young before fields are planted and continuing to occupy pastures and fields planted to corn, beans, and potatoes well into midsummer. Like that of many other species of grasslands and open spaces, its gradual decline coincides with patterns of declining agriculture and regrowth of forests described by other researchers (Caslick 1975; Nicholson 1985; Marks et al. 1992; B. E. Smith et al. 1993), and it has been recommended that it be added to the NYSDEC list of Species of Special Concern.

Nonbreeding Large, nomadic flocks may be seen from Nov to Mar, along the coast of LI and inland, especially along the Great Lakes Plain. They occur most often in open, rural, agricultural areas, foraging in both plowed and uncultivated fields. In suburban areas, beaches, golf courses, and airports are used. CBC data from 1960 to 1989 show that annual totals in excess of 5000 birds across the state are not uncommon, and individual counts in excess of 1000 birds have been reported from the Oak Orchard (1981), Letchworth (1986), and Chatham (1967, 1981) CBCs.

Remarks Two subspecies occur in NY. The breeding form is *praticola*, the "Prairie" Horned Lark; transient and winter birds typically represent the "Northern" Horned Lark, *alpestris*. These two subspecies usually can be separated in the field, with optimum birds. With such individuals, *praticola* will show a white supercilium, but possibly some yellow in the throat, whereas *alpestris* will be yellow in both areas.
Charles R. Smith

SWALLOWS—HIRUNDINIDAE

Purple Martin *Progne subis*

Range Nearctic, breeding from south-central Canada to northern Mexico and the Gulf states; absent from higher mountains in the west. Winters in northern South America to Bolivia and southeastern Brazil.

Status Locally common but widespread breeder at lower elevations. Locally abundant migrant, locally very abundant in late summer roosts.

Breeding A colonial breeder and aerial insectivore, nesting near and feeding over wetlands, its breeding is concentrated along major rivers, lake shores, and coasts, especially the shores of Lakes Erie, Ontario, Oneida, and Champlain, the Finger Lakes, and LI. Recorded in 963 Atlas blocks (18%) and Confirmed in 614, it is generally absent from areas of the Adirondacks, Catskills, and Tug Hill Plateau higher than 1000 ft in elevation. It nested historically in crevices and cornices of buildings in major cities, and continued doing so into the early 1970s in Buffalo. Current breeding is dependent on martin houses and prevention of nest competition by the Tree Swallow, European Starling, and House Sparrow (Atlas 1988).

Populations have decreased markedly in recent decades. On 18 BBSs in the Niagara Frontier, breeding martins decreased 67% during 1967–1993 (KB 43:312). Eaton and Eaton (1990) reported on censuses at

Canandaigua L., Ontario Co. and reviewed evidence and causes of nesting failure in NY. They attributed the low population in 1967, and a 74% decline in breeding pairs between 1968 and 1989, primarily to repeated cold and wet nesting seasons. Benton and Tucker (KB 18:71) reported similar declines in western NY following the cold, wet spring of 1966. In addition, loss of wetlands bodes ill for the future of the Purple Martin.

Nonbreeding The mean spring arrival date is 10 Apr, ranging from 29 Mar on the coast and 2 Apr in the Niagara Frontier to 29 Apr in the Adirondacks. Fall flights take place from late Aug through Sep. Away from breeding localities, Purple Martins are rare migrants but very abundant at key staging areas, and spectacular tree roosts are found from late Aug through Sep. Since 1980, numbers are 10–90% smaller than those of the past. In addition to deterioration of habitat in North America, migrants face loss of wintering habitat in Brazil.

   Spring maxima: 1000 Derby Hill, Oswego Co. 26 Apr 1960. *Fall maxima:* 2000 Lake Ronkonkoma, Suffolk Co. 30 Aug 1952; 1000 INWR 23 Aug 1993. *Roosts:* 100,000 Jamestown, Chautauqua Co. 29 Aug 1960, decreasing to just 200 on 23 Sep; 100,000 Strawberry I., Erie Co. 30 Aug 1970; 35,000 Buffalo, Erie Co. 25 Aug 1978; 6000–10,000, Niagara R. 23 Sep 1991. *Extreme dates:* 24 Feb (1996) Bridgehampton, Suffolk Co. and 28 Oct. Ordinarily rare before mid-Apr and after Sep.
Kenneth L. Crowell

Tree Swallow   *Tachycineta bicolor*

Range Nearctic, breeding widely from Alaska and Labrador south to southern California and southern Maryland. Winters along the coast from Virginia to Florida; also in Cuba and northern Central America.

Status Widespread breeder throughout the state. Common to very abundant migrant, especially in fall along the outer coast. Rare in winter on the coast, and rarer inland.

Breeding Widely distributed, absent only from the innermost areas of NYC, it nests wherever natural or human-made cavities are available, most often in the vicinity of open water. Preferred sites include woodpecker holes and cavities in dead trees in or near lakes, marshes, or wooded swamps, where it can find flying insects on which to feed. Although common in upstate NY at least since the early 1800s, it did not occur in many areas on LI until the early 1900s. Griscom (1923) reported that it was not known to breed in the NYC area, although it was a fairly common though local summer resident of the eastern half of LI. Ten years later, there was only one known breeding locality in Dutchess Co. (Griscom 1933). According to Siebenheller (1981), it did not become a regular breeder on SI until about 1950. It can now be found across most of the state and is missing only from the innermost areas of NYC (Atlas 1988). It is more numerous upstate, reaching maximum numbers in the eastern Ontario and St. Lawrence plains. Numbers can vary from year to year because of weather. Severe weather on the wintering grounds in the southern United States can kill thousands, and cold periods during the nesting season can cause high mortality. Eighty-two eggs were frozen in 70 nests in bluebird boxes in Erie and Cattaraugus counties in late May 1992 (KB 42:156).

As with other hole-nesting species that are unable to excavate their own cavities, population size is believed to be limited by the availability of nest sites (Stutchbury and Robertson 1985). The Tree Swallow has benefited from increasing numbers of boxes placed for Eastern Bluebird, as in Allegany Co., where 75 pairs nested in bluebird boxes in 1991 (KB 41:258). The BBS detected no significant trend in NY populations 1966–1994 (Peterjohn 1995).

Nonbreeding This is the first swallow to arrive in the spring, usually appearing by the third week of Mar in much of the state and as late as 1 Apr in the northern regions. Fall departures take place over a longer period, with the last date ranging from early Sep to mid-Nov (or rarely into Dec), but most often in Oct. Extraordinary numbers of Tree Swallows move along the coast in fall, with estimates of 50,000–100,000 or more on the South Shore of LI reported in the mid-1960s. No recently published counts approach those numbers, but "exceptionally large groups of migrant Tree Swallows all fall" were noted in the LI region report for fall 1993 (KB 44:77). Huge tornado-shaped flocks (an estimate of 300,000 by Proctor) were seen diving into their nighttime roost in phragmites near the mouth of the Connecticut R., not far from the eastern end of LI, in mid-Oct 1994. This regularly occurring spectacle occurs near dark and is presumably a way to avoid predation by Merlin and Northern Harrier (R. T. Peterson, pers. comm.).

At inland locations the numbers recorded are smaller but still impressive: 20,000 flying south at Cayuga Marsh in fall 1978 (KB 29:40); 8000 at Sandy Pond, Oswego Co. 21 Sept 1974 (KB 25:46); 7000 at Greece, Monroe Co. 8 Sep 1990 (KB 41:34).

LI CBCs recorded this species in the majority of years between 1965 and 1993, whereas upstate the only CBC records occurred at MNWR in 1960 and 1988 and at Jamestown, Chautauqua Co. in 1978. Jan reports include 13 at JBWR 12 Jan 1992 (KB 42:128) and two Monroe Co. records in 1983: one at Braddock Bay 6 Jan and eight at Spencerport 13–17 Jan (KB 33:119).

Remarks Tree Swallows from the East Coast and Great Lakes areas migrate along the Atlantic Coast to winter in Florida, Cuba, and Central America (Butler 1988), but some are able to winter farther north, including to LI in some years, because of their unusual ability to digest waxy bayberries (*Myrica* sp). Erskine (1979) suggested that in Canada, nest boxes are responsible for just a small proportion of the annual production of young, certainly not enough to counterbalance the loss of natural tree sites due to forest cutting during the past 200 years. It has been suggested that forest management in which dead snags are left standing is extremely important to Tree Swallows (Robertson et al. 1992).

Valerie M. Freer

Northern Rough-winged Swallow *Stelgidopteryx serripennis*

Range Nearctic, breeding from southeastern Alaska and southern Canada south to Baja California, the Middle American highlands, southern Texas, the Gulf Coast, and Florida. Winters from southern Texas and Florida south through Mexico and Central America to Panama.

Status Locally fairly common breeder near water throughout most of the state. Fairly common inland migrant, less common on the coast, where it is rarely reported in the fall. More common both spring and fall in western parts of the state.

Breeding Breeding sites are clustered along the lakes and rivers of the state, with fewer in the Adirondack and St. Lawrence regions. It is not found in NYC and most of Nassau Co. but breeds in many locations in the eastern half of LI (Atlas 1988). It was not recorded in NY before 1870. The first known breeding records came from the lower Hudson Valley and LI in 1872. Since that time it has extended its range northward, following rivers and lake shores, becoming nearly statewide in distribution by 1900, although never abundant anywhere. It was still considered rare and irregular on LI in 1923, and by 1933 in Dutchess Co. it was considered to be uncommon along the Hudson R. but rare and local farther inland (Griscom 1923, 1933). Bull (1974) postulated arrival routes via rivers into the central Adirondacks in the mid-1960s.

Cruickshank (1942) suggested that humans may have played a major role in the recent range expansion of this species by unintentionally providing nest sites in structures or excavations. In a study of 725 nests in Canada, Erskine found that 68% were in natural sites and 32% in human-made sites such as gravel pits, roadcuts, or holes in cement, brick, or stone walls. The human-made sites were most common near the northern edge of the range in ON, where there is the densest human population. About 370 of the natural sites were in BC, where the bird is more common than in NY (Erskine 1979). Turner and Rose (1989) believed that humans have had little impact on its populations but, particularly at the edge of the range, have contributed to its spread.

The BBS did not demonstrate any significant change in the NY population 1966–1994, but the number of routes reporting this species is relatively small (Peterjohn 1995). On a larger scale, the BBS showed the population to be increasing in the eastern and central regions of the United States (Robbins et al. 1986). Population size is probably limited by the availability of suitable nest sites. In Lunk's study (1962) this swallow responded readily to sites intentionally placed for it, building complete nests in 90% of the tubes he inserted in sandpits.

There are no reports of more than two or three pairs nesting near each other in NY.

Nonbreeding It is surprisingly scarce where it does not nest. Spring arrivals of this swallow are regularly noted and reported. The average arrival is from 15 to 21 Apr, and sightings before 10 Apr are uncommon. Fall departures are much less often recorded than are those of the other swallows, perhaps because they are rarely seen in large flocks, because of the difficulty of identification in the fall, or because they leave earlier. Cruickshank (1942) believed that most depart for the South immediately after the breeding season and that a sighting after mid-Aug was exceptional; Lunk (1962) also gave evidence that in MI they leave shortly after nesting is completed. *The Kingbird* records show very few sightings after mid-Sep.

Lunk found no evidence of flocking, but he quoted a record of one flock of 200 in PA on 1 Sep. There are just four published examples of fall flocks in NY, three of which are from the Niagara R., and all probably consisted of birds that nested in Canada, where the species is more numerous. Bull reported 500 on the Niagara R. near Buffalo on 10 Oct 1948 and 150 on 17 Oct 1948; more recently, a flock of 200 was seen at Seneca R. inlet, Seneca Co. on 10 Oct 1976 (KB 27:39) and another of 200 at Goat Island, Niagara R. on 23 Sep 1990 (KB 41:31).

Remarks The Northern Rough-winged Swallow is so named because of the presence of stiff projections on the outer web of the outer primary feathers, straight in the female and recurved in the male. The function of these roughened barbs is unknown, but they may be used to produce a noise during displays (Lunk 1962).
Valerie M. Freer

Bank Swallow   *Riparia riparia*

Range Holarctic, breeding in North America from central Alaska to Newfoundland south to southern California, Tennessee, and Virginia. Winters in South America to Peru and Argentina.

Status Widespread but local breeder. Very common spring migrant inland, less commonly reported along the coast; abundant fall migrant along the L. Ontario Plain.

Breeding Our smallest swallow nests in colonies in river or lake banks or human-made sites often but not exclusively near water. The Atlas demonstrated that they were scattered across the state (in 37% of the blocks), missing only from NYC and portions of the Catskills and Adirondacks. Since they excavate their own burrows, their distribution is dependent upon the availability of exposed banks of soils of proper physical characteristics. Fine soils are preferred to coarse, and fine loamy sands are selected most often (Spencer 1964). In many places in the state, natural sites along river or lake banks are used. Glacial deposits often contain proper material, and where they recently have been exposed by the activities of humans, these swallows are likely to be found. Sloping or overgrown banks are not suitable. Therefore, colony locations, especially in human-made sites such as sand and gravel pits, are used for a few years and then abandoned unless they are newly excavated (Freer 1979).

Colonies may consist of only a half-dozen pairs, but when adequate space is available they may contain large numbers of burrows. Bull (1974) mentioned a colony of 1000 near Falconer, Chautauqua Co. in 1956 and an unusually large colony of at least 2000 pairs near Sandy Pond, Oswego Co. in 1966. More recently, a colony near South Dresden, Yates Co. contained 1000 nests in 1982 and 1983 (KB 32:276, 33:270). *The Kingbird* records since the mid-1980s mention no colonies of more than 100 pairs.

Before the widespread use of mechanized excavation equipment in NY, Bank Swallow colonies must have been restricted for the most part to natural sites along riverbanks, lakesides, and coastal cliffs, and their populations may well have been at a low level. They benefited during this century from the excavation of sandbanks associated with construction and road building, and their numbers may have peaked from the 1950s to the 1970s. Their dependence on humans was shown by Erskine (1979), who found that 40% percent of more than 27,000 nests were in natural sites in Canada and that 60% percent were in human-made sites. The stagnation of the economy along with decreased construction and less excavation of sandpits could well be a factor in their recent decline, as could recent laws requiring landowners to grade inactive sandbanks to a gradual slope. The BBS shows a significant decrease of 4.1% annually in Bank Swallow populations in NY 1966–1994 (Peterjohn 1995). The importance of this decrease is underscored by NY's prominence in their distribution. According to Turner and Rose (1989) the Bank Swallow breeds throughout most of North America but is most abundant in PQ, NB, the St. Lawrence Plain, and the eastern Great Lakes Plain.

Nesting sites are in short supply, and some swallows may be unable to nest because no site is available, as shown by Freer's observations near Ellenville, Ulster Co. On 27 May 1976 a colony of seven nests in a mostly overgrown bank was destroyed by the removal of several truckloads of sand, leaving a large clear vertical surface. The swallows at nearby colonies were well into the nesting cycle, either incubating or just starting to feed young. Within a few days, many appeared from unknown sources and began to dig burrows at the new site. The seven destroyed burrows were replaced by more than 100 new ones. Over 80% of them fledged young (Freer 1977). Late nestings such as this have led some authors to believe that Bank Swallows occasionally produce a second brood. Stoner (1936) is widely quoted on this point. He thought that a few birds produced a second brood but provided no evidence that those that were still feeding young in July had reared an earlier brood. A late first nesting, or renesting after a failed first nest, may be a more likely explanation.

Nonbreeding The average spring arrival is during the third week in Apr. It is rare before 10 Apr. Most birds leave by mid-Aug, and the last stragglers are usually gone by mid-Sep, although there are a few early Oct records. They leave the nesting sites shortly after the young fledge and join others in loose flocks that forage over streams and lakes. The flocks can reach remarkable size. One of 27,000 at Braddock Bay, Monroe Co. on 26 Jul 1969 was said to be "not unusual" (KB 19:216). At the same location on L. Ontario a flock of more than 50,000 on 18 Jul 1980 was said to be a "typical peak concentration" (KB 30:230). Sandy Pond, Oswego Co. is another important gathering place of Bank Swallows. On 11 Aug 1957, 15,000 were seen (KB 7:130), and on 17 Aug 1975, 13,500 were reported (KB 25:223).

By the mid-1980s, however, the flocks were smaller. At Clay Marsh WMA, Onondaga Co. there were 11,000 on 3 Aug 1985 (KB 35:277); 15,000 were seen along the west lake shore of Region 2 on 12 Jul 1986 (KB 36:218). The numbers continued to decline into the 1990s. At Sandy Pond the maximum number seen in 1992 was 830 on 9 Aug (KB 42:253), and at Braddock Bay the 1993 maximum of only 1600 was found on 29 Jul (KB 43:317).

An estimate of 400 at JBSP 28 Aug 1953 is the highest coastal figure known.

Valerie M. Freer

Barn Swallow   *Hirundo rustica*

Range Cosmopolitan, in North America breeding nearly throughout, from southeastern Alaska to southern Newfoundland and south to Mexico and the Gulf states. Winters from Mexico south to South America; also in the Caribbean.

Status Widespread breeder in open areas, common to abundant migrant.

Breeding Barn Swallows breed as single pairs or in small groups in open areas throughout the state, preferring open country such as farmland where buildings are available for nesting and where water is nearby. The mud and straw nest is placed on beams or rafters of open buildings or under bridges. Found in 92% of Atlas blocks, missing only from some urban areas and from forested areas lacking human habitation, especially in parts of the Adirondacks, they usually have two broods a year and often use the same nest for the second brood. They also reuse the nest in successive years (Turner and Rose 1989). Before European settlement, the nests were built in caves or overhanging cliffs, so this swallow was not nearly so common or widespread as it is today. As it adapted to nesting in human habitations, its numbers greatly increased. Nests in natural sites are rare today. A shale outcrop near Lakeview on L. Ontario had several nests in 1967, 1970, and 1971 (ph in Bull 1974) with a maximum of five in 1972. Also in 1972 there were nine nests on shale cliffs in another location about two miles away at Ninemile Point, Oswego Co. (KB 22:181; Speich et al. 1985). A study of nearly 5000 nests in Canada showed only 49 (1%) to be in natural sites (Erskine 1979).

Colonies usually contain only a few pairs, although when nesting conditions are excellent, there can be more. Colonies of 50 or more nests have been recorded (Turner and Rose 1989). From 1979 to 1983 Shields (1984) studied their nesting ecology at Cranberry L. in the Adirondacks, where there were colonies of up to 25 pairs in boathouses. He found that most breeding adults tended to return in subsequent years to previously used colonies and to clusters within colonies, to the same nests, and even to previous mates, if the bird was available.

In an analysis of coloniality in this species, Shields and Crook (1987) could not find any obvious benefits to group living. On the contrary, they found that nest success was lower in the larger colonies because of increased parasitism by blow flies. They concluded that they should be considered "passive aggregators," nesting near each other as a result of shortages of nesting habitat. Unlike their close relative the Cliff Swallow, Barn Swallows are seldom bothered by House Sparrows, which prefer a fully enclosed nest site (Erskine 1979). National BBS data indicated that they were still increasing through 1979 in the eastern region, and the highest counts in North America came from the St. Lawrence Plains (Robbins et al. 1986). More recently, however, the BBS detected a significant decrease of 2.8% per year in NY during 1980–1994 (Peterjohn 1995). The BOS May Count found 2693 Barn Swallows in 1990 (NY data only), but the numbers dropped to 140 in 1991, 134 in 1992, and 101 in 1993 (G. Rising, pers. comm.). Little is known about causes for these decreases. A recent decline is also reported in Britain and much of Europe, but increases are recorded in some other parts of the world (Turner and Rose 1989).

Nonbreeding Barn Swallows arrive early in the spring, on average between 8 and 15 Apr in most of the state, with extremes of 14 Mar (coastal) and 17 Mar (inland). The average departure is usually during the third week of Sep, but sightings in Oct are not uncommon. They are rare after Oct, but there have been a few Nov sightings, and two Dec dates are in the records: 19 Dec 1937 at JBSP and 15 Dec 1980 at JBWR. The mild winter of 1974 produced two remarkable upstate records: two at Ithaca 27–29 Jan and one at Kirkwood, Broome Co. for several days in early Feb.

Maxima: Summer flocks going to roost in the evening can be very large. At Clay Marsh, Onondaga Co. there were estimates of 20,000 on 24 Aug 1965; 30,000 on 5 Aug 1978; 25,000 on 3 Aug 1980; and 12,000 on 3 Aug 1985. Since the mid-1980s much smaller numbers have been recorded there. For example, the maximum for 1995 was 1450 on 9 Aug. On the coast, 25,000 were seen at JBSP 23 Aug 1958. Although no comparable numbers have been recorded there in recent years, flocks of many thousands appear at the beaches every fall (E. Levine, pers. comm.).
Valerie M. Freer

Cliff Swallow   *Petrochelidon pyrrhonota*

Range Nearctic, breeding widely in the west from Alaska to central Mexico and, in the east, more locally from southern Canada to the mountains of North Carolina; near the coast to New Jersey and Delaware, but absent from the coastal plain. Winters in southern South America.

Status Locally common colonial breeder upstate. Common inland migrant, rare to uncommon on the coast.

Breeding Cliff Swallows build a gourd-shaped nest of pellets of mud or clay, which they plaster on a rough surface under a protective overhang. In addition to an appropriate nest location with unobstructed view and flight path, the habitat must contain open areas for foraging, preferably including open water, and a source of mud for nest building.

This swallow was found in 23% of the Atlas blocks, fewer than any swallow except the Purple Martin. Breeding locations are curiously clustered in four main areas: the western Catskills and Delaware Hills, the Tug Hill Transition and Oswego Lowlands, the St. Lawrence Plains and the L. Champlain Valley. Elsewhere they are scattered thinly across the state, with a cluster in the southwest, where they are dramatically increasing (KB 42:235). They are absent from LI, NYC, and Rockland Co., uncommon in the rest of the lower Hudson region and Dutchess Co., and absent from Niagara and most of Erie counties.

Cliff Swallows have always been most numerous in western North America, where cliffs provide nest sites. Bull (1964) knew of only one relatively recent nesting on cliffs, that of six pairs found on a small cliff near Cornwall, Orange Co. in 1932.

Following their acceptance of buildings as nesting sites in the early 1800s, there was a rapid initial spread in range and increase in numbers in the East. As they began to use barns as substitutes for cliffs, they became quite common in portions of the state, but the increase was not uniform. According to Eaton (1914) they were most common in the Catskills and Adirondacks but "where it was very common 40 years ago it has almost disappeared." Griscom (1923) described it as "the rarest of our swallows" in the NYC region. The last recorded breeding on LI was in 1924 at Cutchogue, Suffolk Co. (Bull 1964).

Their nests are very attractive to House Sparrows, which are common around farms, and which usurp the swallow nests. The importance of this competition was shown by Krapu (1986), who found that the swallow population in one area of ND increased at an annual rate of 87% when the local House Sparrows were removed.

Another problem surfaced as old barns with rough siding were replaced with new ones having smooth siding and inadequate roof overhang, resulting in the species' disappearance from many former nesting locations. Dams and highway bridges provide good nest sites, usually without the House Sparrows of farms, and the swallows are now using them with success, once more reversing the population trend in some portions of the state.

Records from dams in the Massena area, St. Lawrence Co. illustrate their importance for this species: 840 nests in 1977 (KB 27:230); 1200 nests in 1979 (KB 29:228); 2000 pairs in 1983 (KB 33:208). Although there is no information on average colony size in NY, most are not that large. In a major study of nest sites in Canada, Erskine (1979) found that colonies there consisted of an average of 30 birds.

Breeding distribution is probably not related to elevation as was thought earlier. The importance of coloniality to this species was demonstrated by Brown (1986). He found that swallows that are unsuccessful on a foraging trip return to the colony, locate a successful forager, and follow that individual to a food source. Thus the colonial habit facilitates finding food.

Nonbreeding Most migrate farther than our other swallows, moving via Central America, Colombia, and Venezuela to spend the winter in southern South America. They are rarely seen in the Caribbean (Turner and Rose 1989). They are often the latest of the swallows to arrive in the spring, and their arrival date is more variable than that of the others. They usually appear during the last week in Apr, although the first sightings can occur any time from early Apr to late May. Most probably leave by the third week in Aug, but fall departure often goes unnoticed, probably because they do not commonly form huge flocks as do some other swallows. A flock of 650 at Robert Moses Power Dam, St. Lawrence Co. on 20 Aug 1992 is the largest reported in recent years, although a few larger flocks were found in the past: 1000 near Lake Placid, Essex Co. 19 Aug 1940 and 800 at Cranberry Lake, St. Lawrence Co. 17 Aug 1957. A record late date was at Sandy Pond, Oswego Co. 18 Oct 1984.

Remarks In the Catskills, the large forest-ringed reservoirs built for NYC provide important new habitat for this species, and incidentally, for Bald Eagles. On the Rondout Reservoir, for example, a Cliff Swallow colony is located under a bridge over a river emptying into the reservoir, and there is another under the eaves of a stone building next to the water at the other end of the reservoir. The birds benefit from the expanse of open water for foraging, the excellent and undisturbed nest sites, and the absence of House Sparrows. Ashokan, Neversink, and other NYC reservoirs in the Catskills also support colonies. The numerous bridges along Route 17 provide many similar sites, also unattractive to House Sparrows because of the forested habitat.

Another and probably less important Catskill site is the resort hotel. For many years the main building at Brown's Hotel served as a successful substitute for a cliff. More recently, at Monticello, Sullivan Co. a strip mall with a roofed-over walkway was used for nesting by these swallows. A shopping center site was also reported at Potsdam, St. Lawrence Co. in 1987 (KB 37:232).

No matter what the location, populations fluctuate dramatically. At Brown's Hotel, for example, there were at least 25 pairs in the 1980s, but in 1995 there were only three or four. The cause of these fluctuations is not known. Brown and Brown (1986) suggested that parasitism is important in this species. They found that in NB the nests can become infested with swallow bugs, which cause the death of significant numbers of nestlings and decrease the likelihood of the use of that site the following year.
Valerie M. Freer

Cave Swallow *Petrochelidon fulva*

Range Nearctic and Neotropical, expanding in North America. Disjunct breeding with populations in the American Southwest, Florida, Mexico, and Greater Antilles. Vagrant north to Canadian Maritime Provinces and Ontario.

Status Accidental.

Occurrence There is one sight record, JBWR, 23 May 1990, accepted by NYSARC (1992) (Kaufman, Drennan, LeBaron) (AB 44:404).

To see the Spruce Grouse in New York, one has to go to the Adirondacks. These mountains are also the exclusive New York breeding territory for several other species.

Remarks Concurrent with the first NY record was the first NJ record of this species at Cape May, 20 Apr–4 Jun 1990. Historically, there have been five records from NS, with the most recent definite one in 1982; two sightings included up to nine birds. There is one ON record, 21 Apr 1989 at Point Pelee, and one unconfirmed report from NB. Recently (1992–1995) there have been annual fall occurrences at Cape May, NJ, involving as many as four birds. Both the Caribbean subspecies *fulva* (the NY bird appeared to be of this subspecies) and the Southwestern breeding subspecies *pelodoma* have had dramatic population and breeding range expansions over the past 20 years.

Geoffrey S. LeBaron, Kenn Kaufman, and Susan Roney Drennan

CHICKADEES AND TITMICE—PARIDAE

Black-capped Chickadee *Poecile atricapillus*

Range Nearctic, breeding from Alaska and Newfoundland south, in eastern North America to central Kansas and east to central New Jersey, and locally in the Appalachian Mountains to Tennessee and North Carolina. Northern populations are irregularly migratory but generally do not go farther than the southern limits of the breeding range.

Status Common and widespread resident. Occasionally abundant in fall irruptions.

Breeding Breeding in open woodland, parks, and neighborhoods throughout the state, it was found in 97% of the Atlas blocks; absent only from NYC. It is most abundant in the Adirondacks, where its density is among the highest in North America (Robbins et al. 1986). It excavates a nest cavity in a dead tree (or dead limb) by pecking and tearing away rotting wood. It sometimes uses an old woodpecker hole or a bird box and is more likely to use boxes if natural cavities are scarce and if the box is partially filled with sawdust. It has one brood a season.

Cowbird parasitism is rare, as very few chickadee nest cavities have entrances large enough for a female cowbird to enter, but DeBenedictis watched two Black-capped Chickadees feeding a young Brown-headed Cowbird near Warners, Onondaga Co. 19 Jun 1983 (KB 33:277).

Statewide BBS data indicated that populations were increasing 1966–1994 (Peterjohn 1995), but a survey of birds at feeders in Sullivan Co. showed no significant change 1981–1993 (Freer and Visconti 1996).

Nonbreeding Long-distance movements, generally by young in the first year, occur irregularly every few years. Many of these irruptions are strongly correlated with years of low seed crops in northern boreal forest trees (Bock and Lepthien 1976). Fall movements tend to be to the south or southwest

(Smith 1991); spring movements, sometimes aimless, are generally north-easterly (Brooks 1987). In contrast with most migrating passerines, they make their long-distance movements during the day, especially in the morning, and thus are easily seen (Smith 1991). Movements are sometimes of single birds or small groups. Occasionally, irrupting chickadees form large flocks, which can be conspicuous along shores of large bodies of water and which have been most often reported from the NY shore of L. Ontario. For example, in the vicinity of Rochester 27,000 were seen flying from west to east on three dates in Oct 1954, and more than 42,000 flew east to west at nearby Oklahoma Beach 6–12 Oct 1961. More recently, 8000 were individually tallied along L. Ontario 29 Aug–7 Oct 1968; 2280 were at Braddock Bay 15 Oct 1975; and at least 10,000 were recorded 24–31 Oct 1977 moving along the lake shore.

Remarks Perhaps the most familiar bird at winter feeding stations, it is now known to have several traits that allow it to survive the severest winters. A long-known aid to survival is the habit of roosting in dense vegetation or cavities. Chaplin (1976) found that it can enter a state of regulated hypothermia on cold winter nights, dropping its body temperature 10°–12°C below their ordinary daytime body temperature, thereby saving significant overnight energy expenditure. Other recent research demonstrated that it stores food (particularly in autumn) under bark or dead leaves or in knotholes and is able to recover this food after as many as 28 days (Hitchcock and Sherry 1990). It benefits also from our handouts of sunflower seed. Brittingham and Temple (1988) showed that feeding stations increased chickadee overwinter survival, especially in periods of severe weather.
Valerie M. Freer

Boreal Chickadee   *Poecile hudsonicus*

Range Nearctic, resident in boreal forests of North America; in the east to extreme northern United States from New York to Maine. Irregularly irrupts south as winter visitant to Maryland and Pennsylvania.

Status Fairly common breeder in the Adirondacks. Sedentary, rarely occurring anywhere else except during periodic irruptions.

Breeding Boreal Chickadee (formerly known as Brown-capped Chickadee) was recorded in 123 Atlas blocks, mainly in Essex, Franklin, Hamilton, Herkimer, and St. Lawrence counties, from lowland bogs to the High Peaks. Yunick (1984) reported a marked increase in breeding reports between 1950 and the mid-1980s, in part due to greater observer activity but also to establishment of the Adirondack SP and the "forever wild" Forest Preserve, which protects suitable habitat.

Nonbreeding It occasionally irrupts southward from its boreal conifer and mixed conifer-deciduous breeding grounds north of the Adirondacks. In winter, it forms mixed-species flocks with other chickadees, kinglets, nuthatches, and small woodpeckers. On 66 NY CBCs 1960–1989, totals ranged from none in 1960 and 1961 to a high of 31 in 1983. Yunick analyzed irruptions in 1950–1982 and noted major irruptions roughly every six to eight years, including 1954–1955, 1961–1962, 1969–1970, 1975–1976, and 1983–1984. The spring return flight after these irruptions is never as intense as the late Oct–Nov flight, but a distinct lakeshore flight has been observed in Apr–May at Derby Hill, Oswego Co.

The species is rarely reported in the extreme southeastern portion of the state, and especially LI. The irruption of 1954–1955 produced an unusual record of five birds that spent Dec–Feb at a Norway spruce plantation in Albertson, Nassau Co. (P. Buckley, pers. comm.). The flight of 1961–1962 saw some 35–40 birds in the metropolitan NYC area, with most occurring in adjacent northern NJ but others scattered out as far as Montauk.

Maxima: 15 Westmoreland, Oneida Co. 11 Nov 1965; 8 Franklin Co. 4–10 Feb 1985; 6 Limekiln L., Hamilton Co. 24 Sep 1989.
Elizabeth W. Brooks

Tufted Titmouse *Baeolophus bicolor*

Range Eastern Nearctic, resident from southeastern Minnesota to Maine, south to the Gulf Coast and southern Florida.

Status Common to very common resident in the lower Hudson Valley and LI. Expanding its range upstate in central NY. Scarce or absent in the mountains.

Breeding A fairly common to common breeder in deciduous forests associated with riparian areas, it is uncommon or absent at higher elevations. These active, noisy birds were easily located by observers for the Atlas.

Titmice occur in two disjunct geographical populations in NY. The center of distribution is in the lower Hudson Valley and LI. A separate, more scattered population occurs throughout central NY in the geographical corridor from the Susquehanna R. northward through the Finger Lakes and Genesee R. regions to L. Ontario. There are scattered populations along the Great Lakes Plain, with resident populations in Buffalo, Rochester, Oswego, and Watertown. It is scarce or absent in the Allegheny, Catskill, and Adirondack mountains, as well as the St. Lawrence Valley. The pattern of range expansion is to the north and east in the state. BBS data showed a strong, increasing population trend 1966–1994.

Breeding typically is confined to elevations below 1000–1500 ft (Atlas 1988). It appears that Tufted Titmouse, as a breeding bird, is intolerant of the colder temperatures at higher elevations, although it has been observed (1994–1996) throughout the year at 1500–1650 ft elevation south of Dryden in Tompkins Co. (pers. obs.). Field observers should be alert to documenting the elevation ranges at which this species is found breeding as it expands its range in NY.

In the latter half of the twentieth century it has been a rapidly increasing, wide-ranging species, in contrast to a single breeding report from SI in 1914. In the NYC area it began appearing with increasing frequency in the 1950s. The Atlas reported its presence in 36% of the blocks. The increasing population trend was characterized by its virtual absence as a breeding species at the turn of the century, followed by expanding resident populations in the NYC, lower Hudson Valley, and LI regions, and apparent movement into western NY via the Susquehanna R.–Finger Lakes corridor. This species' preference for large deciduous trees and riparian bottomlands is reflected in the geographical patterns of its distribution over time.

Nonbreeding CBC data reported increasing numbers, with diminished numbers of individuals in severe winters during the 1970s, as expected. The lower Hudson and LI CBCs do not show the influence of severe winter weather.

Claudia K. Melin

NUTHATCHES—SITTIDAE

Red-breasted Nuthatch *Sitta canadensis*

Range Nearctic, breeding in eastern North America from central Manitoba and northern Michigan east to southern Labrador and south; in the east to the Berkshires, Catskills, and Poconos, and in the higher mountains to Tennessee and North Carolina. Irregularly migratory, with some birds reaching the Gulf Coast in winter after major flights.

Status Common breeder in the Adirondacks. Rare to fairly common breeder throughout the rest of the state. As a migrant, variously rare to common as befits an irruptive species.

Breeding This nuthatch is a common breeder in the coniferous forests of the Adirondacks. Breeding elsewhere may be rare to fairly common, depending on the availability of conifer trees. It has exhibited a breeding range expansion from its former concentration in the Adirondack and Catskill coniferous forests, with new populations developing during the twentieth century in the Appalachian Plateau, Rensselaer Hills, Taconic Mountains, Manhattan Hills, SI, and LI. It is now found in every region of the state except the boroughs of NYC and the Triassic Lowlands. The expansion may be attributed to the twentieth-century reforestation trend in NY providing more numerous and widespread coniferous forest habitats (Atlas 1988).

An analysis of 1966–1994 BBS data showed an average annual increase in the Red-breasted Nuthatch population of 3.7%. A feeder survey in Sullivan Co. Dec–Mar 1981–1994 showed no significant changes in that county's population (Freer and Visconti 1996).

Nonbreeding An irruptive species, dependent on the conifer seed crop at higher latitudes, it is very erratic and unpredictable, sometimes rare or almost absent in fall, in other years very numerous. Single-day counts of more than 100 in Sep and Oct have been reported from LI in some years. An invasion was reported during the winter of 1975–1976 (KB 26:98). The 1976 Saranac L., Essex Co. CBC reported 311 (KB 38:101). During the fall of 1990 a major flight was observed in the spruce-pine plantations in Region 5, with one observer in southern Onondaga Co. reporting up to 250 a day (KB 40:39). The species is scarce in summer (late Jun–Aug); greatest concentrations occur during the winter. It is not common in the southern part of the state until late Sep or early Oct except for infrequent years, when it arrives as early as Jul or mid-Aug.

Good spring flights usually follow fall irruptions, such as 28 banded at Fire I. Lighthouse 9 May 1970 (Buckley et al.).

An assessment of CBCs by Yunick (1988b) indicated that Red-breasted Nuthatch abundance in NY was one-fifth to one-tenth of that of the White-breasted Nuthatch. He found that long-term trends appeared to be positive, with the pattern of variations in abundance consistent with the bird's irruptive nature. CBC data indicated it is most abundant in the Adirondacks, where it is a common breeder, followed by LI, where it is primarily a migrant and winter visitant and a breeder to a much lesser degree.

Remarks It is cavity nester in both coniferous and deciduous trees. Both adults smear pitch from conifers around the cavity entrance hole. The purpose of this activity is not clearly understood. Some have suggested that the pitch may act as a deterrent to predators; others believe it may simply be a nonfunctional evolutionary relict behavior. That the nuthatches themselves brush against the pitch is evidenced by the reported increasingly disheveled appearance of their plumage during the nesting period. One was found dead stuck to the pitch around the entrance hole in a dead stub of a paper birch (Kilham 1972).

Chad E. Covey

White-breasted Nuthatch

Sitta carolinensis

Range Nearctic, resident from southern Canada to the Gulf states and the mountains of Mexico. Absent from the Great Plains.

Status A widespread breeder, absent only at higher elevations lacking deciduous forests. Sedentary and migratory.

Breeding It is a widespread common breeder in deciduous woodlands throughout the state; during Atlas work the species was found in 80% of all blocks. It was not found in parts of the mountain spruce-fir forest of the Adirondacks or in parts of the spruce–fir–northern hardwood forests and successional northern hardwoods of northern and western NY. It has expanded its range in the NYC area, throughout LI, and in Albany Co. It is now much more common in those areas than reported in the first part of the twentieth century. Found primarily in open woodlands, it is also common in dense deciduous and deciduous-conifer woodlands as well as in open areas containing large deciduous trees, such as parks, orchards, and urban and suburban areas. It is an early breeder, with most nest building in Apr and egg laying from mid-Apr to early Jun (Atlas 1988).

Its status appears fairly stable, but there are some questions. The Atlas indicated that it may have expanded its range in recent years but pointed out that Robbins et al. (1986) discovered a significant decrease in numbers on BBS routes 1965–1979. However, an analysis of NY BBS data 1966–1994 showed no significant trend. A feeder survey in Sullivan Co. Dec–Mar 1981–1994 showed no significant changes in that county's population (Freer and Visconti 1996).

Nonbreeding Although it is considered a resident species that is commonplace at winter feeding stations, a portion of the population is migratory. For instance, one banded 13 Nov 1959 at Huntington, Suffolk Co. was found dead 2 May 1960 near Portland, ME, some 400 mi distant. It is difficult to ascertain migration parameters for a common resident, but evidence seems to indicate that a spring flight occurs in mid-Apr through mid-May, with the return flight beginning in mid-Sep. The largest concentrations are reported during the winter, when birds arriving from more-northern areas supplement the local population. The greatest numbers are reported around Christmas, when many observers are afield and numerous feeding stations are well stocked.

CBC maxima: 308 in 1996 Ithaca, Tompkins Co.; 281 in 1981 Ithaca; 260 in 1964 Peekskill, Westchester Co. White-breasted Nuthatch outnumbered Red-breasted Nuthatch on CBC reports 1960–1989 by six to one.

An assessment of the species on NY CBCs 1960–1985 showed wide, erratic fluctuations in annual abundance, with a long-term negative trend suggesting a decline of 17–34%, depending on the method of treating the data (Yunick 1988b).

Chad E. Covey

Brown-headed Nuthatch   *Sitta pusilla*

Range Eastern Nearctic, resident throughout southeastern United States north to southern Delaware.

Status Accidental.

Occurrence The only record in NY is that of an adult male collected near Elmira, Chemung Co. 24 May 1888 (Swift) CUM 13512. This is a most surprising record of a sedentary species of southern pine forests.

Remarks An 1876 feeder record and two other nonspecific or doubtful records in NJ were noted by Leck (1984), and three single-observer sight reports in CT 1954–1962 were noted by Zeranski and Baptist (1990).

Stanley R. Lincoln

CREEPERS—CERTHIIDAE

Brown Creeper   *Certhia americana*

Range Nearctic, breeding from Alaska to Newfoundland and south; in the east to southern Illinois, in the mountains to North Carolina, and on the coastal plain to Virginia. Sedentary and migratory, withdrawing in winter from the more northern portions of the range.

Status Common breeder at high elevations; less common at lower elevations but has increased in all wooded areas of the state, extending its range south to the lower Hudson Valley and LI. Common to very common migrant. Uncommon to fairly common in winter; somewhat decreased in recent years.

Breeding It was always a common breeder in the higher elevations of the Adirondack and Catskill mountains but was considered rare and local anywhere else in the state (Eaton 1914; Griscom 1923; Beardslee and Mitchell 1965). A nest was found in Bronx Co. in 1926 and another on LI in 1947 (Cruickshank 1942; Bull 1964), with more records in the 1950s and 1960s. By 1975, there were 12 pairs at Connetquot River SP, Suffolk Co., with other records from Nassau and Suffolk counties. It was not recorded as nesting in Rockland and Westchester counties until the mid-1960s. Two decades later, Atlas workers had Confirmed it in 11 blocks in Westchester, 15 on LI, and in every county in the state except for Niagara and the five of NYC. There were particular concentrations in the Tug Hill Plateau, the Cattaraugus Highlands and Allegany Hills, western Mohawk Valley, Finger Lakes Highlands, eastern Appalachian Plateau, lower Hudson Valley, Rensselaer Hills, Taconic and Hudson highlands, and Manhattan Hills.

Initially, range expansion was attributed to the depredations of Dutch elm disease, which provided both a food supply and nesting sites. This cause cannot apply to places like LI, where pitch pine stands in swampy areas provide the principal breeding sites, so reforestation and maturation of the eastern forests provide a more likely general explanation (Atlas 1988).

As is the case with several range expansions of the 1970s and 1980s, the initial buildup of populations has leveled off or even declined in some areas. Whether this trend reflects a consolidation of population in a new range or an actual retraction of short-lived territorial gains remains to be seen.

Nonbreeding Migrating birds arrive in mid-Sep, occasionally earlier, and sometimes in considerable numbers. These thin out after mid-Nov as migrants depart, leaving smaller overwintering populations. They return in early Apr, and nonbreeding birds depart by mid-May. Fairly large numbers of wintering birds have been reported in the past from certain areas, mostly in southern NY: 40 on the 1980 Central Suffolk CBC; 19 on the 1982 Southern Nassau count; Bull (1974) reported 20–50 individuals present in the MNWR area during Jan 1966–1968, feeding on diseased or dying elms. Much lower numbers have been reported on CBCs in widely separated parts of the state in the past decade, suggesting that more birds are passing through to winter in the South or are remaining north of NY or that, even as the southern range expands, northern populations are down. Brown Creepers, like other winter visitants, are subject to long-range cyclical variations.

Fall maxima: 150 Fire I. Lighthouse, Suffolk Co. 9 Oct 1971; 78 Sandy Pond, Oswego Co. 30 Sep 1976. *Spring maxima:* 75 Manitou, Monroe Co. 14 Apr 1960; 60 Selkirk Shores, Oswego Co. 22 Apr 1961; 50 Syracuse, Onondaga Co. 28 Apr 1956; 35 Far Rockaway, Queens Co. 6 May 1950. There are no comparable numbers from recent years.
Eric Salzman

WRENS—TROGLODYTIDAE

Rock Wren   *Salpinctes obsoletus*

Range Western Nearctic and northern Neotropical, breeding from southern British Columbia east to the Dakotas, and south to southern Arizona and Texas; also in Central America to Costa Rica. Winters from northern California, southern Utah, and north-central Texas south through the southern portions of the breeding range.

Status Accidental.

Occurrence The only record is of one at Fredonia, Chautauqua Co. 29 Nov–3 Dec 1986 (Mahoney), accepted by NYSARC (1987). A full account of this discovery, with photograph, was published (Mahoney 1987).

Remarks There are two records from MA (Veit and Petersen 1993), one from NJ (Halliwell 1995), and four from ON (James 1991). William C. D'Anna

Carolina Wren   *Thryothorus ludovicianus*

Range Eastern Nearctic, resident throughout southeastern United States and northeastern Mexico, north to southeastern Minnesota, southern Ontario, and Massachusetts.

Status Locally common resident in the lower Hudson Valley and LI. Scattered resident populations throughout the Susquehanna drainage north to the Finger Lakes, with isolated populations along the L. Erie and L. Ontario shores.

Breeding Carolina Wren has been a breeding species in southeastern regions of the state for some time. Referring to it as the "Mocking Wren," DeKay (1844) considered it a rare visitant to the state but suspected its breeding in Westchester and Rockland counties. Upstate, this species has been present for more than 100 years, but in smaller numbers, which are regularly decimated by severe winter weather. Eaton (1914) considered it a common resident only in the lower Hudson and LI regions. All other records from the interior of the state were of individual birds or pairs, except the Ithaca, Tompkins Co. records, where some clarification of the historical record may be in order.

The first Ithaca breeding record from 1878, attributed to King by Eaton, apparently is an error. The report of King referenced by Eaton from *Bulletin of the Nuttall Ornithological Club* is actually a report of Winter Wren not Carolina Wren, nesting in the Ithaca area. The first documentation of nesting Carolina Wren in the Cayuga Lake basin is that of Fuertes in 1890, with a second report in 1903 (Reed and Wright 1909). These reports confirm that the species bred at the southern end of Cayuga L. and that it was found from year to year in the same locality. In addition to these observations, Eaton (1914) commented that "it is probable that (Carolina Wren) breeds in other localities of . . . New York."

The distribution of this species follows closely the waterways of the state and is limited to lower elevations, and its breeding range today has not changed much since Bull's 1974 assessment. It is still found mainly on LI, except for the densely populated southwestern end, in the lower Hudson Valley, along the Mongaup R. in Sullivan Co. and Esopus Creek in Ulster Co. The Atlas recorded it in the Susquehanna Valley and watershed, in areas adjacent to PA, north through the Finger Lakes corridors to L. Ontario, and along the southern shore of L. Erie. The northernmost (and very isolated) Confirmed Atlas record was along L. Champlain in Essex Co.

This species is very sensitive to severe winters, being decimated by ice storms, heavy snows, and long periods of subzero weather. With a succession of mild winters, it gradually recovers and reestablishes itself. These observations are consistent with populations elsewhere in its range (Brauning 1992).

Nonbreeding During the 1970s, after a series of severe winters, populations were decimated in their upstate localities, and numbers plummeted (Atlas 1988), sometimes requiring as much as a decade to recover to former levels of abundance. Ithaca CBC data show that, after falling to near zero detectability from a record high of 11 birds in 1977, Carolina Wren did not return to a comparable level of detectability until 1989 (C. R. Smith, pers. comm.). Statewide CBC data show population decreases after the winters of 1976–1978, followed by gradual increases until 1989, when numbers approximated former levels on CBCs.

These numbers continued to rise for another four years and then took a nosedive in 1994, reflecting the severe winter of 1993–1994. The CBCs of the 1994–1995 season seemed to show an uncharacteristically quick recovery, which was short-circuited by the particularly devastating winter of 1995–1996. Perhaps, with the apparent increasing entrenchment of this species even in small suburban backyards, this boom and bust cycle may be leveled out.

Claudia K. Melin

Bewick's Wren   *Thryomanes bewickii*

Range Nearctic, breeding from southwestern British Columbia east to southern Ontario and south to central Mexico, central Texas, the northern portions of the Gulf states and central Georgia. Winters from the northern limits of the breeding range south to the Gulf Coast, central Florida, and to the limits of the breeding range in Mexico.

Status One confirmed breeding record. Very rare vagrant.

Breeding The only confirmed and documented nesting (Smiley and Stapleton 1974) was 6 ft up between the rafters and roof of a rustic pagoda at Mohonk L., Ulster Co. Observations included both adults feeding the two- to four-day-old nestlings on 8 Jul 1974, the fledging of three young on 17 Jul, and continued observations of fledglings 22 Jul–11 Aug. The nesting represented a very considerable, and apparently aberrant, range extension of what was supposedly a strictly sedentary species, which previously had bred only as far northeast as southern PA and very rarely in extreme southeastern ON (Bull 1976).

Nonbreeding There are two documented state records: (1) a male collected at Riverhead, Suffolk Co. 21 Sep 1930, NYSM 25297 and (2) one color photographed at an Auburn, Seneca Co. feeder and present there Nov 1953 to late Feb 1954 (on file at the Laboratory of Ornithology, Cornell University).

Six reports, which Bull believed to be correct, from New York, Westchester, and Monroe counties between 1928 and 1954, were all spring occurrences. The last sightings, published without details, were in the mid-1970s: 1 Braddock Bay, Monroe Co. 26–27 Sep 1974 (J. Skelly, Henderson) (KB 25:35); 2 Cuba, Allegany Co. 1 Oct–30 Nov 1975 (*fide* D. Burton) (KB 26:35).

Remarks It was extirpated as a breeder in PA in the 1970s and is no longer even an annual visitant; it was last seen in 1977 (Brauning 1992). There are three convincing fall sight records from coastal MA, in 1975, 1976, and 1986 (Veit and Petersen 1993). The half-dozen modern records in NJ are split between spring and fall (Halliwell 1995). There is one fall record in RI (Conway 1992).
Elizabeth W. Brooks

House Wren *Troglodytes aedon*

Range Nearctic and Neotropical, breeding across southern Canada and throughout most of the United States and south to southern South America. In the east, winters north to North Carolina, rarely to coastal Maryland and southern New York.

Status Common breeder throughout except for portions of the Adirondacks. Fairly common migrant.

Breeding It breeds in rural and suburban areas, in dense thickets, forest clearings, and swampy woodlands, rarely at elevations above 1500 ft and never above 2100 ft. Although it is frequently found around human habitation, it cannot survive in densely populated areas. Around the turn of the century there was a reported decline of this species owing to the expanding populations of the introduced House Sparrow and European Starling, which created competition for nest cavities (Griscom 1923). The Atlas indicated that this decline was temporary, a fact current BBS data and field observations substantiate.

This wren is very adaptable in its nesting habits. Its messy nests are found in an astonishing assortment of crannies and cavities. The widespread program of bluebird restoration has benefited it, for it will readily occupy artificial nest boxes, often displacing current occupants. This aggressive songster frequently destroys the eggs of other House Wrens and other species nesting nearby. In a further effort at survival the male will often build crude "dummy" nests. This tiny songbird appears to be thriving throughout most of the state.

Nonbreeding Although widespread, the House Wren is not reported in large numbers during migration. Arrival is rare before late Apr, and it usually departs by mid-Oct. A review of early 1990s records indicated that the early arrival date stated by Bull, 9 Apr, is still valid, but the departure date was found to be as late as 14 Nov (KB 44:27). Winter occurrences are rare, and no adequate documentation exists for any having survived the winter. A review of 1960–1989 CBCs revealed numerous sightings in the southern portions of the state and two reports from as far north as the Mohawk Valley and the Great Lakes Plain. With few exceptions, the House Wren's wintering grounds are found in warmer latitudes where temperatures average above 30°F.

Joan L. Quinlan and John J. Fritz

Winter Wren *Troglodytes troglodytes*

Range Holarctic, breeding in eastern North America from Alaska, central Manitoba, eastern Quebec, and Newfoundland south to northern Michigan, southern New York, Connecticut, and in the Appalachians to northern Georgia. Winters throughout except the more northern portions of the breeding range, south to the Gulf Coast and Florida.

Status Fairly common breeder in the mountains, local elsewhere at higher elevations or in Canadian life zone type habitat. Uncommon migrant throughout. Uncommon to rare in winter at lower elevations, more common during mild winters.

Breeding Considered by some to be the finest singer in the state, it occupies two distinct nesting habitats. One is the montane evergreen forest consisting primarily of spruce and balsam fir in the Adirondack and Catskill regions and in the Tug Hill Plateau. The other is in more lowland areas in "cold" bogs and swamps, especially hemlock–white cedar bogs upstate, and even more rarely in hemlock-rhododendron ravines in the lower Catskills and to the southeast. There is a single recorded nesting on LI at Connetquot River SP, Suffolk Co. (KB 26:200). Atlas work found some evidence of breeding in 23% of all blocks, primarily in the Adirondacks and Catskills but with a scattering elsewhere, including the Great Lakes Plain.

Nonbreeding During migration and in winter this secretive species frequents brush piles and dense thickets but may be "squeaked" out of hiding to be more easily observed. Frequently only one or two birds are seen, but sometimes more are recorded at the peak of its migration. Normal dates for arrival and departure of migrants are about 30 Mar to 15 May in the spring and 22 Sep to 2 Nov in the fall. Statewide, it is frequently encountered on CBCs that include good Winter Wren habitat and that get good coverage by birders, there being more records downstate than in the northern parts. Numbers of individuals on these counts over the past 20 years have remained about the same.

Spring maxima: 14 Sandy Pond, Oswego Co. 25 Apr 1954; 13 Manitou, Monroe Co. 20 Apr 1954. *Fall maxima:* 105 Sandy Pond, Oswego Co. 6 Oct 1980; 40 Buck Pond, Monroe Co. 4 Oct 1987. Robert G. McKinney

Sedge Wren   *Cistothorus platensis*

Range Nearctic and Neotropical, breeding in North America locally from central Manitoba and southern Quebec south to Arkansas and West Virginia; also on the Delmarva Peninsula and erratically in southern New England, New York, and New Brunswick; also from southern Mexico to extreme southern South America. Northern populations winter from Maryland and Tennessee south to Mexico and east to Florida.

Status A rare to uncommon local breeder and migrant.

Breeding As its name implies, it is a bird of wet sedge meadows, pastures and hayfields, upland edges of ponds and streams, and coastal brackish and tidal marshes. Inland habitats are typically dominated by a variety of graminoid species, whereas in coastal marshes, saltmeadow cordgrass *(Spartina patens)* predominates. All breeding habitats have scattered shrubs and an absence of standing water, but the birds seem sensitive to habitat conditions, abandoning sites that succeed into shrubland or that become too wet or too dry. Because they breed opportunistically in ephemeral habitats, they seldom occupy the same site for more than a few years (Gibbs 1992).

DeKay (1844) described this wren as not numerous, and Eaton (1914) found it to be local and uncommon throughout the state except for the lower Hudson Valley and parts of central and western NY. Bull (1964) noted a decline in the NYC area in the preceding 15 years. In 1974, in apparent agreement with Eaton's account, he described the bird as rare to uncommon throughout the state, absent from the mountains of the Catskills and Adirondacks, and least rare in the southeast and parts of central and western NY. He went on to note, however, that at least some of the breeding colonies occupied in the 1960s along the South Shore of LI and the lower Hudson R. were destroyed. The last breeding record on SI was 1943 (Atlas 1988). During the Atlas it was not recorded from LI or the lower Hudson area, and Swift (1987) did not report this species from any of his study sites in the Hudson R. marshes in the 1980s. In fact the only Atlas record from southeastern NY was of a single singing, nest-building male in Westchester Co. This compelling evidence suggests that Sedge Wren has been extirpated from a substantial portion of its historical range in the state.

Today this bird is most often found in the Great Lakes and St. Lawrence plains, with apparent strongholds in St. Lawrence and Jefferson counties. In the summer of 1993 DiTomasso reported 30 singing males in uncut hay fields at 11 sites in the St. Lawrence Co. towns of Morristown, Oswagatchie, and Lisbon (KB 43:331). In 1994 Leone obtained similar numbers in Jefferson Co. when he conducted night surveys of uncut hay fields in the towns of Brownville, Orleans, and Pamelia (KB 44:320).

Nonbreeding It is seldom reported during migration, and in some years it is not reported at all away from the breeding ground (KB 33:43). Scattered specimens, believed to represent birds killed during migration, have been collected in late Sep and early Oct.

The bulk of the population winters along the Gulf Coast in TX and LA and also along the Atlantic Coast from the Carolinas to FL (Root 1988). Rarely reported in NY in winter, there is one record from Jones Beach, Nassau Co. in 1913 and another from Westhampton Beach, Suffolk Co. in 1980 (KB 31:120). The earliest spring migrants reach NY in mid-Apr.

Bull (1964) attributed the decline of this species in the NYC area to loss of habitat through development and the burning of coastal marshes. Observers in St. Lawrence and Jefferson counties, where the wrens nest in unmowed hay fields, noted losses to mowing and grazing (KB 44:320). Like many species that occupy ephemeral habitats it is probably vulnerable to habitat fragmentation. Because it is mobile and opportunistic, a mosaic of wetlands representing different stages of succession may provide adequate habitat for this species. Its continued existence in the more rural and agri-cultural parts of the state suggest that this habitat is still readily available, but at these sites the birds are vulnerable to incompatible agricultural practices. It is currently listed as a Species of Special Concern in the state, and the NYSDEC has recommended that it be elevated to Threatened status. Kathryn J. Schneider

Marsh Wren

Cistothorus palustris

Range Nearctic, breeding in southern Canada and throughout most of northern and central United States. Winters along the Gulf Coast from Florida to Texas, along the south Atlantic Coast to Maryland, and occasionally north along the coast to Massachusetts.

Status Fairly common to abundant breeder and migrant in appropriate habitat.

Breeding It breeds colonially in NY's larger marshes; it is much less numerous northward and rare at higher elevations. The Atlas found breeders well distributed in the Coastal Lowlands, Hudson Valley, Great Lakes and St. Lawrence plains, L. Champlain Valley, and the Finger Lakes but rare or absent elsewhere. No widespread change in abundance has been documented, but many local populations have been adversely affected by the destruction of wetlands. Inland, it is found most frequently in tall reeds and dense cattail beds. Downstate, phragmites and cattails are preferred nesting sites.

Nonbreeding The Marsh Wren is rare to uncommon in winter. This bird's secretive nature during the day and its preference for migrating at night makes its status as a migrant difficult to determine. It has been determined to arrive from late Apr to early May, departing the state throughout Oct.

Remarks Three subspecies of Marsh Wren occur in NY. The nominate form *palustris* breeds, in general, in coastal and estuarine marshes. The second form that breeds in NY, *dissaeptus*, is found inland, where it prefers

large cattail marshes. The third form, *iliacus*, like many other Midwestern birds, has a southeast-northwest migration route and may be found during migration within the breeding range of *dissaeptus* and casually as far east as LI. A single specimen of *iliacus* (AMNH 66451) was collected 13 Oct 1888 at the Montauk Lighthouse (Parkes 1952). There are four specimens of *iliacus* in the Cornell collection, all from Tompkins Co.: 13179, 3 Oct 1923; 13186, 18 May 1924; 13177, 17 May 1940; 21657, 10 Oct 1948 (K. C. Parkes, in litt.).
John J. Fritz and Joan L. Quinlan

KINGLETS—REGULIDAE

Golden-crowned Kinglet   *Regulus satrapa*

Range Nearctic, breeding from Alaska to Newfoundland and south, in the west to the mountains of Guatemala, in the east to the mountains of Tennessee and North Carolina. Winters nearly throughout the breeding range and southward. Sedentary and migratory.

Status Common breeder at higher elevations in the Adirondacks and Catskills; in recent years greatly increased at lower elevations outside the mountains in mature spruce plantations. Variously uncommon to very common migrant and winter visitant.

Breeding Before 1950 this species was limited in breeding season to bogs, swamps, and natural conifer forests at higher elevations (1970–3930 ft) of the Adirondacks and Catskills, with a scattering of records in contiguous counties. As Norway and white spruce matured in the massive state reforestation tracts planted in the early 1930s, ideal breeding habitat was created in a number of southwestern counties as well as in the Finger Lakes and the Tug Hill Plateau, most at much lower elevations. Andrle found that habitat with cool, moist, and densely shaded stands of spruce was the critical factor in determining suitable breeding sites (Atlas 1988).

By the early 1980s it was recorded in 973 Atlas blocks, 18% of the total, and was Confirmed in 232. The only areas in the state in which the bird does not breed are the Coastal Lowlands and the Great Lakes Plain. BBS data indicated an upward trend 1966–1994 of 7.9% annually. Breeding continues to be confirmed in additional locations, but as lumbering and selective logging expand in state reforestation and privately owned spruce plantations, the population may very well decline.

Nonbreeding This species is subject to marked fluctuations, with massive concentrations sometimes followed by population crashes, often after severe winters. In winter, it frequents conifers and is usually more prevalent inland than along the coast. In migration, it is often in the company of chickadees, nuthatches, and creepers. It is somewhat hardier than Ruby-crowned Kinglet, migrating earlier in spring and later in fall.

Spring maxima: 130 Oswego 14 Apr 1991; 100 Bronx Park, Bronx Co. 3 Apr 1946; 69 banded, Manitou, Monroe Co. 26 Apr 1989 (Brooks). *Fall maxima:* 450 (estimate) Selkirk Shores, Oswego Co. 20 Oct 1967; 400 Fire I., Suffolk Co. 7 Oct 1971, a record for the coast; 410 Sandy Pond Inlet, Oswego Co. 6 Oct 1981. *Winter maxima:* On the 66 NY CBCs 1960–1989, totals ranged from a low of 138 in 1982 to a high of 1411 in 1985. Winter flocks of more than 30 are unusual. There is one record of 85 at Bear Mtn., Rockland Co. 27 Dec 1952. Elizabeth W. Brooks

Ruby-crowned Kinglet   *Regulus calendula*

Range Northern Nearctic, in eastern North America breeding from northern Manitoba to central Labrador and Newfoundland and south to the extreme northern portions of the United States. In the east, winters north occasionally to New York and Massachusetts and south regularly to Florida, the Gulf Coast, and most of Mexico.

Status Fairly common breeder in the Adirondacks. Fairly common to very common spring migrant, occasionally abundant in fall; rare winter visitant.

Breeding Unknown as a breeder in NY a century ago, this species, like Golden-crowned Kinglet, has enjoyed remarkable success during the twentieth century. The reasons are not clearly understood.

This tiny but active bird breeds almost exclusively in the Adirondacks. It prefers medium to mature spruce, sometimes mixed with balsam fir, but tolerates considerable variation in habitat, from boreal bog forest to mixed woodlands with a strong spruce component (Atlas 1988).

Bull (1974) considered this a very rare breeder and listed 11 known breeding sites in Franklin, Essex, Hamilton, and Herkimer counties. Atlas workers Confirmed breeding in 15 blocks in those counties, plus two blocks in St. Lawrence Co. and one on the Franklin-Clinton county line, but the Atlas also listed it as Possible or Probable in 169 other blocks.

A very rare summer visitant elsewhere in NY. There is only one documented record of breeding outside the Adirondacks. A nest was found on an island in Red House L., Allegany SP, Cattaraugus Co. in Jul 1977 (Andrle 1978).

Nonbreeding It arrives earlier in fall and departs later in spring than Golden-crowned Kinglet. In spring it usually arrives early to mid-Apr and departs by mid-May; in fall it is rare before mid-Sep and usually departs by mid-Nov.

Spring maxima: 200 Syracuse, Onondaga Co. 27 Apr 1957; 125 on the

L. Ontario littoral, Oswego Co. 26 Apr 1992; 121 banded at Kaiser-Manitou Beach, Monroe Co. 10 May 1995, during an exceptional fallout of migrants. *Fall maxima:* 530 Sandy Pond and Selkirk Shores SP, Oswego Co. 30 Sep 1976; 500 Brockport, Monroe Co. 4 Oct 1987. *Extreme dates:* early fall arrivals 10 Aug (inland) and 22 Aug (coastal); late spring departures 31 May (coastal) and 19 Jun (inland).

This is a rare but regular winter visitant near the coast; it is much rarer inland, where scattered single birds are usually reported, sometimes coming to feeders for suet. Record or near record counts of 24 and 28 were tallied respectively on the Northern Nassau Co. and Bronx-Westchester CBCs, 22 and 23 Dec 1984, during a very mild December. Fifteen on the Rockland Co. CBC on 20 Dec 1981 was a record for that count.

Robert E. Marcotte

OLD WORLD WARBLERS AND GNATCATCHERS—SYLVIIDAE

Blue-gray Gnatcatcher   *Polioptila caerulea*

Range Nearctic, breeding widely in southern Canada and the United States; in the east from southeastern Minnesota to central Maine and south to Texas, the Gulf Coast, southern Florida, and the Bahamas. Winters on the Atlantic Coast from Virginia south and throughout the southern parts of the Gulf states and from southern California to central Texas south throughout Mexico to Guatemala.

Status Local uncommon breeder at low elevations. Uncommon to fairly common spring migrant, less common in fall.

Breeding During the nineteenth century and the first half of the twentieth this diminutive species was a rare visitant to the state. There was a single nineteenth-century breeding report from Coldwater, Monroe Co. in Jun 1890 (Short 1896). The species increased as a casual migrant from 1915 through the 1930s (Griscom 1923; Cruickshank 1942). In 1943 it bred along L. Erie in Chautauqua Co. (Beardslee and Mitchell 1965). An unprecedented, huge spring flight took place in 1947. This was followed over the next 15 years by large flights in 1954, 1956, and 1963 (Ellison 1993). By the early 1950s this species was established along the Great Lakes Plain (Parkes 1952). Establishment in southeastern New York occurred in the 1960s (Bull 1964). A series of major spring flights in the 1970s led to its spread into northern NY (Ellison 1991, 1992).

Since 1974 it has filled in gaps in its range in the Mohawk Valley and eastern LI. It first bred on SI in 1982 (Siebenheller and Siebenheller 1982b). It has also spread in small numbers into the L. Champlain lowlands and the plains along the east shore of L. Ontario and the St. Lawrence R. It remains a rare migrant in the central Adirondacks and is absent as a breeder from the Tug Hill Plateau and higher elevations (above 2000 ft) in the Catskills, Taconics, and Appalachian Plateau.

This tiny but feisty bird nests in both young and mature hardwood forest, often where it is wet, as in elm-maple swamps, and cottonwood, willow, sycamore, box-elder, and silver maple along streams and lake shores. It also may occur in upland oak-hickory forest, generally near brooks and small ponds.

Nonbreeding This species is an early spring migrant, arriving in numbers during the latter half of Apr. It is less conspicuous in fall and departs early, with the bulk of migration completed by late Aug. A few may be seen in late autumn, especially along the outer coast. These are presumably reversed migrants following a northerly heading instead of the expected southerly one (Veit and Petersen 1993).

Spring maxima: 20 Central Park, Manhattan 20 Apr 1974; 20 Dunkirk, Erie Co. 3 May 1974; 20 Ithaca, Tompkins Co. 12 May 1958. *Fall maxima:* 6 Montauk, Suffolk Co. 18 Sep 1948; 5 Central Park, Manhattan 24 Aug 1953. *Extreme dates: Coastal:* 3 Apr and 2 Dec. *Inland:* 6 Apr and 1 Dec. Rare before mid-Apr and after mid-Sep.

Reversed migrants occasionally occur on the coast from mid to late Dec. In Dec 1984 reverse migration took the form of a flight, with reports scattered in northeastern North America, mostly on the coast, from NY to NF. There have been five mid to late Dec reports for NY; three of them arose from the 1984 flight. The latest was one 15–30 Dec 1984 at Croton Point, Westchester Co. (Weissman) (NYSARC 1985). One on the Central Suffolk Co. CBC 27 Dec 1986 has not been submitted to NYSARC.

Remarks Only one subspecies has been documented in NY, the nominate *caerulea*. The western subspecies, *amoenissima*, is a long-distance Neotropical migrant and could occur in NY. Specimens of late-autumn gnatcatchers should be examined with this possibility in mind. *Amoenissima* is duller above and shows slightly more black in the outer rectrices than *caerulea*; it can only be identified in the hand.
Walter G. Ellison

THRUSHES—TURDIDAE

Northern Wheatear   *Oenanthe oenanthe*

Range Holarctic, in North America breeding in the northwestern corner, and separately, in the northeastern corner from Ellesmere Island south to northern Quebec and Labrador. The two populations winter in Asia and

Africa, respectively. Casual or accidental in both coastal and interior locations of North America.

Status Rare vagrant, but becoming increasingly regular.

Occurrence A study of the literature revealed more than 40 records, starting with four specimens taken in the nineteenth century. Then, after a hiatus of 50 years, between 1934 and 1978 there were an additional 16 sight records (Bruun 1981). Observers in the next 18 years then doubled the previous sightings. These numbers probably more correctly reflect the huge increase in field birder numbers than an increase in the species' occurrence.

An examination of the records showed that fully 65% have taken place in Sep, some 20% later in the fall, and the balance in the spring. The Coastal Lowlands accounted for twice as many as the rest of the state.

Remarks There is some speculation as to whether this species should be categorized as a rare "vagrant" or a rare "migrant." As you will note from the range description, breeding on this continent takes place in the far northern portions, with the wintering grounds in tropical Africa and Asia. Possibly, with an increase in breeding populations, there is or will be an increase in records as more birds return to their breeding grounds from Africa, crossing to the East Coast from Africa. Through 1996 there were no South American records of the species, but if the above speculation is correct, it may be recorded there as well. If this hypothesis has no merit, then all the birds recorded are true vagrants.

Records in the adjoining states with ocean coastlines reflect our own picture fairly closely.
Anthony J. Lauro

Eastern Bluebird *Sialia sialis*

Range Eastern Nearctic, breeding from southern Quebec, New Brunswick, and Nova Scotia, south to the Gulf states and, in the mountains, to northern Nicaragua. Winters mainly in the southeastern United States northeast to southern New England.

Status Generally an uncommon but widespread breeder and uncommon spring migrant; common to locally very common, and occasionally abundant, fall migrant. Variously rare to locally common in winter.

Breeding Bluebirds are cavity nesters, preferring open areas and farmlands as well as swamps and drier forest openings (KB 32:6). They use natural cavities or holes excavated by woodpeckers but must compete with other hole nesters.

Their history in NY is closely linked to the development of farming. Bluebird was not a common summer resident until forests were cleared to be replaced by fields and orchards. At the turn of the century and through the 1930s it was reported in most rural areas of the state (Atlas 1988), but, as farming began to decline and competition from other species, became more intense, the population suffered. By 1960, the falloff was serious, and an 8% decrease, to a degree weather related, in the breeding population was reported during 1966–1979 (Peterjohn 1995).

This problem was offset to some extent by the activities of concerned enthusiasts who build and maintain nestbox trails. The Ralph T. Waterman Bird Club of Dutchess Co. reported "a banner crop of over 700 young from a 28-year-old trail of 200 boxes in 1989" (KB 39:246). A trail of 453 boxes in Oswego Co. successfully fledged 580 young in 1991 (KB 41:271), and an Allegany Co. trail of 125 boxes had 37 nesting pairs, which fledged 177 young in 1987 (KB 37:218). The New York State Bluebird Society proposed a trail of nest boxes across the state along Route 20 from the MA border to PA. By March 1996, the trail was 50% complete. Upon completion, it will have approximately 2500 boxes, placed in suitable habitat and maintained by members of the Society (K. Colton, pers. comm.).

The NYS Bluebird Society reported 2000 young hatched in nest boxes maintained by its members in 1991, with a total of 6000 young statewide. By 1994, a positive trend in the population prompted the NYSDEC to consider removing the Eastern Bluebird from the list of Species of Special Concern.

Breeding is reduced in the higher forested areas of the Adirondacks, central Tug Hill Plateau and northern Tug Hill Transition, the St. Lawrence Plains, and the Coastal Lowlands (Atlas 1988). In all regions, weather has a significant effect, with spring snows and late frosts adversely affecting nesting success. In a good season, three nestings may occur, with young from the previous brood assisting the parents. Nests with young have been reported as late as 23 Sep in Chemung Co. (KB 26:39).

Nonbreeding Small resident populations are reported throughout the nonbreeding season (*The Kingbird*, vols. 26–44). Depending on weather conditions, migrants arrive from late Feb to mid-Mar, with the northern regions seeing them in early May. A "split migration" occurs in Region 2, with arrivals in Mar and a later group passing through at the end of May (KB 37:136). In the fall they usually depart by late Nov, except for wintering birds.

Ordinarily this species is observed only in very small numbers during spring migration. In fall, however, large flocks may be seen and heard passing overhead. On 26 Oct 1962, 200 were reported at Brocton,

Chautauqua Co. In 1944, there was an unprecedented flight over LI, with 500 at Long Beach, Nassau Co. 24 Oct (Komorowski) and 400 at Orient, Suffolk Co. 5 Nov (Latham). On 24 Feb 1934, 200 were seen at Rye, Westchester Co. (Drescher).

CBC records show bluebirds most numerous in the east and south in the areas near the Hudson R. A high of 114 birds was reported on the Peekskill, Westchester Co. CBC in 1988. In 1993, there were 104 on the Catskill-Coxsackie, Greene Co. CBC and 109 on the Albany Co. CBC. The Brooklyn CBC reported 65 in 1995, an unusual number for a coastal location.

Remarks Officially recognized as the New York State bird, and a lovely herald of spring, the Eastern Bluebird has benefited from the attention of conservation-minded people throughout the state.
Phyllis R. Jones

Mountain Bluebird   *Sialia currucoides*

Range Western Nearctic, breeding from central Alaska, southern Yukon, and western Manitoba south to southern California and southern New Mexico. Winters south to northern Mexico; vagrant to the East Coast.

Status Casual vagrant.

Occurrence There are seven records: three winter, two spring, two fall. The first was observed and photographed by numerous people 20 Dec 1974–2 Mar 1975, at Coxsackie, Greene Co. (Guthrie and Davis 1975). A photo is on file at the AMNH. A sight report only came from Newark, Wayne Co. 15 Jan 1977 (KB 27:100). One was photographed by Beyer 15 Nov 1977 at JBSP (KB 28:62). Another was photographed during 17–21 Mar 1978 near Schultzville, Dutchess Co. (Van Auken) (NYSARC 1979). One was at North Tarrytown, Westchester Co. 20 Apr 1990 (Lewis) (NYSARC 1992), and one at JBSP 20 Oct 1990 (Machover and Saphir) (NYSARC 1992). One was photographed at Point Peninsula, Jefferson Co. 21 Jan 1993 (Chamberlaine) (NYSARC 1995).

Remarks This species hybridizes with Eastern Bluebird at the eastern edge of its range in MN (AB 44:1137), and the progeny are fertile. It is considered irruptive, and when it shows up in NY there are usually others in the Northeast and Canada. A review of records since 1988 for adjacent states and provinces revealed: one, MA May 1994; one, PA Dec 1988–Mar 1989; one, NJ Nov 1988, the second state record; one, PQ, fall 1993 and two, spring 1994; one ON Apr 1991, the sixth spring record and eleventh since 1978. The winter of 1995 produced a significant number of records, with three each in MA, CT, ON, and NS.
Lee B. Chamberlaine

Townsend's Solitaire   *Myadestes townsendi*

Range Western Nearctic, breeding from central Alaska to western Manitoba south to southern California and east to the western portions of South Dakota and Nebraska. Winters south to northern Mexico. Vagrant to the East Coast.

Status Casual vagrant.

Occurrence Six individuals of this species have been recorded, three of them in Dutchess Co. The first state record was a specimen taken at Kings Park, Suffolk Co. 25 Nov 1905 (Weber) AMNH 377452. The second specimen came from Amenia, Dutchess Co., a female present 14–16 Mar 1953 (George) AMNH 707718. After another long hiatus, the third state record was observed in New Berlin, Chenango Co. 20 Dec 1986 (Covey, Daigle) (KB 37:173; NYSARC 1987). The fourth was found in Dover, Dutchess Co. 7 Jan 1990 (Van Wagner et al.) (KB 40:123, NYSARC 1992) and was last seen 13 Mar 1990 (KB 40:200). Record five was from JBWR 25 Nov 1994 (Nugent) (KB 45:146) and 3 Dec 1994 (Jaslowitz) (NYSARC 1996). (The date given in the NYSARC report is erroneous.) The sixth occurrence and third county record, submitted to NYSARC, was at Pawling, Dutchess Co. 2–3 Jan 1995 (Gilbert) (KB 45:141).

Remarks A popular field guide describes this species as casual in winter as far east as NF and NY (National Geographic Society 1987). That description tends to be supported by several records from 1989–1995 in PA, NJ, CT, MA, and NH.

Robert W. Brock

Veery   *Catharus fuscescens*

Range Nearctic, breeding from southern Canada, in the west to the mountains of northern Arizona and in the east to northern Illinois, southern Pennsylvania, and northern New Jersey, and in the mountains to northern Georgia. Winters in tropical South America south to central Brazil.

Status Widespread, generally common breeder. Common migrant, best detected by call overhead at night.

Breeding Although widespread in NY, this unobtrusive forest bird with its ethereal spiraling song is local on the Coastal Lowlands and Great Lakes Plain and absent from the highest elevations in the Adirondacks (above 3000 ft) and Catskills (above 3600 ft).

It inhabits moist or wet forest, often in lowlands. Dilger (1956:177) observed that it "reaches its greatest concentrations in rather damp areas, either deciduous or coniferous. Moist bottomland woods with a lush understory of ferns and other plants seem to provide optimum conditions." This thrush can be very common in favored locations; for example, Axtell (1947) estimated that there were 66 pairs in the half-mile between Alpine and Odessa, Schuyler Co. They are even sometimes numerous on LI, where they are very local. One hundred singing males were counted at Connetquot River SP, Suffolk Co. on 14 June 1975.

As have many other long-distance migrants to the Neotropics, this species has declined over the last 30 years. The average annual decline on NY BBS routes 1966–1994 was 1.1% (C.R. Smith and B. Peterjohn, pers. comm.)

Nonbreeding They are shy and quiet migrants, thus few are encountered by day during passage, but their characteristic calls are heard as they pass over at night. According to upstate surveys of nocturnal migration, they are at maximum abundance 27 Aug–6 Sep during autumn migration, with very few detected after 8 Sep. There appear to be two important corridors, with the largest numbers between Alfred and Cuba, Allegany Co. and fewer over the eastern Appalachian Plateau over Norwich, Chenango Co. (W. Evans, pers. comm.).

Spring maxima: 50 Goat Island, Niagara Co. 21 May 1943; 25 Central Park, Manhattan 4 May 1950; 25 Massena, St. Lawrence Co. 14 May 1993. *Fall maxima:* nocturnal counts: 700 Far Rockaway, Queens Co. 10 Sep 1946 and 500 at the same place 3 Sep 1949; 100 in one hour, Syracuse, Onondaga Co. 19 Sep 1966 (Scheider); a very late high count was of 29 that struck the Fire I. Lighthouse, Suffolk Co. 30 Sep 1883 (Dutcher). *Extreme dates:* 18 Apr (coastal) and 20 Apr (inland); 8 Nov (coastal). Rare before the first week of May and after the fourth week of Sep.

Although several Dec and Jan reports exist, only one has been satisfactorily documented and accepted: 13 Dec 1993 at JBSP (Fritz) (NYSARC 1995). For out-of-season reports of this species to be acceptable they must be accompanied by complete, not simply pertinent, descriptive details. It is preferable that a salvaged winter corpse be preserved in a museum collection or a good color photograph be taken and shared with NYSARC.

Remarks Three subspecies have been recorded. Nominate *fuscescens* is the breeding form; *fuliginosus* of NF occurs in migration in the eastern part of the state (Parkes 1952). Phillips (1991) split *salicicola* of the northern Midwest and points westward into two subspecies, *salicicola* and *levyi*, with the latter ranging farthest to the east. A Veery collected on LI has been attributed to *levyi* (possibly *salicicola*) by Phillips (1991). The existence of dark Veery subspecies showing little or no rust should be taken into account by observers confronted with possible Bicknell's and Gray-cheeked thrushes.

Walter G. Ellison

Gray-cheeked Thrush   *Catharus minimus*

Range Northern Nearctic and extreme eastern Palearctic, breeding from eastern Siberia east to northern Quebec, Labrador, and Newfoundland, south, in North America, to the northern areas of British Columbia, Alberta, Saskatchewan, Manitoba, and Ontario and in the east to southeastern Quebec. Winters chiefly in South America, south to northern Peru and northwestern Brazil.

Status Fairly common to uncommon migrant, more common on the coast in spring than at other times of the year. Most often heard calling overhead at night.

Occurrence This subarctic thrush had been considered conspecific with the locally nesting Bicknell's Thrush until recent studies by Ouellet (1993) were accepted by the AOU (1995) as conclusively proving that these very similar birds are discrete species. The combination of difficulty in identification with a shy and unobtrusive nature, makes its status hard to assess. Abundance is best determined through banding or counts of calls produced by birds as they pass overhead at night. Their nasal flight calls are subtly distinct from those of the closely related Bicknell's Thrush (Evans 1994). Migrants may occur in any wooded site but are most often encountered in dense upland thickets, alder and willow swamps, and woods with a thick, shrubby understory. Save for Bicknell's, this is the least common migrant *Catharus* thrush. It constituted 10% of all *Catharus* banded at Huntington, Suffolk Co. 1958–1969 (Lanyon et al. 1970). Counts of migrants from nocturnal recordings made with automated sound equipment showed that the peak of autumn migration is 14–28 Sep, and extreme dates are from the last week of Aug to the last week of Oct. The greatest numbers have been detected from Richford, Tioga Co. westward (W. Evans, pers. comm.).

Spring maxima: Counts from Bull 1974 are repeated here with the caveat that some Bicknell's Thrushes may be included in coastal counts. 50 Central Park, Manhattan 20 May 1924 (Helmuth), an unusually large number for spring; 11 Manitou, Monroe Co. 28 May 1993. *Fall maxima:* 300 Far Rockaway, Queens Co. 20 Sep 1953 (Bull) and "hundreds" Syracuse, Onondaga Co. 16 Sep 1965 (Scheider), both were counts of calls from nocturnal migrants; 29 Colden TV tower, Erie Co. 29 Sep 1962; 16 Braddock Bay, Monroe Co. 26 Sep 1990. *Extreme dates:* Counts are uncertain given its great similarity to Bicknell's. *Spring:* 25 Apr (coastal); 8 Jun (inland) and 12 Jun (coastal). *Fall:* 25 Aug (coastal) and 1 Sep (inland); 21 and 28 Nov (coastal specimens). Accidental to 16 Dec 1910 Brooklyn Botanic Garden, Kings Co. (specimen AMNH).

It is rare before mid-May and after late May, and before mid-Sep and after early Oct. Midwinter reports are unacceptable without very careful documentation.

Remarks Two subspecies occur in NY. The wide-ranging *aliciae* of the subarctic mainland from eastern Siberia to Labrador migrates throughout the state, probably in greatest numbers in western upstate counties, and *minimus* of insular NF almost exclusively occurs on the coast, although interior specimens exist for other states (Wallace 1939; Phillips 1991). Given a detailed and close look, *aliciae* is distinguishable from Bicknell's Thrush in the field. Distinguishing *minimus* from Bicknell's appears to present serious identification problems if not measured in the hand (McLaren 1995).
Walter G. Ellison

Bicknell's Thrush   *Catharus bicknelli*

Range Eastern Nearctic, breeding from northern Nova Scotia and the north shore of the Gulf of St. Lawrence south through the mountains of New England and the Adirondacks and Catskills of New York. Winter distribution apparently restricted to a narrow area within the Caribbean basin, with its major stronghold likely in the Dominican Republic.

Status Fairly common breeder at high elevations (above 3000 ft) in the Catskills and Adirondacks. Uncommon migrant in eastern and coastal portions.

Breeding The Catskills of southeastern NY are at the southernmost edge of the range of this breeding endemic of northeastern North America. There it is found at the summits of the highest peaks (above 3300 ft). In the Adirondacks it ranges as low as 2700 ft at L. Colden in the High Peaks (Atlas 1988), but even in these northern mountains it is most numerous on the highest ridges up to treeline at 4500 ft.

The breeding range parallels that of Blackpoll Warbler. This shy and often quiet thrush is most common in young or stunted, closely ranked stands of balsam fir. It is less frequent in young and stunted spruce and heavy second growth of fir, birch, and cherry. Details of this species' ecology and nesting habits are found in Wallace 1939, Dilger 1956, and Noon 1981.

There are nesting season reports from 38 mountains: 14 in the Catskills and 24 in the Adirondacks (C. C. Rimmer, pers. comm.). It probably occurs on many other suitable mountains in the Adirondacks, but reports are lacking. Slide Mtn., Ulster Co. is the type locality of the species. USNM 95545, collected on the summit by Eugene Bicknell on 15 June 1881, served as Robert Ridgway's type in his description of the new form in 1882.

Nonbreeding Bicknell's Thrush has only recently been considered separate from the closely related and widespread subarctic-breeding Gray-cheeked

Thrush (AOU 1995). A public proposal of Bicknell's Thrush as a distinct species from Gray-cheeked was first made by Ouellet and Seutin in separate papers presented at the AOU Annual Meeting in 1991, outlining morphological, vocal, and biochemical differences between these thrushes (Ouellet 1993). Phillips (1991) also provided a cogent argument in favor of splitting Gray-cheeked and Bicknell's thrushes, emphasizing differences in bill coloration and the discrete wintering ranges of the two. The recency of this split combined with the continuing difficulty of separating these species in the field, currently the most difficult challenge in a difficult genus (McLaren 1995), makes it hard to assess the status of Bicknell's Thrush during migration.

It is the least numerous *Catharus* in migration. It constituted less than 2% of all *Catharus* banded at Huntington, Suffolk Co. 1958–1969 (Lanyon et al. 1970). It is apparently found in migration almost entirely in eastern NY from the central Adirondacks and southeastward to eastern LI. It is very rare in western NY. There are no published specimen records for upstate west of the Adirondacks. W. Evans (pers. comm.) has not detected it on upstate nocturnal surveys with automated recording equipment at a battery of stations on the Appalachian Plateau. Less than 4% of nearly 160 "gray-cheekeds" banded at Braddock Bay, Monroe Co. and Alfred, Allegheny Co. over a 20-year span showed wing lengths strongly consistent with Bicknell's Thrush (E. Brooks, pers. comm.). This finding is reasonable, given that the Bicknell's must migrate southeastward to its Greater Antillean wintering range. Some sight reports exist for western NY, but it is best to base identification on in-the-hand measurements or preserved specimens. Any "gray-cheek"-type *Catharus* with a wing less than 94 mm is probably a Bicknell's. Photographs are likely to be misleading because "Newfoundland" Gray-cheeked Thrushes *(C. m. minimus)* are similar to Bicknell's (McLaren 1995).

On LI this species occurs over about the same range of dates in spring and autumn migration as Gray-cheeked Thrush. Bicknell's passes through LI in spring at a much more rapid pace than Gray-cheeked, with stays at an Elmhurst, Queens Co. banding station never exceeding the date of capture (Beals and Nichols 1940).

Maxima: Uncertain; high seasonal counts from the cited banding operation in Queens were 5 on 27 May 1935 and 9 on 3 Oct (year unspecified). *Extreme dates:* Beals and Nichols (1940) reported a spring arrival of 11 May and a late date of 27 May, although the birds are likely to occur into Jun in many years. In fall they captured this species from 7 Sep to 8 Nov.

Remarks Wallace (1939) considered the species to be polymorphic, exhibiting brown and olive morphs. These morphs may show some geographical separation, with brown birds in the south, olive birds in the north,

and overlap occurring in the Adirondacks, northern Green Mtns., and White Mtns. There is also a size cline, with birds being larger to the north (Ouellet 1993; pers. obs.). Todd (1963) suggested that the large northern olive morph of southern PQ may belong to a separate subspecies.
Walter G. Ellison

Swainson's Thrush *Catharus ustulatus*

Range Nearctic, breeding from central Alaska east in Canada to southern Labrador and Newfoundland and south to southwestern United States, and, in the east, to northern Minnesota, Wisconsin and Michigan, southern Ontario and Quebec, southern New England and New York, and, in the higher mountains, to West Virginia and western Virginia. Winters from central Mexico to Argentina, Peru, and Bolivia.

Status Common breeder in the Catskills, Adirondacks, and Tug Hill Plateau. Uncommon and local in the northern Taconics and the Appalachian Plateau. Fairly common to common migrant, occasionally very common overhead at night.

Breeding In the Adirondacks it reaches its greatest abundance mainly below the stunted subalpine haunts of Bicknell's Thrush. Overlap with Hermit Thrush is greater, but Swainson's generally inhabits more mature and open forests (Noon 1981). Overlap is greater in the Catskills; all three boreal *Catharus* may be heard in chorus in nearly adjacent territories atop such mountains as Slide and Hunter (pers. obs.).
　　Dilger (1956) and Hough (1964) stated that red spruce–balsam fir forests are preferred at higher elevations in the Adirondacks and Catskills. At lower elevations the species also occupies northern hardwoods mixed with either red spruce or hemlock and black spruce–tamarack bogs.
　　Breeding records are sparse outside the Catskills, Adirondacks, and Tug Hill. There are persistent populations in the Alleghenies from southeastern Chautauqua, through Cattaraugus, to southwestern Wyoming counties and in northwestern Chenango Co. around Pharsalia WMA. A few also nest in the northern Taconics of Rensselaer Co.

Nonbreeding This species has traditionally been the most numerous member of its genus during migration, generally outnumbering Veery, and by far more common than Gray-cheeked Thrush. Since the mid-1980s it has declined considerably, and over the last decade the Hermit Thrush has often been more numerous. Upstate autumn migration peaks 10–25 Sep, with the heaviest flights west of Richford, Tioga Co. (W. Evans, pers. comm.).
　　Spring maxima: 200 Central Park, Manhattan 11 May 1914, early for

so many; 175 Buffalo, Erie Co. 20 May 1957; 100 Rochester, Monroe Co. 29 May 1974. **Fall maxima:** nocturnal counts of birds heard calling over-head: 2000 Far Rockaway, Queens Co. 7 Sep 1953 (Bull); "thousands," Syracuse, Onondaga Co. 16 Sep 1965 (Scheider); 188 (TV tower kills) Elmira, Chemung Co. 20 Sep 1977 (Welles 1978); 173 Colden, Erie Co. 29 Sep 1962. A good late count was 25 at Island Cottage Woods, Monroe Co. 5 Oct 1981. **Extreme dates: Spring:** 24 Apr (coastal) and 26 Apr (inland); 11 Jun (coastal). It rarely occurs away from nesting areas in mid to late Jun; for example, one spent Jun 1979 at Glen Cove, Nassau Co. (KB 29:243). **Fall:** there are at least nine late Jul arrival dates for nonbreeding areas upstate, with the earliest 19 Jul. The late date is 10 Nov both inland and coastal.

It is occasionally reported in late Dec, especially on CBCs. These reports are seldom supported by sufficient details to safely rule out other *Catharus*, the most likely of which is the very similar Hermit Thrush. One seen by Davis et al. at JBWR 29–30 Dec 1978 was accepted by NYSARC (1980).

Remarks Subspecies limits in this species, indeed throughout the genus *Catharus*, are under debate. Ramos, in Phillips 1991, proposed that our breeding subspecies is the newly described *appalachiensis*. The common migratory subspecies is the widely distributed *swainsoni* of boreal Canada, of which *appalachiensis* may be a variant. Parkes (in litt.) concluded that *appalachiensis* is most likely based on a reddish morph of the widespread *swainsoni*. The Newfoundland subspecies *clarescens*, proposed by Burleigh and Peters (1948), is generally considered synonymous with *swainsoni* (Bull 1964; Phillips 1991; K. C. Parkes, in litt.).
Walter G. Ellison

Hermit Thrush *Catharus guttatus*

Range Nearctic, breeding from Alaska east to northern Ontario and southern Labrador and Newfoundland, south to southwestern United States and, in the east, to southern New England, New York, including the coastal plain of Long Island, and in the mountains to Maryland, West Virginia, and western Virginia. Winters irregularly in the northern portions of the breeding range south to southern Florida, the Gulf Coast, southern Texas, and through interior Mexico to Guatemala and El Salvador.

Status Fairly common to common but often localized breeder. Common to abundant coastal migrant, less common inland. Uncommon in winter in the southeast; rare elsewhere.

Breeding One of the state's finest singers, it is widely distributed, ranging from the cool wooded slopes of the Adirondacks and Catskills to the hot, dry, sandy pine-oak woodlands of LI. It is found at elevations in excess of 500 ft, except in LI and upstate pine barrens.

It nests in open, dry to mesic, mixed and coniferous woodlands. These include northern hardwoods with a generous admixture of hemlocks and white pine, spruce-fir forest with either a moss or blueberry and lichen carpeted floor, and pitch pine with scattered scrub oak in the understory. Despite this broad array of habitats the species shows large gaps in its NY breeding range and further areas of sparse distribution. Noteworthy gaps include the Great Lakes and St. Lawrence plains, much of the lower Hudson Valley, and the Mohawk Valley. It is sparsely distributed from the Finger Lakes westward on the Appalachian Plateau save for the Allegany Hills, where it is common. The highest populations are in the northern Adirondacks; for example, nearly 58 a year were counted on one BBS route from 1985 to 1991 (Price et al. 1995). On LI the Hermit Thrush occurs most commonly in southeastern Suffolk Co., but it ranges westward on the North Shore to northern Nassau Co. (Atlas 1988).

Recent BBS population trends in NY have been positive (C. R. Smith, B. Peterjohn, pers. comm.). There was a relatively brief but sharp decline after the exceptionally cold winters of 1977–1978 and 1978–1979 (Robbins et al. 1986).

Nonbreeding Migrants are most numerous during Oct and Apr. In fall, they are most common along the coast. It is rarely seen in summer away from known nesting haunts.

Fall maxima: 350 Prospect Park, Kings Co. 15 Oct 1950; 300 Orient, Suffolk Co. 12 Oct 1952; 66 Sandy Pond-Selkirk Shores, Oswego Co. 30 Sep 1976. *Spring maxima:* 250 Far Rockaway, Queens Co. to Woodmere, Nassau Co. 6 May 1950; 75 Braddock Bay, Monroe Co. 20 Apr 1954.

Some birds overwinter, either where shrubs and vines retain persistent fruit or at well-stocked feeding stations in the southeast, including LI and the lower Hudson Valley north to Greene and Columbia counties. As many as five wintered near New Rochelle, Westchester Co. 1939–1940. CBC totals, because they occur early in the winter, necessarily overestimate the wintering population. Nonetheless, the winter of 1976–1977 was apparently particularly favorable, with 48 recorded on CBCs upstate and 287 on the coast. They only rarely overwinter upstate, although they are regular in late Dec. Records suggesting successful overwintering exist northward to Henderson, Jefferson Co. and Stillwater, Saratoga Co. The species is very rare in Dec in the Adirondacks and has never been known to overwinter there.

Walter G. Ellison

Wood Thrush

Hylocichla mustelina

Range Eastern Nearctic, breeding from southeastern North Dakota, east through extreme southern Canada and northern United States to Nova Scotia and central Maine, and south to eastern Texas, northern Florida, and the Gulf states. Winters from southern Texas to Panama.

Status Widespread breeder, common in the south but gradually becoming uncommon to the north. Fairly common to common spring migrant; fairly common but easily overlooked autumn migrant inland.

Breeding This fine singer and familiar forest bird is found virtually throughout the state except above 3000 ft in the Catskills and 2500 ft in the Adirondacks and in urban southwestern LI. It occurs in mesic forests and woodlands, both mixed and deciduous, but seems to prefer open, moist deciduous forest with a well-developed midstory of saplings and small tree species and little herb and shrub cover. Smaller woodlots and urban parks may harbor a few pairs, but they apparently cannot breed successfully in such places because of high nest predation, brood parasitism, and competition with common edge-dwelling birds such as American Robin (Hoover et al. 1995; Robinson et al. 1995). Recent BBS data indicate a precipitous population decline in NY and throughout the species' range (C. R. Smith, B. Peterjohn, pers. comm.; Price et al. 1995). Despite this decline, it occurs farther north in NY than it did at the beginning of the twentieth century because of a midcentury range expansion.

Nonbreeding It is less numerous in migration than other spotted thrushes, which breed much farther to the north. Monitoring of nocturnal migration with automated sound equipment on the Appalachian Plateau suggested a major migratory corridor between Ithaca, Tompkins Co. and Norwich, Chenango Co. on the eastern Appalachian Plateau and two peak periods of movement, the second week of Sep and from late Sep to the first week of Oct (W. Evans, pers. comm.).

Spring maxima: Good numbers sometimes occur in migratory fallouts,

439

such as 5–6 May 1950, when 40 were counted in Central Park, Manhattan and there were counts of 35 at each of two other NYC parks; 46 HIWMA, Cayuga Co. 13 May 1995. *Fall maxima:* 108 struck the Elmira TV tower, Chemung Co. 20 Sep 1977 (Welles 1978); 100 Whiskey Hollow, Onondaga Co. 5 Sep 1994. *Extreme dates:* 14 Apr and 3 Dec. Rare before the last days of Apr and after mid-Oct.

Bull (1974) expressed some doubt about the validity of six winter reports he previously cited (1964) because no documentation was ever submitted in support of them. Since then, several additional reports have been published for Dec and later. The most plausible of these are for birds overwintering in Central Park and on Park Avenue, Manhattan 28 Jan–8 Mar 1993 (KB 43:163) and 13 Jan–15 Mar 1995 (KB 45:146), respectively. These birds were seen by many observers who seem to have concurred on their identity, but no reports were submitted to NYSARC in support of these extraordinary observations.

Remarks The Wood Thrush was first described by Gmelin in 1789 from the description of a specimen taken at Hempstead, Nassau Co. (Phillips 1991). Walter G. Ellison

Fieldfare   *Turdus pilaris*

Range Palearctic, breeds from southern Greenland and Scandinavia east to northern Siberia and south to central Europe, central Russia, and southern Siberia. Winters from Iceland, the British Isles, southern Scandinavia, and central Europe south to the Mediterranean regions, Asia Minor, and north-western India; casual in North America.

Status Accidental.

Occurrence An individual found by Lehman at Larchmont, Westchester Co. 3–12 Feb 1973, represents the only record of this species for NY. Although not supported by specimen or photographic evidence, the record is well documented and was accepted by NYSARC (1981).

Remarks Veit and Petersen (1993) listed one record for MA. Zeranski and Baptist (1990) relegated the single CT record to the Hypothetical list because of its questionable origin. It has also occurred in DE and in PQ, ON, and the Maritime Provinces. Dates range from late fall through spring. Michael F. Cooper

Redwing   *Turdus iliacus*

Range Palearctic, breeding from Iceland across northern Eurasia to central Siberia. Winters south to the Mediterranean region. Casual in migration to Greenland.

Status Accidental.

Occurrence An individual was seen and color photographed at JBWR 20–24 Feb 1959. This record constituted the first for continental North America. Because of the proximity of JBWR to JFK Airport, where many caged birds enter the United States, it remained on NY's Hypothetical list until 1981, when it was accepted by NYSARC (1981).

Remarks This species has been recorded a number of times in the Maritime Provinces.
Michael F. Cooper

American Robin *Turdus migratorius*

Range Nearctic, breeding from Alaska and northern Manitoba to Newfoundland and south, in the east, to central Florida, the Gulf states, Texas, and Mexico. Winters throughout Mexico and north, at least irregularly, to Newfoundland, southern Ontario, and Michigan, and in the west to southern Alaska.

Status Very common and widespread breeder; abundant to very abundant migrant. Uncommon to very abundant in winter, increasingly numerous locally in response to good berry crops and a series of mild winters.

Breeding Easily the most adaptable of our native breeding species, the robin is ubiquitous. It nests from city parks and suburban yards to forest clearings in the Adirondack wilderness. Its gregarious character together with its widespread occurrence make its Atlas range map the most complete of all species; it has been recorded in 97% of all blocks, with breeding Confirmed in 90%. However, in many communities, lawn, garden, and mosquito spraying may be the cause of decreased local breeding populations. An analysis of 116 NY BBS 1966–1994 showed a significant 15% decline in numbers (Peterjohn 1995), but BBS are mostly rural counts and penetration of urban areas may offset some of this downturn (E. Salzman, pers. comm.).

Nonbreeding Migrants usually arrive in late Feb or early Mar downstate, about a week later upstate; they depart by late Nov. Great flocks pass through in both spring and fall, their numbers often increasing dramatically in spring at barriers such as Lakes Erie and Ontario. On 10 Apr 1970, for example, 5000 were recorded at Manitou, Monroe Co. In late summer through early winter they occasionally congregate in enormous roosts: a remarkable "50,000 plus" was reported near Coxsackie, Greene Co. late 1984–Jan 1985 (Guthrie) (KB 35:143). Even in winter, American Robins are widely distributed across the state. CBC totals show a steady increase:

the average annual statewide total for the 1960s was 905; for the 1970s, 2826; for the 1980s, 4837. These census increases are evenly distributed statewide (Salzman 1994).

Remarks The nominate subspecies breeds in our area. The darker *nigrideus* of northeastern Canada is rare but is regularly recorded in winter and early spring.

Gerry Rising

Varied Thrush   *Ixoreus naevius*

Range Western Nearctic, breeding from Alaska south to northern California and east to northwestern Montana. Winters chiefly south of the breeding range to northern Baja California. Casual in central and northeastern North America.

Status Rare vagrant.

Occurrence In Bull (1974) there were 29 records, 18 of them from LI: 4 specimens and 25 sight records. Nearly all were from feeding stations. Since then, an additional 44 have been reported, mostly at feeders: 6 downstate and 38 upstate. Most occurred in Dec and Jan, with the largest number in 1977, when seven birds were recorded. Five were found in 1979, four in 1986, and three in 1978, 1983, 1984, 1990, and 1991. There were no birds recorded, except spring carryovers, in 1974 and 1976. The earliest date is 20 Sep and the latest 24 May. Most of the birds, when sex was indicated, were males (14 males and 3 females).

North of LI and NYC, it has been seen in 26 counties, from Westchester in the southeast, north to St. Lawrence, and west to Cattaraugus and Niagara. Monroe has had the most sightings, with six records, five of which have been in Durand-Eastman Park, Rochester. Erie is second with four; Jefferson and Tompkins each had three.

Remarks In winter 1993–1994 there were seven individuals in MA, one in VT, two in CT, one in ME, and five in ON (NASFN 48:183, 205). It is thought by some that vagrant birds wander east from SA to southwestern PQ, northern NY, LI, New England, and NJ. However, an analysis of data gathered by Project FeederWatch of the Cornell University Laboratory of Ornithology showed that there is no correlation between high numbers of the species at feeders and high numbers of vagrants in the same year. This finding may suggest that vagrant birds come from a portion of their range not readily sampled in that survey, such as interior AK and the Northwest Territories (Wells and Rosenberg 1996).

Lee B. Chamberlaine

MOCKINGBIRDS, THRASHERS, AND ALLIES—MIMIDAE

Gray Catbird   *Dumetella carolinensis*

Range Nearctic, breeding from southern British Columbia east to Nova Scotia and south to Oregon, the central portions of Arizona, New Mexico, the Gulf states, and northern Florida. Winters along the southeastern coast from Long Island south, in the Mississippi Valley north to southern Illinois, and elsewhere from the southern parts of its breeding range south through Central America; also in Bermuda and the West Indies.

Status Widespread breeder, absent only in the high elevations of the Adirondacks. Common to very common migrant. Uncommon to fairly common in winter on LI and the lower Hudson Valley, rarer upstate.

Breeding One of the most widely distributed breeding birds in the state, it was found in 92% of the Atlas blocks. It is found wherever low dense shrubs and thickets occur, from swamp borders and streamsides, forest edges, farmland, and roadsides to surburban yards, city parks, and even coastal sand dunes. It has been common in NY at least since the early 1900s (Eaton 1914). The BBS found no significant trend in NY populations 1966–1994 (Peterjohn 1995). Breeding density from 1985 to 1991 was greatest in the lower Hudson Valley and LI and lowest in the L. Champlain Valley and Adirondacks (Price et al. 1995).

It is double brooded; one nest is started in early May, the young fledge in mid-Jun, and the second nest is built in late Jun to mid-Jul. Even though 44% of catbird nests in ON were found to contain Brown-headed Cowbird eggs (Scott 1977), cowbird parasitism is rarely successful because catbirds regularly throw out the foreign eggs. Catbirds are one of only about a dozen species known to recognize and eject cowbird eggs (Cimprich and Moore 1995).

Nonbreeding Catbirds arrive on average during the last week in Apr, and a few can appear as early as the first week in Apr. Major migratory movements are nocturnal. Fall departure occurs by the third week in Oct on average, but there are many Nov sightings, and a few winter every year on LI and in other parts of NY, most often near large bodies of water. Cruickshank (1942) noted that they regularly brave the winter in sheltered thickets near the coast, where they can be "astonishingly secretive." Catbird is now common on CBCs from LI, NYC, and the lower Hudson, where the total from combined counts reached a few dozen in the 1960s and increased to a hundred or more in the 1980s. One or two are sometimes found on CBCs in Rochester, Syracuse, Ithaca, Schenectady, and Dutchess Co., but it shows no increase in those places since the 1960s.

Remarks This is a hardy and adaptable species and an important component of our native avifauna that seems likely to continue to thrive. The

familiar threats to other migratory songbirds—cowbird parasitism, forest fragmentation, loss of habitat on the winter range, hazards of migration over the Gulf of Mexico, increasing human populations—have little effect on this bird, which shows great flexibility in its nest sites, tolerates human presence, likes forest edges, often detours around the Gulf of Mexico or winters in the United States, and recognizes cowbird eggs and ejects them from the nest. It is not without enemies, of course, and is preyed upon by cats, snakes, crows, jays, and other common predators, but losses from these apparently are replaced and the population continues to remain relatively steady.
Valerie M. Freer

Northern Mockingbird *Mimus polyglottos*

Range Southern Nearctic and Neotropical, resident from northern California generally east to southern New England, sporadically and locally farther north, and south to Baja California, through Mexico, and to southeastern Texas, the Gulf Coast, southern Florida, and the Greater Antilles. Northern populations partially migratory.

Status Common resident throughout the Coastal Lowlands, Hudson Valley, Finger Lakes region, and Genesee R. at Rochester, and increasing in other areas.

Breeding The Northern Mockingbird has been increasing and expanding its resident range in NY since the 1950s, when the first birds were found nesting on LI. This expansion is not readily explained, but several possible reasons have been suggested, such as climatic warming favoring northward movement, the increase of residential areas providing additional suitable habitat, and the exploratory drive of individual birds and pairs to strike out in search of suitable breeding habitat (Atlas 1988; Brauning 1992). Cadman et al. (1987) suggested the possibility that the first occurrences of mockingbirds in ON may have been escaped individuals, since the species was commonly kept as a cage bird in the nineteenth century. A comparison of Bull's (1974) map with the Atlas shows a striking range expansion northward along the Hudson R. into the L. Champlain region from the 1970s to 1980s.

Like other species with southeastern ranges, the mockingbird has increased its range in NY along three riparian geographical zones. It has moved into the state by way of the NYC and LI regions, then up the Hudson R. corridor to the shores of L. Champlain. The Mohawk R. then serves as a secondary corridor for movement west to the interior of the state. A second route into the state follows the Susquehanna R. north through the Finger Lakes and Genesee R. corridor. The third pattern is along the Great Lakes shores, with population clusters at Niagara and Rochester. Indeed, mockingbirds may be somewhat more common west of the Niagara R., rather than east of it, because relatively mild winters west of the river may favor them.

BBS data showed a strong increasing population trend in NY since the 1960s. In the Atlas, mockingbirds were located in 46% of the blocks, with nearly half in the Confirmed category.

Nonbreeding Before the mid-1950s, when they began to occupy downstate year-round, mockingbirds were regular fall migrants along the coast, but the extent to which birds withdraw in fall from the summer range and return to the same territories in spring is unclear (Brauning 1992). Mockingbirds are observed at all months of the year but are less common after Jan upstate. Outside the downstate regions, they were scarce and not consistently observed on CBCs until the 1970s. They have been present, although often in small numbers, on CBCs in northern NY since 1970, most notably in the areas of Watertown, Canton, and Massena along the St. Lawrence R., where winter conditions are harsh.
Claudia K. Melin

Sage Thrasher *Oreoscoptes montanus*

Range Western Nearctic, breeding from southern British Columbia east to southeastern Wyoming and south throughout the Southwest to northern Texas. Winters south to northern Mexico and southern Texas. Casual east to the Great Plains, vagrant to New York and Massachusetts.

Status Casual vagrant.

Occurrence The four substantiated New York records, two from upstate, two from LI, are: (1) a female collected at Braddock Bay, Monroe Co. 12 Apr 1942 (Meade) CUM 12789; (2) one banded, color photographed, and released at Shinnecock Inlet, Suffolk Co. 18 Oct 1958 (Wilcox and Terry, confirmation by Eisenmann and Bull by comparison of the color slide with AMNH study skins), ph in AMNH; (3) one at Massena, St. Lawrence Co. 27 Dec 1971 (photographed by Allen and also identified by comparison with AMNH study skins), ph in AMNH; (4) one at JBWR 13–17 Jan 1973, photographed (Davis 1973). No Sage Thrasher has been reported in the state since 1973.

Remarks The Massena bird was originally misidentified and published locally as an even rarer Bendire's Thrasher, a sedentary species of the arid Southwest.

There are records in at least five other eastern states, including two in NJ, 1949 and 1990 (Leck 1984; Halliwell 1995), and a single 1965 MA

record with photograph (Veit and Peterson 1993). Zeranski and Baptist (1990) cited no CT records.
Gerry Rising

Brown Thrasher *Toxostoma rufum*

Range Chiefly central and eastern Nearctic, breeding from southern Canada south to eastern Texas, the Gulf states, and Florida. Winters chiefly in the southeastern United States but also north to Massachusetts.

Status Widespread breeder except at higher altitudes, with populations declining sharply. Common coastal migrant; uncommon migrant upstate.

Breeding This handsome songster is a bird of hedgerows in dry open country at lower elevations. It was recorded in 63% of Atlas blocks. Bonney and Burrill summarized it as "widespread . . . except in portions of the Allegany Hills, Catskill Peaks and adjacent ecozones, the Adirondacks, and the Tug Hill Plateau. Presumably these areas are too high and too heavily forested to support the species" (Atlas 1988).

Despite this broad distribution, it is a species in serious trouble in NY. Data from 111 BBSs statewide 1966–1994 showed a highly significant and precipitous decline of 87% in the breeding population. Further analysis of these data indicated that this decline accelerated in the later years of that period (Peterjohn 1995) and that it is widespread throughout the state. Rising (1994a) discussed the decline over 18 western BBS routes, and Raynor (1976b) noted similar declines on two LI BBSs, recording a 90% drop in their numbers between 1967 and 1976.

Nonbreeding It usually arrives in mid-Apr and remains until mid-Oct, but the season is shorter upstate by as much as one week, both spring and fall.
Spring maxima: 23 Prospect Park, Kings Co. 12 May 1945. *Fall maxima:* 50 Far Rockaway, Queens Co. 17 Sep 1949.

Comparable maxima are not available for single upstate locations, but the regional Niagara Frontier May Counts have dropped from 380 in 1966 to fewer than 40 each year since 1989. As with the BBS results cited above, these data also suggest imminent local elimination (Rising 1995). The corresponding Oct counts (taken after some birds have migrated) have dropped from 21 in 1966 to 5 or fewer in each year since 1979 (Rising 1994b).

The increase in wintering Brown Thrashers, which Bull (1974) correlated with the increase in bird feeders, continued through the 1960s and 1970s, but populations have declined since then. Average statewide CBC totals for the 1960s were 35; for the 1970s, 50; and for the 1980s, 31. This pattern of rise and then fall was uniform across the state except in central NY, where the small numbers showed a steady decrease (Salzman 1994).

Remarks A literature review and discussions with experienced birders disclosed no satisfactory reasons for the tragic decline of this attractive species. Friedmann (1929) referred to it as "a decidedly uncommon victim of the cowbird." It is in fact the largest species so parasitized, and even when such parasitism occurs Friedmann (1963) noted that it had 50–60% success in bringing off its own brood. Nickell (1955) cited three instances of nests with chicks of both species, in one of which the cowbird died.

Bent (1948) provided a lengthy roster of mammalian, avian, and reptilian nest predators. (Audubon's Brown Thrasher portrait includes a threatening black snake.) It is also true that many abandoned farms have passed through scrubland to forest, but extensive open farmland and scrub remain. The other mimids Gray Catbird and Northern Mockingbird have similar breeding habits and similar enemies, but they show increasing NY populations.

Raynor (1976b) said that his winter "observations suggest that Mockingbird is displacing Brown Thrasher at feeders, berry-bearing plants and other winter food sources." But, these species coexist throughout the southern United States, and the small number of mockingbirds in western NY, despite their population increase there, cannot account for the steep decline in thrasher numbers.

It is distressing to note that the Brown Thrasher is not listed of at least Special Concern by the NYSDEC.

Gerry Rising

STARLINGS AND ALLIES—STURNIDAE

European Starling *Sturnus vulgaris*

Range Originally Palearctic; widely introduced into various parts of the world, including North America in the late 1880s. Now breeds throughout North America; in the east, north to central Ontario and Quebec and southern Labrador. Retreats from northernmost areas in winter.

Status Introduced. Very abundant throughout, except in the densely forested portions. Sedentary and migratory. Probably the most numerous bird in NY.

Breeding The Atlas showed Confirmed breeding in 4082 blocks out of 4622 (88% of the total) in which it was recorded. It does not breed in heavily forested areas or in the higher elevations of the Adirondacks, Allegany Hills, Catskills, or Tug Hill (Atlas 1988). An analysis of BBS data 1966–1994 showed that the NY population was leveling off from a three-decade decline. In 1966–1979 the decline averaged 3.8% per year. In 1980–1994 it was only 0.7% (Peterjohn 1995).

Nonbreeding The state population is pulling out of a decline and seems to be leveling off, as shown by an analysis of CBC data, which corroborates the BBS data. During the winter months, starlings tend to congregate in large roosts, which sometimes contain massive numbers of birds. Winter roosts tend to confound population interpretations because enormous concentrations of birds are packed into very small geographical areas. When these roosts appear within CBC circles, they can disproportionately inflate the state totals. For this reason, the median gives a better expression of the typical count than does the average. The state totals tend to fluctuate in synchrony with the numbers from large roosts. The medians, which are less distorted by the extreme numbers, reveal a fairly stable, albeit highly variable, long-term population level.

The largest statewide tally was on the 1978–1979 CBC, when 55 counts reported 1,809,383 starlings. The median was 1803. The seven highest counts that year were: Rochester 800,000; Lower Hudson 750,000; Buffalo 98,842; Queens Co. 14,600; SI 13,376; southern Rensselaer Co. 12,051; Syracuse 10,829.

On the 1993–1994 CBC, the statewide tally from 65 counts was 395,395 starlings with a median of 1547.

Remarks After two failed attempts, the European Starling was first successfully introduced with the release of 60 birds in Central Park, Manhattan in 1890. Spreading rapidly, it was distributed throughout the state within the next 30 years. It is so successful because it can readily exploit opportunities offered by humans through both agriculture and urban developments. It also gains a competitive advantage with its unique bill, which can exert a powerful opening force once it is in the ground, enabling it to pry out invertebrates (Martin 1987).

Where abandoned farms are reverting to forests, starling populations have been declining, but where both farms and forests are being subdivided into housing and commercial developments, populations are rising. Since urban development seems to be outpacing the reversion to forests, a population increase can be expected.

Donald A. Windsor

WAGTAILS AND PIPITS— MOTACILLIDAE

American Pipit *Anthus rubescens*

Range Holarctic, breeding in arctic North America, in the Rocky Mountains, and south; in the east, to Newfoundland, with peripheral populations on the Gaspe Peninsula and at Mt. Katahdin, Maine and Mt. Washington, New Hampshire. Winters in the southern United States, north occasionally to Massachusetts on the East Coast.

Status Uncommon to abundant migrant throughout; usually rare and irregular winter visitant on LI and in lower Hudson Valley. Erratic and unpredictable in occurrence, numbers fluctuating widely.

Occurrence It inhabits open treeless country and frequents recently plowed fields, lake and river shores, inland and coastal beaches, shortgrass areas such as airports, and subalpine tundra. There are three recent fall records for above 4000 ft elevation in the Adirondacks (KB 36:42, 43:70, 45:51). Flocks of 50–200 individuals are often encountered during migration. Rare before late Aug and after mid-Nov upstate, it winters regularly in small numbers on the coast but only rarely inland. During 1960–1995, only nine pipits were reported for 42 upstate CBCs, whereas several hundred were logged on 24 southeastern counts. Spahn suggested that the spring migration occurs as an early wave in late winter and a later one in early May (KB 37:133). It is very rare after late May.

Spring maxima: all at Braddock Bay, Monroe Co.: 500 on 1 May 1954, 1000 on 12 May 1954, 230 on 16 Apr 1993. *Fall maxima:* 800 near Tully, Onondaga Co. 28 Oct 1965; 500 MNWR 24 Sept 1985. *Winter maxima:* 125 Jamaica Bay, Queens Co. 25 Dec 1934; 20 Ghent, Columbia Co. 15 Dec 1990. *Extreme dates:* 10 Jun and 23 Jul.

Remarks A bird collected at Miller Place, Suffolk Co. 10 May 1882 (AMNH 25964) was found by Parkes to belong to the subspecies *alticola*, the Rocky Mountain subspecies, rather than the nominate *rubescens*, which is our regular migrant. Parkes (in litt.) advised that *alticola* can be identified in the alternate plumage by the virtual lack of ventral streaking.
Kenneth L. Crowell

WAXWINGS—BOMBYCILLIDAE

Bohemian Waxwing   *Bombycilla garrulus*

Range Holarctic, breeding in North America from Alaska east to northern Manitoba and south to central Washington and southern Alberta. Winters south irregularly to northwestern United States and southwestern Canada but wanders eastward with increasing regularity to central Maine, Pennsylvania, and New York and more rarely to New Brunswick and Nova Scotia.

Status Highly erratic winter visitant, subject to irruptive flights in certain years. Since the late 1970s seen more regularly upstate, particularly in the northern and western regions. Casual on LI.

Occurrence Described by Bull (1974) as "one of the very rarest of winter visitors," this species now occurs annually. It is typically seen alone or in small numbers, often with the more numerous Cedar Waxwing. Flocks of more than 300 birds have been reported, and as the maxima listed below indicate, these observations do not necessarily correspond to flight years. In addition to this species' regular occurrence in the state, it has apparently expanded its winter range eastward, notably in Region 7, where in the last 15 years it has been recorded almost annually (KB 40:46). The only LI observation since a 1918 specimen record was an individual first recorded on the Southern Nassau CBC and seen 3–7 Jan 1993 at Tackapausha Preserve, Wantagh (Jones, Joost) (KB 43:160): the winter of 1993–1994 was a flight year for the species.

Years in which it occurred in considerable numbers were 1879–1880, 1919–1920, 1961–1962, 1969, 1980–1981, 1985–1986, 1993–1994.

Maxima: 1200–1500 near Watertown, Jefferson Co. 9 Apr 1994, an unprecedented number; 500 Dry Hill, St. Lawrence Co. 3 Apr 1984; 450 Keeseville to Port Douglas, Essex Co. 11 Jan 1987. *Extreme dates:* 28 Oct and 28 Apr.

Ken Feustel

Cedar Waxwing   *Bombycilla cedrorum*

Range Nearctic, breeding across much of the northern United States and southern Canada and, in the east, south to southern New Jersey and in the mountains to northern Georgia. Moves about erratically during migration and is recorded in winter from New England south to Panama and the Greater Antilles.

Status Common breeder throughout the state, except in heavily urbanized areas. Sedentary and migratory. Very common spring and fall migrant.

Breeding A widespread breeder in NY, it is found both coastally and inland at most elevations, especially near water. This species prefers open areas with scattered vegetation in rural areas, usually near fruiting trees or bushes, but it avoids dense forest. Only 11 species were recorded more frequently in the Atlas. It was recorded in 92% of all blocks and was Confirmed in 31% of those. On BBS routes in the Adirondacks, it was more abundant than anywhere else in North America (Robbins et al. 1986). During the Atlas project it was not found in the developed sections of western LI or NYC. It was last recorded breeding on SI in 1967. Despite its absence from urbanized areas, it has increased slightly as a breeder in the state since the 1970s.

It nests later in the season than all other passerines with the exception of the American Goldfinch. In NY it does not usually commence breeding until early Jun and has been known to nest as late as Oct. One of the few North American passerines that nest semicolonially, this species will travel in small flocks even during the nesting season.

Nonbreeding Although feeding chiefly on fruit through much of the year, it supplements this diet with insects during the warmer months, especially in late summer, often flycatching along the edges of lakes and streams. Bull (1974) described the Cedar Waxwing as "very common throughout the state in spring." It has apparently increased significantly inland in late spring, as the inland maxima illustrate.

   Coastal maxima: Fall: 1000 Far Rockaway, Queens Co. 8 Sep 1953 and 10 Sep 1969; 1000 Riis Park, Queens Co. 28 Sep 1975. *Inland maxima: Spring:* These records exceed by 2 to 5 times the maxima in Bull 1974, 1976. 5000 Braddock Bay, 22 May 1977; 3000 Point. Breeze, Orleans Co. 30 May 1994; 1913 Hamburg, Erie Co. 5 Jun 1984. *Fall:* 4500 Braddock Bay, Monroe Co. 31 Aug 1993, an impressive number. *Winter maxima:* 600 near Rochester, Monroe Co. 26 Feb 1955; 600 near Syracuse, Onondaga Co. 28 Feb 1964; 300 East Hampton, Suffolk Co. 28 Dec 1946.

Remarks Upstate observers have increasingly reported Cedar Waxwings with orange, as opposed to the normal yellow, tail tips. This orange variant has been referred to by some as typical of the Japanese subspecies. Parkes (1983) pointed out that there is no Japanese subspecies of the Cedar Waxwing, which is a purely North American species. Parkes further stated that the Japanese Waxwing, *B. japonica*, is a highly distinctive species, differing from both the Cedar Waxwing and the Bohemian Waxwing in having bright red, not orange, tail tips. A review by Parkes of 207 nonalbinistic study skins in the collection of the CMNH indicated that six had orange tail tips. Peterson (KB 39:185) raised the possibility that this is a recent mutation spreading through the waxwing population. However, recent experimentation seemed to indicate that the color of the Cedar Waxwing's tail is influenced by what the bird eats while the feathers are growing (Witmer 1996).
Ken Feustel

WOOD WARBLERS—PARULIDAE

Blue-winged Warbler   *Vermivora pinus*

Range Eastern Nearctic, breeding from eastern Nebraska and Iowa east locally to extreme southeastern Ontario, central New York, and Massachusetts; south to Arkansas, the mountains of northern Georgia, and the coast of Delaware. Winters from Mexico to Panama.

Status Common breeder in most of state but absent from higher elevations. Fairly common to common migrant.

Breeding Historically it probably bred along the prairie-forest ecotone in the south-central United States (Short 1963; Gill 1980). Farmland abandonment and the appearance of early successional shrubland provided suitable habitat (Confer and Knapp 1981) for the expansion of the Blue-winged to the east and north (Gill 1980). Both the Blue-winged and the Golden-winged warbler nest in shrubby fields and into the edge of forests. In central and north-central NY the Blue-winged tends to use slightly later stages of succession, including young second-growth forests (pers. obs.).

The Blue-winged was established in southern NY and LI around the turn of the century (Eaton 1914). Throughout the 1900s it consistently expanded northward. It appeared in Tompkins Co. in central NY in 1942, reached the Syracuse area by the 1960s, expanded to the Lake Ontario Plain by the 1980s (Atlas 1988), and reached Clinton Co. in the extreme northeastern corner of the state by 1994 (KB 44:236). It is now common as a breeder throughout most of the state except the higher elevations of the Catskills and Adirondacks and the northernmost portions. The northward expansion is correlated with farmland abandonment, which progressed from south to north across the state. The slightly more southern distribution of the Blue-winged, in comparison to the Golden-winged, is correlated with the blue-wing's use of later stages of succession. In NY the northern limit of the breeding range of the Blue-winged has lagged 30–50 mi behind the Golden-winged population as both have expanded northward throughout this century.

Nonbreeding It is difficult to distinguish migrants from residents. The Region 1 count on 16 May 1993 detected 106. A few of them might have been migrants. However, most males have established territories by that date in north-central NY at the same latitude (pers. obs.). Bull (1974) noted an extreme record of 17 Apr 1947 West Falls, Erie Co., the same date as a Hooded Warbler, after a heavy storm in the OK-TX region. Typical dates for arrival are 28–30 Apr and for departure are late Aug to mid-Sep. There is only one report as late as Oct in the last 20 years: 20 Oct in Region 2 (KB 39:32). Bull, however, cited records for 29 and 30 Nov.

Remarks Its abundance has increased greatly as it has expanded northward. Within the appropriate habitat it is now fairly common. In Tompkins Co. it was a decade before the species became established after its first appearance in 1942. Yet a May count there in 1995 found 67 in 230 party-hours, making it the seventh most abundant warbler species. BBS reports show that the Blue-winged has begun to decline in the more southern parts of its range, although not in NY. Declines have occurred in areas where mature forests have become established. This decline may result from a loss of habitat, which we may soon see in NY.

John L. Confer

Golden-winged Warbler   *Vermivora chrysoptera*

Range Chiefly northeastern Nearctic, breeding locally from southeastern Manitoba (rarely), northeastern North Dakota, and southeastern Iowa east to central and northwestern New York and Massachusetts, south on the coast to New Jersey and in the mountains to northern Georgia. Ranges farther north and at higher altitudes than *V. pinus*, and not as far south in the Midwestern states or along the Atlantic coastal plain. Winters from southern Mexico to northwestern South America.

Status Localized breeder throughout but absent from LI and higher elevations. Rare to uncommon migrant.

Breeding The historical and current distribution of the Golden-winged Warbler in the eastern United States has been highly influenced by human alterations of its habitat. Most breeding sites in upstate NY are abandoned farmland in early stages of succession that have patches of grasses and shrubs but few trees. Most territories in north-central (J. L. Confer, unpub. data), central (Confer and Knapp 1981), and southern (Frech and Confer 1987) NY had less than one-third forest canopy. As succession progresses with a regional increase in forest cover and a decrease in shrubland, nesting habitat declines, and the species has been recommended for inclusion on NYSDED's list of Species of Special Concern.

The southern population, which commonly nests along the edges of swamp forests in the Ramapo Mtns., appears to be stable. This part of NY and adjacent NJ is the only known area in the entire range in which Golden-winged and Blue-winged warblers have been able to coexist for nearly a century. (Gill 1980; Confer and Knapp 1981; Atlas 1988).

It has been expanding northward in NY for nearly a century. By 1972 it was noted as a common breeder in the eastern portions of the Great Lakes Plain, with occasional reports from the St. Lawrence Valley. Now reported regularly, but in low numbers, from northeastern NY in the lower elevations surrounding the Adirondacks.

During this century, as its range expanded northward, it declined and even disappeared from much of its former range (Confer et al. 1991). For example, in Region 3 the bird was common from the 1930s through the early 1980s, but no breeding male was reported from 1992 to 1995. In Region 1 it outnumbered the Blue-winged Warbler in the 1970s, but a 1993 "count day" revealed only five Golden-winged compared with 106 Blue-winged warblers (KB 43:211).

In NY, and throughout the eastern United States as well, declines in the regional abundance are correlated with two factors: a regional decline in early successional habitat as the growth of secondary forests prevails (Confer and Knapp 1981) and expansion of the Blue-winged Warbler into its range (Gill 1980). Gill noted that in most locations in the east, expansion of the Blue-winged into the Golden-winged range was followed by the disappearance of the latter within 50 years. Perhaps hybridization with blue-wings favors replacement of the golden-wing phenotype by the blue-wing phenotype (Short 1963) because of some as yet unexplained selective factor.

Will (1986) compiled observations of interactions between males of the two species in central MI at a site where about 50% of the male golden-wings were not mated. He found that blue-wing dominated golden-wing and suggested that golden-wing might be driven into inferior nesting habitat. In contrast, observations in central NY, based on a larger sample from sites where most males had mates, showed that golden-wing dominated blue-wing (pers. obs.). Territorial overlap is frequent and extensive, as noted in many studies of the breeding biology of these two species (Ficken and Ficken 1968; Gill and Murray 1972; Murray and Gill 1976). These studies reported that interactions between males of the two species are infrequent, even when males have territories that overlap. One recent study showed that male golden-wings generally did not expand their territory into areas vacated by the removal of adjacent blue-wings (pers. obs.). Most evidence suggests that golden-wings are not driven from their optimal habitat by blue-wings.

Nonbreeding It is rarely seen outside of breeding sites. The earliest arrival date is 26 Apr both coastally and inland; most arrival dates are 3–5 May. Most males have arrived on territory by 14 May in north-central NY unless the spring is unusually cold (J. L. Confer, unpub. data). Typical departure dates are late Aug to late Sep, with extreme dates of 10 Oct and 17 Oct.

Golden-winged and Blue-winged Hybridization Usually golden-wings and blue-wings behave as distinct species; golden-wings mate with golden-wings and blue-wings with blue-wings. However, hybridization between Golden-winged and Blue-winged warblers is not rare in areas of range overlap. Hybridization produces two distinct phenotypes, the "Brewster's" and the "Lawrence's" warblers. Parkes (1951) provided an excellent description of the genetics of these phenotypes. The black throat patch may be due to a single recessive gene. The extension of the chest color, either golden-wing white or blue-wing yellow, into the throat region appears to be due to a dominant allele and is fully expressed even in heterozygous individuals. The white belly, plus the gray back and the yellow wing patch of the golden-wing may each be due to separate genes, both of which are incompletely expressed in a heterozygous individual. Parkes (1951) and Gill (1980) noted that many individuals have a yellowish white combination in the chest, whereas others may have semiseparate wing bars that are yellow-ish white. These intermediate phenotypes indicate that body color and wing bar color and pattern are due to genes that are incompletely dominant. The fact that some rare individuals will have the blue-wing body color and the golden-wing wing pattern, or vice versa (Parkes 1951; Gill 1980), suggests that these phenotypes are due to two separate but closely linked genes.

Hybrids are fertile, although there is a suspicion that hybrids have greater difficulty obtaining mates than do pure phenotypes of either species. Hybridization might contribute to the golden-wing decline following expansion of the blue-wing into a portion of the golden-wing range. We do not know why hybridization might be more deleterious for golden-wings than for blue-wings. In north-central NY, golden-wing males frequently mate with "Brewster's" females, but blue-wings do not (pers. obs.). Perhaps this difference in mating pattern is related to the loss of the golden-wing phenotype.

Remarks The Golden-winged Warbler is very inconspicuous when not singing, and its absolute abundance may be underestimated by general birding activities. For example, 0–12 were reported in Region 5 from 1990 to 1994, but studies of their breeding ecology located about 30 resident males yearly from only a dozen sites in the same region. However, birding reports conducted in a similar manner for many years may accurately depict population trends.
John L. Confer

Tennessee Warbler *Vermivora peregrina*

Range Nearctic, breeding from southern Alaska and central Canada to Labrador and western Newfoundland, south to southern Canada, Nova Scotia, and northern United States from Minnesota to Maine. Winters from southern Mexico to northern South America.

Status Rare breeder in the Adirondacks. Regular but cyclically uncommon to very common migrant. Usually most common in spring in central and western NY.

Breeding Before Atlas work from 1980 to 1985, there was only one instance of confirmed breeding in the state: an adult feeding two recent fledglings at North Elba, Essex Co. in Jul 1926. The Atlas provided an additional five Confirmed breeding records, but no nest has yet been found in NY. This warbler is widely distributed but scarce in the Adirondacks, occupying second-growth habitats in boreal forest including young aspen, birch, alder, and willow, usually intermixed with sapling fir, spruce, and tamarack. Counties with reports of Confirmed or Probable breeding included Essex, Franklin, Hamilton, St. Lawrence, and Warren. Given that some males seen after 25 Jun are actually transients, it requires care to determine if birds seen after that date are indeed nesters.

Nonbreeding This warbler's great fluctuations in numbers are apparently in response to insect outbreaks in the boreal forest, especially those of spruce budworm *(Choristeneura fumiferana)*. It was very common most recently from the mid-1970s to the early 1980s. It has been much less common since the mid-1980s. Continental BBS data indicate how volatile population fluctuations are. Although numbers were 171% higher in 1993 than in 1966, counts showed no significant upward or downward trend because of extreme variation in totals from year to year (Price et al. 1995).

　Spring maxima: On 22 May 1983 a huge, and unprecedented, coastal count of 250 at Forest Park, Queens Co. coincided with a count of 67 at Letchworth SP, Wyoming Co.; 12 was an early high count at Syracuse, Onondaga Co. 5 May 1955. *Fall maxima:* 243 struck the Elmira TV Tower, Chemung Co. 20 Sep 1977 (Welles 1978); 90 Venice, Cayuga Co. 1 Sep 1982; 28 Pompey, Onondaga Co. 3 Oct 1980, very late for so many. *Extreme dates: Spring:* 29 Apr (coastal) and 30 Apr (inland). There are reports of singing males at inland, non-Adirondack localities on three mid-Jun dates. There are at least 31 late Jun and Jul reports of this species away from the Adirondacks, mostly of singing males. These may be unsuccessful Canadian nesters that undertake a molt migration into the northeastern United States (C. C. Rimmer, pers. comm.). *Fall:* one banded and present 22–26 Nov (inland). Usually rare before mid-May and after early Oct. *Winter:* An adult present at an Ossining, Westchester Co. feeding station 12–30 Jan 1955 was found dead and preserved as a specimen AMNH 788901 (Bull 1961). Other reports after the first of Dec lack archival documentation.

Walter G. Ellison

Orange-crowned Warbler　　*Vermivora celata*

Range Nearctic, breeding from Alaska to Labrador and south, in the east to central Ontario and western Newfoundland. Winters from the southern United States south to Guatemala. Migrates primarily west of the Appalachians, rarely in the east.

Status Rare migrant and winter visitant.

Occurrence Dull-colored and skulking, the Orange-crowned Warbler undoubtedly occurs more often than the infrequent reports indicate. Look for it in scrubby areas and weedy fields throughout the state from mid-fall to early winter, when most other warblers have gone. In western NY it is a rare but regular spring migrant, when it should be looked for in the taller trees. Elsewhere in the state it is very rare in spring.

Spring maxima: 3 Syracuse, Onondaga Co. 7 May 1962; 3 Geneva, Ontario Co. 18 May 1958. *Fall maxima:* 5 North Pompey, Onondaga Co. 2 Oct 1979; 5 Montauk, Suffolk Co. 27 Oct 1979. *Winter maxima:* 3 at a feeder in Babylon, Suffolk Co. all Jan 1955, one of these wintering. *Extreme dates:* 29 May (1926 specimen, Cayuga Co. CUM 16026) and 6 Jun; 7 Sep (earliest specimen). Rare before Oct.

Bull (1974) reported four additional cases of individuals wintering at feeders in Chemung, Nassau, Richmond, and Yates counties. Another was at the Helgesen feeder, Richmond Co. for two months in the winter of 1982–1983, feeding mainly on grape jelly. A bird found dead at Tobay Beach, Nassau Co. 17 Jan 1975 (Friton) was the first state winter specimen (AMNH 811309).

Also unusual was one found dead on a fishing boat, approximately 30 m southeast of Montauk 6 Oct 1967 (Jensen and Livingstone 1969).

Remarks Aug records have not been included because of possible confusion with dull or immature Yellow and Tennessee warblers.
Joseph DiCostanzo

Nashville Warbler   *Vermivora ruficapilla*

Range Nearctic, breeding from southern British Columbia east to Nova Scotia and south, in the east to northern Illinois, northeastern West Virginia, New York, and southern New England. Winters from Mexico to Guatemala.

Status Locally numerous breeder in the mountains and in central NY but uncommon in most of the far western portions and rare on the lake plains and southeastward. Fairly common migrant inland but only uncommon to fairly common along the coast.

Breeding Uncommon to common breeder in the Adirondacks and Catskills. In the former region Beehler (1978) reported it as an inhabitant of "old pastures, recent burns, bogs, anywhere that the predominant growth is low and young," and Saunders (1929) stated that this bird showed a preference for alder, willow, and birch thickets in old burns and at the edges of tamarack swamps. Over much of the central portions of the state, however, spruce-sphagnum or tamarack-sphagnum bogs are often its choice. In Allegany SP, Cattaraugus Co. mixed aspen-cherry groves seem to be favored. Bull (1974) listed some samples of breeding densities based chiefly on singing males: 25 in bogs of the Rome Sand Plains, Oneida Co. 9 Jun 1956; 15 at the edge of a spruce-fir planting in Highland Forest, Onondaga Co. 19 Jul 1960 (both by Rusk and Scheider); 18 in 50 acres, Edwards, St. Lawrence Co. 30 Jun 1960 (Allen).

It is almost absent as a breeder in the Great Lakes Plain but does nest in a few bogs within 20 mi of L. Ontario. It is totally absent as a breeder east of the Hudson R. south of Columbia Co. and on LI. Atlas workers found this species to be fairly widespread within the limitations listed above. It was recorded in 1469 blocks, and breeding was Confirmed in 18% of those. BBS data indicate a fairly constant breeding population.

Nonbreeding Generally more numerous upstate than along the coast. As with many of our Neotropical migrants, it has gone through a definite decline as a migrant in the past two decades or so. Statewide spring arrival dates range from 26 Apr to 1 May. In fall it is a rare migrant before mid-Aug. Statewide fall departure dates range from 4 Oct to 12 Oct. There are winter records of one at Van Cortlandt Park, Bronx Co. 16 Dec 1917–9 Jan 1918; one coming to a feeder in Penn Yan, Yates Co. through the winter of 1979–1980; and one at a feeder in Lloyds Neck, Suffolk Co. 5 Jan–7 Feb 1967. One found freshly dead 24 Feb 1997 in Bronx Co. (Wallstrom) was delivered to AMNH. There are also a very few scattered records of this bird's being observed on CBCs in the southern part of the state, including two in Dec 1996.

Spring maxima: 18 Buffalo area, Erie Co. 15 May 1993; 17 De Witt, Onondaga Co. 2 May 1992; 14 banded, Fire I. Lighthouse, Suffolk Co. 9 May 1970. *Fall maxima:* 18 struck the Empire State Building, Manhattan 27 Sep 1970; 10 L. Ontario shore, Oswego Co. 1 Oct 1976.
Robert G. McKinney

Northern Parula *Parula americana*

Range Primarily eastern Nearctic, breeding from southern Canada to southern Florida, the Gulf Coast, and Texas. Winters south through Middle America to Costa Rica and from southern Florida through the West Indies.

Status Fairly common but local breeder in the Adirondacks, very rare elsewhere. Common to very common coastal migrant, especially in spring; uncommon inland.

Breeding Formerly locally uncommon throughout the state; formerly very common on eastern LI but extirpated by the early 1950s. The Northern Parula usually builds its nest in *Usnea* lichen. Until the early years of the twentieth century it was a locally common breeder wherever this lichen was abundant. Apparently as a result of air pollution, *Usnea* has disappeared from everywhere in the state except the Adirondacks, and the parula has disappeared as a breeder to the same extent (Atlas 1988). A bird with young seen 27 Jun 1993 at Van Buren, Onondaga Co. (Rusk) (AB 47:1095) is one of the few cases of breeding outside the Adirondacks in recent times.

Nonbreeding Rare before late Apr and after mid-Oct. Coastal migrants in fall usually appear by late Aug.

Spring maxima: 200 Prospect Park, Kings Co. 14 May 1950; 12 Far Rockaway, Queens Co. 28 May 1967, a very late spring. *Fall maxima:* 34 struck the Westhampton Air Force Base tower, Suffolk Co. 5 Oct 1954; 15 Cornell University Wildflower Garden, Tompkins Co. 16 Sep 1994.

Extreme dates: 1, 6, and 9 Apr (coastal, some storm driven) and 27 Apr (inland in 1994, a year with many early warbler arrivals); 3 Dec (inland specimen) and 17 Dec 1993 (coastal).

The first known winter occurrence in the state was one that ate suet at a feeding station in Noyack, Suffolk Co. 1–23 Dec 1965.

Remarks Lindsay and Vezo (1995) reported a male seen feeding a Brown-headed Cowbird chick in a nest being tended by a female Cerulean Warbler in East Hampton, Suffolk Co. in Jun 1994. No actual evidence of hybridization between the two warbler species was found.
Joseph DiCostanzo

Yellow Warbler   *Dendroica petechia*

Range Nearctic, breeding from Alaska east through Canada to Newfoundland and south, in eastern North America, to central Georgia, the northern part of the Gulf states, and on the coast to Virginia. Winters from Mexico and the West Indies to northern South America.

Status Widespread breeder except at higher elevations in the Adirondacks. Very common migrant.

Breeding The Yellow Warbler is quite adaptable in its breeding locations. It nests in shrubbery in rural and suburban gardens, in bushes and smaller trees, and often in willows along streams, lakes, swamps, and marshes. It has been known to nest in thickets of poison ivy and bayberry on coastal sand dunes. There are a few records of this species nesting in conifers where conifers are the predominant vegetation (KB 43:26). It is more frequently parasitized by the Brown-headed Cowbird than any other species in NY.

Atlas workers found it to be widely distributed, with some evidence of breeding in 86% of the blocks. It is found commonly in all parts of the state except the Central Adirondacks. In the Adirondacks it is usually found only at the lowest elevations, often along waterways, where it can be found nesting in willow and alder thickets. BBS data showed evidence of a slight increase statewide in recent years.

Nonbreeding This is a very common migrant. Statewide spring arrival dates range from 25 Apr to 1 May, with LI arrivals about five days earlier. This is one of the very earliest species to migrate south after the breeding season. It can be seen at that season in large numbers along the L. Ontario shore, where 40–65 individuals have been banded in one day in mid to late July. Statewide fall departure dates range from 8 Sep to 22 Sep.

Spring maxima: 120 Sandy Pond, Oswego Co. 19 May 1977; 25 Central Park, Manhattan 23 May 1954. *Fall maxima:* 1000+ Braddock Bay, Monroe Co. 28 Jul 1979; 50 Syracuse, Onondaga Co. 23 Aug 1964. *Extreme dates:* 17 Apr and 24 Oct.

Remarks (By K. C. Parkes) There are some 35+ subspecies of Yellow Warbler, at least two of which occur in NY. Our common migrant and breeder is *aestiva*. The darker, greener northern subspecies *amnicola* has been collected in NY many times. It is a late migrant both in spring and fall and passes through NY when the local *aestiva* has already begun nesting; dates of five Ithaca specimens are 14–21 May, and five Westchester Co. and LI specimens range from 17 to 22 May. Late fall records in NY are most likely *amnicola* but possibly one of the other northern subspecies. Field observers should limit themselves to noting only that such birds were of a non-*aestiva* subspecies.
Robert G. McKinney and Kenneth C. Parkes

Chestnut-sided Warbler   *Dendroica pensylvanica*

Range Nearctic, breeding from east-central Alberta and Nova Scotia south to southern Michigan, Pennsylvania, and New Jersey and in the mountains to northern Georgia, but along the coast only to central New Jersey and Long Island. Winters from southern Mexico to Panama.

Status Common breeder over much of NY. Common migrant.

Breeding The fifth most common warbler breeding in NY, it was recorded in 68% of Atlas blocks and was Confirmed in 32% of those. It is uncommon on the Great Lakes Plain and other areas where modern agriculture is practiced. It is rapidly being displaced by urban sprawl in central Suffolk Co. and is absent in urban areas such as western LI and Buffalo, in the Adirondack High Peaks above 3000 ft, and in extensive mature forest. This is a species of the forest edge, brushy pastures, and neglected roadsides. The BBS found a significant decrease of 2.95% per year in the eastern region from 1966 to 1988 (Sauer and Droege 1992). This slow downward trend is probably due to changes in land management on the Appalachian Plateau, with fewer small farms and the cleaning out of hedgerows and edges. The maturation of the forest and the overbrowsing by deer on the understory have also had an adverse effect on this warbler's habitat. In 1930–1931 in Quaker Run Valley of Allegany SP, it was estimated that 161 pairs nested. By 1983–1985 the same area was estimated to contain 22 pairs (Saunders 1936; Baird 1990). It was a dominant warbler of the Rome Sand Plains, with 60 singing males along a mile and a half of road (KB 6:98). In

DeKay's time (1844) this warbler was considered rare, but following the cutting of the forests in the 1800s the resulting scrub favored its breeding. By the early 1900s, as succession advanced, the bird was especially common in the brushy pastures of eastern, central, and western NY and the outskirts of the Adirondacks. It was only local in the southeast and uncommon on LI (Eaton 1914). By the 1980s (Atlas 1988) it was common across the Appalachian Plateau and had increased in the southeast and in suitable habitat in eastern Nassau and central and eastern Suffolk counties.

Nonbreeding Average arrival and departure statewide 1966–1988 was 6 May and 28 Sep (KB 37:12).

Spring maxima: 45 Central Park, Manhattan 23 May 1954; 25 Syracuse, Onondaga Co. 14 May 1962. *Fall maxima:* 50 Pompey, Onondaga Co. 11 Sep 1969; 47 struck the Colden TV tower, Erie Co. 24 Sep 1970. *Extreme dates:* 16 Apr and 13 Nov (both Central Park, Manhattan). Rare before May and after early Oct.

Stephen W. Eaton

Magnolia Warbler

Dendroica magnolia

Range Nearctic region, breeding in central and southern Canada, in the west entirely north of the United States, in the east south to the Berkshires, Catskills, and Poconos and in the higher mountains to Virginia; rarely at high elevations in New Jersey. Winters mainly in Middle America and the West Indies, rarely north to southern Florida; casually in Virginia (specimen).

Status A common breeder in the Adirondacks and Tug Hill areas and a fairly common breeder in the Catskills and on the Appalachian Plateau above 1000 ft. Common to very common migrant.

Breeding On the Appalachian Plateau and Tug Hill it breeds in hemlock–northern hardwoods and now has expanded into plantations of spruce and red pine (Rosche 1967; Andrle 1971). In the Adirondacks it is found primarily in the spruce–fir–northern hardwoods forest. Across the Appalachian Plateau and other areas at that latitude it nests above 1000 ft. Farther north in Oswego, Jefferson, Lewis, and Clinton counties, Atlas workers recorded several Probable and a few Confirmed below 1000 ft. This is one of several species that was not found on the east side of the Hudson R. south of the Rensselaer Hills. It is often found nesting with Blackburnian and Black-throated Green warblers at different strata in the conifers, with Blackburnian inhabiting the tops of mature trees, Black-throated Green the intermediate levels of the canopy, and Magnolia the young trees seeded below. It is essentially a bird of early succession.

In most areas of NY it appears to be on the increase. NY BBS data showed a significant 2.9% annual increase 1966–1994 (Peterjohn 1995). In Region 1, populations were generally on the increase (Klaubunde 1986), particularly in Allegany Co. (Klingensmith and Hoover 1986), but in certain areas there have been declines. In the Finger Lakes region, the small populations that inhabited the ravines entering Keuka, Owasco, and Canandaigua lakes, present to the 1940s, have disappeared (Eaton 1914; Benton 1949). The Brown-headed Cowbird, with elevated populations surrounding these ravines, could well have eliminated them (Atlas 1988). The warbler had an 83% nesting density decline between 1930–1931 and 1983–1985 in Allegany SP, which probably is related to local conditions where the forest has matured but the understory has been severely over-browsed by deer, eliminating much of its preferred habitat (Baird 1990).

Nonbreeding At times this is the most numerous of our warblers on migration. The average statewide arrival is 6 May and departure 8 Oct (KB 37:9).

Spring maxima: 75 Rochester, Monroe Co. 24 May 1917; 70 Prospect Park, Kings Co. 10 May 1948; 51 banded at Fire I. Lighthouse, Suffolk Co. 8 May 1970. *Fall maxima:* 64 hit the Empire State Building, Manhattan 27 Sep 1970 and 63 on 14 Sep 1964; 60 struck the TV tower at Colden, Erie Co. 24 Sep 1970; 30 Syracuse, Onondaga Co. 7 Oct 1968. *Extreme dates: Spring:* 26 Apr (inland) and 23 Jun (coastal). *Fall:* 25 Jul (coastal) and 30 Nov (coastal); exceptionally to 12–13 Dec 1954 Westernville, Oneida Co. and 15–18 Dec 1984 Endwell, Broome Co. "eating suet and feeding on millet with Dark-eyed Junco" (KB 34:120). The only NY CBC record 1960–1989 was on the 1970 Hidden Valley, Putnam Co. count.
Stephen W. Eaton

Cape May Warbler   *Dendroica tigrina*

Range Nearctic, breeding from northeastern British Columbia to Nova Scotia and south, in the east to northern Minnesota and northern New

England. Winters in Florida and the West Indies, casually to Middle America.

Status Rare breeder in the Adirondacks. Uncommon to common migrant.

Breeding The rarest of NY's spruce-nesting warblers, it was not Confirmed by Atlas workers, although Probable breeding was noted in six blocks in Essex, Franklin, and St. Lawrence counties and Possible breeding was noted in 12 blocks in Hamilton, Essex, Franklin, and St. Lawrence counties. Elevations ranged from 1200 ft along the Sacandaga R. to almost 3000 ft along the shores of Avalanche L. Essex. Its apparent rarity may be due in some measure to failure to locate it during nesting.

Eaton (1914) reported that "we have been unable as yet to record it positively as a breeding species in the Adirondack district" The first confirmation of nesting in NY occurred on 4 Jul 1947, when an adult female was discovered feeding two young in North Meadow, Essex Co. at 1900 ft (Carleton et al. 1948). Carleton and others found it still frequenting North Meadow during the Atlas project, and it was heard singing there in Jun 1992 (KB 42:267). A second confirmation came on 23 Jun 1962, when Scheider, Rusk, and others (Scheider 1962) saw a female feeding recently fledged young at Madawaska, Franklin Co. at an elevation of 1600 ft. Even today the nest and eggs of the species have not been documented in NY. This lack of documentation is understandable because the bird, during nesting, forages and nests in the tops of spruce, fastening its nest close to the trunk in the terminal spire. Further, the parents do not fly directly to the nest but enter the tree far below and make their way up, branch by branch near the trunk (Harrison 1984).

It has been found breeding elsewhere in stands of medium-aged spruce, about 25–75 years old, usually with some regeneration of younger balsam fir. Along with the Tennessee and Bay-breasted warblers, it favors areas infested by spruce budworm *(Choristoneura fumiferana)* (Morse 1989). Much of the million acres of the Adirondacks that burned between 1880 and 1913 may now be good Cape May Warbler habitat (Atlas 1988). The 1947 first breeding record was in an area that Saunders (1929) described in 1925 as an area of charred stumps covered with a growth of aspen and fire cherry and a few young maples, spruces, and balsams.

Nonbreeding Numbers fluctuate from season to season in apparent response to spruce budworm abundance. Most birds appear in the first two weeks of May and again in early Sep to the first week in Oct. The average statewide arrival date is 7 May, and average departure 4 Oct (DeBenedictis 1987).

Spring maxima: 32 Mexico, Oswego Co. 22 May 1973; 23 Syracuse, Onondaga Co. 8 May 1959; 15 Far Rockaway, Queens Co. 16 May 1954. *Fall maxima:* 112 banded at Fire I. Lighthouse, Suffolk Co. 6 Sep 1971; 45 East Hampton, Suffolk Co. 15 Sep 1946; 9 Spring Brook, Erie Co. 4

Oct 1967; 6 Cape Vincent, Jefferson Co. 3 Sep 1995. *Extreme dates:*
Spring: 23 Apr and 6 June; casual 3 July 1960 Arkwright, Chautauqua Co.
singing male (Rew). *Fall:* 3 Aug and 16–22 Nov (coastal, banded); excep-
tionally to 5 Dec. *Winter:* Dec records, all single males, include: at a
Geneva, Ontario Co. feeder early to 28 Dec 1918; collected at a feeder,
Poughkeepsie, Dutchess Co. early to 31 Dec 1946 (MCZ 275788); well
observed at Point Lookout, Nassau Co. 30 Dec 1956 (Bull and
Eisenmann); well described at Ossining, Westchester Co. 21 Dec 1996
(Roberto). There are no records after Dec.

Remarks An amazing 3000 Cape Mays were precipitated out of the eye of
Hurricane Gloria 27 Sep 1985 into a relatively small area at the west end of
JBSP as the hurricane passed over that spot (Wollin 1986; KB 36:48).
Totally exhausted and disoriented, many fell prey to gulls and raptors or
simply expired. Others lingered for several days before apparently continuing their southward movement. The question is whether any made it to
their wintering grounds; birders in western Nassau Co. did not record the
species for some four springs hence. This event vividly demonstrates how
vulnerable Neotropical migrants are to natural phenomena such as hurricanes, when they apparently travel en masse.
Stephen W. Eaton

Black-throated Blue Warbler *Dendroica caerulescens*

Range Primarily eastern Nearctic, breeding from western Ontario east to
Nova Scotia and south to northeastern Minnesota, southern New York, and
southern New England; also in the Appalachians south to Georgia. Winters
from southern Florida south through the West Indies.

Status Widespread breeder at higher elevations, but local in the southeast.
Variously uncommon to common migrant.

Breeding A common breeder at higher elevations throughout the state
with centers of abundance in the Adirondacks and Catskills. Except for a
handful of isolated records, it is absent from all low elevations and the
Coastal Plain (Atlas 1988).

Nonbreeding It is very variable in numbers from year to year; very
common migrant some years, uncommon others.
Spring maxima: 100 Rochester, Monroe Co. 24 May 1917, a very late
spring; 50 Bronx Park, Bronx Co. 6 May 1953. *Fall maxima:* 51 hit the
Empire State Building, Manhattan 27 Sep 1970; 41 hit the TV tower in
Elmira, Chemung Co. 20 Sep 1977, another 40 the next night (Welles
1978). *Extreme dates: Spring:* 11 Apr (coastal) and 14 Jun (coastal). *Fall:*

7 Aug and 21 Nov (coastal); exceptionally to 12 Dec (inland). Rare before and after May, before late Aug and after mid-Oct. ***Winter:*** There have been six winter occurrences, five of them males and all but one at feeders: Northport, Suffolk Co. 13 Nov 1954–13 Jan 1955; Brookhaven, Suffolk Co. 27 Dec 1962; Brookhaven, 1–24 Dec 1972; Smithtown, Suffolk Co. 18 Nov 1979–9 Mar 1980; a female seen on the Orient, Suffolk Co. CBC 2 Jan 1993. Most astonishing was a male wintering inland mid-Nov 1985–14 Feb 1986 at a feeder in Endwell, Broome Co. The bird disappeared after a snowstorm on the latter date.

Remarks The overwhelming proportion of males in the winter records probably has more to do with the distinctiveness of the male's plumage compared with the female's than with a greater hardiness in males. This is one of the few warblers in which males appear the same in fall as in spring and young birds molt directly into an adult-appearing plumage in their first fall.

Joseph DiCostanzo

Yellow-rumped Warbler *Dendroica coronata*

Range Nearctic, breeding from Alaska across Canada to Labrador and Newfoundland and south, in the east to the north-central United States, New York, and New England. In the east, winters from southern Ontario and New England south through the southern states and to Middle America and the West Indies.

Status Common breeder at higher elevations upstate and uncommon breeder at lower elevations. Common to abundant migrant throughout and abundant to uncommon in winter.

Breeding Historically it was known to breed in the Adirondacks and the Catskills. In addition, Bull (1974) mapped 25 breeding locations outside of those mountains. Atlas workers added more than 100 Confirmed and more than 200 Probable sites to that total, again all outside of the historical locales. This range expansion, whether a natural phenomenon or the result of more diligent observation, is ongoing and generally limited to higher elevations, with the exception of the St. Lawrence Plains and transition areas. Breeding does not take place in the lower Hudson Valley or Coastal Lowlands, with the exception of one, probably anomalous, nesting on LI.

Nonbreeding It is perhaps the most abundant passerine migrant. Spring numbers inland and upstate are larger than those on the coast; in the fall numbers on the coast are larger. A brisk October northwest wind brings birds in uncountable numbers along the barrier beaches of LI. Davis reported that "as many as 10,000 or more visit the Jones Beach strip during the peak of the fall migration in mid-October" (Bull 1976).

Although terms such as *superabundant, incredible numbers,* and *unprecedented numbers* are frequently used by reporters, maximum numbers published since Bull have not exceeded 2700 on any one date or at any place.

Able to subsist on berries, weed seeds, and other wild grains, it is suited to winter throughout, when it is always present in low to abundant numbers on barrier beaches and in smaller numbers upstate. Winter abundance on the coast is closely related to the bayberry crop on which it feeds. A remarkable winter status change has taken place since 1974, when Bull termed it "usually rare inland." Since then, hundreds have been repeatedly reported, with the largest numbers coming from the western portion of the state.

As a migrant, it usually arrives in mid-Apr and departs in mid-Nov.

Remarks Of the five subspecies generally recognized, there are three known to occur or to have been recorded in NY. The nominate, *coronata,* is the common migrant. Its western counterpart, *auduboni,* recognizable in the field because of its yellow throat (rather than white), was first recorded by A. Lauro 28 Nov 1970, and again on 6 Nov 1971, at his banding station at the John F. Kennedy Wildlife Sanctuary, Nassau Co. Both were mistnetted, banded, color photographed, and then released. Since then, *auduboni* has been recorded 16 additional times in the state: six were on LI, four in fall and two in spring; 10 were upstate, four in spring, four in fall, and two in winter. These records in the last 25 years perhaps reflect an awareness of their possible presence rather than a true change in status.

A third subspecies, *hooveri,* the white-throated Alaska population, is darker, larger, and longer-winged and is best identified with the bird in the hand through measurements. Four such individuals were mistnetted and banded by Lauro at his banding station, the first on 12 Nov 1975. Subsequently, Robert Dickerman inspected the *coronata* skin collection at the AMNH and identified seven specimens taken in NY as *hooveri,* either migrant or wintering individuals, as they were collected between 22 Oct and 5 May.

Anthony J. Lauro

Black-throated Gray Warbler *Dendroica nigrescens*

Range Western Nearctic, breeding from southwestern British Columbia and southern Wyoming south to southeastern Arizona and southern New Mexico and east to central Colorado. Winters in central and western Mexico. Vagrant east to New York and Massachusetts (specimens).

Status Very rare vagrant.

Occurrence Bull (1974) acknowledged six sight records in addition to the specimen collected in Ithaca, Tompkins Co. on 15 Nov 1932. There are three new records, all accepted by NYSARC. A female 13 Oct 1991 JBWR (Boltson) (NYSARC 1993; AB 46:72); one 14 Dec 1991 Flushing Meadow Park, Queens Co. (Dieterich, Kondratiev) (NYSARC 1994); a male photographed 14 Sep 1992 RMSP (Quinlan 1993; NYSARC 1994).

Remarks In adjacent states, there are at least 40 records, about half occurring since 1975. Most were in fall but, curiously, of six in RI, four were in spring (Conway 1992).
John J. Fritz and Joan L. Quinlan

Townsend's Warbler   *Dendroica townsendi*

Range Western Nearctic, breeding from Alaska, western Canada, and northwestern United States, southeast to Montana and Wyoming. Casual or accidental widely outside the breeding range. Winters in California and in the highlands of Mexico and Central America, south to Costa Rica.

Status Very rare vagrant

Occurrence Bull (1974) listed six sight reports 1947–1970 (five spring, one fall, all males, all downstate) that he believed were correct, but he put the species on his Hypothetical list in the absence of a specimen or photo.

The evidence he sought came on 7 May 1978, when an adult male was banded and photographed on Great Gull I., Suffolk Co. (DiCostanzo et al. 1978). Four days later, 11 May 1978, another was photographed at New Haven, Oswego Co. and accepted by NYSARC (1979). It was the first upstate record.

Since then there have been five additional records accepted: Braddock Bay, Monroe Co. 20 Apr 1980 (NYSARC 1981); HLSP 29–30 Apr 1981 (NYSARC 1982); Forest Park, Queens Co. 14 May 1988 (NYSARC 1990); Verona Beach SP, Oneida Co. 8 Sep 1991 (NYSARC 1993); Alley Pond Park, Queens Co. 9 May 1993 (NYSARC 1995).

Three other published sight reports were not reviewed by NYSARC: Montauk, Suffolk Co. 2 Oct 1976 (KB 27:60); HLSP 15 Apr 1977 (KB 27:175); Alley Pond Park, Queens Co. 9 May 1981 (KB 31:196). Altogether there are 16 reports: seven substantiated; three in fall and 13 in spring; three upstate and 13 downstate; all adult males. Spring sightings ranged from 15 Apr to 14 May.

Remarks Townsend's Warbler has occurred as a vagrant in many eastern states. The 16 NY reports outnumber the total of all records combined in NJ, PA, RI, CT, and MA.
Dominic F. Sherony

Black-throated Green Warbler *Dendroica virens*

Range Nearctic, breeding from eastern British Columbia to southern Labrador and Newfoundland and south to north-central United States and in the mountains to northern Georgia; also locally on the coastal plain from Virginia to South Carolina. Winters from southern Florida and Texas to Panama and the Greater Antilles, rarely farther north.

Status Fairly common to common breeder. Fairly common to very common migrant.

Breeding It is common in the Adirondacks, Tug Hill, and Catskills; fairly common on the Appalachian Plateau above 1000 ft; uncommon in the Hudson Highlands; and essentially absent on the Great Lakes Plain, in the Mohawk Valley, the Hudson Valley, and LI (Atlas 1988). On the Appalachian Plateau and Tug Hill Transition it occurs in hemlock-hardwoods forest and in conifer plantations planted in the 1930s (Saunders 1942; Kendeigh 1945; Rosche 1967). In the Adirondacks and Tug Hill it nests in spruce, fir, and other conifers mixed with hardwoods (Saunders 1929; Atlas 1988). On LI it formerly nested in pitch pine but had not been found there in about 50 years until 1993 and 1994, when it was located in eastern Suffolk Co. in white pine, pitch pine, tupelo, and oak (E. Salzman, in litt.).

On the Appalachian Plateau it is often found nesting with Blackburnian and Magnolia warblers (see the Magnolia Warbler account). In upland mixed pine-spruce-hardwood plantations it is often more common than in native hemlock-hardwood stands. In 41 acres in Allegany Co. 17 Black-throated Green, 11 Magnolia, and 10 Blackburnian singing male warblers were recorded in Jun 1980 (Brooks 1981).

Breeding evidence was found in 45% of Atlas blocks, and breeding was Confirmed in 19%. The BBS in the eastern United States 1978–1988 showed a significant annual decrease of 3.2% (Sauer and Droege 1992). The cause of this decline has not been determined. In Quaker Run Valley, Allegany SP, it was the most abundant breeding bird in 1930–1931 (Saunders 1936). In 1983–1985 in this same valley, populations in all types of forest were reduced by 64%, and in its preferred forest of hemlock-hardwoods by 75% (Baird 1990). Similar losses, although not so drastic, occurred in NH, other areas of NY, and NC (Wilcove 1983; Holmes et al. 1986; Klingensmith and Hoover 1986). Its rank, however, as to relative susceptibility to extinction on a scale of 1 to 8 is 5 on its breeding grounds and 8 on its wintering grounds. It is more of a habitat specialist on its breeding grounds and a generalist on its tropical wintering area (Reed 1992).

Nonbreeding One of the more numerous warblers on migration, average arrival statewide is 1 May, average departure 9 Oct (DeBenedictis 1987).

Spring maxima: 100 Rochester, Monroe Co. 24 May 1917; 100 Sandy Pond, Oswego Co. 25 May 1960. *Fall maxima:* 135 Pompey, Onondaga Co. 19 Sep 1969; 60 Sandy Pond, Oswego Co. 15 Sep 1960. *Extreme dates: Coastal:* 30 Mar and 10 Dec. *Inland:* 3 Apr. Rare before late Apr and after Oct.
Stephen W. Eaton

Blackburnian Warbler *Dendroica fusca*

Range Nearctic, chiefly central and eastern North America, breeding from Saskatchewan to Nova Scotia and south to central Minnesota and Michigan, Pennsylvania, Massachusetts, southeastern New York, and in the mountains to northern Georgia and South Carolina. Winters from Guatemala to Peru but chiefly in northern South America.

Status Common breeder above 1000 ft; local or absent elsewhere. Common migrant inland, uncommon to fairly common coastal.

Breeding Common in the Adirondacks, Tug Hill Plateau, Catskills, Appalachian Plateau, Rensselaer Hills, and Taconic Mountains above 1000 ft. It is local below 500 ft on the Great Lakes and St. Lawrence plains, north of the Adirondacks in the St. Lawrence and Champlain transitions, in the Mohawk, upper Hudson, and Champlain valleys. It was found in 32% of Atlas blocks and was Confirmed in 22% of those (Atlas 1988). It was not Confirmed south of Columbia Co. or southeast of Orange Co. Its distribution appears to be slightly more boreal than that of the Black-throated Green Warbler and very similar to that of the Magnolia Warbler (see the Magnolia Warbler account).

On the Appalachian Plateau it favors stands of mature hemlock but is often common in plantations of mixed pine, spruce, and hardwoods. Consequently, it has increased, because of lumbering, particularly in Chenango, Otsego, and Delaware counties (Atlas 1988). In the Adirondacks it inhabits hemlock, balsam fir, and red and black spruce; on the Tug and Taconic hills, it is in hemlock and spruce, and in the Champlain Valley in open stands of white pine (Saunders 1929). It is also found in primarily deciduous forest where there are occasional tall pines or hemlocks. These tall scattered trees, left by the lumbermen, seem to accommodate localized pairs or colonies (Baird 1990).

Nonbreeding Average statewide arrival is 5 May, average departure 29 Sep (DeBenedictis 1987). It is more numerous inland than on the coastal plain.

Coastal maxima: Spring: 15 Bronx Park, Bronx Co. 6 May 1953; 15 Woodmere Woods, Nassau Co. 23 May 1954. *Fall:* 17 hit the Empire State Building, Manhattan 14 Sep 1964. *Inland maxima: Spring:* 200

Rochester, Monroe Co. 24 May 1917; 55 Camillus Valley, Onondaga Co. 19 May 1966. *Fall:* 35 Pompey, Onondaga Co. 11 Sep 1969; 21 found dead, Albany airport ceilometer 15 Sep 1956. *Extreme dates: Inland:* 16 Apr and 17 Nov (found dead). *Coastal:* 19 Apr and 18 Jun (banded); 3 Aug and 13 Nov.

Remarks It is a long-distance migrant most abundant in winter in the sub-tropical zone of the Andes of Colombia, South America. There, it is often the only member of its genus and perhaps avoids, in this way, competition with other warblers that are often its competitors on the breeding grounds (Chipley 1980; Morse 1989). But the fact that it migrates that far may be to its disadvantage because its wintering area of mature forest is in greater jeopardy than that of others in its genus, which winter farther north (Chipley 1980; Reed 1992).
Stephen W. Eaton

Yellow-throated Warbler   *Dendroica dominica*

Range Eastern Nearctic, breeding from southern Wisconsin, northern Ohio, and southern New York south to Texas, the Gulf states, and central Florida. Winters from South Carolina and the Gulf Coast south to Costa Rica and the Greater Antilles.

Status Very rare breeder. A rare but regular spring migrant along the coast; irregular and very rare in fall. Very rare elsewhere.

Breeding During Atlas fieldwork in 1984, two widely separated pairs were Confirmed breeding, the first records in the state (Atlas 1988).

A nest near the top of a red pine near Science L., Allegany SP, Cattaraugus Co. (Baird 1984) was discovered on 9 Jul 1984 and was observed until 29 Jul; it was later collected and is now in the BMS. The species was first observed in Allegany SP in Jun 1979, without breeding evidence, and was seen regularly through 1994 (KB 33:260; 37:143; 38:231, 259; 39:170; 43:312; 44:296).

Another nest was discovered on 6 June 1984 on Catskill Creek in South Cairo, Greene Co. (Atlas 1988; KB 34:223, 266) with nest building, incubation, and feeding of young observed. The nest was collected and is in the AMNH. No further nesting attempts have been reported at this site.

A pair was found during summer 1994 in the Arnot Forest, Tompkins and Schuyler counties (KB 44:305), but no evidence of nesting was uncovered. Two males were found in mid-May 1997 where the border of Sullivan and Orange counties meets the Delaware R. As of 29 Jun, both males were still singing vigorously at this location, but no evidence of nesting was observed (V. Freer, pers. comm.). It is possible that the species is expanding its breeding range.

Nonbreeding It is recorded annually in spring in the NYC-LI area, with 69 records for the past 20 years. The peak number of occurrences in Region 10 in recent years was 10 in 1977 and 1984 (KB 34:210; 27:174) but three to five would be average. Bull (1974) mentioned a statewide season high of 12 in 1956. Ninety percent of all records in the past 20 years occurred 14 Apr–18 May, with two peaks in the coastal migration: 14–27 Apr and a weaker peak 5–18 May. These birds, which rarely linger for more than a day, are, no doubt, coastal migrant overshoots.

It is rare along the coast in fall, with one record 31 Aug 1991 (KB 41:290) and four in Sep.

In the inland Regions, it is rare in spring. If one sets aside reports from Allegany SP, since these probably represent breeders, there is a geographical trend for a higher number of occurrences in the western part of the state (Regions 1, 2) and the fewest in the north-central part (Regions 5, 6, 7). There were 33 inland spring records 1975–1994 (excluding Allegany SP), with peak dates 5–18 May.

Fall records are rare, but, surprisingly, most are from Nov and Dec and are concentrated in the western part of the state. Inland fall records span a wider date range than do those of the coast, with 10 inland records ranging from 4 Sep (KB 27:37) to 26 Dec (KB 39:110). The latter was found on the 1988 Conesus-Hemlock-Honeoye Lakes CBC and the bird remained into Jan 1989. These late-occurring birds tend to linger at feeders and may be migrants that have moved in the wrong direction.

Extreme dates: Coastal: 6 Apr and 25 May. ***Inland:*** 11 Apr and 13 Jun. Bull (1974) noted two Jul specimens taken in Suffolk Co. many years ago.

Remarks There are four known subspecies of Yellow-throated Warbler (Curson et al. 1994). The two that have been confirmed in NY are *dominica*, the form of the eastern coastal plain, and *albilora*, of the Appalachians and central United States. The latter subspecies has a supercilium white throughout its length and a slightly shorter bill. Parkes (1953) pointed out that the two forms are difficult or impossible to correctly identify in the field because the yellow lores of *dominica* can be so faint that they are only visible in the hand.

Bull (1974) gave a synopsis of eight specimens taken in NY. Five collected in the NYC-LI area are of the nominate race. The other three are *albilora*: from Albany, Nassau, and New York counties. Bull (1976) also cited two additional specimens of *albilora* collected in 1974 and 1975 on LI. Dominic F. Sherony

Pine Warbler *Dendroica pinus*

Range Eastern Nearctic, breeding chiefly from southern Manitoba east to central Maine and south to Texas, the Gulf Coast, and Florida. Winters in the southeastern United States, casually north to New York and New England and in Mexico.

Status Common breeder in the LI pine barrens in mature stands of pitch pine; uncommon and localized breeder in pine forests elsewhere. Uncommon migrant on the coast, rare but regular in winter. Rare but increasing upstate as a migrant and in winter.

Breeding In 1974, Bull noted four disjunct populations: the LI pine barrens, the Hudson and L. Champlain valleys, the Great Lakes Plain, and the Finger Lakes region, all lowland areas. Writers on the NY avifauna from Eaton (1914) to Bull (1974) all emphasized that this species was absent from the mountains and higher elevations generally. Atlas workers found breeding evidence not only in lowland locales but also in a wide area of the Adirondacks, from the High Peaks region to the foothills and adjacent valleys, as well as south and west of the Finger Lakes in the Appalachians; notable concentrations were also found in the St. Lawrence Plains from Massena south. In the Catskills, Mongaup Hills, Neversink Highlands, and Westchester and Putnam counties, many sites were in plantations around the NYC and other reservoir systems (B. Lincoln, pers. obs.). All of these rather localized breeding sites were in pine forests or smaller stands, and many, perhaps most, continued to be occupied throughout the 1980s and into the 1990s.

The author of the Atlas account thought that this was a difficult species for workers to locate and expressed the opinion that mapping was probably incomplete. Even so, Atlas work indicated that this species, whose traditional stronghold lay in the southeastern pine forests, had extended its range, in suitable habitat, northward and to higher elevations. Regional *Kingbird* correspondents have continued to report similar patterns since the Atlas. Breeding was Confirmed in Region 1 in 1994 (KB 44:202, 296; 45:285).

In its pine barrens strongholds, the verdict is mixed. It disappeared from the Albany Pine Bush by the 1980s (Kerlinger and Doremus 1981), and both Bull (1974) and Salzman (1977) thought that it was considerably diminished in the LI pine barrens because of development. Atlas work showed little or no recovery in the Albany area but indicated that breeding populations on LI had expanded to a range that now included northern Nassau Co. and large areas of Suffolk Co., with the exception of the North Fork, where there are no suitable pine forests. Fairly large stands of pine have matured in the past decades owing to the virtual cessation of logging, the establishment of substantial protected areas (mostly now within the Pine Barrens Preserve), and effective fire suppression. Such areas are often invaded by oaks, but Pine Warblers will use mixed habitat, even where oak has replaced all but a few large pines.

Nonbreeding Arrival dates are difficult to determine because of over-wintering birds, but it often appears in coastal areas in mid to late Mar, upstate by early to mid-Apr (KB 39:164). Schiff (1989) reported a mean average date of 7 Apr in southern Nassau Co. It is uncommon but regular in the NYC parks at about the same time. It is much less often noted in the fall, perhaps because it molts in late summer into a confusing fall plumage that only gradually brightens through feather wear (Curson et al. 1994). Departure dates are also difficult to determine because birds linger to the end of the year and beyond. Although traditionally described as "very rare" in winter, it now appears annually on LI CBCs from Brooklyn to Montauk and, somewhat less frequently, in the lower Hudson Valley.

It is increasingly reported as an upstate migrant, particularly in western NY and over a wide area of the St. Lawrence Plains. Most upstate birds leave between late Sep and early Oct but are now occasionally noted in Nov (e.g., Saranac Lake, Franklin Co. 23 Nov 1994), and it is rare but increasing in winter. Bull (1974) gave only five upstate winter occurrences, but birds are now recorded almost annually at feeders in Regions 1 and 2 and somewhat less regularly in widely scattered areas of central and northern NY.

Remarks This is the only warbler whose summer and winter ranges lie entirely in North America. In NY it is largely migratory, but most other populations are sedentary. This fact may suggest that the acquisition of migratory habits and associated colonization of northern pine forests is a rather recent and still-evolving behavioral strategy.
Eric Salzman

Prairie Warbler *Dendroica discolor*

Range Eastern Nearctic, breeding from eastern Nebraska, southern Ontario, and southern New Hampshire south to east Texas, northern Louisiana, and Florida. Winters from central Florida, the Bahamas, and West Indies to Caribbean islands off Middle America.

Status Common breeder in LI, the Hudson Valley, and the Appalachian Plateau; rapidly expanding northward except at higher elevations. Locally common to rare migrant.

Breeding The Atlas found expansion of the breeding range since Bull 1974. Bull stated it was confined to the southern portion of the state. Since the Atlas, it has been found to be regular on rare grassland communities called alvars and limestone barrens called calcareous pavement communities on TNC preserves in northwestern Jefferson Co., about 100 mi north of known breeding populations at the time of the Atlas fieldwork (Smith,

1988). Rossell and DiTomasso (1992) found it along a nine-mile power line right-of-way in northern Lewis Co. in 1991. Probable Ft. Drum locations are considerably farther east in Jefferson Co. and not far from the Lewis Co. site. Much of the Ft. Drum area is an outwash sandplain with pitch pine, white pine, and various pine species planted to reduce wind erosion. Military maneuvers and management practices keep much of the area in grassland and semi-open conditions with pioneer species of conifers and hardwoods as well as various shrubs, ideal habitat for this species. Further field investigations will no doubt find additional breeding sites in Jefferson and Lewis counties. There are areas in St. Lawrence, Essex, and Clinton counties of sandstone pavement barrens, power rights-of-way and various pineland-shrub communities that should be surveyed.

Although rare at higher elevations, this species does breed at Connecticut Hill WMA, Tompkins Co. at an elevation of about 2100 ft. This location suggests that many other WMAs and state forests in northern and central NY could provide suitable habitat. It is also increasing in the west and in the Appalachian Plateau as more habitat becomes available. How long this habitat will be viable for Prairie Warbler before passing into old field and forest is unknown.

Maxima: 17 singing in one mile of the Upper Mine Road, USMA, Orange Co. 6 May 1981; 16 near Alfred, Allegany Co., summer 1983; 12 Bornt Hill, Binghamton, Broome Co. 7 Jun 1993.

Nonbreeding Because it is basically at the northern limits of its breeding range here, its status as a migrant will depend on how far and how fast its northward expansion takes place. Although it is a common migrant in the southeast and Appalachian Plateau, it is still uncommon to rare in the north and west. Rare before late Apr and after Oct.

Remarks A review of field records indicates some form of scouting for new sites before actual breeding takes place. There are singing males seen Jul–Sep at various locations in the type of habitat usually associated with nesters. In many of them, singing males have been seen for years but breeding has never been proved. Sometimes birds appear in alternate years or are just a one-time occurrence. It would be worthwhile to revisit some of these locations for a more thorough survey.

Lee B. Chamberlaine

Palm Warbler   *Dendroica palmarum*

Range Nearctic, breeding from Mackenzie and northern Alberta east to Newfoundland and south, in the east, to central Michigan, Nova Scotia, and central Maine. Winters from northern Texas, the Gulf Coast, Florida, and the West Indies south to coastal Honduras and Nicaragua.

Status Accidental or casual breeder before 1995. Uncommon to very common migrant; especially numerous along the coast; in winter rare to locally uncommon on LI, very rare elsewhere.

Breeding On 23 Jun 1983, during Atlas fieldwork, Stiles found a pair of Palm Warblers in Bay Pond Bog in Waverly, Franklin Co. On 6 Jul, Stiles, Nickerson, and Peterson returned to find a nest under construction on a sphagnum hummock. It was woven "around the woody stems of Labrador tea" at the bog edge near a clump of spruces. On 8 Jul, Stiles found the nest completed, feather lined, and containing a single "small creamy egg blotched with brownish markings." Thus the first Confirmed NY breeding record of this species was established. The empty nest was collected on 24 Aug by Peterson and Johnson and is in the AMNH (Peterson 1984), together with a photograph of habitat and nest.

Three years later, on 1 Jul 1986, Barnett, Chase, and Randorf found a pair on neighboring Spring Pond Bog. Although no nest was located, this find added a probable second breeding record (KB 36:232). Then, remarkably, in the summer of 1995, DiTomasso, Leone, and others found about 20 pairs, many with young, in Massawepie Mire and another two pairs in nearby Hitchins Bog, St. Lawrence Co. This impressive discovery was in an area closed to Atlas surveys (KB 45:309), so it is not known whether the numbers represented a buildup over some years or a sudden explosion of breeding birds in that area. In 1996, the only available data indicated the presence of seven singing males at this location (KB 46:264), as physical entry to the Mire was not possible during the breeding season. On 15 Jun 1997, Long, Fritz, and DiTomasso again surveyed the Massawepie Mire and recorded 22 males, either observed or heard singing, in a 1.5 m stretch.

The two Franklin Co. bogs where breeding was recorded were threatened in 1981 by a proposal to harvest sphagnum moss mechanically for sale as a horticultural medium. Happily, the Adirondack Conservancy intervened in time to purchase and save these bogs and the surrounding square mile of woodlands. This area will in turn become part of the 75,000 acre Boreal Heritage Preserve being established by TNC. Atlas observers recorded 130 breeding species in this preserve, including Spruce Grouse (KB 36:233).

Nonbreeding This species is an early spring warbler migrant, preceded only by Yellow-rumped and Pine warblers and Louisiana Waterthrush. It first appears in early to mid-Apr in southern NY, in the third or fourth week of Apr farther north. Peak numbers move through 21 Apr–6 May (coastal) and 29 Apr–16 May (inland).

Annual Niagara Frontier May Counts of this species 1935–1995 averaged six, with a maximum of 41, suggesting both wide variation from year to year and the mid-May count date too late for the peak of its migration (Rising 1995).

Fall migration runs from mid-Sep to mid-Oct, with lingering individuals occasionally recorded upstate through mid-Nov and a few birds remaining through the winter downstate. By mid-Oct, when the Niagara Frontier October Count is mounted, most have left, as indicated by decade maxima for the 1930s–1990s: 2, 0, 0, 0, 3, 2, 1 (Rising 1994b).

The average annual Palm Warbler totals for all southern (mostly LI) CBCs were: in the 1960s, 6; 1970s, 19; 1980s, 24. Over that same 30-year period, only four were recorded on CBCs across the rest of the state (Salzman 1994).

Spring maxima: Coastal: 300 Van Cortlandt Park, Bronx Co. 1 May 1950. *Inland:* 36 in one hour, Derby Hill, Oswego Co. 4 May 1963. *Fall and winter maxima: Coastal:* 30 Quoque CBC, Suffolk Co. 1972; 30 Central Suffolk CBC 1986. *Inland:* 18 State University at Albany 29 Sep 1994.

Remarks The yellower subspecies, *hypochrysea* (formerly called Yellow Palm Warbler), breeds from eastern ON to northeastern New England and is the commoner migrant through eastern portions of NY. The NY breeding birds are this subspecies. The whiter, nominate subspecies, *palmarum* (formerly Western Palm Warbler), breeds from northern MI west to the Rockies but migrates eastward through western NY and even to LI. Clearly they overlap in NY in both spring and fall. They also intergrade, thus further confusing subspecific identification (Parkes 1952).

In the Finger Lakes region in 1994, the Gregoires banded 22 *palmarum* 1 Sep–25 Oct and 4 *hypochrysea* 22–25 Oct, suggesting a later passage for the Northeastern subspecies (KB 44:47).
Gerry Rising

Bay-breasted Warbler *Dendroica castanea*

Range Chiefly eastern Nearctic, breeding from northern Alberta to Nova Scotia and south, in the east from northern Minnesota to northern New England. Winters from Panama to northwestern South America.

Status Very rare to rare but widely distributed breeder through the Adirondack and Tug Hill regions. Fairly common to common migrant in western NY, rare to fairly common elsewhere.

Breeding The Bay-breasted Warbler was not established as a breeding species in NY until 23 Jul 1926, when Weber found a female feeding young near North Hudson, Essex Co. (Auk 44:111). Earlier, Merriam (1881) and Eaton (1914) had searched for breeders unsuccessfully, but by 1974 Bull was able to note 11 nest sites.

In the face of this paucity of early records, some breeding evidence was found in 32 Atlas blocks, still less than 1% of the total. These blocks were distributed among the various Adirondack zones: Central (12), High Peaks (6), Western Foothills (5), Eastern Transition (5), Western Transition (1), and Sable Highlands (1), as well as in the Tug Hill Central (1) and Transition (1) areas. All were located below 2800 ft. Peterson suggested reasons for not finding more: "Hard to find amid dense spruces, the Bay-breasted Warbler is equally difficult to hear" (Atlas 1988).

Nonbreeding Average spring arrival is about 10 May, but in some years birds appear as early as late Apr. No difference is noted between downstate and upstate arrivals. The migration peak is about 20 May, with almost all gone by the end of the month. In western NY, where it is more plentiful in migration, it is among the half-dozen commonest warblers for a few days in mid-May. On 23 May 1984 in Webster, Monroe Co. Spahn counted more than 200 in a half-hour (KB 34:100).

An indication of the spotty distribution of migrants is given by reports for spring 1993: Region 1, absent to common in various locales; Region 2, "good numbers"; Region 4, "scarce"; Regions 5 and 6, "fairly common"; Region 7, "abundant migrant above 1800 ft at Duck Hole"; and Region 9, "depressed numbers reported" (KB 43:216).

Annual Niagara Frontier May Counts 1935–1995 averaged 67 per year, rising above 125 only twice: 457 in 1947 and 388 in 1978. Even with those two unusual years included, the decade averages showed reasonable variation with no recent decline: 1930s, 44; 1940s, 103; 1950s, 64; 1960s, 34; 1970s, 86; 1980s, 59; 1990s, 63 (Rising 1995).

Fall migration begins in mid-Aug and runs through mid-Oct, with most birds passing through in the first half of Sep. Bull (1974) noted two Jul records and a male retaining rufous sides in Riis Park, Queens Co. 25 Nov–1 Dec 1956.

Fall maxima: 175 Hamburg, Erie Co. 15 Sep 1953. Tower kills included 63 at the Empire State Building, Manhattan 26 Sep 1953 and 43 at the Elmira TV Tower, Chemung Co. 26 Sep 1968.
Gerry Rising

Blackpoll Warbler   *Dendroica striata*

Range Northern Nearctic, breeding from Alaska east to northern Ontario, northern Labrador, and Newfoundland south to central Manitoba, central Ontario and Quebec and locally at higher elevations to New York and Massachusetts. Winters in northern South America.

Status Fairly common breeder only at higher elevations in the mountains. Common migrant throughout, especially in the southeast, where it is often abundant in fall.

Breeding Historically, this species was thought to breed only at the highest elevations in the Catskills and in the Adirondacks only at or above 3500 ft. It was long thought to be restricted to the upper slopes and summits of the highest mountains. Eaton (1914) stated that it was "found on all the higher peaks . . . where there are stunted spruces and balsam firs." More recently, Beehler (1978) reported it locally below 2500 ft. Atlas surveyors found numerous singing males in appropriate habitat at elevations around 1500–1600 ft and rarely as low as 1000 ft. This discovery extended the known Adirondack range westward into the Western Adirondack Foothills of Franklin, Hamilton, Herkimer, Lewis, and St. Lawrence counties. Its preference for small growth, however, usually leads this species higher on the mountainsides than other warblers associated with coniferous forests. Atlas work found some breeding evidence in 125 (2%) of all blocks.

Nonbreeding It is one of the most numerous and latest members of the family in migration, especially in the southeastern part of the state, although since about 1970 numbers have decreased. Statewide spring arrival dates are 8–16 May. Fall migrants begin arriving the end of Aug or early Sep. Statewide fall departure dates are 26 Sep–7 Oct. It is rare after mid-Oct.

   Spring maxima: 130 Prospect Park, Kings Co. 17 May 1945; 100 Woodmere Woods, Nassau Co. 16 May 1953; 30 Manitou Beach, Monroe Co. 1 Jun 1968. *Fall maxima:* all Suffolk Co.; 356 struck Fire I. Lighthouse 23 Sep 1887, as did 230 on 30 Sep 1883; 123 Great Gull I. 23 Sep 1977. *Extreme dates:* 28 Apr and 26 Jun; 21 Aug and 3 Dec. Robert G. McKinney

Cerulean Warbler   *Dendroica cerulea*

Range Chiefly eastern Nearctic, breeding from southeastern Minnesota and southern Ontario to Vermont and south; in the east to North Carolina and the central portion of the Gulf states. Winters in South America, east of the Andes, to Peru.

Status Locally common breeder. Rare to uncommon spring migrant, casual in fall.

Breeding This species has been slowly but steadily expanding its breeding range in the Northeast for decades. As a result, it has a complex history of distribution and status changes in NY.

   Eaton (1914) knew it to be a locally common breeder in the western and central portions, in the lowland plain south of L. Ontario and in the Finger Lakes region, and these localities still hold the most extensive concentrations today.

   In 1922 breeding was confirmed in Dutchess Co. (Griscom 1923), and three or more colonies were subsequently located there. Cruickshank (1942) reported a slight increase, citing 11 pairs at Tivoli in 1932.

In the 1950s and 1960s, additional isolated sites were discovered. Notable, if slight, range expansion was evident, especially south of the L. Ontario Plain in Erie and Cattaraugus counties and south and north of the Hudson Valley area. Far to the north, a breeding record was established in Jefferson Co., well isolated from the main areas in NY, although the species had been known to breed in ON, to the northwest, since 1961, and quite possibly this pair originated from there. Singing males found on three dates in Jun 1974 near Muskalonge L. near the St. Lawrence Co. border, may also be indicative of northward expansion.

Curiously, it was many years before the Dutchess Co. population showed any signs of overflow to the west bank of the Hudson R., except for a short-lived occurrence in Ulster Co. in 1939. Bull (1964) wrote of increased spring sightings in Rockland Co. since 1952 and predicted that it might breed there in the future. Speiser (1982) noted an increase in the Hudson Highlands since the mid-1970s, and the Atlas project in the 1980s reported a widespread but localized expansion west of the river, including a thriving population in the highlands. New summer breeding counts in 1994 located additional sites in the lower Hudson Valley, also harboring healthy populations (NASFN 48:930).

The Atlas also documented range expansion southward along the Genesee R. and near the Alleghany R., eastward to Chemung Co.; in the upper Mohawk Valley; in the Indian River Lakes area; and east along rivers in St. Lawrence Co. A singing male at Moriah, Essex Co. near L. Champlain on 11 Jun 1983 suggested possible breeding at this distant and isolated site and was a first record for this northeast region (Atlas 1988; KB 33:284, 287). This record is augmented by a small isolated breeding colony near the lake in VT. Some historical sites, such as the Niagara R. region, were unreported in the Atlas, probably owing to loss of habitat. An increase in reports in the 1990s from formerly unoccupied areas of the state con-tinues to illustrate the trend of expansion eastward and northward, espe-cially into the eastern Appalachian Plateau.

In the NYC area and on LI, few historical summer records exist. In 1962 and 1963, one or two birds were said to have "summered" on eastern LI but did not breed (Bull 1964). It was not until 10 Jul 1983, during the Atlas survey, that a breeding record was finally established, in Sag Harbor, Suffolk Co. (Salzman 1983). There were no further reports of nesting activity there until 1992, when a small population was discovered and sus-pected to be breeding in East Hampton (Lindsay and Vezo 1992). In 1993 and 1994 breeding was confirmed at this site (Lindsay and Vezo 1994, 1995).

The Cerulean Warbler has been recommended to the NYSDEC for listing as a Species of Special Concern. Although its range is expanding in the Northeast, there is an overall, severe, long-term population decline, particularly in the heart of its breeding range in the Mississippi and Ohio valleys. Perhaps the main reason is that the Cerulean Warbler is especially sensitive to habitat loss due to forest fragmentation. Loss of breeding habitat is compounded by problems on the wintering grounds. The wintering range is restricted to an extremely narrow ecological zone in the Andean foothills that is severely threatened by agricultural development (Robbins et al. 1992).

Nonbreeding Because NY is near the northern and eastern limits of its breeding range, it is casual to uncommon on migration. In spring, it normally arrives in early to mid-May, moving singly or in small groups, even on "wave" days. A bird on a jetty in the Jones Inlet, Nassau Co. 21 Apr 1995 was notable both for its early date and odd location (KB 45:236).

It is rarely reported in fall, probably because of its very early departure. The birds begin to disperse by early to mid-Jul and have usually departed by the latter part of Aug. Many fall reports are probably of misidentified drab, first-fall female Blackburnian Warblers, and the validity of such records is questionable (Lehman 1987).

Extreme dates: 21 Apr and 8 Oct, but misidentification is possible as noted above. Rare before May and casual after late Aug.

Remarks Consistent with the species' gradual increase throughout the Northeast are reports of breeding from the New England states. Zeranski and Baptist (1990) reported on the expansion into CT, probably starting in the 1960s, with a first confirmed breeding in 1972. VT had its first breeding record in 1977; four to six pairs were known to nest in only one location as of 1985 (Ellison 1985b). Four possible new sites were found in 1994 (NASFN 48:926). MA had reports of birds in suitable habitat as early as 1956. Breeding was first documented in 1989 and had been "more or less continuous" since then, but only 5–10 pairs were found in the state (Veit and Petersen 1993). A single site in NH held the species for the fourth consecutive year in 1995 (NASFN 49:910).
Patricia J. Lindsay

Black-and-white Warbler   *Mniotilta varia*

Range Chiefly central and eastern Nearctic, breeding from southern Canada to the southern United States. Winters from coastal South Carolina and Texas south to northern South America, very rarely farther north along the Atlantic Coast.

Status Uncommon to common breeder, common to very common migrant.

Breeding Its breeding distribution is unique. It breeds from eastern LI to timberline on Mt. Marcy, mainly in the eastern half of the state. It is common in the southeast, in the Adirondacks, Tug Hill, Oswego Lowlands, and Central Appalachians. It is uncommon and local in highly agricultural areas of fertile soils and low relief, such as the Great Lakes Plain and the Mohawk, upper Hudson, and Wallkill valleys. On the Appalachian Plateau it is also uncommon in northern Madison and Onondaga counties and the portion west of the Finger Lakes.

The largest populations appear to be where forest cover is more than 66%, as in the Hudson Highlands, Catskills, Adirondacks, and Tug Hill. But on the eastern half of the Appalachian Plateau, Central Appalachians, and St. Lawrence Plains it is well-distributed where forest cover is only 50%. In neighboring VT it occurs in high densities in stands of medium-aged second growth with well-developed understories rather than more mature, closed-canopy forests (Ellison 1985a). In NY it is found in a great number of forest types, from pitch pine–scrub oak on LI, to various types of northern hardwoods on the Appalachian Plateau, to spruce–fir–northern hardwoods in the Adirondacks. It is found even in alpine krummholz on Mt. Marcy (Atlas 1988).

Because it is essentially a forest bird requiring tracts of more than 60 acres, it is rare in parts of NY where forests have been fragmented. In MD and PA it has disappeared from many such forests (Galli et al. 1976; Whitcomb et al. 1977; Schwalbe 1992). NY BBS data showed a significant annual decline from 1966 to 1994 of 1.9% (Peterjohn 1995) but in the Northeast generally showed a nonsignificant annual increase from 1966 to 1988 (Sauer and Droege 1992). Over the species' breeding and wintering ranges it is not considered to be Threatened at this time (Reed 1992).

Nonbreeding Early to arrive and late to depart, it is a common migrant both inland and coastal, with average statewide arrival 27 Apr and average departure 2 Oct (DeBenedictis 1987).

Spring maxima: 100 Woodmere Woods, Nassau Co. 6 May 1950; 50 Rochester, Monroe Co. 24 May 1917. *Fall maxima:* 66 struck the Empire State Building, Manhattan 27 Sep 1970; 40 JBSP 10 Sep 1969. *Extreme dates:* 3 Apr and 20 Dec. One was killed at a window in Westport, Essex Co. 17 Dec. *Winter:* CBC reports include: Rochester, Monroe Co. 1975; Putnam Co. 1978; on four LI counts 1965–1994.
Stephen W. Eaton

American Redstart

Setophaga ruticilla

Range Nearctic, breeding locally from southeastern Alaska to Newfoundland and south to Arizona and Texas, the Gulf states, and northern Florida. Winters from central Florida and the Bahamas south through the West Indies and Middle America to Brazil and Ecuador.

Status Widespread common breeder, fewer only in areas of intensive agriculture and urban sprawl. Common spring and fall migrant inland; along the coast fairly common in spring, very common to abundant in fall.

Breeding This species was noted on 81% of the Atlas blocks. Suitable breeding habitat is widely diversified and includes, for example, river flats and high peaks. That their nesting can reach high densities is suggested by Scheider's 11 Jun 1960 report of 60 singing males distributed along 4 mi of logging road at the edge of the Tug Hill region.

Despite this abundance, it is another species with a declining statewide breeding population. NY BBS 1966–1989 data showed a decline of 29%, with 19% since 1980. That this reduction may be a regional phenomenon, however, is suggested by the 18 western NY BBSs, which showed a slight increase in total numbers over the same period (Rising 1994c).

Nonbreeding It usually arrives about 3 May, but in some years there is a scattering of Apr records, especially downstate. Bull (1974) cited a spring maximum of 125 in Rochester, Monroe Co. 24 May 1917. On Niagara Frontier May Counts 1935–1995, American Redstart is outnumbered among warblers only by Yellow and Yellow-rumped warblers and Common Yellowthroat. On this census the average count is 287, with a maximum of 923 on 19 May 1946. Decade averages have stayed at about 250 since the 1960s, down from 400 in the 1940s and 350 in the 1950s (Rising 1995).

Fall numbers decline after about 20 Sep, with average state departures by the end of the month. Individuals, however, have been recorded in Oct,

Nov, and even Dec, including three CBC records: Peekskill, Westchester Co. 1973 and Rockland Co. and Lower Hudson 1985 (Salzman 1994).

Fall maxima: 200 Mamaroneck, Westchester Co. 10 Sep 1969; 111 struck the Empire State Building, Manhattan 14 Sep 1964.
Gery Rising

Prothonotary Warbler   *Protonotaria citrea*

Range Southeastern Nearctic, breeding from central and eastern Minnesota to southern Ontario, New York, and Massachusetts and south to Florida, the Gulf Coast, and Texas; also west to Kansas and Oklahoma. Winters from Mexico to Venezuela.

Status Localized breeder and rare but regular migrant.

Breeding This species is a very localized breeder in west, central, and southeastern NY. Attempted breeding was first noted in 1910 in a marsh at the head of Cayuga L., Tompkins Co. (Allen 1911). It was not until 1931 that it was first recorded as successful at Oak Orchard Swamp, Genesee Co. (Beardslee 1932), where four breeding pairs were found. Up to 10 individuals were observed there on 15 June 1961 (Beardslee and Mitchell 1965), and this colony was still extant during the Atlas period. Breeding was first observed at MNWR in 1948 (KB 2:56), and Atlas workers found it still active. A third "permanent colony" (Bull 1974) existed only until 1968 at Oneida L., Onondaga Co. (KB 32:284), where nests had been found at Short Point (Bull 1974) and nearby Muskrat Bay (KB 7:99). Other upstate nesting localities included: Ashville and Riverside Marsh, both in Chautauqua Co.; Delta L., Oneida Co.; INWR; Alma Pond, Allegany Co. Breeding at LeRoy, Genesee Co. and Riverside Marsh, Chautauqua Co. (Bull 1974) was never confirmed (Beardslee and Mitchell 1965). Breeding in the southeastern part of the state was first suspected in 1970, when singing males were observed in Jun on LI, but it was not confirmed until 1979 when a nest was found at Nissequogue River SP, Suffolk Co. (KB 29:190). Other sites were subsequently discovered in Suffolk Co. at Belmont Lake SP (KB 33:298) and Wyandanch (Atlas 1988).

Nonbreeding It is a rare but regular spring migrant and is scarcer in the fall. It is recorded as far north as Saratoga and Oswego counties, but more commonly in western, central, and southeastern NY, generally from the last week of Apr through late May. A spring maximum count of 16 on 26 May 1936 is given by Beardslee and Mitchell (1965) without a locality. Maximum seasonal counts in the NYC area are topped by 18 in 1973 from 9 Apr to 2 Jun, two-thirds of these from 24 Apr to 4 May. In 1984 up to 10 were recorded, with four in Prospect Park, Kings Co. on 16 Apr.

Extreme dates: 27 Mar; 30 Sep (inland) and 15 Oct (coastal). There are no substantiated CBC or winter records.

Remarks The Prothonotary Warbler is one of several southeastern species whose ranges have been gradually moving northward. Eaton (1914) considered it an accidental or rare visitant, with only eight records by 1914. Griscom (1923) considered that "it has occurred far too often in the Northeast in recent years to be regarded as accidental," but it was not until the late 1920s or early 1930s that it was reported with any degree of regularity.
Paul R. Sweet

Worm-eating Warbler *Helmitheros vermivorus*

Range Eastern Nearctic, breeding throughout much of the eastern United States from northeastern Kansas to southeastern New York, northern Connecticut, western Massachusetts, and south to northeastern Texas, the Gulf states, and northern Florida. Winters from southern Florida and the West Indies south through Middle America to Panama.

Status Locally common breeder in the lower Hudson Valley, with a scattering of records elsewhere. Rare to uncommon migrant in both spring and fall along the coast; very rare to casual upstate.

Breeding In 1974 Bull recorded only 28 breeding localities for the Worm-eating Warbler. This number was extended by the Atlas to 225 blocks, a remarkable 4% of the total. The concentrations are suggested by approximate county block totals: Westchester 59, Orange 38, Ulster 32, Putnam 32, Dutchess 24, Sullivan 7, Chemung 5, Delaware 5, Nassau 4, Suffolk 4, Chenango 4, Broome 3, Cortland 2, Tompkins 1, Schuyler 1, Onondaga 1, Schoharie 1, Greene 1, and Columbia 1. The Columbia report was a county first.

The distribution does not speak to the concentration of birds within blocks. Observations by Hickey of 10 pairs on a 40-acre tract in Grassy Sprain (Yonkers), Westchester Co. in 1941 and by Axtell of 12 pairs along the Chemung R. near Elmira in 1943 suggest intensive nesting. No state records published since the 1940s compare with those. Outside the lower Hudson Valley, this species remains a rare local breeder in the Susquehanna-Chemung R. watershed from Binghamton to Elmira and on the North Shore of LI.

The Atlas suggested reasons why it is not more widely reported: It is wary and difficult to see. It is also quiet, and when it does sing, "it sounds very much like a Chipping Sparrow."

Nonbreeding Most arrive in early May and depart by mid-Sep, with extreme dates 10 Apr and 17 Oct.
Spring maxima: 12 Prospect Park, Kings Co. 5 May 1950; 10 Van Cortlandt Park, Bronx Co. 6 May 1950. *Fall maxima:* 7 Inwood Hill

Park, Manhattan 2 Aug 1963; 5 killed, Fire I. Lighthouse, Suffolk Co. 28 Aug 1898.

Despite the dearth of nesting records beyond the southern counties, a few are recorded with some regularity north of these regions during migration periods. Between 1976 and 1995 these reports averaged 1.5 per year, almost all during spring migration. The highest number of these "overshoot" records was in 1976, when a total of nine were recorded in Regions 1, 2, 3, and 5. Even farther north, there are two records from Essex Co.: a bird banded in Wadhams 10 May 1979, the first record for Region 7, and another seen just 3.5 mi east of there 11–12 May 1993. There are also two 1992 records for Region 6: at Harrisville, Lewis Co. 16 Jun and at Cape Vincent, Jefferson Co. 29 Aug. Although the Harrisville bird was reported as a Region 6 first, Parkes (1952) had claimed an earlier Watertown record.

Remarks The idea of overshooting migrants raises interesting questions, but questions that surely defy investigation. Are they birds that fly too far north and then retreat? Are they thinly represented in isolated breeding spots north of their normal breeding range, or do they spend their summer isolated from breeding partners? Do they represent the pioneers to new breeding territories?
Gerry Rising

Swainson's Warbler   *Limnothlypis swainsonii*

Range Southeastern Nearctic, breeding locally only from southern Ohio and Indiana east to coastal Delaware and south to eastern Texas, the Gulf Coast, and northern Florida. Winters in the Bahamas, the Greater Antilles, and in the Yucatan Peninsula and Belize. Casual both north and west of the breeding range.

Status Very rare migrant overshoots.

Occurrence The first was discovered in Prospect Park, Kings Co. 5–6 May 1950, and the second in 1963. Bull (1974) placed it on the state list with a bird netted, banded, and photographed by Lauro at Tobay, Nassau Co. 20 May 1973. The first upstate bird was netted and photographed at the Burgeson Sanctuary, Chautauqua Co. 13 May 1975 by the Richardsons (Sundell 1975).

An individual in Central Park, Manhattan 7, 9, and 11 May 1979 was photographed and published (Post 1980). Post's account included a summary of previous reports in NY and NJ.

Only two subsequent reports were submitted to and accepted by NYSARC; both were upstate. One was at Portage, Livingston Co. 14–15 May 1990 (Reinhardt, Cass, VanderWerf) (NYSARC 1992); the other was at Elmira, Chemung Co. 29 Apr 1993 (Scrocarelli) (NYSARC 1995).

There are about 11 other published reports, some of which may be correct. All are of individual birds in late Apr or May, and most are from the NYC area.

Remarks CT, RI, and MA have very few records, but PA and NJ have many, as might be expected, given the proximity of those states to the limits of the breeding range.
Gerry Rising

Ovenbird *Seiurus aurocapillus*

Range Nearctic, chiefly the eastern portions, breeding from central Canada south throughout the northeastern United States and, in the mountains, to northern Georgia. Winters in Florida, the West Indies, Middle America, and northern South America.

Status Common breeder and common to very common migrant.

Breeding It is common across the Appalachian Plateau, Catskills, Adirondacks, Tug Hill, the southeast, and eastern LI. It has been displaced by agriculture where there is productive soil: for example, the Great Lakes Plain and the Mohawk, Black, upper Hudson, and Wallkill valleys. In these areas populations exist but are scattered. On western LI it has been displaced by urban sprawl. Found in 76% of Atlas blocks and Confirmed in 29% of those, it is the fourth commonest warbler breeding in the state after Common Yellowthroat, Yellow Warbler, and American Redstart (Atlas 1988).

It nests and feeds on the forest floor, where it is most often observed walking deliberately, with head bobbing and tail up, much like a small hen. It seeks cover in the lower canopy. Usually it is found in mature forest, either deciduous or mixed, with little underbrush and an abundance of fallen leaves, logs, and rocks (DeGraff et al. 1980). It may be found in deciduous forests of beech-maple, red maple–gray birch, maple-oak, and mixed forest of pitch pine–oak, spruce, hemlock, and beech (Atlas 1988).

NY BBS 1966–1994 data showed a significant average annual increase of 2.6% (Peterjohn 1995), but in some areas losses were reported. In Quaker Run Valley of Allegany SP the population in 1930–1931 ranked third of all species in the valley (1196 pairs), but by 1983–1985 in the same area, it had slipped to sixth place (506 pairs), behind Red-eyed Vireo, American Redstart, Black-throated Green and Blackburnian warblers and Dark-eyed Junco (Saunders 1936; Baird 1990). A survey in Allegany showed a slight drop in the population between 1971 and 1977 but then a sharp rise between 1978 and 1984 (Klingensmith and Hoover 1986).

Nonbreeding The Ovenbird is one of our best known and most numerous Neotropical, long-distance, migrant warblers. The average statewide arrival is 4 May; average departure is 1 Oct (DeBenedictis 1987). The maximum date of passage in western NY is 20 Sep; immature birds migrate the same time as adults (Eaton 1981).

Spring maxima: 200 Central Park, Manhattan 11 May 1914; 200 Madison Square Park, Manhattan 15 May 1921; 200 Goat I., Niagara R. 21 May 1943. *Fall maxima:* 175 hit the Colden TV tower, Erie Co. 24 Sep 1970; 85 hit the Empire State Building, Manhattan 28 Sep 1970. *Extreme dates:* 5 Apr (coastal specimen 10 Apr) and 24 Nov (coastal). *Winter:* There were many reports at feeders in the 1970s to 1990s; most were in Dec and most did not remain or survive past that month. One overwintered at Southhold, Suffolk Co. 7 Jan–16 Mar 1980, eating seed on the ground (KB 30:131). Other published dates range only to 16 Jan, and most were not submitted to NYSARC. There were several records on LI CBCs.

Remarks (By K. C. Parkes) Contra Bull (1974), *furvior* of Newfoundland is considered a valid subspecies. Its ventral streaks are heavier than those of the nominate subspecies, its back tends to be darker, the olivaceous color of the flanks is deeper and more extensive, and the axillars and wing linings are olive instead of pale greenish yellow. The black crown streaks are often broader, and the crown patch tends to be browner, less orange. The fact that its breeding range is apparently confined to the southern two-thirds of Newfoundland probably explains the relative scarcity of migrant specimens in collections. Parkes examined two from NY: Turkey Hill, near Varna, Tompkins Co. 4 Oct 1951 (caught in a mousetrap) and Ithaca, Tompkins Co. 6 Sep 1952 (flew into window of Bailey Hall on the Cornell University campus).
Stephen W. Eaton and Kenneth C. Parkes

Northern Waterthrush *Seiurus noveboracensis*

Range Nearctic, breeding from central Alaska east to northern Ontario, Labrador, and Newfoundland and south to southern Ontario and the northern United States, in the east as far south as Pennsylvania, northern New Jersey, southeastern New York, and southern New England; in the mountains to West Virginia and Maryland. Winters from Florida and Texas south through Central America and the West Indies to Peru.

Status Fairly common local breeder and fairly common to common migrant.

Breeding It was reported in 21% of Atlas blocks and was Confirmed in 17% of those. It probably breeds in the majority of our undisturbed, wooded swamps more than 30 acres in size, south to the Hudson Highlands and northeastern Westchester Co. (Eaton 1957; Speiser 1982).

Outside the Adirondacks, concentrations occur in Oswego, northern Cayuga, Madison, Onondaga, Chenango, Otsego, Tompkins, Tioga, Sullivan, and Columbia counties, all areas where small or large wetlands are in abundance. It is less widespread west of the Finger Lakes, as are suitable wetlands. In the Adirondacks it appears to follow the rivers flowing in all directions from the central highlands, but this distribution may reflect the fact that rivers provide Atlas workers relatively easy access to its nesting habitat. In reality the species is probably more widespread. Eaton (1914) said it was commonly found in the Mt. Marcy area in swamps up to 2750 ft. This shy bird, which stops singing early and breeds in wetlands seldom penetrated by humans, was probably underreported in the Atlas.

It is found in red maple–hardwood swamps of the Great Lakes Plain and hemlock-hardwood swamps of the valleys and uplands of the Appalachian Plateau. In the Adirondacks and Tug Hill Plateau it frequents black spruce–tamarack and spruce–balsam fir, as well as northern white cedar and alder thicket swamps. Some of these on the Great Lakes Plain and on the Appalachian Plateau have been drained for peat mining and vegetable growing and have reduced habitat for breeding. But, because the species breeds across Canada to Alaska, its overall breeding range appears to be secure for the present. It is on its wintering grounds where there is some concern. It commonly inhabits mangrove swamps, which have been reduced in some areas for fuel wood, shrimp culture, and golf courses (Terborgh 1989).

Nonbreeding It is widespread during migration but commoner near the coast than inland. The average arrival statewide is 30 Apr; average departure is 21 Sep (DeBenedictis 1987).

Spring maxima: 25 Manitou, Monroe Co. 30 Apr 1960; 21 banded, Huntington, Suffolk Co. 28 May 1967. *Fall maxima:* 55 Prospect Park, Kings Co. 13 Sep 1964; 38 hit the Westhampton Air Force Base tower, Suffolk Co. 5 Oct 1954. *Extreme dates:* 7 Apr (coastal, banded), 19 Apr (inland, specimen), and 7 Jun (coastal). In fall it is one of the first warblers to appear along the coast: 12 Jul to 30 Nov (coastal) and 6 Nov (inland). *Winter:* One at Tifft Nature Center, Erie Co. 4–24 Jan 1947 and one at the same locality 5 Jan 1980; one at a Mill Neck, Nassau Co. feeder 26–27 Dec 1965; one along a spring-fed pond Mastic, Suffolk Co. 26 Dec 1968. Reported on several LI CBCs.
Stephen W. Eaton

Louisiana Waterthrush *Seiurus motacilla*

Range Eastern Nearctic, breeding from eastern Nebraska and southeastern Minnesota to central New York and central New England and south to eastern Texas, the Gulf states, and northern Florida. Winters in southern Florida and the West Indies and from Mexico to northern South America.

Status Fairly common breeder along streams south of the Adirondacks, rare to uncommon migrant.

Breeding It was found in 20% of Atlas blocks and was Confirmed in 34% of those. Although still essentially a bird of the southeastern part of the state, it is increasing its range north. It is well distributed across the Appalachian Plateau and the Mohawk Valley. It has even invaded the Central Adirondacks, occurring along the south and north branches of the Moose R. in Herkimer and Hamilton counties, along tributaries of the Boquet R., Essex Co., and in the Tug Hill Plateau. It is now found in the L. Champlain Valley to Plattsburgh, Clinton Co., and still breeds on LI's North Shore (Atlas 1988).

Its distribution distinctly follows major rivers and their tributaries of moderate grade, but it is absent from slow-moving, deeper, and muddy streams of the Great Lakes, Eastern Ontario, and St. Lawrence plains. After the removal of the forest from the Appalachian Plateau in the nineteenth century, this species was undoubtedly greatly reduced in numbers because of the drastic changes in the streams from sawdust and increased water temperatures, which affected the aquatic insect life. Saunders (1942) did not find the bird nesting in Allegany SP in the 1920s and 1930s, but with the return of the forest and clear-flowing streams the bird returned (Eaton 1981). Like many riparian birds, it depends on the health of both its aquatic habitat and the surrounding forest. Because it winters in Caribbean and Central American streamside forests, its populations may depend on the health of those habitats just as much as on those in its breeding range.

Nonbreeding Being at the northern limits of its range in NY, with no large populations to the north, it is uncommon on migration inland and rare along the coast. In 10 years of banding (1960–1969) near Huntington, Suffolk Co., of more than 400 waterthrushes processed by Lanyon and his assistants, only 13 were Louisianas. It is one of the earliest warblers to appear in breeding areas and earliest to leave in the fall. Dates after Aug can be suspected as being its sibling Northern Waterthrush, widespread on migration into mid-Sep. The Louisiana is rare before 15 Apr and after mid Aug.

Maxima: 3–4 Central Park, Manhattan mid-Apr (Bull 1964). *Extreme dates:* 25 Mar (coastal) and 31 Mar (inland); 25 Aug (coastal). Stephen W. Eaton

Kentucky Warbler *Oporornis formosus*

Range Eastern Nearctic, breeding from eastern Nebraska and southern Wisconsin to southwestern Connecticut and south to Texas, the Gulf Coast, and central Georgia. Winters from southern Mexico to northern South America.

Status Uncommon and local breeder in the southeast and probably breeding in river valleys along the PA border. Rare spring and fall migrant through breeding area and very rare anywhere else.

Breeding One of a few southern species that was more common in NY a century ago than today, this was a common nineteenth-century breeder in the lower Hudson Valley from Riverdale, Bronx Co. north and an uncommon "summer resident" of LI. Nests were also found in Taylor and Cincinnatus, Cortland Co. in 1903 and 1906 (Fisher 1878; Eaton 1914). It disappeared from all these locales in the first three or four decades of the twentieth century, becoming little more than a vagrant or migratory overshoot. Then, in 1973, it bred at Huntington, Suffolk Co., the first state breeding record in over 30 years. Subsequent records were obtained in several areas of LI, mostly on or near the North Shore, and in Westchester, Rockland, Putnam, Orange, and Dutchess counties (Atlas 1988), approximately the same areas where it had bred a century earlier. Starting in the late 1970s it was also recorded during breeding season in river valleys north of the PA border along the Appalachian Plateau from western NY to the Susquehanna R., all south-facing drainages that provide habitat and routes north for southern species. Although confirmation was not obtained during Atlas work, these populations have persisted and they undoubtedly represent established breeding populations. At least one of these sites is close to the area where nests had been found in 1903 and 1906.

Nonbreeding Regarded by Bull (1974) as "one of our rarest warblers" but now a rare but regular coastal migrant in the spring, it is often observed in the NYC parks and in the lower Hudson Valley. It is rare in the fall in these areas and very rare anywhere in the state away from its breeding grounds at any time.

Extreme dates: 18 Apr and 7 Oct. It generally appears in late Apr or early May and, as a fall migrant, from mid-Aug to the third week of Sep. Eric Salzman

Connecticut Warbler *Oporornis agilis*

Range Central Nearctic, breeding from British Columbia east to Quebec and south to the northern portions of Minnesota, Wisconsin, and Michigan. Migrates in spring through the Mississippi Valley, in fall mainly along the Atlantic Coast. Winters in South America, from Colombia south to Amazonia and central Brazil.

Status Rare spring migrant. Uncommon fall migrant in the southeastern and western portions, very rare in the north, with the number of occurrences declining.

Occurrence Before 1910, it was a fairly common fall coastal migrant. Bull (1974) noted the following accounts: Dutcher, in his field notes, reported that 57 struck the Fire I. Lighthouse, Suffolk Co. on 23 Sep 1883; in Sep 1900, Cherrie collected 10 south of Jamaica, Queens Co.; on 5 Oct 1954, Wilcox picked up 13 dead at the Westhampton Air Force Base tower, Suffolk Co. Occurrences with such numbers are unheard of today, and it appears that the decline continues. The number of fall sightings reported annually in *The Kingbird* has dropped from about 16 per fall in the late 1970s to about six per fall in the 1990s. Virtually all occurrences today are single individuals, with very rarely two to four being seen in a single area. An unusual record of four came from Ithaca, Tompkins Co. 17 Sep 1983 (KB 34:39).

This warbler shows a distinctive geographical pattern in its occurrences both spring and fall. In the fall, it is seen in the western portions of the state (Regions 1, 2, 3, 4, 5) and in the southeast (Regions 9, 10); it is very rare in the other Regions. It is regular but uncommon in Region 10, which accounts for about 25% of all fall records, and is regular but rare in the other Regions cited, with a frequency of occurrence in each about half that of NYC-LI. It appears to migrate east-southeast across Buffalo and L. Ontario to the coast, but it is very rare on the eastern edge of L. Ontario. Most fall records occur 25 Aug–5 Oct, with a peak in the week of 15–22 Sep. It is very rare after mid-Oct.

It is rare in spring, with an average of two or three reports a year; 75% of all spring sightings are from the western side of the state, from Buffalo to Syracuse, with the highest concentration in the Rochester area, and 80% occur 14–31 May. The majority of spring migration is through the Mississippi and Ohio valleys, but a small fraction of that migration must move northeast.

Extreme dates: 3 May and 8 Jun; 15 Aug and 30 Oct (coastal specimen). There are six reports before 7 May, five of them after 1986. These are early when compared with FL arrival dates and earliest dates for ON. Although these spring reports may be credible, early sightings should be documented with photographs. There is one very unusual summer record of a singing male at Indian L., Hamilton Co. 1 Jul 1978, where an immature had been banded the year before (KB 28:255). Bull (1964) mentioned four Nov records, all in 1938 from East Hampton, Suffolk Co., the latest occurring on 26 Nov.

Dominic F. Sherony

Mourning Warbler   *Oporornis philadelphia*

Range Nearctic, breeding from central Alberta to Newfoundland and south, in the east to northern Ohio, northern Pennsylvania, and western Massachusetts; also at higher elevations to Virginia and West Virginia. Winters from Nicaragua south to Panama and in northern South America.

Status Locally common breeder; absent in the central Appalachian Plateau and south and east of the Catskills. Rare to uncommon but regular migrant.

Breeding Showing a preference for nesting in dense thickets that cover old clearings and cutover lands, this species benefited from the clear-cutting of forests in the early nineteenth century. Evidence from early observers, however, does not indicate how the population has changed over time. Bull (1974) stated that it was recognized as a locally common nesting bird in the 1880s. The Atlas recorded it in 26% of the blocks, with Confirmed and Probable breeding in 62% of those. Its range is extensive in NY, showing concentrations in the Adirondacks, the Appalachian Plateau east of the Finger Lakes, the Allegany Hills, the Cattaraugus Highlands, and the Great Lakes Plain from Central Tug Hill westward. It is not found south and east of Sullivan Co., is very rare to absent in the Central Appalachian Plateau (Chemung, Tioga, and Broome counties), and is uncommon in the western L. Ontario Plain.

Densities of 4–13 pairs per 100 acres were found in areas that had been clear-cut four to five years earlier, but no birds were found in areas that had been clear-cut three years previously (Atlas 1988). A six-year survey estimated an average of 110 breeding pairs in Letchworth SP, Wyoming and Livingston counties (Bassett 1994). BBS data indicated that the population remained stable over the 15 years before 1994.

Nonbreeding In spring it is an uncommon migrant in the western and central regions and a rare migrant on the eastern side, with an arrival date of 17 May, although it can occur in early May. Although it is a notable "skulker," its distinctive song gives it away.

Fall reports are scarce throughout, and almost all are of single individuals. It is exceedingly difficult to observe because of the dense vegetation at that season and because the bird does not sing then. Fall migrants can be found in Aug, but most reports are in Sep, with the latest records in mid-Oct.

Spring maxima: 18 BOS May Count, 16 May 1993; 16 banded, Manitou, Monroe Co. 24 May 1993. *Fall maxima:* 12 banded, Huntington, Suffolk Co. 20 Aug–10 Sep 1964; 4 Rye, Westchester Co. 1 Sep 1984. *Extreme dates:* 6 May and 19 Oct.
Dominic F. Sherony

Common Yellowthroat   *Geothlypis trichas*

Range Nearctic and northern Neotropical, breeding from southern Alaska to southeastern Newfoundland south to northern Mexico, southern Texas, the Gulf Coast, and southern Florida. In the east, winters from South Carolina, and casually farther north, south to the Gulf Coast, the West Indies, and Panama.

Status A common breeder, as well as a common migrant. In winter, annual but uncommon on the coast, rare inland.

Breeding It prefers to nest in old fields with extensive shrubbery or in cattail marshes and is also found in margins of swamps and secondary growth bordering woodlands, with a preference for moist or wet locations. It was recorded in 97% of the Atlas blocks and was Confirmed in 56% of those. It is always found in low-level vegetation and forages at or near the ground; although secretive, it will respond to a variety of noises. It is sometimes double brooded, and late nesting may begin mid-Jul. By mid-Jul, some may begin their southbound migration, but most do not leave until late Aug or Sep. Although susceptible to brood parasitism by Brown-headed Cowbirds, the population remained constant from 1979 to 1994, according to BBS data.

Nonbreeding It is a common spring migrant throughout. The average spring arrival is 24 Apr on the coast and 1 May inland; the full range of arrival dates between 1988 and 1995 was 11 Apr–11 May. Peak numbers are usually encountered about mid-May. At that time, one should be able to find 10–30 in a day in a single location.

Fall migrants begin to appear by late Jul and are routinely found from Sep until mid to late Oct. They are rare inland past Nov but will linger if weather conditions remain mild. On the coast, they are uncommon but regular in small numbers in Dec and Jan and are frequently found on CBCs.

Spring maxima: 250 Central Park, Manhattan 11 May 1914; 200 JFK Airport, Queens Co. 17 May 1960. Multiple observers covering extensive territories counted: 600 on the BOS May Count 16 May 1993; 106 Tompkins Co. 14 May 1994. *Fall maxima:* 71 struck the Empire State Building, Manhattan 14 Sep 1964; 50 Erieville, Madison Co. 12 Sep 1991. *Winter:* 8 Montauk CBC 15 Dec 1984. *Extreme dates:* 7 Apr and 4 Jan. Dominic F. Sherony

Hooded Warbler   *Wilsonia citrina*

Range Eastern Nearctic, breeding from southeastern Nebraska, southern Ontario, and southern New England south to Florida and the Gulf states. Winters in Middle America.

Status Fairly common breeder west of the Finger Lakes. Uncommon on the eastern Appalachian Plateau, Great Lakes Plain, and southeastern NY. Absent in the Adirondacks, Catskills, and Hudson Valley north of Ulster and Dutchess counties. Rare to uncommon migrant except near breeding areas.

Breeding It was found in 421 Atlas blocks and was Confirmed in 25% of those. In the southeast it was reported mainly in the Hudson Highlands and Manhattan Hills, probably spilling over from populations in northern NJ. It was also found in isolated blocks in Ulster and Sullivan counties but no farther up the Hudson Valley. It is a rare breeder on LI. No reports came from Greene and only a few from Wayne, Monroe, and Orleans counties, where it was formerly fairly generally distributed. There was only one confirmation in Madison Co., where it had been widely distributed (Eaton 1910). Breeding sites in Onondaga Co. shown in Bull (1974) have largely disappeared, but it has expanded its range onto the Tug Hill Plateau and has maintained populations in the eastern Drumlins and Oswego Lowlands. Populations southeast of Buffalo, Erie Co., referred to by Bull, have survived, and the Atlas documented three new areas of concentration in Wyoming—especially Letchworth SP, where an estimated 534 pairs occur (D. Basset, *fide* D. Sherony)—southern Cattaraugus, and Chautauqua counties. These last three areas have apparently been colonized by birds moving north from large populations in extreme northwestern PA (Ickes 1992). It is uncommon across the Appalachian Plateau south and east of the Finger Lakes, but some populations appear to be increasing along with the forest in the Finger Lakes Highlands—i.e., Finger Lakes National Forest (KB 42:265)—and Dryden, Tompkins Co. (KB 33:195).

It is a bird of large forest tracts where there is a partially open canopy with a thick understory of shrubs or saplings. The density of the population depends not just on the size of the forest but also on the type. In Quaker Run Valley of Allegany SP, density was 0.7 pairs per 100 acres in mature northern hardwoods, but it was five per 100 acres in oak–northern hardwoods (Baird 1990). In Westchester Co. it is found on wooded slopes containing an understory of mountain laurel. In three very distinct areas of central NY it is found in well-drained, open maple woods containing a thick undergrowth of maple saplings (Scheider 1959).

Because it is a forest bird on its wintering grounds as well, it is threatened there (Rappole et al. 1983) but is not a conservation priority at this time (Reed 1992).

Nonbreeding Rare to uncommon migrant except near large breeding populations, where it is difficult to categorize. It arrives the second week of May throughout and departs mid-Sep.

Maxima: 49 Letchworth SP, Wyoming Co. 22 May 1989; 5 Prospect Park, Kings Co. 12 May 1945. *Extreme dates:* 4 Apr and 7 Nov; exceptionally, 3–7 Dec 1954 Northport, Suffolk Co. **Extralimital:** 1 Massena, St. Lawrence Co. 14 May 1990; 1 Colonie, Albany Co. 24 May 1990. Stephen W. Eaton

Wilson's Warbler   *Wilsonia pusilla*

Range Nearctic, breeding in the east from northern Ontario, central Labrador, and Newfoundland south to northern New England and northern New York. Winters from southern Texas south through Middle America to Panama.

Status One confirmed breeding record. Rare summer records from the Adirondacks. Uncommon to fairly common migrant, more numerous inland than on the coast.

Breeding Nickerson (1978) discovered a nest in North Elba, Essex Co. on 1 Aug 1978 in an open evergreen forest of white and red spruce, tamarack, and firs; the open areas were grown over with spiraea to a height of 1–5 ft. The area was an overgrown pasture, partially flooded by beaver activity, at an elevation of 1900 ft. The nest was on the ground beneath a hummock of moss.

Before this discovery, there had been three summer reports in Essex and Franklin counties (Nickerson 1978). The BBS also recorded three singing males in the same two counties (Atlas 1988; KB 34:262) in 1984, but there have been no summer reports since then. This bog-inhabiting species breeds through western ME and the northern sections of NH and VT; the NY records are probably an extension of that population.

Nonbreeding It is an uncommon to fairly common spring migrant upstate and uncommon along the coast. The average spring arrival throughout is 11 May; peak migration ranges from 12 to 22 May, and it is rare before 6 May. It is annual but uncommon in fall, with most records in Sep and early Oct; it is extremely rare after 15 Oct. There are a few records for Dec.

Spring maxima: 35 Sandy Pond, Oswego Co. 20 May 1969; 24 banded, Manitou, Monroe Co. 24 May 1993 (Brooks). *Fall maxima:* 22 struck the Elmira TV tower, Chemung Co. 21 Sep 1977; 20 Sandy Pond 3 Sep 1960. *Extreme dates:* 29 Apr and 10 Jun; 14 Aug and 22 Dec. Bull (1974) mentioned an early coastal fall record of 26 Jul. The latest banded record is 4 Nov.
Dominic F. Sherony and Elizabeth W. Brooks

Canada Warbler   *Wilsonia canadensis*

Range Nearctic, chiefly central and eastern, breeding across southern Canada from Alberta to Nova Scotia south to the north-central United

States to northern New Jersey and southeastern New York, and in the higher mountains to northern Georgia; rarely to the coast of southern New England. Winters from Colombia to Peru.

Status Fairly common breeder at higher elevations and common to very common migrant.

Breeding It was found in 32% of Atlas blocks and was Confirmed in 25% of those. It is most widely distributed in the Adirondacks, Tug Hill, Catskills, and the Appalachian Plateau east of the Finger Lakes, above 1000 ft. There are gaps in its distribution on the plateau west of the Finger Lakes, but it is fairly common again in the Allegany Hills. It is rare on the Great Lakes and St. Lawrence plains, Mohawk and Hudson valleys, and LI. Its overall breeding range has changed little since the early 1900s except for its spread into the Taconics, Hudson Highlands, and Manhattan Hills (Atlas 1988).

It breeds in varied forest types with dense understory in cool, moist microhabitats. In the Adirondacks it is found along streams in thickets of willow, alder, and elderberry and in old burns of aspen and cherry (Saunders 1929). In the Allegany Hills it nests along wet stream borders running through hemlock-hardwoods, wooded swamps, and on dry oak slopes with shrubby understory (Eaton 1981). In central NY it breeds in spruce bogs, alder swamps, hemlock glens, and weedy ravines. In the Catskill region it occurs in hemlock-rhododendron swamps, and in the Hudson Highlands in moist woodland with understory of mountain laurel.

NY BBS 1966–1994 data showed a significant annual 4.6% decline (Peterjohn 1995), and the BBS throughout the Northeast also showed this trend (C. R. Smith et al. 1993). The cause of this decline is not known, but studies in Allegany SP point to a loss of habitat due to maturation of the forest, coupled with overbrowsing of the understory by deer. In 1930–1931 Saunders (1936) estimated that there were 282 pairs in Quaker Run Valley; in 1983–1985 Baird (1990), in the same valley, recorded seven pairs.

Nonbreeding It appears in greatest numbers in late May and again in Aug and is more numerous along the coast than inland. The average statewide arrival is 10 May, and average departure is 20 Sep (DeBenedictis 1987).

Spring maxima: 75 Central Park, Manhattan 23 May 1954; 75 Selkirk Shores, Oswego Co. 25 May 1960; 49 banded, Huntington, Suffolk Co. 28 May 1967. *Fall maxima:* 74 banded, Huntington 20 Aug 1964; 35 Far Rockaway, Queens Co. 23 Aug 1958. *Extreme dates:* 23 Apr and 12 Jun; 1 Jul and 31 Oct, exceptionally to 13 Nov (coastal).
Stephen W. Eaton

Painted Redstart   *Myioborus pictus*

Range Southwestern Nearctic and Neotropical, breeding from western Arizona and western Texas south to Nicaragua. Winters from Mexico to Nicaragua.

Status Accidental.

Occurrence A single bird has been observed in NY. It was first noticed at the Dilgards' feeder in Dansville, Livingston Co. on 14 Dec 1979, then on 22 Dec, and daily 25 Dec–24 Jan 1980. On 25 Jan, feathers and parts were found under the feeder, indicating loss to a predator. The bird was reported to and verified by the birding community on 6 Jan and had been seen and photographed by hundreds until its demise (Spahn 1980; NYSARC 1981).

Remarks At the time of this occurrence, it was the fifth record east of the Mississippi R.; the others were in MA, WI, OH, and ON. Since then, there have been an additional three records east of the Mississippi: MI in 1983; GA in 1984; MS in 1987. There are also records from MO in 1986 and MN in 1992.
Robert G. Spahn

Yellow-breasted Chat

Icteria virens

Range Nearctic, breeding from southern British Columbia across southern Canada to central New York and southern New England and south, in the east to the Gulf Coast and Florida. Winters chiefly in Middle America, but also regularly in small numbers north to the Great Lakes, New York, and New England.

Status Local breeder in the southeastern portion. Uncommon in migration in coastal areas; rare in winter.

Breeding Formerly a common breeder on LI, SI and in the lower Hudson Valley, it is now much reduced and localized on LI, with breeding records concentrated on the North Shore, Fishers and Gardiners islands, Montauk, and the Shinnecock Hills; all are areas with heath or pastureland grown up to dense tangles of shrubs, briars, and vines. It declined on SI after 1950 but was rediscovered by Atlas workers in three or four locales. It is "greatly decreased in numbers" in the Hudson Highlands (Speiser 1982), with relatively few Atlas records for Westchester Co. and none at all for Rockland Co. The bird had been historically common in those areas. The loss of old-field habitat as former farm and pastureland was cleared for development or grew back into forest appears to be responsible for the bird's decline. There were, however, a number of Atlas records from Orange Co., where the development process is in a different phase, with more recently abandoned farm and pastureland providing the necessary habitat. It was entirely absent from the Hudson and Lake Champlain valleys, and from the Catskills, Adirondacks, Tug Hill, and northern regions of the state. This species has been recommended for inclusion on NYSDEC's list as a Species of Special Concern.

In western and central NY, its distribution has changed little during the twentieth century. The bird was reported by Eaton (1914) to be a localized breeder in the river valleys along the Appalachian Plateau and in the Finger Lakes and a very rare breeder in the Niagara region. This distribution was confirmed by Atlas workers, who also found it to be fairly widespread in the L. Ontario Plain. All of these are lowland areas with extensive patches of overgrown old-field habitat.

Nonbreeding It is an uncommon migrant, rare away from coastal areas, usually noted singly or in very small numbers. Bull (1974) gave maxima of four to six birds, all between 11 Sep and 7 Oct. His extreme dates were 26 Apr and 29 Nov. He described it as rare before mid-May and after mid-Oct and rare but regular along the coast in winter. This timetable has probably not changed a great deal since then except that it is now being reported annually in late fall and winter on LI, on CBCs and otherwise, from Brooklyn to Montauk, and in Bronx and Westchester counties as well.

Upstate, it is rare to extremely rare in migration and winter, with a handful of fall records to 24 Oct and a single recent winter record at Conesus L., Livingston Co. 13 Dec 1981–3 Jan 1982 (KB 32:115). Eric Salzman

TANAGERS—THRAUPIDAE

Summer Tanager *Piranga rubra*

Range Nearctic, breeding chiefly in the central and southern United States and northern Mexico and, in the east, north to the central portions of Ohio and to Maryland and southern New Jersey. Winters from Mexico and Middle America into South America.

Status Uncommon migrant.

Breeding There are no accepted breeding records, but persistent singing males, pairs on territory, a growing number of Jun and Jul records, and a reported pair feeding young suggest that breeding may have already taken place or is likely to do so in the near future. A carefully detailed report of adults feeding young in Jun 1990 in the LI pine barrens (KB 40:277; J. Clinton, pers. comm.) was not accepted by NYSARC (1992).

Nonbreeding It has been annually reported in the spring since 1947 in NYC, LI, and the lower Hudson Valley. It became increasingly common in the 1980s, with up to 30 individuals in 1983 and regular reports at slightly lower levels since. It arrives in late Apr, exceptionally from 25 Mar, with birds observed to mid-Jun and, less commonly, into late Jun and early Jul. It is much less often observed in fall, with reports from 28 Aug to early Oct.

In 1974 Bull (1974) called it "extremely rare" upstate, but it has since become more common, with more than a dozen reports ranging from the Appalachian Plateau to the Great Lakes Plain, Finger Lakes, and L. Champlain Valley, mostly in May. There is a single published fall record, a female seen at Webster, Monroe Co. 21 Sep 1973 (Bull 1976). Spring records are fairly equally divided among singing males, mature and immature, and females. Since there is no accepted state breeding record and no known breeding population to the north, these birds must be put in the category of extralimital wanderers or migrational overshoots.
Eric Salzman

Scarlet Tanager *Piranga olivacea*

Range Eastern Nearctic, breeding from southeastern Manitoba to New Brunswick and south to eastern Oklahoma, central Arkansas, and the northern part of the Gulf states and Georgia and to central Virginia. Winters from Panama to Bolivia.

Status Common breeder in deciduous or mixed forests. Common and widespread migrant.

Breeding Breeding throughout in deciduous and mixed forests from sea level on LI to nearly 5000 ft in the Adirondacks, it has apparently increased in the more southerly parts of the state. Eaton (1914) considered it to be less common in southern, central, and eastern NY, and Bull (1974) described it as "rare and local over much of the sandy coastal plain, even where oaks predominate." Atlas workers found it to be common throughout most of western, central, and southeastern NY, ranging into NYC, on the North Shore of LI, and on the South Shore in oak and mixed oak-pine forests throughout the pine barrens and South Fork. On SI it was a regular breeder until the 1950s and was rediscovered by Atlas workers in several locations. Notably high population densities have been found in western NY, where the BOS recorded 91 birds on its 1993 May count.

All of this evidence suggests that its population has been steadily increasing over a broad band in the western and southern parts of the state. Like other species that favor second-growth woodlands, Scarlet Tanager benefited from the regrowth of the eastern deciduous forest that followed extensive nineteenth-century logging. The particular increases of recent decades may be due to insect outbreaks in oak forests, notably the gypsy moth, whose early larval stages are taken by a number of insectivorous species including this one. Local population declines, reportedly due to insect declines, cold weather during breeding season, and forest fragmentation (Atlas 1988), appear to be more than balanced by positive factors, including habitat increase and availability of alternate prey. As is the case with other insectivores, some cyclical patterns of increase and decrease may be involved.

Nonbreeding It is most common in fall, when aggregations of as many as 50 have been observed (South Nyack, Rockland Co. 6 Oct 1959); up to 25 have been reported in several localities in mid-May.

Extreme dates: 11 Apr and 13 Dec. Normally rare before May and after mid-Oct.

Eric Salzman

Western Tanager   *Piranga ludoviciana*

Range Western Nearctic, breeding east to central Saskatchewan and western Nebraska. Winters chiefly from northern Mexico to Costa Rica. Vagrant east to the Atlantic Coast from Nova Scotia to Maryland.

Status Very rare vagrant.

Occurrence This species has been reported in NY approximately 30 times, predominantly in the southeast, with specimen records ranging from 1881 to 1970 as outlined in Bull (1974).

Only two of the more recent sight records were submitted to and accepted by NYSARC: Croton Point, Westchester Co. 7–14 Dec 1985 (Weissman, Askildsen) (NYSARC 1987); Brighton, Monroe Co. 9 May 1993 (Browning) (NYSARC 1995).

Other reports include: Montauk, Suffolk Co. 9 Dec 1983 (KB 34:143); JBSP 9 Oct 1986 (KB 36:49); RMSP 3 Dec 1988 (KB 39:128); RMSP

9–12 Nov 1990 (KB 45:83); Ft. Tilden, Queens Co. 12 and 29 Dec 1991 (AB 46:72, 243); RMSP 19 Nov 1995 (KB 46:93).

Upstate records are decidedly fewer. In addition to those in Bull, and the accepted record above, another was reported at Vine Valley, Yates Co. Aug 1981 (KB 31:243).

Remarks It occurs almost annually in MA (Veit and Petersen 1993), as well as in NJ (Leck 1984). PA has about a dozen records (Santner et al. 1992), CT a half dozen (Zeranski and Baptist 1990), and RI five (Conway 1992). The great majority of these were fall and winter birds.
Robert W. Brock

NEW WORLD
SPARROWS—EMBERIZIDAE

Green-tailed Towhee *Pipilo chlorurus*

Range Western Nearctic, breeding primarily in mountains from Washington east to Wyoming and south to southern California and western Texas. Winters south to central Mexico.

Status Casual fall or winter vagrant; no reports since 1977.

Occurrence There are three confirmed records: one at the Anderson feeder Ithaca, Tompkins Co. mid-Dec 1962–25 Apr 1963 (color ph by Allen, examined by Bull); a specimen netted 19 Oct 1971 died of "unknown causes" 3 Nov 1971 Scarsdale, Westchester Co. (Haeni), retained as AMNH 808899; an adult associated with White-throated Sparrows at the Adamo feeder in Wading River, Suffolk Co. 9 Dec 1976–22 Apr 1977, ph in AMNH, recognizable but not suitable for publication (Raynor 1977).

Another individual was observed 10–14 May 1969 south of Cazenovia, Madison Co. (KB 19:166).

Remarks In winter it is casual at NJ feeders (Leck 1984) and very rare at MA feeders (Veit and Petersen 1993). These visitants occasionally remain for weeks.
Gerry Rising

Eastern Towhee *Pipilo erythrophthalmus*

Range Primarily eastern Nearctic, breeding from southern Manitoba and southeastern North Dakota east to southwestern Quebec and northern New England and, in the east, south to northeastern Texas, the Gulf Coast, and southern Florida. Winters south to southern Texas, the Gulf Coast, and southern Florida.

Status Common breeder throughout. Common migrant, rare to uncommon in winter.

Breeding Habitats containing low, shrubby vegetation such as abandoned farmland, thickets, hedgerows, and pine barrens are preferred for breeding. In particularly favorable habitats it is the most numerous avian species, as found by Kerlinger and Doremus (1981) in the LI and Albany pine barrens and by Baird (1990) in the thicket habitat of Allegany SP. Baird replicated a study of breeding birds of part of the Allegany SP done in 1930–1931. He found the largest decline in forest species that build nests less than 2 m above the ground, including a major decline in Eastern Towhee. Yet, thicket habitat (land reverting from agriculture to forest) contained 12 pairs per 100 acres, the most abundant species in that habitat.

It is found breeding throughout the state, but in varying abundance. The Coastal Lowlands and lower Hudson Valley host the greatest density but also show the most significant decline in numbers. BBS data showed 18 birds per route 1975–1979 and four to six birds per route 1990–1994. This is a continuation of the decline in central LI 1967–1976 noted by Raynor (1976b). The lowest density in the state, fewer than one bird per route, occurs in the Great Lakes Plain.

The Adirondacks had exhibited increasing numbers of breeding towhees during the 1960s and early 1970s. BBS numbers have declined since then, with three birds per route in 1975–1979 down to 0.5 per route in 1990–1994. Yet Peterson (KB 44:234, 45:216) noted an increase in May reports for the Adirondacks during 1994 and 1995.

The St. Lawrence River Plains is the only area with a stable breeding population, with five birds per BBS route in 1975–1994. The rest of the state experienced a more moderate, but still steady, decline from five to seven birds per route to fewer than three. (The means cited above were calculated from the BBS routes that reported towhees at least once.)

Nonbreeding Normal spring arrival dates are mid to late Apr. The bulk of the population departs during the last half of Oct. There are a number of Nov records; the most unusual, owing to its northern location, is 10 at Lake Alice, Clinton Co. 2 Nov 1985 (KB 36:38).

Spring maxima: 200 Lawrence to Woodmere, Nassau Co. 6 May 1950; 110 Central Park, Manhattan 30 Apr 1947. Multiple-observer, large-area counts: 265 Allegany migration count May 1974 (126 participants); 109 BOS May Count 16 May 1993. *Fall maxima:* 65 Pompey, Onondaga Co. 9 Oct 1983. *Winter:* 177 Montauk, Suffolk Co. CBC 17 Dec 1994.

Eastern Towhee is reported in small numbers each winter from the southeastern and southwestern areas of the state, with the highest counts on LI and the lower Hudson Valley. A number of the LI CBCs normally report 10–20, with occasional counts of 50 and more. There are very few winter reports from the northern counties and none from the Adirondacks. For the remainder of the state, a few birds are found at feeders, regularly, but not every year. Winter occurrences have remained at this level over the last two decades, but they show a seasonal expansion over earlier times.

Remarks Significant declines in Eastern Towhee populations have occurred throughout the northeastern states (Hagan 1993). Hagan examined several factors, such as forest maturation, forest management practices, and white-tailed deer populations, all of which contribute to a reduction in the low, thick vegetation favored by towhees. He also speculated that the towhee is returning to the population levels of a pre-agricultural, forested Northeast. Towhee nests are frequently parasitized by Brown-headed Cowbirds (Harrison 1978).

The English name was formerly Rufous-sided Towhee. The name change was part of the AOU decision to elevate the former western form *maculatus* to a full species: Spotted Towhee, *P. maculatus* (AOU 1995).
Barbara A. Butler

Spotted Towhee *Pipilo maculatus*

Range Nearctic, breeding from southern British Columbia to southern Saskatchewan and south to southern California east to the central Dakotas and north-central and western Nebraska; also in west-central and southern Arizona, eastern New Mexico, and western Texas, and in Central America to Guatemala. Winters throughout much of breeding range and to south-central Texas. Casual in the east.

Status Very rare vagrant.

Occurrence There are seven records: (1) immature female discovered by Grant, JBSP 28 Dec 1956, collected by Buckley on 16 Feb 1957 (NYSM 19019); (2) immature female found by Peszell in the Bronx Zoo, along the Bronx R. 30 Nov 1957, collected by Buckley on 23 Dec 1957 (AMNH 707778); (3) male at a Bellport, Suffolk Co. feeder 3 Dec 1964–1 Feb 1965 (Puleston, Wilcox, et al.) color photo in AMNH; (4) male at a Chili, Monroe Co. feeder "for about three weeks during Feb 1976" (J. Skelly, R. D. Coffee, et al., pers. comm.; KB 26:101); (5) male at a Maspeth, Queens Co. feeder 28 Nov 1982 only (E. Polgar and E. Polgar, pers. comm.; KB 33:76); (6) male at a Greenville, Greene Co. feeder "late Dec 1984 through Feb 1985" (C. Ketham, R. Guthrie, et al., pers. comm.; KB 35:143); (7) male found on the Conesus-Honeoye-Hemlock CBC, Livonia, Livingston Co. 22 Dec 1990 (J. Skelly and D. Sherony, pers. comm.; KB 41:103).

Remarks Vagrants are known from the Canadian Maritimes south to at least NC; most records are coastal. Spotted Towhee was merged with the former Red-eyed Towhee, both becoming Rufous-sided Towhee, in the fifth

edition of the AOU Check-list in 1957 and was resplit in 1995 in the fortieth Supplement (AOU 1995). In the course of trying to determine which of the approximately 12 subspecies of Spotted Towhees had occurred in NY, Buckley examined the only NJ specimen, an immature female, collected in Metuchen, Somerset Co. on 23 Dec 1952 by James Baird (USFWS 421001) and published as *montanus* (Baird 1957). He determined that bird, as well as his two New York specimens, to be *arcticus* (Buckley 1959), which is the only subspecies ever taken anywhere in eastern North America. Apart from the 1957 and 1958 specimens, the age and subspecies of the other New York Spotted Towhees are unknown, although it is most likely all were immature *arcticus*.
Paul A. Buckley

Bachman's Sparrow *Aimophila aestivalis*

Range Eastern Nearctic, breeding, at least formerly, from Illinois, Ohio, Pennsylvania, and Maryland south to eastern Texas, the Gulf Coast, and south-central Florida; now generally absent as a breeder in the Northeast, north of southern Kentucky and North Carolina. Winters throughout the breeding range.

Status Casual vagrant, not recorded since 1948.

Occurrence There are three records: (1) a male collected at Greenport, Suffolk Co. 4 Jun 1930 (Latham) NYSM 25683 examined by Bull; (2) a singing bird at Mendon Ponds Park, Monroe Co. 8–12 May 1940 (Meade, Hall, et al.) (Auk 58:103); (3) one observed in Prospect Park, Kings Co. 21–22 Apr 1948 (Carleton, Jacobson, et al.) (KB 2:82).

Remarks This species has been recorded only twice in NJ, in 1918 and 1957 (Leck 1984). Until about 1920 it bred in OH and southwestern PA, where it was then regularly recorded (Todd 1940).
Gerry Rising

American Tree Sparrow *Spizella arborea*

Range Nearctic, breeding from northern Alaska across central Canada to Labrador and south to northern British Columbia and northern Quebec. Winters from southern Canada south to northern California, central Arizona and Texas, and to Tennessee and North Carolina.

Status Common to abundant winter visitant, especially numerous in the interior.

Occurrence It occurs in or near open country, preferring weedy, brushy fields but also found in marshes, hedgerows, and woodland edges, usually in flocks of a few individuals to, occasionally, more than 100. It is a frequent visitor to feeders. Although it is always common in winter, numbers vary greatly from year to year. Bull (1974) suggested that it is less common during mild, open winters. CBCs suggest a slight decrease in the state.

Coastal maxima: 280 Orient, Suffolk Co. 25 Dec 1909. **Inland maxima:** 600 Tully, Onondaga Co. 19 Dec 1968; 500 Wilson, Niagara Co. 11 Feb 1968; 500 Point Peninsula, Jefferson Co. 13 Dec 1994. **Extreme dates:** 20 Sep and 22 May; exceptionally 9 Jun and 28 Jun. Usually rare before late Oct and after late Apr.

William C. D'Anna

Chipping Sparrow *Spizella passerina*

Range Nearctic, breeding from Alaska to Newfoundland and south to northern Florida, the Gulf states, and to Nicaragua. Winters in the southern portion of the breeding range and, in the east, north along the coast and occasionally inland to New York and New England.

Status Widespread breeder. Common to very common migrant, occasionally more numerous. Rare but regular in winter, most frequently on the coast.

Breeding It breeds around farms, gardens, orchards, clearings in woods, suburban yards, city parks, estates, and in much of the settled rural country. Its nest is placed in trees, bushes, vines, and often in low ornamental conifers. Breeding occurs throughout the state except in some of the northern forests, where there is insufficient appropriate habitat. It was recorded in 91% of the Atlas blocks and was Confirmed in 67% of those, making it the eighth most commonly confirmed species. BBS data are somewhat difficult to interpret. For the period 1966–1994, there was no significant change in population size, although 1966–1979 did exhibit a decline that was statistically significant. The species seems to be in no immediate danger, given its ability to breed in human-altered landscapes. With continued forest clearing in the Adirondacks for recreational development, it may eventually colonize even that area.

Nonbreeding Very fond of lawns and shortgrass fields with areas of bare ground, during migration it is often found in such places, feeding with other sparrows. Individuals are reported every year at scattered locations throughout, although misidentifications are not uncommon. Some remain at feeders all winter, such as the one banded in Belmont, Allegany Co. (KB 30:160). The highest number reported on a CBC between 1960 and 1989 was 20 in Herkimer Co. 1981. It is rare before mid-Apr and after Oct.

Spring maxima: 200 Prospect Park, Kings Co. 2 May 1945; 160 Selkirk Shores, Oswego Co. 6 May 1961. **Fall maxima:** 250 Bronx Park, Bronx

Co. 15 Oct 1950; 200 Lima, Livingston Co. 15 Sep 1970; 172 Lysander, Onondaga Co. 6 Oct 1987.

Remarks At least two poorly defined subspecies may occur in NY. A northern and western subspecies, *boreophila*, occurs across Canada north of the range of the nominate *passerina* (Zink and Dittman 1993). Although *passerina* is the only one that breeds in NY, *boreophila* presumably occurs as a migrant.

At least three occurrences of Chipping Sparrows hybridizing with Clay-colored Sparrows have been reported in New York (McIlroy 1961; KB 34:263; KB 31:165).

William E. Cook

Clay-colored Sparrow *Spizella pallida*

Range Nearctic, chiefly central North America, breeding from southern Canada to the central United States east of the Rockies; locally east to southeastern Ontario and casually to western New York since 1960. Winters from southern Texas south to southern Mexico. Regular fall migrant on the Atlantic Coast from Massachusetts to New Jersey.

Status Formerly casual breeder, but now established in Allegany and Franklin counties. Rare but regular fall migrant along the coast, casual inland; rare but regular spring migrant, primarily in the Great Lakes Plain.

Breeding The first breeding record was obtained in 1960 with an apparent mating between a male Clay-colored and a female Chipping Sparrow at Ithaca, Tompkins Co., where a nest with three eggs was found in a red cedar in an open field, and both birds were subsequently observed feeding nestlings (McIlroy 1961). The next confirmed records occurred a decade later when a pair of Clay-colored Sparrows nested in a Scotch pine plantation at Alfred, Allegany Co. in 1971 (Brooks 1971), and a single adult was observed feeding young near Rochester, Monroe Co. 1972 (Claffey 1972). A possible hybridization with a Field Sparrow in 1974 near Millbrook, Dutchess Co. (Bull 1976) and another mixed mating with a Chipping Sparrow in 1984 near Harlemville, Columbia Co., where a nest with young was located by Atlas fieldworkers (KB 34:263), represent the only subsequent breeding records documented by nests or adults with young.

Although it has not been reported annually, four Probable and three Possible Atlas records, and subsequent summer reports from Elm Valley in 1988 (KB 38:256) and Andover in 1992 (KB 42:233), strongly suggest that it has become established as a regular breeder in the vicinity of Alfred, Allegany Co. since 1971. In addition, the Hogansburg-Ft. Covington-Westville area of northern Franklin Co. and the Ft. Drum Military Reservation, Jefferson Co. are areas with multiple Atlas records and subsequent summer sightings and where this sparrow appears to be established. Rare-species surveys conducted by the New York Natural Heritage Program at Ft. Drum during 1992 found Clay-colored Sparrows in several areas, including some of the same locations where it was recorded during the Atlas. A followup survey conducted in 1995 by researchers at Ft. Drum recorded an incredible total of 18 singing birds (Johnson, pers. comm.) The occupation of these areas in recent years is surely an extension of the sparrow's range expansion in the nearby Kingston and Ottawa areas of southeastern ON (Cadman et al. 1987). It is possible that some of the occasional summer records from elsewhere in the state may in fact represent breeding attempts, perhaps masked in some cases by its ability to pair with Chipping Sparrows.

Nonbreeding The first state specimen was not obtained until Apr 1935 at Ithaca, Tompkins Co. As a migrant, it was nothing more than a vagrant before 1950, after which it was reported annually in fall on the coast of LI, where it prefers sandy fields with short grass and scattered bushes. Its increase as a migrant between 1950 and 1971 continued into the 1990s and is the result of its breeding range extension. It is rare but regular in spring inland, and fall records are almost entirely from LI. Virtually all records, spring and fall, are of single birds; a record of three males at the Watertown Airport, Jefferson Co. 27 May 1977 (KB 27:166) is an exception.

Extreme dates: 16 Mar and 15 Apr (all other spring records are from May); 9 Sep and 21–23 Nov; rare before mid-Sep and after Oct. *Winter:* Two records, both Suffolk Co.: Montauk 10 Dec 1978; Ditch Plains 14 Dec 1992.

Paul G. Novak

Field Sparrow   *Spizella pusilla*

Range Chiefly eastern Nearctic, breeding from northern Montana east through southern Canada to New Brunswick and south to northern Florida, the Gulf states, and eastern Texas. Winters nearly throughout, except the more northern portions.

Status Widespread breeder at lower elevations, but rare northward and absent in the higher mountains. Common to very common fall migrant. Uncommon to common in winter.

Breeding This species breeds in open country on or near the ground, in brushy fields, thickets, overgrown pastures, and thorn scrub throughout, except for the northern forests and portions of the Catskills and in Bronx and New York counties, where suitable habitat does not exist. During the Atlas, it was recorded in 73% of the blocks and was Confirmed in 36% of those; it was, coincidentally, the thirty-sixth most commonly Confirmed species. BBS 1966–1994 data recorded a significant decline. With the conversion of brushy fields into shopping malls, tract housing, or woodland since the beginning of the twentieth century, breeding areas have been greatly reduced, yet this species is still common.

Nonbreeding It is a common migrant, both inland and along the coast. Small flocks are occasionally noted in swampy thickets during the winter. The number of individuals reported on 1960–1989 NY CBCs ranged from 155 to 635 per year, with the highest concentrations along the coast. It is rare after mid-Nov and before mid-Mar.

Spring maxima: 20 Otselic, Chenango Co. 23 Apr 1993; 12 Derby Hill, Oswego Co. 3 May 1979. *Fall maxima:* 60 Selkirk Shores, Oswego Co. 13 Sep 1967; 55 East Hampton, Suffolk Co. 2 Nov 1930; 50 Allegany, Cattaraugus Co. 16 Oct 1965. *Winter maxima:* 50 Warwick, Orange Co. 9 Jan 1986; 24 at a manure pile, Clinton, Oneida Co. 30 Dec 1967. The highest number reported on a CBC between 1960 and 1989 was 150 at Bronx-Westchester 1961.
William E. Cook

Vesper Sparrow   *Pooecetes gramineus*

Range Nearctic, breeding from central British Columbia to Nova Scotia south to California, Arizona, Missouri, and North Carolina. Winters in the east from southern Illinois and Connecticut south to central Florida, the Gulf Coast, southern Texas, and Mexico.

Status Widespread breeder, concentrated in agricultural areas. Common to very common inland migrant, much less numerous on the coast. Rare to uncommon in winter on LI, very rare inland.

Breeding This species, found in agricultural regions throughout, is absent only in the higher elevations of the Adirondacks and Catskills. During the Atlas project, it was often found in association with plantings of corn and potatoes, as at the edges of hilltop fields around Dansville, Livingston Co. and in potato fields near Lake Placid, Essex Co. Near Ithaca, Tompkins Co. It can be found in cornfields in summer.

Its preference for agricultural fields most likely is a reflection of the apparent requirement of this species for bare ground somewhere in its breeding territory. In his classic study of grassland birds, Wiens (1969) reported that Vesper Sparrow preferred the shortest grass among the species he studied, which included Savannah, Grasshopper, and Henslow's sparrows, and that bare ground typically was found within its breeding territory.

Quite likely, it was more common during the period shortly after 1900, when sheep were more common as grazing animals on NY pastures

(Nicholson 1985). The sheep's habit of closely cropping growing vegetation and a tendency toward overgrazing probably created optimal habitat for this species early in the twentieth century.

BBS 1966–1994 data showed a significant decline, with most of the decline occurring between 1966 and 1979.

Nonbreeding CBC 1960–1989 data indicated that this species is uncommon upstate and common on LI in winter. The 1971 winter season was a "peak" year for the southeast and LI, with 62 and 52 individuals reported on the Bronx-Westchester and Central Suffolk Co. counts, respectively, while the highest upstate count was eight birds at Chatham, Columbia Co. Since then, LI CBCs have shown remarkable decreases in numbers and sometimes total absence. In addition, it has become "decidedly uncommon" as a coastal migrant (E. Levine, pers. comm.). During spring and fall migration, it can be very common, with occasional counts of more than 100 birds inland. Migrants typically arrive by late Mar and depart by late Nov.

Remarks Like the Horned Lark, the Vesper Sparrow benefits from agricultural activities in NY. The decline of this species as a breeding bird coincides with a general decline in agricultural acreage and a pattern of afforestation across NY during the past 75 years (Nicholson 1985; Marks et al. 1992). In describing changes in the breeding bird populations of Allegany SP, Baird (1990) reported the complete disappearance of this species between 1930 and 1985, coincident with a decline of open, grassy areas. Similar patterns are reported from PA (Brauning 1992). Because of its preference for areas of short grass and bare ground, this species most likely was less common before settlement and the advent of agriculture than it is now and probably was confined to a few areas of native grassland on LI and to areas that were recovering from natural fires or had been scoured by extensive flooding in other parts of the state. Because of the documented decline of its breeding population in NY, it is considered a Species of Special Concern by the NYSDEC.

Charles R. Smith

Lark Sparrow *Chondestes grammacus*

Range Nearctic, breeding from southern British Columbia east to southern Ontario, south to northern Mexico and Texas; locally and irregularly east of the Mississippi Valley to North Carolina and western Virginia. Winters from the southern United States south to southern Mexico; occasionally north to southern New England in the east.

Status Rare but regular fall vagrant; occasional in winter and very rare in spring.

Occurrence The Lark Sparrow prefers dry sandy fields along the outer coast during fall migration. It has occurred in every month, with 90% of records from LI between mid-Aug and the end of Oct. As many as 10 individuals have been seen in one fall season (KB 27:57); three is the maximum for one day. There are five fall records from the western part of the state.

More than half of the 24 spring records are from May, mostly from western and southeastern NY. It is virtually unrecorded in central and northeastern NY in any season. Exceptional were a bird at North Elba, Essex Co. 8 Sep 1981 (KB 32:321) and one at Point Pleasant, Jefferson Co. 14 May 1984 (KB 35:228). It is rare in winter in the southeast and unrecorded in the interior then.

Remarks Predictions by Eaton (1914) and Griscom (1923) that the Lark Sparrow "might become a common bird in New York State sometime in the future" have not been realized. Griscom characterized it as a "casual visitant," and essentially it still is.
Dale Dyer

Lark Bunting *Calamospiza melanocorys*

Range West-central Nearctic, breeding in the Great Plains from southern Alberta to southwestern Minnesota and south, east of the Rockies, to eastern New Mexico, northern Texas, and northwestern Missouri; sporadically elsewhere. Winters in southwestern United States and northern Mexico. Vagrant on the Atlantic Coast from Nova Scotia to Florida and on the Gulf Coast.

Status Very rare vagrant.

Occurrence Of the 25 records, 17 are from the southeast in the fall, most of them from LI, and most in Sep, with the earliest fall record 31 Aug 1939. Some were photographed, and there are at least four early specimens. All three winter records are of birds that lingered at feeders: a male at Belmont, Allegany Co. 30 Nov 1966–13 May 1967; one at East Northport, Suffolk Co. 4 Jan–3 May 1978 (KB 28:128), and another the same year 25 Feb–12 Apr at Stony Point, Rockland Co. (KB 28:197). The eight spring occurrences include those lingerers and several other birds at feeders. The latest spring date was 6 Jun 1959. The only upstate records are the Allegany Co. bird, one at Stissing, Dutchess Co. 12–13 May 1970, and one at Wampsville, Madison Co. 19–22 May 1977.

From 1964 to 1978, Lark Bunting was almost annual in NY, a significant increase over the six pre-1960 records. Since 1978, there has been only one record: RMSP 14 Sep 1992 (NYSARC 1994).
Dale Dyer

Savannah Sparrow

Passerculus sandwichensis

Range Nearctic and northern Neotropical, breeding from Alaska and northern Canada to Newfoundland and south, in the east, to Missouri and northern New Jersey. Winters from southern Illinois and southern New England south to El Salvador and the West Indies.

Status Widespread but local breeder, most prevalent on the coast. Very abundant fall coastal migrant; very common spring inland migrant. Occasionally abundant in winter on the coast, uncommon inland.

Breeding It is the most widespread and numerous of our breeding grassland sparrows (Atlas 1988), a pattern that has changed significantly since Eaton's period, when the Vesper Sparrow was regarded as more widespread and numerous (Eaton 1914). Like Vesper, it is generally absent from the Adirondack and Catskill regions. A further comparison of the two species shows Savannah recorded in 56% of all Atlas blocks, with Vesper found in only 21%. Savannahs are more accepting of a wider range of grassland and early successional habitat types than are other grassland sparrows. At Finger Lakes National Forest, studies (Smith and Smith 1992) showed that this species occurs in a wider range of cover types and can occupy smaller areas of suitable habitat (as small as 20–25 acres) than are preferred by other grassland birds, suggesting that it is more of a generalist than the other species.

On the basis of changing patterns of agricultural land use in NY over the past 100 years, one can speculate about the changing relationships of Savannah and Vesper sparrows. Most likely, both species were very rare in our region before the land was cleared for agriculture, beginning in the late 1700s. Both likely occurred on the Hempstead Plains of LI, but Savannah probably was more widespread upstate than Vesper because of its ability to use the kinds of grassy areas that might remain after abandonment of beaver meadows by beaver. As grazing customs shifted from an economy based predominantly on sheep to one of mostly dairy cattle on NY farms, the close-cropped pastures of sheep, interspersed with occasional patches of bare, overgrazed ground, began to disappear, leaving less suitable habitat for Vesper Sparrow but favoring Savannah, as Peterson suggested (Atlas 1988). Since the late 1920s, the shifting patterns of agriculture have largely favored Savannah Sparrow, but the continuing pattern of afforestation and decline of agriculture will reduce suitable habitat for both species throughout most of NY. On LI, suburban development will have the same effect.

BBS 1966–1994 data showed a moderate, but significant pattern of decline of 2.9% per year, with a greater decline during the period 1966–1979 than more recently. Among the declining species that favor open lands and grassy or early successional habitats (Horned Lark, Vesper, Grasshopper, and Henslow's sparrows, and Eastern Meadowlark), the Savannah Sparrow shows the least decline over the period 1966–1994.

Nonbreeding CBC 1960–1989 data showed that this species can be very common to abundant in winter in southeastern counties and on LI. In 1983, 421 were counted on the Lower Hudson CBC, and counts of 50 or more birds are typical for LI CBCs. Upstate, it is decidedly uncommon in winter, where one or two on a CBC is typical. Migrants usually arrive in late Mar and depart by mid-Nov.

Remarks Three subspecies occur in NY. The breeding form throughout is *savanna. Princeps*, a regular winter visitant to the coastal dunes of LI, was known as the Ipswich Sparrow, a separate species, until 1973, when it was merged with Savannah Sparrow by action of the AOU Check-list Committee (AOU 1973) on the recommendation of Peters and Griscom (1938). Typical individuals are readily recognizable, although observers should be aware that limited interbreeding with mainland Savannahs has recently been detected in NS opposite the Sable I. home of the "Ipswich" Sparrow (K. C. Parkes, in litt.). A third subspecies, *labradorius*, is "probably a regular transient in small numbers" with occasional wintering individuals on LI (Parkes 1952). Charles R. Smith

Baird's Sparrow *Ammodramus bairdii*

Range Central Nearctic, breeding from southeastern Alberta to southern Manitoba south to central Montana and east to western Minnesota. Winters in southwestern United States and northern Mexico.

Status Accidental.

Occurrence There is one substantiated occurrence, a bird taken at Montauk, Suffolk Co. 13 Nov 1899 AMNH 802438. Several sight records in southeastern NY were not substantiated, but birds that may well have been this species were identified as such in Central Park, Manhattan 24 Oct 1949 and at JBSP 31 Oct 1949 (Bull 1974).

Remarks There are no records of Baird's Sparrow from any other north-eastern state. The closest modern records are from OH (Halliwell 1995) and MD, the latter a specimen from 14 Oct 1966 (*Maryland Birdlife* 23:87).
Dale Dyer

Grasshopper Sparrow   *Ammodramus savannarum*

Range Nearctic and Neotropical, breeding, locally, from southern British Columbia and eastern Washington to southern Quebec and central New England and south to California, Texas, and Florida; also resident in Greater Antilles, Middle America, and northern South America. Winters, in the east, north to Tennessee and North Carolina, casually farther north.

Status Fairly common but local breeder on LI and the interior lowlands of the Appalachian Plateau and the Great Lakes Plain. Absent from the Alleghenies, Adirondacks, and Catskills. Rare migrant anywhere.

Breeding Eaton (1910) called it "a fairly common breeder" and showed a distribution map with populations on LI, in the Hudson Valley, and on the southern parts of the Great Lakes Plain and Appalachian Plateau. Bull (1974) advised that it was numerous only on LI, was widely distributed at low elevations upstate, and was local in the St. Lawrence and Lake Champlain valleys.

The Atlas basically mirrored Eaton and Bull but extended the range northward to Oswego, Jefferson, St. Lawrence, Franklin, and Clinton counties and recorded nesting up to 2000 ft. Gretch (1995) reported a colony at the Plattsburgh Air Force Base, Clinton Co. that had been active since 1980 but was inaccessible to Atlas workers. On 16 Jun 1994, he located 17 birds and a nest with downy young (KB 45:242).

BBS data for the period 1966–1994 showed a statistically significant annual rate of decline of 10.2%, with most of the decline occurring from 1966 to 1979. This apparent gradual disappearance coincides with patterns of declining agriculture and regrowth of forests (Caslick 1975; Nicholson 1985; Marks et al. 1992; C. R. Smith et al. 1993).

Comparative studies of Grasshopper and Henslow's sparrows nesting in active pastures of Finger Lakes National Forest showed that Grasshopper Sparrow accepts pastures of smaller size with shorter grasses than those preferred by Henslow's (Smith, in press; Smith and Smith 1992), suggesting that Grasshopper is a greater generalist than Henslow's, which may account for the fact that it was recorded in more than twice as many blocks during the Atlas project.

Grassland habitat in NY is generally transitional and unstable. The cutting of forest for pasture, conversion of pasture to other agriculture, extensive use of pesticides, abandonment of farms and pasture, and subsequent regeneration of forest have produced a complex landscape mosaic for this species. Fire, grazing, or mowing is needed to keep grasslands from turning into shrublands or woods and there by provide a stable habitat.

Nonbreeding Secretive and not known to flock, it is a rarely reported migrant at any season. The extreme dates of 20 Mar and 23 Nov reported by Bull (1974) remain unchanged. Bull's maxima of eight in Madison Square Park, Manhattan 15 May 1921 and six at East Hampton, Suffolk Co. 14 Oct 1933 will undoubtedly survive for the foreseeable future. Although it is extremely rare in winter, there are two such recent records: Great Kills, Richmond Co. 10 Jan 1977 (KB 27:116) and Montauk, Suffolk Co. 16 Dec 1989 (KB 40:127). There were none reported on 1960–1989 CBCs.

Remarks Because of its specialized habitat requirements, declining breeding population, and limited distribution, Grasshopper Sparrow is listed as a Species of Special Concern by the NYSDEC.
Eric Salzman and Charles R. Smith

Henslow's Sparrow   *Ammodramus henslowii*

Range Eastern Nearctic, breeding from eastern South Dakota, southern Ontario, northern New York, and New England south to Missouri, northern Kentucky, and east-central North Carolina. Winters mainly in coastal states from South Carolina to southern Texas, casually farther north.

Status Rare to uncommon and local breeder at lower elevations. Rare and little-known migrant.

Breeding The earliest documented breeding reports are from LI (DeKay 1844), where it no longer breeds, and the Cayuga L. basin in 1916 (Wright 1919).

It was recorded in only 7% of all blocks, and the Atlas showed it breeding primarily through the Mohawk. Valley, then west and south of Oneida L. across western NY, and totally absent anywhere that its very specific nesting requirements are not met. Absent from the Atlas map, due to the fact that the area was not open to birders at the time, is the concentration at the Ft. Drum area in Jefferson and Lewis counties, where 100 territorial males were reported in 1995 (R. LeClerc, pers. comm.).

Even with recent declines, it is probable that the species is now more abundant and widespread than it was at the turn of the century. BBS data for 1966–1994 showed a significant declining population trend of 12.1%, with much of this decline occurring between 1980 and 1994. The pattern of decline in NY is typical for the species throughout most of its breeding range. It requires open lands that result from abandonment of agricultural activities but is able to use both active and inactive pastures (Peterson 1983; Smith 1992; Smith and Smith 1992). The decline at Galeville Airport, Ulster Co. from 15 birds in 1982 (KB 32:221) to 1 in 1987 (KB 37:240) is not an unusual pattern of change at many breeding localities, although populations on public grazing lands at Finger Lakes National Forest appeared to be stable during 1989–1995 (pers. obs.). The ephemeral nature of local populations is typical of the species and has been commented upon by many authors (reviewed in Smith 1992). The decline in NY parallels a decline in agricultural activity and increasing afforestation of the state, well described by others (Caslick 1975; Nicholson 1985; Marks et al. 1992; C. R. Smith et al. 1993). The widespread prevalence of grass hayfields and the reversion of lands used for row and field crops to early old-field succession following abandonment in the early twentieth century all contributed to a widespread availability of suitable habitat for Henslow's Sparrow and other grassland birds. Those habitats, essential for breeding, have declined throughout NY and the Northeast with suburban development and regrowth of forests.

Among the grassland bird species studied by Smith and Smith (1992) on Finger Lakes National Forest, Henslow's Sparrow preferred pastures of the largest size and best quality. In that context, it was tolerant of grazing by cattle and would not have occurred there in the absence of the open grass-lands maintained by grazing. Similarly, it occurs on sites at Ft. Drum, where its nesting habitats also are maintained by periodic disturbance, in this case resulting from military training exercises (R. LeClerc, pers. comm.).

Whether Henslow's Sparrow existed in NY and the Northeast before set-tlement by Europeans and subsequent extensive clearing of forests is unknown. In other parts of its range, Henslow's uses wet meadows for nesting (Smith 1992). Such habitat was widespread across the NY landscape before settlement, because of the succession of habitats following the aban-donment of impounded areas by beaver (Marks et al. 1992). Those preset-tlement wet meadows may have been suitable for the species, since their average size of 70–80 acres in central NY (Marks et al. 1992) is within the range of habitat areas that appear favorable to Henslow's (Peterson 1983; Smith 1992; Smith and Smith 1992). Even with recent declines, it is proba-ble that it is still more abundant and widespread than it was at the turn of the century.

Limited breeding distribution and population have led to its being identified as a Species of Special Concern by NYSDEC, with the recommen-dation pending that its status be changed to Threatened. Nationally, it is being considered for listing under the Endangered Species Act.

Nonbreeding The extreme migration dates of 2 Apr and 27 Nov, reported by Bull (1974), still stand. In general, it appears to settle on its breeding grounds by mid-May and depart by mid-Aug. The only winter record is the observation of a bird visiting a feeder in Suffolk Co. 26 Dec 1963–14 Jan 1964.

Remarks Two subspecies have traditionally been identified (AOU 1957). The original description of the eastern subspecies, *susurrans*, by Brewster (1918) was based on an examination of only 52 specimens, 27 of which were believed to be *susurrans*, from localities in New England and the southeastern United States. No measurements were reported by him except for his type specimen, although he described *susurrans* as larger than the nominate subspecies *henslowii*. The number of specimens upon which Brewster based his subspecific determination is modest by modern standards, and the variation described by him for *susurrans* might well be within the range for what one might expect for a species showing a north-to-south or west-to-east clinal variation.

As for distribution in NY, most of the state is occupied by intermediates. The range of true *henslowii* extends into the state from the west. A good series of specimens from Crawford Co., PA, just southwest of the southwestern corner of NY, is almost completely typical of *henslowii* except for one with a fractionally larger bill; another has a bill small even for *henslowii* but dorsal coloration more nearly typical of *susurrans*. In NY, a specimen from Franklinville, Cattaraugus Co. (CUM) and one from Hilton, Monroe Co. (NYSM) are both typical of the western subspecies. Most of central NY is occupied by a variably intermediate population; most tend to resemble *henslowii* in color but have bills too large for that subspecies but not as large as the largest-billed *susurrans*. A series of five collected by Parkes from one colony at Chaumont, Jefferson Co. is highly variable. One matches *susurrans* both in color and bill size; two are too slender-billed for *susurrans* although like it in color; one matches the blackest (i.e., most *henslowii*-like) topotype of *susurrans*; and one is *henslowii* in color but is too large billed. Charles R. Smith

Le Conte's Sparrow   *Ammodramus leconteii*

Range Nearctic, breeding from southern Mackenzie, central Manitoba, northern Ontario, and southern Quebec south to central Montana and northern Michigan. Winters mainly in southeastern United States from South Carolina to northern Florida and southern Texas; also north to southern Illinois and western Kansas.

Status Very rare vagrant.

Occurrence The first record for the twentieth century was of a bird mist-netted, banded, photographed, and released by Lauro at Tobay, Nassau Co. 18 Oct 1970. Before that, the only other record was a bird collected near Ithaca, Tompkins Co. 11 Oct 1897 CUM 29455.

NYSARC has accepted four records. The first was in Hanover, Chautauqua Co. 10 Oct 1991 (J. Goetz and T. Goetz) (NYSARC 1993). The next was found and photographed in New Haven, Oswego Co. 7 May 1992 (Koeneke 1992; NYSARC 1994). The others were at: State University of NY at Oswego 28 Apr 1993 (Fosdick) (NYSARC 1996) and Braddock Bay, Monroe Co. 3 May 1994 (Griffith) (NYSARC 1996).

Several later reports to NYSARC have not yet been reviewed. The most interesting are a singing male that spent a month in a grassy field in Lisbon, St. Lawrence Co. 23 Jun–20 Jul 1995 (KB 45:313), raising the possibility of future breeding, and one photographed 15 Mar 1996 in a most unlikely place, Battery Park, Manhattan (KB 46:287).

Altogether since the 1970 record, there have been approximately 16 reports: three in the 1970s, three in the 1980s, and the balance in the 1990s. They have been scattered statewide.

Remarks This is an extremely secretive sparrow, elusive even during migration. An increase in accepted records in NY is possibly due in part to the increase in active birders. MA has documented 14 records, 10 since 1980, and most frequently from habitat similar to that in which the bird breeds, dense grassy meadows (Veit and Petersen 1993). In NJ there have been only two documented records, in 1964 and 1968 (Leck 1984), with 10 more that may be valid (Halliwell 1995; NASFN 48:95, 191; 50:30). CT has only one definitive record, 27 Dec 1987–9 Jan 1988 (Zeranski and Baptist 1990). PA had six records from 1959 to 1992 (Santner et al. 1992). Mary Alice Koeneke

"Sharp-tailed Sparrows" *Ammodramus caudacutus* and *A. nelsoni*

(See also Saltmarsh Sharp-tailed Sparrow and Nelson's Sharp-tailed Sparrow accounts, which follow.)

For many years, the Sharp-tailed Sparrow *(Ammodramus caudacutus caudacutus)*, Acadian Sharp-tailed Sparrow *(A. c. subvirgatus)*, and Nelson's Sharp-tailed Sparrow *(A. c. nelsoni)* were illustrated in the popular field guides and sought by earlier generations of birders as distinctive subspecies of a single species. The recognition of two additional subspecies, *diversus* and *alterus*, further complicated the matter. Many writers pointed to the difficulty of separating these forms, and field identification of subspecies was, in general, discouraged.

Recent studies (Greenlaw 1993; Rising and Avise 1993) have affirmed the distinctiveness of northern and southern sharp-tailed sparrow populations, which are in the process of speciating. In the modern view, they constitute a superspecies made up of two allopatric species, Nelson's

517

Sharp-tailed *(A. nelsoni)* and Saltmarsh Sharp-tailed *(A. caudacutus)* spar-rows, which replace each other geographically. Nelson's Sharp-tailed Sparrow now includes the northern plains, Hudson and James bays, and Atlantic maritime populations, comprising three subspecies, *nelsoni*, *alterus*, and *subvirgatus*, respectively. Saltmarsh Sharp-tailed Sparrow is made up of the nominate form, *caudacutus*, and the southern coastal *diversus* (Sibley 1995). A relatively small amount of interbreeding takes place between these two species where their ranges meet in coastal ME.

Both species are on the NYS checklist as of the Fortieth Supplement to the AOU Check-list (AOU 1995). Bull (1974) recognized that four of the five subspecies have occurred in the state. Because of the confused history, the following accounts rely heavily on specimen evidence.

Field identification of the nominate *nelsoni* subspecies of Nelson's Sharp-tailed Sparrow is usually possible, but the visual separation of the other northern populations is more difficult (see Sibley 1996). The assumption is that most, perhaps all, of the upstate records, especially those accepted by NYSARC, refer to one or the other of the two inland races *(nelsoni* and *alterus)*, and they are so treated here. For recent views of this situation see DeBenedictis 1995, Sibley 1995, and Sibley 1996. For the status of the various subspecies in NY see Parkes 1952 and Bull 1974.

Note: The author and editor thank Jon S. Greenlaw for reviewing the sharp-tailed accounts and for the many helpful suggestions he made to clarify some of the confusion arising from the recent split.
Eric Salzman

Saltmarsh Sharp-tailed Sparrow *Ammodramus caudacutus*

Range Nearctic, breeding along the Atlantic Coast from southern Maine south to North Carolina. Winters mainly along the coast from Massachusetts south to north-central Florida, rarely on the Gulf Coast.

Status Common to uncommon localized breeder. Common, occasionally abundant, fall migrant; fairly common in spring, and uncommon but regular in winter.

Breeding It is a common breeder in coastal salt marshes on the South Shore of LI from Brooklyn to East Hampton, Suffolk Co. and in the Peconic–Gardiners Bay system. It is more localized on the North Shore, on the LI Sound coastline of Bronx and Westchester counties (Pelham and Rye), and in SI marshes. It formerly bred in the marshes of the Harlem R., Bronx Co. and north on the Hudson R. to Piermont, Rockland Co. (Bull 1964). Although Bull suggested that, as of 1974, it still bred in Hudson R. and SI marshes, Atlas fieldworkers did not find any breeding evidence in those localities. However, in 1992, four breeding pairs were discovered on Saw Mill Creek, Richmond Co. (KB 42: 278).

The males of this species are not territorial (Greenlaw and Rising 1994), and, in suitable habitat, loose breeding aggregations are formed, often with Seaside Sparrow. Bull (1974) recorded 13 pairs in 15 acres in a ditched marsh at Tobay, Nassau Co. in 1970, and similar or larger numbers could easily be duplicated on other LI marshes. The largest known population, some 200 pairs, was on the present site of JFK Airport, Queens Co.

It should be added that the use of the term *pairs* is inappropriate for this species, which practices a mating system that has been described as a "scramble competition polygyny" in which males occupy large overlapping home ranges and seek promiscuous matings with receptive females who tend to occupy and return to small, nest-centered home ranges (Post and Greenlaw 1982; Greenlaw and Rising 1994).

Nonbreeding It is most numerous in fall migration when it is or was common to abundant in some coastal marshes. After the 1938 hurricane, Latham saw 1000+ in the Orient area, many of them dead. Counts in the hundreds have been recorded on a number of occasions in Sep and Oct. Most birds have left NY salt marshes by the end of Oct, but lingerers remain at least through Dec, when they regularly appear on LI CBCs. A high of 26 was on the 1981 Central Suffolk CBC, and up to 32 were reported as overwintering in the Jones Beach area in 1940–1941. These reports may include individuals or numbers of Nelson's Sharp-tailed Sparrow as well (J. Greenlaw, pers. comm.) as pre-1996 records of Sharp-tailed Sparrow are species indeterminate. Spring migration takes place between late Apr and mid-May.

Saltmarsh Sharp-tailed Sparrows are very rare away from salt marsh. The specific identity of the half-dozen sharp-tailed sparrows reported in the NYC parks over the years is unknown.

Remarks The only breeding sharp-tailed sparrow in NY is *A. caudacutus*, which also accounts for the majority of migrants, but, despite a lack of winter specimens it is now believed that *A. nelsoni* occurs in winter as well. Except for one western PA specimen (Parkes 1992), there is no evidence that this bird has ever occurred anywhere outside of the coastal region and the lower Hudson Valley.

Although it has hybridized with the Seaside Sparrow, the frequency of hybridization is considered to be low (Greenlaw and Rising 1994), and there are no recent records from NY. The two species commonly inhabit the same marshes on LI, often nesting within a few meters of each other (pers. obs.).

For many years, NY marshes were routinely drained and filled for garbage dumps, airports, and housing developments, destroying large areas of breeding habitat. The destruction of coastal marshes from ME south may account for the lower numbers reported in migration and winter in recent decades when compared with the historical record. Wetlands protection in recent years appears to have stabilized the remaining populations at all seasons.

Eric Salzman

Nelson's Sharp-tailed Sparrow   *Ammodramus nelsoni*

Range Nearctic, breeding in freshwater marshes from central British Columbia southeast to South Dakota and Minnesota and from Hudson Bay south to the St. Lawrence River and on the Atlantic Coast from Nova Scotia to Maine. Eastern birds winter mainly along the Atlantic and Gulf coasts from the Carolinas to Texas, occasionally farther north.

Status Uncommon fall migrant in both coastal and inland marshes, regular in small numbers in winter on LI. Rare spring migrant.

Occurrence This species is found in the state most frequently during migration, when it is moving to and from its wintering grounds on the southern Atlantic and Gulf coasts; it is now also believed to winter on LI in small numbers (J. Greenlaw, pers. comm.). The maritime populations of Nelson's Sharp-tailed, *subvirgatus*, move exclusively along the coast. The inland birds, *nelsoni* and *alterus*, breeding south to SD and MN and east to ON and PQ, mostly migrate on an inland route to the west of NY, but a few, especially in fall, move across the western and southern parts of the state and some reach the lower Hudson Valley and LI coast on their way south. This movement appears to be the source of an increasing number of fall sight records in the Greece, Monroe Co. area (Region 2 reports 1982–1993) and in Oswego Co. from 29 Aug to 28 Oct (Region 5 reports, 1960–1991). Thirty specimens, including both inland subspecies, have been taken at Ithaca, Tompkins Co. Other documented occurrences include tower kills at Colden, Erie Co. 25 Oct 1983 (KB 34:36) and at Scriba, Oswego Co. 9 Oct 1991 (KB 42:14). All three subspecies have been taken in Hudson R. marshes as far north as Highland Falls, Orange Co., as well as on SI and LI, with dates ranging from the third week of Sep to 24 Nov (Bull 1964).

There are fewer spring records. A bird banded at Manitou Beach, Monroe Co. 1 Jun 1993 was said to be the fifth Region 2 spring record, all of which fell between 30 May and 2 Jun (KB 43:315); a sight record the same year from Canton, St. Lawrence Co. on 7 and 9 Jun was unusually far north (KB 43:336). There are specimens from Dunkirk, Chautauqua Co. 29 May 1930, from SI 30 May 1908, and from a handful of other coastal locations taken between 26 May and 8 Jun.

Remarks As presently understood, this species consists of three subspecies, *nelsoni, alterus,* and *subvirgatus,* which breed respectively, in the upper Midwest, the Hudson Bay area, and the coastal marshes from ME north. Reports of nominate *nelsoni* have increased in recent years. The other two subspecies are much harder to separate in the field (Sibley 1996).

Both *nelsoni* and *alterus* pass through central NY, as shown by the specimen record from Ithaca (Parkes 1952). Although Bull (1974) stated that "the only known New York winter specimens [of sharp-tailed sparrows] are of *caudacutus* from Long Island," Parkes (1952) believed that *subvirgatus* wintered in NY in small numbers, and, at one time, the AOU Check-list carried the statement that this form winters "casually north to New York (Long Island)." These assumptions are confirmed by Greenlaw (pers. comm.), who, on the basis of netting experience on LI, has expressed the belief that *nelsoni* may actually be somewhat more common than *caudacutus* in early winter in some marshes. Winter specimens of both species have been collected on Cape Cod (Griscom and Snyder 1955). Careful fieldwork and limited collecting can help establish the actual winter status of *nelsoni* in New York. Bull and Parkes agreed that no bona fide record of *subvirgatus* has ever been identified in NY any farther north or inland than Ossining, Westchester Co. Therefore all upstate records, including a number accepted by NYSARC, should be *nelsoni* or *alterus.*

As there are few specimens of any sharp-tailed sparrows for western and northern NY, the striking increase in reports in both spring and fall along the Great Lakes and St. Lawrence plains is notable. These apparently represent a recent phenomenon: the regular passage of at least one of the inland subspecies of Nelson's Sharp-tailed Sparrow at the eastern edge of its migration route. The whole situation needs further study.

To further complicate an already complex situation, hybrids are known between one or both of the inland subspecies *(nelsoni* and *alterus),* and the closely related Le Conte's Sparrow, which overlaps both in range and habitat (Murray 1968; Pyle and Sibley 1992). Greenlaw and Rising (1994) suggested that the frequency of known hybrids is low and comparable to that seen in most other related pairs of sparrows.
Eric Salzman

Seaside Sparrow *Ammodramus maritimus*

Range Eastern Nearctic, breeding along the Atlantic and Gulf coasts from southern New Hampshire south to northern Florida and west to southern Texas. Winters primarily within the southern parts of the breeding range and to southern Florida and southern Texas.

Status Formerly locally common breeder in Regions 9 and 10 but nowhere else in the state. Numbers now declining. Regular but uncommon in winter in the same areas.

Breeding It is a bird of coastal salt marshes. Within the marsh it chooses sites that provide adequate elevation for protection from flooding and that offer proximity to openings in the vegetation, for foraging. These habitat requirements for nesting and feeding are found in both high and low salt marsh and are patchily distributed within the marsh itself. In high salt marshes the birds avoid uniform stands of saltmeadow grass and nest on edges dominated by marsh elder. Low-marsh nests occur near tufts or clumps of smooth cordgrass (Greenlaw 1983).

Within the patchy microhabitat of a high-quality salt marsh, breeding densities may be very high. Small populations of one or two pairs can persist in marginal habitats for many years.

Historically, it bred in brackish marshes and salt marshes on SI, LI, and the lower Hudson R. to Piermont, Rockland Co. (Eaton 1914). It had disappeared from the east end of LI by the 1940s, but in 1942 Cruickshank still reported it from the south shore of SI and marshes east of Bronx Co. as well as sites in Westchester Co. and on the South Shore of LI. Bull (1964, 1974) reported the bird to be locally common to very common on the coast but rare at the east end of LI and along LI Sound. Breeding records from Orient and Sag Harbor, Suffolk Co. and Piermont were considered historical, and there was no mention of a population on SI. In 1973 it was once again reported breeding at Piermont (Bull 1976).

It was recorded in 48 blocks in the Atlas. Of these, 43 were located on the barrier islands that line southern LI. The other five records included one from Westchester Co. on LI Sound, one each from Fishers and Gardiners islands, and two on the North Shore of western LI. It was not recorded from SI or marshes on the Hudson R. during the Atlas project.

Since the Atlas, this species has been consistently reported from its stronghold in the salt marshes of LI from Jamaica Bay east to Shinnecock and Mecox bays. Greenlaw (1992) reported that numbers in Jamaica Bay were greatly reduced and noted a few birds in the small marshes at the heads of Little Neck and Hempstead bays on the North Shore. It has been reported breeding annually since 1990 at the Westchester Co. locale, and in 1992 six pairs bred at Saw Mill Creek on SI (KB 42:282). The latter record is believed to be the first from this location in at least 30 years.

Nonbreeding Postbreeding birds disperse locally to take advantage of seasonal changes in the food supply. Greenlaw (1992) reported them inhabiting tall stands of fruiting cordgrass along the perimeter of bays. They typically migrate during mid-Oct but are recorded regularly in small numbers on LI CBCs. Root (1988) documented concentrations of wintering Seaside Sparrows in coastal areas off northeastern FL, GA, the Carolinas, and the Gulf Coast, but it is not known where NY's breeding birds spend the winter (Greenlaw 1992). Early arrivals reach NY in mid-Apr, with the majority arriving in late Apr.

Post et al. (1983) demonstrated that predation by Norway rats and flooding cause substantial nest mortality. Distributional changes in NY over the last seven decades are more likely the result of habitat alteration. Ditching and filling of salt marshes in conjunction with coastal development are common practices, and there is substantial evidence that unaltered marshes support higher densities than ones that have been ditched or filled (Reinert et al. 1981; Greenlaw 1983). The NYSDEC has recommended listing as a Species of Special Concern.
Kathryn J. Schneider

Fox Sparrow   *Passerella iliaca*

Range Nearctic, breeding from Alaska to northern Labrador and south, in the east, to northern Ontario, central and southeastern Quebec, and Newfoundland. Winters on the East Coast from Maine south to central Florida and to the Gulf Coast, Texas, and northern Mexico.

Status A regular migrant throughout, variously common to uncommon.

Occurrence This species is noted for its rather rapid passage through the state, particularly in spring, often remaining only a few days. Ordinarily rare before mid-Oct and after Apr upstate and before late Oct and after early Apr downstate. There are numerous CBC records statewide, and it is not rare at feeders near the coast nor uncommon along the coast in winter; it is much rarer inland at that season. It does not occur today in the numbers recorded in the 1930s, such as: 150 Suffern, Rockland Co. 18 Nov 1934 and 100 Central Park, Manhattan 31 Mar 1933.

Spring maxima: all multiple-observer, large-area counts: 43 Allegany Co. 8 Apr 1979; 31 Niagara Frontier 1982 season; 24 Susquehanna region 1982 season. *Fall maxima:* 34 Pompey, Onondaga Co. 30 Oct 1983; 25 same place 30 Oct 1987. *Extreme dates:* 9 Aug and 3 Jun.

Remarks Of the approximately 20 subspecies, the nominate *iliaca* is our regular migrant. An adult female mistnetted at RMSP 12 May 1971 (Buckley 1979b) was confirmed as *altivagans* by Johnson, Laybourne, and Weske, specimen USNM 566277. This subspecies breeds in the southern Rockies and Canada, winters chiefly in California, and is casual in Manitoba. This is the first known record of this subspecies for eastern North America. In addition, the northwestern subspecies *zaboria* probably occurs in NY as a rare migrant, since there are several specimens as well as intergrades from PA in the CMNH collection (K. C. Parkes, pers. comm.). This subspecies is similar to *iliaca* but is darker and less brightly rufescent.
Lee B. Chamberlaine

The Saratoga National Historic Park, Saratoga Co., where this family of Henslow's Sparrows is being raised, is one of the few remaining open grasslands left in the state. Bobolinks breed there as well and probably Upland Sandpiper too.

524

Song Sparrow   *Melospiza melodia*

Range Nearctic, widespread throughout most of North America, breeding in the east from northern Manitoba to southwestern Newfoundland and south to central Arkansas, northern Georgia, and coastal South Carolina. Winters throughout most of the breeding range south to southern Florida and southern Texas.

Status Widespread resident and very common breeder. Common to abundant migrant and locally very common in winter, especially near the coast.

Breeding Recorded in more Atlas blocks than any other species, it nests in a wide variety of habitats from coastal scrub, roadside edges, brushy areas, thickets, hedgerows, woodland clearings, edges of waterways and wetlands, suburban and urban yards, gardens, and parks. It is absent only from open fields, marshes, and heavy woodland, where shrubs, bushes, and thickets are missing. An early nester (arrives in Mar or early Apr) with a long breeding season, it is often triple brooded in NY. Although declines have been recorded on some BBSs (Allegany Co. 1970–1984 and several 1995 Region 1 surveys), most populations of this adaptable bird have remained stable or, after the cutting of woodlands, have increased in numbers and range.

Nonbreeding The highest counts are recorded during migration, from late Mar to early May and, in particular, in Oct, when large numbers pass through the state. It is regular in winter, often at feeders, with the largest counts in the south. As is the case with other common year-round residents, this species is underreported.

Spring maxima: 1228 BOS Spring Count 4 Apr 1993; 230 Nine Mile Point, Oswego Co. 10 Apr 1993; 125 Flushing, Queens Co. 30 Mar 1940. *Fall maxima:* 400 East Hampton to Montauk, Suffolk Co. 14 Oct 1929; 100 Beatty Point, Monroe Co. 7 Oct 1990; 75 Central Park, Manhattan 13 Oct 1953. *Winter maxima:* 634 Southern Nassau CBC 30 Dec 1990; 185 Orient region, Suffolk Co. 22 Dec 1918.

Remarks There are three subspecies of Song Sparrow in the Northeast: the nominate *melodia* of New England, inland *euphonia*, and south coastal *atlantica*. According to Parkes (1952, 1954), most of NY is in a "broad area of intergradation" between the first two of these poorly differentiated forms.

Typical *atlantica*, as represented by birds from coastal MD and DE south to NC, is a very gray form with a large, somewhat swollen bill and is often identifiable in the field. Most available specimens from the lower Hudson Valley and LI represent variable intergrades between *atlantica* and *melodia*, with the *atlantica* influence greater on LI; two breeding-season specimens from Shelter I. confirm the inclusion of that locality in the range of *atlantica* in the fifth edition of the AOU Check-list (AOU 1957). Outside the breeding season, some typical *atlantica* may be found on LI. Eric Salzman

Lincoln's Sparrow   *Melospiza lincolnii*

Range Nearctic, breeding from Alaska and northeastern Manitoba to Newfoundland south to the mountains of California, Arizona, and New Mexico in the west, but in the east only as far as northern Minnesota and Michigan, Nova Scotia, northern New York, and central New England. Winters in the south-central United States north to central Missouri and northern Georgia, also south to El Salvador and Honduras.

Status Fairly common breeder in the Adirondacks, rare in the adjacent transition areas. Rare to uncommon but regular migrant, occasionally more numerous, very rare in winter.

Breeding Until the Atlas project, it was considered a rare breeder, largely confined to bogs in the Adirondacks. By 1983, the fourth Atlas year, it was clear that this was not the case. Where Bull (1974) noted just 20 breeding localities, virtually all within the Central Adirondacks and Western Adirondack Foothills, the Atlas documented the species in 277 blocks, including 108 with Confirmed breeding. The vast majority of the records still come from the Central Adirondacks and Western Adirondack Foothills, although it is now known to breed in the outlying Western Adirondack and Champlain Transition areas and possibly the Central Tug Hill as well. A record of probable breeding from appropriate bog habitat in the Rensselaer Hills, east of Albany, in 1995 (KB 45:325) is also especially notable. Although sphagnum bogs and fens with tamarack and spruce remain the primary habitat, the Atlas found this sparrow breeding in other habitats as well, including lake borders and openings with scattered conifer edge. Although it is likely that the abandonment of farms and resulting early successional growth in some parts of the Adirondacks and adjacent areas over the last several decades have led to an increase in population and distribution, the relative lack of summer reports both before the Atlas project and since suggests that the perception of this bird as rare was probably due mostly to its secretive nature and birders' infrequent visits to its primary habitat during the breeding season.

Nonbreeding Bull (1974) described it as most prevalent in spring inland and on the coast in fall. The former is still true, but it is now reported as a fall migrant inland at least as regularly, if not more so, as on the coast. Although there are no winter specimens, Bull (1974) reported several observations that he believed to be correct, including: Greece, Monroe Co. 1 Jan–30 Mar 1960; Baychester, Bronx Co. 22 Dec 1963; Cropseyville, Rensselaer Co. 27 Jan–10 Feb 1966. Some recent winter observations come from Ghent, Columbia Co., where it was recorded for three consecutive years on a CBC (KB 28:122); Wellsville, Allegany Co. 19 Dec 1979–17 Jan 1980 (KB 30:105); 2 Pawling, Dutchess Co. CBC 1 Jan 1992 (KB 42:123), as well as several records from LI. Many of the winter observations come from feeders.

Spring maxima: An extraordinary count of 70 West Lakeshore, Monroe Co. 15 May 1979; 35 Hamlin, Monroe Co. 13 May 1978. *Fall maxima:* 13 Hannibal-Sterling, Cayuga-Oswego counties 1 Oct 1988; 8–12 West Lakeshore, Monroe Co. 10 Oct 1981; 11 Clay, Onondaga Co. 24 Sep 1983. *Extreme dates:* 16 Mar (coastal) and 1 Apr (Adirondacks); 15 Aug (downstate) although confusion with immature Song Sparrow is possible. Rare before and after May; rare in Aug and after Oct.
Paul G. Novak

Swamp Sparrow   *Melospiza georgiana*

Range Nearctic, breeding from northern Saskatchewan to Newfoundland and south, in the east to central Ohio, Maryland, and Delaware. Winters south to Florida, the Gulf Coast, and Texas and north to New York, Massachusetts, and the Great Lakes.

Status Widespread breeder. Common to very common migrant, especially in fall; uncommon but apparently increasing in winter.

Breeding This species of primarily fresh wetlands has been recorded as breeding in every county in the state except New York (Atlas 1988). On LI, it has been reported to nest at the edges of salt marsh. The coastal upper marsh, formerly fresh or brackish, has virtually disappeared because of draining and filling and also as ditching, inlet stabilization, and sea-level rise have pushed tidal movements inland. Species that utilized this habitat, including both bitterns, Virginia Rail, Sedge Wren, Henslow's Sparrow, and Swamp Sparrow have vanished or become rare. Elsewhere in the state, where wetlands survive, this species remains common, with particularly dense concentrations in all the counties of the lower Hudson region, the upper Hudson and L. Champlain valleys, the Oneida L. and upper Finger Lakes regions, around the edges of the Adirondacks and Tug Hill, and on the Great Lakes and St. Lawrence plains.

Like other species of specialized habitat, it can be semicolonial in its nesting habitats, with local densities as high as one pair per acre. It has been noted as an "abundant" nester in the floodplain of Lakes Erie and Ontario, in the MNWR marshes, in the Oneida L. region and, formerly, on the now-destroyed site of JFK Airport, Queens Co. One of the few areas where, in recent years, actual numbers have been surveyed is Clay Marsh in Region 5: 54, 28 May 1990; 44, 28 Apr 1990; 31, 4 Jul 1991; 33, 22 Jul 1992; 38, 12 May and 41, 13 Jul 1993. These numbers suggest a dense and fairly consistent breeding population. Breeding birds are on territory by late Mar or early Apr in most parts of the state.

Nonbreeding Swamp Sparrows are most common and easiest to locate in fall passage, when they utilize a variety of habitats; in summer and winter they prefer deep marsh. Spring migrants arrive in late Mar or early Apr; most fall migrants arrive in Sep and are gone by early Nov. As is the case with other sparrows, wintering numbers are highly variable from year to year.

Spring maxima: 84 BOS May Count 16 May 1993; 44 Guilderland, Albany Co. 13 May 1995; 40 Central Park, Manhattan 14 May 1933. *Fall maxima:* 219 banded, Brookhaven, Suffolk Co. 19 Oct 1964; 200 Cuba Marsh, Allegany Co. 1 Oct 1966. *Winter maxima:* 71 Southern Nassau CBC 1963; 58 Brooklyn CBC 1990.

Remarks (By K. C. Parkes) Bull (1974) did not recognize the northern subspecies *ericrypta* (originally described as a western form), stating that it "is poorly differentiated, the differences in color being only of average quality." The Swamp Sparrow exhibits great individual variation, including sexual dichromatism in crown color undescribed in any field guide. Oberholser described *ericrypta* on the basis of minor size differences and alleged differences in dorsal coloration. With respect to the latter, Bull was correct; the excellent Carnegie series does not uphold Oberholser's characters at all. However, there is a color character not mentioned by Oberholser that serves to uphold *ericrypta*, although it is manifested almost entirely in fresh basic plumage. Northern birds are heavily suffused with rusty on the underparts, especially on the sides, flanks, and under tail coverts, but to some extent on the breast as well. This rusty color is much less intense on the sides and flanks of nominate *georgiana*, and it is absent on the breast. These color differences are present but inconspicuous in breeding birds. Fall migrants in the eastern United States that appear heavily rusty on the underparts are probably *ericrypta*.

Eric Salzman and Kenneth C. Parkes

White-throated Sparrow *Zonotrichia albicollis*

Range Nearctic, breeding from central Canada to the northern United States, in the east from central Quebec, southern Labrador, and Newfoundland south to northern Ohio, Pennsylvania, and New Jersey, rarely to the mountains of West Virginia and Maryland. Winters north to southern Canada, rarely, and south to the Gulf Coast and northern Mexico.

Status Common breeder in the mountains, uncommon and sporadic elsewhere. Common to abundant migrant throughout. In winter uncommon in the far north, varying from fairly common to abundant elsewhere; most abundant in coastal region.

Breeding Early avian records for NY name the Adirondacks as the center of the breeding range. By the 1980s, Atlas workers recorded it in fully 47% of all Atlas blocks and Confirmed it in 31% of those. It was now widespread throughout the general Adirondack and Catskill mountain areas, as well as the Rensselaer Hills. It is also now found more widely in other parts of the state, mainly at elevations of 1000–2000 ft. It was still nearly absent from the Mohawk Valley and the Great Lakes Plain and was not found southeast of the Catskills or on the east side of the Hudson R. south of the Taconics. West and south of the Finger Lakes area, there were only about 20 blocks with Confirmed breeding, those mostly in the Finger Lakes Highlands and Allegany Hills.

NY BBS 1966–1994 data indicated an overall downward trend. Most of the decline occurred from 1966 to 1979; 1980–1994 numbers showed no change.

Unquestionably, changes in available nesting habitat, particularly those caused in recent decades by changing agricultural and land use patterns have influenced both population and range. In the mountain regions, it prefers openings in the taiga and in mixed evergreen-deciduous woodlands; in other areas a key factor is its preference for bogs and openings and edges where its nest can be concealed by bushes and undergrowth.

Nonbreeding It is probably the most numerous sparrow on migration, often occurring in very large flocks in both spring and fall. How many of the unconfirmed reports during the Atlas project might be a result of late spring migrants is unknown.

The species is also found throughout in winter. CBCs from all Regions normally list White-throated Sparrows, although their numbers are fewer in the northern mountain areas. The Saranac Lake, Essex Co. CBC reported six individuals on 30 Dec 1989. The year before, on 18 Dec 1988, the tally on the Rochester, Monroe Co. CBC was 101. In central NY, 158 were reported on the 1986 CBC at Ithaca, Tompkins Co. In the southernmost regions, on 27 Dec 1984 the Central Suffolk Co. CBC recorded 789 individuals. In the same year the Bronx-Westchester count on 23 Dec topped the list with 1949.

Spring maxima: 2500 Manitou, Monroe Co. 30 Apr 1960; 2000 JBSP May 1973; 1000 Washington Park, Albany 5 May 1941. *Fall maxima:* 1200 JBSP 5 Oct 1963; 1000 Prospect Park, Kings Co. 15 Oct 1950; 700 Sterling-Hannibal-Clay Swamp, Onondaga Co. 13 Oct 1976.

Remarks The White-throated Sparrow is polymorphic, having two color morphs unrelated to either age or sex. The chief difference between the two lies in the color of the median head stripe, which is white in one and tan in the other. In general, the coloring of the rest of the body in the white morph is brighter and the streakings are fewer than in the tan. Normally, a nesting pair will consist of one individual of each morph. Nests in which the female has a white head stripe tend to be located in more-secluded sur-

roundings than are nests in which the female has a tan head stripe (Atlas 1988).
Harriet T. Marsi and Gail M. Kirch

Harris's Sparrow *Zonotrichia querula*

Range Nearctic, breeding from west-central Canada south to northeastern Saskatchewan and northern Manitoba. Winters south and east to southern Texas, Louisiana, and Tennessee. Wanders, rarely but regularly, on migration to both coasts.

Status Very rare vagrant.

Occurrence This species was first confirmed in NY and collected for NYSM in 1931. Since then it has been observed more than 50 times. The increase in sightings seems largely attributable to the popularity of bird feeders. About 30% of sightings occur in winter; the rest are divided between fall and spring. About 20% of the individuals are known to have overwintered (KB 33:187, 40:180). Inland records are five times as frequent as coastal ones. Frequency of occurrence is irregular; there were no reports from Apr 1983 to Mar 1990. Birds have been photographed or banded, or both at least six times (Bull 1974; KB 28:41, 31:45, 45:74). Three birds that over-wintered at feeders in 1964–1965 molted into breeding plumage in May and were photographed.

   Extreme dates: 28 Sep and 23 Jun. Most occur between late Oct and mid-May.

Remarks Seasonal distribution in neighboring states is similar to that in NY. Veit and Petersen (1993) commented that, in MA, "Mid fall occurrences suggest that individuals wander about until settling in at feeding stations."
Kenneth L. Crowell

White-crowned Sparrow *Zonotrichia leucophrys*

Range Nearctic, breeding from northern Alaska to Labrador and south, in the east to central Manitoba, central and southeastern Quebec, and northern Newfoundland. In the east, winters coastally from Massachusetts to Florida and the West Indies, also to the Gulf Coast, Texas, and northern Mexico.

Status Uncommon to very common migrant, particularly in fall. Rare to uncommon but regular in winter.

Occurrence This species is most numerous in the fall, arriving in early to mid-Sep. Most birds depart by early Nov, but numbers regularly linger into

Dec, with some remaining through the winter. Spring migration takes place between mid-Apr and late May, with stragglers lingering along the Great Lakes Plain into Jul. Early dates are hard to determine because of wintering birds.

Spring maxima: 682 L. Ontario littoral 13 May 1995; 150 Syracuse, Onondaga Co. 12 May 1956; 80 Central Park, Manhattan 10 May 1956. *Fall maxima:* 1500 Pompey, Onondaga Co. 13 Oct 1974; 300 L. Ontario littoral 13 Oct 1992; 160 RMSP 12 Oct 1974. *Winter maxima:* 100 Newfane, Niagara Co. 23 Jan 1965; 25 Avon, Livingston Co. 14 Jan 1995; 20 Old Brookville, Nassau Co. 31 Dec 1968.

Remarks Two of the five recognized subspecies occur in NY. They are the commonly seen nominate form, *leucophrys*, which breeds in eastern Canada, and, rarely, *gambelii*, which breeds in AK and northwestern Canada. They are separable in the field, and there are a number of reports, mostly coastal, of *gambelii*, including: a hybrid, specimen taken at Ithaca, Tompkins Co. 30 Apr 1898 (Eaton 1914; Parkes 1952); a specimen taken at Tobay, Nassau Co. 26 Sep 1974 (Bull 1976); two sight reports from Tobay, 9 May 1975 and 24 Oct 1980; one photographed by Vezo, JBSP 15 May 1994 (NASFN 48:283); Orient Point, Suffolk Co. 25 Mar 1995.
Eric Salzman

Golden-crowned Sparrow *Zonotrichia atricapilla*

Range Western Nearctic, breeding from western Alaska and central Yukon south to northern Washington and southern Alberta. Winters mainly along the Pacific Coast to southern California. Casual locally throughout much of North America.

Status Casual vagrant.

Occurrence There are two records, at almost the same location in JBSP, Nassau Co. The first was found by Carleton, 31 Jan 1954, and remained until 24 April. Although it was seen by many competent observers, including Bull, the lack of a specimen or satisfactory photo caused the relegation of the species to the Hypothetical list (Bull 1974). NYSARC (1984) subsequently reviewed and accepted the record. The second bird was photographed by Dignan on 17 Oct 1987 and remained until the next day (Bull 1988a).

Remarks It is considered hypothetical in CT and a vagrant in MA, where there have been nine records, and in NJ, which has four records.
Emanuel Levine and Richard O'Hara

Dark-eyed Junco *Junco hyemalis*

Range Nearctic, breeding from Alaska and Canada to the mountains of the southwestern United States and Baja California, in the east to the mountains of northern Georgia and at lower elevations, to the northern and northeastern United States. Winters through much of the breeding range, except in the extreme north, south to northern Mexico, the Gulf Coast, and northern Florida.

Status Common breeder in forest at higher elevations. Common to abundant migrant and common to abundant winter visitant.

Breeding It was found in 43% of Atlas blocks and was Confirmed in 41% of those. This arboreal member of the sparrow tribe is found throughout the Adirondacks, Tug Hill, Catskills, and across the Appalachian Plateau. Although mostly confined to altitudes above 1000 ft, it is occasionally found at lower elevations in cool, forested ravines or swamps. The bird is rare to absent on the Great Lakes and St. Lawrence plains and in the Mohawk and Hudson valleys, and it is absent on LI (Atlas 1988). In the Allegany Hills it is suspected that small flocks of these birds found in large forest tracts throughout the winter are permanent residents and not winter visitants. They sing on territory from the tops of trees as early as 21 Mar, before the migrants arrive (Eaton 1981).

It inhabits the more open deciduous, mixed, and coniferous forests and forest edges. Its territory usually includes an opening in the forest canopy surrounding a rock outcrop or an exposed soil bank, as along a woodland road (Eaton 1965).

Juncos have continuously expanded their range from the early 1900s to the 1970s and 1980s (Eaton 1910; Bull 1974; Atlas 1988). This expansion appears to be in response to increased forest habitat. Additional counties in southeastern NY added to its breeding distribution by the Atlas included Putnam and Orange. This southeastern range now includes Harriman SP in Rockland Co., where birds have probably extended their range from northwestern CT along the Reading Prong (Speiser 1982).

Nonbreeding It is one of the most numerous sparrows on migration, appearing in open spaces in large flocks, smaller groups in wooded habitat, and often at feeders. Large migrant flocks appear about 15 Apr to early May and in fall 15 Oct to early Nov.

Spring maxima: 1000 Karner, Albany Co. 2 Apr 1957; 350 Tully, Onondaga Co. 19 Apr 1962. *Fall maxima:* 1000 Riis Park, Queens Co. 25 Oct 1953; 1000 Waterloo, Seneca Co. 17 Oct 1966; 850 East Hampton, Suffolk Co. 2 Nov 1930. *Winter maxima:* 512 along 15.6 m of road Allegany SP 13 Jan 1985, feeding on hemlock seeds; 500 Wilson, Niagara Co. 11 Feb 1968.

Remarks (By G. F. Barrowclough) Several species of juncos that had long been recognized by ornithologists were lumped by the AOU Committee on Classification and Nomenclature in 1983. Through this action, the Slate-colored, White-winged, Gray-headed, and Oregon (including Pink-sided) juncos were united as the Dark-eyed Junco. The justification largely consisted of data published in a monograph by Miller (1941); these data were interpreted and cited in subsequent taxonomic treatments by other authors (e.g., Mayr 1942; Phillips et al. 1964) but were never used by Miller himself to justify lumping.

The actual data leading to the consolidation of the taxa were the occurrence of hybrid individuals in several regions of contact between the various species. However, although hybridization appears to be rampant in areas of contact between species, the geographical extent of such zones is quite limited in most cases. For example, hybridization between Oregon and Gray-headed juncos is restricted to a few patches of forest at high elevation in small, dry mountain ranges straddling the CA-NV border. In other cases, areas of hybridization may be ephemeral; White-winged Juncos were thought to hybridize with Pink-sided Juncos in ponderosa pine forests along sand ridges in southeastern MT, on the basis of a few specimens collected in the 1950s. However, this author was unable to find any area of contact during a 1985 survey of the region and instead noted that fires and cattle grazing had eliminated much of the potential habitat for juncos in this crucial area. In general, the actual pattern of junco hybridization among the well-marked forms consists of restricted areas of intergradation connecting vast regions of relatively uniform populations. Given this situation, it is likely that the current trend toward splitting and the recognition of phylogenetic species will eventually lead ornithologists to return to recognizing five separate species of juncos that are all currently called the Dark-eyed Junco. Therefore, until such time as the expected revision occurs, possibly with the publication of the long-awaited seventh edition of the AOU Check-list, we may refer to Dark-eyed Junco as a "superspecies" consisting of the following complexes: Slate-colored Junco, three subspecies; Oregon Junco, eight subspecies; Pink-sided Junco, one subspecies; Gray-headed Junco, two subspecies; White-winged Junco, one subspecies. In anticipation of the likely split of Dark-eyed Junco into five species, we review the status of these birds in NY.

Slate-colored Junco. The breeding juncos of NY all belong to the slate-colored complex, which consists of three subspecies: *hyemalis, carolinensis,* and *cismontanus.*

PA, NJ, and NY are in the region where a transition occurs between *carolinensis* and the nominate Slate-colored Junco, *hyemalis.* Pure *carolinensis* are larger than *hyemalis* and have bluish bills, versus pink in *hyemalis.* The breeding juncos of southern NY are members of an intermediate series of populations and cannot be allocated unambiguously to either subspecies.

However, breeding juncos from the Adirondacks are inseparable from nominate *hyemalis*. Hybrid populations of Oregon and Slate-colored Juncos from western Alberta and northern British Columbia are named *J. h. cismontanus*. Members of this subspecies, particularly first-year birds, frequently have at least some brown or pinkish feathers on their sides and can be mistaken for Oregon and Pink-sided juncos. Because of their southeastward migration pattern, they can be expected to occur in NY in winter on occasion.

Oregon Junco. Oregon Juncos, *oregonus*, have been reported frequently in NY during winter and migration periods (sight records from Oct through Apr). Only rarely have they been collected (e.g., Bull 1974). Although Oregon Juncos undoubtedly do occur from time to time, sight records of juncos must be evaluated with great care because of the exceptionally variable plumages of Slate-colored Juncos (Miller 1941); for example, many first-year and female Slate-colored Juncos bear a resemblance to Oregon Juncos in appearing to have a relatively dark "hood" and a relatively brown back due to brownish edges on freshly molted back feathers. In addition, they occasionally have feathers suffused with buff and brown on the back and sides. All of this can be confusing to observers who do not have substantial experience with actual populations of Oregon and other juncos.

Pink-sided Junco. The closest breeding populations of Pink-sided Juncos occur in central Wyoming and Montana. There are several sight records and one banded bird from NY (KB 35:142; 43:147). These reports have to be viewed as questionable without specimens or photographs; immature Oregon and the *cismontanus* subspecies of Slate-colored juncos could be misidentified as Pink-sided. In addition, individuals of nominate *hyemalis* occasionally have buff-colored feathers on the flanks; Pink-sided Juncos have uniformly broad pink sides and flanks.

Gray-headed Junco. Gray-headed Juncos breed in Colorado and west through the Great Basin. A 1990–1991 report from NY (KB 41:35) is surprising given the normal migration path of this species. A specimen or photograph is required to document the record.

White-winged Junco. At this time, no records of White-winged Juncos from NY are known to this author. Geographically, this form is most proximal to our region and thus might be expected to occur. However, White-winged Juncos appear to have a relatively restricted wintering area in the southern and western Great Plains and adjacent mountain states. In addition, its identification is not trivial because white wingbars are frequently found within Slate-colored Junco populations. For instance, Miller reported in his 1941 monograph that 2–3% of Slate-colored Juncos have white on the wings. On the other hand, not all White-winged Juncos have white in the wing; Miller found that 5% of male and 22% of female White-winged Juncos have no white wingbar. In the hand, White-winged Juncos can usually be separated from Slate-colored Juncos by their larger size and the much greater amount of white in the tail, but these characteristics are not easily observed in the field.

Stephen W. Eaton and George F. Barrowclough

Lapland Longspur   *Calcarius lapponicus*

Range Holarctic, in eastern North America breeding south to the northern parts of Ontario, Quebec, and Labrador. Winters from southern Canada south to Maryland.

Status Winter visitant, varying from uncommon to locally abundant. Most numerous near L. Ontario.

Occurrence A bird of the Arctic tundra, in NY the Lapland Longspur frequents open-country habitats: shortgrass fields, airports, golf courses, coastal beaches, and the like. When found, it is frequently in the company of Horned Larks and Snow Buntings. Most winters few or none will be found, but in some years it appears in large flocks.

   Coastal maxima: 200 JBWR 10 Feb 1974; 150 Sagaponack, Suffolk Co. 12 Jan 1975; 120 Rockaway, Queens Co. 4–18 Jan 1981; all are exceptional numbers for the coast. *Inland maxima:* 880 Braddock Bay, Monroe Co. 28 Mar 1954; 400 Ransomville, Niagara Co. 14 Feb 1975; 50 Peru, Clinton Co. mid-Feb 1994, a Regional record. *Extreme dates:* 6 Sep (inland) and 29 Sep (coastal); 9 May (inland and coastal); exceptionally to 31 May (inland). Rare before mid-Oct and after early May.

Remarks Most, when seen in NY, are in their drab basic plumage, but some individuals occasionally linger late into the spring, giving birders a chance to see the male's bright and very distinctive alternate plumage.

Joseph DiCostanzo

Smith's Longspur   *Calcarius pictus*

Range Nearctic, breeding from Alaska southeastward across arctic Canada to extreme northern Ontario. Winters in the Great Plains from Kansas and Iowa south to east-central Texas and northwestern Louisiana.

Status Accidental.

Occurrence There is one record. An individual was found, netted, and collected 22 Sep 1974 at RMSP, Suffolk Co. (Davis 1976). The bird, a female with a partially ossified skull, is specimen AMNH 811078.

Remarks There are very few East Coast records and only a handful in the Northeast: NJ 1991 (Sibley 1993) and 1995 (NASFN 50:30); CT 1968

and 1982 (Zeranski and Baptist 1990); VT 1981 (AB 35:822); MA 1968 (Veit and Petersen 1993); RI 1965 (Conway 1992).
Joseph DiCostanzo

Chestnut-collared Longspur   *Calcarius ornatus*

Range Central Nearctic, breeding east to southwestern Minnesota. Winters from northern Louisiana and northern Arizona south to northern Mexico. Vagrant along the Atlantic Coast from New Brunswick to Virginia.

Status Casual vagrant.

Occurrence There are five accepted records for NY, all from LI. Bull (1974) listed four: (1) male, collected, Long Island City, Queens Co. 16 Feb 1889 (Hendrickson) AMNH 65626; (2) female, collected, Miller Place, Suffolk Co. 14 Sep 1891 (Helme) AMNH 802440; (3) male in nearly full alternate plumage, Orient, Suffolk Co. 21–27 Apr 1923 (Latham) NYSM 25664; (4) male in alternate plumage, observed, Dyker Beach, Kings Co. 29 Apr 1944 (Grant).

The fifth record, a male in alternate plumage, was discovered and photographed at Bay County Park, Nassau Co. 6–8 Jun 1982 (Lindauer 1982).

Remarks Surprisingly, this is the longspur recorded most frequently in the summer months in the Northeast. Summer records in neighboring states are: 18 Jun 1980 in NJ (Leck 1984); 28 Jul 1876 in MA (Veit and Petersen 1993); 29 Aug 1968 in CT (Zeranski and Baptist 1990); Stratford, CT 7 Jun 1994 (NASFN 48:926). Not even the Lapland Longspur, the regularly wintering East Coast longspur, has appeared that many times in the warm months. It is possible that the Chestnut-collared is overlooked in winter because of its similarity in basic plumage to the Lapland in basic. Bull (1974) considered all reports of Chestnut-collareds in basic plumage unsatisfactory because of the possible confusion between the species. Any wintering individual would have to be very critically identified.
Joseph DiCostanzo

Snow Bunting

Plectrophenax nivalis

Range Holarctic, breeding in North America from northern Alaska east to Ellesmere Island and, in the east, south to Hudson Bay and northern Labrador. In the east, winters south to North Carolina and northern Kentucky, casually farther south.

Status Uncommon to very abundant visitant from early fall to late spring.

Occurrence This species usually occurs in flocks of varying size from Sep to May, chiefly in lowlands but also in upland areas. The largest numbers have been recorded in the Great Lakes Plain. It frequents farm and other fields and grasslands, mostly in open country, as well as Great Lakes and maritime shores and beaches. Recently, it has been reported in lower numbers in the Coastal Lowlands than heretofore.

It usually moves rapidly along shores and through an area in the initial and last portions of the occurrence period. During the winter, it frequently ranges for varying periods in more restricted areas where seeds and other foods are sufficient to support it. It has been reported in small numbers at feeders in seven counties; many of them probably are locations where the feeders are adjacent or close to the types of habitat it normally frequents.

Coastal maxima: 1500 Orient, Suffolk Co. 10 Feb 1956; 1000 Long Beach, Nassau Co. 27 Dec 1919. *Inland maxima:* 10,000 near East Aurora, Erie Co. 24 Mar 1962; 9000 lake plain west of Rochester, Monroe Co. 24 Jan 1983; and 7500 in the same location 22 Jan 1978. *Extreme dates:* 5 Sep and 23 May (both inland).

Robert Andrle

GROSBEAKS AND BUNTINGS—
CARDINALIDAE

Northern Cardinal   *Cardinalis cardinalis*

Range Nearctic and Neotropical, resident, in the east from eastern South Dakota, southern Ontario, and central Maine south to central Texas, the Gulf states, and Florida. Range gradually expanding northward.

Status Common resident throughout, except in the Adirondacks and Tug Hill.

Breeding The history of this species as a breeder in NY is difficult to document. Eaton (1914) advised that it bred in the lower Hudson Valley, SI, and LI. Griscom (1923) told of its apparent disappearance in the 1920s, using the word *extirpation*. Then Cruickshank (1942) wrote of its reestablishment as a nester in the 1930s and of its gradual movement northward. Evidently, there was a separate movement from the Ohio Valley into western NY, where it became established as a breeder in the 1920s (Atlas 1988). The rest, as they say, "is history," with the phenomenal spread of the bird virtually throughout the state, with the exception of the Adirondacks and Tug Hill.

The range of this species with respect to elevation would be worth noting. Bull observed its preference for lower elevations during its decades-long range expansion. The Atlas reported that "it seems to have largely avoided land above 1000 ft except in well-settled communities." However, the bird's population increase may lead to movement into higher elevations. For example, a breeding pair has been present since 1990 at 1500–1650 ft, south of Dryden, Tompkins Co., where feeding stations are available (pers. obs.). It would be useful if future CBC and Atlas sampling would include a reference to elevations where cardinals are found, to help determine the range tolerated by this steadily increasing species. Once it is established at low elevations, it is reasonable to expect it to move to higher elevations if population growth continues, especially in the presence of widespread supplemental winter feeding.

Once established as a breeding species, it is relatively sedentary and rarely leaves its territory even in harsh winters. The cardinal's ability to double brood or triple brood in a single season probably also has contributed significantly to its expansion in NY and the entire Northeast.

Nonbreeding More than any other species, its increase and spread coincide with the availability of feeding stations. Also, changes in land use from agricultural to suburban communities rich in shrubby cover provide opportunities for summer food and nesting and protective winter cover (Atlas 1988). Decades of milder winters in the last 100 years have favored this resident species, which expands its range during the fall after the breeding season. CBC data from Rochester, Monroe Co. show an explosive population increase from 1950 to 1980.

Claudia K. Melin

Rose-breasted Grosbeak *Pheucticus ludovicianus*

Range Primarily eastern Nearctic, breeding from northeastern British Columbia across southern Canada to Nova Scotia, south to eastern Nebraska, northern Oklahoma, northern Ohio, New York, and southern New England; in the mountains to northern Georgia. Winters from Mexico to northern South America.

Status Widespread breeder and fairly common migrant throughout. Rare in winter.

Breeding It nests in mature, primarily deciduous, woodlands, in second-growth deciduous woodlands, in wooded gardens and parks, and in forested swamps. Atlas workers found it well distributed throughout the state; it occurred in 88% of the blocks and was Confirmed in 26% of those. Atlas work indicates that there has been a range expansion since the early twentieth century into the lower Hudson Valley and LI, except for southwestern LI, where it has never been present. BBS data indicate a significant population decrease statewide from 1979 to 1994.

Nonbreeding Statewide spring arrival dates are 27 Apr–4 May, with the earliest being 1 Apr; fall departure dates are 27 Sep–11 Oct. There are numerous records in Nov and Dec. Although it is not normally considered a species encountered in winter, there are many CBC reports and many other records of individuals' persisting for several weeks or longer with food available at feeders. There has been no significant change in numbers of individuals reported on CBCs.

Spring maxima: 500 Braddock Bay, Monroe Co. 12 May 1978; 369 on the Buffalo area, Erie Co. count 16 May 1993. *Fall maxima:* 45 Buckhorn I. SP, Niagara Co. 6 Sep 1977; 40 Elmira, Chemung Co. 1978.
Robert G. McKinney

Black-headed Grosbeak *Pheucticus melanocephalus*

Range Western Nearctic, breeding from southeastern British Columbia east to northwestern North Dakota and south to eastern California, western Texas, and central Kansas. Winters chiefly in Mexico. Vagrant east to the Atlantic Coast from Massachusetts to South Carolina.

Status Very rare vagrant.

Occurrence There are more than 15 reports of this western stray, mostly from feeding stations, with several substantiated by photographs. The first fully documented record was a male at a Watertown, Jefferson Co. feeder 30 Apr 1959. Next was a female at a Holland, Erie Co. feeder 1 Jan–20 Apr 1962. Unlike most western strays recorded in NY, it is more likely to occur in winter and spring than in fall. About half the reports are from the Coastal Lowlands, and most of those are from NYC.

Remarks A review of the literature of surrounding states shows occurrences closely approximating those of NY.
William C. D'Anna

Blue Grosbeak   *Guiraca caerulea*

Range Nearctic and Neotropical, breeding from southern California, southern Colorado, central Illinois, and southeastern New York south, in the east to northern Florida, and in Central America to Costa Rica. Winters from Mexico to Panama.

Status Two breeding records. Uncommon spring and fall visitant to LI, rare spring and summer farther north.

Breeding There was one confirmed nest, in Latourette Park, Richmond Co. 17 Jun 1982, on a weedy hillside (Siebenheller and Siebenheller 1982a), where breeding was suspected the previous year. Three eggs were laid and two young fledged. Also, during the Atlas survey, a female was reported carrying food, June 1984, at Pine Island, Orange Co. Two Possible sites, in Orange and Westchester counties, were also recorded. No nesting has been confirmed since the Atlas period. Breeding evidence should be carefully looked for in weedy edges on LI and in the lower Hudson Valley, since this species is quiet and discreet around the nest. A pair was present at Muttontown, Suffolk Co. 22 Jun–18 Jul 1995, but no nest or other evidence of breeding was found (KB 45:332).

Nonbreeding Although recorded in NYC as early as 1838 (Cruickshank 1942), it was a rare bird in the state before the late 1940s. It has become regular in southern NY since then, as its breeding range spread steadily northward, reaching the Hackensack Meadows of northern NJ in 1973. It has bred there regularly since. Most records are from the South Shore of LI in Apr and May and again in Sep and Oct; three to six in a season there is normal. It is still rare north of Orange and Westchester counties, although reliably described as far north as Livingston, Monroe, Essex (KB 14:215) and Lewis counties (KB 41:276). It is rare before mid-Apr or after mid-Oct.

  Extreme dates: 25 Mar and 28 Nov, exceptionally to 15 Dec. Maximum one-day total 13, along the JBSP strip 11 Apr 1993. There is one winter record: Freeport, Nassau Co. 7–13 Jan 1977.

Remarks This southern species has moved north only gradually; Audubon discovered the first NJ nest near Camden in 1829 (Leck 1984). It seems to require extensive brush in truly rural settings and has not taken to suburbia. Robert O. Paxton

Indigo Bunting   *Passerina cyanea*

Range Eastern Nearctic, breeding from southeastern Saskatchewan to New Brunswick and south to Texas, the Gulf Coast, and central Florida. Winters in tropical America south to Panama and north to Florida, casually north to Massachusetts.

Status Widely distributed, fairly common breeder, absent from higher elevations. Uncommon to fairly common migrant.

Breeding From colonial times up to the recent past, it showed a slow but steady increase in population over most of the state. This positive trend was attributed to the opening of the dense precolonial forest by logging, burning, and agriculture, practices that created large areas of suitable habitat (Atlas 1988).

Since 1980, however, that trend seems to be reversing. NY BBS data showed that a significant increase in population from 1966 to 1979 was followed by a significant decrease between 1980 and 1994. The numerous references in the Kingbird Regional Reports to a decline in numbers in many areas of the state, starting around 1986, support the conclusion that the population is declining.

Perhaps subsequent reforestation of the state, as well as increasing development, have had a bearing on the species' recent negative trend. Payne (1992) reported that, although it was increasing in range and densities on a continental basis, local decreases and disappearances occurred in areas of increased forest growth, urbanization, and intensive agriculture where second growth is precluded.

It can be found almost everywhere in the state, but population densities are greatest in the southern and westernmost portions inland. Eaton (1914) stated that the bird did not enter the Canadian Zone, but in 1952 Parkes noted an increase at higher elevations where it apparently was not found before 1947. Atlas observers found the bird absent from the higher elevations of the Catskills, Adirondacks, and Central Tug Hill.

On the coastal plain, intense urban development has usurped much of the species' habitat. Giraud (1844) and Chapman (1906) considered it a common summer resident there, and Eaton (1914) described it as characteristic of the coastal district. But Griscom (1923) called it uncommon on the west end and rare and local elsewhere on LI. By 1942, that description had changed to "scarce to unknown" around NYC and rare and irregular on LI (Cruickshank 1942). In the 1980s the bird was "sparsely represented" on LI (Atlas 1988).

Nonbreeding It arrives in early to mid-May throughout, somewhat earlier in Regions 9 and 10. Fall departures range from early Sep through Oct. Once considered casual in Oct, the bird is now seen regularly in that month, and there are numerous records for Nov as well.

In fall, it is often seen on lawns that have scattered shrubs, such as city parks or just behind the beaches. An interesting observation by Griscom (1923), and repeated by Cruickshank (1942), was of its "marked preference for borders of swamps and marshes where it is seldom seen in spring." Usually seen singly or in small groups of two or three, it sometimes occurs in larger numbers.

Spring maxima: 65 along the barrier beaches, Nassau and Suffolk counties 27 Apr 1983; 18 JBSP 26 Apr 1983; 16 Derby Hill, Oswego Co. 12 May 1964. *Fall maxima:* 15 JBSP 30 Sept 1951; 8 Prospect Park, Kings Co. 10 Oct 1947. *Extreme dates:* 22 Mar and 14 Nov, casual to 7 Dec.

There are four winter reports: at a Riverhead, Suffolk Co. feeder throughout Dec 1957; Pleasant Valley, Dutchess Co. 13–19 Dec 1975; Bronx Park, Bronx Co. 21 Dec 1975; Newburgh, Orange Co. 12 Feb–31 Mar 1975.

Patricia J. Lindsay

Painted Bunting   *Passerina ciris*

Range Nearctic and Neotropical, breeding from southern New Mexico and southern Missouri east to southeastern North Carolina and south to central Florida, the Gulf Coast, and central Mexico. Winters from Florida and the Gulf states south to Panama and in the Greater Antilles.

Status Very rare vagrant.

Occurrence There are approximately 30 records, dating back to at least 1875. Early records were suspected to be escapes. Griscom (1923) wrote that the species should be removed from the state list and considered hypothetical, because all records had occurred during the time it was a popular cage bird. The practice of caging the bird was outlawed in 1913, but illegal possession by some dealers in the NYC area caused sightings there to be treated with suspicion into the 1960s (Bull 1964).

The majority of records, both early and recent, are from the coastal region. Of the dates available, nearly all early records (1875–1949) are from Jul to Dec, whereas the overwhelming majority of more recent sightings (1952–1993) occurred Apr to Jun.

Of the 10 most recent records, some were photographed and seven were accepted by NYSARC: female, West Monroe, Oswego Co. 7 Jun 1978 (NYSARC 1979); male, Richmond Co. 2 May 1983 (Siebenheller and Siebenheller 1983; NYSARC 1984); male, Pine City, Chemung Co. 6–7 May 1983 (NYSARC 1984); male, Preble, Cortland Co. 5–6 May 1984 (NYSARC 1985); immature male at feeder, Richmond Co. 18–20 May 1985 (NYSARC 1987); Lafayetteville, Dutchess Co. 10 Aug 1992 (NYSARC 1994); female, Montauk, Suffolk Co. 19–28 Dec 1992 (NYSARC 1994; KB 43:161).

Other reports were: Olean, Cattaraugus Co. 28 Apr–15 May 1981 (KB 31:160); male, Afton, Chenango Co. 15–16 Aug 1985 (KB 35:273); pair, Manhattan 25 May 1993 (KB 43:272).

Remarks MA has more than 20 records dating from 1957 (Veit and Petersen 1993). In recent years, it has shown up with surprising regularity in the winter months there. Of the 14 records since 1989, 12 are from Oct to Dec, with a few birds remaining throughout the winter at feeders (AB 1985–1995). In CT there are four records (Zeranski and Baptist 1990; AB 1990–1993), as well as several published but uncorroborated reports. There were 12 NJ sightings from 1958 to 1995 (Leck 1984; AB 1986–1995) and seven records in RI from 1953 to 1983 (Conway 1992).

Patricia J. Lindsay

Dickcissel   *Spiza americana*

Range Nearctic, chiefly central North America, breeding from extreme southern Canada to the Gulf states; sporadically east to southern Ontario, west-central New York, Ohio, Pennsylvania, southern New Jersey, and Maryland. Before 1880, bred on the Atlantic coastal plain from Massachusetts to South Carolina. Winters from southern Mexico to northern South America, rarely north to the Gulf states; since 1952, regular in small numbers at feeding stations north to New York and New England.

Status Casual breeder. Rare but regular fall migrant, primarily coastal and in the lower Hudson Valley; much less frequent in spring and at any time inland. Regular winter visitant at feeders.

Breeding This species formerly ranged widely in the breeding season over the Atlantic states from MA to SC. Specific information regarding its abundance in the early and middle nineteenth century is lacking, although early writers called it "common" or "abundant." It was primarily found in lowland areas, where it nested on or near the ground in grassy fields and meadows.

The last of the pre-1900 breeding records in NY was from Junius, Seneca Co. in 1875 (Eaton 1914). The first modern breeding occurred in May 1937 in a hayfield in Meridian, Cayuga Co. After two eggs were collected, the pair renested and raised four young (Benton 1949). A nest with four eggs was located near Victor, Ontario Co. on 29 Jun 1955, but the nest was destroyed when the field was mowed. A small colony resided in an abandoned field in Pomfret, Chautauqua Co. during Jun and Jul 1976. As many as 8–10 males and five females were present and copulation was observed. Several birds captured for banding were in breeding condition, and one female was observed carrying nesting material (Slack and Baumgartner 1977). However, adults were not observed carrying food, no fledged young were seen, and, despite some searching, no nests were located. These observations certainly suggested attempted breeding, but by Atlas criteria they represented a record of Probable rather than Confirmed breeding. No breeding records were obtained during the Atlas, but soon after, in Jun 1988, breeding was finally documented again in NY when a female was flushed from a nest with five eggs in a Christmas tree plantation in Andover, Allegany Co. (Brooks 1988). The eggs failed to hatch, perhaps because of disturbance from tree-maintenance activities. A second record of probable breeding was in South Lansing, Tompkins Co. in 1992, when four males and one female were present 18 Jun–15 Aug; again, no evidence of nesting was found (KB 42:243).

Although these recent records suggest that the Dickcissel is on that the verge of becoming reestablished as a more regular breeder in NY, that may not be the case. This species is noted for its unpredictable presence near the edge of its range, and 1988, the year of Brooks's nest record, has been noted as a year when many extralimital regions were "invaded," perhaps as a result of drought conditions in the species' Midwestern breeding range (Brauning 1992).

Nonbreeding It is recorded during every month of the year but much less frequently in spring than in fall and winter. Fall migration records occur throughout Sep, Oct, and Nov, with the majority from Oct. A 3 Aug 1991 record from JBSP (KB 41:290) surely represented an exceptionally early migrant. Most observations come from the lower Hudson Valley and LI; birds have been observed at JBSP almost annually since 1980. Dickcissels have become regular as a winter visitant to feeders, with individuals reported from most upstate regions as well as coastal areas.

Maxima: A literal invasion at Fire I. Lighthouse, Suffolk Co. during the fall of 1969—with 53 individuals recorded 6 Sep–8 Nov and maxima of 5 on 27 Sep, 13+ on 29 Sep, and 8 on 9 Oct (Buckley and Davis et al.)—has never been repeated, and one or two individuals per locality is the rule. Paul G. Novak

BLACKBIRDS—ICTERIDAE

Bobolink *Dolichonyx oryzivorus*

Range Nearctic, breeding from southern British Columbia to Nova Scotia and south to the central United States; in the east, to northern Missouri east to central New Jersey and locally in the mountains to North Carolina. Winters chiefly in southern South America.

Status Widespread breeder, except for higher elevations and LI. Common to very abundant fall migrant, much less so in spring, although locally abundant inland.

Breeding With the urbanization of much of downstate and the decline in farming upstate, open habitat, particularly grasslands, has been much reduced, with a resultant drop in breeding numbers for this species. The Atlas recorded it in 63% of all blocks and Confirmed breeding in 38% of those. A glance at the Atlas map shows distribution generally throughout, with the exception of the Adirondacks and the Catskills and most of the Coastal Lowlands. Nesting success is lowered by intense haying practices. Early haying has the benefit of increased protein content of the hay, but, unfortunately, it must take place before the young have fledged.

Nonbreeding Bobolinks are both diurnal and nocturnal migrants, the diagnostic call being heard in flight during the fall passage. Spectacular numbers may be observed on the southbound flight, particularly on the South Shore of LI. Nocturnal migration listening stations established by Evans throughout upstate NY have found that peak migration is from mid-Aug through the first week of Sep. Larger flights have been in the eastern part (Oneonta, Otsego Co.) of the monitoring transect, typically at the end of Aug or early Sep.

The return passage in spring is much less impressive, with relatively small numbers observed or heard at any one time and rarely in big flocks. The dates of the maxima possibly indicate a decline in numbers in the last few decades.

Spring maxima: 400 Derby Hill, Oswego Co. 6 May 1966; 258 Ithaca, Tompkins Co. 17 Jun 1995; 100 Lattingtown, Nassau Co. 16 May 1967. *Fall maxima:* 8000 Mastic, Suffolk Co. 24 Aug 1912; 5000 Far Rockaway, Queens Co. 8 Sep 1953.

There are two winter records, both from Onondaga Co. The first was of a bird that visited a feeder at Salina from early Dec 1971 to late Feb 1972; it was discovered dead on 23 Mar and was discarded. The mummified corpse was retrieved by Spies a week later, and it is now CUM 34904, possibly the first winter specimen for North America (Bull 1976). The second, also a feeder bird and apparently injured, was photographed at De Witt 16 Jan and 2 Feb 1992 (Crumb 1992).
Steve Kelling

Red-winged Blackbird *Agelaius phoeniceus*

Range Nearctic and Neotropical, breeding from south-central Alaska to southwestern Newfoundland, south throughout the United States to Costa Rica; also in the Bahama Islands and Cuba. Winters from southern British Columbia, Iowa, the southern Great Lakes region, and New England south throughout the breeding range.

Status Widespread breeder. Common to very abundant migrant. Locally very common to very abundant in winter, especially in the southeast.

Breeding Estimates of relative abundance from BBSs indicate that this is the most abundant breeding bird in NY, although it declined significantly between 1966 and 1994. The Atlas recorded it in 95% of the blocks, and breeding was Confirmed in 74% of those. Various nesting habitats are used, from marshes and open swamps to upland fields and pastures. Breeding red-wings tend to be polygamous; one male mates with multiple females within its territory. Howard (1977) reported that nesting productivity of marsh and upland populations near Ithaca, Tompkins Co. were essentially the same.

There is evidence that it has expanded its range of acceptable nesting habitats in NY during this century. The classic study by Allen (1914) described this species as a bird of freshwater marshes and open swamps, with little mention of its use of other habitats for nesting. More-recent studies by Howard (1977) suggested that a movement of Red-winged Blackbird from lowland marshes into upland fields occurred in the wake of widespread clearing of land and draining of wetlands across the state for agricultural purposes, reflecting the adaptability of this species to landscapes dominated by humans. Its decline since 1966, according to BBS data, prob-ably is indicative of a response to the widespread, natural reforestation of upland sites (Caslick 1975; Stanton and Bills 1996) that appears to be affecting many bird species of successional grassland and shrubland habitats throughout NY.

Nonbreeding During winter, CBC data show this species to be most numerous in the western and southeastern parts of the state, with total counts of 1500–3000+ birds reported from the west and counts of 8000–11,000+ reported from the Lower Hudson CBC.

Premigratory flocking in late summer and fall is typical. At two tradi-tional fall roost sites at the north end of Cayuga L. in 1970 and 1971, Cutright (1973) reported a peak count of 764,870 in the Cayuga Marsh on 26 Aug 1970. The roosting flocks studied by Cutright also included Common Grackle, Brown-headed Cowbird, and European Starling, with a peak count for all four species of 971,805 birds in Cayuga Marsh on 14 August 1970, possibly the largest roosting aggregation of its kind ever reported from NY.

The species returns to the state starting mid-Feb.

Remarks Two subspecies occur in NY (AOU 1957; Parkes 1952). The common, widespread, breeding form is *phoeniceus*. A larger, Midwestern form, *arctolegus*, reported to occur regularly in winter as far east as central OH and WV, was added to the NY list on the basis of the seven specimens listed by Parkes (1952), who considered it a "casual migrant in western and central New York." No subsequent work has been reported on the status and relationships of these two subspecies in NY. In view of research by Ball et al. (1988), reporting that observed "morphological differentiation among redwing populations apparently has occurred in the context of relatively little phylogenetic separation," a careful review of the status of NY sub-species might prove interesting.

Charles R. Smith

Eastern Meadowlark   *Sturnella magna*

Range Nearctic and Neotropical, breeding from southwestern South Dakota and southern Canada east to central Nova Scotia and south to central Arizona and the Gulf states and from Mexico to northern South America. Winters nearly throughout the breeding range, generally withdrawing from the more northern portions.

Status Widespread breeder, sedentary and migratory. Common to locally abundant migrant. Fairly common inland and coastally in winter in the milder districts.

Breeding Meadowlarks nest on the ground in grassy fields and meadows, building a domed or arched nest. It is a common breeder throughout the state except in forested portions of the Adirondacks, Catskills, and Allegany Hills and in the metropolitan counties of the NYC region. Populations have declined in recent years throughout the Northeast, as suitable nesting habitat has been lost to urbanization, reforestation, and intensive agricultural practices. The mean number of birds per BBS route in NY dropped from 20.8 in 1966 to 4.6 in 1993.

Nonbreeding It is sometimes seen in impressive numbers on spring passage along the L. Ontario shore. It was formerly more numerous on the coastal salt meadows in winter than it is now. Smaller concentrations in recent years reflect the widespread decrease in populations. Migrants usually arrive in early to mid-Mar and depart by late Oct. Note that with a few exceptions, the maxima shown are before the 1980s.

Spring maxima: all Derby Hill, Oswego Co.: 550, 4 Apr 1969; 465, 27 Mar 1968; 350, 16 Apr 1960; 350, 24 Mar 1988. *Fall maxima:* 200 JBSP 20 Oct 1964; 200 Holland Patent, Oneida Co. 24 Oct 1967; 100 Millerton, Dutchess Co. 14 Nov 1992. *Winter maxima:* 375 Orient region, Suffolk Co. 25 Dec 1911; 50 Wellsville, Allegany Co. 20 Dec 1963; 48 Skaneateles CBC, Onondaga Co. 29 Dec 1974; 41 Catskill-Coxsackie CBC, Greene Co. 19 Dec 1989.
Wesley E. Lanyon

Western Meadowlark   *Sturnella neglecta*

Range Chiefly western Nearctic, breeding from central British Columbia east to northwestern Ohio, very rarely to western New York, and south to southern California and southwestern Tennessee. Winters in the southern portion of the breeding range and south to Mexico. Mostly sedentary.

Status Has bred at least twice. Rare to very rare spring and summer visitant in western NY, casual in the southeastern portion, and unreported on LI.

Breeding Where male Western Meadowlarks have been reported singing at the same localities for consecutive years, breeding is possible or even probable. Confirmation is difficult, however, and apparently there are only two such breeding records: (1) The first was between Manitou and Braddock Bay, Monroe Co. 1957 (Miller 1957). The male was seen in company with a presumed female giving the species-specific call note, and the pair was present throughout the summer. In late Aug one of the adults, identified by its call, was observed feeding young at the nest. (2) The second was near Bangall, Dutchess Co. 1962 (Jones 1963). A male Western Meadowlark with characteristic songs and calls paired with a female Eastern Meadowlark with calls of her species. Both adults and their five hybrid young, taken from the nest on 26 Jun, were placed in an aviary for subsequent analysis of morphology and vocalizations and were used in a captive breeding program to further study hybridization in these sibling species (Lanyon 1966, 1979).

Nonbreeding Observers must rely principally on distinctive vocalizations to separate it from its sibling species, the Eastern Meadowlark; hence, most reliable records are for the months of Apr through Jul. There is virtually no information on the presence of Western Meadowlark in the state during the nonbreeding months.

Remarks The Western Meadowlark, native of the grasslands of western North America, underwent a dramatic northeastward range expansion during the first half of the 1900s and became established as a breeding bird in southern ON (Lanyon 1995). Entry into NY presumably was via the Niagara Frontier corridor. The first definite record for NY was a specimen collected near North Hamlin, Monroe Co. 18 Apr 1948 (Klonick 1951). Since then there have been reports of singing males almost on an annual basis at localities throughout the Great Lakes Plain, mainly within the counties of Chautauqua, Erie, Niagara, Orleans, Monroe, Wayne, Oswego, and Onondaga. There are less frequent records for the lower Hudson Valley.

Singing males have been reported irregularly in MA, CT, and NJ, principally during the 1950s and 1960s, but such records have been scarce or absent since 1974. Atlas fieldwork in PA resulted in two Possible breeding records, one in 1985 and one in 1987.
Wesley E. Lanyon

Yellow-headed Blackbird *Xanthocephalus xanthocephalus*

Range Western Nearctic, breeding from British Columbia and central Washington east to extreme southern Ontario and south, in the east to northern Texas and northwestern Indiana and Ohio. Winters from central

California and central Texas south to Mexico. Casual east to the Atlantic Coast from Nova Scotia to Florida.

Status Rare but increasingly regular vagrant, occurring in all seasons.

Occurrence Since Bull (1974) reported "at least two dozen occurrences of this very striking and conspicuous species" and added two more through 1975, another 80 observations have been reported from every section of the state and every month of the year. Yellow-headed Blackbird was recorded in all but one year between 1976 and 1994; the maximum occurred in 1984, when a statewide total of 10 appeared in seven of the Regions.

Contrary to Bull's half upstate–half coastal summary, the newer records are less than a quarter coastal, with almost half coming from areas along L. Ontario, not unexpected given the western range of this species. The fewest records (four) came from the nine northernmost counties.

Of those individuals, 42% occurred during spring migration and 21% during fall. Whereas Bull reported "the only known winter report," a full quarter of the more recent sightings were in winter. Only 12% were observed during the summer months.

As might be expected, most were adult males, whose striking coloration made them conspicuous even when flying with other blackbirds. Yet the ratio of males to females (of those identified to sex) was only 14:9. Pairs were observed in Monroe Co. in successive years: in Chili, 10 and 22 Jan 1987 (KB 27:98), and in Irondequoit, Jan 1988 during a storm (KB 28:106). In two other instances a male and a female were seen in the same area within a short time period: a female 5 Jun and a male 15 Jun 1985 in Ellisburg, Jefferson Co. (KB 35:281); a female 7 Apr and a male 15 Apr 1986 near Braddock Bay, Monroe Co. (KB 36:147). These events, rare though they are, suggest the possibility of NY breeding in the foreseeable future.

Gerry Rising

Rusty Blackbird   *Euphagus carolinus*

Range Nearctic, breeding in northern Alaska and northern Canada to Newfoundland and south to central Manitoba, southern Ontario, and the northern parts of New York and New England (chiefly in the mountains). Winters from southern North Dakota, southern Michigan, and southeastern New York south to Florida.

Status Uncommon breeder in Adirondacks, but evidently increasing. Very common to locally very abundant migrant in western NY; much less numerous eastward and relatively uncommon in southeastern portions. Rare and local but regular in winter, chiefly near the coast.

Breeding This blackbird reaches the southern limits of its breeding range in the Adirondacks, where it nests in or near bog forest, alder and willow thickets, beaver ponds with standing dead timber, and wooded shores of lakes. It was recorded in 151 Atlas blocks and was Confirmed in 51, but much apparently suitable habitat is as yet unoccupied by this species. Probable breeding was reported from Central Tug Hill. The apparent recent extension of NY distribution appears to be due to both the intensive effort of Atlas work and the reestablishment of the beaver population, which creates ideal nesting habitat.

Nonbreeding It is generally found in wooded swamps and other wetlands on migration and in wintering areas, but occasionally visits feeders in winter. Fall migration is between early Sep and mid-Dec. It is irregular and uncommon on upstate CBCs, but 1–300 were reported on various coastal counts from 1969 to 1974. It winters irregularly in flocks of 10–50 in the lower Hudson Valley and on the coast. Increasing numbers upstate throughout the winter obscure the distinction between migrants and wintering birds (KB 45:111). Spring migrants usually arrive after early Feb, and fall migrants depart by mid-Dec. It is rare before mid-Sep and after mid-May.

    Spring maxima: 1000 Clay Swamp, Onondaga Co. 23 Apr 1959; 500 Saratoga L., Saratoga Co. 24 Apr 1993. *Fall maxima:* 10,000 Hague, Warren Co. 31 Oct–4 Nov 1990; 2078 BOS Count 13 Oct 1990; 500 Black R. plains, Lewis Co. 26 Oct 1995. *Winter maxima:* 58 Patterson Swamp, Putnam Co. 1 Jan 1992 (KB 42:124); 30 Mendon Ponds, Monroe Co. 1 Jan 1992.

Remarks There are two subspecies recognized, the nominate *carolinus,* which breeds in NY, and *nigrans,* which breeds in NF, the Magdalen Islands, and NS. According to Parkes (1952), fall adult males of *nigrans* are identified by "the very dark chocolate brown feather edging, especially on the dorsum." He suggested that it is probably not uncommon as a migrant along the coast, but he had identified only one NY specimen, from Brooklyn, Nov 1861 (AMNH 440946).
Kenneth L. Crowell

Brewer's Blackbird   *Euphagus cyanocephalus*

Range Chiefly western Nearctic, breeding from central British Columbia to western Ontario and south to southern California east to northwestern Indiana. In migration and winter, east to western North Carolina and south to central Mexico. Vagrant to New York and Massachusetts.

Status Uncommon vagrant, especially inland, formerly very rare. Very rare in winter and casual in summer.

Occurrence It is found in open country, particularly pastures, but also grassy areas such as sod farms and lawns. There are several records at feeding stations. The one specimen is a male collected in Hamburg, Erie Co. 14 Dec 1966 BMS 5077. Only six other records were mentioned by Bull (1974). Since then there have been more than 60 reports, with at least a dozen accepted by NYSARC. This change in status coincides with the eastward expansion of its breeding range in ON. It has been found in fall most frequently in Oct and Nov, with about half the reports from the southeast, including LI.

In spring it is almost strictly an inland migrant, with western regions garnering most of the records. Mar and, particularly, Apr are the most frequent months of occurrence. One pasture site in Hamlin, Monroe Co. has attracted this species almost yearly since 1981, and it is from this site that our only summer reports come: two, 3 Jun 1983; one, 4 Jun 1983 (KB 33:268); one, 14 Aug 1984 (KB 34:244); one, 14 Jun and two, 1–12 Jul 1992 (KB 42:240). These reports and the fact that it has bred in ON within 75 mi of Buffalo (Mitchell and Andrle 1970) suggest possible breeding in NY.

In winter it has been recorded in several regions. The most northerly were at Adirondack feeders: Essex 6–14 Dec 1984; Tupper L., Franklin Co. 7–16 Jan 1993.

Spring maxima: all from the Hamlin, Monroe Co. site: 2–23 birds, 2–30 Apr 1981, especially notable as the previous maximum was only 2; 24 birds, 21 Apr 1982; 2–22 birds, 16 Mar–30 Apr 1983. Away from western NY the maximum is only three. *Fall maxima:* 13 Big Flats, Chemung Co. 14 Nov 1995 (KB 46:54), unprecedented and the only count over two, submitted to NYSARC. *Extreme dates:* 8 Oct (coastal); 10 May and 11 Oct (inland). There are several sightings after 10 May at the Hamlin site. William C. D'Anna

Common Grackle   *Quiscalus quiscula*

Range Nearctic, breeding in southern Canada from British Columbia to southwestern Newfoundland and south, in the east to central Texas and southern Florida. Winters in southern portions of its range north to southern Minnesota, southern Ontario, and southern New England; casually farther north.

Status Common to very common breeder throughout, rare or absent only at high elevations and in heavy forest. Common to very abundant migrant, especially upstate. Increasing throughout in winter.

Breeding It is a widespread breeder in all localities but absent from the higher peaks of the Adirondacks and Catskills and uncommon in heavily forested areas, where it is more or less restricted to openings. This species was Confirmed in the largest cities as well as in smaller towns and in suburban and rural areas throughout.

Nonbreeding Wandering postbreeding flocks are widely noted in early and midsummer, often entering woodlands and urban areas, where they do not breed. These coalesce into much larger agglomerations in late summer and fall, moving south in large numbers. Huge flocks are regularly reported at inland hawkwatches and along the Great Lakes in both spring and fall migration, with counts not uncommonly in the tens of thousands. Increasing numbers are present through the winter with the largest counts at or near the coast.

Maxima: Maxima reported by Bull (1974) were in the range of 75,000–100,000 in the 1960s. More-recent maxima include up to 200,000 Derby Hill, Oswego Co. 19–20 Mar 1993; 25,000 birds every five minutes, with a total of more than 175,000 Cayuga L., Tompkins Co. 11 Oct 1991; "huge icterid flights" along L. Ontario, spring 1977, with 100,000 on 6 Apr and hundreds still passing 27 May. *Winter maxima:* Bull reported 200+ on the Northern Nassau CBC 29 Dec 1968 and 9 each at Buffalo, Erie Co. and Watkins Glen, Schuyler Co. in late Dec 1968. Since then, the upstate numbers have consistently been surpassed: 50 Union Springs, Cayuga Co. 3 Jan 1995; 32 Plattsburgh, Clinton Co. CBC 20 Dec 1992; up to 22 Oneida, Madison Co. 22 Dec 1990. Downstate, Region 10 high counts include: 4500+ Bronx-Westchester CBC 1982; 2000+ Orient, Suffolk Co. CBC 1984; and winter roosts of 1000–3000 in mixed flocks in eastern Suffolk Co. 1985–1995. Birds recorded in late Dec and early Jan may be late fall lingerers, but the recent appearance of large numbers of mixed blackbirds in Suffolk Co. represents overwintering flocks of resident birds.

Remarks (Based on personal observations as well as discussions with L. Penny and L. Miller of the East Hampton Department of Environmental Resources, P. Stoutenberg, and J. Ash.) Two subspecies, *versicolor* and *stonei*, occur in NY. For a period of four years, they were regarded as separate species, known as Bronzed and Purple, respectively, until the AOU Check-list Committee, in 1948, reversed its 1944 decision. The NYC area is, or was, on the line of hybridization. *Versicolor* is the breeding bird in most of the state, and the majority of migratory flocks that occur throughout belong to this subspecies. *Stonei* breeds on LI, in NYC and vicinity, and in the lower Hudson Valley. Intermediates occur (or have occurred in the past) in the Hudson Valley north to Troy, Rensselaer Co., in the interior from the Delaware and Susquehanna valleys north to Tompkins and Monroe counties, and on eastern LI, although the birds now breeding in the latter location appear to be largely *stonei*. Some of these birds show strong bronzy tints on their body plumage in good light, possibly repre-

senting some lingering genetic influence of *versicolor*. This breeding population and most wintering birds are quite distinct from the migratory flocks,
which are dominated by pure *versicolor*. The recent appearance of winter
flocks on eastern LI, consisting largely of *stonei* with Red-winged Blackbirds
and Brown-headed Cowbirds, also seems to be connected with this shift in
breeding range as "purple" grackles appear to be more sedentary than
"bronzed." A review of the status of these taxa is needed; the line between
the breeding populations appears to have moved farther north, with migratory *versicolor* traveling from wintering to breeding grounds by leapfrogging
over the weakly migratory *stonei*.

That the relative distribution of these forms of *Q. quiscala* has been
undergoing dynamic change is supported by the situation in western PA,
where the "purple" grackle was historically no more than accidental (Todd
1940). Among specimens salvaged from large flocks of poisoned grackles in
the Pittsburgh area during the fall migrations of 1974 and 1984, individual
birds ranged from typical *versicolor* to typical *stonei*, with the majority
showing various degrees of intermediacy (K. C. Parkes, pers. comm.).
Eric Salzman

Boat-tailed Grackle *Quiscalus major*

Range Nearctic, resident along the Atlantic Coast from New York south to
Florida and along the Gulf Coast to southeastern Texas.

Status Breeds in coastal marshes on LI and SI, where it is resident most of
the year; rare to very rare anywhere else.

Breeding This species began nesting on the NJ shore of Delaware Bay in
1952, but it was casual in NY well into the 1970s. By the mid-1970s,
however, there was a marked increase in sightings in and around JBWR and
in Hempstead, Nassau Co. A fully grown immature was seen on Pearsall's
Hassock, southeast of Hewlett Bay, Nassau Co. 29 Jun 1979; adult females
with begging young were seen in 1981 in Hewlett Bay 23 Jun and Jamaica
bay 18 Jul; and two nests were found on 31 May 1982 at Pearsall's
Hassock (Davis 1981a; Gochfeld and Burger 1981; Zarudsky and Miller
1983). It has also been nesting at Great Kills, Richmond Co. since at least
1990 (KB 40:207). Since then it has established itself as far east as
Shinnecock Inlet, Suffolk Co., with breeding in that area since at least 1994
(Salzman 1995).

Nonbreeding It is increasingly observed on the South Shore of LI east to
East Hampton and on the Atlantic coast of SI. Mixed flocks of foraging
adults and juveniles tend to remain on or near the breeding grounds
throughout most of the year, moving out only in extremely adverse weather
conditions (pers. obs.; KB Region 10 reports 1971–1995). The few pub-

lished sightings away from the immediate Atlantic Coast include: Oakland L., Queens Co. (KB 30:131) and Van Cortlandt Park, Bronx Co. (KB 32:224). There are also two upstate records: a male photographed at Greece, Monroe Co 29–30 Oct 1980 (Spahn) (NYSARC 1981); one at Braddock Bay, Monroe Co. 19 Sep 1981 was apparently not submitted to NYSARC (Anonymous 1985a); otherwise it is unreported away from NYC and LI.

Remarks It has been reported along the CT shore since 1985 (Zeranski and Baptist 1990); nesting was attempted in 1995. It was also reported in 1985 and 1986 in RI and MA (Veit and Petersen 1993).
Eric Salzman

Brown-headed Cowbird   *Molothrus ater*

Range Nearctic, breeding widely from southern Alaska to southern Newfoundland and south to the Gulf states and northern Mexico. Winters, in the east, from the southern Great Lakes region and southern New England south to Florida, the Gulf Coast, and southern Mexico.

Status Widespread common breeder. Common to very abundant migrant; regular winter visitor.

Breeding The sight of a harried warbler struggling to feed a young cowbird twice its size has become all too familiar and ominous. At least 77 species in NY, mainly passerines, are parasitized by cowbirds, which lay their eggs in other birds' nests and let the host parents raise the young (Atlas 1988). Bull (1974) listed Yellow Warbler, Red-eyed Vireo, and Song Sparrow as the most frequent victims.

Cowbirds favor open areas. BBS data suggest that their numbers may be declining somewhat, perhaps as abandoned farmland reverts to forest. Nonetheless, cowbirds continue to exact a costly toll on other species. Development continues to fragment forests into smaller woodlots. This fragmentation allows cowbirds to penetrate these areas and find nests of woodland species that have not developed the defense strategies used by edge and field species.

In some areas, host species raise as many or more cowbirds as they do their own young. Parasitism by cowbirds compounds the problems faced by Neotropical migrants, already hard pressed by loss of habitat here and on their Central and South American wintering grounds.

The impact of this species was illustrated in a study of Eastern Phoebes that nested in ammunition storage structures at Seneca Army Depot, Seneca Co. (Jones 1975). Cowbirds caused half of all nesting losses by interfering with one-third of nests. Among 20 parasitized nesting pairs, 27 phoebe young were lost to produce 15 cowbirds. "Most bird lovers," the author noted, "wouldn't think that is much of a trade."

Nonbreeding Depending on the severity of winter, cowbirds can over-winter in at least small numbers throughout NY, often coming to feeders, even in the heart of the Adirondacks. In spring, migrants begin to appear in late Feb or early Mar, with exceptional counts at roosts or during heavy flights, usually in conjunction with other blackbirds. A staggering 175,000 was estimated in a roost of nearly 2.5 million blackbirds at Gates, Monroe Co. 28 Mar 1978 (KB 28:172). Spring flights along the L. Ontario shore-line at Derby Hill, Oswego Co. include 90,000 on 19–20 Mar 1995 (KB 45:208) and 50,000 on 6 Apr 1978 (KB 28:185). An estimated 70,000 were at a roost in Clay Swamp, Onondaga Co. 12 Oct 1960; 1400 spent the 1964–1965 winter at a roost in Syracuse.

Remarks Eradication of cowbirds may be necessary to protect endangered host species with limited geographical range, much as was done to protect Kirtland's Warbler *(Dendroica kirtlandii)* on its breeding grounds in MI. However, Robinson (1995) argued against mass eradication, noting that it does not address the underlying problem of habitat fragmentation. Restoration and maintenance of large forest tracts of 50,000 acres or more, he contended, would provide sufficient surplus young to compensate for losses to cowbirds in other areas.

Robert E. Marcotte

Orchard Oriole *Icterus spurius*

Range Primarily eastern and central Nearctic, breeding from southeastern Saskatchewan to southern Ontario, central New York, and northern Massachusetts south to northern Florida, the Gulf states, western Texas, and northeastern Mexico. Winters from southern Mexico to northern South America.

Status Uncommon local breeder, absent from areas over 2500 ft elevation. Uncommon migrant.

Breeding Although the Orchard Oriole was reported as numerous and widespread in southeastern NY in the nineteenth century, a decline began about 1920 that progressed for 50 years. A noticeable increase throughout the Northeast became evident in the 1970s. The Atlas reported it in 224 (4%) blocks, half located in the southeast. Most others were in the Finger Lakes region, near the mid-Hudson, and along the shores of the Great Lakes. The Atlas map is almost blank above the Mohawk Valley except for a few blocks on the eastern border along L. Champlain. Since that project, the first confirmed Region 6 breeding record was established with a nest found at the Point Peninsula of Chaumont Bay, Jefferson Co. in 1994 and again in 1995 (KB 44:326 and 45:313).

Nonbreeding Orchard Orioles migrate to NY from southern Mexico and northwestern South America, and a few pass through to New England and southern ON. The total number of individual birds (including young) reported each year in Kingbird Region accounts peaked in the early 1980s at 48; by 1995 only a third that number were noted.

Western NY May census records offer additional evidence of decline with annual count data for each decade: 1950s, 32 maximum and 9 average; 1960s, 16 and 5; 1970s, 15 and 3; 1980s, 7 and 1; 1990s, 6 and 2 (Rising 1995).

The average arrival date in the south is 8 May, and in more-northern sections 5–10 days later. There were five Apr records downstate and an equal number upstate during 1975–1995; the earliest was 20 Apr in Dutchess Co. (KB 30:192). There was one 20 Apr coastal record before 1975.

Immediately after nesting, this species joins the Yellow Warbler in their headstart southward. From 1975 to 1995, 68 late dates for Kingbird Regions averaged 4 Jul. Among them were only four downstate and nine upstate after 31 Jul. Three of them, however, were well into Sep. Two were downstate: JBSP 19 Sep 1982; Clove Lake Park, Richmond Co. 28 Sep 1992. The other was at Ghent, Columbia Co. 12 Sep 1981.

Unlike its congener, the Baltimore Oriole, this species has never been recorded in NY between Oct and mid-Apr.

Remarks Thinking of the Orchard Oriole as a southern species does not convey the whole story. Flood (in Cadman et al. 1987) pointed out that the center of its range "lies in the Mississippi River valley in the central US." That western influence helps explain why this species' breeding density in lower Canada north of L. Erie is greater than in nearby NY.
Gerry Rising

Baltimore Oriole

Icterus galbula

Range Eastern Nearctic, breeding from central Alberta to Nova Scotia and south, from the western edge of the Great Plains to the southern United States. Winters chiefly from Mexico to northern South America, more rarely in the southern states, very rarely but regularly north to Massachusetts.

Status Widespread common breeder and common to occasionally abundant migrant. Rare but regular in winter, especially near the coast.

Breeding It breeds generally throughout the state but is absent from large portions of the Adirondacks and the Tug Hill Plateau. Especially numerous in lowland regions and valleys, it avoids only those places with unbroken forest, high elevation, and urban areas. It usually nests in tall trees along roads and waterways, in orchards, or in scattered trees in fields, towns, parks, and woodland edges (Atlas 1988). It has lost its favorite nesting tree, large American elms, to Dutch elm disease but readily uses other species. NY BBS 1980–1994 data showed a 1.5% annual drop.

Nonbreeding It arrives during the last week of Apr or first week of May. Most depart by mid-Sep. The largest numbers are found along the Great Lakes in spring and in coastal areas during fall. It is unusual among our breeding species in that it is one of the earliest to depart in fall and yet is now recorded annually in winter, when it is usually found at feeders, more frequently on LI than elsewhere. It has been recorded in winter from every Region of the state.

Spring maxima: Derby Hill, Oswego Co.: 860, 14 May 1976; 550, 16 May 1966; 365, 12 May 1982. Away from the Great Lakes: 100 Montour Falls, Schuyler Co. 28 May 1994; 93 netted and banded, RMSP 8 May 1970. *Fall maxima:* about 500 in one hour, JBSP 1 Sep 1985; 300 in two hours, Far Rockaway, Queens Co. 10 Sep 1969. *Winter maxima:* 9 at an East Meadow, Nassau Co. feeder Dec 1973–Jan 1974 (Bull 1976) was unprecedented.

Remarks An interesting article by Parkes (1993) discussed erythrism in the Baltimore Oriole. Erythrism is "the abnormal occurrence of red, mostly confined to originally yellow or orange feathers, occasionally produced by abnormal food (Newton and Gadow 1896)." There are only four records in the Northeast of erythristic Baltimore Oriole with locality known; three were collected on LI, and the other was netted and banded on nearby Block I., RI. This unique and localized phenomenon caused Parkes to speculate that these four individuals were migrants that had all originated from the same area where a particular red-pigmented food was available.
William C. D'Anna

Bullock's Oriole *Icterus bullockii*

Range Western Nearctic, breeding from southern British Columbia east to the western edge of the Great Plains and south, east of the coastal areas, to northern Mexico and southern Texas. Winters in coastal California and south through western Mexico to Costa Rica, with small numbers in the Gulf Coast area east to southern Florida. Vagrant in northeastern North America.

Status Very rare vagrant in the coastal regions, casual inland.

Occurrence There are three substantiated records. An immature male at an Eastport, Suffolk Co. feeder 12 Dec 1963–4 Mar 1964 was banded and photographed by Wilcox. The color photos were compared with skins at the AMNH. An adult male at a feeder in Woodmere, Nassau Co. early Jan–2 Apr 1966 was photographed by Dignan; photos in AMNH. An immature female netted at Fire I. Lighthouse, Suffolk Co. by Davis, 30 Nov 1969, now AMNH 793547, was identified as *bullockii*, although the presence of some *galbula* alleles could not be entirely ruled out (Buckley 1974). There are several undocumented reports from LI and the vicinity of NYC and two from the L. Ontario shoreline. The coastal sightings range from 6 Oct to 24 Jan. The two inland reports occurred 7–9 May (KB 29:147) and 21 Aug (KB 37:223); the latter is a very unusual date. Considering the possibility of hybrids *(I. bullockii × I. galbula)*, all undocumented reports should be regarded with caution.

Remarks The taxonomic status of Bullock's Oriole and Baltimore Oriole has been unclear for some time. The fifth edition of the AOU Check-list (1957) carried both species. The sixth edition (1983) lumped them under the name Northern Oriole *(I. galbula)*. The Fortieth Supplement to the AOU Check-list (1995) separated them again.
William C. D'Anna

FRINGILLINE AND CARDUELINE FINCHES—FRINGILLIDAE

Brambling   *Fringilla montifringilla*

Range Palearctic, breeding in northern Eurasia. Winters from the British Isles and the southern edge of its breeding range south to northern Africa and from the Middle East to Japan. Vagrant in North America but more regular in the Aleutian Islands and western Alaska.

Status Accidental.

Occurrence NYSARC (1985) accepted the photographed record from Pleasant Valley, Dutchess Co. 13–27 Mar 1984 (KB 34:214) as the first for NY. Documentation for a 1962 report from Tupper Lake, Franklin Co. (AFN 16:393) has been lost. A male seen at JFK Airport, Queens Co. 11 Feb 1965 was believed to have been an escape from an air shipment.

Remarks Leck (1984) noted 1958 and 1965 NJ records; the 1958 one was the first for eastern North America. Veit and Petersen (1993) listed three MA records: winter of 1961–1962, 1962, and 1979. There are no CT records, and there is a single accepted record in PA (Santner et al. 1992). Bull (1974) considered all Northeast records to be suspect, including the 1958 NJ specimen, citing the possibilities of escaped cage birds or assisted ship passage.
Stanley R. Lincoln

Pine Grosbeak *Pinicola enucleator*

Range Holarctic, breeding in North America from western Alaska to northern Labrador and south, in the east to southern Ontario and southern Quebec; sporadically to northern New England. Wanders south during irruptions, in the east to the Carolinas.

Status Irregular, rare to very common winter visitant.

Occurrence The irruptions of this northern finch are unpredictable, yet eagerly anticipated by birders. Usually it is the rarest of all "winter finches" in NY except for Hoary Redpoll. During major irruptions, however, it can be among the most numerous; its movements do not necessarily correspond with those of other irruptive species.

The "feast or famine" nature of this species' visits is reflected in the statewide total counts on NY CBCs from 1960 to 1989. There were 1842 recorded on counts during the winter of 1961–1962, 641 in 1965–1966, 1805 in 1968–1969, 2003 in 1972–1973, 695 in 1977–1978, 897 in 1980–1981, 1367 in 1981–1982, and 1493 in 1985–1986. The statewide CBC tally was fewer than 210 for 22 other years, including fewer than 20 for 10 of those years. It is usually found in small groups, occasionally in flocks of 40 or more, and occasionally is reported at feeders.

Maxima: 302 Plattsburgh CBC, Clinton Co. 17 Dec 1995; 269 Massena CBC, St. Lawrence Co. Dec 1985; 200 Indian L., Hamilton Co. 3 Feb 1979. *Extreme dates:* 15 Sep (inland) and 8 Oct (coastal); 18 May (inland) and 25 Apr (coastal). This late coastal date is made more remarkable by the fact that this species was found only very rarely in coastal areas through 1982, and it has not been reported there since. It is generally rare before Nov and after Mar. No summer occurrences have been substantiated, although it has been known to breed in ME and northern NH.

Remarks There are a dozen or so subspecies, two of which occur in NY. They are *eschatosus* and the larger *leucura*; they are not separable in the field. *Eschatosus* breeds as far south as central ME and northern NH; *leucura* breeds farther north. As expected, examination of museum skins

showed the majority to be *eschatosus,* no doubt mirroring the actual distribution of our visitants (Bull 1974).
Robert E. Marcotte

Purple Finch   *Carpodacus purpureus*

Range Nearctic, breeding from northern British Columbia east to Newfoundland and south, in the east to central Minnesota and Wisconsin, southern Michigan, northern Ohio, West Virginia, Pennsylvania, and southeastern New York. Winters in the southern portion of its range south to Arizona, Texas, and Florida.

Status A widespread and common breeder upstate, especially at higher elevations, but uncommon downstate and rare on LI. Erratic and unpredictable migrant and nomadic winter visitant, common to abundant in fall on the coast and sometimes numerous in the interior. Usually scarce in winter, except in "winter finch" irruption years.

Breeding The Atlas showed Confirmed breeding in 691 blocks (22%) out of 3148 in which it was recorded. It favors cool, forested, high elevations, with the key habitat requirement being the presence of coniferous trees. Thus, it breeds most commonly in the Adirondacks, the Catskills, and the Appalachian Plateau. Breeding occurs in many other sites where coniferous trees and cool summers obtain. It is uncommon in the lower river valleys, the Great Lakes Plain, and most notably, downstate below its southern breeding limit through Sullivan, Ulster, and Dutchess counties. BBS data showed a wide tongue of nonbreeding in central NY, from the PA border to L. Ontario (Price et al. 1995), whereas Atlas fieldwork showed otherwise. This discrepancy is probably due to the more intensive searching done by Atlas observers. It is rare in the NYC area and on much of LI, although some breeding activity has been noted on the eastern end (Atlas 1988). An analysis of BBS 1980–1994 data showed that the NY population has been decreasing by 1.2% per year (Peterjohn 1995).

Nonbreeding Fall migration starts in Sep and peaks in Oct, but some birds persist into early winter. Spring migrants usually arrive in Mar, peaking in Apr. Analysis of CBC 1967–1994 data showed that it has been slightly decreasing overall, with peak years 1976–1977, 1982–1983, and 1992–1993. Those data also showed the erratic nature of the Purple Finch in winter, with many counts reporting none one year and several dozen the next; during peak years, more counts report this species. In the peak 1982–1983 count, only 5 out of 63 counts reported none; the median was 22. In 1981–1982, a more typical year, 20 out of 62 counts reported none; the median was 3.

Spring maxima: 8200 Derby Hill, Oswego Co. 18 Apr 1985 (Scheider and Crumb 1985). *Fall maxima:* 400 Larchmont, Westchester Co. 3–4 Nov 1973. *CBC maxima:* 1033 Saranac L., Essex-Franklin Co. 2 Jan 1977; 610 Elizabethtown, Essex Co. 26 Dec 1976.

Remarks Problems in differentiating Purple Finch from its congener House Finch in the early years of the latter's expansion may be reflected in some of the data (Mundinger and Hope 1982). The Purple Finch and House Finch may compete during the warmer seasons but not as much in the winter, when the Purple Finch migrates or becomes nomadic. Habitat partitioning may be occurring as a result of their interactions. Although the House Finch also competes with the House Sparrow, there is no competition between the Purple Finch and the House Sparrow (Wootton 1987). Donald A. Windsor

House Finch *Carpodacus mexicanus*

Range Nearctic, originally breeding from British Columbia and Idaho east to Kansas and south to Texas and central Mexico. Since introduction on Long Island in the 1940s, it has spread throughout most of the eastern United States and southern Canada.

Status Introduced, abundant resident, except in heavily forested portions. Its population is increasing throughout the state but may be leveling off.

Breeding The Atlas showed Confirmed breeding in 1629 blocks (57%) out of 2871 in which it was recorded. Breeding was not Confirmed in much of the North Country or in many areas in the western and Catskill regions (Atlas 1988). An analysis of BBS 1966–1994 data showed that the NY population is increasing but not as much as formerly. From 1966 to 1979 it was increasing by an average of 50.8% per year. From 1980 to 1994 that average had dropped to 12.3% (Peterjohn 1995).

Nonbreeding Analysis of CBC 1975–1994 data showed that the NY population had been progressively increasing, but it was almost level for the last four counts. On the 1974–1975 CBC, no House Finches were reported on half (27) of the 52 counts. The 1985–1986 CBC was the first to report House Finch on all of the 64 counts in the state. Burtt's monthly (Oct–May) feeder surveys in the *Syracuse Herald American* showed a rapid increase of House Finch from about 1980 to 1983, with a peak during the 1988–1989 season and then a decline with a leveling off since.

Winter maxima: 2022 Syracuse, Onondaga Co. CBC 20 Dec 1986; 2169 per 100 feeders in the Syracuse area 4–10 Jan 1987.

Remarks During the past half-century, the House Finch has successfully established itself virtually all over NY. First released on LI in 1940, these illegally captured birds, which were sold as "California Linnets," spread to the mainland and then up the Hudson Valley. Radiating outward in a "jump-dispersal" mechanism (Mundinger and Hope 1982), they then spread west, simultaneously across the Great Lakes Plain and the Appalachian Plateau. By 1965 they were in Buffalo. Now their population growth finally seems to be stabilizing, although they still seem to be moving into new locations in the higher elevations.

The first sight record was at JBSP 11 Apr 1941, and the first breeding record was in May 1943 at Babylon, Suffolk Co., about 2 mi north (Elliott and Arbib 1953).

Early recognition was hampered because the House Finch was not listed in Peterson's eastern field guide before the 1980 fourth edition. Many birders, especially feeder watchers, were still using older editions and were reporting Purple Finch instead (Cant 1962), much to the discomfort of CBC compilers. Serious birders, however, recognized the differences early and documented the spread. The pivotal paper by Elliott and Arbib (1953) established a foundation for careful tallies. Bull (1964) provided a comparative diagnosis, which contrasted the House Finch with the Purple Finch. A concise chronicle by Wilkins (1988) provided a neat one-page history up to 1987. Perhaps the most readily available single-source, quantitative documentation of the House Finch's spread across NY lies in the CBC data, even though they tend to lag behind other observations by several years. The first report was on the Southern Nassau Co. CBC in 1947 (AFN 2:41). The next year that count reported 104, but it was still alone. In 1949 the Western LI count reported three as Southern Nassau went down to 33. In 1952, the Port Chester, Westchester Co. count, on the CT border, joined in by reporting 30. From then on the number of counts reporting House Finch steadily increased. It took six years to achieve 10% of NY counts reporting the species, an additional 23 years to reach 50% (CBC 1975), and 14 more years to attain 100% (CBC 1989). The CBCs at Old Forge, Herkimer Co. and Elizabethtown, Essex Co. were the holdouts, reporting their first House Finches in 1984 and 1985, respectively. One can see by just looking at the first reports on the CBCs that the birds went up the Hudson R. corridor and then turned west across the entire stretch, virtually simultaneously across the Great Lakes Plain and the Appalachian Plateau. The sharp contrast between CBC and other reports deserves critical attention. The first record in Buffalo was in 1965, with confirmed breeding in 1971, whereas the first report on a Buffalo CBC was in 1977. Likewise, the first record in Rochester was in 1956, with confirmed breeding in 1971; the first report on the CBC was in 1975. For a feeder bird, this lag remains puzzling, especially since there is an apparent bias on CBCs toward feeder birds (Butcher and Dunn 1995).

The rise of the House Finch did not go unnoticed in the Kingbird

Regional Reports. In the mid to late 1970s it was listed in some regions with the rarities (KB 25:164). Many reports for the next decade chronicled first appearances in various places at various seasons. Reference to it as a "pest" began to sprinkle reports through the 1980s (KB 33:56; 36:230). The 1990s brought appraisals of its decline (KB 43:72).

The spread of the House Finch occurred by two mechanisms: diffusion, or the gradual outward enlargement of its residence areas, and jump-dispersals, flying over undesirable habitat to start diffusing colonies elsewhere (Mundinger and Hope 1982). In its early dispersion over the Northeast, coastlines and rivers were followed, probably because of human settlements along those areas. Now that the House Finch has saturated NY, its population is stabilizing.

NY habitat is not itself stable. There is a dynamic tension between abandoned farms reverting to forests and deforestation to clear space for human housing and commercial developments. Bird feeders surely play a key role, perhaps more so than with any other bird, because virtually any residential feeder offering black sunflower seeds will bring in House Finches. Their constant presence at the feeders further encourages the owners to keep their feeders stocked, a mutual reward system that is truly win-win. The upshot seems to have been: the more humans, the more House Finches. Other stabilizing factors, such as diseases, are beginning to exert themselves. An outbreak of a fatal conjunctivitis, caused by *Mycoplasma gallicepticum*, in NY and other eastern states appeared, by 1996, to be having a significant impact on populations. Because the feeder is an accommodating place to spread disease, this key to the House Finch's success may also be pivotal in its population control.

As the House Finch increased, the House Sparrow decreased and a causal relationship has been proposed (see the House Sparrow account). Perhaps the decrease of the House Sparrow, for other reasons, enabled the House Finch to move into the human habitation niche. Moreover, the House Sparrow decline was already under way before the House Finch arrived, although in states with both species the House Sparrow decline has been steeper (Kricher 1983). Although they have been living together for about a century out West, their competitive interactions have yet to play out here in the East. The House Finch's interactions with its congener the Purple Finch are even less understandable than are those with the House Sparrow, because most Purple Finches migrate south for the winter and are not apt to be near human dwellings. However, some decline in the summer population of Purple Finch has been noted since the House Finch was introduced (Wootton 1987). Along an urban-suburban gradient, the House Sparrow seems to have chosen the urban and the House Finch the suburban habitat (Cody 1974).

Even though the House Finch is so common that many birders tend to ignore it, its population dynamics in the coming years should make it one of the most fascinating of all birds to watch. It is now reported in every state except Alaska. It is back in touch with its Western forebears. Donald A. Windsor

Red Crossbill   *Loxia curvirostra*

Range Holarctic, breeding, in North America, from southern Alaska to Newfoundland, south widely and irregularly throughout the United States and the highlands of Mexico and Middle America; in the east to New York and Massachusetts and in the mountains to northern Georgia. Wanders erratically south to the southeastern United States, mainly during winter.

Status Uncommon breeder and irregular resident. Occurs as part of nomadic movements, chiefly as a winter visitant, but recorded in all months of the year.

Breeding Breeding occurs in forests that have ripe conifer cones, predominantly in an extended season between Jan and Aug. Virtually all species of conifers native to NY are used, but different conifers attract different forms of the Red Crossbill. Early-nesting birds (Jan–Apr) use open, brown cones that ripened the previous summer. Late-summer nests are associated with new green cones that begin to open during the period of nestling development. Historically, most nesting records were immediately after large winter influxes, with egg dates around Mar–Apr. The Atlas map may not be truly representative, because the last year of the fieldwork coincided with a major irruption, which started in the winter of 1984. Like White-winged Crossbill breeding, most breeding takes place in the Adirondacks and on the Appalachian Plateau east of the Finger Lakes, with additional breeding Confirmed during the Atlas period in Sullivan and Suffolk counties. Historically, the first Suffolk Co. nesting was recorded in 1883 (Atlas 1988). Summer breeding probably occurs regularly, but these events are less conspicuous than those in winter.

Before the massive harvest of conifers in the late nineteenth and early twentieth centuries, Red Crossbills must have been common, yet ephemeral, breeders throughout NY in appropriate habitat (Dickerman 1987). Recent maturing of second-growth conifers may allow more frequent breeding in many areas, including the Adirondacks and the Alleghany Plateau (Messineo 1985).

Nonbreeding The extended breeding season makes the separation of breeding and nonbreeding observations difficult. Birds seen in Sep–Dec are generally nonbreeders, but crossbills seen at other times may be breeding.

Most Red Crossbills seen on CBCs are probably nonbreeders and may be the result of winter irruptions. Reasons for these irregular invasions are not certain, but cone crop failures in areas of high crossbill abundance in the northern Rocky Mountains and Pacific Northwest may impel the birds to move south and east. Numbers seen on counts fluctuate dramatically from year to year, and it is not unusual for fewer than 100 birds to be recorded on combined counts for the entire state. For all counts since 1960, including the major flight years of 1964–1965, 1973–1974, and 1984–1985, fewer than half of all count areas reported the Red Crossbill. Winter irruptions, such as the ones documented for 1960–1961 and 1984–1985, occurred after the count period and were therefore not recorded on CBCs. There seems to be no pattern as to where in the state they appear in flight years. In some years, including 1964–1965, 1970–1971, 1974–1975, and 1976–1977, the birds were far more numerous along the coast than in upland areas. The pattern for high CBCs in coastal areas ended around 1980.

Remarks The Red Crossbill is a complex of reproductively isolated sibling species (Groth 1993). These forms differ in bill and body size measurements and vocalizations. At least four occur and breed in NY, and each of these also occurs and breeds in western North America. Contrary to earlier accounts of the subspecific taxonomy, there is no evidence for an eastern form confined to the Appalachian or Great Lakes region.

The nomenclature for the *L. curvirostra* complex has undergone numerous changes over the years (Dickerman 1986a) and will require another revision in the light of new data. Nevertheless, four forms of Red Crossbill, in three size classes, are known to occur in NY and may be summarized as follows:

1. A small form ("Type 3" of Groth 1993), variously referenced as *minor* and *sitkensis*. This is the smallest North American crossbill and is generally found in association with hemlock and spruces. Most of the breeding crossbills in 1985 in Chenango Co. (Messineo 1985) may have been of this form.

2. Two medium-sized forms ("Type 1" and "Type 4" of Groth 1993), nearly identical in measurements and known to differ only in vocalizations. The forms have been referred to as *minor, neogaea, bendirei,* or *pusilla.* The names *minor, bendirei,* and *pusilla,* however, cannot correctly be applied to either medium-sized form because the type specimens are not within the appropriate size range. It is not clear which of the two forms is most common in NY, nor is it certain to which form the name *neogaea* should apply. Either Type 1 or both Type 1 and Type 4 may constitute the "Old Northeastern" subspecies (Dickerman 1986b). Medium-sized crossbills were once common in NY and were found in association with white pine and hemlock forests before the forests were destroyed around 1900.

3. Large-billed crossbills ("Type 2" of Groth 1993), variously classified as *bendirei, benti, pusilla,* or *percna.* Although ecological observations are

lacking, in NY these crossbills are probably most strongly associated with various species of pine, including pitch pine and red pine. Examination of museum specimens and analysis of vocalizations indicate that large-billed NY crossbills are identical to many collected in western North America. Contrary to earlier assumptions that crossbills migrate south for the winter, large-billed NY specimens are morphologically unlike Newfoundland birds. Jeff Groth

White-winged Crossbill   *Loxia leucoptera*

Range Holarctic, breeding in North America from central Alaska to northern Labrador and Newfoundland south, in the east to northern Minnesota, New York, and New England. Chiefly sedentary but wanders irregularly south in winter to Missouri and North Carolina.

Status Uncommon breeder and irregular resident. Occurs as part of nomadic movements.

Breeding Unlike the Red Crossbill, which uses virtually all conifers native to NY for breeding, the White-winged Crossbill is primarily a bird of spruce, fir, and larch forests. There is evidence for breeding of this species, in both winter and summer, in the Adirondacks and on the Appalachian Plateau east of the Finger Lakes. The only recorded nest for the state (Peterson 1975) was initiated in late Feb 1975. Large numbers bred on the Appalachian Plateau in early 1985 (Messineo 1985) and again in early 1990 (Messineo 1990). Numerous summer records from the Adirondacks of singing males, including one near L. Placid with fully enlarged testes, collected 19 July 1987 (MVZ 171431), provide strong evidence for at least irregular breeding in NY.

Nonbreeding Although breeding may occur in any month, White-winged Crossbills seen on CBCs are probably nonbreeding. Major flight years documented on CBCs include the winters of 1964–1965, 1966–1967, 1984–1985, and 1985–1986. However, as in the Red Crossbill, large influxes or irruptions may occur in spring or summer and are not evident from CBC data. Causes for these irruptions are not known, but they may be related to patterns of conifer cone abundance.
Jeff Groth

Common Redpoll   *Carduelis flammea*

Range Holarctic, in North America breeding from northern Alaska to Baffin Island south, in the east to James Bay and Newfoundland. Winters in most of the breeding range and south to the northern United States, irregularly or casually farther south, in the east to Missouri, Kentucky, and South Carolina.

Status Irregular winter visitant, absent or very rare some years, common to occasionally very abundant in others.

Occurrence Like the abundance of many species of northern finches, the abundance of redpolls is governed by the availability of preferred foods (birch, alder, and spruce seeds) in their northern breeding and wintering grounds (Cramp and Perrins 1994). On a continental scale, redpolls, like other northern species, show a two-year cycle of southerly irruptions from their circumboreal breeding range (Bock and Lepthien 1976). These large-scale irruptive events are noted less regularly in NY, although some redpolls occur within the state almost every year. During irruptions, flocks can reach well over 100 individuals at many locations; some sites report flocks as large as 500–1000.

In nonirruption years, singles and flocks numbering fewer than 20 individuals may be reported from a small number of localities. Within the last 25 years, large-scale irruptions have occurred in 1973–1974, 1975–1976, 1977–1978, 1980–1981, 1981–1982, 1993–1994, and 1995–1996. Redpoll flocks are often observed feeding in birches and weedy fields as well as at bird feeders. Their use of feeders appears to increase as the season progresses.

Coastal maxima: 2000 JBSP 30 Jan 1960; 2000 Fire I., Suffolk Co. Feb 1974. *Inland maxima:* 4000 Point. Peninsula, Jefferson Co. 9 Dec 1993; 3000+ near Rochester, Monroe Co. 17 Nov 1991; 2500 Pomona, Rockland Co. 7 Feb 1960; 1500 Point Peninsula, Jefferson Co. 2 Jan 1982.

Although Common Redpolls typically arrive in early to mid-Nov, since 1975 there have been six years when birds have arrived as early as Oct. Surprisingly, only three of the six were irruption years. The earliest recorded arrival dates are of single birds: 5 and 9 Oct 1977, both in western NY. In irruption years, peak numbers are normally recorded in late Mar and early Apr as large flocks move rapidly north. At Derby Hill, Oswego Co., for example, counts of 500–800 per day have been noted during this period (Smith and Ryan 1978). However, an unusually large fall movement was recorded in mid-Nov 1991, along western L. Ontario, with an estimated 3000+ passing near Rochester (KB 42:30). This movement was particularly notable since few birds were observed in NY during the remainder of that winter. Most birds depart by late Apr, although individuals were recorded in May in three years since 1975, all in irruption years. The latest recorded departure dates involve single birds: 30 May 1978 Wurtsboro, Sullivan Co. and 22 May 1982 Delhi, Delaware Co.

Remarks The species limits within the redpoll complex have historically been controversial (Knox 1988). The current view is that there are two

species: Common Redpoll *(C. flammea)* with four subspecies and Hoary
Redpoll *(C. hornemanni)* with two subspecies. Recent published work has
failed to resolve whether that view is correct. For example, Seutin et al.
(1992, 1993) examined plumage and morphological variability in redpolls
from Churchill, Manitoba and concluded that there were two relatively
well-differentiated types but that such a finding might represent some form
of polymorphism rather than two species. A mitochondrial DNA analysis of
redpolls showed no consistent differences corresponding to described
species and subspecies (Seutin et al. 1995). The authors pointed out,
however, that such a result is possible if the two forms recently diverged or
if some hybridization had occurred. Further work will be required before
the species limits within the redpoll complex become clarified.
Jeffrey V. Wells and Allison Childs Wells

Hoary Redpoll *Carduelis hornemanni*

Range Northern Holarctic, breeding in North America in northern Alaska
and northern Canada south to the extreme northern portions of Manitoba
and Quebec. Winters mainly in the breeding range but occasionally south,
in the east to southern Michigan and New Jersey.

Status Very rare winter visitant.

Occurrence Hoary Redpoll, like Common Redpoll, varies greatly in abundance from year to year, although it is typically a very rare winter visitant,
even in seasons of greatest Common Redpoll abundance. In winters of large
Common Redpoll irruptions, Hoary Redpoll may or may not be present in
very small numbers, and this unpredictability may have to do with the geographical origin of the Common Redpoll in a given year or with the origin
of (or taxon of) Hoary Redpoll involved in the flight.

Invariably, many more reports of Hoary Redpoll come from upstate than
down. No Hoary has ever been reported in NY outside the context of a
Common Redpoll flight or flock. It should be considered rare or very rare
anywhere in NY until a strong body of data proves otherwise and should
always be documented thoroughly. Hoary Redpolls often accompany
Common Redpolls at feeding stations that offer sunflower or niger seed,
but both species frequent weedy fields also favored by American Goldfinch,
as well as white birch, American tamarack (or larch), and northern white
cedar (Peterson 1974), whose buds are eaten.

Bull (1974) expressed reservations about sight records of multiple Hoary
Redpolls in NY, but with the advent of improved field identification information, better morphometric keys, and multitudes of bird enthusiasts (especially feeder watchers, and banders in the case of this species), reliable
photographic evidence and in-hand studies of Hoary Redpoll have become

available. Older records included herewith (but not in Bull 1974) suggest that Hoary have made up a small part (perhaps 1–2%) of most redpoll irruptions overall this century. CBCs in the state reported a total of only five between 1960 and 1988.

Coastal maxima: 3 Rye, Westchester Co. 25 Feb–31 Mar 1978 (AB 32:330); otherwise, only single birds have been reported. **Inland maxima:** 10 Rochester CBC 22 Dec 1946; 6 Lyndonville, Orleans Co. 25 Mar 1939; 6 Elizabethtown, Essex Co. 29 Dec 1993–8 Feb 1994.

Remarks Only one subspecies of Hoary Redpoll is known from NY, *exilipes*, a form often very difficult to distinguish from Common Redpoll in worn or immature plumages. The nominate subspecies of Hoary, *hornemanni*, which nests in Greenland as well as on Bylot, Ellesmere, and Baffin islands, has not been conclusively documented in NY, but it may be found in the future, as it has been documented in other northeastern states (Veit and Petersen 1993). Redpoll taxonomy is still controversial, with authors advocating from one to four species. The most thorough analysis is that of Knox (1988), who showed that the supposed existence of "intermediates," identified as *C. h. exilipes* and *C. f. flammea*, was an artifact of insufficient appreciation of the range of variation within each of the two species. The supposed frequent interbreeding in areas of sympatry was shown to be unproved, although Knox admitted that such interbreeding may occur rarely.

Careful documentation of all apparent Hoary Redpolls in NY is still very much warranted, especially for suspected nominates, for which no NY specimen exists. For information on identification, see Lansdown (1991). Note that leucistic Common Redpolls have presented an ongoing obstacle in obtaining accurate data on Hoary Redpolls away from the nesting areas. Some such birds have been photographed in central NY. It is quite conceivable that a leucistic *exilipes* Hoary Redpoll would present field identification difficulties in its possible resemblance to the paler nominate form, but *hornemanni* is substantially larger than *exilipes*.
Edward S. Brinkley

Pine Siskin *Carduelis pinus*

Range Nearctic, widespread in the west, breeding from Alaska and northern Canada to the mountains of Guatemala but in the east only from southern Canada to the northern United States, rarely and erratically as far as northern Pennsylvania, southern New York, and southern New England. Winters throughout the breeding range except for the extreme northern portions.

Status Rare to uncommon breeder upstate, often in the Adirondacks, but even there it is unpredictable, absent some years but widely distributed after some irruptions. Extremely erratic, rare to very common fall migrant with a corresponding echo the following winter and spring.

Breeding The Atlas's 102 Probable and 20 Confirmed blocks outside the Adirondacks compare strikingly with the 13 "presumed" nesting records outside the Adirondacks reported by Bull (1974). Because 1985 was an exceptional year for siskin nesting in NY and also fell within the Atlas period, that volume showed a patchy breeding distribution throughout the state, including records from the Catskills, the Great Lakes Plain, the Cattaraugus Highlands, and LI. On SI a nest was found in 1982 (Siebenheller and Siebenheller 1982b). However, the usual breeding picture is far closer to that suggested by Bull.

Although siskins are not quite as erratic in their breeding times as cross-bill are, extreme records include nest building near Syracuse, Onondaga Co. on 19 Feb (Crumb 1985) and a nest with a single egg near Elmira, Chemung Co. on 20 Jul (CUM collection).

Nonbreeding During those years when siskins reach NY, most are observed from Oct to mid-May, but a few Sep and early Jun dates have been recorded. The largest flights have been noted in fall downstate and in spring upstate. On 19 Oct 1969, 5000 passed Fire I. Lighthouse, Suffolk Co. and 4000 flew over Riis Park, Queens Co. that same day. On 11 May 1988, 4000 were seen at Braddock Bay, Monroe Co.; that number was eclipsed by the 5000 there on 23 May 1990. The buildup of numbers in an irruption year was documented by Yunick's remarkable Schenectady Co. banding totals in 1988: 67 in Feb, 74 in Mar, 1999 in Apr, and 1012 in May (KB 38:216).

State CBC 1960–1989 totals range from decade lows of 78 (1965), 66 (1971), and 15 (1980) to decade highs of 6551 (1964), 4028 (1978), and 6565 (1988). Figure 6 suggests no simple pattern.

For example, a sequence of low counts (fewer than 200 birds) that began in 1963 and continued every fourth year until 1983 suddenly ran into a count of 3969 in 1987 (Salzman 1994).

Remarks As they do for other irruptive visitants, Pine Siskin data present more questions than answers. For example, why are some irruptions such as those of the autumns of 1981 and 1982 not followed by more-widespread nesting? An early study in Nebraska by Swenk (1929) suggested that below-normal spring temperatures may discourage birds from leaving their winter-ing territories, thus encouraging them to stay and breed. Statistics for L. Placid, Essex Co. comparing spring 1982 and 1983 (few nesting records) with spring 1985 (widespread nesting) offered no support for that conjecture.

Comparison of 49 years of western NY May count data for siskin and three other irruptive species (Evening Grosbeak and Red and White-winged crossbills) yielded a correlation of only 0.11, suggesting that what retains

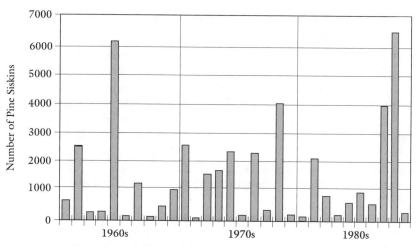

Figure 6. Number of Pine Siskins on New York State Christmas Bird Counts, 1960–1989

siskins is essentially different from what causes those other species to delay their exit from the region (Rising 1995).

The underlying and probably very complex dynamics and scheduling of Pine Siskin irruptions from their population center in the northwestern United States and western Canada and their subsequent breeding remain a challenging enigma.

Gerry Rising

American Goldfinch

Carduelis tristis

Range Nearctic, breeding from southern Canada south to the southern Great Plains, central Georgia, and South Carolina. Winters nearly through-out the breeding range and south to Florida and northern Mexico.

Status Widespread breeder. Sedentary and migratory, variously common to very abundant during migration and winter; subject to marked fluctuations.

Breeding It is a common breeder throughout the state except for some densely forested areas in the Adirondacks and heavily populated areas of NYC and LI. It nests later than any other breeder in the state, usually late Jun into late Sep. This late nesting affords the goldfinch less susceptibility to brood parasitism by the Brown-headed Cowbird than earlier nesting species. Nesting is most common in active or abandoned agricultural areas with nests generally located along edges of woodlands or hedgerows, in trees, or in shrubs in brushy areas (Atlas 1988). Nesting is often associated with maturation of thistles, which the goldfinch uses for food and nesting material.

An analysis of NY BBS 1966–1994 data indicated a statistically significant average annual rate of decline of 2.2%. This decline may well be attributed to the increase in the percentage of forested land during the period. A Dec–Mar feeder survey in Sullivan Co., 1981–1994, showed no significant changes in that county's population (Freer and Visconti 1996).

Nonbreeding Although common in spring and summer it is notably erratic in fall and winter, common to occasionally very abundant in some years, and rare in others. The 1980 Rochester, Monroe Co. CBC reported 5416 goldfinches. Except for that, fall and winter maxima given by Bull (1974) have not been surpassed: 4000 Retsof, Livingston Co. 9 Feb 1964; 2000 Atlantic Beach, Nassau Co. 10 Nov 1946.

Between 29 Dec 1992 and 23 Feb 1993, 1084 were banded near Elizabethtown, Essex Co. (KB 43:147). Its presence in winter is largely dependent upon the available food supply, chiefly weed seeds and the fruit of birch, alder, pine, and other trees; it is common at feeders. In some years, large flights are observed at Derby Hill, Oswego Co. In May 1978, flocks of hundreds to thousands were observed throughout the month, with a count of 6000 on 19 May (KB 28:185). Migrants usually arrive in late Mar and depart in Nov.

Chad E. Covey

European Goldfinch *Carduelis carduelis*

Range Palearctic, resident throughout much of temperate Eurasia. Unsuccessfully introduced into various parts of the United States.

Status Introduced, but probably extirpated since the late 1950s. Temporarily established in Manhattan and later on LI, where it was resident.

Occurrence This species was first found in 1879 in Central Park, Manhattan, where it increased for some time but had disappeared by 1907.

In 1910 it was discovered in Nassau Co., in the vicinity of Massapequa, where it soon increased and spread to surrounding areas and east into Suffolk Co. to Amityville and Babylon. It was principally in the Massapequa-Seaford sector that it prospered; as many as a dozen pairs were found there in the mid-1940s. With the boom in real estate after World War II and resultant destruction of its haunts, it finally disappeared by the late 1950s. See Bent et al. 1968 for a detailed account of these introductions. The AOU (1983) mentioned that other introductions were made in North America, including NJ and MA, adding that the species was not presently established in any of those localities.

The LI birds were found in cultivated country, including gardens, orchards, nurseries, and shade trees and hedgerows along village streets. Nests were most commonly in Norway maples. In winter they resorted to weed fields but were not usually found at feeding stations.

Remarks The European Goldfinch is common in captivity and is frequently imported and caged. It is generally considered that most, if not all, sightings since the late 1950s are of released or escaped birds. *The Kingbird* 1961–1992 had 17 reports, all of single individuals, most at feeders in winter. Each of these was at a different location, spread across the state. One LI sighting in April 1976 was traced to an individual who released his birds because they were "nervous cage birds and difficult to breed." In July 1986 some 20 pairs were reported to have been released in Delaware Co. Stanley R. Lincoln

Evening Grosbeak   *Coccothraustes vespertinus*

Range Nearctic, breeding across southern Canada from British Columbia to Nova Scotia south, in the western mountains to central California and southern Mexico and in the east to northern Minnesota and northern New England. Winters throughout the breeding range and south, sporadically, to the central United States and casually to the Gulf Coast and central Florida.

Status Fairly common but local breeder in and near the Adirondacks, very rare to rare elsewhere. Irregular, locally common to abundant migrant and winter visitant; most numerous inland.

Breeding Outside of an exceptional record in 1882, the first summer reports were not until 1942, when at least five pairs were seen. The first breeding evidence was not obtained until 1946, when young birds were found near Bay Pond, Franklin Co. on 3 Aug. It has been recorded every summer since. It is most frequently found in the Adirondack High Peaks, Central Adirondacks, and Western Adirondack Foothills, with breeding extending outward (Atlas 1988). The southernmost locale for confirmed breeding was Stissing, Dutchess Co. in 1962; westernmost was Frewsburg,

Chautauqua Co. in 1976. Nesting habitat is northern coniferous and mixed coniferous-deciduous woodlands, second growth, and occasionally parks. It tolerates a greater variety of habitats than other northern finches and is more common around hamlets than wilderness areas in the Adirondacks (Atlas 1988). Nests are difficult to locate, with only about a half-dozen found in the state.

Nonbreeding Best known as a prodigious consumer at sunflower seed feeders, it is also notably fond of seeds of the ash-leaved maple. It shows preference for higher-elevation interior regions, more noticeably so in winter than in migration. It can be abundant in some locales one year and absent the next, although it is always present in the Adirondacks. Before the twentieth century it was rare in NY, but as it spread eastward as a breeder through ON to NS and ME, it became abundant during the 1950s and 1960s. High numbers continued into the 1970s, but since the early 1980s wintering numbers have fallen off and irruptions, which occur mainly in Oct and May, have been less frequent. During some recent winters it has actually been rare in several Regions.

Spring maxima: all Derby Hill, Oswego Co.: 2550, 1 May 1986; 1300 on 7 May and 1200 on 8 May 1969; 2450, 6 May 1982. *Fall maxima:* about 2000 in 25 flocks of 50–100 Newark Valley, Tioga Co. 18 Oct 1985; 500 in one flock, Webster Park, Monroe Co. 7 Oct 1961. *Winter maxima:* 1300 banded at a feeder, Deposit, Broome Co. 1959–1960 season; 1200 banded at a feeder, Amsterdam, Montgomery Co. 1955–1956 season.

Extreme dates: 22 Aug and 7 Jun, both coastal, where it does not breed; 9 Sep and 3 Jun, both near Buffalo, Erie Co., where it is not known to breed. Extraordinary was one in lower Manhattan 4–16 Jul 1975 (ph in AMNH collection).

William C. D'Anna

OLD WORLD SPARROWS—PASSERIDAE

House Sparrow   *Passer domesticus*

Range Originally Palearctic, Oriental, and northern Ethiopian, now Cosmopolitan, having been widely introduced into various parts of the world. Sedentary.

Status Introduced. Abundant resident.

Breeding The Atlas showed Confirmed breeding in 3412 blocks (81%) out of 4196 in which it was recorded. Breeding does not occur in heavily forested regions or in the higher elevations of the Adirondacks, Allegany Hills, Catskills, or Tug Hill (Atlas 1988).

An analysis of BBS 1966–1994 data showed that the NY population is in a three-decade decline. In 1966–1979 it declined by an average of 1.5% per year. In 1980–1994 that accelerated to 3.1% (Peterjohn 1995).

Nonbreeding Analysis of NY CBC 1976–1995 data showed that it was steadily declining, from a high in 1976 of 44,571 individuals on 52 counts (average 857) to a low in 1993 of 28,673 individuals on 65 counts (average 441). The population was fairly stable between 1991 and 1995, averaging 476. The overall decline is corroborated by both the CBC and the BBS data. Burtt's monthly (Oct–May) feeder surveys in the *Syracuse Herald American* also show a progressive decline.

Maxima: 7541 Lower Hudson CBC, Manhattan 18 Dec 1993; 2056 per 100 feeders, Syracuse area 6–12 Dec 1981.

Remarks The House Sparrow was first introduced in the United States in early spring of 1851 in Brooklyn. Those eight pairs did not survive, so about 50 more were released in 1852 and another 50 in 1853. Their early spread was about 25 mi in five years, 50 mi in 10 years, and 100 mi in 15 years. During 1865–1869 more were released in Rochester, Monroe Co. It was also released in other states (CT, MA, ME, OH, PA, RI, and TX) during that period. Most of the birds came from England, although some originated in Germany (Robbins 1973). By 1888 it was found throughout the state.

The House Sparrow population has been declining since 1914 (Peterson 1948). The following traditional reasons have been postulated: the disappearance from the streets of horse manure, which contains undigested seeds these sparrows eat; the lack of nooks and crannies in modern architecture, thereby depriving them of nest sites; and competition with the European Starling for nest sites.

Recently, another reason has been added, the introduction and spread of the House Finch. Although the House Sparrow and House Finch have been living together for about a century in the West (Robbins 1973), their competitive interactions are new in the East. The result of interspecific competition is often a coexistence wherein each species successfully obtains its own favored habitat and the squabbling is confined to the intergrade zones. In the West the partition is along an urban-suburban-rural gradient, where the sparrow has the more urban and the finch the more suburban areas (Cody 1974).

"If in some way the American house finch could be induced to come east and the English sparrow could be given papers of extradition, the exchange would be a relief and benefit to the whole country." This prophetic lament was published by Keyser (1902). Beneficial relief is not materializing, however, as we are now stuck with both. But this fortuitous pairing is providing an excellent opportunity to watch interspecific competition in action, as it is happening in our own backyards.

Much of the interpretation of the competition depends on the scale being considered. In some Western urban areas the House Sparrow has been responsible for a decline in the House Finch population. In the East the new sympatry does not appear to be well settled. For example, although the accelerated decline of the House Sparrow occurred simultaneously in both the NYC and Boston regions, the House Finch was already abundant in NYC in 1965 but had just begun to appear in Boston. Competition is certainly occurring, but effects on the populations may depend on whether a local, regional, or continental scale is being assessed (Bennett 1990).

Drawing on CBC 1958–1979 data, Kricher (1983) concluded that the House Finch increase was correlated very closely with the House Sparrow decline. However, he cautioned that that correlation only suggests possible relationships; it never proves cause and effect. In fact, he postulated that the very presence of House Sparrow may have provided the selection pressures that stimulated the House Finch to become a superior competitor. In the West it was the sparrow that invaded the finch range and the sparrow seems to dominate. In the East, just the opposite occurred; the finch was the invader. Perhaps not enough time has elapsed here for the House Finch and the House Sparrow to attain some sort of mutually advantageous sympatry—all the more reason for birders to pay attention to these common species.
Donald A. Windsor

Bibliography

Able, K.P. 1982. Ivory Gull visits a bird feeder in Saratoga Springs. Kingbird 32:74–77.

Aldrich, J.W. 1946. The United States races of the Bob-White. Auk 63:493–508.

———. 1951. A review of the races of the Traill's Flycatcher. Wilson Bulletin 63:192–197.

———. 1953. Habits and habitat differences in two races of Traill's Flycatcher. Wilson Bulletin 65:8–11.

Alerich, C.L., and D.A. Drake. 1995. Forest statistics for New York: 1980 and 1993. USDA Forest Service, Northeastern Forest Experiment Station, Resource Bulletin NE-132. Radnor, PA.

Allen, A.A. 1911. A note on the Prothonotary Warbler. Auk 28:115.

———. 1914. The Red-winged Blackbird: a study in the ecology of a cattail marsh. Proceedings of the Linnaean Society of New York 24–25:43–128.

———. 1947. Ornithology laboratory notebook, 5th ed. Comstock Publishing Associates, Ithaca, NY. P. 52.

American Birds. Journal of the National Audubon Society. 1971–1993. Volumes 25–47. [Replaced Audubon Field Notes with vol. 25 in 1971; became National Audubon Society Field Notes after 1993.]

American Ornithologists' Union (AOU), Washington, DC. 1957. Check-list of North American Birds, 5th ed. Port City Press, Baltimore.

———. 1973. Thirty-second supplement to the American Ornithologists' Union Check-list of North American birds. Auk 90:411–419.

———. 1982. Thirty-fourth supplement to the American Ornithologists' Union Check-list of North American birds. Auk 99:1cc–16cc.

———. 1983. Check-list of North American Birds, 6th ed. Allen Press, Lawrence, KA.

———. 1985. Thirty-fifth supplement to the American Ornithologists' Union Check-list of North American birds. Auk 102:680–686.

———. 1987. Thirty-sixth supplement to the American Ornithologists' Union Check-list of North American birds. Auk 104:591–596.

———. 1989. Thirty-seventh supplement to the American Ornithologists' Union Check-list of North American Birds. Auk 106:532–538.

———. 1991. Thirty-eighth supplement to the American Ornithologists' Union Check-list of North American birds. Auk 108:750–754.

———. 1993. Thirty-ninth supplement to the American Ornithologists' Union Check-list of North American birds. Auk 110:675–682.

———. 1995. Fortieth supplement to the American Ornithologists' Union Check-list of North American birds. Auk 112:819–830.

———. 1997. Forty-first supplement to the American Ornithologists' Union Check-list of North American birds. Auk 114:542–552.

Anderson, W.C., and R.E. Duzan. 1978. DDE residues and eggshell thinning in Loggerhead Shrikes. Wilson Bulletin 90:215–220.

Andrle, R.F. 1969. Thayer's Gull in the Niagara Frontier region. Auk 86:106–109.

———. 1971. The birds of McCarty Hill, Cattaraugus County, NY. Prothonotary 37:90.

———. 1977a. Gulls on the Niagara Frontier. Miscellaneous. Contributions no. 20. Buffalo Society of Natural Sciences.

———. 1977b. Gulls on the Niagara River. Kingbird 27:119–134.

———. 1978. Ruby-crowned Kinglet breeding in Cattaraugus County. Kingbird 28:29–30.

Andrle, R.F., and J.R. Carroll, eds. 1988. The atlas of breeding birds in New York State. Cornell Univ. Press, Ithaca, NY.

Anonymous. 1985a. The birds of Monroe County, New York, annotated list. Proceedings of the Rochester Academy of Sciences 16:56.

——. 1985b. Annual Report 1984. Orange Co. Chapter, New York State Archaeological Association of Middletown, NY.

——. 1994. 1993 Eskimo Curlew record is erroneous. Cotinga 3:69.

——. 1995. Regional News. Endangered Species Technical Bulletin 19:18. USFWS, Washington, DC.

Atlas of breeding birds in New York State. 1988. R.F. Andrle and J.R. Carroll, eds. Cornell Univ. Press, Ithaca, NY.

Audubon, J.J. 1834. Ornithological biography, vol. 2. A. Black, Edinburgh.

Audubon Field Notes. Journal of the National Audubon Society in collaboration with the USFWS. 1947–1970. Volumes 1–24. [Became American Birds with vol. 25].

Auk, The. Journal of the American Ornithologists' Union. 1884–1996. Volumes 1–113.

Axtell, H.H. 1947. Distribution of the vertebrate animals of Chemung and Schuyler counties, New York. Ph.D. dissertation, Cornell Univ. Ithaca, NY.

Bagg, E. 1911. Annotated list of the birds of Oneida County, NY and the West Canada Creek Valley. Transactions of the Oneida Historical Society 12:17–86.

Bailey, H.H. 1941. An undescribed race of the eastern Ruffed Grouse. Bulletin no. 14. The Bailey Museum and Library of Natural History, Miami, FL.

Bain, M. 1994. Ontario bird records committee report for 1993. Ontario Birds 12:41.

Baird, J. 1957. A western representative of the Rufous-sided Towhee collected in New Jersey. Condor 59:401.

Baird, T.H. 1984. A first record of nesting Yellow-throated Warblers in New York State. Kingbird 34:221.

——. 1990. Changes in breeding bird populations between 1930 and 1985 in Quaker Run Valley of Allegany State Park, New York. New York State Museum Bulletin no. 477.

Ball, R.M., Jr., S. Freeman, F.C. James, E. Bermingham, and J.C. Avise. 1988. Phylogeographic population structure of Red-winged Blackbirds assessed by mitochondrial DNA. Proceedings of the National Academy of Sciences of the United States of America 85:1558–1562.

Banks, R.C. 1977. The decline and fall of the Eskimo Curlew, or why did the curlew go extaille? American Birds 31:127–134.

Bannon, P. 1983. First nesting of the Little Gull *(Larus minutus)* in Quebec. American Birds 37:838.

Bartram, J. 1751. Observations on the inhabitants, climate, soil, rivers, productions, animals, and other matters worthy of notice. Made by John Bartram in his "Travels from Pensilvania to Onondago, Oswego and the Lake Ontario, in Canada." J. Whiston and B. White, London.

Bassett, D.K. 1989. Wintering Turkey Vultures in Letchworth State Park. Kingbird 39:74–79.

——. 1994. Letchworth State Park breeding bird survey. Unpublished data.

Beals, M.V., and J.T. Nichols. 1940. Data from a banding station at Elmhurst, Long Island. Birds of Long Island 3:57–76.

Bean, M.J. 1983. The evolution of national wildlife law. Praeger, New York.

Beardslee, C.S. 1932. Prothonotary Warblers nesting near Buffalo, NY. Auk 49:91.

Beardslee, C.S., and H.D. Mitchell. 1965. Birds of the Niagara Frontier region. Bulletin of the Buffalo Society of Natural Sciences, vol. 22.

Bednarz, J.C., and J.J. Dinsmore. 1982. Nest-sites and habitat of Red-shouldered and Red-tailed Hawks in Iowa. Wilson Bulletin 94:31–45.

Beehler, B. 1978. Birdlife of the Adirondack Park. Adirondack Mountain Club, Glens Falls, NY.

Belknap, J.B. 1955. The expanding range of the Ring-billed Gull. Kingbird 5:63.

——. 1968. Little Galloo Island—a twenty-year summary. Kingbird 18:80.

Bellrose, F.C. 1976. Ducks, geese, and swans of North America. Stackpole Books, Harrisburg, PA.

Bennett, W.A. 1990. Scale of investigation and the detection of competition: an example from the House Sparrow and House Finch introductions in North America. American Naturalist 135:725–747.

Benning, W. 1980. The shorebirds of Montezuma National Wildlife Refuge. Kingbird 30:68–71.

Bent, A.C. 1937. Life histories of North American birds of prey: part 1. Smithsonian Institution U.S. National Museum Bulletin no. 167. [Republished by Dover Publications, New York, in 1961.]

——. 1939. Life histories of North American woodpeckers. Smithsonian Institution U.S. National Museum Bulletin no. 174. [Republished by Dover Publications, New York, in 1964.]

——. 1942. Life histories of North American flycatchers, larks, swallows and their allies. Smithsonian Institution U.S. National Museum Bulletin no. 179. [Republished by Dover Publications, New York, in 1963.]

——. 1948. Life histories of North American nuthatches, wrens, thrashers, and their allies. Smithsonian Institution U.S. National Museum Bulletin no. 195. [Republished by Dover Publications, New York, in 1964.]

——. 1953. Life histories of North American wood warblers: part 1. Smithsonian Institution U.S. National Museum Bulletin no. 203. [Republished by Dover Publications, New York, in 1963.]

Bent, A.C., et al. 1968. Life histories of North American cardinals, grosbeaks, buntings, towhees, finches, sparrows, and allies. Compiled and edited by O.L. Austin Jr. [Originally published by Smithsonian Institution Press as U.S. National Museum Bulletin no. 237. Republished by Dover Publications, New York, in 1968.]

Benton, A.H. 1949. The breeding birds of Cayuga County, NY. M.S. thesis, Cornell Univ., Ithaca, NY.

Bergtold, W.H. 1927. The Carolina Paroquet in western New York. Auk 44:252.

Bevier, L.R., ed. 1994. The atlas of breeding birds of Connecticut. State Geological and Natural History Survey of Connecticut Bulletin no. 113.

Birding. Journal of the American Birding Association. 1978–1996. Volumes 1–28.

Birds of North America. 1992–1996. A. Poole and F. Gill, eds. Species accounts published by the Academy of Natural Sciences, Philadelphia, and the American Ornithologists' Union, Washington, DC. Numbers 1–240.

Bishop, P.G., Jr. 1980. The history and recent breeding of the Common Raven in New York State. M.S. thesis, State Univ. of New York, College of Environmental Sciences and Forestry, Syracuse.

Blair, R. 1990. Water quality and the summer distribution of Common Loon in New York. Kingbird 40:10–18.

Blokpoel, H., and G.D. Tessier. 1986. The Ring-billed Gull in Ontario: a review of a new problem species. Canadian Wildlife Service Occasional Paper no. 57. Ottawa, ON.

Blokpoel, H., and D.V. Weseloh. 1982. Status of colonial nesting birds on Little Galloo Island, Lake Ontario. Kingbird 32:149–157.

Blumton, A.K., J.D. Fraser, R.W. Young, S. Goodbred, S.L. Porter, and D.L. Luukkonen. 1990. Pesticide and PCB residues for Loggerhead Shrikes in the Shenandoah Valley, Virginia, 1985–1988. Bulletin, Environmental Contamination Toxicology 45:697–702.

Bock, C.E., and L.W. Lepthien. 1976. Synchronous eruptions of boreal seed-eating birds. American Naturalist 110:559–571.

Bollinger, B.P. 1985. Status of the Common Tern population breeding on Oneida Lake in New York. New York Cooperative Wildlife Research Unit, Cornell Univ., Ithaca, NY. Mimeo.

Bollinger, E.K., and T.A. Gavin. 1992. Eastern Bobolink populations: ecology and conservation in an agricultural landscape. *In* Ecology and conservation of Neotropical migrant land birds. J.M. Hagan III and D.W. Johnston, eds. Smithsonian Institution Press, Washington, DC.

Bosakowski, T., and R. Speiser. 1984. Highway observations of Great Horned Owls in New York State. Kingbird 34:16.

Bouta, R.P., and R.E. Chambers. 1990. Status of threatened Spruce Grouse populations in New York: a historical perspective. New York State Museum Bulletin no. 471.

Bowman, M.C. 1974. Common Crows as commensals of Common Mergansers. Kingbird 24:60–61.

Brauning, D.W., ed. 1992. Atlas of the breeding birds in Pennsylvania. Univ. Pittsburgh Press, Pittsburgh.

Brewster, W. 1918. An undescribed race of Henslow's Sparrow. Proceedings of the New England Zoological Club 6:77–79.

Brittingham, M.C., and S.A. Temple. 1988. Impacts of supplemental feeding on survival rates of Black-capped Chickadees. Ecology 69:581–589.

Brock, R. 1994. Photographs of New York State rarities 59: Slaty-backed Gull. Kingbird 44:82–86.

Brodkorb, P. 1964. Catalogue of fossil birds, part 2. Bulletin of the Florida State Museum, Biological Sciences 8:195–335.

——. 1967. Catalogue of fossil birds, part 3. Bulletin of the Florida State Museum, Biological Sciences 11:99–220.

Brooks, B.L., and S.A. Temple. 1986. The breeding distribution of the Loggerhead Shrike in Minnesota. The Loon 54:151–155.

Brooks, E.W. 1971. A nesting record of Clay-colored Sparrow in Allegany County. Prothonotary 37:99.

——. 1981. Breeding bird survey no. 64. Upland mixed pine-spruce-hardwood plantation. American Birds 35:65.

——. 1987. A summary of Black-capped Chickadee recoveries during spring migration. North American Bird Bander 12:19–20.

——. 1988. A third post-1875 nesting of Dickcissel in New York State. Kingbird 38:237–239.

Brown, C., J. Kelley, J. Penman, and J. Sparling. 1973. Faunal analysis of the Cole Quarry Archaic Site. New York State Archaeological Association Bulletin 58:25–40.

Brown, C.R. 1986. Cliff Swallow colonies as information centers. Science 234:83–85.

Brown, C.R., and M.B. Brown. 1986. Ectoparasitism as a cost of coloniality in Cliff Swallows (*Hirundo pyrrhonota*). Ecology 67:1206–1218.

Brown, M.K., and G.R. Parsons. 1979. Waterfowl production on beaver flowages in a part of northern New York. New York Fish and Game Journal 26:142–153.

Browne, S. 1975. Hooded Mergansers breeding in New York. New York Fish and Game Journal 22:68–70.

Bruun, B. 1981. Photographs of New York State rarities 40: Wheatear. Kingbird 31:123.

Bryant, A.A. 1986. Influence of selective logging on Red-shouldered Hawks *(Buteo lineatus)*, in Waterloo Region, Ontario, 1953–1978. Canadian Field-Naturalist 100:520–525.

Buckley, F., M. Gochfeld, and P.A. Buckley. 1978. Breeding Laughing Gulls return to Long Island. Kingbird 28:203–211.

Buckley, P.A. 1959. Recent specimens from southern New York and New Jersey affecting AOU Check-list status. Auk 76:517–520.

———. 1974 Recent specimens of western vagrants at Fire Island National Seashore, Long Island, New York. Auk 91:181–185.

———. 1979a. Photographs of NY rarities 20: Bell's Vireo. Auk 91:181.

———. 1979b. Recent specimens of western vagrants at Fire Island National Seashore, Long Island, NY. Auk 91:181–185.

Buckley, P.A., and F.G. Buckley. 1979. Roseate Tern: our newest threatened species? Abstracts: Proceedings of the Second Conference of Scientific Research National Parks, San Francisco, November 1979.

———. 1980. Population and colony-site trends of Long Island waterbirds for five years in the mid 1970s. Transactions of the Linnaean Society of New York 9:23–56.

———. 1981. The endangered status of North American Roseate Terns. Colonial Waterbirds 4:166–173.

Buckley, P.A., F.G. Buckley, and M. Gochfeld. 1975. Gull-billed Tern: New York State's newest breeding species. Kingbird 25:178.

Buckley, P.A., and P. Post. 1970. Photographs of NY State rarities 20: Bell's Vireo. Kingbird 20:57.

Bull, J. 1961. Wintering Tennessee Warblers. Auk 78:263–264.

———. 1964. Birds of the New York area. Harper and Row, New York.

———. 1970. Supplement to birds of the New York area. Proceedings of the Linnaean Society of New York no. 71.

———. 1974. Birds of New York State. Doubleday/Natural History Press, Garden City, NY. [Reprinted by Cornell Univ. Press, Ithaca, NY, 1985.]

———. 1976. Supplement to the Birds of New York State. Special Publication of the Federation of New York State Bird Clubs. Wilkins Printers, Cortland, NY. [Reprinted in Birds of New York State by Cornell Univ. Press, Ithaca, NY, 1985.]

———. 1981. Double-crested Cormorants breeding at Fishers Island. Kingbird 31:83.

———. 1988a. First substantiated record of Golden-crowned Sparrow from New York State. Kingbird 38:8–9.

———. 1988b. Photographs of New York State rarities 49: Vermilion Flycatcher on Long Island: a first New York State record. Kingbird 38:2.

Bump, G., R.W. Darrow, F.G. Edminster, and W.F. Crissey. 1947. The Ruffed Grouse: life history, propagation and management. New York State Conservation Dept., Albany.

Burger, J. 1996. Cedar Beach Roseate Tern report. Unpublished report to NYSDEC.

Burger, J., and M. Gochfeld. 1995. Cedar Beach Roseate Tern report. Unpublished report to NYSDEC.

Burke, T.W. 1991. Photographs of New York State rarities 52: Wood Sandpiper at Marshlands Conservancy. Kingbird 41:70–72.

Burleigh, T.D., and H.S. Peters. 1948. Geographic variation in Newfoundland birds. Proceedings of the Biological Society of Washington 61:111–124.

Burtt, H.E., and B.P. Burtt. 1984. Changes in the House Finch population in central New York. Kingbird 34:8–10.

Busbee, E.L. 1977. The effects of dieldrin on the behavior of young Loggerhead Shrikes. Auk 94:28–35.

Butcher, G.S., and E.H. Dunn. 1995. Bird feeders and Christmas Bird Counts: a cautionary tale. Kingbird 45:79–85.

Butler, R.W. 1988. Population dynamics and migration routes of Tree Swallows *(Tachycineta bicolor)* in North America. Journal of Field Ornithology 59:395–402.

Cadman, M.D., P.F.J. Eagles, and F.M. Helleiner, eds. 1987. Atlas of the breeding birds of Ontario. Univ. Waterloo Press, Waterloo, ON.

Campbell, J.M. 1965. An impressive Gray Jay migration. Canadian Field-Naturalist 79:157–158.

Campbell, W.W. 1849. The life and writings of De Witt Clinton. Baker and Scribner, New York.

Cant, G. 1962. The House Finch in New York State. Kingbird 12:68.

Carleton, G.C. 1958. The birds of Central and Prospect parks. *In* Proceedings of the Linnaean Society of New York 66–70, L.S. Pearl, ed. Pp. 1–60.

Carleton, G., H.H. Poor, and O.K. Scott. 1948. Cape May Warbler breeding in New York State. Auk 65:607.

Carroll, J.P. 1993. Gray Partridge *(Perdix perdix)*. *In* The birds of North America, no. 58, A. Poole and F. Gill, eds. The Academy of Natural Sciences, Philadelphia, and the American Ornithologists' Union, Washington, DC.

Carroll, J.R. 1988. Status and breeding ecology of the Black Tern in New York. Kingbird 38:159–172.

Caslick, J.W. 1975. Measuring revegetation rates and patterns on abandoned agricultural lands. Cornell Univ. Agricultural Experiment Station Search 5(6):1–27. New York State College of Agriculture and Life Sciences, Ithaca, NY.

Castro, G., D. Blanco, R. Banchs, and P. Canevari. 1994. Searching for the endangered Eskimo Curlew in South America. Endangered Species Update 11:5. USFWS, Washington, DC.

Chamberlain, D.R. 1964. New York State crow roost survey. Kingbird 14:208–210.

Chamberlaine, L.B. 1994. Mourning Dove with ice ball on bill. Kingbird 44:289.

Chaplin, S. 1976. The physiology of hypothermia in the Black-capped Chickadee *(Parus atricapillus)*. Journal of Comparative Physiology B 112:335–344.

Chapman, F.M. 1906. The distribution and relationships of *Ammodramus maritimus* and its allies. Auk 16:1–12.

——. 1917. The warblers of North America. D. Appleton and Company, New York.

Chartier, A. 1994. Sharp-shinned Hawk declines: an inland perspective. Winging It 6(6):8–9.

Chipley, R.M. 1980. Nonbreeding biology of the Blackburnian Warbler. *In* Migrant birds in the Neotropics: ecology, behavior, distribution and conservation, A. Keast and E.S. Morton, eds. Smithsonian Institution Press, Washington, DC. Pp. 309–317.

Cimprich, D.A., and F.R. Moore. 1995. Gray Catbird *(Dumetella carolinensis)*. *In* The birds of North America, no. 167, A. Poole and F. Gill, eds. The Academy of Natural Sciences, Philadelphia, and the American Ornithologists' Union, Washington, DC.

Claassen, C. 1994. Summary of the results of research at the archaic Dogan Point Site, Westchester Co., New York. Bulletin of the New York State Archaeological Association 107:26–37.

Claffey, J. 1972. Clay-colored Sparrow *(Spizella pallida)*. Goshawk 28(7):50–52.

Clark, R.C., and S.W. Eaton. 1977. The breeding biology of the Eastern Phoebe [abstract]. American Ornithologists' Union Annual Meeting, Berkeley.

Claypoole, K. 1988. First nesting of the Double-crested Cormorant at Oneida Lake, NY. Kingbird 38:235–236.

Clermont, R. 1979. Photographs of New York State rarities 33: Mississippi Kite. Kingbird 29:178–180.

Clum, N.J. 1986. The effects of prey quantity on reproductive success of Osprey

(Pandion haliaetus) in the Adirondack Mountains. M.S. thesis, Cornell Univ., Ithaca, NY.

Cobb, T.L. 1993. Fostering environmental stewardship—a first report on managing and protecting the natural and cultural resources of the New York State Park System. Office of Parks, Recreation and Historic Preservation, Albany, NY.

Cody, M.L. 1974. Competition and the structure of bird communities. Princeton Univ. Press, Princeton, NJ. Pp. 134–135, 169–170.

Coghlan, A. 1990. Pigeons, pests and people. New Scientist 128(1745):48–51.

Confer, J.L., and K. Knapp. 1981. Golden-winged Warblers and Blue-winged Warblers: the relative success of a habitat specialist and a generalist. Auk 89:108–114.

Confer, J.L., K. Knapp, D. Coker, M. Armstrong, and J. Doherty. 1991. The rapidly changing status of the Golden-winged Warbler *(Vermivora chrysoptera)* in central New York. Kingbird 41:5–10.

Conolly, B. 1971. Bar-tailed Godwit at Moriches, L.I. Kingbird 21:142–143.

Considine, T.J., Jr. 1984. An analysis of New York's timber resources. USDA Forest Service Bulletin NE-80. Broomall, PA.

Converse, H.M. 1908. Myths and legends of the New York State Iroquois. New York State Museum Bulletin no. 125.

Conway, R.A. 1992. Field-checklist of Rhode Island birds, 2nd ed. Rhode Island Ornithological Club Bulletin no. 1.

Cooper, D., H. Hays, and C. Pessino. 1970. Breeding of the Common and Roseate terns on Great Gull Island. Proceedings of the Linnaean Society of New York 71:83–104.

Cormons, P. 1992. A rare find. Linnaean News-Letter 46(3).

Courtney, P.A., and H. Blokpoel. 1983. Distribution and numbers of Common Terns on the lower Great Lakes during 1900–1980: a review. Colonial Waterbirds 6:107–120.

Cramp, S., ed. 1983. Handbook of the birds of Europe, the Middle East and North Africa. Volume 3: Waders to gulls. Oxford Univ. Press, Oxford.

Cramp, S., and C.M. Perrins, eds. 1994. Handbook of the birds of Europe, the Middle East, and North Africa. Volume 7: Crows to finches. Oxford Univ. Press, Oxford.

Crocoll, S.T., and J.W. Parker. 1989. The breeding biology of Broad-winged and Red-shouldered Hawks in western New York. Journal of Raptor Research 23:125–139.

Crowe, D.M. 1983. Comprehensive planning for wildlife resources. Wyoming Game and Fish Department, Laramie.

Cruickshank, A.D. 1942. Birds around New York City. American Museum of Natural History Handbook no. 13. American Museum Press, New York.

Crumb, D.W. 1982. Photographs of New York State rarities 43: Say's Phoebe. Kingbird 32:147–148.

———. 1985. Nesting finches in the highlands of southern Onondaga and Madison counties. Kingbird 35:238–240.

———. 1992. Bobolink wintering near Syracuse, NY. Kingbird 42:141.

Crumb, D.W., and C. Smith. 1980. Some observations on the fall migration of water-birds at the east end of Lake Ontario. Kingbird 30:6–10.

Curson, J., D. Quinn, and D. Beadle. 1994. Warblers of the Americas, an identification guide. Houghton Mifflin, Boston.

Cutright, N.J. 1973. Summer and fall flocking and roosting activities of the Red-winged Blackbird in central New York. Ph.D. dissertation. Cornell Univ., Ithaca, NY.

D'Anna, W. 1995. The migration of Red-throated Loon on Lake Ontario. Kingbird 45:86.

Davis, M.B., ed. 1996. Eastern old growth forests: prospects for rediscovery and recovery. Island Press, Covelo, CA.

Davis, T.H. 1968. Willet nesting on Long Island. Wilson Bulletin 80:330.

——. 1973. Photographs of New York State rarities 23: Sage Thrasher. Kingbird 23:72–74.

——. 1975. Bar-tailed Godwit at Moriches Inlet, Suffolk Co., New York. Kingbird 25:27–28.

——. 1976. First record of Smith's Longspur in New York. Auk 93:838–839.

——. 1977. The Burrowing Owl in New York State. Kingbird 27:69.

——. 1979a. Photographs of New York State rarities 31: White Ibis. Kingbird 29:74.

——. 1979b. Photographs of New York State rarities 32: Wilson's Plover. Kingbird 29:118.

——. 1980. Photographs of New York State rarities 34: White-faced Ibis. Kingbird 30:3–5.

——. 1981a. Boat-tailed Grackles breeding at Jamaica Bay Wildlife Refuge. Kingbird 31:214.

——. 1981b. Photographs of New York State rarities 41: Sharp-tailed Sandpiper. Kingbird 31:198–201.

——. 1982. The 1981 fall shorebird season at Jamaica Bay Wildlife Refuge. Kingbird 32:85–96.

——. 1984. The 1983 fall shorebird season at Jamaica Bay Wildlife Refuge. Kingbird 34:75.

Davis, T.H., and A.J. Lauro. 1978. Anhinga in Nassau County. Kingbird 28:3–4.

Davis, T.H., and B. Trimble. 1967. Photographs of New York State rarities 10: Lapwing. Kingbird 17:126–127.

Davison, J.L. 1889. Birds of Niagara County, N.Y., Part 1. Forest and Stream, September 19 and September 26, with corrections November 7. Unpaged.

Dean, F.C., P. Valkenburg, and A.J. Magoun. 1976. Inland migration of jaegers in northeast Alaska. Condor 78:271.

DeBenedictis, P.A. 1977. Buff-breasted Sandpiper in Oswego County in May. Kingbird 27:140–141.

——. 1987. Editorial: Regional boundaries and migration dates. Kingbird 37:9–24.

——. 1989. Photographs of New York State rarities 50: Black-necked Stilt in upstate New York. Kingbird 39:195.

——. 1995. Sharp-tailed Sparrow: a parable of field ornithology. Birding 27:312–314.

Deed, R. 1982. Frigatebird in Rockland County. Kingbird 32:256–257.

DeGraaf, R.M., G.M.Witman, J.W. Lanier, B.J. Hill, and J.M. Keniston. 1980. Forest habitat for birds of the Northeast. USDA Forest Service, Washington, DC.

DeGraff, L.W. 1974. The Mourning Dove. New York State Conservationist 29:34–35.

DeKay, J.E. 1844. Zoology of New York; or, the New York fauna. Part 2: Birds. D. Appelton, and Wiley and Putnam, New York.

Delehanty, C. 1978. Photographs of New York State rarities 29: Western Grebe. Kingbird 28:208.

Dempsey, S.B., A. Lauro, and B. Lauro. 1975. Long-billed Curlew on Long Island. Kingbird 25:207.

Derven, P. 1986. A Wilson's Storm-Petrel sighting from Rockland County, NY. Kingbird 36:207.

Devillers, P. 1977. The skuas of the North Pacific Coast. Auk 94:104.

Dickerman, R.W. 1986a. A review of the Red Crossbill in New York State. Part 1: Historical and nomenclatural background. Kingbird 36:73–78.

——. 1986b. A review of the Red Crossbill in New York State. Part 2: Identification of specimens from New York. Kingbird 36:127–134.

——. 1987. The "Old Northeastern" subspecies of Red Crossbill. American Birds 41:189–194.

———. 1991. Specimens of subarctic nesting population of Great Horned Owl from NY, NJ, and CT. Kingbird 41:154–157.

Dickerman, R.W., and K.C. Parkes. 1987. Subspecies of Red-tailed Hawk in the Northeast. Kingbird 37:57.

DiCostanzo, J.A. 1993. Anhinga in New York City. Linnaean News-Letter 47(1).

DiCostanzo, J.A., R.E. Harrison, and J.O. Biderman. 1978. Photographs of New York State rarities 28: Townsend's Warbler. Kingbird 28:150.

Dilger, W.C. 1956. Adaptive modifications and ecological isolating mechanisms in the thrush genera *Catharus* and *Hylocichla*. Wilson Bulletin 68:171–199.

Drumm, J. 1963. Mastodons and mammoths: ice age elephants of New York. New York State Museum and Science Service Educational Leaflet 13.

Duncan, B. 1993. Merlins: population changes. Journal of the Hawk Migration Association of North America 19(1):8–13.

Duncan, C.D. 1996. Changes in the winter abundance of Sharp-shinned Hawks in New England. Journal of Field Ornithology 67:254–262.

Dunn, E.H., and D.J. Agro. 1995. Black Tern *(Chlidonias niger)*. *In* The birds of North America, no. 147, A. Poole and F. Gill, eds. The Academy of Natural Sciences, Philadelphia, and the American Ornithologists' Union, Washington, DC.

Dutcher, W. 1893. Notes on some rare birds in the collection of the Long Island Historical Society. Auk 10:267–277.

Dwight, J. 1917. The status of *Larus thayeri*, Thayer's Gull. Auk 34:413–414.

Eaton, E.H. 1910. Birds of New York State, part 1. State Univ. of New York, Albany.

———. 1914. Birds of New York State, part 2. State Univ. of New York, Albany.

Eaton, S.W. 1953. Birds of the Olean and Salamanca quadrangles, New York. St. Bonaventure Univ. Science Studies 15:1–27.

———. 1957. A life history study of *Seiurus noveboracensis*. St. Bonaventure Univ. Science Studies 19:7–36.

———. 1965. Juncos of the high plateaus. Kingbird 15:141–146.

———. 1967. Recent tower kills in upstate New York. Kingbird 17:142–146.

———. 1981. Birds of Cattaraugus County, New York, Bulletin of the Buffalo Society of Natural Sciences, vol. 29.

———. 1992. Wild Turkey *(Meleagris gallopavo)*. *In* The birds of North America, no. 22, A. Poole, P. Stettenheim, and F. Gill, eds. The Academy of Natural Sciences, Philadelphia, and the American Ornithologists' Union, Washington, DC.

Eaton, S.W., and E.E. Eaton. 1990. Purple Martin at Canandaigua Lake: behavioral notes and census. Kingbird 40:154–157.

Eaton, S.W., F.M. Evans, J.W. Glidden, and B.D. Penrod. 1976. Annual range of the Wild Turkey in southwestern New York. New York Fish and Game Journal 23:20–33.

Eckert, K. 1993. Identification of Western and Clark's Grebes: the Minnesota experience. Birding 25:304–310.

———. 1995. Western and Clark's Grebes: further notes on identification. Birding 27:54–55.

Elliott, J.E., and P.A. Martin. 1994. Chlorinated hydrocarbons and shell thinning in eggs of *(Accipiter)* hawks in Ontario, 1986–1989. Environmental Pollution 86:189–200.

Elliott, J.J. 1962. Sharp-tailed and Seaside sparrows on Long Island, New York. Kingbird 12:115–123.

Elliott, J.J., and R.S. Arbib. 1953. Origin and status of the House Finch in the eastern United States. Auk 70:31–37.

Ellison, P.T. 1980. Habitat use by resident screech owls *(Otus asio)*. M.S. thesis, Univ. Massachusetts, Amherst.

Ellison, W.G. 1985a. Black-and-white Warbler. *In* The atlas of breeding birds of Vermont. S.B. Laughlin and D.P. Kibbe, eds. Vermont Institute of Natural Sciences. Univ. Press of New England, Hanover. Pp. 310–311.

——. 1985b. Cerulean Warbler. *In* The atlas of breeding birds of Vermont. S.B. Laughlin and D.P. Kibbe, eds. Vermont Institute of Natural Sciences. Univ. Press of New England, Hanover, NH. Pp. 308–309.

——. 1991. The mechanism and ecology of range expansion by the Blue-gray Gnatcatcher. M.S. thesis, Univ. Connecticut, Storrs.

——. 1992. Blue-gray Gnatcatcher *(Polioptila caerulea)*. *In* The birds of North America, no. 23, A. Poole, P. Stettenheim, and F. Gill, eds. The Academy of Natural Sciences, Philadelphia, and the American Ornithologists' Union, Washington, DC.

——. 1993. Historical patterns of vagrancy by Blue-gray Gnatcatchers in New England. Journal of Field Ornithology 64:358–366.

Emlen, J.T. 1938. Midwinter distribution of the American Crow in New York State. Ecology 19:264–275.

Emslie, S.D. 1987. Age and diet of fossil California Condors in Grand Canyon, Arizona. Science 237:768–770.

Erskine, A.J. 1977. Birds in boreal Canada: communities, densities and adaptations. Canadian Wildlife Service Report Series no. 41. Minister of Supply and Services, Ottawa, ON.

——. 1979. Man's influence on potential nesting sites and populations of swallows Hirundinidae in Canada. Canadian Field-Naturalist 93:371–377.

Erwin, R.M. 1979. Coastal waterbird colonies: Cape Elizabeth, Maine to Virginia. USFWS, Office of Biological Services FWS/OBS-79/10. Washington, DC.

Erwin, R.M., and C.E. Korschgen. 1979. Coastal waterbird colonies: Maine to Virginia, 1977. An atlas showing colony locations and species composition. USFWS, Office of Biological Services FWS/O85-79/08. Washington, DC.

Estel, B.L. 1989. Habitat use and nesting success of dabbling ducks in western New York State grasslands. M.S. thesis, Cornell Univ., Ithaca, NY.

Evans, F.M. 1983. The Wild Turkey: trap and transfer. New York State Conservationist 38:38.

Evans, W.R. 1994. Nocturnal flight call of Bicknell's Thrush. Wilson Bulletin 106:55–61.

Evans, W., R. Meade, T. Nix, and S. Kelling. 1994. The fall flight of Common Loons over Cayuga Lake. Kingbird 44:164–169.

Faanes, C.A., and S.E. Senner. 1991. Status and conservation of the Eskimo Curlew. American Birds 45:237–239.

Fain, J.J., T.A. Volk, and T.J. Fahey. 1994. Fifty years of change in an upland forest in south-central New York: general patterns. Bulletin of the Torrey Botanical Club 121:130–139.

Federation of New York State Bird Clubs. 1996. Checklist of the birds of New York State.

Fenton, W.N. 1955. The maple and the Passenger Pigeon in Iroquois Indian life. New York State Education Dept. School Bulletin (March).

Ficken, M.S., and R.W. Ficken. 1968. Territorial relationships of Blue-winged Warblers, Golden-winged Warblers and their hybrids. Wilson Bulletin 80:442–451.

Fisher, A.K. 1878. Kentucky Warbler *(Oporornis formosus)* at Sing Sing, NY. Bulletin of the Nuttall Ornithological Club 3:191–192.

Fisher, D.W. 1955. Prehistoric mammals of New York. New York State Conservationist 9:18–22.

Fisher, R.G. 1993. The great albatross day. Birding 25:78.

Flickinger, E.L. 1995. Loggerhead Shrike fatalities on a highway in Texas. *In* Shrikes

(Laniidae) of the world: biology and conservation, R. Yosef and F.E. Lohrer, eds. Proceedings of the Western Foundation of Vertebrate Zoology 6(1):67–69.

Forness, M. 1979. Photographs of New York State rarities 30: Wood Stork. Kingbird 29:2–4.

Frech, M.H., and J.L. Confer. 1987. The Golden-winged Warbler: competition with the Blue-winged Warbler and habitat selection in portions of southern, central and northern New York. Kingbird 37:65–72.

Freer, V.M. 1973. Sparrow Hawk predation of Bank Swallows. Wilson Bulletin 85:231–233.

——. 1977. Colony structure and function in the Bank Swallow, *Riparia riparia* L. Ph.D. dissertation, State Univ. of New York at Binghamton, Binghamton.

——. 1979. Factors affecting site tenacity in New York Bank Swallows. Bird-Banding 50:349–357.

Freer, V.M., and J. Visconti. 1996. Population trends of birds at feeders in Sullivan County, NY, 1981–1994. Kingbird 46:4–11.

Friederici, P. 1994. *In* Call to action, by M. Rands and M. Kelsey. American Birds 48:37.

Friedmann, H. 1929. The cowbirds: a study in the biology of social parasitism. Charles C. Thomas, Springfield, IL.

——. 1963. Host relations of the parasitic cowbirds. Smithsonian Institution, Washington, DC.

Fritz, R.S. 1979. Consequences of insular population structure: distribution and extension of Spruce Grouse populations. Oecologia 42:57–65.

Funk, R.E. 1973a. The Garoga Site (Las. 7). *In* Aboriginal settlement patterns in the Northeast, W.A. Ritchie and R.E. Funk, eds. New York State Museum and Science Service Memoir 20. Pp. 313–332.

——. 1973b. The Scaccia Site (Cda 17-3). *In* Aboriginal settlement patterns in the Northeast, W.A. Ritchie and R.E. Funk, eds. New York State Museum and Science Service Memoir 20. Pp. 99–116.

——. 1976. Recent contributions to Hudson Valley prehistory. New York State Museum and Science Service Memoir 22.

——. 1988. The Laurentian concept: a review. Archaeology of Eastern North America no. 16. Eastern States Archaeological Federation, Bethlehem, CT.

——. 1991. Late Pleistocene and Early Holocene human adaptation in the Lower Hudson Valley. *In* The archaeology and ethnohistory of the lower Hudson Valley and neighboring regions. Essays in honor of Louis A. Brennan, H.C. Kraft, ed. Occasional Publications in Northeastern Anthropology no. 11. Pp. 49–67. Archaeological Service, Bethlehem, CT.

——. 1992. Some major wetlands in New York State: a preliminary assessment of their biological and cultural potential. Man in the Northeast 43:25–41.

——. 1993. Archaeological investigations in the upper Susquehanna Valley, New York State, vol. 1. Persimmon Press, Buffalo.

Funk, R.E., and D.W. Steadman. 1994. Archaeological and paleoenvironmental investigations in the Dutchess Quarry Caves, Orange County, New York. Persimmon Press, Buffalo.

Funk, R.E., G.R. Walters, and W.G. Ehlers Jr., eds. 1969. The archaeology of Dutchess Quarry Cave, Orange County, New York. Pennsylvania Archaeologist 39:7–22.

Galli, A.E., C.F. Leck, and T.T. Forman. 1976. Avian distribution patterns in forest islands of different sizes in central New Jersey. Auk 93:356–364.

Gaston, A.J., and R. Decker. 1985. Interbreeding of Thayer's Gull, *Larus thayeri*, and Kumlien's Gull, *Larus glaucoides kumlieni*, on Southampton Island, Northwest Territories. Canadian Field-Naturalist 99:257–259.

George, C.J. 1991. A sad day for the "Quawks": destruction of a Black-crowned Night-Heron colony in the lower Mohawk Valley. Kingbird 41:83–87.

Gibbons, D.W., J.B. Reid, and R.A. Chapman. 1993. The new atlas of breeding birds in Britain and Ireland: 1988–1991. T. & A.D. Poyser, London.

Gibbs, J. 1992. Sedge Wren. *In* Migratory nongame birds of management concern in the Northeast. K.J. Schneider and D.M. Pence, eds. USFWS, Newton Corner, MA.

Gibson, D.D., and B. Kessel. 1989. Geographic variation in the Marbled Godwit and description of an Alaskan subspecies. Condor 91:436–443.

Gibson, S.J. 1968. The Oran-Barnes Site. Bulletin of the Chenango Chapter of the New York State Archaeological Association 10:1–22.

Gill, F.B. 1980. Historical aspects of hybridization between Blue-winged and Golden-winged warblers. Auk 97:1–18.

Gill, F.B., and B.G. Murray. 1972. Discrimination behavior and hybridization of the Blue-winged and Golden-winged warblers. Evolution 26:282–293.

Gingrich, T. 1995. Montezuma National Wildlife Refuge annual waterfowl production. Seneca Falls, NY. Unpublished data.

Giraud, J.P., Jr. 1844. Birds of Long Island. Wiley & Putnam, New York.

Gochfeld, M., and J. Burger. 1981. Boat-tailed Grackles in Hewlett Bay, Long Island. Kingbird 31:214.

Godfrey, W.E. 1986. The birds of Canada, rev. ed. National Museums of Canada, Ottawa.

Goodrich, L.J., S.T. Crocoll, and S.E. Senner. 1996. Broad-winged Hawk *(Buteo platypterus). In* The birds of North America, no. 218, A. Poole and F. Gill, eds. The Academy of Natural Sciences, Philadelphia, and the American Ornithologists' Union, Washington, DC.

Gordon, A.L., and J.L. Confer. 1996. Do Downy Woodpecker abandon their breeding territories in winter and relocate near a permanent food source? Kingbird 46:111.

Goslin, R.M. 1955. Animal remains from Ohio rock shelters. Ohio Journal of Science 55:358–362.

Gosselin, M., and N. David. 1975. Field identification of Thayer's Gull *(Larus thayeri)* in eastern North America. American Birds 26:1059–1066.

Graham, R.W., and E.L. Lundelius Jr. 1984. Coevolutionary disequilibrium and Pleistocene extinctions. *In* Quaternary extinctions, P.S. Martin and R.G. Klein, eds. Univ. Arizona Press, Tucson. Pp. 223–249.

Granger, J.E., Jr. 1978. Meadowood phase settlement pattern of the Niagara Frontier region of western New York State. Museum of Anthropology Paper no. 65. University of Michigan, Ann Arbor.

Granlund, J. 1994. The winter season: Western Great Lakes region. National Audubon Society Field Notes 48:209–211.

Grant, P.J. 1986. Gulls: a guide to identification. Buteo Books, Vermillion, SD.

Greenlaw, J.S. 1983. Microgeographic distribution of breeding Seaside Sparrows on New York salt marshes. *In* The Seaside Sparrow: its biology and management, T.L. Quay, J.B. Funderburg Jr., D.S. Lee, E.F. Potter, and C.S. Robbins, eds. Occasional Papers of the North Carolina Biological Survey 1983–1985, Raleigh, NC. Pp. 99–114.

——. 1992. Seaside Sparrow, *Ammodramus maritimus. In* Migratory nongame birds of management concern in the Northeast, K.J. Schneider and D.M. Pence, eds. USFWS, Newton Corner, MA.

——. 1993. Behavioral and morphological diversification of Sharp-tailed Sparrows *(Ammodramus caudacutus).* Auk 110:286–303.

Greenlaw, J.S., and R.F. Miller. 1982. Breeding Soras on a Long Island salt marsh. Kingbird 32:78–84.

Greenlaw, J.S., and J.D. Rising. 1994. Sharp-tailed Sparrow *(Ammodramus caudacutus)*. *In* The birds of North America, no. 112, A. Poole and F. Gill, eds. The Academy of Natural Sciences, Philadelphia, and the American Ornithologists' Union, Washington, DC.

Greenway, J.C. 1958. Extinct and vanishing birds of the world. American Committee for International Wildlife Protection, New York.

Gretch, M. 1995. Grasshopper Sparrow at Plattsburgh Air Force Base. Kingbird 45:243.

Gretch, M., H. Booth, and R. Booth. 1982. Red-headed Woodpecker breeding in Clinton County. Kingbird 32:176.

Griscom, L. 1923. Birds of the New York City region. American Museum of Natural History Handbook no. 9. American Museum Press, New York.

——. 1933. The Birds of Dutchess County, NY. Transactions of the Linnaean Society of New York 3.

Griscom, L., and D. Snyder. 1955. The birds of Massachusetts. Peabody Museum, Salem, MA.

Gross, A.O. 1928. The Heath Hen. Memoirs of the Boston Society of Natural History 6:487–588 + 12 plates.

Groth, J.G. 1993. Evolutionary differentiation in morphology, vocalizations, and allozymes among nomadic sibling species in the North American Red Crossbill *(Loxia curvirostra)* complex. Univ. California Publications in Zoology 127.

Grubb, T.C., and R. Yosef. 1994. Habitat-specific nutritional condition in Loggerhead Shrikes *(Lanius ludovicianus)*: evidence from ptilochronology. Auk 111:756–759.

Guilday, J.E. 1969. Faunal remains from Dutchess Quarry Cave No. 1. *In* The archaeology of Dutchess Quarry Cave, Orange County, New York, by R.E. Funk, G.R. Walters, and W.F. Ehlers Jr. Pennsylvania Archaeologist 39:7–22. Pp. 17–19.

——. 1973a. Faunal remains from the Nahrwold No. 1 Site. *In* Aboriginal settlement patterns in the Northeast, W.A. Ritchie and R.E. Funk, eds. New York State Museum and Science Service Memoir 20. Pp. 288–290.

——. 1973b. Vertebrate remains from the Garoga Site, Fulton County, NY. *In* Aboriginal settlement patterns in the Northeast, W.A. Ritchie and R.E. Funk, eds. New York State Museum and Science Service Memoir 20. Pp. 329–330.

——. 1980. Bone refuse from the Lamoka Lake Site. *In* The Archaeology of New York State by W.A. Ritchie. Harbor Hill Books, Harrison, NY. Pp. 54–59.

Guilday, J.E., and P.W. Parmalee. 1965. Animal remains from the Sheep Rock Shelter (36 Hu 1), Huntingdon County, Pa. Pennsylvania Archaeologist 35:34–49.

Guillion, G.W., and W.H. Marshall. 1968. Survival of Ruffed Grouse in a boreal forest. Living Bird 7:117–167.

Guthrie, R.P., and J.A. Davis. 1975. Photographs of New York State rarities 24: Mountain Bluebird. Kingbird 25:68–70.

Hagan, J.M., III. 1993. Decline of the Rufous-sided Towhee in the eastern United States. Auk 110:863–874.

Halliwell, T. 1995. Major rarities near N.J. Personal compilation.

Haney, J.C., and C.P. Schaadt. 1996. Functional roles of eastern old growth in promoting forest bird diversity. *In* Eastern old-growth forests, M.B. Davis, ed. Island Press, Washington, DC. Pp. 76–88.

Hansen, L. 1960. Krydsning mellem Solvmage *(Larus argentatus* Pont.*)* og Sildemage *(Larus fuscus* L.*)* fundet ynglende sammen med en Solvmage. [Hybrid Herring × Lesser Black-backed Gull found breeding with a Herring Gull.] Dansk Ornitologisk Forenings Tidsskrifter 54:85–87.

Haramis, G.M. 1974. Cinnamon Teal sighted at Montezuma National Wildlife Refuge. Kingbird 24:172–173.

Harper, L.H. 1993. Status and reproductive success of the threatened Common Tern *(Sterna hirundo)* on the upper St. Lawrence River, 1993. Final Project Report for NYSDEC.

Harris, M.P., C. Morley, and G.H. Green. 1978. Hybridization of Herring and Lesser Black-backed gulls in Britain. Bird Study 25:161–166.

Harrison, C. 1978. A field guide to the nests, eggs and nestlings of North American birds. Collins, Glasgow, Scotland.

Harrison, H.H. 1984. Wood Warblers' world. Simon and Schuster, New York.

Harrison, P. 1983. Seabirds: an identification guide. Houghton Mifflin, Boston.

———. 1985. Seabirds: an identification guide, rev. ed. Houghton Mifflin, Boston.

Hayman, P., J. Marchant, and T. Prater. 1986. Shorebirds: an identification guide. Houghton Mifflin, Boston.

Hays, H. 1984. The vole that soared. Natural History 93(5):7–6.

———. 1995. Fort Tyler Report—1995. Unpublished report to NYSDEC.

Hedrick, U.P. 1966. A history of agriculture in the state of New York. Hill and Wang, New York. [Reprint of original publication of 1933.]

Herbert, R.A., and K.G.S. Herbert. 1965. Behavior of Peregrine Falcons in the New York City region. Auk 82:62–94.

———. 1969. The extirpation of the Hudson River Peregrine Falcon population. *In* Peregrine Falcon populations: their biology and decline. J.J. Hickey, ed. Univ. Wisconsin Press. Madison. Pp. 133–154.

Hickey, J.J. 1935. The ornithological year in the NYC region. Proceedings of the Linnaean Society of New York 47:103–104.

High Peaks Audubon Society. 1984. Proposal for study and management of colonial waterbirds of the Four Brothers Islands, Lake Champlain. Unpublished Research Proposal to NYSDEC.

Hitchcock, C.L., and D.F. Sherry. 1990. Long-term memory for cache sites in the Black-capped Chickadee. Animal Behavior 40:701–712.

Holmes, R.T., T.M. Sherry, and F.W. Sturges. 1986. Bird community dynamics in a temperate deciduous forest: long-term trends at Hubbard Brook. Ecological Monographs 56:201–220.

Hoover, J.P., M.C. Brittingham, and L.J. Goodrich. 1995. Effects of forest patch size on nesting success of Wood Thrushes. Auk 112:146–155.

Horning, N.M., L.D. McBrayer, T.D. White, and S.W. Calhoun. 1995. Reproductive status of Common Tern *(Sterna hirundo)* colonies on the Niagara Frontier during the 1995 breeding season. Final Project Report for NYSDEC.

Hotopp, K.P. 1986. Status of Common Terns on the Buffalo Harbor and upper Niagara River. NYSDEC, Buffalo, NY. Mimeo.

Hough, A.F. 1936. A climax forest community on East Tionesta Creek, northwestern Pennsylvania. Ecology 17:9–28.

———. 1965. A twenty-year record of understory vegetational changes in a virgin Pennsylvania forest. Ecology 46:370–373.

Hough, F.N. 1964. The thrushes (Turdidae): their occurrence in Ulster County, NY. Burroughs Natural History Society Bulletin 7:19.

Howard, R.A. 1977. Habitat structure, polygyny, and the evolution of upland nesting in Red-winged Blackbirds *(Agelaius phoeniceus)*. Ph.D. dissertation Cornell Univ., Ithaca, NY.

Hunter, M.L., Jr. 1990. Wildlife, forests, and forestry—principles of managing forests for biological diversity. Prentice Hall, Englewood Cliffs, NJ.

Hyde, A.S. 1939. The ecology and economics of the birds along the northern boundary of New York State. Roosevelt Wild Life Bulletin 7:61–215.

Ickes, R. 1992. Hooded Warbler. *In* Atlas of breeding birds in Pennsylvania. D.W. Brauning, ed. Univ. Pittsburgh Press, Pittsburgh. Pp. 352–353.

Irving, F.H. 1953. Record of the nesting of a pair of phoebes in West Nyack, NY. Kingbird 3:35.

Jackson, S.T. 1989. Postglacial vegetational changes along an elevational gradient in the Adirondack Mountains (New York): a study of plant macrofossils. New York State Museum Bulletin no. 465.

James, R.D. 1991. Annotated checklist of the birds of Ontario. Royal Ontario Museum, Toronto.

Jaramillo, A., R. Pittaway, and P. Burke. 1991. The identification and migration of breeding plumage dowitchers in Southern Ontario. Birders Journal 1:8–27.

Jensen, A.C., and R. Livingstone. 1969. Offshore records of land birds. Kingbird 19:5–10.

Johnsgard, P.A. 1978. Ducks, geese, and swans of the world. Univ. Nebraska Press, Lincoln.

——. 1988. North American owls: biology and natural history—Eastern Screech-Owl. Smithsonian Institution Press, Washington, DC. Pp. 113–118.

Johnson, G., and R.E. Chambers. 1994. Breeding ecology of the Red-shouldered Hawk in north central New York. Kingbird 44:87–95.

Jones, A.D. 1963. Dutchess County's singular Eastern-Western Meadowlark successful hybridization. Kingbird 13:152.

Jones, I.L. 1989. First record of Mew Gull *(Larus canus brachyrhynchus)* in New York State. Kingbird 39:2–6.

Jones, M.V., III. 1975. Brown-headed Cowbird brood parasitism on the Eastern Phoebe. Kingbird 25:119–122.

——. 1980. The New York State waterfowl count—a quarter century report. Kingbird 30:210–216.

Jonsson, L. 1993. Birds of Europe with North Africa and the Middle East. Princeton Univ. Press, Princeton.

Karwowski, K. 1994. Food study of the Double-Crested Cormorant, Little Galloo Island, Lake Ontario, NY, 1992. USFWS, Cortland, NY.

Karwowski, K., J.E. Gates, and L.H. Harper. 1995. Common Terns nesting on navigational aids and natural islands in the St. Lawrence River, New York. Wilson Bulletin 107:423–436.

Kaufman, K. 1990. A field guide to advanced birding. Houghton Mifflin, Boston.

Keller, J.K. 1980. Species composition and density of breeding birds in several habitat types on the Connecticut Hill Wildlife Management Area. M.S. thesis, Cornell Univ., Ithaca, NY.

——. 1982. From Yellowthroats to Woodpeckers—how forest succession affects bird life. New York State Conservationist 37:31–35.

Keller, J.K., and C.R. Smith. 1983. Birds in a patchwork landscape. Living Bird 2:20–23.

Kendeigh, S.C. 1945. Community selection by birds on the Helderberg Plateau of New York. Auk 62:418–436.

Kerlinger, P. 1993. Sharp-shinned Hawk populations in free-fall. Winging It 5(9):10–11.

Kerlinger, P., and C. Doremus. 1981. The breeding birds of three pine barrens in New York State. Kingbird 31:126–135.

Key, M.C., and J.W. Key. 1983. Black-shouldered Kite visits Dutchess County: a first record for New York State. Kingbird 33:151–152.

Keyser, L.S. 1902. A pretty House Finch. Birds and Nature 12:24–25.

Kiester, A.R., J.M. Scott, B. Csuti, R.F. Noss, B. Butterfield, K. Sahr, and D. White. 1996. Conservation prioritization using GAP data. Conservation Biology 10:1332–1342.

Kilham, L. 1972. Death of Red-breasted Nuthatch from pitch around nest hole. Auk 89:451–452.

Kingbird, The. Journal of the Federation of New York State Bird Clubs. 1950–1996. Volumes 1–46.

Kinsey, W.F., III. 1989. Susquehannock zoomorphic images; or, why the seasons change. *In* New approaches to other pasts. W.F. Kinsey III and R.W. Moeller, eds. Archaeological Services, Bethlehem, CT. Pp. 71–88.

Klaubunde, W. 1986. USFWS breeding bird surveys for western New York. Prothonotary 52:102–108.

Klingensmith, C., and D. Hoover. 1986. The Allegany County breeding bird survey. Kingbird 36:114–126.

Kllnowski, S., and M. Richmond. 1992. Breeding and fledging success in the Common Tern *(Sterna hirundo)* on Oneida Lake, NY. 1992. Final Project Report for NYSDEC.

Klonick, A.S. 1951. Western Meadowlark, *Sturnella neglecta*, in New York State. Auk 38:107.

Knox, A.G. 1988. The taxonomy of Redpolls. Ardea 78:441–458.

Koeneke, M.A. 1992. Photograph of New York State rarities 55: Le Conte's Sparrow. Kingbird 42:131.

——. 1994. Photograph of New York State rarities 61: Scissor-tailed Flycatcher. Kingbird 44:255.

Krapu, G. 1986. Pattern and causes of change in a Cliff Swallow colony during a 17 year period. Prairie Naturalist 18:109–114.

Kricher, J.C. 1983. Correlation between House Finch increase and House Sparrow decline. American Birds 37:358–360.

Krueger, W. 1993. Wilson's Phalarope, a new nesting species for New York State. Kingbird 43:274–277.

Kuhn, R.D. 1994. The Cromwell Site (NYSM 1121) including a brief treatise on early seventeenth-century Mohawk pottery trends. Journal of the New York State Archaeological Association 108:29–38.

Kuhn, R.D., and R.E. Funk. n.d. Boning up on the Mohawk: an overview of Mohawk faunal assemblages. Typescript.

Kutz, H.L., and D.G. Allen. 1947. Double-crested Cormorant nesting in New York. Auk 64:137.

Lansdown, P. 1991. Identification of Arctic Redpoll. British Birds 84:41–56.

Lantz, B.J. 1994. Red-necked Grebes in Delaware. Delmarva Ornithologist 26:10–13.

Lanyon, W.E. 1966. Hybridization in meadowlarks. Bulletin of the American Museum of Natural History 134:1–26.

——. 1979. Hybrid sterility in meadowlarks. Nature 279:557–558.

——. 1995. Western Meadowlark *(Sturnella neglecta)*. *In* The birds of North America, no.104, A. Poole and F. Gill, eds. The Academy of Natural Sciences, Philadelphia, and the American Ornithologists' Union, Washington, DC.

Lanyon, W.E., R.G. Van Gelder, and R.G. Zweifel. 1970. The vertebrate fauna of the Kalbfleisch Field Research Station. American Museum of Natural History, New York.

Laporte, P., and M. Robert. 1995. The decline and current status of the Loggerhead Shrike in Quebec. *In* Shrikes (Laniidae) of the world: biology and conservation, R. Yosef and F.E. Lohrer, eds. Proceedings of the Western Foundation of Vertebrate Zoology 6(1):85–87.

Laub, R.S. 1994. The Pleistocene/Holocene transition in western New York State: fruits of interdisciplinary studies at the Hiscock Site. *In* Great Lakes archaeology and paleoecology, R.I. MacDonald, ed. The Quaternary Studies Institute, Univ. Waterloo, ON. Pp. 155–167.

Laub, R.S., M.F. DeRemer, C.A. Dufort, and W.L. Parsons. 1988. The Hiscock site: a rich late Quaternary locality in western New York State. *In* Late Pleistocene and early Holocene paleoecology and archaeology of the eastern Great Lakes region, R.S. Laub and D.W. Steadman, eds. Bulletin of the Buffalo Society of Natural Sciences 33:67–81.

Lauro, A.J. 1977. Photographs of New York State Rarities 26: Mew Gull: a first for New York State. Kingbird 27:179–180.

Lauro, A.J., and B.J. Spencer. 1980. A method for separating juvenal and first-winter Ring-billed Gulls *(Larus delawarensis)* and Common Gulls *(Larus canus)*. American Birds 34:111–117.

Leck, Charles F. 1984. The status and distribution of New Jersey birds. Rutgers Univ. Press, New Brunswick, NJ.

Lehman, P. 1980. Identification of Thayer's Gull in the field. Birding 12:198–210.

——. 1987. Immature Blackburnian and Cerulean Warblers: a cautionary note. Birding 19:22–23.

Leuchner, P., and K. Roblee. 1996. Noteworthy records—addenda. Prothonotary 62:5.

Levine, E. 1995. Photographs of New York State rarities 62: Ross' Gull in Nassau County. Kingbird 45:3–4.

Lindauer, M.R. 1982. Photographs of New York State rarities 44: Chestnut-collared Longspur. Kingbird 32:326.

Lindberg, A.J. 1978. Overwintering and nesting of Long-eared Owl at Muttontown Park and Preserve, East Norwich, Long Island. Kingbird 28:77.

Lindsay, P., and T. Vezo. 1992. Probable breeding of Cerulean Warbler on Eastern Long Island. Kingbird 42:213–215.

——. 1994. Cerulean Warbler confirmed breeding and Acadian Flycatcher probable breeding on eastern Long Island. Kingbird 44:108.

——. 1995. Cerulean Warbler and Northern Parula tending the same nest. Kingbird 45:160–161.

Litwin, T.S., A. Ducey-Ortiz, R.A. Lent, and C.E. Liebelt. 1993. 1990–1991 Long Island Colonial waterbird and Piping Plover survey. NYSDEC, Stony Brook, NY.

Lucas, F.A. 1890. The expedition to Funk Island, with observations upon the history and anatomy of the Great Auk. U.S. National Museum Report for 1888:493–529.

Lundelius, E.L., Jr., R.W. Graham, E. Anderson, J. Guilday, J.A. Holman, D.W. Steadman, and S.D. Webb. 1983. Terrestrial vertebrate faunas. *In* Late-Quaternary environments of the United States, vol. 1. The Pleistocene, H.E. Wright Jr., ed. Univ. Minnesota Press, Minneapolis. Pp. 311–353.

Lunk, W.A. 1962. The Rough-winged Swallow: a study based on its breeding biology in Michigan. Nuttall Ornithological Club Publication no. 4. Cambridge, MA.

Luukkonen, D.L. 1987. Status and breeding ecology of the Loggerhead Shrike in Virginia. M.S. thesis, Virginia Polytechnic Institute and State University, Blacksburg.

Lymn, N., and S.A. Temple. 1991. Land-use changes in the Gulf Coast region: links to declines in midwestern Loggerhead Shrike populations. Passenger Pigeon 53:315–325.

Lynch, P.J., and D.G. Smith. 1984. Census of Eastern Screech-Owls *(Otus asio)* in urban open-space areas using tape-recorded song. American Birds 38:388–391.

MacNamara, E.E., and H.F. Udell. 1970. Clapper Rail investigations on the south shore of Long Island. Proceedings of the Linnaean Society of New York 71:120–131.

MacPherson, A.H. 1961. Observations on Canadian arctic *Larus* gulls and the taxonomy of *L. thayeri*. Arctic Institute of North America Technical Paper 7:1–40.

Madge, S. 1994. Crows and jays: a guide to the crows, jays and magpies of the world. Houghton Mifflin, Boston.

Mahoney, T.P. 1987. Photographs of New York State rarities 48: Rock Wren in Chautauqua County: a first New York State record. Kingbird 37:55.

Marcotte, R. 1995. Photographs of New York rarities 63: Ancient Murrelet. Kingbird 45:149.

Marks, P.J., S. Gardescu, and F.K. Seischab. 1992. Late eighteenth century vegetation of central and western New York State on the basis of original land survey records. New York State Museum Bulletin no. 484. State Education Dept., Albany, NY.

Marshall, W.B., and W. Dutcher. 1892. A specimen of *Numenius arquatus* said to be taken on Long Island, N.Y. Auk 9:390–392.

Martin, G. 1987. The world through a starling's eyes. New Scientist 28:114(1562):49–51.

Martin, P.R., and B. Di Labio. 1994. Identification of Common × Barrow's Goldeneye hybrids in the Field. Birding 26:104–105.

Martin, P.S. 1990. 40,000 years of extinction on the "planet of doom." Palaeogeography, Palaeoclimatology, Palaeoecology 82:187–201.

Maurer, B.A., and M. Villard, eds. 1996. Continental scale ecology and Neotropical migratory birds: how to detect declines amid the noise. Ecology 77:1–68.

Mayfield, H.F. 1972. Bird bones identified from Indian sites at western end of Lake Erie. Condor 74:344–347.

Mayr, E. 1942. Speciation in the junco. Ecology 23:378–379.

Mazzocchi, I.M., and S. Muller. 1991. Black Tern counts from eastern Lake Ontario. Kingbird 41:250.

——. 1992. A White-winged Tern nests in New York State. Kingbird 42:210.

——. 1995. Black Tern *(Chlidonias niger)* investigations in New York, 1994. NYSDEC, Division of Fish and Wildlife, Delmar, NY.

McAtee, W.L. 1926. Relation of birds to woodlots in New York State. Roosevelt Wild Life Bulletin 25:7–148.

McBrayer, L.D., J.M. Arnold, T.D. White, and S.W. Calhoun. 1995. Reproductive status of Common Tern *(Sterna hirundo)* colonies on the Niagara Frontier. Final Report, Fiscal Year 1993–1995 for NYSDEC.

McCaskie, G., J.L. Dunn, C. Roberts, and D.A. Sibley. 1990. Notes on identifying Arctic and Pacific loons in alternate plumage. Birding 22:70–73.

McIlroy, M. 1961. Possible hybridization between a Clay-colored Sparrow and a Chipping Sparrow at Ithaca. Kingbird 11:7–10.

McKinley, D. 1959. On the arrival of parakeets at Albany, New York, in the eighteenth century. Kingbird 8:105.

McLaren, I.A. 1995. Field identification and taxonomy of Bicknell's Thrush. Birding 27:358–366.

McNeely, J.A., K.R. Miller, W.V. Reid, R.A. Mittermeier, and T.B. Werner. 1990. Conserving the world's biodiversity. International Union for the Conservation of Nature, Gland, Switzerland: World Resources Institute, Conservation International, World Wildlife Fund–United States, and the World Bank.

Meanley, B. 1992. King Rail *(Rallus elegans). In* The birds of North America, no. 3, A. Poole, P. Stettenheim, and F. Gill, eds. The Academy of Natural Sciences, Philadelphia, and the American Ornithologists' Union, Washington, DC.

Meng, H. 1951. The Cooper's Hawk. Ph.D. dissertation, Cornell Univ., Ithaca, NY.

Merriam, C.H. 1878–1879. Remarks on some of the birds of Lewis County, northern New York. Bulletin of the Nuttall Ornithological Club 3:52–56, 123–128; with Remarks by A.J. Dayan, 4:1–7.

——. 1881. Preliminary list of birds ascertained to occur in the Adirondack region, northeastern New York. Bulletin of the Nuttall Ornithological Club 6:225–235.

Meskill, K.J., L.A. Sommers, M.L. Alfieri, and R.L. Miller. 1995. 1994 Long Island colonial waterbird and Piping Plover survey. A Research Report of NYSDEC. Stony Brook, NY.

Messineo, D.J. 1985. The 1985 nesting of Pine Siskin, Red Crossbill and White-winged Crossbill in Chenango County, NY. Kingbird 35:233–237.

———. 1990. White-winged Crossbill breeding in Chenango-Cortland-Madison counties 1989–1990. Kingbird 40:230–231.

Miller, A.H. 1941. Speciation in the avian genus *Junco*. Univ. California Publications in Zoology 44:173–434.

Miller, H.S. 1957. The Western Meadowlark in Monroe County. Kingbird 7:115.

Miller, N.G. 1973a. Late glacial plants and plant communities in northwestern New York State. Journal of the Arnold Arboretum 54:123–159.

———. 1973b. Late-glacial and post-glacial vegetation changes in southwestern New York. New York State Museum Bulletin no. 420.

———. 1988. The late Quaternary Hiscock Site, Genesee County, New York: paleoecological studies based on pollen and plant macrofossils. Bulletin of the Buffalo Society of Natural Sciences 33:83–93.

Minor, W.F., and M.L. Minor. 1981. Nesting of Red-tailed Hawks and Great Horned Owls in central New York suburban areas. Kingbird 31:68.

Mitchell, H.D., and R.F. Andrle. 1970. Birds of the Niagara Frontier region supplement. Buffalo Society of Natural Sciences.

Mitchell, J.G. 1987. A man called Bird. Audubon 89:81–104.

Mithun, M. 1984. The proto-Iroquoians: cultural reconstruction from lexical materials. *In* Extending the rafters: interdisciplinary approaches to Iroquoian studies, M.K. Foster, J. Campsi, and M. Mithun, eds. State Univ. of New York Press, Albany. Pp. 259–281.

Montgomery, W. 1992. First record of Merlin nesting in New York State. Kingbird 42:206.

Morris, A. 1985. The fall shorebird season at Jamaica Bay Wildlife Refuge, New York City. Kingbird 35:79–89.

———. 1986a. An account of New York State's first Rufous-necked Stint. Kingbird 26:3–5.

———. 1986b. The fall shorebird season at Jamaica Bay Wildlife Refuge, New York City. Kingbird 36:54.

———. 1987. The fall shorebird season at Jamaica Bay Wildlife Refuge, New York City. Kingbird 37:110.

———. 1988. The fall shorebird season at Jamaica Bay Wildlife Refuge, New York City. Kingbird 38:86.

———. 1989. The fall shorebird season at Jamaica Bay Wildlife Refuge, New York City. Kingbird 39:82.

———. 1990. The fall shorebird season at Jamaica Bay Wildlife Refuge, New York City. Kingbird 40:133.

Morse, D.H. 1989. American Warblers. Harvard Univ. Press, Cambridge.

Moser, J. 1982. Waterfowl population study. New York federal aid in wildlife restoration project W-39-R (final report). NYSDEC, Albany. Mimeo.

Muhlstein, A. 1994. La Salle—explorer of the North American Frontier. Arcade Publishing, New York.

Muller, E.H., and P.E. Calkin. 1988. Late Pleistocene and Holocene geology of the eastern Great Lakes region: geological setting of the Hiscock paleontological site, western New York. *In* Late Pleistocene and early Holocene paleoecology and archaeology of the eastern Great Lakes region, R.S. Laub and D.W. Steadman, eds. Bulletin of the Buffalo Society of Natural Sciences 33:53–63.

Mundinger, P.C., and S. Hope. 1982. Expansion of the winter range of the House Finch: 1947–1979. American Birds 36:347–353.

Murphy, R.C. 1933. Probable records of the Eskimo Curlew *(Numenius borealis)* at Montauk Point, New York. Auk 50:101–102.

——. 1936. Oceanic birds of South America, 2 vols. Macmillan for the American Museum of Natural History.

Murray, B.G., Jr. 1968. The relationships of sparrows in the genera *Ammodramus, Passerculus* and *Ammospiza* with a description of a hybrid Le Conte's × Sharp-tailed Sparrow. Auk 85:586–593.

Murray, B.G., Jr., and F.B. Gill. 1976. Behavioral interactions of Blue-winged and Golden-winged warblers. Wilson Bulletin 88:231–254.

Nadareski, C.A. 1992. Prey selection by urban nesting Peregrine Falcons *(Falco peregrinus)* and contaminant analysis of prey in their diets along the lower Hudson River estuary. Poster presented at the 1992 New York Natural History Conference in Albany, NY.

National Audubon Society Field Notes. Publication of the National Audubon Society. 1994–1996. Volumes 48–50. [Replaced American Birds with vol. 48 in 1994.]

National Geographic Society. 1987. Field guide to the birds of North America, 2nd ed. National Geographic Society, Washington, DC.

Neumann, T.W. 1989. Human-wildlife competition and prehistoric subsistence: the case of the eastern United States. Journal of Middle Atlantic Archaeology 5:29–57.

Newton, A., and H. Gadow. 1896. A dictionary of birds. A.&C. Black, London.

New York Birders. Newsletter of the Federation of New York State Bird Clubs. 1972–1996.

Nicholson, A.G. 1985. The development of agriculture in New York State. Natural Resources Research and Extension Series no. 23. Dept. of Natural Resources, Cornell Univ., Ithaca, NY.

Nickell, W.P. 1955. Notes on Cowbird parasitism of four species. Auk 72:88–92.

Nickerson, D. 1978. Wilson's Warbler nests in New York State. Kingbird 28:215.

Nisbet, I.C.T. 1980. Status and trends of the Roseate Tern *(Sterna dougallii)* in North America and the Caribbean. Unpublished report to the USFWS, Office of Endangered Species.

Noon, B.R. 1981. The distribution of an avian guild along a temperate elevational gradient: the importance and expression of competition. Ecological Monographs 51:105–124.

Norris, C.A. 1947. Report on the distribution and status of the Corn Crake. Part 2—a consideration of the causes of the decrease. British Birds 40:226–244.

Noss, R.F., E.T. LaRoe III, and J.M. Scott. 1996. Endangered ecosystems of the United States. Biological Report no. 28. U.S. Dept. of Interior, National Biological Service, Washington, DC.

Novak, P.G. 1989. Breeding ecology and status of the Loggerhead Shrike *(Lanius ludovicianus)* in New York State. M.S. thesis. Cornell Univ., Ithaca, NY.

——. 1990. Population status of the Black Tern in New York State—1989. NYSDEC Division of Fish and Wildlife, Nongame Unit, Delmar, NY.

——. 1992. Black Tern, *Chlidonias niger. In* Migratory nongame birds of management concern in the Northeast, K.J. Schneider and D.M. Pence, eds. USFWS, Newton Corner, MA.

Nye, P. 1996. Where eagles soar . . . in New York State. New York State Conservationist 51:2–6.

NYSARC. 1979. Report of the New York State Avian Records Committee. Kingbird 29:120.

——. 1980. Report of the New York State Avian Records Committee. Kingbird 30:201.

——. 1981. Report of the New York State Avian Records Committee. Kingbird 31:202.

——. 1982. Report of the New York State Avian Records Committee. Kingbird 32:228.

——. 1983. Report of the New York State Avian Records Committee. Kingbird 33:246.

——. 1984. Report of the New York State Avian Records Committee. Kingbird 34:216.

——. 1985. Report of the New York State Avian Records Committee. Kingbird 35:224.

——. 1987. Report of the New York State Avian Records Committee. Kingbird 37:200.

——. 1988. Report of the New York State Avian Records Committee. Kingbird 38:226.

——. 1990. Report of the New York State Avian Records Committee. Kingbird 40:209.

——. 1991. Report of the New York State Avian Records Committee. Kingbird 41:241.

——. 1992. Report of the New York State Avian Records Committee. Kingbird 42:5.

——. 1993. Report of the New York State Avian Records Committee. Kingbird 43:18.

——. 1994. Report of the New York State Avian Records Committee. Kingbird 44:3.

——. 1995. Report of the New York State Avian Records Committee. Kingbird 45:71.

——. 1996. Report of the New York State Avian Records Committee. Kingbird 46:296.

NYSDEC. 1993. Fact sheet: Mute Swans in New York.

——. 1994–1995. Wild Turkey hunting seasons and regulations.

——. 1996. Field visit to Little Galloo Island, Lake Ontario. Field Notes.

O'Brien, M., and R. Askins. 1985. The effects of Mute Swans on native waterfowl. Connecticut Warbler 5:27–31.

O'Connor, R.J. 1981. Habitat correlates of bird distribution in British census plots. Studies in Avian Biology 6:533–537.

Odom, R. 1977. Sora *(Porzana carolina). In* Management of migratory shore and upland game birds in North America, G.C. Sanderson, ed. International Association of Fish and Wildlife Agencies, Washington, DC. Pp. 57–65.

Ouellet, H. 1993. Bicknell's Thrush: taxonomic status and distribution. Wilson Bulletin 105:545–571.

Palmer, R.S. 1976. Handbook of North American Birds, vols. 1–3. Yale Univ. Press, New Haven. [Volume 1 originally published in 1962.]

——. 1988. Handbook of North American birds, vol. 4. Yale Univ. Press, New Haven, CT.

Panko, D. 1990. Decline of migrant Sharp-shinned Hawks. Hawk Migration Studies 15(2):3–13.

Parker, K.E. 1987. An apparent prefledged Common Loon chick found at Montezuma National Wildlife Refuge. Kingbird 37:189–191.

Parkes, K.C. 1951. The genetics of the Golden-winged × Blue-winged warbler complex. Wilson Bulletin 63:4–15.

——. 1952. The birds of New York and their taxonomy, 2 vols. Ph.D. dissertation, Cornell Univ., Ithaca, NY.

——. 1953. The Yellow-throated Warbler in New York. Kingbird 3:4.

——. 1954. Birds of the Adirondacks and Catskills. Annals of the Carnegie Museum 33:173–174.

——. 1983. Letter to the editors. Kingbird 33:251.

——. 1992. The subspecies of the Sharp-tailed Sparrow and the re-identification of a western Pennsylvania specimen. Pennsylvania Birds 6:13–14.

——. 1993. Erythristic Northern Orioles. Kingbird 43:13–17.

Parmalee, P.W. 1967. Additional noteworthy records of birds from archaeological sites. Wilson Bulletin 79:155–162.

Paulson, D. 1993. Shorebirds of the Pacific Northwest. Univ. Washington Press, Seattle.

Payne, R.B. 1992. Indigo Bunting *(Passerina cyanea)*. *In* The birds of North America, no. 4, A. Poole, P. Stettenheim, and F. Gill, eds. The Academy of Natural Sciences, Philadelphia, and the American Ornithologists' Union, Washington, DC.

Peck, G.K., and R.D. James. 1983. Breeding birds of Ontario. Vol. 1: Non-Passerines. Royal Ontario Museum, Toronto.

Penrod, B., and J. Hill. n.d. Landowners' manual for Ring-necked habitat improvement. NYSDEC, Albany, NY.

——. 1983. In quest of the Ringneck. NYSDEC, Albany, NY. Pamphlet.

Peteet, D.M., R.A. Daniels, L.E. Heusser, J.S. Vogel, J.R. Southon, and D.E. Nelson. 1993. Late-Glacial pollen, macrofossils and fish remains in northeastern U.S.A.—the Younger Dryas oscillation. Quaternary Science Reviews 12:597–612.

Peterjohn, B.G. 1995. 1995 breeding bird survey trend statistics for New York State. Mimeographed compilation.

Peterjohn, B.G., J.R. Sauer, and S. Orsillo. 1995. Breeding bird survey: population trends 1966–92. *In* Our living resources—a report to the nation on the distribution, abundance, and health of U.S. plants, animals, and ecosystems, E.T. LaRoe, G.S. Farris, C.E. Puckett, P.D. Doran, and M.J. Mac, eds. U.S. Dept. Interior, National Biological Service, Washington, DC.

Peters, J.L., and L. Griscom. 1938. Geographical variation in the Savannah Sparrow. Bulletin of the Museum of Comparative Zoology 80(13):445–478.

Peterson, A. 1983. Observations on habitat selection by Henslow's Sparrow in Broome County, New York. Kingbird 33:155–164.

Peterson, J.M.C. 1974. Here come the redpolls. Adirondack Life 6(1):28–30.

——. 1975. Attempted nesting of the White-winged Crossbill in New York State. Kingbird 25:191–193.

——. 1976. Greater Shearwater flies up the Hudson River to Lake Champlain. Kingbird 26:148.

——. 1984. First record of Palm Warbler nesting in New York State. Kingbird 34: 2–7.

Peterson, J.M.C., and S.T. Crocoll. 1992. Red-shouldered Hawk, *Buteo lineatus*. *In* Migratory nongame birds of management concern in the Northeast, K.J. Schneider and D.M. Pence, eds. USFWS, Newton Corner, MA.

Peterson, R.T. 1948. Birds over America. Dodd, Mead & Co., New York.

——. 1980. A field guide to the birds, 4th ed. Houghton Mifflin, Boston.

Phillips, A.R. 1975. Semipalmated Sandpiper: identification, migration, summer and wintering ranges. American Birds 29:799–806.

——. 1991. The known birds of North and Middle America. Part 2. A.R. Phillips, Denver, CO.

Phillips, A.R., W.E. Lanyon, and M.A. Howe. 1966. Identification of the flycatchers of eastern North America, with special emphasis on the genus *Empidonax*. Bird-Banding 37:153.

Phillips, A.R., J. Marshall, and G. Monson. 1964. The birds of Arizona. Univ. Arizona Press, Tucson.

Phillips, J.C. 1986. A natural history of the ducks, vols. 1 and 2. Dover Publications, New York.

Pitelka, F.A. 1950. Geographic variation and species problems in the shore-bird genus *Limnodromus*. Univ. California Publications in Zoology 50:46.

Poole, A.R. 1989. Ospreys a natural and unnatural history. Cambridge Univ. Press, Cambridge.

Post, P.W. 1966. Photographs of New York State rarities 4: Smew. Kingbird 16:2–3.

——. 1967. Photographs of New York State rarities 9: Hoary Redpoll. Kingbird 17:66.

——. 1968. Photographs of New York State rarities 13: Yellow-nosed Albatross. Kingbird 28:66.

——. 1980. Photographs of New York State rarities 36: Swainson's Warbler. Kingbird 30:134–137.

Post, P.W., and F. Enders. 1969. Reappearance of the Black Rail on Long Island. Kingbird 19:189.

——. 1970. Notes on a salt marsh Virginia Rail population. Kingbird 20:61–67.

Post, P.W., and R.H. Lewis. 1995a. The Lesser Black-backed Gull in the Americas. Part 1: Taxonomy, distribution, and migration. Birding 27:283–290.

——. 1995b. The Lesser Black-backed Gull in the Americas. Part 2: Field identification. Birding 27:370–381.

Post, P.W., and G. Raynor. 1964. Recent range expansion of the American Oystercatcher into New York. Wilson Bulletin 76:339–346.

Post, P.W., and D. Riepe. 1980. Laughing Gulls colonize Jamaica Bay. Kingbird 30:11–13.

Post, W., and J.S. Greenlaw. 1982. Comparative costs of promiscuity and monogamy; a test of reproductive effort theory. Behavioral Ecology and Sociobiology 10:101–107.

Post, W., J.S. Greenlaw, T.L. Merrian, and L.A. Wood. 1983. Comparative ecology of northern and southern populations of the Seaside Sparrow. *In* The Seaside Sparrow: its biology and management, T.L. Quay, J.B. Funderburg Jr., D.S. Lee, E.F. Potter, and C.S. Robbins, eds. Occasional Papers of the North Carolina Biological Survey 1983–1985, Raleigh, NC. Pp. 123–136.

Potts, G.R. 1980. The effects of modern agriculture, nest predation, and game management on the population ecology of partridges *(Predix perdix* and *Alectoris rufa)*. Advances in Ecological Research 11:2–79.

——. 1986. The partridge: pesticides, predation and conservation. Collins, London.

Powers, K.D., and J. Cherry. 1983. Loon migration off the coast of the northeastern United States. Wilson Bulletin 95:125.

Prescott, D.R.C. 1987. Yellow Rail. *In* Atlas of the breeding birds of Ontario, M.D. Cadman, P.F.J. Eagles, and F.M. Helleiner, eds. Univ. Waterloo Press, Waterloo, ON.

Price, I.M., and D.V. Weseloh. 1986. Increased numbers and productivity of Double-crested Cormorants, *Phalacrocorax auritus*, on Lake Ontario. Canadian Field-Naturalist 100:474–482.

Price, J., S. Droege, and A. Price. 1995. The summer atlas of North American breeding birds. Academic Press, London.

Pyle, P., and D. Sibley. 1992. Juvenal-plumaged Le Conte's Sparrows on migration. Birding 24:70–76.

Quilliam, H.R. 1965. History of the birds of Kingston, Ontario. Privately printed. 216 pp.

Quinlan, J. 1993. Photographs of New York State rarities 57: Black-throated Gray Warbler. Kingbird 43:86–87.

Rappole, J.H., E.S. Morton, T.E. Lovejoy III, and J.L. Ross. 1983. Nearctic avian migrants in the Neotropics. USFWS, Washington, DC.

Raynor, G.S. 1976a. Brown Boobies on Long Island. Kingbird 26:23–26.

——. 1976b. Decrease in breeding Brown Thrashers and Rufous-sided Towhees on central Long Island. Kingbird 26:190–193.

———. 1977. Green-tailed Towhee on Long Island. Kingbird 27:139–140.

———. 1979. Distribution and abundance of some common breeding species in mixed habitats. Kingbird 29:20–26.

Records of New Jersey's Birds. Publication of New Jersey Audubon Society, Franklin Lakes, NJ.

Reddall, J. 1988. First record of a Ross' Gull for New York State. Kingbird 38:5–7.

Reed, H.D., and A.H. Wright. 1909. The vertebrates of the Cayuga Lake basin, New York. Proceedings of the American Philosophical Society 48, no. 193.

Reed, J.M. 1992. A system for ranking conservation priorities for Neotropical migrant birds based on relative susceptibility to extinction. *In* Ecology and conservation of Neotropical migrant land birds, J.M. Hagan III and D.W. Johnston, eds. Smithsonian Institution Press, Washington, DC.

Reiger, J.F. 1986. American sportsmen and the origins of conservation. Univ. Oklahoma Press, Norman.

Reilly, E.M., and K.C. Parkes. 1959. Preliminary annotated checklist of New York State birds. New York State Museum and Science Service, Albany.

Reinert, S.E., R.C. Golet, and W.R. DeRagon. 1981. Avian use of ditched and unditched salt marshes in southeastern New England: a preliminary report. *In* Proceedings of the Twenty-seventh Annual Meeting of the Northeastern Mosquito Control Association, Newport, RI. Pp. 1–23.

Remsen, J.V., Jr., and T.A. Parker III. 1990. Seasonal distribution of the Azure Gallinule *(Porphyrula flavirostris),* with comments on vagrancy in rails and gallinules. Wilson Bulletin 102:380–399.

Reschke, C. 1990. Ecological communities of New York State. New York Natural Heritage Program, NYSDEC, Latham, NY.

———. 1993. Estimated numbers of EOs, acreage, trends, and threats for selected New York natural communities. Unpublished report. New York Natural Heritage Program, NYSDEC, Latham, NY. [As cited by Noss et al. 1996.]

Richard, A. 1988. Burrowing Owls on Long Island. Kingbird 38:116–117.

Richards, H., and S. Chevalier. 1978. Brown Boobies at Riis Park, Queens County. Kingbird 28:32.

Ridgway, R. 1895. The ornithology of Illinois, vol. 2. Natural History Survey of Illinois, Bloomington.

Riepe, D. 1994. A Forster's Tern colony at Jamaica Bay, New York City. Kingbird 44:10–13.

Riexinger, P., W.T. Corbett, and W. Sharich. 1978. Hooded Merganser breeding in Schoharie County. Kingbird 28:30–31.

Rimmer, C. 1996. A closer look: Bicknell's Thrush. Birding 28:119.

Ripley, S.D. 1977. Rails of the world. Godine, Boston.

Rising, G. 1994a. Buffalo Ornithological Society Christmas Count Records, 1929–1994. Unpublished computer data.

———. 1994b. Buffalo Ornithological Society October Count Records, 1935–1994. Unpublished computer data.

———. 1994c. Summary of 18 western New York breeding bird censuses, 1967–1994. Unpublished computer data.

———. 1995. Buffalo Ornithological Society May Count Records, 1935–1995. Unpublished computer data.

Rising, J.D. 1996. A guide to the identification and natural history of the sparrows of the United States and Canada. Academic Press, London.

Rising, J.D., and J.C. Avise. 1993. Applications of genealogical-concordance principles to the taxonomy and evolutionary history of the Sharp-tailed Sparrow *(Ammodramus caudacutus).* Auk 110:744–756.

Ritchie, W.A. 1928. An Algonkian village site near Levanna, New York. Research Records of the Rochester Museum of Arts and Sciences no. 1.

———. 1946. A stratified prehistoric site at Brewerton, New York. Research Records of the Rochester Museum of Arts and Sciences no. 8.

———. 1947. Archaeological evidence for ceremonialism in the Owasco culture. Research Transactions of the New York State Archaeological Association 11(2).

———. 1971. A typology and nomenclature for New York projectile points. New York State Museum Bulletin no. 384.

———. 1973a. The Bates Site (Grn. 1). *In* Aboriginal settlement patterns in the Northeast, W.A. Ritchie and R.E. Funk, eds. New York State Museum and Science Service Memoir 20. Pp. 226–290.

———. 1973b. The Nahrwold no. 1 Site (Shr. 51–4). *In* Aboriginal settlement patterns in the Northeast, W.A. Ritchie and R.E. Funk, eds. New York State Museum and Science Service Memoir 20. Pp. 276–290.

———. 1973c. The Sackett or Canandaigua Site (Can. 1). *In* Aboriginal settlement patterns in the Northeast, W.A. Ritchie and R.E. Funk, eds. New York State Museum and Science Service Memoir 20. Pp. 213–225.

———. 1980. The archaeology of New York State. Harbor Hill Books, Harrison, NY.

Ritchie, W.A., and R.E. Funk, eds. 1973a. Aboriginal settlement patterns in the Northeast. New York State Museum and Science Service Memoir 20.

———. 1973b. The Kelso Site (Bwv. 12). *In* Aboriginal settlement patterns in the Northeast, W.A. Ritchie and R.E. Funk, eds. New York State Museum and Science Service Memoir 20. Pp. 253–275.

Ritchie, W.A., D. Lenig, and P.S. Miller. 1953. An early Owasco sequence in eastern New York. New York State Museum Circular no. 32.

Robbins, C.S. 1973. Introduction, spread, and present abundance of the House Sparrow in North America. *In* Ornithological Monographs 14, S.C. Kendeigh, ed. American Ornithologists' Union, Washington, DC. P. 9.

Robbins, C.S., D. Bystrak, and P.H. Geissler. 1986. The breeding bird survey: its first fifteen years, 1965–1979. USFWS Resource Publication no. 157, Washington, DC.

Robbins, C.S., J.W. Fitzpatrick, and P.B. Hamel. 1992. A warbler in trouble: *Dendroica cerulea*. *In* Ecology and conservation of Neotropical migrant land birds, J.M. Hagan III and D.W. Johnston, eds. Smithsonian Institution Press.

Robertson, R.J., B.J. Stutchbury, and R.R. Cohen. 1992. Tree Swallow *(Tachycineta bicolor)*. *In* The birds of North America, no. 11, A. Poole, P. Stettenheim, and F. Gill, eds. The Academy of Natural Sciences, Philadelphia, and the American Ornithologists' Union, Washington, DC.

Robinson, S. 1995. Looking at the big picture. Living Bird 15:2.

Robinson, S.K., F.R. Thompson III, T.M. Donovan, D.R. Whitehead, and J. Faaborg. 1995. Regional forest fragmentation and the nesting success of migratory birds. Science 267:1987–1990.

Roosevelt, T., Jr., and H.D. Minot. 1877 [reprint 1923]. The summer birds of the Adirondacks in Franklin County, NY. Roosevelt Wild Life Bulletin 5:501–504.

Root, T. 1988. Atlas of wintering North American birds, an analysis of Christmas Bird Count data. Univ. Chicago Press, Chicago.

Rosche, R.C. 1967. Birds of Wyoming County, NY. Bulletin of the Buffalo Society of Natural Sciences 23.

Rosenburg, C. 1992. Barn Owl, *Tyto alba*. *In* Migratory nongame birds of management concern in the Northeast, K.J. Schneider and D.M. Pence, eds. USFWS, Newton Corner, MA.

Rossell, C.R., Jr., and D.J. DiTomasso. 1992. Prairie Warbler colonization of a right-of-way in Lewis County, NY. Kingbird 42:142.

Salzman, E. 1977. Some notes on breeding birds in the eastern Long Island pine barrens. Linnaean News-Letter 31(4).

——. 1983. Cerulean Warbler breeding in Suffolk County. Kingbird 33:105.

——. 1994. Christmas Bird Counts for New York State: 1960–1989. Unpublished computer data.

——. 1995. Boat-tailed Grackle at Shinnecock, Long Island. Kingbird 45:169.

Salzman, L., and E. Salzman. 1993. Photographs of New York State rarities 56: Roseate Spoonbill on Staten Island, New York. Kingbird 43:2.

Santner, S., D. Brauning, H. Schwalbe, and P. Schwalbe. 1992. Annotated list of the birds of Pennsylvania. Pennsylvania Biological Survey.

Sauer, J.R., and S. Droege. 1992. Geographic patterns in population trends of North American Neotropical migrants. *In* Ecology and conservation of Neotropical migrant land birds, J.M. Hagan III and D.W. Johnston, eds. Smithsonian Institution Press, Washington, DC.

Sauer, J.R., B.G. Peterjohn, S. Schwartz, and J.E. Hines. 1996. The North American breeding bird survey Home Page. Version 95.1. Patuxent Wildlife Research Center, Laurel, MD.

Saunders, A.A. 1929. The summer birds of the northern Adirondack Mountains. Roosevelt Wild Life Bulletins 1:239–354; 3:324–475; 5:327–499.

——. 1936. Ecology of the birds of Quaker Run Valley, Allegany State Park. New York State Museum Handbook no. 16.

——. 1942. Summer birds of the Allegany State Park. New York State Museum Handbook no. 18.

Schaeffer, F.S. 1968. Saw-whet Owl nesting in Tobay Sanctuary, Long Island. Kingbird 18:143–144.

Scheider, F. 1959. Warblers of southern New York. Kingbird 9:13–19.

——. 1962. Cape May Warbler breeding in the Adirondacks. Kingbird 12:140.

——. 1966. Hooded Merganser × Common Goldeneye hybrid at Fulton, Oswego County. Kingbird 16:149–150.

Scheider, F.G., and D.W. Crumb. 1985. Spectacular flight of Purple Finches at Derby Hill. Kingbird 35:115.

Schiff, S. 1989. Spring arrivals in southern Nassau Co. Kingbird 39:21–23.

Schmidt, K.P. 1938. Herpetological evidence for the postglacial eastward extension of the Steppe in North America. Ecology 19:396–407.

Schorger, A.W. 1952. Introduction of the domestic pigeon. Auk 69:462–463.

——. 1955. The Passenger Pigeon. Univ. Wisconsin Press, Madison.

——. 1964. The Trumpeter Swan as a breeding bird in Minnesota, Wisconsin, Illinois, and Indiana. Wilson Bulletin 76:331–338.

——. 1966. The Wild Turkey, its history and domestication. Univ. Oklahoma Press, Norman.

Schwalbe, P.W. 1992. Black-and-white Warbler. *In* Atlas of breeding birds in Pennsylvania, D.W. Brauning, ed., Univ. Pittsburgh Press, Pittsburgh. Pp. 330–331.

Scott, D.M. 1977. Cowbird parasitism on the Gray Catbird at London, Ontario. Auk 94:18–27.

Scott, J.M., B. Csuti, and F. Davis. 1991. Gap analysis: an application of geographic information systems for wildlife species. *In* Challenges in the conservation of biological resources, D.J. Decker, M.E. Krasny, G.R. Goff, C.R. Smith, and D.W. Gross, eds. Westview Press, Boulder, CO. Pp. 167–180.

Scott, J.M., F. Davis, B. Csuti, R. Noss, B. Butterfield, C. Groves, H. Anderson, S. Caicco, F. D'Erchia, T.C. Edwards Jr., J. Ullman, and R.G. Wright. 1993. Gap analysis: a geographic approach to protection of biological diversity. Wildlife Monograph no. 123.

Seutin, G., P.T. Boag, and L.M. Ratcliffe. 1992. Plumage variability in redpolls from Churchill, Manitoba. Auk 109:771–785.

——. 1993. Morphometric variability in redpolls from Churchill, Manitoba. Auk 110:832–843.

Seutin, G., L.M. Ratcliffe, and P.T. Boag. 1995. Mitichondrial DNA homogeneity in the phenotypically diverse redpoll finch complex (Aves: *Carduelis:* Carduelinae: *flammea-hornemanni*). Evolution 49:962–973.

Sharrock, J.T.R. 1976. The atlas of breeding birds in Britain and Ireland. T. & A.D. Poyser, Calton, England.

Sheldon, W.G. 1971. The book of the Woodcock. Univ. Massachusetts Press, Amherst.

Sherony, D. 1994. The status of Long-billed Dowitcher in western New York. Kingbird 44:258–267.

Shields, W.M. 1984. Factors affecting nest and site fidelity in Adirondack Barn Swallows *(Hirundo rustica)*. Auk 101:780–789.

Shields, W.M., and J.R. Crook. 1987. Barn Swallow coloniality: a net cost for group breeding in the Adirondacks? Ecology 68:1373–1386.

Shipman, J. 1995. A summary of Christmas Bird Count data from 1960–1989, compiled by John Shipman, obtained by Gerry Rising and reworked into tabular format for easy analysis of the New York data by Ajay Shekhawat of the University of Buffalo. Letter and tables.

Short, E.H. 1896. Birds of western New York. F.H. Lattin, Albion, NY.

Short, L.L. 1963. Hybridization in the wood warblers *Vermivora pinus* and *V. chrysoptera*. Proceedings of the Thirteenth International Ornithological Congress, Ithaca, NY. American Ornithologists' Union, Baton Rouge, LA. Pp. 147–160.

Sibley, C. 1995. Birds of the world. Version 1.5. Thayer Birding Software, Cincinnati, OH.

Sibley, C., and J.E. Ahlquist. 1990. Phylogeny and classification of birds. Yale Univ. Press, New Haven, CT.

Sibley, C.G., and B.L. Monroe Jr. 1990. Distribution and taxonomy of birds of the World. Yale Univ. Press, New Haven, CT.

Sibley, D. 1993. The birds of Cape May. Cape May Bird Observatory, NJ.

——. 1996. Field identification of the Sharp-tailed Sparrow complex. Birding 28:196–208.

Siebenheller, N. 1981. Breeding birds of Staten Island, 1881–1981. Staten Island Institute of Arts and Sciences, Staten Island, NY.

Siebenheller, N., and W. Siebenheller. 1982a. Blue Grosbeak nesting in New York State: a first record. Kingbird 32:234–238.

——. 1982b. Some noteworthy breeding records on Staten Island in 1982. Kingbird 32:258.

——. 1983. Photographs of New York State rarities 45: Painted Bunting on Staten Island. Kingbird 33:230.

Skelly, S.M. 1992. Photographs of New York State rarities 53: White-winged Tern. Kingbird 42:2.

Slack, R.S., and C.A Baumgartner. 1977. A possible New York State Dickcissel breeding colony. Kingbird 27:26–27.

Smiley, D., and J. Stapleton. 1974. First breeding record of Bewick's Wren in New York State. Kingbird 24:174–175.

Smith, B.E., P.L. Marks, and S. Gardescu. 1993. Two hundred years of forest cover changes in Tompkins County, NY. Bulletin of the Torrey Botanical Club 120:229–247.

Smith, C.R. 1989. An analysis of New York State breeding bird surveys 1966–1985.

Final Project Report, Contract no. C001667, New York State Dept. of Environmental Conservation, Albany.

——. 1990. Relationship of landscape patterns to summer and winter bird species diversity in New York State. Final Project Report, National Fish and Wildlife Foundation, Washington, DC.

——. 1991a. Building partnerships for bird conservation: some examples from New York State. *In* The Neotropical migratory bird conservation program, D.M. Finch, ed. Second Annual Meeting, 21–23 October 1991. USDA Forest Service, Forest Products Laboratory, Madison, WI. Pp. 71–74.

——. 1991b. Challenges in the conservation of biological resources—an epilogue. *In* Challenges in the conservation of biological resources, D.J. Decker, M.E. Krasny, G.R. Goff, C.R. Smith, and D.W. Gross, eds. Westview Press, Boulder, CO. Pp. 367–380.

——. 1992. Henslow's Sparrow. *In* Migratory nongame birds of management concern in the Northeast, K.J. Schneider and D.M. Pence, eds. USFWS, Newton Corner, MA.

——. In press. Use of public grazing lands by Henslow's Sparrow, Grasshopper Sparrow, and associated grassland species in central New York. *In* Ecology and management of grasslands and heathlands of the Northeast, P. Vickery, ed. Massachusetts Audubon Society, Lincoln, MA.

Smith, C.R., D.M. Pence, and R.J. O'Connor. 1993. Status of Neotropical migratory birds in the Northeast: a preliminary assessment. *In* Status and management of Neotropical migratory birds, D.M. Finch and P.W. Stangle, eds. USDA Forest Service, Rocky Mountain Forest and Range Experiment Station, Fort Collins, CO. Pp. 172–188.

Smith, D.G., and R. Gilbert. 1984. Eastern Screech-Owl home range and use of suburban habitats in southern Connecticut. Journal of Field Ornithology 55:322–29.

Smith, D.J., and C.R. Smith. 1992. Henslow's Sparrow and Grasshopper Sparrow: a comparison of habitat use in Finger Lakes National Forest, NY. Bird Observer 20(4):187–194.

Smith, G.A. 1988. Prairie Warbler as a regular breeder at alvar sites in Jefferson County. Kingbird 38:247.

——. 1989. Point Peninsula, Jefferson County: mouse raptor mecca during the winter of 1987–1988. Kingbird 39:7–20.

Smith, G.A., and J.M. Ryan. 1978. Annotated checklist of the birds of Oswego County and northern Cayuga County, NY. Rice Creek Biological Field Station Bulletin no. 5. State Univ. of New York at Oswego.

Smith, N.G. 1963. Evolution of some arctic gulls *(Larus)*: a study of isolating mechanisms. Ph.D. dissertation, Cornell Univ., Ithaca, NY.

——. 1966a. Adaptations to cliff-nesting in some arctic gulls *(Larus)*. Ibis 108:68–83.

——. 1966b. Evolution of some arctic gulls *(Larus)*: an experimental study of isolating mechanisms. Ornithological Monographs 4. American Ornithologists' Union, Washington, DC.

——. 1967. Visual isolation in gulls. Scientific American 217:94–102.

Smith, S.M. 1991. The Black-capped Chickadee: behavioral ecology and natural history. Cornell Univ. Press, Ithaca, NY.

——. 1993. Black-capped Chickadee *(Parus atricapillus)*. *In* The birds of North America, no. 39, A. Poole, P. Stettenheim, and F. Gill, eds. The Academy of Natural Sciences, Philadelphia, and the American Ornithologists' Union, Washington, DC.

Snell, R.R. 1989. Status of *Larus* gulls at Home Bay, Baffin Island. Colonial Waterbirds 12:12–23.

Snow, D.R. 1995. Mohawk Valley archaeology: the sites. State Univ. New York Press, Albany.

Snyder, D.E. 1961. First record of the Least Frigate-bird *(Fregata ariel)* in North America. Auk 78:265.

Sommers, L., and M. Alfieri. 1997. 1996 Long Island colonial waterbird and Piping Plover survey. A Research Report of NYSDEC. Stony Brook, NY.

Sommers, L., M. Alfieri, K. Meskill, and R. Miller. 1996. 1995 Long Island colonial waterbird and Piping Plover survey. A Research Report of NYSDEC. Stony Brook, NY.

Sommers, L., K. Meskill, R. Miller, and M. Alfieri. 1994. 1992–1993 Long Island colonial waterbird and Piping Plover survey. A Research Report of NYSDEC. Stony Brook, NY.

Spahn, R. 1980. Photographs of New York State rarities 35: Painted Redstart. Kingbird 30:67.

Spear, R., Jr. 1976. The birds of Vermont. Green Mountain Audubon Society, Burlington, VT.

Speck, F.G., and J. Witthoft. 1947. Some notable life-histories in zoological folklore. Journal of American Folklore 60:345–349.

Speich, S.M., H.L. Jones, and E.M. Benedict. 1985. Review of the natural nesting of the Barn Swallow in North America. American Midland Naturalist 115:248–254.

Speiser, R. 1982. Recent observations on breeding birds in the Hudson Highlands. Kingbird 32:97.

———. 1992. Notes on the natural history of the Northern Goshawk. Kingbird 42:133–137.

Spencer, B.J. 1982. Photographs of New York State rarities 42: Purple Gallinule. Kingbird 32:2–5.

Spencer, S.J. 1964. Some physical characteristics of nesting sites used by Bank Swallows. EBBA News 27:219–227.

Spitzer, P.R. 1978. Osprey egg and nestling transfers: their value as ecological experiments and as management procedures. *In* Endangered birds: management techniques for preserving threatened species, S.A. Temple, ed. Univ. Wisconsin Press, Madison. Pp. 171–82.

———. 1980. Dynamics of a discrete coastal breeding population of Ospreys in the northeastern USA, 1969–1979. Ph.D. dissertation, Cornell Univ., Ithaca, NY.

Spofford, W.R. 1971a. The breeding status of the Golden Eagle in the Appalachians. American Birds 25:3–7.

———. 1971b. The Golden Eagle-rediscovered. New York State Conservationist 26: 6–8.

Stallcup, R. 1990. Ocean birds of the nearshore Pacific. Point Reyes Bird Observatory, Stinson, CA.

Stanton, B.F., and N.L. Bills. 1996. The return of agricultural lands to forest—changing land use in the twentieth century. Dept. of Agricultural, Resource, and Managerial Economics, College of Agriculture and Life Sciences, Cornell Univ., Ithaca, NY.

Starna, W.A., G.R. Hamell, and W.L. Butts. 1984. Northern Iroquoian horticulture and insect infestation: a cause for village removal. Ethnohistory 31:197–207.

Steadman, D.W. 1980. A review of the osteology and paleontology of turkeys (Aves: Meleagridinae). Contributions in Science, Natural History Museum of Los Angeles County 330:131–207.

———. 1988a. Prehistoric birds of New York State. *In* The atlas of breeding birds in New York State, R.F. Andrle and J.R. Carroll, eds. Cornell Univ. Press, Ithaca, NY. Pp. 19–24.

——. 1988b. Vertebrates from the late Quaternary Hiscock Site, Genesee County, New York. Bulletin of the Buffalo Society of Natural Sciences 33:95–113.

——. 1996a. . . . And live on pigeon pie [extinction of the Passenger Pigeon]. New York State Conservationist 50:20–23.

——. 1996b. Human-caused extinction of birds. *In* Biodiversity II: understanding and protecting our resources, M. Reaka-Kudla, D.E. Wilson, and E.O. Wilson, eds. Joseph Henry Press, Washington, DC. Pp. 139–161.

Steadman, D.W., L.J. Craig, and J. Bopp. 1993a. Diddly Cave: a new late Quaternary vertebrate fauna from New York State. Current Research in the Pleistocene 9:110–112.

Steadman, D.W., L.J. Craig, and T. Engel. 1993b. Late Pleistocene and Holocene vertebrates from Joralemon's (Fish Club) Cave, Albany County, NY. Bulletin of the New York State Archaeological Association 105:9–15.

Steadman, D.W., and R.E. Funk. 1987. New paleontological and archaeological investigations at Dutchess Quarry Cave No. 8, Orange County, NY. Current Research in the Pleistocene 4:118–120.

Steadman, D.W., R.S. Laub, and N.G. Miller. 1986. The late Quaternary Hiscock Site, Genesee County, NY. Progress report. Current Research in the Pleistocene 3:22–23.

Steadman, D.W., and P.S. Martin. 1984. Extinction of birds in the late Pleistocene of North America. *In* Quaternary extinctions, P.S. Martin and R.G. Klein, eds. Univ. Arizona Press, Tucson. Pp. 466–477.

Steadman, D.W., and N.G. Miller. 1987. California Condor associated with spruce-jack pine woodland in the late Pleistocene of New York. Quaternary Reserach 28:415–426.

Steadman, D.W., T.W. Stafford Jr., and R.E. Funk. 1997. Nonassociation of Paleoindians with AMS-dated late Pleistocene mammals from the Dutchess Quarry Caves, New York. Quaternary Research 47:105–116.

Stein, R.C., 1958. The behavioral, ecological, and morphological characteristics of two populations of the Alder Flycatcher. New York State Museum Bulletin no. 371.

——. 1963. Isolating mechanisms between populations of Traill's Flycatchers. Proceedings of the American Philosophical Society 107:25–27.

Stoddard, H.L. 1917. The Roseate Tern *(Sterna dougalli)* on Lake Michigan. Auk 34:86.

Stoner, D.1932. Ornithology of the Oneida Lake region: with reference to the late spring and summer seasons. Roosevelt Wild Life Annals 2:271–764.

——. 1936. Studies on the Bank Swallow, *Riparia riparia*, in the Oneida Lake region. Roosevelt Wild Life Annals 4:126–233.

Strickland, D., and H. Ouellet. 1993. Gray Jay *(Perisoreus canadensis)*. *In* The birds of North America, no. 40, A. Poole, P. Stettenheim, and F. Gill, eds. The Academy of Natural Sciences, Philadelphia, and the American Ornithologists' Union, Washington, DC.

Stutchbury, B.J., and R.J. Robertson. 1985. Floater populations of female Tree Swallows. Auk 102:651–654.

Sundell, R.A. 1975. A record of Swainson's Warbler in southwestern New York State. Kingbird 25:204–205.

Swenk, M.H. 1916. The Eskimo Curlew and its disappearance. Smithsonian Report for 1915: Publication 2393.

——. 1929. The Pine Siskin in Nebraska: its seasonal abundance and nesting. Wilson Bulletin 41, N.S. 36:77–92.

Swift, B.L. 1987. An analysis of avian breeding habitats in Hudson River tidal marshes. New York State Dept. of Environmental Conservation, Delmar, NY.

Sykes, P. 1974. Fla. Burrowing Owl collected in North Carolina. Auk 91:636–637.

Tabb, E.C. 1973. A study of wintering Broad-winged Hawks in southeastern Florida 1968–1973. EBBA News (Supplement) 36:11–29.

Tate, G.R. 1992. Short-eared Owl, *Asio flammeus*. *In* Migratory nongame birds of management concern in the Northeast, K.J. Schneider and D.M. Pence, eds. US-FWS, Newton Corner, MA.

Temple, S.A., and B.L. Temple. 1976. Avian population trends in central New York 1935–1972. Bird Banding 47:238–257.

Terborgh, J. 1989. Where have all the birds gone? Princeton Univ. Press, Princeton, NJ.

Terres, J.K. 1980. The Audubon Society encyclopedia of North American birds. Alfred A. Knopf, New York.

Thompson, D.G., and R.H. Smith. 1970. The forest primeval in the Northeast—a great myth? Proceedings of the Annual Tall Timbers Fire Ecology Conference. Pp. 255–265.

Thompson, J.H., ed. 1977. Geography of New York State. Syracuse Univ. Press, Syracuse, NY.

Thomson, A.L. 1964. A new dictionary of birds. Nelson, London.

Tinbergen, N. 1929. A breeding pair of Herring-Gull *(Larus a. argentatus* Pont.*)* and Lesser Black-backed Gull *(Larus fuscus* subspec.*)*. Ardea 18:1.

Tiner, R.W., Jr. 1984. Wetlands of the United States: current status and recent trends. USFWS National Wetlands Inventory, Washington, DC.

Titus, K., and M.R. Fuller. 1990. Recent trends in counts of migrant hawks from northeastern North America. Journal of Wildlife Management 54: 463–470.

Tobish, T. 1986. Separation of Barrow's and Common goldeneyes in all plumages. Birding 18:17.

Todd, W.E. Clyde. 1940. Birds of western Pennsylvania. Univ. Pittsburgh Press, Pittsburgh.

——. 1963. Birds of the Labrador Peninsula and adjacent areas. Univ. Toronto Press, Toronto.

Tove, M.H. 1993. Field separation of Ring-billed, Mew, Common, and Kamchatka gulls. Birding 25:386–401.

Treacy, E.D. 1981. Photographs of New York State rarities 39: Ivory Gull. Kingbird 31:62.

——. 1983. Ross' Goose added to New York State list. Kingbird 33:153–154.

Trouern-Trend, J., and L.R. Bevier. 1992. Bird species reported in the Northeast but not in Connecticut. The Connecticut Warbler 12(2):33–57.

Tuck, J.A. 1971. Onondaga Iroquois prehistory. Syracuse Univ. Press, Syracuse, NY.

Turner, A., and C. Rose. 1989. Swallows and martins: an identification guide and handbook. Houghton Mifflin, Boston.

Ulrich, E.C. 1938. "Notes." Prothonotary 4:6.

Van Camp, L.F., and C.J. Henny. 1975. The screech owl: its life history and population ecology in northern Ohio. USFWS, North American Fauna no. 71.

Vargo, J., and D. Vargo. 1983. The Rabuilt Cave Site—Pke 4-1 site report. Bulletin of the New York State Archaeological Association 87:13–39.

Veit, R., and L. Jonsson. 1984. Field identification of the smaller sandpipers within the genus *Calidris*. American Birds 38:853.

Veit, R., and W. Petersen. 1993. Birds of Massachusetts. Natural History of New England Series. Massachusetts Audubon Society, Lincoln, MA.

Verhovek, S.H. 1994. Bush son misfires on hunt for publicity in Texas race. New York Times, September 2. P. A21.

Versaggi, N.M., J.M. McDonald, A.T. Mair II, and S.C. Prezzano. 1982. The southside treatment plant site, SuBi-672 Village of Owego. Cultural Resource Survey Report to Village of Owego, NY.

Vickery, P.D., and R.P. Yunick. 1979. The 1978–1979 Great Gray Owl incursion across northeastern North America. American Birds 33:242–244.

Vohs, P.A. n.d. Fisheries and Wildlife Research and Development 1991/1992. U.S. Dept. of Interior, National Biological Service, Washington, DC.

Voous, K.H. 1946. Sur un casd'hybridation naturelle entre *Larus fuscus* L. et *Larus argentatus* Pont. dans les pays-bas. [On a case of natural hybridization between Lesser Black-backed and Herring gulls in the low countries.] Alauda 14:21–32.

———. 1962. Another presumed hybrid of Lesser Black-backed Gull and Herring Gull in the Netherlands. Ardea 50:171–172.

Walkinshaw, L.H. 1991. Yellow Rail. *In* The atlas of the breeding birds of Michigan, R. Brewer, G.A. McPeek, and R.J. Adams Jr., eds. Michigan State Univ. Press, East Lansing.

Wallace, G.J. 1939. Bicknell's Thrush: its taxonomy, distribution, and life history. Proceedings of the Boston Society of Natural History 41:211–402.

Walsh, T. 1988. Identifying Pacific Loons: some old and new problems. Birding 20:12.

Warren, P.H. 1979. Birds of Clinton County, NY. Northern Adirondack Chapter, National Audubon Society, Plattsburg, NY.

Watson, G.E., D.S. Lee, and E.S. Backus. 1986. Status and subspecific identity of White-faced Storm-Petrels in the western North Atlantic Ocean. American Birds 40:401–408.

Watson, W. 1995a. Early fledging Common Terns—a "new" state record. Prothonotary 61:110–111.

———. 1995b. First successful nesting of Double-crested Cormorant in the Niagara Frontier Region. Kingbird 45:168.

Watts, B.D. 1995. Yellow-crowned Night-Heron *(Nyctanassa violacea)*. *In* The birds of North America, no. 161, A. Poole and F. Gill, eds. The Academy of Natural Sciences, Philadelphia, and the American Ornithologists' Union, Washington, DC.

Webster, D.W. 1980. De Witt Clinton's ". . . Fishes of the western waters of the state of New-York" reexamined. Fisheries 5:5–12.

Weinman, P.L., and T.P. Weinman. 1969. The Moonshine Rockshelter. Bulletin of the New York State Archaeological Association 46:11–15.

Weissman, B.B. 1980. Photographs of New York State rarities 37: California Gull. Kingbird 30:198–200.

Weissman, B.B., and W. Howe. 1976. Yellow-nosed Albatross at Croton Point, Westchester County. Kingbird 26:200.

Weller, M.W. 1964. Distribution and migration of the Redhead. Journal of Wildlife Management 28:64–103.

Welles, M. 1978. TV tower kill at Elmira. Kingbird 28:159.

Wells, J.V., and K.V. Rosenberg. 1996. Birdscope 10, no. 2. Cornell Laboratory of Ornithology, Ithaca, NY.

Weseloh, D.V., and H. Blokpoel. 1993. Caspian Tern nesting at Little Galloo Island: a new nesting species for New York State. Kingbird 43:6.

Weseloh, D.V., and B. Collier. 1995. The rise of the Double-crested Cormorant on the Great Lakes: winning the war against contaminants. Great Lakes Fact Sheet. Canadian Wildlife Service, Environment Canada, Burlington, ON.

Weseloh, D.V., and P.J. Ewins. 1994. Characteristics of a rapidly increasing colony of Double-crested Cormorants *(Phalacrocorax auritus)* in Lake Ontario: population size, reproductive parameters and band recoveries. Journal of Great Lakes Research 20(2):443–456.

Weseloh, D.V., P.J. Ewins, J. Struger, P. Mineau, C.A. Bishop, S. Postupalsky, and J.P. Ludwig. 1995. Double-crested Cormorants of the Great Lakes: changes in population size, breeding distribution and reproductive output between 1913 and 1991. Colonial Waterbirds 18 (Special Publication 1):48–59.

Wheeler, B.K., and W.S. Clark. 1995. A photographic guide to North American raptors. Academic Press, London.

Whitcomb, B.L., R.F. Whitcomb, and D. Bystrak. 1977. Island biogeography and "habitat islands" of eastern forest. Part III: long-term turnover and effects of selective logging on the avifauna of forest fragments. American Birds 31:17–23.

Whitcomb, R.F., et al. 1981. Effects of forest fragmentation on avifauna of the eastern deciduous forests. *In* Forest island dynamics in man-dominated landscapes, R.I. Burgess and D.M. Sharpe, eds. Springer-Verlag, New York.

White, R.P. 1983. Distribution and habitat preference of the Upland Sandpiper *(Bartramia longicauda)* in Wisconsin. American Birds 37:16–22.

Whitney, B., and K. Kaufman. 1985. The *Empidonax* challenge. Part I: introduction. Birding 17:151–158.

——. 1986. The *Empidonax* challenge. Part III: Willow and Alder flycatchers. Birding 18:153–159.

Whittaker, R.H., S.A. Levin, and R.B. Root. 1973. Niche, habitat and ecotope. American Naturalist 107:321–338.

Wiens, J. 1969. An approach to the study of ecological relationships among grassland birds. Ornithological Monographs no. 8.

Wilbur, S.R. 1983. The status of vultures in the Western Hemisphere. *In* Vulture biology and management, S.R. Wilbur and J.A. Jackson, eds. Univ. California Press, Berkeley. Pp. 113–123.

Wilcove, D.S. 1983. Population changes in the Neotropical migrants of the Great Smoky Mountains: 1947–1982. Unpublished report to the World Wildlife Fund–United States.

Wilcox, L. 1959. A twenty year banding study of the Piping Plover. Auk 76:129–152.

Wilds, C.P., and D. Czaplak. 1993. Yellow-legged Gulls *(Larus cachinnans)* in North America. Wilson Bulletin 106:344–356.

Wilds, C.P., and M. Newlon. 1983. The identification of dowitchers. Birding 15:151–165.

Wilkins, C.N. 1988. The House Finch explosion. New York Birders 17(1):6.

Will, G. 1981. Gray Partridge in Essex Co. NY. Kingbird 31:152.

Will, T.C. 1986. The behavioral ecology of species replacement: Blue-winged and Golden-winged warblers in Michigan. Ph.D. dissertation, Univ. Michigan, Ann Arbor.

Winging It. Newsletter of the American Birding Association, Colorado Springs, CO.

Winkler, H., D.A. Christie, and D. Nurney. 1995. Woodpeckers: an identification guide to the woodpeckers of the world. Houghton Mifflin, Boston.

Witherby, H.F., F.C.R. Jourdain, D.F. Ticehurst, and B.W. Tucker. 1941. Handbook of British Birds, rev. ed. Witherby, London.

Witmer, M. 1996. The telltale tail. Living Bird 15:16–20.

Wollin, A. 1986. Out of the eye of the storm. Kingbird 36:205.

——. 1994. Species limits in the Fox Sparrow *(Passerella iliaca)*. Evolution 48:96–111.

Wootton, J.T. 1987. Interspecific competition between introduced House Finch populations and two associated passerine species. Oecologia 71:325–331.

Wray, C.F. 1963. Ornamental hair combs of the Seneca Iroquois. Pennsylvania Archaeologist 33:35–50.

——. 1964. The bird in Seneca archaeology. Proceedings of the Rochester Academy of Sciences 11:1–56.

Wright, A.H. 1919. Henslow's Sparrow in New York and Virginia. Auk 36:574–575.

Wunz, G.A. 1973. Evaluation of game-farm and wild-trapped turkeys in Pennsylvania. *In* Wild Turkey management, current problems and programs, G.C. Sanderson and H.C. Schultz, eds. Missouri Chapter of the Wildlife Society, Univ. Missouri Press, Columbia. Pp. 199–209.

Yosef, R. 1994. Evaluation of the global decline in the true shrikes (family Laniidae). Auk 111:228–233.

Yrizarry, J. 1993. Photographs of New York rarities 58: a Spotted Redshank winters in Brooklyn. Kingbird 43:167.

Yunick, R.P. 1978. Photographs of New York State rarities 27: Black Guillemot. Kingbird 28:67–69.

——. 1979. A review of New York State Boreal Owl records. Kingbird 29:181–189.

——. 1980. The 1978–79 Great Gray Owl invasion in New York State. Kingbird 30:85–98.

——. 1984. An assessment of the irruptive status of the Boreal Chickadee in New York State. Journal of Field Ornithology 55:27–31.

——. 1988a. An assessment of the Downy Woodpecker and Hairy Woodpecker on recent New York State Christmas Counts. Kingbird 38:147–158.

——. 1988b. An assessment of the White-breasted Nuthatch and Red-breasted Nuthatch on recent New York State Christmas Counts. Kingbird 38:95–104.

Zarudsky, J. 1981. Forster's Tern breeding on Long Island. Kingbird 31:212–213.

——. 1985. Breeding status of the American Oystercatcher in the town of Hempstead. Kingbird 35:105–113.

Zarudsky, J.D., and R. Miller. 1983. Nesting Boat-tailed Grackles on Pearsall's Hassock. Kingbird 33:3–5.

Zeranski, J.D., and T.R. Baptist. 1990. Connecticut birds. Univ. Press of New England, Hanover, NH.

Zeuner, F.E. 1963. History of domesticated animals. Harper and Row, New York. Pp. 460–462.

Zimmer, K.J. 1991. Plumage variation in "Kumlien's" Iceland Gulls. Birding 23:254–270.

Zimmerman, J.L. 1977. Virginia Rail *(Rallus limicola)*. *In* Management of migratory shore and upland game birds in North America, G.C. Sanderson, ed. International Association of Fish and Wildlife Agencies, Washington, DC. Pp. 46–56.

Zink, R.M., and D.L. Dittman. 1993. Population structure and gene flow in the Chipping Sparrow and a hypothesis for evolution in the genus *Spizella*. Wilson Bulletin 105:399–413.

Index of English Bird Names

Pages listed in this index refer only to the location of individual species accounts. The names of the birds and the systematic order used throughout the text follow the *A.O.U. Check-list of North American Birds*, Sixth Edition (1983), and all subsequent Supplements published in *The Auk* through 1997.

Index of Scientific Bird Names

Pages listed in this index refer only to the location of individual species accounts. The names of the birds and the systematic order used throughout the text follow the *A.O.U. Check-list of North American Birds*, Sixth Edition (1983), and all subsequent Supplements published in *The Auk* through 1997.